P9-DWN-372

THE TOP OF HIS GAME

THE TOP OF HIS GAME

THE BEST SPORTSWRITING

EDITED AND WITH AN INTRODUCTION BY **BILL LITTLEFIELD**

A Special Publication of  The Library of America

Volume compilation of *The Top of His Game* copyright © 2015 by
Literary Classics of the United States, Inc., New York, N.Y.
Essays by W. C. Heinz copyright © 1947, 1948, 1949, 1951, 1953, 1954, 1955, 1958,
1959, 1961, 1965, 1979, 1982, 2000, 2001 by W. C. Heinz,
used by permission of Gayl Heinz.
Introduction copyright © 2015 by Bill Littlefield.
All rights reserved.

www.loa.org

No part of this book may be reproduced commercially
by offset-lithographic or equivalent copying devices without
the permission of the publisher.

Distributed to the trade in the United States
by Penguin Random House Inc.
and in Canada by Penguin Random House Canada Ltd.

Book design by David Bullen

Library of Congress Control Number: 2014946643
ISBN 978-1-59853-372-9

First Printing

Printed in the United States of America

Contents

Introduction

True to the Way It Happens

Sixty-odd years ago, the sides of the trucks delivering the New York *Sun* to newsstands were decorated with a large and colorful banner. The banner read:

W. C. HEINZ

Read His
Human Interest Stories On Sports
Daily In

The Sun

Buy It Today

To the left of the copy was a picture of W. C. Heinz himself, dapper in a bow tie, smiling a little ruefully, perhaps at the celebrity he had achieved. Or perhaps he was bemused that he was still alive. He'd recently returned from duty as a war correspondent in Europe. Half a century later he would talk with quiet gratitude about the soldiers who'd kept him safe during World War II while he walked with them and huddled with them in foxholes and wrote about their days for readers at home.

One morning as he was crossing a Manhattan street, one of the trucks advertising his work came hurtling around the corner. W. C. Heinz, Bill to his friends, jumped back out of the street just in time to avoid becoming a sad and ironic headline on the sports page of the newspaper for which he was writing.

I got that story from Bill's daughter, Gayl Heinz. She told me Bill had enjoyed telling it. Gayl is the sort of daughter all writers should have, or at least all writers who deserve to stay in print, because she has devoted a lot of energy and time to ensuring that generations of readers will have the opportunity to appreciate the work her father did.

The work that appeared in the *Sun* under the byline "W. C. Heinz" can be categorized as "human interest stories" in the same sense that the work of William Faulkner, Flannery O'Connor, Kurt Vonnegut, and Ernest Hemingway can be so categorized.

Like Faulkner, Bill Heinz understood the significance of place. For him the place was not an imaginary county in Mississippi but a very real boxing gym on Eighth Avenue, or a racetrack in the rain, or a tavern in the middle of a clumsy hold-up.

Like O'Connor, he understood that the people at the edges of any endeavor offered, by necessity, original perspectives on a culture into which they would never fit.

Like Vonnegut, he wrapped his darkest observations in humor. Often the humor was exceptionally gentle.

Like Hemingway, he never wasted a word. Hemingway recognized that quality in Heinz. When, in 1958, he was invited to comment on Bill's novel *The Professional*, Hemingway sent a telegram in which he called it "the only good novel I've ever read about a fighter and an excellent first novel in its own right."

They were more than passing acquaintances. Both had worked as correspondents in Europe during World War II. Apparently numbers of correspondents would regularly crash at whatever house Hemingway had secured as his headquarters. On at least one occasion, Bill was one of them. According to Gayl, her father brought a bottle of scotch as "a true gift of admiration for the master," in return for which Hemingway said he wouldn't allow Bill to spend the night on the floor with the others. Hemingway was prepared to give up his bed.

"I couldn't," Heinz said, "I wouldn't sleep a wink," and, again according to his daughter, he slept with the rest of the journalists.

As it happened, Bill's visit coincided with the breakdown of Hemingway's typewriter, perhaps from overwork. That night he borrowed the 1932 Remington portable Bill had been hauling around from battlefield to battlefield, and in the morning he said, "That machine has a nice mill. It writes very well."

"Sure," Bill said, "but it writes a hell of a lot better for you than it does for me."

Heinz was wrong. The machine didn't write better for Hemingway, only differently. But the comparison serves to highlight one of the qualities that distinguish the body of work he left behind from the work of his fellow newspaper and magazine journalists. Bill Heinz wrote from the war and from the ball field and from the racetrack, the gym, and the arena. He wrote *The Professional*, which is more Hemingway than Red Smith, and co-wrote another novel, *M*A*S*H*, which provided Elliott Gould and Donald Sutherland with employment in the movies and Alan Alda with a career on TV. He also wrote about medicine and civil rights and popular culture, all of which may not be pertinent to a collection of his best sportswriting, but my point is that Heinz brought to his writing about games a wide-ranging curiosity not just about athletes but about people. They fascinated him. He took pains to capture the way they talked, the way they cheated and cherished one another, the way they did what they had to do to make it through each day without surrendering more blood or dignity than necessary.

Heinz's work is also characterized by integrity, which cannot be said of the work of a lot of the fellows writing about sports in the middle of the twentieth century. Back then baseball writers traveled by train with the ball clubs and the bar car was generally open, the tab picked up by the home team. Not so many years earlier, Babe Ruth had allegedly run naked through one of those railroad cars pursued by a young woman, equally naked except for the carving knife in her fist. The chase is said to have provoked one New York beat writer to turn to the fellow beside him and say, "There goes another story we won't write."

According to Gayl Heinz, Bill was presented opportunities to profit financially from his position, all of which he refused. She told me that one night Jake LaMotta, who had once been the middleweight champion of the world, tucked a twenty-dollar bill into Bill's shirt pocket with the understanding that he would write something likely to sell tickets to LaMotta's next bout. Heinz plucked the money from his pocket and, at considerable risk to his person, tucked it into LaMotta's pocket, saying, "I am disgusted that you thought you could buy me, and insulted that you thought twenty dollars would do it." It's a funny story but also one that underscores certain principles that Bill brought to his work. Yes, he chronicled the schemes and scams of the trainers and promoters, and was frequently amusing about it, and he wrote sports profiles for newspapers and magazines that sometimes helped the athletes and their handlers at the gate. But he wasn't primarily a humorist or even an entertainer, and was never a paid publicist. His calling was to present the people he wrote about not as cartoon swindlers or noble warriors or any of the other sportswriting clichés but as flesh-and-blood individuals with their own voices and with stories worth telling accurately, so that his readers would recognize them and come to know them. And he cared enough about the subjects of his stories to get them right.

Heinz also addressed the powers and circumstances that conspired against the athletes he wrote about—race and class and who got paid for the work they performed. In several pieces he denounced the hypocrisy of the NCAA, and he recognized Major League Baseball's reserve clause as unjust in an era when many baseball writers were mere mouthpieces for club owners who argued that free agency for players would destroy the national pastime.

All of Heinz's work is marked by integrity of a still-higher order. He was loyal to the people he came to know. He listened to them, and in the columns and articles and essays he wrote, he presented their humanity. He appreciated what was funny about them, and what was sad, and he never forgot that they deserved to be treated with respect.

Necessarily, he developed all the skills and resources that any craftsman writing several columns a week requires. Bill used to tell a story about how one day he was heading to a gym, probably Stillman's, in search of a boxing guy, probably Jack Hurley, of whom Damon Runyon is alleged to have said: "There are two honest managers in boxing.

The one is Jack Hurley, and I can't remember the name of the other." Hurley, like many of his associates, could always be counted on as a source for the kind of talk that makes a good column. Bill Heinz knew that. On this particular day, on his way to the gym, Bill ran into a friend who, having nothing of his own that especially needed doing, asked if he could tag along. Bill shrugged and said "Sure."

Together the two men spent the better part of the afternoon listening to tales of used-up pugs, reigning champs, and promising lads who would no doubt wow the world one day if they could just learn to duck and to avoid women.

Bill's column in the next day's paper was an account of his visit with Hurley. That evening, he ran into the friend who had accompanied him to the gym. The fellow was astonished.

"Bill," he said, "I don't know how you do it. At the gym, you didn't take a single note. Yet in today's column, you had everything that manager said, word for word. You must have the greatest memory in the world."

Telling the story many years later, Bill smiled. "He didn't get it," he said. "I couldn't have written everything the guy had said in a column. A column is eight hundred fifty words. We were there for a couple of hours. What I did was get the rhythm of what the manager said, the sound and the feel of it. But that guy thought I'd remembered it all."

None of this is to suggest that Bill's friend wasn't paying attention, only that Bill was a master reporter. He had a great eye, an even better ear, and an exceptional sense of what mattered.

He was also his own harshest critic. For a wonderful profile written for *Sports Illustrated*, Jeff MacGregor read through Heinz's scrapbooks of his columns from the *Sun* and discovered that "none of them were bad." MacGregor was right about that, though Heinz would not have agreed. In the scrapbooks, under those few columns of which he was most proud, Heinz wrote lightly in pencil, "Good." Sometimes he wrote a little more. The column that ran on October 17, 1949, is followed by this notation: "Good description at end." This suggests that perhaps Bill was not entirely happy with the rest of the column. It's an account of a football game in the Yale Bowl. Cornell won it by thirty-four points, which means it can't have generated much suspense. Toward the end of the column, Bill listens in as young Bob Jablonski, one of the Yale ball carriers, muses on the fact that he "can't remember anything that happened" during the game. The days of worry about football-induced brain injury and lives cut short by chronic traumatic encephalopathy were still decades away, so that sad fact about football gets short shrift. Bill's penciled note refers instead to the final three paragraphs of the column:

> *In the parking areas an hour after the game the cars still stood, congested. On some the luggage racks were still open, and the people stood around them, the evening starting to darken now, the people still laughing, the glasses again in their hands.*
>
> *The headlights were on by the time the last of the cars crowded out. In the West the dark clouds were starting to open, the sky to glow a little, the first star to show. The red tail-lights strung as far as you could see, the cars moving in a great company, the dead leaves swirling behind the cars, dancing in the headlights of the ones behind.*
>
> *Those who had heard the rumor had heard it right. The football season had, indeed, started.*

Devotees of the work of W. C. Heinz seem to agree that the column titled "Death of a Race Horse" is not only his finest column but perhaps the best sports column ever written. If it's not, it is, as they say, among 'em. It ran on July 28, 1949, has been anthologized many times, and is used by teachers of writing, presumably to convince students they should quit the writing dodge and find a day job, because they will never write anything half as good as "Death of a Race Horse." It is a brilliant and brilliantly understated demonstration of a writer's determination to stay out of the way of a story that will be powerful and moving if he can tell it without fanfare. If he read the *Sun* that morning, Hemingway smiled.

Lots of other writers have loved the work of W. C. Heinz. One story has it that Damon Runyon, age sixty-six and dying of throat cancer, was approached by an editor to do a piece that, Runyon regretted, he was too ill to write. He was also unable to speak, but when the editor asked him to suggest another man for the job, Runyon wrote on a cocktail napkin, "W. C. Heinz very good." He then underlined "very good" three times.

David Halberstam agreed. When, in 1999, he served as guest editor of *The Best American Sports Writing of the Century*, he included three of Bill's stories. Nobody else rated more than two. One of those three stories is "Brownsville Bum," which Jimmy Breslin regarded as the best sports story ever to appear in a magazine.

And of course "Brownsville Bum" is no more a sports story than *Moby-Dick* is an account of a fishing trip. In a letter written last winter to nominate W. C. Heinz for the PEN/ESPN Lifetime Achievement Award for Literary Sports Writing, John Schulian, who numbers himself among the many writers who learned from Heinz's work and benefitted from acquaintance with him, says of the subject of "Brownsville Bum" that "the short, violent life of 'Bummy' Davis was nothing less than the American version of a Greek tragedy." He's right. Al "Bummy" Davis is a boxer, sure, and a boxer who, likely as not, will respond to a rabbit punch with a low blow or eleven, but in Bummy's circumstances Bill Heinz saw an opportunity to explore a realm beyond boxing. He figured, correctly, that telling Bummy's story would provide him with the chance to say something about what it is like to be alive on this planet, which is why the story begins not with the day Bummy Davis was born or a celebration of his first bout, but with this extraordinary paragraph:

> *It's a funny thing about people. People will hate a guy all his life for what he is, but the minute he dies for it they make him out a hero and they go around saying that maybe he wasn't such a bad guy after all because he sure was willing to go the distance for whatever he believed or whatever he was.*

Who could stop reading there? Nobody, I think.

There is a pattern in the writing of W. C. Heinz that suggests that he was seldom satisfied with the work he'd done, and that his curiosity and his imagination were too large to be contained within a column or a magazine piece or perhaps any form.

Even before 1950, when the *Sun* went out of business, Bill was writing stories for magazines. Jeff MacGregor has suggested that by doing so he taught such worthies as Gay Talese, Tom Wolfe, and Frank Deford the trade. Lots of Heinz's magazine stories feature the same people he wrote about in his columns: Beau Jack and Rocky Graziano and Jack Hurley, for example, and Pistol Pete Reiser, the Brooklyn Dodgers outfielder who'd have made the Hall of Fame if he hadn't been so inclined to keep running after fly balls until he'd crashed into an outfield wall and knocked himself unconscious. In 1979, some thirty years after his first magazine feature, Bill brought out a book titled *Once They Heard the Cheers* in which he revisited a lot of the same characters from his early days, or at least revisited their stories. The columns had been brilliant gems. The magazine stories had given Heinz a greater opportunity to talk with the family, teammates, and acquaintances of the subjects, and with people who'd been at the few great events Bill had missed. Then, in the chapters of *Once They Heard the Cheers*, Heinz found the space to say what wouldn't fit in the magazine stories. His fascination with the people he wrote about never waned, and perhaps he knew on some level that there is always more to any person's story than any writer can finally pin down. So he kept going back, and the stories just got richer and better.

The Top of His Game is a collection of Bill's nonfiction writing set in sports, so there is no room here for even a chapter of *The Professional*, much as Mr. Hemingway might have wished otherwise. But there's room for something Bill Heinz said in relation to that novel, because it applies to the integrity apparent in everything he wrote. I'd just finished reading *The Professional* when I met W. C. Heinz for the first time. I'd felt in the novel the writer's admiration for Eddie Brown, his fictional fighter—an amalgam, it is said, of the boxers Billy Graham and Rocky Graziano. In creating Eddie Brown, Heinz was praising honest fighters for the discipline and intelligence they brought to their work, and in creating Doc Carroll, he was praising every trainer—or, at least, Jack Hurley—who understood and taught boxing as science and strategy. But things don't go as well as any reader is bound to hope they will for Eddie Brown, and I asked the author if he'd been tempted at any point during the writing of the book to take Eddie Brown to the top.

"No," Bill said.

"Why not?" I asked.

"Because," he said, "that's not the way it happens."

Bill Littlefield
Boston, Massachusetts
August 2014

★ OUT OF THE WAR ★

Transition

Autumn 1945

THOSE WERE the good years, right after the war. I mean that if you got out of it alive and all in one piece, and if you did not lose anyone close to you, and if you had done honest work during that time, no matter what it was or where it was, you knew that the next years, after all that had happened, had to be the good ones, as long as your luck held out.

It was early in the fall after the war ended, and I was standing in the sports department by Wilbur Wood's desk. Wilbur Wood was the sports editor of the paper, and before that he had been its boxing writer. He was rather large-boned and balding, and because at some time his nose had been hit he looked tough, but he was a soft and sentimental man. During the war he used to write me V-mail letters, giving me the gossip of the office and recounting something that he had found memorable or amusing in sports. Once he described a block that Doc Blanchard, the Army fullback, had thrown in the Yankee Stadium on Tree Adams, a six-foot seven-inch Notre Dame tackle. I can still see it the way Wilbur described it in the letter—which I got after we had crossed the border into Germany—with Adams going up in the air and turning a somersault and landing on his head. In all his letters Wilbur said he liked what I was writing, and several times he added that he guessed now he would never be able to get me into sports.

I had been wanting to get into sports since I had been in high school, and trying, with time out for the war, for the eight years I had been on

---

Introduction to *Once They Heard the Cheers*, 1979.

the paper. In high school I weighed 118 pounds, and my heroes were the football players, the ones who ten thousand came out to see in a big game, filling the concrete stands and, across the field, the wooden bleachers, and lining the sidelines. Several of them were six feet tall, or more, and must have weighed 180 or 190 pounds, and I felt that I was fortunate when I was in the same class with one or another of them.

I would sit near the back of the room, so that I could watch them in their letter sweaters lolling behind the desks, their legs out into the aisle. They made their desks seem small, and the books seemed small in their hands, and at the end of the class, when we all stood up and walked out, they towered not only above the rest of us but above the teacher. They seemed to me to be men, and as we all walked out of the class I felt that they could walk right out of the school and be men out there in the world too.

Many years later, when I came to live in training camp and travel with the New York Football Giants and then the Green Bay Packers in their great years, they still seemed big to me, those heroes of my youth. Remembering them, in a Giant or a Packer dressing room, I still had to tell myself that Tommy Mallon and Eddie Williams and Ernie Jansen had been only teenagers, really, and that they were never such superb football players as Andy Robustelli or Alex Webster or Frank Gifford, with the Giants, or Bart Starr, Paul Hornung, Jimmy Taylor, Forrest Gregg, Jerry Kramer, or Willie Davis of the Packers.

That was how bad I had it in high school, when I was too frail for football and afraid of a baseball thrown near the head and had been a reluctant starter and worse finisher in street fights. Once, when we were both eight years old, they put the shoemaker's son and me together in the school playground with gloves on us, and he punched me around for three one-minute rounds.

"You know," I said, a long time after that, to Sugar Ray Robinson, the greatest fighter I ever saw, "you and I fought the same guy. When we were little kids he punched my head off in a playground fight."

"Who was that?" Robinson said.

"Vic Troisi," I said.

"Vic Troisi?" Robinson said. "Did I fight him?"

"Yes," I said, "you fought him in the Eastern Parkway, and knocked him out in the first round."

"Is that so?" Robinson said.

It was the same with Frank Boucher, another hero of my youth, when he centered a great forward line of the New York Rangers, with the Cook brothers, Bill at right wing and Bun on the left, and they won the Stanley Cup twice. The year after the war ended, Boucher was coaching the Rangers, and he and I got on the subway at the Garden to ride out to Brooklyn, where the team was to practice, and I told him about a remembered youthful embarrassment that I still carried with me after thirteen years.

"In high school," I said, as we sat together on the subway, "I played on the hockey team. We were a terrible team. We won one game and tied one in two years, and one night we played between the periods of a Bronx Tigers game in the Bronx Coliseum. You were refereeing, and in one scramble after a face-off I knocked you down."

Turned toward him, I was watching Boucher's face. I was waiting for some sign of recollection to invade it, to start with a quickening in the eyes and then around them, but nothing was happening.

"When I knocked you down," I said, "the crowd roared, and I wanted to melt into the ice, because I was so ashamed that I had knocked Frank Boucher down, and people were laughing. Do you remember me knocking you down?"

"No," Boucher said, smiling now but shaking his head. "In fact, I don't even remember refereeing that game."

There was no way I could ever be one of them—first the football heroes of high school and then, as I projected myself into manhood, those paragons of the professional sports. When I read the sports pages, though, I discovered that the sportswriters rode on the same trains and lived in the same hotels with the ballplayers and visited the training camps of the prizefighters and knew them man to man. Now the sportswriters acquired an eminence of their own by association with those whom, if my mother had known anything about sports, she would have referred to as "the higher-ups." If you were a German-American family that had survived World War I in this country, when they called sauerkraut "Liberty Cabbage" and changed the name of Wittenberg Place in the Bronx to Bradley Avenue, and if you were not of that arrogant type that had always made trouble for themselves and the world, then you were so humble that all you hoped for your offspring was that he would get a steady job on which he would come to know those who hired and fired.

"He has a very good job," my mother said once, after I had started on the paper and she was telling me about one of my former high school classmates. "He works for the telephone company."

"What does he do?" I asked, wondering if he climbed poles or sat in an office half the size of a gymnasium with half a hundred others, all of them at desks, all of them poring over open ledgers.

"I don't know," she said, "but he's getting to know the higher-ups."

They do not run newspapers the way they run ball clubs, though, because there is a paternalism that contravenes their professionalism. There is no place to trade off old baseball writers who can no longer go into the hole or get the bat around in time to meet the fastball, and so they go on beyond their best days, while their replacements wait in vain to get into the lineup. For two years after college I ran copy, and when I was twenty-four they were still calling me "Boy." For the next four years, before they sent me to report the war, I covered and wrote almost everything from pushcart fires on the Lower East Side to political campaigns, but when I came back from the war I figured I finally had the leverage to get into sports.

We were in Weimar, the birthplace of the Republic that had failed, and it must have been about seven o'clock when I was awakened that morning by a rooster crowing. They had us in two small hotels, and the sun was coming into the room, bright on the flowered rug, and I lay in bed and looked out the open window into the May morning. I could see treetops, the new leaves yellow-green and clean, and through them house tops. I could hear Germans talking and working in the yard below, and I lay in the soft bed between the clean sheets and for the first time in a long time I was empty of fear. On the morning that peace came again to Europe I lay in that bed and it came to me that all of the rest of my life, for however long it would go on, would derive from this morning.

Some years later I asked the oldest son of a Massachusetts shoe worker what it had been like for him when he had awakened in that hotel room in Philadelphia on what must have been his own great and beginning morning. The night before, in the thirteenth round of one of the most vicious of heavyweight title fights, Rocky Marciano had knocked out Jersey Joe Walcott with a single right hand.

"You know how it is when you wake up in a strange place and you don't know where you are?" Marciano said. "I thought to myself, 'Something nice happened to me.' Then I remembered. 'That's right. Last night I won the heavyweight championship of the world.'"

We had the best duty in the war, those of us who by the accidents of age and occupation were picked to report it. The Army provided our transportation and our keep, and we who otherwise might have been carrying rifles and sleeping in foxholes, carried typewriters and slept under roofs even as we pursued our profession. We saluted no one physically, and figuratively only those we felt deserved it. We never had that responsibility that came down from generals to noncoms of sending others where they knew some of them would be killed and others maimed, and so we would never have to live with that for the rest of our lives. Our only responsibility was to order ourselves to go where we could see it, and then to try to tell it as it really was, as those who were being killed and maimed would have wanted to tell it if they could, and not as some of the big-name writers wrote it, or told it on lecture tours, after they came back from junkets on which they were briefed at any Army headquarters or maybe even at some division command post.

"It was a marvelous speech," Harry Markson was telling me, some months after I came back. "You should have heard it."

We had had lunch at Lindy's and were walking west on Fiftieth Street back to Madison Square Garden. Harry was doing publicity then for Mike Jacobs when Jacobs was running boxing in this country, and later Harry would run the boxing at the Garden.

"You know he was a big Roosevelt man," Harry was saying, talking about the writer, "and this was at a Democratic fund-raising luncheon at the Waldorf. I'll never forget it because at one point he said, 'And when your son, your brother, or your husband lands on that foreign beach under fire, and when he finally finds a moment of respite from the shelling and the horror and opens his K-ration, do you know what he finds therein? Among the other things, he finds four cigarettes. Now someone must have thought of those cigarettes. Could it have been F.D.R.?'"

What I said I don't want in this book, and then I said, "If he'd ever landed on a beach or made an attack and opened a K-ration during his moment of respite, he'd have found that the cigarettes were Avalons or Wings, and he wouldn't have mentioned them."

You see, if they didn't get the cigarettes right they weren't going to get any of it really right for the sons and the brothers and the husbands, and for all those who also served by waiting. We despised them while they were doing it, and there was one of us, who tended to be irascible anyway, who became absolutely irate one night when he read in a letter from his wife that she had spent three dollars to listen to a lecture by one of them who had been with us for five days, and that she had found what he had said fascinating. After it was over though, and I was introduced to the cigarette shill, he was so impressed by a magazine piece I had written about Rocky Graziano and so humble and obviously ashamed of all his own work that, reasoning that it was too late to do any good, anyway, I found that I didn't have the heart to level on him.

So we knew what the cigarettes were in the same breakfast issue with the insipid pork-and-egg-yolk, and we learned the mechanics of how war was made on the ground, how attacks were mounted, and how men behaved under stress and great danger—and what they did and how they did it and why. We learned early, of course, the rules of self-preservation, how to analyze a situation map in order to decide where to go and where not to go, and our ears became attuned to the sounds of shelling, the difference between the incoming and the outgoing, so that we were not constantly cowering. When, in late afternoon, we would come back from the front on a day when we had really been out, and not just covering something from the perimeter around regiment or battalion, we would be joyous in the jeep, sometimes even singing, so exalted were we to be still alive.

"What's the matter with you?" John Groth said to me one evening. He had come into my room where I had been trying for more than an hour to write my piece about what I had seen that day. He was doing his drawing and his watercolors then for the Marshall Field publications, and two years later I would take him into Stillman's Gym for the first time and then introduce him to the baseball and thoroughbred-racing people, and he would do those fine things he did on sports.

"The matter?" I said.

"You look terrible," he said. "What's going on?"

"I'm coming apart," I said.

It was late September, and we were inside Germany now. That day several of us had gone up to the Ninth Infantry Division, and a captain named Lindsey Nelson had taken us up to a battalion command post in the Hürtgen Forest. Nineteen years later I was driving north out of Manhattan one night, and when I got on the Major Deegan Expressway in the Bronx, I could see, across the Harlem River, the lights of the Polo Grounds. That was after the Giants had gone to San Francisco and the Mets had moved in, and I turned on the car radio and I heard Lindsey doing the game.

There were two hundred square miles of it in the Hürtgen, the fir trees sixty feet tall and planted ten feet apart in absolutely straight rows. It was a picture forest, and there in the cool, soft, and shaded dampness, in a place that had once known the cathedral quiet that is a forest's own, they were dying between the trees and among the ferns.

"I don't think I can do it any more," I said to John.

"You have to," he said.

"Day after day," I said, "I see those kids going out and sacrificing themselves. They haven't even had a chance to live yet. They're eighteen and nineteen and twenty, and they're giving their lives, and what am I doing for them? They deserve the best writers we have, and except for Hemingway, they're not here."

John had just come back from living for several days with Hemingway in a house he had taken over in the Siegfried Line. They had become friends, and later John would illustrate the Living Library edition of *Men Without Women*.

"I try," I said, "but it isn't any good."

"You can't write *War and Peace* every night," John said. "Nobody can."

"I'm not trying to," I said. "I'm just trying to get it right, but I can get so little of it in."

"Just do the best you can for today," John said, "and tomorrow try again."

"And then every afternoon," I said, "we wave them a hearty farewell, and we leave them up there. We run around with our little notebooks and pencils making a living, and then come back here and leave them to die up there."

"Gee," John said, "you've got it bad. I don't know."

"I don't know, either," I said. "The whole thing is wrong."

"I mean I don't know about you," John said. "You'd better pull yourself together. You know what's going to happen to you if you don't pull yourself together?"

"Who knows?" I said.

"I know," John said. "They'll come around and wrap you up and send you home."

"I'm no psycho," I said.

"You will be if you don't pull yourself together," John said. "You want to be sent home? Then you better stop this. You better just write your piece for today and say to yourself, 'That's that for today and there's another day tomorrow.'"

"There isn't for a lot of them," I said.

"You've got to do that," John said. "You really have to do that."

We talked for another half hour or so, and then John left, telling me again to just take it one day at a time, and I finished my piece, such as it was. It was about how the Germans had all the main roads, and all the crossroads in the forest zeroed in for their artillery, and about how they had the pillboxes hidden among the trees and about the land mines that would explode at knee height and take a man's legs and his masculinity and about the almost invisible trip wires they had strung from tree to tree so that, when they were touched, they would set off a whole chain of explosives.

When I finished I took the piece across the street to where the censors were set up, and I handed it to one of them and I came back and went to bed. I was fortunate that night because there was no way I could have known then that it would take more than three months to get the Germans out of what remained of that forest, and that five infantry divisions and parts of four others would be chewed up and we would suffer thirty-three thousand casualties in there. I was fortunate, too, that I had John Groth for a friend and that he scared me about being sent home, and I lay in bed that night thinking about that and about how odd it was that he should be fathering me because we were always fathering John.

John was the most impressionable of all of us, and he saw everything through the wide, unspoiled eyes of a child. He knew little about the martial art, about troop dispositions or unit actions, and when, now and then, the others of us would get into an argument about where we were going, John would never put in but just come along.

"Wherever you guys are going," he'd say, "it's all right with me."

When we got up to where we were going, and the rest of us were trying to cover our ignorance with professional poses, the way insecure outsiders do when they want to seem to belong, John would ask the simple civilian questions that were the best, but that gave the impression that he had no idea of what was going on.

"But I don't understand," John would ask some major or captain who was filling us in. "Why are you fellows going to do that?"

It was the same two years later, when I took him to Stillman's Gym the first time. After I introduced him to Lou Stillman, I left him standing behind the two rings on the main floor while I went back to the dressing rooms to interview some fighter, probably one who would be fighting in the Garden that Friday night. When I came back out a half hour or so later, John was still standing there and sketching, with the fighters shadowboxing around him and sparring in the raised rings above him.

"How are you doing?" I said.

"I don't know," he said, showing me his notebook and riffling through the pages.

"Hold it a second," I said. "Go back a couple of pages. There. That's Rocky Graziano's right leg, isn't it?"

Graziano toed in with his right foot, and his right leg was slightly bowed. I always figured that that was one of the reasons he was such a great right-hand puncher, and now, with a few quickly scrawled lines on a notebook page, John had captured with absolute definition the one leg that was distinctively different from all the other legs in that gym.

"Who's Graziano?" John said.

"He's the leading contender for the middleweight title," I said. "He's the hottest fighter in years."

"Gee," John said. "He is?"

"Yes," I said, "and he's the reason most of this crowd is here in those chairs and up in the balcony."

"Oh," John said, and then pointing, "it's that fella over there."

"Right," I said. "That's Rocky Graziano."

The next week, when I stopped off at the gym again, Lou Stillman spotted me as I came in. He hollered at me and motioned for me to come over to where he was sitting on the high stool under the time clock and from where he ran the traffic in and out of the two rings.

"Listen," he said, growling at me in what someone once described in print as that ash-can voice, which Lou resented. "You know that beard you brought in here last week?"

"John Groth?" I said.

"Yeah," Lou said. "You know what he done? Two days later he come in here with a whole gang of beards."

"He teaches at the Art Students League," I said.

"Up on my balcony there's a whole gang of beards, all of them drawin'," Lou said. "What are they tryin' to turn this place into, anyway?"

"I don't know," I said. "Ask them."

"You ask them," Lou said. "I ain't got time to bother with them."

The next time I saw John, I told him what Stillman had said. I told him that Stillman had all the fighters cowed, which was the way he kept order in the gym full of them, and I said that some of that carried over to the way he talked to everyone.

"Oh, we get along fine," John said. "You know what Stillman does at home on Sundays? He paints in oil, and we talk about that."

"There are some fighters I know," I said, "who won't believe it."

Lying in that bed, though, that night after John had fathered me, I remembered the time he showed up without his bedroll and slept in my trench coat. I remembered the time I had found him in a barn behind a château in France, drawing in ink with a goose quill. The dampness had affected his drawing paper, so that he couldn't get the lines he wanted with his pens, and he had run down a goose and plucked a couple of quills and sharpened them with a penknife.

"Now I can draw thin lines, thick lines, any kind of lines I want," he said, "but with everything that's going on over here, I don't get enough chance to draw the lines."

There was the time, too, when he was worried that he was going to lose his accreditation because he was supposed to be back at Army Group instead of up with us. Then I remembered the day he was so obviously depressed that I asked him what was wrong, and he showed me the letter he had just received from a friend back home in New York.

"I play volleyball for the Grand Central 'Y,'" John said, "and this guy is on the team, too. He writes here, see, that they got into the semi-finals of the Nationals at Kansas City, and look at this."

With his index finger he pointed out the sentence ending one paragraph: "Al Burwinkle says that if you had been with us we would have won the national championship."

"He's got to be kidding," I said.

"No he's not," John said. "Al Burwinkle is our captain, and if he says we could have won it if I was there, we could have won it."

"Those guys must be on another planet," I said. "They're playing volleyball in Kansas City and you're covering a war in Germany, and they're blaming you because they lost?"

"That's what Al Burwinkle said," John said, and he walked away still depressed.

So each day after the night John scared me about being sent home, I would tell myself that I would just try to do the best I could for that day, and then hope I could get more of it in, and right, the next day. I always lived, though, as most of us did, with that suppressed guilt about the way it was at the front and the way we had it, and with that growing personal fear. Man is born with the illusion that he is immortal, and as every good writer who has gone into man's reactions in war has written, he goes under fire the first time shielded by that illusion and believing that others will be killed but that it will not happen to him. Then it happens, not to him, but so close to him that it could have been to him, and that is the beginning of the fear.

"A good soldier does not worry," Hemingway wrote in his introduction to *Men at War*, the anthology he edited. "He knows that nothing happens until it actually happens and you live your life up until then. Danger only exists at the moment of danger. To live properly in war, the individual eliminates all such things as potential danger. Then a thing is only bad when it is bad. It is neither bad before nor after. Cowardice, as distinguished from panic, is almost always simply a lack of ability to suspend the functioning of the imagination. Learning to suspend your imagination and live completely in the very second of the present minute with no before and no after is the greatest gift a soldier can acquire. It, naturally, is the opposite of all those gifts a writer should have."

That was the problem we had, we who were not soldiers but writers, we who were not ordered by others but had to order ourselves. Each day, two or three to a jeep and with a G.I. driver from the motor pool, we would go up toward the front and stop off at Corps to be briefed on what the divisions were doing, and then we would split up by jeeps and go to one division or another. At Division they would fill us in about what the regiments were doing, and at Regiment what the battalions were doing. Then we would go up to a battalion and sometimes to a company or a platoon until we got what we thought were our stories.

At first, and functioning behind that illusion of immortality, we all bore ourselves as if we were brave, but then, depending upon what happened around us, and to us, and upon our separate abilities to suspend our imaginations, we all came to live in fear. Then it became more difficult to go beyond battalion, and we went less often, and there wasn't a one of us who lived through it who could honestly say to himself that he had covered the war the way he should have. Two I knew, who had been in it too long and whose pieces had become irrational, were called home, and I heard later that, months after it was over, one of them was still walking around New York in uniform and carrying his musette bag. Then, when the Germans broke through during the Bulge, scattering our troops and us in panic, several of us, including the one who had been so irate about his wife buying that lecture by the Five-Day Wonder, took off for Paris and London, and the rest understood. When their replacements arrived, we watched them sally forth behind the shields of their own illusions, as we once had, and then always that thing happened, whatever it was, near them and thus to them, and they too became, like us, cautious in their fear.

The soldier fights the enemy and his fear, and exercises that fear, if it is not so big that he can't handle it, against the person of the enemy. For the writer, implanted weaponless in war, his two personal enemies are his guilt and his fear, and after a while it was only our guilt that sent us out against our fear. We did whatever we did because, knowing what those we left at the front were doing, we were ashamed not to, and if we were honest with ourselves, we knew that all we were doing was trying not just to go on living, but to go on living with ourselves.

If ever there is a time to die in a war, it is not after the issue has been decided. That time came after the bridge across the Rhine was captured at Remagen, and we broke out of the bridgehead on the east bank, and one day, five years later, I was sitting in the Yankee dugout at the Stadium watching batting practice and talking with Ralph Houk. This was when Houk was a second-string catcher with the Yankees and, of course, before he managed them and later the Detroit Tigers, and I knew what he had done in the war. Among other things, during the Bulge he had taken a night patrol in to Bastogne while the Germans had it surrounded, and he had brought out the plans for the defense of the town. During the last week of the 1949 baseball season, though, with the Yankees and the Red Sox wrestling for the pennant in a game at the Stadium, Johnny Pesky had slid home under Houk's tag with the winning run. The next day, all of the New York newspapers, and I suppose the Boston papers as well, carried a photo sequence of the play intended to let the reader make up his own mind as to whether Pesky had been safe or out, and now a lot of people finally knew Houk's name because an umpire had said he had missed a tag in a game.

"You remember Remagen?" Houk was saying in the dugout. We had been talking about the war that had just started in Korea, and Houk had said that he couldn't tell much about it from what he read in the paper, and that got him onto our war.

"Remagen?" I said. "Sure I remember it."

"You remember," Houk said, "how, in the town, there was one road that turned right along the river?"

"I know where you mean," I said. "One day I came back across the river and I was driving along our side, and somebody was working south along the other side. You know the river's nowhere near as wide there as the Hudson, and I could see and hear a firefight going on over there in the trees just south of the bridge."

"You saw that?" Houk said, looking right at me.

"Yes."

"That was me," Houk said. "We had a hell of a firefight there. I'll be damned."

"So will I," I said, sitting there and watching Joe DiMaggio, Yogi Berra, Phil Rizzuto, Hank Bauer, and the others taking their batting practice.

Once they broke out of that bridgehead, though, and the tanks started east, the infantry rode on the tanks or in trucks for miles before they had to dismount, cursing, to clear out the scattered pockets of resistance. Now it was obvious that the Germans were finally beaten, and now the dying seemed sadder than ever. In the residential suburbs of Halle, the birthplace of Handel, they fell among the fallen petals of magnolias, when there was no longer any reason for it. Now the fear, suppressed for so long, of not surviving swept the troops themselves, whole units, and we were all of us one as the time wore down slowly to that new morning.

As I lay in that bed now, on that morning, free again at last, I heard the voices of the Germans in the yard below rising and, although I had no idea what they were saying, I could tell that they were arguing, women's voices among men's. Then the voices of two men began to dominate, as if they had singled out each other, and I thought that maybe this would turn into a fistfight, and I would enjoy seeing Germans fighting among themselves. When I got up and looked down, though, I couldn't see them through the leaves and branches of the trees, and even as I tried to make them out, the intervals between the verbal exchanges became longer and the two voices less assertive, so I went across the hall and washed and shaved. When I came back there were no sounds at all in the yard below, and I dressed and went downstairs and walked, in the cool, clear morning, around the corner to the other hotel where they fed us. We sat there, eating and then smoking with our coffee, and we were all of us loose and lazy and dull, like men who have slept themselves out for the first time in a long while.

Several of us walked back to our hotel together. We got a jeep and a driver from the motor pool, and we drove out of Weimar into the

Thuringian countryside. The lilacs were blooming in the farmyards, and under the yellow of the morning sun the apple trees were white and pink along the sides of the roads. In the rich brown fields the Germans were walking along the furrows, sowing their grain, and we went out to get a story of V-E Day in Germany because it would be the last story and it was a way to end a job.

We drove for almost an hour, following our map and looking for the Third Armored Division, until we saw the tanks in a field on the left. There were four or five divisions that we had come to know well and for whom we had the highest admiration. The Third Armored was one, and so we had decided that we would end the war with them—or what was left of them.

There were seventeen of the tanks parked in the field on the left and along the partial cover of a long gray barn. Across the road on the right the land rose, and on the flat of the rise and forming a quadrangle there were some low, brown wooden barracks of what had been a Nazi youth camp. We could see the tankers walking about and lolling in the sun on the plot of winter-browned grass in the middle of the quadrangle, so we drove up the rise and into the quadrangle.

The lieutenant was the eighth commanding officer the company had had in ten months of fighting, which will give you an idea of what they had been through, and he had the Silver Star and the Bronze Star and the Purple Heart with cluster. His name was Thomas Cooper and he was from Henderson, Kentucky, and we asked him how I Company of the First Battalion of the Thirty-third Regiment of the Third Armored Division had heard the news of the German surrender.

"I got a telephone call from Battalion headquarters at nine ten last night," he said. "I told the first sergeant. He had an old nickel-plated horn from a Kraut car, and he went to the door and blew the horn a couple of times. Then he hollered, 'The war is over. The war is over, you guys. It's official now.'"

"Then what happened?" one of us said.

"Nothing much," the lieutenant said. "We knew for a long time it was gonna be over."

Some of the kids from the company were standing around us as we talked with the lieutenant. Out of the eighty-five who had started out with the I Company in Normandy, there were only six originals left on the day that peace came, and one of the best was a staff sergeant named Juan Haines from Gatesville, Texas.

"This tank of yours," I said to Haines. "What's its name?"

At the beginning, almost all of them gave their tanks names. I wanted to find out if the soldier who went through the war with a tank had any affection for it, if he felt anything about his tank on the day the war ended.

"I don't rightly know," Haines said. "This is the fourth tank we had. We lost three."

"When did your tank fire its last shot?" another of us asked, trying to establish when the war in Europe had really ended for the sergeant and the others in his tank.

"I'll have to think," Haines said.

He was tall and thin and with reddish hair. He stood looking at the ground at his feet.

"It was on the outskirts of Dessau a week or so ago," he said.

"It was April twenty-second," one of the other kids listening said. "We were firing on a pillbox."

"Was the pillbox built against a building," I asked him, "or was it out in the open?"

"It was out in the open," the kid said, "covering a field."

"Did you get the pillbox?"

"Hell, we got 'em all," one of the other kids said.

We turned back to the lieutenant. He had been standing and listening, a little bored by our questions.

"What will you people do now?" I said. "After all, it's V-E Day, and are you going to do anything special?"

"Well," the lieutenant said, "at noon we're going to drink a toast to General Eisenhower. He sent the division champagne after we crossed the Rhine, and there's enough for one glass for each man."

"Then what?"

"We have a ball game on this afternoon," the lieutenant said, "and there's some German museum near here, and one of the platoons will visit that."

We walked around with the lieutenant for a while, looking in at the kids in the barracks. Most of them were lying on their bunks in the barracks, brown uniforms on the brown Army blankets, reading or writing letters, and when we stopped to talk with them they wanted to know if we knew where they were going next, and if they could get home soon. It was strange, having them ask us the questions, and there was one who wanted me to put his lieutenant's name in the paper. He said his lieutenant's name was Loren Cantrell and that the lieutenant came from Springfield, Illinois, and that the kids under him wanted to get him a citation.

We got back into the jeep, and as we started to drive out of the quadrangle we could hear a guitar being played, and we could hear the voice of a G.I. singing. The G.I. was singing that song they retitled "Those Eighty-eights Are Breaking Up That Old Gang of Mine."

They had been a great outfit, the Third Armored, and suddenly in one day they weren't anything that was important any more. Riding along, I thought about how great they had been at Mons where, with the First Infantry Division, "The Big Red One" that had been in it since Africa, they cut off the Germans trying to get back to the Siegfried Line and killed nobody knew how many and took eight thousand prisoners, including three generals. On the day we crossed the German border with them and they took Roetgen, they were the first to capture a German town since Napoleon, and when they breached the Siegfried Line and were pinned down by the shelling on a hillside outside of Stolberg, their general came up, erect, immaculate, and handsome, and got them out of their holes and up the hill.

I remembered them, with their tanks painted white, in the snow and fog of the Ardennes, and then driving across the brown-gray Cologne plain in the mist and the rain and then taking the city, fighting around the cathedral, and knocking out a German tank at the cathedral steps. After they broke out of the bridgehead across the Rhine, I was with them the day they went more than ninety miles behind the German lines. It was the longest single combat advance in the world's military history, and the next evening, in the dusk and on a dirt road outside of Paderborn, their general was killed.

"It can't be him," the young lieutenant said. "I'm sure it ain't him."

"They've identified the body," the major said.

"I sure hope it ain't him," the lieutenant said.

We had spent the night where they had coiled the tanks and half-tracks in a field next to a wood. It was eight o'clock in the morning, and I was standing, talking with some tankers around a fire, when the major called me over and the colonel told us that they had found the general's body. We got our typewriters out of the jeeps and we walked over to a fieldstone farmhouse and we wrote our pieces. I wrote about what the young lieutenant said, and why at first he couldn't believe it, and about the risks the general had always taken and how, two nights before, he had called us over to his CP to tell us that at six o'clock the next morning we would be starting that drive to the north that took us more than ninety miles.

"This thing is almost over now," one of us had said. "When it is, what are you going to do?"

"I have a son," the general had said. "He's four years old now, and I don't know him. We're going to get acquainted, and that's going to take a lot of time."

Now, in the stone farmhouse, we finished our pieces about the death of the general, and they gave us an armed jeep to escort us back around the pockets of Germans who were still holding out. In places on the way back we left the roads and drove across fields and over low hills, following the tracks the tanks and the half-tracks had made, and when we got to Marburg we found the press camp set up in a big private mansion on a hill. We turned our pieces in to the censors, and then gave the rest of them the word that Major General Maurice Rose was dead.

"He was a Jew, wasn't he?" one of them asked me.

"A Jew?" I said. "How would I know? All I know is that he was a great general, and he's dead."

We learned later that he was the son of a Denver rabbi, and that a congressman from Colorado—so far from it all—had stood up in the House of Representatives and made an impassioned speech calling for a congressional investigation into the general's death. To me he was a great general, as two years later, when Jackie Robinson came up to the major leagues, he was a great ballplayer. It should have been as simple as that, and after the general was killed, the Third Armored linked up with the Second Armored, coming down from the north, and they sealed off the Ruhr pocket with 374,000 German prisoners inside.

So we left them now to have their one drink of warm champagne in their tin cups and to their ball game and the visit to the museum, and we drove back between the same brown fields, with the Germans still working in them, and through the same little towns we had passed through coming out. In all of the towns there were duck ponds, and there were white ducks and geese and small yellow goslings paddling around in them. There were young German women wheeling their babies in the sun, and there were other women and children waiting patiently near the doorsteps of their small stone and stuccoed houses. They were waiting for the American trucks to come through, loaded with the German soldiers on the way back to the prison cages.

In one town we stopped to let the trucks go by. The American trucks came through the town quickly, fast and high, and with the dust rising around them and behind them, and with the grinding of their gearing and the noise of their exhaust loud in the tight aisle of the road lined by the small closely packed houses. Ahead of the convoy the women and children had spread, jumping into their doorways as the trucks passed through at high speed, each truck, after the first, fifteen feet behind the one ahead.

In the open trucks the prisoners stood tightly, seventy packed into each half-ton truck. They stood facing the rear, their gray-green uniforms dirty and dust-covered, all of them rocking together with the motion of the trucks, the rush of air from the forward motion blowing at the backs of their heads.

From some of the doorways the women and children threw bread. Some of the men in the trucks managed to catch some of the hard half-loaves, but more often the bread bounced off their hands or bodies or hit the sides of the trucks and then rolled in the dust under the trucks that followed. The women and children who threw no bread just stood, their heads turning back and forth in the doorways, as they tried to recognize in a second in the seas of faces on the trucks someone of whom they had not heard for many months, because they wanted to know if he was still alive now that peace had come to Europe again.

When we got back to the hotel we went into the press room and wrote our last stories. We wrote them quickly, just telling what it was like where we were on V-E Day in Germany and not trying to tell everything that we wished we could tell. For the last time we turned our stories over to the censors, and then we had lunch. After lunch I went back into the press room, and I wrote a cable to Edmond Bartnett, who was my boss on the *Sun*. The cable said: "Hopefully request permission start homeward shortly." That night I got the answer back: "Gladly grant permission for homeward trip. Bartnett."

We had written so hard every day for so long that it was a strange feeling. We did not know how to kill time. We just sat around a lot and talked some about the best moments, but mostly about our homes and our families and about what we might do now. I said that I had wanted to write sports ever since I had been in high school, and the irate one, who had taken off for London during the Bulge but had joined us again for the easier going after the Rhine crossing, said that he had already done that. He said that he had had enough of games and, as he put it, "the spoiled brats who play them." Then one night the word came.

The next morning we walked across the street under the trees with our blankets and our helmets and our canteens and our mess gear, and we turned them in to a lieutenant behind a table set up just inside the doorway of a small one-family house. He gave us our slips of paper for them, and they put us in a weapons carrier, and we rode out to the small airfield on the top of the raised ground.

While we waited for the C-47 to come in, we stood in the shade under the wing of another plane. There was a major there, and he had with him a young pilot in a leather jacket and dark green dress trousers.

"This man has a hell of a story," the major said to me. "You should write it."

The young pilot told me his story, standing in the shade under the wing of the plane. He said he had been shot down over the outskirts of Berlin, and when he parachuted down he landed in the walled garden of a large estate. As he came down in the garden, the S.S. guards grabbed him and took him into the big stone mansion.

"I was standing in the living room," he said. "It was a great big room with a lot of rich furnishings and oil paintings, when the door opens and the big shot walks in. Who the hell is it but Hermann Göring, himself. I recognized him right away from his pictures—a big fat guy with medals."

The young flier said that Göring treated him very well. He said Göring knew a lot about American planes, and then he told me how he was liberated by the Russians, and I told him it was a good story.

"Are you going to write it?" he said. "What paper will it be in?"

"No," I said. "I'm sorry. The war is over. Two months ago it would have been a real good story, and two weeks ago it would still have been a good story. Now I think it's still a good story, but the war here is over, and the day it ended the people stopped wanting to read these stories from here. My own head is filled with good stories, but no one would print them now. I'm sorry about it."

I don't think the young pilot quite understood why I would not write his story. He flew back in the plane to Paris with us, and I noticed that he was watching Victor Bernstein, who was sitting across from him and who had his typewriter on his lap, trying to write a story.

Victor Bernstein came over late, not really to write about the fighting but to write about post-war Europe. He wrote some of the fighting, but now he was doing what he was meant to do, and I realized this as I watched him typing on his knees until the motion of the plane and his concentration on the lines of his typing became too much for him. Then he put the typewriter down and went to the back of the plane and was sick on the floor, and that meant that, for the moment, now even he could not do any writing.

It took us four hours to get back to Paris by plane, and it had taken us eight months when we were going the other way. We sat in the plane trying to look out of the small windows at the country below, trying to recognize something when we flew over beaten towns, realizing now how rapidly we were putting it all behind us, all of the ground that had been taken so slowly and at that great cost.

"Do you remember," I said to Gordon Fraser, "when we said we would go back the way we came?"

Fraser worked for the Blue Network, and we called him "The Little Colonel." I think he could have taken over a regiment, he knew so much about it, and one day during the Bulge when I went up to a company we had all been with some days before, the captain asked me about him.

"How's that little radio fella who was here with you that time?" he said.

"Gordon Fraser?" I said. "He's fine."

"The day after you two were here," the captain said, "he came up alone, and he made the attack with us. The kid carrying the ammo for the machine gun got hit, so your friend picked up the ammo cases and carried them up to the gun. He's a hell of a guy."

If I hadn't known it before, I knew it then, because Fraser had never mentioned it. Years later, when I used to drop in to see him at NBC in New York, where he was working on *Monitor*, I knew the rest of them in that office didn't know what he was or what he had done in the war.

"What we said we were going to do," I said to him, as we looked down out of that plane flying back, "was follow every side road and stop and walk in particular fields and examine hillsides we remember.

We'd go into houses and cellars we slept in, and go over all of it again so we might understand it better and never forget it."

"I know," Fraser said, "but now let's just get home."

There were ten of us in the room on the ship in officer country, but down in the holds they were stacked in bunks four tiers high. There were seven thousand on what, when the Italians had her and called her the *Conte Grande*, had carried a thousand passengers in luxury. Among the seven thousand there were three thousand of what the Army called RAMPs, for Recovered American Military Personnel. They had been shot down over Berlin or captured at Kasserine or in the Ardennes, and they had survived the prison camps at Sagan and Barth and Hammelburg, and they had bad stomachs. They were supposed to be careful about what they ate, but they stood in the chow lines for hours like everyone else, and they ate everything and were sick.

In that room we were just as we had been back in Weimar. We read and slept and played cards for eleven days. We didn't talk about any of it any more, until the last night out when somebody broke out a bottle we didn't know he had been saving and put it on the table—and we heard some truth.

There was one I had traveled with a lot in the jeep because we wanted to see the same things and because he laughed a lot and relaxed me. If we were behind a wall and had to make a run for it, or if we had to go down a stretch of road, he always said the thing that got us out from behind the wall or down the road.

He was a very good mimic, and at night he was our best entertainment. He turned the things that had happened to us during the day into comedy bits, and we spent much time laughing with him. We knew he had been in the Pacific before he joined us in Europe, and now he was sitting with us around the bottle and his voice was rising and cracking.

"For Tarawa we drew lots," he said, "and I got it. I got it, but then I was afraid to go and they got slaughtered, and because I was afraid to go they sent me home."

We did not know what to say. I had had no idea of what he had been carrying, behind those walls and facing those roads, when he got me out. I tried to say something and somebody else said something but it didn't do any good, and so we just let him try to cry it out in our room on the ship coming home.

The next morning when we came through the Narrows, there was a fog over the Lower Bay, and they were lined four deep along the rails. On the starboard side in the last row there were three kids with First Armored patches on their shoulders, and they were looking over toward where you could just make out the parachute jump at Coney Island, and they said they were trying to see the Statue of Liberty. They said they had been captured at Faïd Pass in Africa in February of 1943, and that one of the German guards at Fürstenberg had told them they would never see the Statue of Liberty again, and I told him that the statue would show up off the other side.

"Look, sir," the Marine guard who was standing there said. "I know they want to see the Statue of Liberty. There are seven thousand guys on this ship who want to see the Statue of Liberty, and if I let them all go on that side, this damn thing will tip over."

"But these guys have been prisoners for more than two years," I said.

"We got three thousand of them that were prisoners," the Marine guard said. "What am I supposed to do?"

"Look the other way," I said.

I led them over to the port side, the big ship listing that way now, and all along the rows at the rail you could hear, "Where? Where?" I could just make it out, just a shadow in the fog, and I tried to point it out to the three kids.

"I think I can see it," the one from Illinois said to the other two. "If you'd ever seen it before, I think you could make it out. You see that something a little dark and kind of sticking up in the gray?"

"Yeah, I think I can see it," the one from North Dakota said. "I'm sure I can."

"I'm sure I can, too," the one from Kentucky said. "That's got to be it there."

"That Kraut has got to be dead now," the one from Illinois said.

"Yeah, and we made a liar out of him, too," the one from North Dakota said.

It was eleven days on the end of a long time, and when I reached out to push the bell in the apartment entrance, my finger shook so that I had to breathe deeply and steady it. When the buzzer sounded I kicked the door open and I held it with my body and moved my old black bag and my barracks bag and my typewriter into the lobby.

I stood at the foot of the stairs and I was shaking. I swung the barracks bag onto my back and took the typewriter in one hand and I left the old black bag and I climbed the three flights of stairs. I climbed the stairs as hard as I could to keep from crying, and my wife stood in the doorway. She looked small and frail, and I could not begin to tell her, no less write it. There was so much that had finally ended.

"We're giving you three months' vacation," Keats Speed was saying. I was sitting in his office off the city room on the day after we came up the Bay and you could barely make out the Statue of Liberty if you had seen it before and knew it was there. "We're also giving you a thousand-dollar bonus."

He was the managing editor, and from all I had heard about him and read about him in one or two memoirs, I knew he had once been a great newspaperman. Like the once-great paper, though, and it was now 112 years old five years before its death, Speed was also getting old.

"I thank you," I said. "I didn't expect this."

"You've earned it," he said.

"About the bonus," I said. "A couple of months ago Mr. Bartnett cabled me six hundred dollars for additional expense money, and I still have about three hundred of that left."

"If I were you," he said, "I'd just keep that, and forget about it."

"I thank you again."

"But I've saved the best for last," he said. "Phelps Adams has asked to have you as the second man under him in the Washington office, and I've approved."

How do you tell them? They have put on the party and raised the toasts and now, with the music rising and everyone standing and applauding they bring it in, all decorated and with the candles on it all ablaze. How do you tell them that they must have been thinking of someone else, because that's not your name on it and it's not your cake?

"I don't know how to say this," I said, "because I appreciate everything you're doing and the Washington offer. The trouble with me is that, since I was a kid, I've always wanted to be around athletes and write sports. Covering the war, where the material was so dramatic, I think I started to learn how to write. I want to continue to learn, and writing sports, where men are in contest, if not in conflict, and where you can come to know them, one can grow as a writer better than anywhere else on the paper."

"But we don't want you to write the hard news in Washington," he said. "We want you to do features."

"I'm sorry," I said, "but for me it just wouldn't be like being in sports."

"There are no openings in the sports department," he said.

"I was afraid of that," I said. "I guess I'll just have to wait and hope."

"When you come back from vacation in September," he said, "report to Mr. Bartnett again in the city room."

He was no longer looking at me. That handsome, aristocratic head, the gray hair smoothed precisely back, was lowered and he was looking at some papers on his desk.

"Yes, sir," I said, "and thank you again for everything."

All that summer, while my wife and I bicycled from New York City to twenty-five miles from the Canadian border, and lived in a cabin on the east shore of Lake Champlain where only the lightning storms that sounded like artillery landing in a town bothered me, I wondered and worried about how I could do it again in the city room. I didn't see how I could stand it, covering the routine court cases and fundraising luncheons and doing rewrite on fires and hold-ups and updating wait-order obits and meeting the Twentieth Century Limited with some Midwestern politician or musical conductor or Hollywood star on it. I would never really get to know any of them or any of it, or get to grow as a writer.

I fully expected that on that first day back in the city room I would find at my desk, as a starter, a sheaf of publicity notices to be ground down, each one, into a B-head, which is what we called a one-paragraph item. There was nothing on my desk, however, and for more than an hour I just sat there, reading the morning papers while around me the others rewrote the publicity or took the phone calls from the leg-men covering the districts or suddenly got up, folding copy paper into a pad as they started for the door.

It occurred to me, sitting there and reading in the morning papers, news that really didn't interest me but that I had to prep myself on in case I should be assigned to the story, that perhaps Ed Bartnett was hesitating to send me out, or to have me take the first phone call, on the first routine story. He was, and still is I am sure, a reserved but kind man, and I wondered if, because I had covered D-Day and then, after the liberation of Paris, all of it on the drive east into Germany and the fighting and the Hürtgen and the Bulge and then, finally, the meeting with the Russians on the Elbe, he was embarrassed and reluctant to reassign me to the prosaic. When, finally, he called me over, he said he wanted me to do a piece on the control tower at La Guardia airport, so I called there and made an appointment for one o'clock that afternoon. I had just hung up, and I was assuring myself that it could be worse, when I felt a hand on my shoulder and it was Wilbur Wood.

"Get out of here," he said. "I've just talked to Speed again, and he's letting me have you. You're now in sports."

"You're not kidding?" I said.

"Follow me," he said. "I'm your new boss."

"In a minute," I said.

I walked over to the City Desk and told Ed Bartnett. He said that he'd just heard it and that he was sorry to lose me but that he knew that was what I wanted. I told him about the one o'clock appointment at La Guardia, and he told me to give that to Millie Faulk, who had the desk next to mine. When I did she said something, kidding, about the cushy jobs in sports. I took my automatic address finder, with the phone numbers of the American Dental Association and the District Attorney's office and the Bronx Zoo that I wouldn't need any more, out of my desk and walked out of the city room and down the hall and into sports.

"You had better go up and see Lou Little," Wilbur Wood was saying now at his desk. "We need some football in the paper, and if you're going to write sports in this town he's one guy you should get to know well."

"That's fine with me," I said. "Whatever you say."

"You won't have any trouble," Wilbur said. "He's a very nice guy."

"From what I've read about him," I said, "I expect so."

I went over to a phone and called Lou Little at Columbia. He said I should come up to see him at the field at three o'clock, and although he was being friendly I could tell that he had never heard of me. While we were writing the war, I guess we all thought that everyone should be reading everything we wrote because we had never had such material and we had never written so well. In New York alone, though, there were nine papers then, and we should have remembered that.

At two o'clock I took the subway and it is a long ride to Baker Field where the Columbia football team practices and where it plays its home games. The subway comes out into the open and goes down into the ground again. You ride to the end of the Eighth Avenue Line, and after I became bored with reading the paper I realized that I was nervous about meeting Lou Little.

After all, he was a famous football coach, and I was just starting to write sports. I did not know the things I should know about him, but I could remember that New Year's Day of 1934, when I was just out of high school and wanting to be a sportswriter, and I sat by the radio in a corner of the living room listening to the Rose Bowl game.

It had said in the newspapers that the California sportswriters had been referring to Columbia as "Pomona High School in light blue jerseys," and when Columbia beat Stanford, 7–0, it became one of the great upsets in football history and, of course, a major professional accomplishment for Lou Little. Almost twelve years later, they were still referring to it, and to KF-79, the naked reverse with which Columbia scored its touchdown.

At the end of the subway I followed the directions they had given me at the office. The afternoon was warm, even for early September, and I walked along the sidewalk with the hilly park on the left. In the park the leaves were turning yellow and the grass drying, and I walked by the small narrow stores and the used car lot and the gas station and turned left up the hill where, across the street and on the right, the chain-link fence runs around the field.

I crossed the street and looked for a gate in the fence until I saw one that was open and walked in past some green wooden barracks. I walked around the end of the barracks and along one side under some elms. There were two college kids with books under their arms walking ahead of me and they went through a doorway into the barracks, and when I came to the doorway I followed them.

There were metal lockers around the walls of the room and there were about a dozen kids undressing in front of them. They were talking in loud voices and kidding back and forth, and I walked around the room and down a hall and looked into a smaller room with white walls and with a rubbing table in the middle and a long wooden bench along one wall.

A couple of kids were sitting naked on the bench and there was another sitting on the rubbing table. There were two men working on the kid on the table, each bandaging an ankle. One of the men was thin, with an Irish face and wearing a white linen cap like Ben Hogan used to wear. The other was rather stout and with white bushy hair and a rather florid face. There was some talk going on in the room.

"You're an athlete?" the large man with the white hair was saying to the kid on the table. "You're an athlete, my elbow. A man of my years and experience and the great athletes I've handled, and at this stage of my life they send me children. You're no athlete."

The kid sitting on the rubbing table was grinning and winking at the kids sitting on the bench along the wall. I waited for the talk to quiet.

"Excuse me," I said, "but is Lou Little around?"

"He hasn't come in yet."

It was the large man with the white hair who answered. He had stopped bandaging, and he had turned his head and was looking at me out of the tops of his eyes. I told him who I was and he said he was Doc Barrett, and I recognized from his name that he was the head trainer. He introduced me to the other whose name was Jimmy Judge.

"How's Will Wedge?" Barrett said.

"He's all right," I said. "He's covering the Yankees."

"Don't you think I know he's covering the Yankees?" Barrett said. He was looking at me again out of the tops of his eyes. "Don't you think I read your paper every night?"

"I'm glad you do."

"How long you been writing sports?"

"I've just started."

"You want to know something?"

"Yes."

"Read Will Wedge," Barrett said. "You'll be all right if you write like Will Wedge. He's a good writer."

"Yes, he is."

"He could write a book. He's a learned man. He's a gentleman. He comes up here a lot. He wrote a good story about me once."

"I'm sure he did."

He looked at me again in that same way, studying me.

"Will Wedge is not a knocker," he said. "He doesn't knock people. There's too many sportswriters knocking people. What do they think they are? You don't have to tell me. I know them. Their noses still run. They come up here and sit around and yes people. They're such timid little men. They ask you for favors, and they can't even wipe their own noses, and you're nice to them and then they go back and knock you."

He tried to show disgust in his face.

"I'd like to punch them in the nose," he said. "If I wasn't associated with a fine and respectable institution, I'd punch them in the nose. Who do they think they are anyway?"

"I don't know," I said.

They had finished with the boy on the table, and he got up and another boy climbed up and lay down. It was quiet in the room for the moment.

"What kind of a team are you going to have this year?" I said.

"How would I know?" Barrett said, looking at me again. "We don't know anything in here. You can come in here if you want, but you won't learn anything. If there's anything you want to know, you'll have to ask Lou Little. Lou Little does the talking around this club."

"That's all right with me," I said.

There was a man standing in the doorway, and I presumed he had been listening. He seemed to be in his mid-forties, but he was well built and only starting to get soft. He had on a dark blue suit and a blue shirt and a dark blue tie.

"Excuse me," he said. "Is Lou Little around?"

"He's not in yet," Barrett said, looking up from his work and at the man.

"I played fullback here in 1921," the man said. He had walked into the room and he was standing in front of Barrett and he put out his hand. "My name's Charley Appleton."

"Don't you think I know?" Barrett said, stopping his work and shaking hands. "I don't forget a face. How are you?"

He introduced the man named Appleton to Jimmy Judge. He went back to his work, and I walked outside and back into the locker room and I waited around there. After a while Appleton came out and stood there until Lou Little came in.

I recognized Lou Little, with his large nose, from all the pictures and cartoons I had seen of him. He had two boys with him, and he led them down the hall to where there was a Dutch door with the top half open, and I could hear him talking in a husky voice to someone in the room beyond the door while the two boys stood in back of him.

"Fit these gentlemen out with uniforms," he was saying. "These gentlemen are going to play a little football for us."

When he walked back toward us Appleton walked up to him. He stuck out his hand and Little took it.

"Can I have a uniform too, coach?" Appleton said.

"Sure," Little said, looking at him, "but you're a little heavy, aren't you?"

"That's right. My name's Charley Appleton, and I played fullback here in 1921. You weren't here then."

"Sure," Little said.

"Next year is our twenty-fifth anniversary," Appleton said. "What I want to know is if I can borrow a jersey to be photographed for a little book we're getting out."

"Sure," Little said. "One of the boys here will fit you with a jersey, and take a helmet too. Want a helmet?"

"Yes. A helmet would be fine too. The photographer is right out here."

"That's all right," Little said.

He started to walk through the locker room, and I stopped him and introduced myself and we shook hands. I could tell that he still thought that maybe he should know me.

"I'm glad to see you," he said. "Come up any time."

I followed him into the small room where several other coaches were getting out of their clothes, and he introduced me to Buff Donelli and Tad Wieman and Ralph Furey and a couple of others. Then he started to undress in front of his locker, and I was impressed by his flawless taste in clothes. Everything was a shade of tan, trousers, sports jacket, shirt, suspenders, tie, shoes, and socks.

"What can I tell you?" he said after a while, looking at me.

I was sitting on a stool near his locker.

"I'm not sure," I said. "I just thought I would come up and write a story telling what a practice is like. I think it might tell some people something they don't know."

"That will be all right."

"You know," I said, "coming up here I was remembering something. I was remembering when I was just out of high school and sitting by the radio in our living room and listening to you beat Stanford in the Rose Bowl. I can still see that radio in the corner. That was a big thrill, and I'll never forget that game."

"I'll never forget it either," he said.

He was pulling on a pair of baseball pants and then a sweatshirt, and I was still ill at ease, because he was Lou Little and I was still new at this. I wanted him to accept me, and I did not want him to be aware of my ignorance, and finally I asked him about his team and he named off some names which I wrote down.

"My line isn't much," he said. "I've got two or three good backs who can run, though, and I like some of the boys I'm getting from our Naval R.O.T.C. They're bigger and better football players than our V-12 boys. Our V-12 boys were all right, but they were mostly pre-med and pre-engineers, which means they were smart enough, but they weren't always football material, if you know what I mean."

"Yes," I said, "I know what you mean."

"Some of our backs are out there now," Buff Donelli said.

He was coaching the Columbia backs then. He was wearing a pair of black shorts and a white T-shirt, football shoes and white woolen sweat socks, and he was standing by the open door that looked out onto the practice field.

"I guess they're ready," Lou Little said. "We might as well go."

He turned to me.

"Come out on the field," he said. "Watch us work as long as you want, and if there's anything else you want to know, you can ask me when we come in."

They left the dressing room, and I followed them out under the elms and onto the field. The sun was starting to get well down now and it was beginning to cool a little. On the field the kids in the light blue jerseys were kicking and passing footballs back and forth. There was the sound of the footballs against shoes and the sound of their shouting, and when Lou Little blew a whistle they stopped what they were doing and ran to him and formed a semicircle in front of him.

Lou Little talked to them for a while in that husky voice, and he kept it low. I did not stand close enough to hear what he was telling them, but after a while they turned from him and joined into groups and spread around the field. I walked to the far end of the field and watched and listened while Little and Donelli worked with the backs.

"Look, look," Little was saying to one of them who had just thrown the ball. "Don't just stand there. When you're not ready to throw it, don't just stand there. Keep moving around. Move around. Move around."

The player was just a kid. He couldn't have been more than five feet nine or have weighed more than 165 pounds. He had his helmet off, and he had dark curly hair and dark eyes. As Little talked to him he listened carefully, nodding his head, and a few minutes later Donelli was shouting at him.

"Hey!" Donelli was shouting, running up to him, when the play had stopped. "What's the reason you're always bumping into him? You've got no reason to be bumping into him. You're supposed to take two steps and then drop back. You're not supposed to be anywhere near him, but you're bumping into him all the time."

After I had watched for a while longer I walked over to the bench at the sideline near midfield, where Doc Barrett and Jimmy Judge were sitting. Doc Barrett introduced me to Dr. Stephen Hudack, the team physician, and I sat down near them. I was listening to their talk when one of the student managers came running across the field.

"Jimmy!" he was calling, "Mr. Little wants to see you, Jimmy!"

Jimmy Judge got up and ran out onto the field. When he came back he had one of the players with him. It was not the little kid with the dark wavy hair and the dark eyes, but an older one, husky and with his black hair starting to thin in the front.

"He's sick," Jimmy Judge said to Dr. Hudack, motioning with his head toward the player.

"You're sick?" the doctor said, standing up and looking at the player. "What's the matter, son?"

"I don't know," the player said. "I get all congested and spit up cotton, and then I start to feel sick to my stomach."

He was standing in front of the bench in his soiled uniform, his face pale and the drops of perspiration on it and on his neck. He had his helmet in his hands.

"Have you been sick lately, or have you had a cold?" the doctor said.

"No," the player said, shaking his head.

"Do you have any idea what it might be?"

"Well," the player said, "I think I may have T.B."

"You think you may have T.B.?" the doctor said. "T.B.? What makes you think you may have T.B.? Is there any T.B. in your family?"

"No, sir, there isn't," the player said.

"Then what makes you think you have T.B.?"

"Well, sir," the player said, "I drank some raw milk."

"You drank some raw milk?" the doctor said, looking right at the player. "Don't you know better than to drink raw milk? Don't you know that you should boil raw milk before you drink it?"

"Yes, sir."

"Then why didn't you boil it? Why didn't you boil the milk?"

"You see, sir," the player said, slowly, "I was in a German prison camp for fifteen months. Once all we had was raw milk."

We were all looking at the player. Then I looked at the doctor.

"Oh," the doctor said, and I could see and hear him soften. "Oh. Is that so?"

"Yes, sir," the player said.

"Were you sick in the camp?"

"Sometimes. I lost forty-one pounds, but I got it all back."

"So," the doctor said. "Well now, you're going to be all right. I think maybe you're just pressing too hard. I think you're just trying to do too much. Too much exercise isn't too good for you. I'll tell you what we'll do. You come in to see me tomorrow morning, and I don't think you should do any more today."

"Yes, sir," the player said. "Thank you."

He started back toward the barracks, but I stopped him and introduced myself and I talked with him for three or four minutes. He said he had been a gunner on a Flying Fortress and that he had been shot down over northern Italy.

"You'll be all right," I said.

"I hope so," he said.

"You'll be fine," I said.

He walked back to the barracks and I walked out onto the field and I found Lou Little. I told him I thought I had better get back to the office, and then it came to me that he might wonder what I would write about. I didn't want him to think that I was lazy or careless, leaving so early during the practice.

"One of your players was just sick," I said. "I mean the one you sent back with Jimmy Judge, and it turns out he was in a German prison camp for fifteen months."

"He was?" Lou Little said. "Is that so?"

"Yes," I said, "and I think I'll write something about that."

"Fine," Lou Little said. "Good. Come up any time."

"Thank you," I said.

"Any time," he said.

Riding back downtown on the subway I started to put together in my mind the piece I would write describing the practice. I would have to work the contrast between the little kid with the curly hair and brown eyes listening so carefully while Little and Donelli lectured him, and the older one coming off the field and, when the doctor asked him what he thought his trouble was, saying he might have T.B. I would have to show somehow without saying it that, at first, the doctor had been a bit patronizing, and then even incredulous when he heard about the raw milk, before he learned that the player had been a prisoner of the Germans, because that should be the way it should come to the reader, too, if I could get that dialogue—the pauses and the emphasis—just right.

The name of the little kid was Gene Rossides, and the older one was Vince Pesature. Rossides was still some weeks away from being eighteen, and during the next four years he became one of the best of all Columbia backs. In his first game he ran eighty yards for one of the three touchdowns he scored, and on a number of Saturday afternoons I sat in press boxes and watched him pull games out. One October afternoon two years later I watched his passes and Bill Swiacki's catches end by 21–20 Army's string of thirty-two games without defeat, and this was almost as important to Columbia and Lou Little as their Rose Bowl game.

Vince Pesature was never much of a football player, and I saw him play only once, late in a one-sided game. What he did in that game I don't remember, but I remember that once he was in a German prison camp and a year later I saw him at Baker Field. He was trying to make the Columbia football team, and he was standing on the sidelines, coughing up a little cotton and saying that sometimes he felt a little sick and that he thought he might have T.B. from drinking raw milk.

And I was writing sports. About a month later I was on the field at the Polo Grounds, where John McGraw, Christy Mathewson, Babe Ruth, Ty Cobb, Honus Wagner, Frankie Frisch, Red Grange, Bronko Nagurski, and dozens of the other heroes of my youth had performed. I was watching the New York Football Giants practice, as I would do every Tuesday morning during the football season. I would be at the Polo Grounds at ten o'clock, and I would stand around there, watching Steve Owen coach the team. I looked forward to those Tuesday mornings because Steve Owen was a big, open, and honest man, and I was trying to appreciate his problems and the problems of his players. After practice I would go into the locker room and talk with him and with his players, and sometimes I would go to lunch with him.

We would sit in a darkened pseudo-Spanish restaurant on Forty-third Street between Fifth and Sixth avenues, with its decorative wall tiles and archways and wrought-iron railings, and he would tell stories about the early days of professional football. After lunch I would walk back with him to Forty-second Street, where he would go up to the Giants' office to work out his problems, and I would take the subway downtown to work on mine.

On this morning it was cold, but the air was clear and the sun was shining. The Giants were running through passing plays in deep right field near the outfield wall with the signs, painted on the dark green, advertising razor blades and hot dogs and ice cream. Steve Owen was standing with his hands in his hip pockets talking to several of us and watching Arnie Herber throw the ball.

Herber threw a pass to an end named Hubert Barker. It was deep and Barker ran for it, but when he was about to run into the wall where the sign advertised Gem blades, he slowed and the pass went over his outstretched hands.

"What are you scared of, Barker?" Owen said, shouting at him. "What are you scared of?"

"He's scared of the five o'clock shadow," Bert Gumpert, who wrote sports for the *Bronx Home News*, said.

Owen turned to Bill Abbott. Abbott was the publicity man for the Giants, and Owen asked him for a copy of the team roster. When Abbott gave it to him Owen ran a finger down the list of players.

"Take this McNamara off the list," Owen said to Abbott, and he was talking about Edmund McNamara, a tackle from Holy Cross. "I just sold him to Pittsburgh."

"In other words," Gumpert said, "McNamara's banned."

"He's a pretty nice kid," Owen said. "He has the Silver Star, and they needed tackles more than we do, and I like to give those war kids jobs."

That was how Abbott got to explaining about Marion Pugh. Marion Pugh was one of Owen's good backs, and before that he had been a star at Texas A&M. I could remember hearing another broadcast of another game, and Ted Husing was doing the game and he talked a lot about Pugh. He kept calling him Dukey Pugh, and Husing had a resonant voice and afterwards the name kept running around in my mind . . . Dukey Pugh . . . Dukey Pugh . . . Dukey Pugh.

"A year ago he was fighting in Europe," Abbott said. "He had a company of tank destroyers. He was wounded twice and got the Bronze Star."

"You should talk to him," Owen said to me. "You might get a story."

After the players had finished running through their plays he had them run up and down the field a couple of times, and then he sent them to the showers. When Pugh came down the old, worn wooden steps from the shower room he was still drying himself, and he walked across the room to his locker. As he started to dress I walked over and introduced myself and stood talking with him.

"They tell me you were in Europe?" I said.

"That's right," he said.

"Where were you?" I said.

"Oh, from France all the way into Germany."

"What outfit were you attached to?"

"The Second Division and the Fourth."

"Is that right? I was with both of them."

"Also the Twenty-eighth."

"Were you with the Twenty-eighth when they were in the Hürtgen Forest?" I said. "I mean that time they were chewed up at Schmidt and Kommerscheidt?"

Marion Pugh was not large for a professional football player. He was rather slim, but nicely muscled. He had started to pull on a pair of slacks, but he stopped and straightened up.

"You know something?" he said, looking at me. "You're the first guy I've met who has even heard of those places."

We stood in the locker room of the Polo Grounds and talked about one of the bad beatings the Americans took in the war. Schmidt and Kommerscheidt were two small towns in a break in the Hürtgen, and the German attack there was a prelude, a first step by which they positioned themselves for their breakthrough later in the Bulge.

"I lost eleven of my twelve T.D.'s in that," Pugh said, and it is what tank destroyers are called. "We were cut off for six days."

"I remember one thing about it in particular," I said. "There were some wounded Americans cut off in a forester's cabin in the woods, and we were trying to get to them. I wrote a story about it, and I also remember that that was the day we had our first snow."

"I was in that cabin," Pugh said, looking at me again. "That's an odd thing. I was in that cabin."

We had been, with Germans between us, not much more than the length of a football field apart, and now he stuck out a finger. He showed me the scar on it.

"They ambushed my jeep," he said, "and we jumped out and hid in some bushes in the dark. A German was probing through the bushes with his bayonet, and it went right through my finger."

"I'd say you're lucky," I said.

"You're telling me?" he said.

"That was just about a year ago, too," I said. "I think it was right about now."

"No," Pugh said. "It was November fifth. I'll never forget that."

Around us the other players had finished dressing and Steve Owen was calling them together. They were preparing to play Boston on the following Sunday, and Owen was going to show them the movies of the Boston game of the previous year.

The players pulled the wooden folding chairs up in front of a small movie screen set up in the middle of the old locker room. Somebody turned out the lights, and when the film started and the titles came on the screen, there was the date. Marion Pugh and I sat side by side in the darkness in the locker room in the Polo Grounds, and we read on the screen that the game had been played the previous year on November 5.

"I'll be damned," Marion Pugh said.

Five weeks later the Giants played the Eagles in the mist and rain in Philadelphia. The Eagles won easily, 38–17, and after the game the Giants, hurting and sullen and silent, had crowded into the bus. Now the bus was moving, halting, and then moving again through the honking traffic of a Sunday evening and over the wet streets between Shibe Park and the North Philadelphia station.

"Kilroy," somebody said. "Kilroy is the guy who did it."

"How bad is it?" somebody else said. "Is it broken?"

"They don't know," one of the players who had been the last to crowd into the bus said. "They're trying to get a cast on it so they can carry him home."

They were talking about Marion Pugh. Near the end of the game he had just completed a pass and Frank Kilroy, the 240-pound Eagle tackle, had hit him. When they had gone down, Pugh had folded forward in a peculiar position so that he was half on top of Kilroy.

Four players had had to carry Pugh off the muddy field. He had been half lying and half sitting in their arms, and from the press box and through my field glasses I had been able to see his face and he had been grimacing with the pain.

When they had brought Pugh into the dressing room they had placed him on one of the rubbing tables, and then they had looked at his leg and had tried to take off his uniform. Every time they had moved him the muscles of his face had tightened and he had shut his eyes, but finally they had got him out of his uniform and dressed him in his street clothes. He had been sitting there with his leg stretched out on the rubbing table when he had looked up and seen me.

"Hey!" he said. "How are you?"

"That's not the question," I had said. "How are you?"

"The way they were coming at me out there," he had said, "I thought I was back at Kommerscheidt."

Behind me now in the crowded bus George Franck was talking. He had been an All-American halfback at Minnesota and he had flown for the Marines in the Pacific, and he was talking to Mel Hein, the All-Pro center.

"When I was shot down over Wotje," Franck was saying, "I was going to kill myself."

"You were going to *kill* yourself?" Hein said.

"Rather than let those bastards get their hands on me," Franck said, "I was going to put a slug through my own head."

"Good God!" Hein said.

I wasn't seeking them, but when I found them I could not ignore them. They were a part of America and of a world in transition, and one Friday night about three weeks later I was walking down the hallway under the main arena seats on the Fiftieth Street side of Madison Square Garden. It was about eight o'clock, with the crowd starting to come in, and Bob Mele, a fight manager from New Haven, was standing outside one of the dressing rooms they used for preliminary fighters. He was smoking a cigarette and he said he had two fighters in the four-round bouts that night, two brothers named Joe and Jimmy Rogers.

"They were on the *Juneau* when she was sunk," he said.

The *Juneau* was a light cruiser, and when it had gone down in the Pacific it had taken the five Sullivan brothers with it, and that had become a part of the history of the war. Mele was saying now that there had been four Rogers brothers on it, too, and that Pat and Louie had been lost and Joe and Jimmy had had to swim for it, and now they were waiting to fight in the Garden.

"It's a good thing for them," he said. "All the time after they came back they kept talking about Pat and Louie. Pat and Louie were better fighters than these two, and they thought about them all the time. Now they've got their minds on this, and it's a good thing."

"Do you mind if I go in and talk to them?" I said.

"No," he said. "They're a little nervous, you know, about being in the Garden, and it'll probably help them relax a little."

There were several other fighters and their handlers in the room. The Rogers brothers, in their ring trunks and blue satin robes, were sitting together on one of the benches and Mele introduced me. I did not want to ask them about the *Juneau*, but if I were going to write about them I would have to, and so I told them I was sorry about their loss and I asked them how the four brothers happened to be on the same ship.

"We enlisted together right after Pearl Harbor," the one named Joe said. "When the war started we said let's get into it together and take care of one another. We didn't know a damn thing about war. How are you gonna take care of one another on a ship like that?"

I was hoping very much that they would turn out to be good fighters, at least good enough to win their bouts. Joe went on first, before the main event, and when they called him, Jimmy walked out with him and then stood at the top of the aisle, trying to see over the heads. It was a slow fight, with the crowd, impatient for the main event to come on, booing, and when Joe lost the decision and came back up the aisle, Jimmy threw an arm around Joe's shoulders.

"You did all right," he said. "You did okay."

"You do it," Joe said. "I couldn't get my hands up in there, but you do it."

Jimmy went on in the walk-out bout after the main event, with the Garden emptying now. For whatever reason, the few who stayed got to rooting for Jimmy's opponent, and when Jimmy lost the decision and came up the aisle where Joe was waiting, there was a loudmouth hollering at him.

"Go back to New Haven," he was hollering. "You're a bum!"

I walked back to the dressing room with them and said I was sorry that they hadn't won, and I wished them luck. They thanked me and we shook hands and I walked out of the dressing room and out of the war again. Some of what I walked into, some of what I came to know about those I came to know, is what follows in the rest of this book.

★ ON THE BEAT ★

Memories of a Great Jockey

George M. Woolf, 1910–1946

IN FRONT of an open fire in a pine-paneled room in Aiken, South Carolina, Ed Christmas was wording the obituary of Georgie Woolf.

Georgie Woolf was killed a year ago at Santa Anita. They used to think something other than blood ran through him and they called him "The Iceman" and he was really one of the best.

"I have never been able to understand that," someone said. "As I read about it he was all alone and there was no one near him so I suppose he must have blacked out."

"No," Ed said. "I can tell you what happened. I can tell you exactly what happened.

"The horse was last," he said. "He had it in behind but you know how he used to ride."

He bent over where he sat on the sofa and he had his hands up close in front of him.

"That boy had a natural seat," he said. "You know what I mean when you see these other boys, but when Georgie rode 'em—hell, he didn't, he didn't lay on 'em and he was over like this—"

He hunched over even more and he tapped his chest.

"There wasn't more than this," he said, indicating with his thumb and his forefinger, "between him and the horse's withers and when

---

New York *Sun*, March 25, 1947.

he brought the horse up—like this—the head come up and it caught him right here."

He straightened up and placed his hand under his chest and looked around.

"When it hit him," he said, "he went right up in the air—like this—and when he come down his head hit the pole right here on the left.

"They knew he was a goner," he said, "when they got to him and picked him up. His wife wanted to go to him but they wouldn't let her see him like that and he never regained consciousness."

"I wondered," someone said. "I wondered about that."

"Man, he could ride," Ed Christmas said, and he waited a moment and shook his head. "You know, people didn't like him, a lot of them didn't."

"I know," someone said.

"They didn't understand him," Ed said. "He was a sick boy."

"I know."

"That boy had diabetes," Ed said. "People didn't know that. Why, when we'd drive out to the track in the morning he'd sit there, with his head down like this, and I'd say, 'Georgie, you all right?' 'Yeah,' he'd say, 'I'm all right.' His wife carried insulin and he'd take that and he'd be all right.

"They used to say," he said, "that he had a swelled head because he wouldn't take this horse or that. Hell, all he wanted to do was ride and he'd take every horse in every race if he could. He was a sick boy.

"He was a peculiar boy in some ways, but I understood him. He used to tell me his troubles and I guess I knew him better than anybody and I guess I understood him.

"You know," he said, smiling, "he come from Canada, and they ask him the date of the Revolutionary War and he said, 'The Revolutionary War? I can't tell you that, but I know the date of the next meeting.'

"I remember," he said, "the day he won the Futurity with Occupy. After the race I see him taking his shower and he says he will see me that night, and that night he comes to my room in the hotel and he's all excited and like a kid.

"It seems they had a pony race that afternoon for some of them older jockeys like Earl Sande and him. He's laughin' and talkin' and tellin' me about this race and I said, 'Hey, what the hell is a pony race when you win sixty-five hundred dollars this afternoon?' 'I'm not talkin' about winnin' money,' he says. 'I'm talkin' about racin'.'

"He knew a guy," he said, "back in the woods was a crack rifle shot. He talked about him all the time and he thought he was the greatest guy in the world."

He looked around at those with him.

"Man, he could ride," he said. "He'd lay back there and he'd kill those other horses in the stretch. You remember? He'd drive with those hands open like this and when you'd see those fingers go out, boy, you knew he was starting to go."

He stopped for a moment as if he were seeking something more to say.

"He was a rider," he said.

Beau Jack Is Good Customer

"Ah'm Buyin' Hats . . ."

THIS IS a prizefighter's dressing room. It is about ten feet long and half as wide and, because he is fighting Terry Young at Madison Square Garden on Friday night, in this case it belongs to Beau Jack.

"Hey!" Chick Wergeles says as he sees a newspaperman standing in the doorway. "The Beau is buying us all hats."

The Beau, in his boxing shoes and wearing a white shirt, is sitting on a stool, a fedora on his head. Sid Bell, his trainer, is leaning against the rubbing table. Chick, his manager, is leaning against the wall. There is one other, in a sweater, standing in the middle of the little room, and he has a pencil and paper in his hands.

"That's right," the Beau says smiling. "Ah'm buyin' hats."

He looks up at the man with the pencil and paper.

"This all right," he says, touching the hat. "This fine."

"All right," the man says. "What color do you want?"

"What color?" the Beau says. "What color kin ah have?"

"Listen," the man says. "You can have any color you want."

"Kin ah have gray?" the Beau says.

"Certainly," the man says. "Do you want gray?"

"Yeah," the Beau says. "Not too light gray."

"Kind of a medium gray," the man says.

New York *Sun*, February 18, 1948.

"Yeah," the Beau says, smiling. "Kind of a medium gray."

"Good," the man says.

"Yeah," the Beau says, looking up at the man, "but you don't have no brown. That right?"

"Brown?" the man says. "Certainly I have brown. I have any color you want. Do you want brown?"

"Yeah," the Beau says, smiling. "Ah like brown. Not too dark brown."

"A medium brown," the man says, writing, "instead of a medium gray."

"Yeah," the Beau says, "but ah want gray, too. One brown and one gray. Kin ah have that?"

"Certainly," the man says. "You can have anything you want. You want two hats, one gray and one brown."

"That right," the Beau says, "but you don't have no green. That right?"

The man looks at Wergeles and at Bell and he shrugs his shoulders. Then he looks at the Beau.

"Certainly I have green," he says. "I said I have any color you want. If you want green you can have green, too."

"Yeah," the Beau says, smiling. "That right."

"Listen," Wergeles says, and he takes the man by the arm. "Don't put that down."

He turns to the Beau, who sits on the stool looking up at him.

"Listen," he says. "You don't want green."

"Oh yeah," the Beau says. "Ah like green. Green ah like."

"Listen," Wergeles says. "You got gray and you got brown. How many hats do you want?"

"Three," the Beau says, smiling. "Ah want three. Ah want one for every suit."

"Listen," Wergeles says. "We won't be getting those suits for a long time. Forget the green."

"Ah get mah suit," the Beau says, smiling. "Ah get mine."

"Okay," Wergeles says, and he turns to the man with the pencil and paper. "Put down three hats, one gray, one brown, and one green."

"Right," the man says, and then he puts the paper and pencil in his pocket and he nods around the room.

"Thanks," he says.

"That all right," the Beau says, smiling. "Thank you, too."

The man goes out and the newspaperman asks the Beau how he feels.

"Me?" the Beau says. "Ah feel fine. Ah'm buyin' hats."

This is, of course, just one of the things that a fighter—Beau Jack—does when he is preparing for a fight.

Down Memory Lane with the Babe

The Ascension of George Herman Ruth

THE OLD YANKEES, going back twenty-five years, were dressing in what used to be the visiting clubhouse in the Yankee Stadium, some of them thin, some of them stout, almost all of them showing the years. Whitey Witt was asking for a pair of size-9 shoes. Mike McNally, bending over and going through the piles of uniforms stacked on the floor, was looking for a pair of pants with a 48 waist.

"Here he is now," somebody said, but when he said it he hardly raised his voice.

The Babe was the last to come in. He had on a dark suit and a cap oyster white. He walked slowly with a friend on either side of him. He paused for a moment and them he recognized someone and smiled and stuck out his hand.

They did not crowd him. When someone pointed to a locker he walked to it and it was quiet around him. When a few who knew him well walked up to him they did it quietly, smiling, holding out their hands.

The Babe started to undress. His friends helped him. They hung up his clothes and helped him into the parts of his uniform. When he had them on he sat down again to put on his spiked shoes, and when he did this the photographers who had followed him moved in. They took pictures of him in uniform putting on his shoes, for this would be the last time.

He posed willingly, brushing a forelock off his forehead. When they were finished he stood up slowly. There was a man there with a small

---

New York *Sun*, June 14, 1948.

boy, and the man pushed the small boy through the old Yankees and the photographers around Ruth.

"There he is," the man said, bending down and whispering to the boy. "That's Babe Ruth."

The small boy seemed confused. He was right next to the Babe and the Babe bent down and took the small boy's hand almost at the same time as he looked away to drop the hand.

"There," the man said, pulling the small boy back. "Now you met Babe Ruth."

The small boy's eyes were wide, but his face seemed to show fear. They led the Babe over to pose him in the middle of the rest of the 1923 Yankees. Then they led him into the old Yankee clubhouse—now the visiting clubhouse—to pose in front of his old locker, on which is painted in white letters, "Babe Ruth, No. 3."

When they led him back the rest of the members of the two teams of old Yankees had left to go to the dugouts. They put the Babe's gabardine topcoat over his shoulders, the sleeves hanging loose, and they led him—some in front of him and some in back in the manner in which they lead a fighter down to a ring—down the stairs and into the dark runway.

They sat the Babe down then on one of the concrete abutments in the semi-darkness. He sat there for about two minutes.

"I think you had better wait inside," someone said. "It's too damp here."

They led him back to the clubhouse. He sat down and they brought him a box of a dozen baseballs and a pen. He autographed the balls that will join what must be thousands of others on mantels, or under glass, in bureau drawers, or in attics in many places in the world.

He sat then, stooped, looking ahead, saying nothing. They halted an attendant from sweeping the floor because dust was rising.

"I hope it lets up," the Babe said, his voice hoarse.

"All right," somebody said. "They're ready now."

They led him out again slowly, the topcoat over his shoulders. There were two cops and one told the other to walk in front. In the third-base dugout there was a crowd of Indians and 1923 Yankees and they found a place on the bench and the Babe sat down behind the crowd.

"A glove?" he said.

"A left-handed glove," someone said.

They found a glove on one of the hooks. It was one of the type that has come into baseball since the Babe left—bigger than the old gloves, with a mesh of rawhide between the thumb and first finger—and the Babe took it and looked at it and put it on.

"With one of these," he said, "you could catch a basketball."

They laughed and the Babe held the mesh up before his face like a catcher's mask and they laughed again. Mel Allen, at the public-address microphone, was introducing the other old Yankees. You could hear the cheering and the Babe saw Mel Harder, the former Cleveland pitcher, now a coach.

"You remember," he said, after he had poked Harder, "when I got five for five off you and they booed me?"

"Yes," Harder said, smiling. "You mean in Cleveland."

The Babe made a series of flat motions with his left hand.

"Like that," the Babe said. "All into left field and they still booed the stuff out of me."

The Babe handed the glove to someone and someone else handed him a bat. He turned it over to see Bob Feller's name on it and he hefted it.

"It's got good balance," he said.

"And now—" Allen's voice said, coming off the field.

They were coming to cheer the Babe now. In front of him the Indians moved back and when they did the Babe looked up to see a wall of two dozen photographers focused on him. He stood up and the topcoat slid off his shoulders onto the bench.

"—George Herman," Allen's voice said, "Babe Ruth!"

The Babe took a step and started slowly up the steps. He walked out into the flashing of flashbulbs, into the cauldron of sound he must know better than any other man.

About Two Guys Named Joe

DiMaggio and Louis Are Picture-Perfect Sportsmen

IF YOU RECALL the sixth game of the 1947 World Series you will remember the long drive that Joe DiMaggio hit and that Al Gionfriddo, running as far as he could, pulled down as it was about to clear the bullpen fence. Had it gone into the bullpen it would have tied the score, and with the Dodgers on the run, the chances were that the Yankees would have won the Series right then and there.

DiMaggio had been deprived of a home run by a miraculous catch, and that night, he said later, he got into his car and drove as far as Mount Vernon and back. While he drove he kept thinking of the catch.

At the moment Gionfriddo made the catch all DiMaggio did, rounding second, was kick the dirt once and then trot out to his fielding position. The next day, before the seventh game, he was sitting in the Yankee dugout watching the Dodgers taking batting practice when a photographer came out and asked him to autograph a photograph of Gionfriddo's catch.

"All right," DiMaggio said, and he signed the picture.

Then they were on him. In the next few minutes, four or five others asked him to autograph their prints of the picture until, finally, when another came up, DiMaggio looked at him and then nodded toward the Dodgers.

"Look," DiMaggio said. "Why don't you get Gionfriddo to sign it?"

New York *Sun*, August 30, 1948.

"Who?" the photographer said.

"Gionfriddo," DiMaggio said. "He made the catch. I didn't."

"What's the matter?" the photographer said. "You're not getting sore are you?"

"No," DiMaggio said, not raising his voice, "but why don't you let up on a guy after a while?"

He signed the picture. The photographer took it, and as he was walking away he stopped beside a reporter who had been listening.

"What's the matter with the guy?" the photographer said.

Thinking of DiMaggio, of his bigness not only on the field but, at a time like this, off it as well, you will also be thinking of Joe Louis and of another picture. It is the picture of the fourth-round knockdown of Louis in the first fight with Jersey Joe Walcott, probably the most humiliating experience in Louis's fighting life.

On the day, several days after that fight, when Louis came out of hiding for the first time, he was seated behind the desk in Mike Jacobs's office and he had been answering questions. Now he stood up to go upstairs with Sol Strauss to see some of the Madison Square Garden executives, and a photographer spoke up.

"Joe," he said, holding out a large blow-up of the knockdown picture, "my office would like me to get a picture of you looking at this."

"Sure," Joe said, and he took the big picture.

"No," Strauss said, shaking his head. "Never mind that. We have to go upstairs."

"That's all right," Louis said, still looking at the picture. "Maybe somebody will make a lot of money with this."

He posed then, looking at the blow-up. It showed him on his back, his feet in the air. It showed Walcott stepping around him, and it showed Ruby Goldstein, the referee, moving in preparatory to starting the count.

"Say," Louis said, looking at the picture. "Ruby looks good, doesn't he?"

The others in the room laughed, which is one of the things you can do when it would be more awkward to applaud openly an exhibition of class.

German Heavyweight Checks In

Hein Ten Hoff Says "Ja" to America

HEIN TEN HOFF is the heavyweight champion of Germany. He arrived in this country on Monday night, and yesterday they brought him and his manager, Emil Jung, to the Twentieth Century Sporting Club, where the boxing writers and the photographers were waiting.

"Now he's here," somebody said, "what are we going to do with him?"

"Take him into Francis Albertanti's office," Harry Markson said. "They can talk to him in there."

"What did Francis ever do?" the other said.

They walked the two of them, then, into Albertanti's office. Francis was sitting behind the desk and he stood up and shook hands with them. Then they seated the two on chairs along one wall, and the reporters stood around, looking Ten Hoff over and waiting for Harry N. Sperber, who was the Army's chief interpreter at the Nuremberg trials and who had been summoned again for this occasion.

Ten Hoff is a big guy, even for a heavyweight. He is tall and broad-shouldered. He has wavy brown hair and blue eyes and is actually handsome. He was hatless, but he had on a light tan coat, belted at the waist, and he was wearing brown suede shoes and there was a silk scarf around his neck. Over one shoulder he carried, on a strap, a small camera in a leather case.

New York *Sun*, January 19, 1949.

"They shouldn't take him to Stillman's," one of them, looking at him, said. "They should take him to Hollywood."

"What does he weigh?"

"He weighs," Lew Burston said, "about two seventeen."

"How tall?" another said, speaking to Ten Hoff and raising his hand to illustrate.

"One hundred ninety-three centimeters," Ten Hoff said.

"That figures about six feet two," Burston said.

"Where does he come from?"

"Hamburg," Burston said. "The same as Schmeling."

"No," one of the writers said. "Schmeling came from Berlin."

"No," Burston said. "He tells me Schmeling was a Hamburger."

"I'll say," another said.

When Sperber came in he walked over to the two and introduced himself in German. Then he sat down next to them, and he told the reporters to start the questions. In the course of the questioning they found out that Ten Hoff has had 149 amateur fights, of which he lost seven, and seventeen professional fights, of which he won all but one draw, and that he is twenty-nine years old.

"Ask him," one of the writers said, "how he happened to get into the fight racket."

"He says," Sperber said, after he had talked with the fighter, "that he has always been interested in it. He said he became interested when he was a boy living in Holland, and that he kept the interest when his parents moved to Germany."

"Ask him what kind of a boxer he is."

"Well," Sperber said, after the fighter had shrugged his shoulders, "he doesn't want to say how good he is."

"I don't mean that. I want to know what style he's got."

"Oh," Sperber said, and then he put the question to the two.

"*Er hat einen eleganten Stil,*" the manager said, "*wie Toonee.*"

"He says," Sperber said, "that he has an elegant style, like Tunney."

"That's what he says," one of the writers said.

"Not only that," Sperber said, "but his manager says that when he is knocked down he gets up and fights like an enraged tiger. He says the customers always go away satisfied when Ten Hoff fights."

"Here's another question I'd like to ask," another said. "At least I'd like to hear the answer to it and I think it's important. When Schmeling was over here and he made a quarter, he ran right back to Germany with it. All the money he made he took back home. I want to know what this guy plans to do with whatever money he makes."

Sperber put the question in German to Ten Hoff. Ten Hoff listened and shook his head and then answered.

"He says," Sperber said, "that as far as he's concerned he'd like to live here for the rest of his life."

"That's a good answer," the one who had asked the question said.

Now more reporters were coming in and one of the photographers had started to take pictures. They were crowding around Sperber and the two Germans and they were finding out that Ten Hoff was in the German Army for three years and that he fought with a Panzer unit on the Russian front.

"He was an *Obergefreiter*," Sperber said. "That's like a corporal."

"No it isn't," Einar Turin, the Swedish newspaperman, said. "Don't try to make him any smaller than he was. That's a sergeant."

"Actually," Sperber said, "it's a private first class, P.F.C.—Poor Foolish Civilian. You can't get any smaller than that."

On the outskirts of the crowd Dan Morgan was craning his neck, trying to get a look. Finally he found an opening and he wedged himself in.

"Ask him if he can count money," Morgan said.

"*Ja*," Ten Hoff said, smiling and nodding his head.

"He's a heady-lookin' gossoon," Morgan said. "Ask him if he likes roadwork."

"*Ja*," Ten Hoff, still smiling, said.

"Then he's all right," Morgan said. "The trouble with most heavyweights is they only know two moves. One, sit down. Two, eat. This guy may do all right."

"They Used to Fight Dogs"

Ringside with William Jennings Bryan

THE MEMBERS of the fight mob, meaning managers and a few hangers-on, are standing around the inner lobby of the Twentieth Century Sporting Club. One of them is Harry Lenny, who, although he does not work at it enough, is one of the game's great trainers, and another is Mike Latzo, who is a brother of Pete Latzo, the old fighter, and who promotes fights now in Scranton.

"You remember Paddy Mullen?" Harry says to Mike. "You remember that Boyle who ran the hotel?"

"Sure," Latzo says. "His partner just died."

"Once I fought after one of Mullen's dogs," Harry says. "Do they still fight dogs out there?"

"No," Latzo says. "Now they fight chickens."

"They used to fight dogs," Harry says. "One day out in Pittston I fought after one of Mullen's dogs. He was fightin' one of Boyle's dogs and Paddy talked to him like he'd talk to me. Before he put him in he said to him, 'Now you're in there with a two-hour dog. Go on the defensive. Fight him on your back, and when I tell you to go then you start to go.'

"So he puts the dog in there and it's just like the dog understands. He goes over on his back, with his four paws up like this, and for two hours he fights off the other dog like a fighter pickin' off punches. Then

---

New York *Sun*, February 28, 1949.

Mullen says, 'All right, go.' That dog gets up and goes for Boyle's dog. He grabs him by the hind leg and he rips it open. He breaks two of the dog's other legs and he almost kills him.

"Boyle thought his dog quit," Harry says, "but he didn't know. The dog almost got murdered, and you should have seen the money around. All new bills like they just come from the mint, and after the dogs got through they put down a canvas and I boxed."

Dan Morgan is making his way through the crowd. He sees Lenny and he walks over to him and sticks out his hand.

"Why don't you quit?" he says to Lenny. "You're done. You don't keep young, like me and like this guy here."

He points to Sol Strauss. Strauss, a cigar in his hand, has been wandering around, but now he sees the others looking at him and he stops.

"What?" he says.

"I'm just after tellin' them," Morgan says, "that that speech you made at the manager's dinner was the greatest since William Jennings Bryan."

"What?" Sol says.

"You're the greatest since William Jennings Bryan," Morgan says.

Strauss shrugs his shoulders and turns and walks away.

"I just tell him that to keep him young," Morgan says. "Bryan was the best. Bryan was the champion until the money interests beat him."

"I'll tell you something," Lenny says. "One day my brother and I are on a train and my brother finds a rock on the floor. He finds a ring with this big rock in it, so we call the conductor. We give it to the conductor and he walks down the car and down about two or three cars. In a few minutes he comes back and he's got this guy with him.

"This guy has one of those big hats on, one of those big hats like La Guardia used to wear. The conductor says, 'These are the men who found the ring.' And the guy says, 'Who are you?' I say, 'This is Eddie Lenny and I'm his brother, Harry Lenny, and we're fighters.' Then the guy says, 'My, even prizefighters are honest.' And do you know who the guy is?"

"No," Morgan says.

"William Jennings Bryan," Harry says. "He says to us, 'Where are you boys from?' And we say, 'Delaware County.' He talks to us for a long time. He gets interested in us and he wants to see us fight. Do you know what we end up doing?"

"No," Morgan says.

"We end up," Harry says, "smuggling him into a fight. One night when we're fighting we smuggle him in. We dress him in a white sweater and a cap so nobody will know who he is. Afterward he tells us if we ever need any help to call on him and he can help us, but we never call on him once."

"That's a story at that," Morgan says. "The man was a great talker. No jokes, just serious speeches, but the greatest until the money licked him."

"Which is very interesting," somebody else says, "but why doesn't Harry Lenny stop talking and get a fighter instead?"

"What fighter?" Harry says.

"Well, a young heavyweight he can teach."

"A young heavyweight?" Harry says. "I've looked at ten of them in the last three months. I really looked at them and do you know what happens?"

"No."

"I say to them, 'Why do you want to be a fighter?' Do you know what they all tell me?"

"No."

"They all say the same thing," Harry says. "They tell me, 'I want to fight to make money.' With me that's enough, and I look some place else."

Rumpus in the Living Room

"Toughie" Brasuhn, Queen of the Roller Derby

STARTING TOMORROW NIGHT and continuing at least two nights a week for the next three weeks a young woman named Marjorie Clair Brasuhn will engage in a campaign of assaulting other young women in many living rooms—even bar rooms—in this section of the country. Miss Brasuhn is the most popular participant in a sporting enterprise known as the Roller Derby, and the Roller Derby will open tomorrow night an eighteen-day stand at the Fourteenth Regiment Armory, Brooklyn, and will be televised at least twice weekly.

The Roller Derby is still new around here, but it has been touring the nation for almost fourteen years. It played this town and surrounding living rooms for the first time last autumn, turning out to be a combination of six-day bicycle racing and professional wrestling while establishing Miss Brasuhn as the most pugnacious female to show here since Katie Jenkins, who, you may remember, used to second and occasionally fight with her husband, Lew, who was then the lightweight champion of the world.

The last time Miss Brasuhn appeared here much had been written but little had been believed about her. Suddenly, however, she erupted before the faces of startled Howdy Doody fans, bumping other women off the roller track, going for their faces with her fists and for their hair with her hands. She spent more time in the penalty box than any other

---

New York *Sun*, March 23, 1949.

skater, engaging in twelve fistfights during the run, and what effect this had on the young of this section is not known because she says she received no complaints.

"I got a lot of letters," she said, "but they were nice letters. A lot of them wanted my picture or my autograph, and a lot wanted me to write to them from other cities, letting them know how the race was going."

Miss Brasuhn—generally referred to as "Toughie"—is twenty-five years old and goes to four feet eleven inches and 120 pounds. She was born and reared in St. Paul, Minnesota, and has been married twice. Her present husband is Ken Monte, three years her junior and a modest, almost bashful young man who is also a competitive skater. She is the mother of a four-year-old son by her first marriage.

"And as a child," someone said to her yesterday, "did you have any brothers and sisters?"

"Two older brothers," she said, nodding her head.

"And did you tag around after them?"

"Do you mean was I a tomboy?"

"Well—"

"Yes, I was a tomboy."

"Does that mean you used to get into fights with other girls?"

"Yes. That's right."

"Why did you get into fights?"

"Well, I had to fight for everything. I was smaller than the other girls. I was an ice skater first, and I was always the smallest in my class. When I began to get as big as the other girls in that class they moved me up into a higher class, so I had a fight on my hands there."

She does not, of course, look like a fighter in her street clothes. Yesterday she was wearing a lightweight red boxcoat and under that a gray fitted jacket with brown lapels, a matching brown skirt, and brown shoes. On her head her brown hair was set in easy, flattering waves.

"And have you," the other said, "been injured since you've been skating?"

"Yes. I broke my ankle in three places. I pulled a muscle in my shoulder. My head was cut and I had a concussion. I've had a lot of bruises."

"And as you've landed in the crowd has anyone in the audience ever tried to fight with you?"

"Oh yes. I've had men try to fight me. Women, too, of course. I've been hit with bottles and sometimes the kids will shoot staples at you. Sometimes someone will throw an egg."

"Do you enjoy watching prizefights?"

"Yes. I like them on the television."

"Has it ever occurred to you that if you learned how to lead with your left hand you might have less trouble in your own scuffles?"

"No. I'm strictly a roundhouse swinger, but I don't care. I'm not interested in fighting. Everyone always makes so much of my fighting, but I'm interested in skating and the fighting just happens when I'm standing up for my rights."

"What do your parents think about it?"

"Well, they don't like it. The last time I was in St. Paul they ran a picture of me taken in Philadelphia with a black eye. My mother didn't like it. It wasn't nice in my own hometown."

"Do you want your son to be a professional skater?"

"Well, if he wants to I suppose so."

"Suppose your next child is a girl. Will you want her to be a skater like her mother?"

"Well, no."

"Why is that?"

"Well, I think a girl should be feminine. I think right from the start they should be feminine. I mean everyone has always called me Toughie since I was a little kid. I don't think that's the way a girl should grow up."

She thought a moment.

"Of course," she said, "a girl should have some spunk. I'd want my daughter to be spunky."

Uncle Mike Is Back

You Can Tell He's All Right, He Won't Listen to Morgan

TWO YEARS AGO last December Mike Jacobs collapsed in the office of his friend Eddie Crozier, the chiropractor. After that he put in a long stretch in the hospital, and since then he has been spending most of his time in Florida, paying only occasional visits to his offices at the Twentieth Century Sporting Club on the second floor of Madison Square Garden.

Mike is in town again now—being driven in from his home in Rumson, New Jersey, each morning and going home each night. They are saying that he is here to sell his interest in the Twentieth Century, and they are saying that he is here to lend the Twentieth Century his support. Whatever are the reasons for his presence, he was sitting yesterday in Francis Albertanti's office with Francis and Crozier and Dan Morgan and one or two others.

"Hey!" someone who had just walked in said, walking up to him. "How do you feel?"

Mike was wearing a tan gabardine suit. He still has only partial use of his right arm and so, when the other walked up to him, he stuck out his left.

"All right," he said, smiling.

"He looks good," the other said, turning to the others in the room. "He doesn't look like a sick man."

New York *Sun*, April 5, 1949.

"Who says he's a sick man?" Crozier said. "Mike's all right, and he'll be even better."

"Certainly," Morgan said. "They're after takin' me into the hospital when I'm weighin' a hundred twenty pounds. Now I'm weighin' one fifty, and I was never in better shape in my life."

They kept coming in that way, seeing Mike and shaking his left hand and asking him how he feels. One of them was Murray Elkins, a manager of fighters.

"So it's good to see you around again," he said to Mike.

Mike didn't say anything. He just smiled and nodded his head.

"Listen to this," Morgan said. "You want to know if he's all right?"

He leaned forward and, raising his voice, he addressed himself to Mike.

"Listen," he said. "You and I can make a lot of money. I mean out in Jamaica. I got a few horses I want to play, and all you gotta do is back me, not over ten thousand bucks."

Morgan laughed then, but Mike said nothing. He just smiled and nodded his head.

"You can tell he's all right," Morgan said, still enjoying it. "You didn't see him goin' for it."

"Anyway," Elkins said, talking to all of them, "I got the young fighter. Eighteen fights. Seventeen knockouts. One win."

"Who?" somebody else said.

"Bill Brennan," Elkins said. "Out of Vancouver."

He saw Mike starting to stand up. Mike stood up slowly, and then slowly he started to walk across the room to the door.

"Eighteen fights," Elkins said, raising his voice. "Seventeen knockouts. One win."

"Ah!" Morgan said, watching Mike walk out the door. "What's the use? What's the use of talkin' about young fighters? You talk about them and they amount to nothin'. What we used to do in the old days was talk about the old-timers until we found out whether the young ones could take a punch in the nose or not."

"Eighteen fights," Elkins said.

"Ah! what's the difference?" Morgan said. "Young fighters. Young fighters make liars out of fight managers."

"What liars?" Elkins said. "Fight managers don't lie, because if they do it comes back."

"Listen," Morgan said. "Don't try to tell me. You put your guy in with some guy with one leg and he looks great. Then you put him in with a guy who can fight and he gets licked. Then you have to lie. You have to say, 'He ate something that didn't agree with him. He's worried about his family. He's got a mortgage.' They make liars out of you."

"Tell him," Irving Rudd said, "about Danny Gardella trying to fight."

"Danny Gardella the ballplayer?"

"That's right," Rudd said. "Murray had Gardella in the gym."

"Sure," Elkins said. "There was this Italian kid who is a friend of Gardella's. Gardella is broke and this kid says, 'Why don't you box?' Gardella says, 'I'd like to fight to make some money, if I had a manager.' So the kid brings him to me and I get him some stuff and put him in up at Mike Mele's gym in the Bronx."

"So what happened?" Morgan said.

"He couldn't hold up his hands," Elkins said. "He's got muscles, though. He's got great big muscles here on his arms and shoulders, but he's goin' like this and like this."

"He can't fight, hey?" Morgan said.

"Well," Elkins said, "if you could ever teach him to hold up his hands. I had him in with a pretty good boy and the guy said, 'Boy, if he ever hit you he'd kill you. Once he missed me and I almost got knocked down with the wind from the punch.' But he was like this—"

He took a wide stance, standing in the middle of the room, his arms spread.

"In other words," Morgan said, "you think he'd make a pretty good minor-league catcher at that."

Late Afternoon on the Harlem

The Columbia Freshmen Are First on the River

THERE HAD BEEN some sun earlier in the afternoon, but it was close to four o'clock before the first of the Columbia crews pushed away from the float and out into the river at Spuyten Duyvil. Now the air and the river were of the same gray, with black clouds scudding across the sky and over the arch of the Henry Hudson Bridge, and when they tried to get out into the Hudson they found it too rough, and so they turned back to work on the Harlem, in the shelter of its banks.

There are eleven crews at Columbia this year—freshmen and lightweights and heavyweights and junior varsities and varsities—and the freshmen, who are first out of classes, are always first on the river. On this day they were out for about forty minutes before the first crew of upperclassmen—tall kids with short haircuts and long, bare legs—paddled down onto the dock in their once-white woolen socks, their shell supported above their heads.

The coxswain is, of course, always a little guy, and he does nothing but think and shout. He walked now behind his crew, carrying nothing but his little light blue megaphone, the straps dangling. He was dressed more warmly against the chill than the rest and, walking behind them, he called their steps. When they slung the shell from overhead into the water, he supervised the act.

New York *Sun*, April 7, 1949.

When this cox had this crew out on the water Walter Raney climbed into one of the launches. It was a blue launch with two crossed oars and the crown of King's College painted on the bow, and Raney is the Columbia crew coach. He is a tall, slim man, and he was wearing, over warm clothing, an old black rubber raincoat, and on his head there was an old felt hat.

"All right," he said, through the big blue megaphone when the launch pulled up to the crew at rest. "Let's do a little work."

"All right," the cox said, shouting it through the little megaphone now strapped to his face. "Let's pick it up. Ready. Row."

When he said that the tall young men in the shell bent to it, and the young man at the wheel of the launch gunned the launch. They moved down the river together—the shell and the launch—the cox shouting in cadence with his men, the men bending together, their blue-tipped oars working together, and Raney, standing well up in the launch, shouting through the megaphone his advice.

"All right, Walter, get those legs in there . . . Go right through, Gomez . . . Don't let that slide jump up . . . If you're gonna row in that boat you're gonna row low . . . Straight through with the hands, Gomez, and don't arch 'em up . . . Press with the feet . . . Draw with the arms . . . Lean together . . . That's it."

It was colder than you might think it would be, and only the rowers could derive any warmth. The water was a cold, dirty gray around them, here and there a little rough. The slim, slick shell, which seemed the only really clean thing on the river, moved past floating bits of lumber and bobbing, half-submerged beer cans, and in the wash of the launch a branch of forsythia bloomed a soiled yellow.

"All right, now . . . A good solid stroke . . . Nobody trying to cheat . . . Do it honest . . . Your legs go down too fast . . . You're losing half your drive . . . That's better . . . That's it."

When they picked up another shell, beyond the Broadway Bridge and going for another, the two shells came to rest. The two crews sat there together, the shells rolling a little, the hands and faces and legs of the young men red from the cold air and from their work, and when they started again they started together, down past the old boathouses crumbling into the river, past the coal yard and the old, decaying docks, and past a tug hauling a barge up.

"Hey!" a man in a blue shirt called from the wheelhouse of the tug. "Why don't you guys buy your own lake?"

They could not hear him in the shells but they could hear him in the launch. They laughed and waved to him and he waved back. Then the tug was gone, and there were only the cries of the two little guys in the sterns, the slapping of the tiller handles against the sides to set a rhythm, the advice of Raney carrying across the rushing water to their work.

"Those legs . . . Those legs . . . Get that squeeze right for the catch . . . Don't slam 'em down . . . Watch the slide . . . Bring that slide up slower . . . Watch those legs."

When they got to the mile-and-three-quarters mark—a stripe painted on the seawall of the Harlem Speedway—they came to rest. There were some kids there on the wall trying to reach them with rocks, but the kids had no success. They must have rested there within sight of the Polo Grounds for about five minutes, and then they jockeyed around slowly, and they were three crews going back.

"Come up fast and then slow down . . . Don't come up slow and then speed up . . . Don't grab too tight with the left hand . . . Elbow in . . . Watch those legs and lean into it . . . All right, now . . . A fast two minutes . . . Let's take 'em in."

By now it was starting to get dark, and here and there along the shores you could see a light. The cars of the New York Central trains were lighted, and the commuters were sitting back, reading their newspapers, as the kids took the shells in. It has been twenty years, you see, since Columbia won at Poughkeepsie, but they are still trying, trying like this.

How They Told Charlie Keller

The Yankees Send a Good Man Down

IT WAS a couple of minutes past noon and there were no more than a half-dozen Yankees on the field. The stands were still almost empty, and Bill Dickey, now a coach with the Yankees, was standing in the batting cage and was hitting them as Charlie Keller, trying hard to work himself back into shape, threw them up to the plate.

"Hey," Keller would holler to Dickey if Dickey got hold of one. "How do you like that?"

Or, if Dickey swung at a pitch and missed or failed to get the best of his bat on it, Keller would shout something else.

"What about that?" he would shout. "Who says I can't pitch?"

He seemed, throwing out there with his cap off, laughing with each pitch, his wavy black hair shining in the sun, to be a kid again. Of course he is not a kid, because ten years have passed since he came up to the Yankees from Newark.

At about one o'clock Casey Stengel climbed up into the dugout. Now there were players all over the field—Yankees on the playing field and the Indians warming up in front of their own dugout—and when Keller came off the field he heard Casey telling a story about Adolfo Luque, and he sat down on the bench near Casey where he could listen to it.

New York *Sun*, May 19, 1949.

"I beat him once at the Polo Grounds," Casey was saying. "On a three-nothing pitch I stood like this with my bat against my shoulder and I was scratching my chest with my other hand. He thought I was gonna take, and he come in with a sucker pitch and I snapped around on it—"

He cast his hand out flat, to show how the ball had gone.

"Did you get a hit on it?" Keller said, smiling at the thought.

"Into the upper deck," Casey said. "A home run. It's in the records."

Casey was still talking when Arthur Patterson, from the Yankee front office, came into the dugout. He walked up to Casey and said something and Casey got up. The two of them walked a couple of steps down the dugout, Arthur talking and Casey listening. When Arthur had finished talking, Casey looked around until he saw Keller. He walked over to him and said something to him, and they sat down together on the dugout steps.

They sat there together, Casey talking and Keller listening, for about five minutes. It was not hard to guess what Casey was talking about, because the rules of major-league baseball state that by midnight of May 18 you may have no more than twenty-five players on your squad. Yesterday the Yankees had twenty-nine on their squad, and Keller has yet to recover from the injuries that have plagued him since the 1947 season.

"What's with Keller?" one of the newspapermen watching said to Patterson.

"We'll make an announcement after the game," Arthur said.

It was a good game for the Yankees to win. The Indians are champions of the world, but Vic Raschi shut them out with only two hits and the Yankees won, 6–0.

"That was easy," someone said to Casey after it was over.

Casey was sitting in his office off the clubhouse. His legs were stretched out in front of him, and he was running a hand through his hair.

"I think it was the easiest game we've had," Casey said.

"What did they announce?" one of the newspapermen said to another who had just come in from the press room.

"They're sending Keller down to Newark on option," the other said. "Houk and Hiller go to Kansas City, and Witek also goes to Newark."

"I guess it wasn't easy telling Keller," the first said to Casey.

"It's never easy," Casey said, sitting up. "It's never easy when they're nice guys and trying hard. I can say I didn't like to do it."

In the clubhouse they were congratulating Raschi and Tommy Henrich. Henrich had hit two home runs and a couple of newspapermen were kidding with him, kidding about the fact that when he broke in they used to call him Baby Face, and now his hair is quite thin.

"I'll admit I'm no kid," Henrich was saying.

"And I guess," another said, "that Keller's going doesn't make you feel any younger."

"It's tough," Henrich said. "It's one of those things. If it wasn't one thing it was another. Just tough breaks, but he was getting in shape. Just the other day he was telling me that he was playing with his kids, and he felt right for the first time in a long while."

When Keller came back from taking his shower he sat down in his dressing booth, which is next to Henrich's. Some of the players stopped to say something to him, but none of them stopped long. When the newspapermen stopped to say something they couldn't seem to find the right thing to say, which in itself was a compliment.

They were talking about that later in the press room. They were looking up the record . . . came up in 1939 . . . hit 181 home runs, plus five in World Series and one in an All-Star game . . . will be thirty-three years old in September.

"What are you going to say to him?" one of them said. "I mean you're talking to a guy who's intelligent. You're talking to a man. You're not going to kid him about it. I know, because I remember the first day he came up."

Jake Steals the Show

Mintz Crowned Heavyweight Manager of the World

THE PUBLIC-ADDRESS ANNOUNCER, a bald man of medium build and wearing summer formal attire, stood in the middle of the lighted ring in the midst of the darkness that enveloped the rest of Comiskey Park. He had in his right hand a telephone, and he started to talk into it, announcing the name of the new heavyweight champion of the world.

"Judge McAdams," he said, his voice booming back from the speakers hidden in the darkness, "votes seventy-eight points to Charles, seventy-two to Walcott."

In the background many people started to cheer. The fighters, each standing in his corner, his robe over him, his handlers around him, went on looking at the floor of the ring and the man went on.

"Judge Marovitz votes seventy-eight points for Charles, seventy-two for Walcott."

At that moment Jake Mintz started to go. He is the man who, by shouting and pleading, joking and cursing, clowning and threatening, had finally led his fighter to the heavyweight title. Now in the moment when he was about to hear that his fighter, Ezzard Charles, had made it, he collapsed.

He is a short, pale, bashed-faced man and he had been standing about ten yards from Charles's corner, leaning on the ropes. When he

---

New York *Sun*, June 23, 1949.

collapsed, his arms tightened around the ropes, and he hung there. His legs bent and loose.

Dave Miller, the referee, was the first to get to him. The announcer was announcing how Miller had voted, and now Miller—a fat man with the sweat streaming off his face—was trying to hold Jake. All over the place there was noise—the announcer speaking, the people roaring—and Jake, Miller still trying to hold him, sliding to the ring floor.

"Jake's heart!" a Pittsburgh sportswriter was hollering in the press row. "He's got a bad heart! He may die!"

Jake didn't die. A couple of men grabbed his legs and they straightened him out on the canvas. A doctor, climbing through the ropes, ran to him. They broke an ammonia capsule under his nose and, in a moment, his eyes opened and they stood him up and they told him, amid the noise and the confusion under the lights in the ring, that his fighter, Ezzard Charles, is the new heavyweight champion of the world.

"But who's the champion?" someone in the press row was shouting.

"Charles," somebody else said, "but Jake stole the show."

He did, too. When he collapsed in the ring he provided more excitement than had been provided at any time during the fifteen rounds it had taken to decide the successor to Joe Louis. As this fight is remembered here the picture will be made up, most of all, of Jake collapsing in the ring, because this is the guy who took an ordinary fighter and schemed him and talked him into the heavyweight title.

Jake was all right in the dressing room. They were using the press room, a place of darkened oak paneling hung with the stuffed heads of boars and buffalo and mountain goats. The fighter stood behind a rubbing table that was draped with a white sheet. His white robe was over him and Jake, still pale, stood at his side.

"Who will you fight next?" The reporters were shouting at Charles.

"Anybody," Charles said.

"Will you fight Walcott again?"

"Let's hope not," another reporter said.

"If my managers want me to," Charles said.

"After you had him hurt in the seventh round," another said, "why didn't you try to finish him in the eighth?"

"He recuperates too fast," Charles said. "He punches pretty hard with his right and you got to watch out for it."

"In other words," Jake said, beaming, "I've got a smart champion."

Let us put it this way. Let us say Jake has a champion, a heavyweight champion. Let us put it the way the man did in the press row. Charles won the fight, but Jake stole the show. In this there is much justice.

Death of a Race Horse

Air Lift, Son of Bold Venture

THEY WERE GOING to the post for the sixth race at Jamaica, two-year-olds, some making their first starts, to go five and a half furlongs for a purse of $4,000. They were moving slowly down the backstretch toward the gate, some of them cantering, others walking, and in the press box they had stopped their working or their kidding to watch, most of them interested in one horse.

"Air Lift," Jim Roach said. "Full brother of Assault."

Assault, who won the Triple Crown . . . making this one, too, by Bold Venture, himself a Derby winner, out of Igual, herself by the great Equipoise. . . . Great names in the breeding line . . . and now the little guy making his first start, perhaps the start of another great career.

They were off well, although Air Lift was fifth. They were moving toward the first turn, and now Air Lift was fourth. They were going into the turn, and now Air Lift was starting to go, third perhaps, when suddenly he slowed, a horse stopping, and below in the stands you could hear a sudden cry, as the rest left him, still trying to run but limping, his jockey—Dave Gorman—half falling, half sliding off.

"He broke a leg!" somebody, holding binoculars to his eyes, shouted in the press box. "He broke a leg!"

Down below they were roaring for the rest, coming down the stretch now, but in the infield men were running toward the turn, running toward the colt and the boy standing beside him, alone. There

---

New York *Sun*, July 28, 1949.

was a station wagon moving around the track toward them, and then, in a moment, the big green van that they call the horse ambulance.

"Gorman was crying like a baby," one of them, coming out of the jockey room, said. "He said he must have stepped in a hole, but you should have seen him crying."

"It's his left front ankle," Dr. J. G. Catlett, the veterinarian, was saying. "It's a compound fracture, and I'm waiting for confirmation from Mr. Hirsch to destroy him."

He was standing outside one of the stables beyond the backstretch, and he had just put in a call to Kentucky where Max Hirsch, the trainer, and Robert Kleberg, the owner, are attending the yearling sales.

"When will you do it?" one of them said.

"Right as soon as I can," the doctor said. "As soon as I get confirmation. If it was an ordinary horse I'd done it right there."

He walked across the road and around another barn to where they had the horse. The horse was still in the van, about twenty stable hands in dungarees and sweat-stained shirts, bare-headed or wearing old caps, standing around quietly and watching with Dr. M. A. Gilman, the assistant veterinarian.

"We might as well get him out of the van," Catlett said, "before we give him the Novocain. It'll be a little better out in the air."

The boy in the van with the colt led him out then, the colt limping, tossing his head a little, the blood running down and covering his left foreleg. When they saw him, standing there outside the van now, the boy holding him, they started talking softly.

"Full brother of Assault." . . . "It don't make no difference now. He's done." . . . "But damn, what a grand little horse." . . . "Ain't he a horse?"

"It's a funny thing," Catlett said. "All the cripples that go out, they never break a leg. It always happens to a good-legged horse."

A man, gray-haired and rather stout, wearing brown slacks and a blue shirt, walked up.

"Then I better not send for the wagon yet?" the man said.

"No," Catlett said. "Of course, you might just as well. Max Hirsch may say no, but I doubt it."

"I don't know," the man said.

"There'd be time in the morning," Catlett said.

"But in this hot weather—" the man said.

They had sponged off the colt, after they had given him the shot to deaden the pain, and now he stood, feeding quietly from some hay they had placed at his feet. In the distance you could hear the roar of the crowd in the grandstand, but beyond it and above it you could hear thunder and see the occasional flash of lightning.

When Catlett came back the next time he was hurrying, nodding his head, and waving his hands. Now the thunder was louder, the flashes of lightning brighter, and now rain was starting to fall.

"All right," he said, shouting to Gilman. "Max Hirsch talked to Mr. Kleberg. We've got the confirmation."

They moved the curious back, the rain falling faster now, and they moved the colt over close to a pile of loose bricks. Gilman had the halter and Catlett had the gun, shaped like a bell with the handle at the top. This bell he placed, the crowd silent, on the colt's forehead, just between the eyes. The colt stood still and then Catlett, with the hammer in his other hand, struck the handle of the bell. There was a short, sharp sound and the colt toppled onto his left side, his eyes staring, his legs straight out, the free legs quivering.

"Aw, ----," someonc said.

That was all they said. They worked quickly, the two vets removing the broken bones as evidence for the insurance company, the crowd silently watching. Then the heavens opened, the rain pouring down, the lightning flashing, and they rushed for the cover of the stables, leaving alone on his side near the pile of bricks, the rain running off his hide, dead an hour and a quarter after his first start, Air Lift, son of Bold Venture, full brother of Assault.

The Psychology of Horse Betting

Hooked on the Thrill of Almost Winning

"I DON'T KNOW where I read it," the man said, "but I read it somewhere. Some psychiatrist said that people don't bet on horse races to win, but to lose."

"But to what?" someone else said.

"To lose," the first said. "I know it sounds silly, and there's more to it than I said. I don't quite get it myself, but the appeal, according to this guy, is in the losing and not the winning."

"I don't get it either," the other said. "I can't make it out."

It was of an evening, and there were others in the room and they talked of other things. Eventually, though, they came back to it, and one of them said:

"You know, I've been thinking about that thing you said a few minutes ago about the psychiatrist and horseplayers. The more I think of it the more I think the guy may have something."

"Why?"

"Well, I haven't quite worked it out in my own mind, but let me say this. I've seen a lot of horseplayers and I've known some of them pretty well. Let's say one of them goes to the track and plays three races. Let's say he wins the second and the fifth and then loses the sixth by a nose. Then he comes back and he meets you, and do you know what he does?"

New York *Sun*, September 19, 1949.

"No."

"Well, he says, 'You know, I win the second and the fifth, but in the sixth—.' He has just brushed off the two races he won, but for the sixth, the one he lost, he gives you everything. He tells you how his horse came out of the gate and how he moved into the turn and down the backstretch. He can tell you exactly how the jockey handled it, and when he gets them into the stretch he's riding it all over again, telling about it, right there on the sidewalk."

"Meaning what?"

"Meaning," the one telling it now said, "that the big excitement for this horseplayer on this afternoon was not in the races he won but in the one race he lost. That was where he got his big thrill."

"I suppose," the other said, thinking.

"Sure, you suppose, but it's right. I've seen it happen over and over again. Listen to some horseplayers talking some evening."

"I was thinking," the other said, "that it might be right, too, for another reason. Horseplayers aren't all stupid. Some of them are very intelligent people—"

"That's right," the first said, interrupting. "I know some very intelligent horseplayers. Some of them are guys with a lot of brains who have made a lot of money in some business, because of their brains, and they keep dumping it at the track. Why, one of the all-time great fight managers, a guy who is as smart as any of them, told me once he has dropped a quarter of a million to the horses in his day."

"That's what I'm saying," the other said. "These aren't stupid people. Therefore they know it to be a practical fact that you can't make money betting the races. That's been proved over and over and they must recognize it, but they still keep going back. Therefore they must be going back—the regulars, that is—not with any real expectation of winning, but for the thrill of losing."

"Well, at least for the thrill of almost winning."

"I suppose."

"Sure. Look, the more you think about it, the more there is to it. There's the basic element of tragedy involved. The nearness of winning and then defeat is one thing all humanity understands. It's been the great force behind our literature, our art. The greatest books, the greatest plays have been tragedies. When they discuss the *Mona Lisa* they don't just talk about her smile. The great thing about it is the sadness of that smile."

"You mean she lost a bet, in other words?"

"Well, maybe she lost a bet. There's something heroic about the ability to accept defeat. It's a role people accept, and enjoy more willingly than they know themselves. For the price of a bet the horseplayer buys a pedestal for himself. Horseplayers are a great fraternity united not by victory but by defeat. There is, between them, something—some understanding of one another that you will never find among the members of any group that knows only success."

"That could be right."

"Sure it could be right," the other said. "That psychiatrist might have something there. It's quite a thesis, and it's something to think about. Remind me, sometime, to think about it."

"The Lost Leader"

Gardella Drops His Suit Against Baseball

"Just for a handful of silver he left us,
Just for a riband to stick in his coat."

Now, a hundred years later, it turns out that Browning was not writing, as literary history holds, of Wordsworth, but of Danny Gardella. Danny Gardella is the onetime Giant outfielder who for the past year or so has been helping to clutter the calendars of our courts while embarked on what was ostensibly a social crusade. He was fighting, it was made to appear, not only for the $300,000 claimed in his damage suit but to end the monopolistic nature of organized baseball, to terminate baseball slavery, to free not only the ballplayers of the present but the ballplayers of the future. He said so himself.

Perhaps you didn't even see what happened. They planned it that way. After the third game of the World Series, when they knew the sports pages would be filled with accounts of the 4–3 victory of the Yankees over the Dodgers, with stories of the relief pitching of Joe Page and of the three Dodger home runs that netted only three runs, they announced it. They announced that Gardella was dropping his suit against baseball, and that he would be given a 1950 contract with the St. Louis Cardinals.

What can the Cardinals do with Gardella? Nothing. This was a wartime ballplayer who never hit better than .272 against the old men,

New York *Sun*, October 12, 1949.

the boys, and the physically disabled, and who turned the catching of the easiest of fly balls into exciting, often disastrous, productions. The Cardinals didn't need him, but baseball did.

Baseball that, except in wartime, didn't need Gardella as a ballplayer now in peacetime needed him as an American citizen. It needed him as an American citizen who, wronged, had stirred up a tempest by turning the white light of publicity on the reserve clause, the foundation of organized baseball.

Was it true that in this country an American citizen had to sign away certain fundamental freedoms in order to earn an honest living at his profession? People all over the country, reading of the Gardella case, had started asking that, had started translating the Gardella case into terms of their own.

So he plays baseball, they were saying, and I sell shoes. I am selling shoes for a shop in New York and I get fired. I go to Mexico and I sell shoes there for a year, and when I come back to the United States I find that all the shoestore owners in the country have banded against me, and I can't get a job anywhere. I like to sell shoes, and I'm good at it and I should have a right to do it, but when I get a job in a small shop away out on Staten Island my old boss finds out about it and he sees that I'm fired. How vindictive can they get? Are they trying to drive me and my wife and my child to starvation? Can this happen in the United States of America?

This did happen, you see, in the United States of America, not to a shoe salesman but to a ballplayer. There is no difference. Danny Gardella and his lawyer, Frederic A. Johnson, were not, unfortunately, as big as the thing they started. It is not known how much they received from baseball to call off their attack. All that is known is that the ideals, the principles, the freedoms for which they professed to fight have a value for which there is no equivalent in money. How could they put a price on the truth they claimed to be seeking?

When they started this fight they enlisted a part of this nation. It was a part that was not primarily interested in whether Gardella got $3 or $300,000. It rallied its interests and its sympathies to their banner because it wanted to know, from the highest court of this country, whether the things they claimed—the monopoly, the slavery, the persecution, the illegality—actually do exist under the guise of the national pastime in the United States of America.

Do they exist? There are many who want to know. Baseball itself should want to know. If it, too, were bigger it would have demanded a decision instead of negotiating a settlement. Why should any enterprise, if it is clear in its own conscience, prefer to continue to operate under suspicion when the opportunity to vindicate itself was present?

They settled so little, you see, in their meeting between lawyers. They had created something that could not be settled by lawyers. Nothing changed, really, just because money changed hands.

"My fight," Gardella said once and they believed him, "is against baseball slavery."

> *"He alone breaks from the van and the freemen,*
> *—He alone sinks to the rear and the slaves."*

Retired Undefeated Heavyweight Champion

Or, How Joe Louis Makes a Living

THIS IS THE THING that Joe Louis does now for a living. He comes to a place called Newark, New Jersey, and he puts up for the afternoon. He eats and naps and they wake him at 8:15 in the evening and he dresses and they drive him to the local armory.

The local armory is almost like all the other armories you have seen. It is a red brick–turreted building and there is a First World War field piece on the front lawn with a light playing on it. There is a crowd around the armory when Joe gets there and they recognize him and you can imagine what it is like because it has been like this for him every place he has gone for the last dozen years.

When Joe gets inside, with the cops leading him, they take him into the basement and into the big locker room with the green metal lockers around the walls and the rubbing table in the middle. Mannie Seaman, who trains him, is waiting there and it is hot in the room and Mannie has stripped to his undershirt.

They start coming into the room—the boxing commissioners and the politicians and the man trying to sell boxing gloves. The town's once-prominent fighter—in Newark it is Steve Hamas—comes in to see him.

New York *Sun*, November 23, 1949.

"Remember me?" he says, shaking hands with Joe. "Steve Hamas."

"Sure," Joe says, taking the hand. "How are you?"

The town's prominent ballplayer—in Newark it is Don Newcombe, the big pitcher of the Dodgers—comes in then. Joe is one who idolizes big-league ballplayers, and so they stand talking, and then the photographers pose them and then the cops hustle them out and they leave Joe and he starts to strip and to get into his ring clothes.

Upstairs the armory is like all other armories. The drill hall is an immense, arched-ceiling place, and it is blue with smoke and filled with people. The people fill the seats and clutter the aisles and the spotlights in the ceiling play on the ring where the preliminary kids slug and grab and break and slug again.

It is that way until 10:00 P.M. At 10:00 P.M. Johnny Addie, the announcer, starts calling ballplayers into the ring—Newcombe and Jackie Robinson and Larry Doby and Monte Irvin and Gene Woodling and Gene Hermanski. They stand awkwardly in the ring while the crowd applauds them, and then, without accompaniment, Addie sings the National Anthem and the crowd helps him.

When the ballplayers leave the ring, the crowd at the back of the hall makes a noise and you can see them starting to stand. Three cops come down the aisle, leading the local fighter who will go ten rounds, if possible, with Joe, with ten-ounce gloves and no decision rendered.

The local fighter in Newark is Joe Cheshul, a twenty-four-year-old heavyweight, and when he comes down the aisle the crowd applauds politely. Then you can hear another noise in the back, and it is Louis and now the crowd cheers.

Louis is wearing a white terrycloth robe and has a white towel over his head and this is familiar. When he climbs into the ring with Seaman and George Nicholson behind him, the crowd cheers again.

He is introduced as "from Detroit, Michigan, wearing purple trunks, a consistent conqueror of all his challengers, the greatest champion of modern times, the undefeated heavyweight champion of the world—Joe Louis."

Now the crowd roars again. It cheers when Cheshul is introduced and then there is a loud sound of surprise when it is announced that Louis weighs 228½ pounds and Cheshul 185.

They go to the center of the ring for their instructions. They go back and the bell rings and they turn. Now you can see that Louis is heavy—through the body and through the legs—and then Cheshul, feinting with his head, starts moving around Louis. He moves clockwise, feinting, feinting. Then he flicks a left and it hits Louis and Louis blinks. Cheshul cuffs with a hook. He seems afraid to hit Louis hard and Louis has not thrown a punch.

"It is Louis–Walcott all over again," someone in the press row says.

It is for the first round. Louis stalks, lands only two jabs, but that is the last round that Cheshul wins. In the second round Louis starts to put more into his jabs and Cheshul's head goes back. Louis brings over a short, chopping right to the side and the crowd groans. He increases the pace as the rounds go on. Cheshul circles faster, afraid to hit back. In the fifth round Louis throws his first right to the head. Cheshul falls inside, but another right opens a cut along the side of his left eye. A hook and a right drop Cheshul to his knees for a nine count. He gets up and grabs, slips down for a no count, and, getting up, runs wildly.

It is the best round. Joe eases off. Not until the tenth does Louis press again and again Cheshul is cornered and hurt. Red is running from his eye and a hook and a right hurt him. He retreats and then, finally, it is over.

The crowd cheers Joe. They lead him back to his dressing room. The reporters ask him the same questions. He feels fine, says he will not fight for the title again, and he tries to think of something nice to say about the local boy. More than five thousand people have paid $15,200 to see this, and next week it will be Kansas City and the following week it will be Chicago.

It is the way a retired, undefeated heavyweight champion makes a living.

★ OUT IN THE WORLD ★

Brownsville Bum

Al ("Bummy") Davis, 1910–1945

IT'S A FUNNY THING about people. People will hate a guy all his life for what he is, but the minute he dies for it they make him out a hero and they go around saying that maybe he wasn't such a bad guy after all because he sure was willing to go the distance for whatever he believed or whatever he was.

That's the way it was with Bummy Davis. The night Bummy fought Fritzie Zivic in the Garden and Zivic started giving him the business and Bummy hit Zivic low maybe thirty times and kicked the referee, they wanted to hang him for it. The night those four guys came into Dudy's bar and tried the same thing, only with rods, Bummy went nuts again. He flattened the first one and then they shot him, and when everybody read about it, and how Bummy fought guns with only his left hook and died lying in the rain in front of the place, they all said that was really something and you sure had to give him credit at that.

"So you're Al Davis?" one of the hoods said. "Why, you punch-drunk bum."

What did they expect Bummy to do? What did they expect him to do the night Zivic gave him the thumbs and the laces and walked around the referee and belted Bummy? Bummy could hook too good ever to learn how to hold himself in, if you want the truth of it.

That was really the trouble with Bummy. Bummy blew school too early, and he didn't know enough words. A lot of guys who fought Zivic used to take it or maybe beef to the referee, but Bummy didn't know how to do that. A lot of guys looking at four guns would have taken the

---

True, June 1951.

talk and been thinking about getting the number off the car when it pulled away, but all Bummy ever had was his hook.

Bummy came out of Brownsville. In the sports pages they are always referring to Brownsville as the fistic incubator of Brooklyn, because they probably mean that a lot of fighters come out of there. Murder, Inc., came out of there, too, and if you don't believe it ask Bill O'Dwyer. If it wasn't for Brownsville maybe Bill O'Dwyer wouldn't have become the mayor of New York.

The peculiar thing about Brownsville is that it doesn't look so tough. There are trees around there and some vacant lots, and the houses don't look as bad as they do over on Second Avenue or Ninth Avenue or up in Harlem. Don't tell Charley Beecher, though, that you don't think it's so tough.

"What's the matter you sold the place?" Froike said to Charley the other day. "It ain't the same, now you sold it."

Charley Beecher used to run the poolroom with the gym behind it on the corner of Georgia and Livonia where Bummy used to train. It was a good little gym with a little dressing room and a shower, and Charley was a pretty good featherweight in the twenties, and his brother, Willie, who was even a better fighter, fought Abe Attell and Johnny Dundee and Jack Britton and Leach Cross and Knockout Brown.

"For seventeen years I was in business," Charley said. "Seventeen times they stuck me up."

He looked at Froike, and then he pointed with his two hands at his mouth and his ears and his eyes.

"I had guns here and here and here," he said. "All I ever saw was guns."

The worst part was that Charley knew all the guys. A week after they'd heist him they'd be back for a little contribution, maybe a C-note. They'd be getting up bail for one of the boys, and they just wanted Charley to know there were no hard feelings about the heist, and that as long as he kept his dues up they'd still consider him friendly to the club. That's how tough Brownsville was.

Bummy had two brothers, and they were a big help. They were a lot older than Bummy, and the one they called Little Gangy and the other they called Duff. Right now Gangy is doing twenty to forty, just to give you an idea, and Bummy took a lot of raps for them too because there were some people who couldn't get back at Gangy and Duff so they took it out on the kid.

When Bummy was about seven his father used to run a candy and cigar store and did a little speaking on the side. In other words, he always had a bottle in the place, and he had Bummy hanging around in case anybody should say cop. When the signal would go up Bummy would run behind the counter and grab the bottle, and he was so small nobody could see him over the counter and he'd go out the back.

One day Bummy was going it down the street with the bottle under his coat and some real smart guy stuck out his foot. Bummy tripped and the bottle broke, and Bummy looked at the bottle and the whiskey running on the sidewalk and at the guy and his eyes got big and he started to scream. The guy just laughed and Bummy was lying right on the sidewalk in the whiskey and broken glass, hitting his head on the sidewalk and banging his fists down and screaming. A crowd came around and they watched Bummy, with the guy laughing at him, and they shook their heads and they said this youngest Davidoff kid must be crazy at that.

Davidoff was his straight name. Abraham Davidoff. In Yiddish they made Abraham into Ahvron and then Ahvron they sometimes make Bommy. All his family called him Bommy, so you can see they didn't mean it as a knock. The one who changed it to Bummy was Johnny Attell.

Johnny Attell used to run the fights at the Ridgewood Grove, a fight club in Brooklyn where some good fighters like Sid Terris and Ruby Goldstein and Tony Canzoneri learned to fight, and Johnny and a nice guy named Lew Burston managed Bummy. When Bummy turned pro and Johnny made up the show card for the fight with Frankie Reese he put the name on it as Al (Bummy) Davis, and when Bummy saw it he went right up to Johnny's office.

"What are you doing that for?" he hollered at Johnny. "I don't want to be called Bummy."

"Take it easy," Johnny said. "You want to make money fighting, don't you? People like to come to fights to see guys they think are tough."

They sure liked to come to see Bummy all right. They sure liked to come to see him get his brains knocked out.

The first time Johnny Attell ever heard of Bummy was one day when Johnny was coming out of the Grove and Froike stopped him. Froike used to run the gym at Beecher's and handle kids in the amateurs, and he was standing there talking to Johnny under the Myrtle Avenue El.

"Also I got a real good ticket seller for you," he said to Johnny after a while.

"I could use one," Johnny said.

"Only I have to have a special for him," Froike said. "No eliminations."

"What's his name?" Johnny said.

"Giovanni Pasconi," Froike said.

"Bring him around," Johnny said.

The next week Johnny put the kid in with a tough colored boy named Johnny Williams. The kid got the hell punched out of him, but he sold $200 worth of tickets.

"He didn't do too bad," Johnny said to Froike after the fight. "I'll put him back next week."

"Only this time get him an easier opponent," Froike said.

"You get him your own opponent," Johnny said. "As long as he can sell that many tickets I don't care who he fights."

The next week Johnny put him back and he licked the guy. After the fight Johnny was walking out and he saw the kid and Froike with about twenty people around them, all of them talking Yiddish.

"Come here, Froike," Johnny said.

"What's the matter?" Froike said.

"What is this guy," Johnny said, "a Wop or a Jew?"

"He's a Jew," Froike said. "His right name's Davidoff. He's only fifteen, so we borrowed Pasconi's card."

"He can sure sell tickets," Johnny said.

Bummy could sell anything. That's the way Bummy learned to fight, selling. He used to sell off a pushcart on Blake Avenue. He used to sell berries in the spring and tomatoes and watermelons in the summer and apples in the fall and potatoes and onions and beans in the winter, and there are a lot of pushcarts on Blake Avenue and Bummy used to have to fight to hold his spot.

"I was the best tomato salesman in the world," Bummy was bragging once.

It was right after he knocked out Bob Montgomery in the Garden. He stiffened him in sixty-three seconds and he was getting $15,000, and when the sportswriters came into his dressing room all he wanted to talk about was how good he could sell tomatoes.

"You go over to Jersey and get them yourself," he was telling the sportswriters. "Then you don't have to pay the middle guy. You don't put them in boxes, because when you put them in boxes it looks like you're getting ready to lam. When you only got a few around it looks like you can't get rid of them, so what you gotta do is pile them all up and holler, 'I gotta get rid of these. I'm gonna give 'em away!'"

The sportswriters couldn't get over that. There was a lot they couldn't get over about Bummy.

When Johnny turned Bummy pro he wasn't impressed by his fighting, only his following. Every time Bummy fought for Johnny in the Grove he'd bring a couple of hundred guys with him and they'd holler for Bummy. Everybody else would holler for the other guy, because now they knew Bummy was Jewish and the Grove is in a German section of Ridgewood, and this was when Hitler was starting to go good and there was even one of those German beer halls right in the place where the waiters walked around in those short leather pants and wearing fancy vests and funny felt hats.

The fight that started Bummy was the Friedkin fight. Bummy was just beginning to bang guys out at the Grove and Friedkin was already a hot fighter at the Broadway Arena and they lived only blocks apart. Friedkin was a nice kid, about three years older than Bummy, kind of a studious guy they called Schoolboy Friedkin, and there was nothing between him and Bummy except that they were both coming up and the neighborhood made the match.

Like one day Bummy was standing in the candy store and a couple of guys told him Friedkin was saying he could stiffen Bummy in two heats. Then they went to Friedkin and said Bummy said Friedkin was afraid to fight. At first this didn't take, but they kept it up and one day Bummy was standing with a dame on the corner of Blake and Alabama and Friedkin came along.

"So why don't you two fight?" the dame said.

"Sure, I'll fight," Bummy said, spreading his feet.

"Right here?" Friedkin said. "Right now?"

"Sure," Bummy said.

"I'll fight whenever my manager makes the match," Friedkin said, and he walked away.

Bummy couldn't understand that, because he liked to fight just to fight. He got right in the subway and went over to see Lew Burston in Lew's office on Broadway.

"Never mind making that Friedkin match," he said to Lew.

"Why not?" Lew said.

"Because when I leave here," Bummy said, "I'm going right around to Friedkin's house and I'm gonna wait for him to come out, and we're gonna find out right away if I can lick him or he can lick me."

"Are you crazy?" Lew said.

By the time Johnny Attell made the fight outdoors for Dexter Park there was really a fire under it. They had show cards advertising it on the pushcarts on Blake Avenue and Friedkin's old man and Bummy's old man got into an argument on the street, and everybody was talking about it and betting it big. Then it was rained out five nights and Johnny sold the fight to Mike Jacobs and Mike put it into Madison Square Garden.

When Bummy started working for the fight Lew Burston came over to Beecher's to train him. When Bummy got into his ring clothes they chased everybody out of the gym, and Lew told Bummy to hit the big bag. Bummy walked up to the bag and spread his feet and pulled back his left to start his hook and Lew stopped him.

"Throw that hook away," Lew said.

"Why?" Bummy said. "What's wrong with it?"

"Nothing's wrong with it," Lew said, "only for this fight you'll have to lose that hook."

Before that Bummy was nothing but a hooker, but for weeks Lew kept him banging the big bag with rights. Then the night of the fight, after Bummy was all taped and ready, Lew took him into the shower off the dressing room and he talked to Bummy.

"Now remember one thing," he said to Bummy. "I can tell you exactly how that other corner is thinking. They've got that other guy eating and sleeping with your hook for weeks. I want you to go out there and I don't want you to throw one right hand until I tell you. If you throw one right before I say so I'll walk right out on you. Do you understand?"

Bummy understood all right. He was like a kid with a new toy. He was a kid with a secret that only Bummy and Lew knew, and he went out there and did what Lew told him. Friedkin came out with his right glued along the side of his head, and for three rounds Bummy just hooked and hooked and Friedkin blocked, and a lot of people thought Friedkin was winning the fight.

"All right," Lew said, after the third round. "Now this time go right out and feint with the left, but throw the right and put everything on it."

"Don't worry," Bummy said.

Bummy walked out and they moved around for almost a minute and then Bummy feinted his hook. When he did Friedkin moved over and Bummy threw the right and Friedkin's head went back and down he went with his legs in the air in his own corner. That was all the fighting there was that night.

Now Bummy was the biggest thing in Brownsville. Al Buck and Hype Igoe and Ed Van Every and Lester Bromberg were writing about him in the New York papers, saying he was the best hooker since

Charley White and could also hit with his right, and he had dough for the first time in his life.

He got $1,400 for the Friedkin fight. When he walked down the street the kids followed him, and he bought them leather jackets and baseball gloves and sodas, just to show you what money meant and how he was already looking back at his own life.

When Bummy was a kid nobody bought him anything and he belonged to a gang called the Cowboys. They used to pull small jobs, and the cops could never find them until one night. One night the cops broke into the flat where the kids used to live with some dames, and they got them all except Bummy, who was with his mother that night.

Sure, Bummy was what most people call tough, but if he felt sorry for you and figured you needed him he couldn't do enough. That was the way Bummy met Barbara and fell in love.

Bummy was nineteen then and one day he and Shorty were driving around and Shorty said he wanted to go to Kings County Hospital and visit a friend of his who was sick, and there was this girl about sixteen years old. They sat around for a while and Shorty did all the talking, and then the next time they went to see the girl Shorty was carrying some flowers and he gave them to her.

"From him," Shorty said, meaning Bummy.

When the girl left the hospital Shorty and Bummy drove her home, and then every day for a couple of weeks they used to take her for a ride and to stop off for sodas. One day the three of them were riding together in the front seat and Bummy wasn't saying anything.

"Say, Bobby," Shorty said all of a sudden. "Would you like to get married?"

The girl didn't know what to say. She just looked at Shorty.

"Not to me," Shorty said. "To him."

That was the way Bummy got married. That was Bummy's big romance.

After the Friedkin fight Bummy won about three fights quick, and then they made him with Mickey Farber in the St. Nick's. Farber was out of the East Side and had a good record, and one day when Bummy finished his training at Beecher's he was sitting in the locker room soaking his left hand in a pail of ice and talking with Charley.

That was an interesting thing about Bummy's left hand. He used to bang so hard with it that after every fight and after every day he boxed in the gym it used to swell up.

"I think I'll quit fighting," Bummy said to Charley.

"You think you'll quit?" Charley said. "You're just starting to make dough."

"They're making me out a tough guy," Bummy said. "All the newspapers make me a tough guy and I don't like it and I think I'll quit."

"Forget it," Charley said.

When Charley walked out Murder, Inc., walked in. They were all there—Happy and Buggsy and Abie and Harry and the Dasher—and they were looking at Bummy soaking his hand in the ice.

"You hurt your hand?" Buggsy said.

"No," Bummy said. "It's all right."

They walked out again, and they must have gone with a bundle on Farber because the day after Bummy licked Farber he was standing under the El in front of the gym and the mob drove up. They stopped the car right in front of him and they piled out.

"What are you, some wise guy?" Buggsy said.

"What's wrong with you?" Bummy said.

"What's all this you gave us about you had a bad hand?" Buggsy said.

"I didn't say I had a bad hand," Bummy said.

"You did," Buggsy said.

"Listen," Bummy said, spreading his feet the way he used to do it, "if you guys want a fight let's start it."

Buggsy looked at the others and they looked at him. Then they all got in the car and drove off, and if you could have been there and seen that you would have gone for Bummy for it.

That was the bad part about Bummy's rap. Not enough people knew that part of Bummy until it was too late. The people who go to fights don't just go to see some guy win, but they go to see some guy get licked, too. All they knew about Bummy was some of the things they read, and he was the guy they always went to see get licked.

Even the mob that followed Bummy when he was a big name didn't mean anything to him, because he could see through that. He could see they were always grabbing at him for what they could get, and that was the thing he never got over about the time he was training in Billy West's place up in Woodstock, New York.

Bummy went up there after he came out of the Army, just to take off weight, and there are a lot of artists around there. Artists are different people, because they don't care what anybody says about a guy and they either like him or they don't like him for what they think he is. They all liked him up there, and Billy used to say that Bummy could have been mayor of Woodstock.

Billy had a dog that Bummy never forgot, either. Bummy used to run on the roads in the mornings and Billy's dog used to run with him. Every morning they'd go out together and one day another dog came out of a yard and went for Bummy and Billy's dog turned and went after the other dog and chased it off.

"Gee, this dog really likes me," Bummy said, when he got back to the house, and he said it like he couldn't believe it. "He's really my friend."

The fight that really started everybody hating Bummy, though, was the Canzoneri fight in the Garden. It was a bad match and never should have been made, but they made it and all Bummy did was fight it.

Canzoneri was over the hill, but he had been the featherweight champion and the lightweight champion and he had fought the best of his time and they loved him. When Bummy knocked him out it was the only time Tony was knocked out in a hundred eighty fights, and so they booed Bummy for it and they waited for him to get licked.

They didn't have to wait too long. After he knocked out Tippy Larkin in five they matched him with Lou Ambers. Just after he started training for Ambers he was in the candy store one day when an argument started between Bummy and a guy named Mersky. Nobody is going to say who started the argument but somebody called Bummy a lousy fighter and it wasn't Bummy. Somebody flipped a piece of hard candy in Bummy's face, too, and that wasn't Bummy either, and after Bummy got done bouncing Mersky up and down Mersky went to the hospital and had some pictures taken and called the cops.

The first Johnny Attell heard about it was the night after it happened. He was walking down Broadway and he met a dick he knew.

"That's too bad about your fighter," the cop said.

"What's the matter with him?" Johnny said.

"What's the matter with him?" the cop said. "There's an eight-state alarm out for him. The newspapers are full of it. He damn near killed a guy in a candy store."

The cops couldn't find Bummy but Johnny found him. He dug up Gangy, and Gangy drove him around awhile to shake off any cops, and finally Gangy stopped the car in front of an old wooden house and they got out and went in and there was Bummy.

Bummy was sitting in a pair of pajama pants, and that was all he had on. There were four or five other guys there, and they were playing cards.

"Are you crazy?" Johnny said.

"Why?" Bummy said, playing his cards, but looking up.

"If the cops find you here they'll kill you," Johnny said. "You better come with me."

After Johnny talked awhile Bummy got dressed and he went with Johnny. Johnny took him back to New York and got him a haircut and a shave and he called Mike Jacobs. Jacobs told Johnny to take Bummy down to Police Headquarters, and when Johnny did that Sol Strauss, Mike's lawyer, showed up and he got an adjournment in night court for Bummy until after the Ambers fight.

The night Bummy fought Ambers there was Mersky right at ringside. He had on dark glasses and the photographers were all taking his picture and when Ambers beat the hell out of Bummy the crowd loved it.

The crowd, more than Ambers, hurt Bummy that night. He didn't like the licking Ambers gave him, but the hardest part was listening to the crowd and the way they enjoyed it and the things they shouted at him when he came down out of the ring.

"I quit," he said to Johnny in the dressing room. "You know what you can do with fighting?"

Johnny didn't believe him. Johnny was making matches for Jacobs in the Garden then and he matched Bummy with Tony Marteliano, but Bummy wouldn't train.

Only Johnny and Gangy knew this, and one day Johnny came out to Bummy's house and talked with Bummy. When that didn't do any good Lew Burston came out and he talked for four hours, and when he finished Bummy said the same thing.

"I don't want to be a fighter," Bummy said. "I like to fight. I'll fight Marteliano on the street right now, just for fun, but when I'm a fighter everybody picks on me. I want them to leave me alone. All I wanted was a home for my family and I got that, and now I just want to hang around my mob on the street."

Johnny still didn't believe it. They put out the show cards, advertising the fight, and one day Bummy saw one of the cards in the window of a bar and he phoned Johnny in Jacobs's office.

"What are you advertising the fight for?" he said, and he was mad. "I told you I'm not gonna fight."

Before Johnny could say anything Jacobs took the phone. Johnny hadn't told him Bummy didn't want to fight.

"How are you, kid?" Jacobs said. "This is Mike."

"Listen, you toothless sonofabitch," Bummy said. "What are you advertising me for? I'm not gonna fight."

He hung up. Mike put the phone back and turned around, and when he did Bummy was suspended and Johnny was out of the Garden and back in the Ridgewood Grove.

When Bummy heard what had happened to Johnny he went over to the Grove to see him. All the time Johnny was in the Garden, Bummy was a little suspicious of him, like he was a capitalist, but now he was different.

"I came over to tell you something," he said to Johnny. "I'm gonna fight."

"Forget it," Johnny said. "You can't fight."

"Who says I can't fight?" Bummy said.

"The New York Boxing Commission," Johnny said. "You're suspended."

"Let's fight out of town," Bummy said. "We'll fight where I'm not suspended."

Johnny did it better. He took Bummy back to Mike and Bummy apologized and Bummy fought Marteliano. For nine rounds they were even, and with ten seconds to go in the last round Bummy landed the hook. Marteliano went down and the referee counted nine and the bell rang and it was another big one for Bummy and he was going again.

It was Johnny's idea to get Marteliano back, but Bummy saw Fritzie Zivic lick Henri Armstrong for the welterweight title and he wanted Zivic. If you knew the two guys you knew this was a bad match for Bummy, because he just didn't know how to fight like Zivic.

There were a lot of people, you see, who called Bummy a dirty fighter, but the Zivic fight made them wrong. The Zivic fight proved that Bummy didn't know how to do it.

When he came out of the first clinch Bummy's eyes were red and he was rubbing them and the crowd started to boo Zivic. In the second clinch it was the same thing, and at the end of the round Bummy was roaring.

"He's trying to blind me," he kept saying in the corner. "He's trying to blind me."

When it started again in the second round Bummy blew. He pushed Zivic off and he dropped his hands and that crazy look came on that wide face of his and they could hear him in the crowd.

"All right, you sonofabitch," he said, "if you want to fight dirty, okay."

He walked right into Zivic and he started belting low. There was no trying to hide anything, and the crowd started to roar and before it was over people were on their chairs throwing things and the cops were in the ring and Bummy was fined $2,500 and suspended for life.

They meant it to be for life—which wouldn't have been very long at that, when you figure Bummy lived to be all of twenty-five—but it didn't work out that way. About three weeks after the fight Bummy walked into Johnny's office with Shorty and Mousie, and they sat around for a time and Johnny could see Bummy was lost.

"You know what you ought to do?" Johnny said. "You ought to join the Army for a while until this blows over."

This was in December 1940, before we got into the war. For a while Bummy sat there thinking, not saying anything.

"Could my buddies go with me?" he said.

"Sure," Johnny said.

So Johnny called up the recruiting officer and Bummy and Shorty and Mousie showed up and there were photographers there and it was a big show. Everybody was for it, and Ed Van Every wrote a story in the *Sun* in which he said this was a great move because the Army would teach Bummy discipline and get him in good physical shape.

That was a laugh. The first thing the Army did was split Bummy and Shorty and Mousie up and send them to different camps. They sent Bummy to Camp Hulen, Texas, and their idea of discipline was to have Bummy cleaning latrines with a toothbrush.

"You got me into this," Bummy used to write Johnny. "I'm going crazy, so before I slug one of these officers you better get me out."

Johnny didn't get him out, but he got Mike Jacobs to get Bummy a leave to fight Zivic in the Polo Grounds for Army Emergency Relief. Bummy used to fight best at about 147 pounds, and when he came back from Texas he weighed close to 200.

"You look sharp in that uniform, Al," Zivic said to him when they signed for the bout.

"I'm glad you like it," Bummy said. "You put me in it."

You can imagine how Bummy was looking to get back at Zivic, but he couldn't do it. He hadn't fought for eight months, and Zivic was a real good fighter and he put lumps all over Bummy and in the tenth round the referee stopped it. They had to find Bummy to take him back to camp. They found him with his wife and they shipped him back, but then the Japanese bombed Pearl Harbor and the Army decided it had enough trouble without Bummy and they turned him loose.

Bummy fought some of his best fights after that. He couldn't get his license back in New York but he fought in places like Holyoke and Bridgeport and Washington and Philadelphia and Elizabeth, New Jersey, and Boston. He didn't like it in those places, but he had to live and so no matter where he fought he would always drive back to Brownsville after the fight and sometimes it would be four o'clock in the morning before he and Johnny would get in.

It's something when you think about Bummy and Brownsville, when you think of the money he made, almost a quarter of a million dollars, and the things he had thrown at him and the elegant places he could have gone. It was like what Lew Burston said, though, when he said the Supreme was Bummy's Opera, and the Supreme is a movie house on Livonia Avenue.

You have to remember, too, that Brownsville is only a subway ride from Broadway, but Bummy had never seen a real Broadway show until Chicky Bogad sent Bummy and Barbara to see *Hellzapoppin* the night before the second Farber fight.

"How long has this been going on?" Bummy said when they came out.

"How long has what been going on?" Chicky said.

"People like that on a stage," Bummy said.

"People on a stage?" Chicky said. "For years and years. For long before they had movies."

"Is that right? I'll have to see more of that," Bummy said, but he never did.

All of those fights Bummy had out of town were murders, too, because Bummy wasn't hard to hit, but the people liked to see him get hit and when the Republicans got back in power in New York, Fritzie Zivic put in a word for Bummy, saying he guessed he had egged the kid on, and Bummy got his license back. That's when they matched him with Montgomery.

"What you have to do in this one," they kept telling Bummy, "is walk right out, throw your right, and miss with it. Montgomery will grab your right arm, and that will turn you around southpaw and then you hit him with the hook."

They knew that was the only chance Bummy had, because if Montgomery got by the first round he figured to move around Bummy and cut him up. They drilled Bummy on it over and over, and they kept talking about it in the dressing room that night.

"Now what are you going to do?" Johnny Attell said to Bummy.

"I'm gonna walk right out and miss with my right," Bummy said. "He'll grab my arm and that'll turn me around southpaw and I'll throw my hook."

"Okay," Johnny said. "I guess you know it."

Bummy sat down then on one of the benches. He had his gloves on and his robe over him and he was ready to go when there was a knock on the door.

"Don't come out yet, Davis," one of the commission guys said through the door. "They're selling some War Bonds first."

When Bummy heard that he looked up from where he was sitting and you could see he was sweating, and then he keeled right over on the floor on his face. Johnny and Freddie Brown rushed over and picked him up and they stretched him on the rubbing table and Freddie brought him to, and now they weren't worried about whether Bummy would do what they told him. All they were worried about was whether they could get him in the ring.

They got him in the ring and Burston had him repeat what he was supposed to do. When the bell rang he walked right out and threw his right and missed around the head. Montgomery grabbed the arm and turned Bummy around, and when he did Bummy threw the hook and

Montgomery went down. When he got up Bummy hit him again and that's all there was to it.

Montgomery was ten to one over Bummy that night and they couldn't believe it. Bummy got $15,000 for that fight and he borrowed $1,500 from Jacobs and the next day when Mike paid him off he told Bummy to forget the grand and a half.

"Take it out," Bummy said, throwing the dough on the desk. "You know damn well if he K.O.'ed me like you thought he would you were gonna take it out."

Bummy thought he'd never be broke again. He got $34,000 the night Beau Jack beat him and $15,000 when Armstrong stopped him. Then somebody sold him the idea of buying that bar and grill and somebody else sold him a couple of race horses and even after Dudy bought the bar and grill from him Bummy was broke.

He should have been in training for Morris Reif the night he was shot. Johnny wanted him to fight Reif, just for the dough and to go as far as he could, but Bummy said that a lot of his friends would bet him and he didn't think he could beat Reif, so instead he was sitting in the back of Dudy's drinking beer and singing.

Bummy used to think he could sing like a Jewish cantor. He couldn't sing, but he was trying that night, sitting with some other guys and a cop who was off duty, when he looked through that latticework at the bar and he saw the four guys with the guns.

"What the hell is this?" he said.

He got up and walked out and you know what happened. When Bummy stiffened the first guy one of the others fired and the bullet went into Bummy's neck. Then the three picked up the guy Bummy hit and they ran for the car. One of the guys with Bummy stuffed his handkerchief in the collar of Bummy's shirt to stop the blood, and Bummy got up and ran for the car. When he did they opened up from the car, and Bummy went flat on his face in the mud.

When the car started to pull away the cop who had been in the back ran out and fired. He hit one guy in the spine, and that guy died in Texas, and he hit another in the shoulder. The guy with the slug in his shoulder walked around with it for weeks, afraid to go to a doctor, and then one night a cop in plain clothes heard a couple of guys talking in a bar.

"You know that jerk is still walking around with the bullet in his shoulder?" the one said.

"What bullet?" the other said.

"The Bummy Davis bullet," the first said.

The cop followed them out, and when they split up he followed the first guy and got it out of him. Then the cops picked up the guy with the bullet and he sang. They picked up the other two in Kansas City and they're doing twenty to life. They were just punks, and they called themselves the Cowboys, the same as Bummy's old gang did.

It was a big funeral Bummy had. Johnny and Lew Burston paid for it. The papers had made Bummy a hero, and the newsreels took pictures outside the funeral parlor and at the cemetery. It looked like everybody in Brownsville was there.

The Day of the Fight

Graziano–Zale, September 27, 1946

THE WINDOW was open from the bottom and in the bed by the window the prizefighter lay under a sheet and a candlewick spread. In the other bed another prizefighter slept, but the first one lay there looking at the ceiling. It was 9:30 in the morning and he would fight that night.

The name of the first prizefighter is Rocky Graziano, but you don't have to remember that. The thing to remember is that he is a prizefighter, because they said this was to be a piece telling what a fighter does, from the moment he gets up in the morning until the moment he climbs into the ring, on the day when he must fight.

"All right, Rock," Whitey Bimstein, his trainer, said. "If you don't want to sleep you can get up."

The suite is on the twelfth floor of a hotel in New York's West Eighties, off Central Park. In the other bedroom Eddie Coco, one of the fighter's managers, still slept. On the soiled striped sofa in the sitting room a young lightweight named Al Pennino lay on his right side, facing the room, a blanket over him and a pillow under his head.

"If he don't feel like sleepin'," Whitey said, "there's no sense of him lyin' there if he wants to get up."

He was walking around the sitting room, picking up newspapers and putting them on the table, fussing around the doors of the closet-like kitchenette. Graziano and Whitey had been living there in the long weeks Graziano had been training for this one. They do not let a fighter live at home when he is in training for a fight.

Cosmopolitan, February 1947.

"What time is it?" Graziano said. He had come out of the bedroom and was standing just inside the sitting room. He was wearing a pair of brown checked shorts and that was all. There was sleep in his face and the black hair was mussed on his head.

"Nine thirty-five," Whitey said.

Pennino and Coco were awake and walking around now. The other fighter, Lou Valles, a welterweight, came out of the bedroom in a shirt and a pair of slacks.

"You sleep?" Coco said to Graziano.

"Yeah," Graziano said. "All right."

"We got a nice day."

Outside the window the sun shone a pale yellow and in the distance over the park there was a blue-gray haze. This one was to be held in Yankee Stadium and the weather is one of the things they worry about when they have an outdoor fight.

As they sat around the small sitting room now they said little, seeming reluctant to break the sleep that was still in their heads. Finally Valles got up and walked over to the table by the wall and picked up the morning newspapers. They were opened to the sports sections because Graziano was going to fight Tony Zale, the middleweight champion, and this one was an important fight.

"You see?" he said, showing one of the papers to Pennino. "That Rocky takes a good picture. Right?"

Graziano did not say anything.

"He's a good-looking guy," Pennino said.

"You know what I'm going to do if I win the title tonight?" Graziano said. "If I win the title, I'm gonna get drunk. You know what I mean by that?"

"Yeah," Whitey said. "I know what you mean. You remind me of another fighter I had. He said if he won the title he'd get drunk. He won the title and he had one beer and he was drunk."

"Who?" Graziano asked.

"Lou Ambers," Whitey said.

Graziano went to the bedroom and when he came out he had on a pair of gray sharkskin slacks, turned once at the cuffs, a basque shirt with narrow blue stripes, and over this a gray-blue sleeveless sweater. He had washed and his hair was combed back. At 10:30 Jack Healy came in. He is another of Graziano's managers, a suave but nervous type they call "The Mustache."

"You all right?"

"Sure," Graziano said. "Relax. I'm all right."

They waited for Pennino and Coco to finish dressing and they sat around talking about Stanley Ketchel, Bob Fitzsimmons, and Joe Dundee, Healy and Whitey talking and the fighters gazing around the room and out the window.

They were ready to leave then because it was 11:15. At the door the maid, in a blue dress with white cuffs and collar, said she wished them luck, and the woman who ran the elevator smiled at them in a way implying that she knew it was a special day.

Graziano's car was waiting in front of the hotel. It is blue and buff, new, and on the front doors the small letters read "Rocky." They got in, Healy driving, Graziano in the middle, and Coco on the outside, Whitey and Pennino and Valles in the back.

When they reached Fifty-fourth Street they turned west and stopped in front of the side door to Stillman's Gym. They got out and left Pennino to watch the car and went upstairs and into the gym, gray and, but for Lou Stillman and a couple of others, deserted.

"Hey," Stillman said, coming across the floor from the front.

"What you guys want anyway?"

"You know what we want," Whitey said.

"I'll punch you in the nose," Stillman said to Graziano. "I'll knock you out before tonight."

"You'll what?" Graziano said, feigning annoyance and taking a fighting pose.

"What's the matter?" Stillman said, smiling. "Can't you take a joke?"

They went back into a small partitioned room in the back. There was a scale and Graziano started stripping and they shut the door. In a couple of minutes they came out, Graziano fastening his belt.

"I'll bet you down there he'll weigh fifty-three and a half," Whitey said. "I'll bet you'll see."

"What did he weigh here?" Healy said.

"A little over fifty-four," Whitey said, "but he'll go to the toilet."

"He looks great," Healy said. "You can tell from his eyes."

In the car again they started around the block. Graziano shut off the radio that Pennino must have turned on while the rest were in the gym.

"You should listen to that," Healy said. "They might tell you about the fight."

Graziano said nothing. They drove west to the West Side Highway and south past the North River docks.

"Rock," Whitey said, "your old man still working down here?"

"No," Graziano said. "He's workin' down at the Fish Market instead."

It was 11:48 A.M. when they were looking ahead down the street to the mob around the rear entrance to the New York State Building where Graziano and Zale would weigh in. There were about two hundred people there, men, kids, photographers, and even a few women standing on and around the steps.

"We'll park down in front of your grandmother's," Healy said.

He drove slowly across the intersection past the park and pulled up at the curb on the right in front of the building where Graziano, as a kid, had lived. This was his neighborhood, and when they got out of the car there was a cop standing there and he stuck out his hand to Graziano and shook his head.

"Well," he said, "you're still the same, aren't you?"

Graziano said something but by now some of the crowd, running, had caught up. They were men, young and middle-aged, and a lot of kids, and one of the men had his left arm in a sling.

"You see this?" he was shouting at Graziano from the back and waving his right fist. "You see this? Think of this tonight."

"All right. All right," the cop was shouting. "Stand back."

They hustled the fighter, then, into the narrow doorway between two stores and, with the fighter leading, they climbed up three flights. He opened a door and there they followed him into the kitchen of an apartment.

"Hello," he said to the man standing there and then pausing and looking around. "Where's Grandma?"

"In the park maybe," the man, Graziano's uncle, Silvio, said. "Maybe shopping. She went out about half an hour ago."

Graziano sat on a chair by the window, his right elbow on the windowsill. He looked around the room and through the door and into one of the bedrooms and his uncle watched him.

"How you feel, Rocky?" Silvio said.

"I feel fine," Graziano said.

That was all they said. He sat there waiting, looking around occasionally, not saying anything to the others who had followed him in. The door to the hall was open and presently a couple of photographers came in.

"Do you mind, Rocky?" one of them said. "We'd just like to get a picture of you and your grandmother."

"That's all right," Graziano said. "She'll be in soon."

He looked out the window again and, leaning forward, at the street below.

"Here she comes now," he said.

An old woman hurried across the street carrying a brown paper bag in one arm. She had been stout once and she had on a gray print house dress and a small black hat and when she came in, breathing heavily from climbing the stairs, she walked across the room, smiling, and took Graziano by the hands and the two of them stood there speaking in Italian and smiling.

Graziano took her then by the arms and led her to the chair by the window and she sat down and put her bundle on the floor and took off her hat. She sat there smiling at Graziano and looking occasionally at the others and nodding her head.

"Do you mind now?" the photographer said to Graziano.

"Oh," Graziano said, and then he turned to the old woman. "They want to take a picture for the newspapers of you and me."

"Picture?" the old woman said, and her face changed. "That's why you come?"

"Oh no," Graziano said, and his own face had changed and he was shaking his head. "Oh no. I'd have come anyway. They just came in."

"I put on black dress," the old woman said.

"No," the photographer said to Graziano. "Tell her no. We'll only take a minute. We haven't got time."

"No," Graziano said to her. "That dress is all right."

"I put on nice black dress," the old woman said.

They took several pictures, then, of Graziano showing his grandmother, in the house dress, his right fist, and then Graziano said goodby to her, taking her by the hands, and he and those who had followed him went downstairs where there was a crowd waiting.

They pushed through the crowd, kids grabbing at Graziano and trying to run along at his side, and men shouting at him, things like: "Hey, Rocky!" . . . "Good luck, Rocky!" . . . "Flatten him for me, Rocky!"

They swarmed, half-running, down the street and the bigger crowd around the steps of the State building shouted and pushed, the cops shoving them back, and the photographers' bulbs flashing and many in the crowd making fists. Inside they hurried into an elevator that was waiting. The room upstairs was a big one. It was crowded with men, some of them standing on chairs, and at the end of the room by the desk there was a scale and around that the crowd was tight-packed.

They pushed the fighter through, the crowd quiet, and when he got to the desk there was some milling around and conversation and then he started taking off his clothes and tossing them on the desk. The crowd stood back and watched him, and he stripped and took off even his wristwatch and his ring, and put on a pair of purple boxing trunks.

Mike Jacobs, the promoter, Nat Rogers, the matchmaker, Eddie Eagan, the chairman of the New York State Athletic Commission, Irving Cohen, another of Graziano's managers, Art Winch and Sam Pian, Zale's managers, Healy and Coco and Whitey—they all were there on the inside of the crowd. Outside of them were newspapermen and photographers and more commissioners, and then Graziano stepped on the scale and Eagan leaned forward and adjusted the weight on the bar and watched the bar settle slowly to rest.

"The weight," Eagan said, announcing it, "is exactly one hundred fifty-four. Graziano, one hundred fifty-four pounds."

Several of the newspapermen were crowding out to find telephones and there was the noise of conversation in the crowd.

"How much did Zale weigh?" Healy asked.

"A hundred and sixty," somebody said.

"Black trunks for Zale," Harry Markson, Jacobs's press agent, said, announcing it. "Purple trunks for Graziano."

Graziano sat on the desk and Dr. Vincent Nardiello, the commission physician, put a stethoscope to Graziano's chest. Then the doctor took the fighter's blood pressure and announced the heartbeat and blood pressure figures to the press.

"All right, Zale," Eagan said, raising his voice. "All right, Zale. Come out."

The other fighter, Zale, who would fight Graziano, came out through a doorway to the left of the desk. He was naked except for the black trunks and tan street shoes. The crowd moved back and he walked to the scales where Graziano stood. They did not look at each other.

"Take a pose. Make them pose," the photographers were hollering and Zale and Graziano faced each other, Graziano's arms cocked wide at the sides of his chest, Zale's arms drawn up in a fighting pose in front of his chest. They stood there holding the pose while the bulbs flashed again and their eyes met. Graziano smiled once and nodded. Zale smiled back.

The photographers were still working away, shouting for one more, swearing at each other, when Eagan stepped between the fighters and moved them over beside the desk.

"Now, I understand you're both good rugged fighters," Eagan said, "but I want a clean fight. I want no hitting in the breaks and that's one rule I'm going to caution the referee to observe."

He talked with them for another moment and then he turned and Zale went back through the door and Graziano went back to the desk and they both dressed. When they were finished dressing they walked, each with his group around him, through the crowd down the hall to another office where, in separate corners of the room, they tried on the gloves and alternate sets of gloves. One of the commissioners marked with a pen each fighter's name on the white lining of his gloves.

"He's got a bad eye," someone said to Graziano, nodding toward Zale who was waiting while the commissioner marked his set. "It's his left."

"No," Graziano said, looking over at Zale. "I noticed that. It's his right, not his left."

There were crowds again in the hall and outside the building, running after him and shouting the same things, a few of them different things, but most of them over and over again: "Hey, Rock!" . . . "Good luck, Rock!" . . . "I prayed for you last night."

They hurried down the street, photographers running ahead of them, and pausing to snap them, and the crowd pushed on behind. They passed the car parked at the curb and went into a small bar and restaurant on the right where a cop stood by the door to keep the crowd out.

They walked through the bar quickly into a small restaurant in the back. There were a half-dozen tables with red and white striped tablecloths on them and Graziano sat down at a table at the right. In the corner at the left there were two men and two women at a table, and one of the men said something to the others and they turned around quickly and watched Graziano as he sat there fingering a fork and waiting while the others, eight or ten, pulled up chairs around the table or stood in back.

"Look, Rock," Healy said, and he shoved a photograph of Graziano in a fighting pose across the table, "autograph this, will you?"

"Okay, Jack," Graziano said, looking at him and then reaching around for the pen someone handed him from in back. "Don't get excited. Relax."

"I know," Healy said, "I'm more excited than you are. I'll relax."

"Autograph it to Pete," someone said. "Pete is his first name. Pasca is the last. P-A-S-C-A."

Graziano wrote something on the photograph and Healy put another down in front of him.

"Sign that to Pat," he said. "P-A-T."

"What is it, a girl or a fella?" Graziano said.

"I don't know," Healy said. "Put 'Best Wishes, Rocky.' It don't matter. That covers it."

In the arched doorway they stood watching, about fifteen or twenty of them, and then the waitress came from the back, carrying on a tray a cup of tea with a slice of lemon on the saucer. She put those down and went away and when she came back she had toast and a soft-boiled egg broken into a cup.

Graziano sat there eating the egg and the toast, blowing on the tea and trying it. They had let those from the bar into the restaurant now and they stood, three and four deep around the table, not saying anything or speaking only in whispers, watching in almost complete silence the fighter as he finished the egg and toast.

There were the crowds outside again, then, shouting the same things, and the cop had to clear a path through them to the car. There were many faces at the windows of the car, faces shouting and fists, and Healy pulled the car away from the curb and drove east and then north on Second Avenue and at Forty-ninth Street he turned west.

On Forty-ninth Street at Seventh Avenue they had to stop for a light. They sat there, not saying anything and waiting for the light to change, when a guy in a white shirt, in his twenties, came off the sidewalk and thrust his face into the open front window of the car where Graziano sat between Healy and Coco.

"Hey, Rock," he said, making a fist, "if you win I get married. If you lose she'll have to wait a couple more years."

He turned as if to leave the car and then he saw them inside starting to smile.

"I ain't kiddin'," he said, turning back and reaching into his pants pocket and coming out with a fist full of bills. "Fresh dough I just got from the bank."

Graziano said nothing. Healy drove over to Ninth Avenue where he had to swerve the car out to avoid a bus pulling wide from the curb.

"You see?" he said. "These bus guys think they got a license to do anything they want."

"Watch," somebody said. "He's gonna yap."

The bus driver was shouting out of the window at his side.

"Hey, Rock!" he was shouting. "Good luck tonight. I know you can flatten that guy."

"What do you make of that?" Healy said. "How do you like that?"

In front of the hotel they sat in the car waiting while Whitey went up to get a leather bag containing Graziano's robe, his boxing shoes, his trunks, and the other things he would need in the fight. While they waited Healy went across the street to a newsstand and came back with the afternoon newspapers. He tossed them down on the front seat and Graziano picked up the first one and turned to the sports page where the banner headline read "Zale Picked to Knock Out Graziano in Eight Rounds."

"Look at this," he said to Healy, flatly, without emotion.

"That's okay," Healy said. "What a guy thinks, he should write."

They drove to Coco's house, which is in the Pelham Bay section of the Bronx. They parked the car in front of the house and walked down the concrete driveway to the back where there were eight or ten men and women and a couple of kids on the back porch.

"Rocky," Mrs. Coco said, "these are friends of ours from Utica. They'd like to meet you and they came down for the fight."

Graziano shook hands with them and they all smiled and tried not to look at him steadily. They studied him furtively, the way some men study an attractive girl on the subway. He sat there on the porch for a few minutes while the others talked around him and they took him downstairs for the dinner on which he would fight.

There is a bar at one end of the wood-paneled room and there was a long table set for twelve. He sat at the head of the table and some of the others sat watching him while they brought him his dish of spinach, his plate of lettuce, his toast, and his steak.

Graziano ate quickly, cutting large pieces, using his fork with his left hand, always holding the knife in his right. When he said he wanted some water, Whitey said he could have a little without ice. He had some hot tea and lemon and then he said he did not want to eat any more, pushing away the plate on which there was still a small portion of steak.

"That's all right," Whitey said. "If you feel satisfied, don't force yourself."

He went upstairs, then, and sat on the porch while the others ate. When they had finished, a half hour later, it was 4:20 and Whitey said they would take a short walk before Graziano took a nap.

They walked—Graziano and Pennino in front and Whitey and Healy in back—down the street and across the street under the elevated to the park. They walked through the park until 4:30 and then Whitey told them it was time to turn back. They walked past a barbershop where they saw Coco sitting down for a shave. Whitey said he would stop in the drugstore down the block and that he would be right back. Graziano and Pennino went into the barbershop and Graziano sat down in the barber chair next to the one in which Coco sat.

"I'll get a trim, Eddie," he said. "Is it all right if I just get a trim in the back?"

"Sure," Coco said. "Why not?"

A couple of girls in their teens and wearing sweaters and skirts came in then and stood by the chair looking at Graziano as he looked back at them.

"Are you Rocky Graziano?" one of them said.

"Yeah," Graziano said. "That's right."

"I could tell by your nose," one of them said. "You gonna win tonight?"

"Sure," Graziano said, smiling. "Why not?"

By now Whitey had come back.

"What are you doin' in the chair?" he said.

"I'm gettin' a trim," Graziano said.

"A what?"

"A trim. A trim just in the back."

"Listen," Whitey said, "get up out of there. It's time for you to rest."

"Look, Whitey," Graziano said, "I'm restin' here."

"C'mon," Whitey said.

When they got back to Coco's house they sat in the living room. At ten minutes to five Graziano went in the next room and phoned his wife and at five o'clock Whitey said it was time for Graziano to go upstairs and lie down.

"What difference does it make?" Healy said. "He'll flatten the guy anyway."

"I know," Whitey said, "but he goes upstairs and takes his nap."

Graziano and Whitey went upstairs then and Mrs. Coco showed them a small room with maple furniture and a single bed. When Mrs. Coco had turned the covers back she left and Graziano stripped down to his shorts and sat on the bed.

"See if they got any comic books, will you, Whitey?" he said. "Go downstairs and see, hey?"

Whitey went downstairs and came back with one comic book. Graziano took it and looked at the cover.

"Go out, hey Whitey?" he said, looking up. "Go out and get some others."

Whitey and Coco walked up the street to a candy store where they picked out ten books from the rack: *Buzzy* . . . *Comic Capers* . . . *Captain Marvel, Jr.* . . . *Whiz Comics* . . . *Sensation Comics* . . . *Ace Comics* . . . *All-Flash* . . .

When they came back and opened the door to the bedroom Graziano was lying on his back under the covers reading the comic book and there was a towel over the pillow under his head.

"Hey!" Coco said. "What about that towel?"

"Yeah," Graziano said. "I got some grease on my hair."

"What of it?" Coco said. "We're gonna wash the sheets and pillow case."

They went downstairs, then, and left him. It was 5:20 and for the next hour and a half the men sat in the driveway at the back on chairs they had brought from the porch and the kitchen and they talked about fights.

At 6:50 Whitey got up and went into the house. He heard someone on the stairs and Graziano came into the kitchen, dressed, his hair combed back.

"Hey," Whitey said. "I was just gonna get you up. You sleep?"

"I don't know," Graziano said. "I think maybe I dropped off a little."

They went out into the back yard, then, and Graziano sat down on one of the chairs. Dusk was setting in, so one of them lighted the garage light so they could see a little better and they sat around waiting and not saying much. At 7:25 Whitey said they had to go.

The driveway, dark, seemed full of people. Some of them wanted to shake his hand and the rest kept calling the word "luck."

"If you hear any noise from section thirty-three," one woman yelled, "that's us."

"We've got an undertaker with us from Utica," another woman said, "so you don't have to worry and you can hit him as hard as you like."

"Excuse me, Rocky," Mrs. Coco said, "but this is my delivery boy and he wants to meet you."

"Sure. Hello," Graziano said.

They walked out the dark driveway and pushed through a lot of kids who had been waiting there all afternoon and got into the car. It took them twenty minutes to drive to Yankee Stadium. On the way Pennino, in the back seat, sang songs and Whitey told a couple of old jokes.

When they reached the Stadium, Healy pulled the car up in front of Gate Four and stopped.

"You can't stop here," a cop said.

"This is Graziano," Healy said.

"I can't help it," the cop said.

Healy did not argue with the cop but eased the car down a few feet in front of another cop. Now someone in the crowd had spotted Graziano in the front seat and the crowd stopped moving forward and started to gather around the car.

"This is Graziano," Healy said to the cop.

"You shouldn't stop here," the cop said.

"I know it," Healy said, "but we gotta stop somewhere. He's fightin' tonight."

"You better see the lieutenant," the cop said.

"C'mon," Whitey said. "Let's get out. Leave it here."

They got out and the cops were pushing the crowd back now and those in the crowd were calling the same things the other crowds had called before. The cops were clearing a way through and Whitey gave Pennino the bag and they pushed through to the gate.

Along the tunnel under the stands they led Graziano now into the clubhouse used by the visiting teams. It was divided lengthwise down the middle by a wood-framed partition covered with cheap lavender cloth. Just inside the door a half-dozen preliminary fighters were in various stages of preparation, getting into their ring clothes, having their hands taped, warming up. They led Graziano past them and, parting a heavy dark blue drape, into his own part of the room.

"What time is it now?" he said, looking around.

"Eight o'clock," somebody said.

He sat down on one of the folding chairs to wait. Whitey had opened the leather bag and was taking out the equipment—the ring shoes, the boxing trunks, the protective cup—and placing them on the rubbing table, when Commissioner Eagan and Commissioner Bruno came in. They shook Graziano's hand as he stood up and stood talking with him for a minute or so and then they left.

"You better warm up, Rock," Whitey said. "Just warm up a little."

Graziano moved around the room, clothed, throwing short punches for about five minutes, and then sat down again.

"Let's go," a voice outside said, calling to the preliminary fighters. "The first two bouts."

Graziano stood up again. He took off his sweater and his basque shirt and went to a locker and hung them up. He came back and sat down on the table, and took off his shoes and socks. He got off the table and put them in the locker and then he took off his trousers and shorts and hung them up. He came back and sat down, naked now, on the table, and Whitey handed him a new pair of white woolen socks. He put them on and then put on his boxing shoes. He started moving around the room again, throwing short punches, weaving and bobbing a little as he went. He did this for a couple of minutes and then Whitey called to him and he went over and tried on a pair of the purple trunks. He took them off and tried on another pair, which he seemed to like better.

Sol Bimstein, Whitey's brother, came in and walked over to the table and picked up a pair of the purple trunks.

"Ain't these a nicer color purple?" he said.

"I like these best," Graziano said.

"Whichever he likes best," Whitey said.

Graziano put on his basque shirt, then, and began shadowboxing around the room again. A couple of deputy commissioners came in to stand there and watch him and then Whitey took Graziano's robe—white with a green trim and with Graziano's name in green block letters on the back—and spread it over half the table. Graziano stopped the shadowboxing and took off his trunks and shirt and walked to the table and lay down on his back.

Whitey worked first over his upper body. He rubbed coco oil on Graziano's chest. Then he put a towel across Graziano's chest and Graziano turned over and lay facedown and Whitey rubbed the oil on his back. Then he sat up and Whitey went over his legs with rubbing alcohol. Whitey was sweating and he took off his own shirt. He worked hard on Graziano's legs and then he went back at his shoulders and chest. When he was finished Graziano got off the table and, once again stripped but for his shoes and socks, moved around throwing punches until Whitey stopped him and took him over to a corner where they talked together quietly and Whitey showed Graziano a move with his left. Then he told Graziano to sit down and put his feet up on the table and he put a towel across Graziano's back and another across his legs.

"What time is it?" Graziano said.

"Eight fifty-five," Sol Bimstein said.

"I thought it was later than that," Graziano said.

"How do you feel?" Whitey said.

"Tired," Graziano said.

At nine o'clock a couple of commissioners and Art Winch, one of Zale's managers, came in.

"Is it time?" Whitey said.

"Yes," Winch said. "We might as well get started."

Graziano got up, then, and Whitey helped him into the white and green satin robe. He sat on the table, his legs hanging over, and Whitey started bandaging Graziano's right hand, Winch and the commissioners watching. It took him about seven minutes to do the right hand. When he was starting the left hand Winch said something and Whitey raised his voice.

"Just what I'm allowed," he said. "No more. No less."

"All right. All right," Winch said.

They stood there watching until the job was done and then Sam Pian, Zale's other manager, came in.

"You stayin'?" Winch said.

"Right," Pian said. He sat down on a chair by the lockers and Winch and the commissioners went out. Graziano, the tape and gauze a gleaming white on his hands now, started moving around, shadow-boxing again.

"I'm spying," Pian said as Graziano passed near him.

"Yeah. Sure," Graziano said. "I know."

He stopped throwing punches.

"This tape stinks," he said, looking at his hands.

"I know it does," Pian said.

"It peels off," Graziano said. He started moving around again, the leather of his shoes squeaking in the quiet room, the satin of his robe rustling. Mike Jacobs came in and Graziano stopped and spoke with him and then Jacobs went out and Healy came in.

"You got half an hour," he said.

"All right," Graziano said. He walked out through the drape.

"Where's he goin'?" Pian asked.

"Some of the preliminary fighters want to see him," Healy said. "They can't come in so he went out to see them."

"Oh," Pian said.

"He's a nice kid, ain't he, Sam?" Healy said.

"Yes," Pian said. "I guess he's a nice kid."

He got up to follow Graziano as Graziano came back in. Healy started out, and put his head back in between the curtains.

"I'll see you after, Rock," he said.

"Scram," Graziano said, looking up from where he was sitting by the table, his feet on the table, his hands on his lap. "Get out."

"I'll punch you in the eye," Healy said. He threw a kiss and pulled his head out as Sol Bimstein came in. "Main bout next," Sol said. "There's two rounds to go in the semifinal."

"Is it warm out?" Graziano said.

"Just nice," Sol said.

Graziano sat there waiting and Whitey came over to him and rubbed a little Vaseline on Graziano's face. It was ten minutes to ten. Whitey said something to him and he got up and went out. In a minute he came back and Whitey helped him off with his robe. He helped him into his protector and his trunks and then Graziano stood there rotating his shoulders, bending at the waist. When he stopped Whitey gave him a short drink from the water bottle. Then Whitey rubbed Graziano's chest and his stomach and his shoulders and Graziano took several deep breaths. Then Graziano began pacing back and forth, throwing short punches, breathing hard through his nose. He was doing this when a couple of the commissioners came in.

"Hey, Rock," one of them said to him. "What are you going to do with all the dough you get? The place is packed."

"All right," a voice shouted in from outside. "Main bout. Main bout."

"All right, Rocky," Whitey said. He moved over to his fighter and put the towel around his fighter's neck, crossing the ends in front, and he helped him back into his robe. Somebody took the pail and Whitey had his first-aid kit and, with Pian still watching them and following them, they moved out.

In the tunnel there were special cops and a couple of preliminary fighters who shouted something at Graziano. They moved quickly through the tunnel and down the steps to the lower level. Whitey's hand was on Graziano's back. Graziano kept exercising his arms, jigging a little now and then. They were close around him and they moved quickly along the lower level and then up the steps of the dugout where they hit him with the sound.

There were 39,827 people there and they had paid $342,497 to be there and when Graziano's head came up out of the dugout they rose and made their sound. The place was filled with it and it came from far off and then he was moving quickly down beneath this ceiling of sound, between the two long walls of faces, turned toward him and yellow in the artificial light and shouting things, mouths open, eyes wide, into the ring where, in one of the most brutal fights ever seen in New York, Zale dropped him once and he dropped Zale once before, in the sixth round, Zale suddenly, with a right to the body and a left to the head, knocked him out.

The Fighter's Wife

Norma Graziano Gets Through the Night

IT WAS 9:30 in the evening, and they would put on the fight shortly after 10:00. There were about a dozen people in the house, all but two of them women, but it was not noisy. They sat in the carpeted, lush living room on the ground floor of the red brick, two-family house. For an hour, on and off, she had taken part in their small talk, but now she went into the kitchen and got out the ironing board.

"I hope he should retire," her grandmother said. "I hope he should win and retire healthy. He must be healthy for his family. Allus hope with my whole heart he should be healthy."

One day, when Norma Unger was seventeen years old, she and her friend Alice and Alice's friend Yolanda were sitting at a table in an ice-cream parlor on the corner of Seventh Street and Second Avenue. They were having sodas and talking about boys. Yolanda said her brother was coming out of the Army, and she reached into a pocket and came out with two snapshots of him.

"I think you'd like him," she said to Norma, while Norma looked at the pictures, "and I think he'd like you. I think it would be fun to arrange a blind date."

That was the first time Norma Unger ever heard of Rocky Graziano, the first time in her life.

"The last time he fought Zale," her mother said, "she had her portable radio, and was walking up and down the street, turning it on and off."

Cosmopolitan, December 1949.

"Once she sat in the bathtub all through the fight," her grandmother said.

So they arranged a blind date for the next Saturday night. On Saturday, she found she wanted to do something else so, still early in the evening, she walked over to Yolanda's house. It was a walkup on First Avenue, and she climbed the steps, rang the bell in the hallway, and waited. There was one bulb burning at the ceiling. After a while Yolanda came downstairs, and Norma explained to Yolanda. While she was explaining, she heard a noise at the top of the stairs, and there he was, hurrying down the stairs. She was embarrassed.

"Oh," Yolanda said, stopping him when he got to the foot of the stairs, "this is Norma Unger. Norma, this is my brother, Rocky."

"Hello," she said looking at him.

"Hello," Rocky said, and then he turned. "I'll see you." He left.

He was wearing a dark blue suit, and he had on a gray hat, porkpie style. He had nice eyes and a nice smile and a nice face—he looked nice altogether. That was the first time Norma Unger ever saw Rocky Graziano, the first time in her life.

"The time he won the title in Chicago," her mother said. "You remember how he was getting beaten, and she ran crying into the bedroom and locked the door. When she came out, he was middleweight champion."

"I don't know," her grandmother said.

"Every time she does something different," her mother said.

They used to see each other around the neighborhood after that. She saw him in the ice-cream parlor a few times. A couple of times they had sodas together. Alice used to go out with Terry Young, the fighter, and he was Rocky's friend, so the first date they had was a double date with Alice and Terry. That was when she found out he was a fighter, but nobody had ever heard of him, and she didn't think much about it. After that they went to the movies a lot. He was always in a happy mood, and he wasn't one of those guys who was always trying to kiss a girl goodnight, and that helped.

"I don't know," her grandmother said. "I wonder what she does tonight."

"I don't know," her mother said, looking around. "Where'd she go?"

It was the first they had missed her. A couple of her friends, one named Lucille and the other named Innocent, got up and walked out into the kitchen and found her ironing.

"So?" Innocent said.

"Oh," she said, "just a blouse for Audrey for school tomorrow. I thought I could sneak it in. You know, anything to keep busy."

"That's right," Lucille said. "That's why we should do the dresses."

It was 9:35.

They were married after they had known each other for three months. For a while they had teased each other about getting married. One day Rocky met her and said Yolanda was getting married. He said Yolanda was going down for her blood test, and they ought to go along to see what it was like. When they got there with Yolanda, they decided to take the blood test themselves. Then, because they had had the blood test, they decided they should get married right away.

She was still only seventeen. They went to City Hall, but a man told them she would have to have her mother's consent. She was afraid to ask her mother or her grandmother, so they took the Hudson Tubes to Hoboken, New Jersey, and then took a bus to Bayonne. They walked along the street and asked some people until they found a place with big windows in the front. It looked sort of like a real-estate office, but it said "Justice of the Peace" on the window. The man said they would have to have the blood test in Jersey and stay there for a while before he could marry them, so they went home.

She doesn't remember exactly how they managed it. A few days later they started going around to buildings downtown. They went around to a hundred buildings, it seemed, and finally a man married them.

It was in an office. She had on a beige suit, and Rocky had on a dark blue suit and a white shirt and dark blue tie. There were a couple of detectives around the building, and Rocky gave them five dollars each to be witnesses. The ceremony seemed so short. She had never thought anything about a big wedding, because they didn't have the money, but still it seemed so short.

A funny thing—after Rocky became famous he was fighting in the Garden one night and after the fight, as he was coming out of the ring, a man stopped him in the aisle.

"Hey," the man said. "Remember me? I'm your best man."

"Who the hell are you?" Rocky said.

"Don't you remember?" the man said, and it was one of the detectives. "I'm the guy who stood up with you on the day you were married, Rock."

She went into one of the bedrooms—quietly, because Audrey, who is five, and Roxie, who is going on two, were sleeping.

When she came out, she had a pile of new dresses in her arms. She dropped them on the table, found the sewing basket, and stood there watching, smoking a cigarette, while Lucille and Innocent began to sort the dresses. Each selected a dress, and began to turn up its hem.

It was 9:40.

"I'll take the radio in," Norma said. "I won't listen."

She went to a closet and took out a small radio and carried it, with its electric cord dangling, to those sitting in the living room. While she was gone the other two sat sewing, not saying anything.

"She's too nervous," Lucille said finally. "I told her to have some brandy around."

"She doesn't drink," the one named Innocent said.

"She could have some brandy around."

When Norma came back they were silent. She stood, leaning on the sideboard, smoking and watching them. She is twenty-three now, slim, dark-haired. She had on a gray-and-green print dress, with short sleeves and a flared skirt.

"I called up my husband," Lucille said, sewing, "and he said the whole place is closed down. Everybody went to the fight. Even the bartender went to the fight."

She used to go to see him fight, but that was at first. One day, while they were still just going together, he asked her to walk over to the gym with him to watch him train. It was the gym on Fourteenth Street, and it was the first time she had ever seen any fighters in a ring. She stood in the gray, dusty-looking gym with all the men, watching Rocky box. Then he always wanted her to go with him when he fought, to Fort Hamilton and the Broadway Arena and the Ridgewood Grove. She liked it less and less, and the first Frankie Terry fight was the last she ever saw. It was such a bad thing to watch, because they were cursing and even kicking. It was a real free-for-all, and after that she wouldn't go any more, although for a while she used to stand outside the clubs and wait for him to come out.

At first, he couldn't understand it. Maybe he thought it meant something else, because he got mad about it once. When she wouldn't go with him for his fight with Leon Anthony, he wouldn't fight. They went to a movie together instead, and Rocky was suspended by the Boxing Commission because of it. After a while, though, she was able to explain it so he saw it, and now he understands why she doesn't even want to watch him train.

"What time is it?" the one named Babe asked.

"It's nine forty-five," Lucille said.

"You people sew so nice," Babe said. Babe was standing in the doorway, watching the two at the table. Then she walked into the kitchen and sat down on one of the high red and white stools.

"The sewing circle," Norma said. "Boys are so much easier."

"Don't say that," Babe said. "You should see my Joseph."

"They make clothes so nice now," Innocent said, sewing.

"I'm getting a nervous stomach," Norma said.

She left them and walked toward the bedrooms and the bath. It was nine fifty by the kitchen clock.

Their first night they spent in a hotel on Fourteenth Street. Then they went to the flat where Rocky's people lived, on First Avenue between Eighth and Ninth streets. They had one bedroom and Rocky's parents had the other. There were only four rooms, so Rocky's brother Lennie slept in the living room, and his sister Ida slept in the kitchen. They lived like that for five months.

For two years after that they lived in Brooklyn with Norma's mother and stepfather. There were only three rooms, so they slept in the living room. When Audrey came a crib was moved into the living room, too.

"Norma," one of those from the living room said, "what's the number on that little radio?"

It was the one named Lee; she was standing in the doorway, leaning against the frame. Norma had come back into the kitchen and was watching the sewing.

"I don't know," Norma said, and the one named Lee left.

"Listen, Norma," Babe said. "He'll come out all right. You know what my husband said, 'We'll carry him home on our shoulders.' Tony says, 'I shouldn't go to the fight, because I get so nervous, but I'm goin' because Rocky is gonna win.'"

"Like my husband," Lucille said. "Dom was cryin' after the last one. Some fellas from Second Avenue found him and said, 'C'mon, we'll take you home.' So tonight he said he didn't care if he was to go or not."

They could hear them tuning in the radio in the living room. Music and then a man's voice came over the radio very loud, and then softer. It was just ten o'clock.

"Say," Norma said, "and what do you think you're doing?"

It was Audrey, standing in the doorway that leads to the bedrooms—a small, dark-haired child in a long white nightgown. She was just standing, blinking in the light, rubbing her eyes with the backs of her hands.

"Aah," Babe said.

"You're makin' too much noise," the child said, still rubbing her eyes, her voice small and whining. "You're makin' too much noise."

"Aah," Babe said. "C'mere."

She reached down and drew the child onto her lap. Audrey continued to rub her eyes.

"How do you like school?" Babe said, bending over to talk to the child.

"She won't be able to stay up," Norma said. "She has to get some sleep."

"She knows something is happening," Innocent said.

"You're makin' too much noise," the child said.

"What's happened?" Norma said, looking up. "You can't get it?"

It was Phil, Lee's husband. He was just standing there, dapper and looking at them and smiling.

"We got it," he said, smiling. "I'm goin' in now."

Now they could hear from the radio the voice of Bill Corum. It was Bill Corum all right, the voice just a little hard and sportslike.

"Bill Corum with Don Dunphy bringing you another major sports event for . . ."

"All right," Norma said softly, getting up and going to the child. She took the child from Babe then, and carried her out of the room.

After a minute, Norma came back. She stood in the doorway and watched the girls sew, and she lighted another cigarette.

"I don't even think it's ten o'clock yet," Lucille said.

"It's after ten," Norma said, "but they have to get the introductions out of the way."

Now, from the radio far off in the living room they could hear the voice of Johnny Addie, the ring announcer. His voice was very clear, but distant, the only sound in the house.

". . . popular middleweight from Cleveland, Chuck Hunter."

"My husband was like this all day," Babe said, moving her hands. "Back and forth, back and forth. He couldn't eat."

". . . middleweight contender from Brooklyn, Vinnie Cidone."

"If anybody wants to go in—" Norma said.

"No," the two at the table said together, shaking their heads.

"I have to go in," Babe said, sliding off the stool.

"If anybody else wants to go in," Norma said, "—because I'm gonna close this door."

"No," her mother, a rather short, trim woman, standing in the doorway, said. "Let's take a walk."

"Wait until it starts," Norma said.

". . . the welterweight king, Sugar Ray Robinson!"

"This is the worst part," Lucille said, "waiting through 'The Star-Spangled Banner.'"

"All right," her mother said. "Let's go."

". . . the ring officials are assigned here by the New York State Athletic Commission . . ."

Norma went to get a fresh pack of cigarettes, and then they hurried, the three of them, each one seeming almost to fall over the one ahead, through the dining room and through the living room. In the living room, those crowded around the small radio looked up and shouted something as the three hurried out the front door.

"We're going for a walk," Lucille said, shouting it back.

". . . from Irvington, New Jersey, wearing black trunks—Charley Fusari!"

It was the last thing she heard, as she rushed out of her own house and into the night.

She had never, at any time, thought marriage would be like this. When she was still so young that she had listened to the words of Frank Sinatra's songs, she had known they were not the truth, and that it would never be like that. She had not thought about it much, just when she did get married it would probably be to some ordinary working guy, and they would live in a little apartment. She could never have known that it would be to a fighter, and that they would have two cars and live in their own house, and that, periodically, she would be driven from her own house by voices like this.

"It's an advantage I have when he fights in the warm weather," Norma said. "I can go for nice long walks."

They stood together for a moment under the tree in front of the house. It was a warm, rather humid evening and the street was busy with traffic, the cars' headlights flooding across the three women standing under the tree and lighting cigarettes and then starting to walk down the block.

"It's not so warm," her mother said. "I'm cold."

"It isn't really cold," Norma said, "but my teeth are chattering."

"Listen," Lucille said, "you can hear the fight even out here on the street. Look at them up there."

They could see them on a second-floor sun porch of one of the brick houses, men sitting around, shirt-sleeved, smoking. Through the open windows they could hear, faintly, the voice of Dunphy. They could tell he was calling the fight, but it was impossible to tell what he was saying, and they walked along under the trees, their heels making hard sounds on the pavement.

"Fusari's! . . ."

They heard that much as they started past another house, and when Lucille heard it she stopped, dropping back. Then she turned into a driveway, her head forward, and stood motionless.

"Let's walk faster," Norma said.

"All I hear is 'Graziano, Graziano,'" her mother said.

"It isn't so much that he wins or loses," Norma said, "but that he doesn't get hurt. Of course, when you win it leaves a better taste, but it's just that he shouldn't get hurt."

Walking along, their heels clicking faster, they could hear Lucille running up behind them, breathing audibly.

"Your husband must be winning," Lucille said. "Your husband must have knocked Fusari down. I heard him say something about the middle of the ring."

"I don't want to hear it," Norma said, walking.

When they came to the corner they stopped for just a moment under the streetlight. Then they turned left and started walking again.

"Who said being a fighter's wife is easy?" Lucille said.

"It's like being in the ring," Norma said.

"She fights right in the ring with him every fight," her mother said, talking to Lucille.

"That's the trouble," Norma said. "You can't get in the ring with him."

"What could you do?" her mother said.

"Well," she said, "if they put Fusari's wife in the ring."

"He just said Fusari's in trouble," Lucille said quickly.

"You heard it?" Norma said.

"Yes."

"I don't know," Norma said. "It's too much."

"That's the funny thing," Lucille said. "Everybody seems to wait for tonight but you."

"I wait for the night after tonight."

They had reached another corner and turned left again. The radio was loud from the house on the corner, the whole first floor lighted beyond the stucco steps. They could hear the hysteria in Dunphy's voice, the crowd noises behind it.

"Shall I ask?" Lucille said. "I could ask here if somebody has been knocked out."

"No," Norma said. "Never mind."

She kept walking, but her mother and Lucille stopped. Lucille started up the steps, toward the loud and frantic radio. When she got to the top of the steps, a dog started to bark in the house, and then the door opened and the dog, wild-looking, stood there barking.

"No," Lucille said to the dog, holding up her hands and starting to back down. "Never mind."

A boy showed behind the dog, a boy of about twelve or thirteen. The boy grabbed the dog and the dog stopped barking.

"We wanted to know—" Lucille said, halfway down the steps, "we wanted to know if one of the fighters was knocked out."

"No," the boy said, "but Fusari is hurt bad. He's gettin' a beating."

"Norma!" her mother said, standing on the sidewalk and hollering it. "Rocky's winning."

"But when?" Norma said, stopping and turning and shouting it back.

The two were running down the block toward her now. They could see her dress, the light from a streetlamp falling on it through the trees.

"It's the fourth round," Lucille said, running up.

"All I hear," her mother said, "is 'a left by Graziano, a right by Graziano.'"

They lighted more cigarettes and started to walk again, Norma between them. A car went by and slowed as it approached the corner, and they could hear the car radio coming through the night.

"It's still going on," Norma said.

"All of a sudden it isn't cold any more," her mother said.

"It got warm," Norma said, trying to laugh.

"That's a funny thing," Lucille said. "Isn't that funny?"

This is a neighborhood of those two-family brick homes. There are small, neat lawns in front of the houses, and low hedges and concrete walks leading up to the front doors.

"We should have gone to a movie," her mother said.

"That's what I did for the Bummy Davis fight," Norma said. "I saw half a movie. You would think you'd get over it."

"Every fight it gets worse," her mother said. "At first we used to be able to go to the fights."

They were back in front of the house. They had slowed down and now they stopped. They could hear, although not distinctly, the radio in the house. They seemed reluctant now to leave the vicinity of the house, to start out on another walk. Suddenly, Babe came running out.

"What?" Norma said. "It's over?"

"No," Babe said, excited, "but Rocky's ahead. He can't seem to get the left, though. They say something on the radio that he can't seem to get the left." She was shaking her left fist.

"Was Fusari down?" Lucille said.

"No, but in one round the bell saved him, so we hear. Now it's four rounds for Rocky and three for Fusari or something, but Fusari's bleeding now."

"Is Rocky hurt?" the mother said.

"In the third round he was bleeding over his left eye, but it doesn't bother him now. You should hear it, because it seems—"

Norma was rocking a little, back and forth, one foot ahead of the other, smoking and looking at Babe and then down the block.

"You should look on it like any other business," Norma said.

"Whatever happens happens," her mother said.

"But you can't do it," Norma said.

Dunphy's excited voice came from the house again. Lucille turned and ran toward the house, and Babe followed her. Norma and her mother began to talk.

"Babe said that Rocky slipped, that he crossed his feet and slipped."

"He always does that," Norma said. "Clumsy."

"Once he fell off a ladder," her mother said.

"Yes, remember?" Norma said, a small smile starting. "Audrey was inside the house watching him through the window, and all of a sudden he disappeared. When he's introduced, he usually manages to fall into the ring."

"It seems such a long time," her mother said.

"Well, it takes forty minutes if it goes ten rounds. That's a long time."

"You're telling me."

"I should go to the dentist when he fights. That way I can't worry about him."

"Oh-oh, it's still on."

"I want to hear it, but I don't want to hear it."

"That's it. You want to hear the good part of it."

"It must be the tenth round pretty soon now."

". . . Fusari's down! . . ."

The phrase, from a car radio, came quickly and loudly, and then was gone. When they heard it they stopped, their feet poised to go on.

"Fusari's down!" her mother said.

"But did he get up?"

". . . a left hook by Graziano. A right by Graziano . . ."

It came from a house and they stood facing the house, their heads turned to hear it. Even then they could hear only some of it.

"Maybe he'll do what he did in the Cochrane fights," Norma said.

"Norma!" It was a scream from down the block. When they heard it, they turned quickly, and they could see figures running, through the light and shadow, out of the house.

"Norma! Rocky wins! He wins! He wins!"

They ran toward the house. As they ran, neighbors came tumbling out of houses, appearing at the low ledges along the sidewalk, shouting to them. The street was all noise now, and when she got to the house she was out of breath, and they were swarming around her, hugging her, kissing her, shouting at her, all of them trying to tell her at once.

Inside now, she hurried to the radio, where the rest were still gathered, and she knelt down in front of it, listening while Corum told again how it had happened. Now she could not get enough.

"What time will he get home?" somebody asked.

"I don't know," she said. "You never can tell."

After the last Zale fight, she couldn't help it. Even when she heard them bringing him into the house, she couldn't stop crying, because that was the first time he had ever really been knocked out like that.

The night in Chicago when he beat Zale was the other kind of night. When he came back to the hotel, with the mob around him, Rocky and she went into the bedroom together to wake Audrey and tell her that her father was the middleweight champion of the world. Audrey was three then, and when they woke her she stood up in the crib and looked at her father and saw the bandages over one eye and the other eye swollen and closed and the welts on his face.

"What happened, Daddy?" Audrey asked sleepily.

"You see what I said?" he said, bending over and pointing his finger at Audrey. "Now stay outta the gutter."

It was three hours before he got home. During those three hours more people had come. The neighbors came in and the men came back from the fight. They congregated in the kitchen, those who had been there and the newcomers, and they fought it all over again for her—swinging their arms, getting more and more excited. They said the same things over and over, and even those who had been in the house all evening, listening to the radio, kept repeating themselves.

"When I was close to the radio," the one named Lee told her twice, "he was losing, and when I walked away he was always winning. I walked away, and Fusari was down. So I stayed away, and Rocky won the fight."

Norma stood out on the terrace for a long time, waiting. A couple of reporters came—Jim Jennings and Harold Weissman from the *Mirror*—and Weissman asked her questions about when she had last seen Rocky fight, and if she had been nervous. In the house, the phone rang again and again and someone finally answered it.

"You should go to bed," her grandmother said to Norma. "The baby will be up early."

At 1:45 a car pulled up, and the mob along the curb and on the sidewalk pressed around it. It was Jack Romeo, and he pushed through them and came up the steps, handing her something in a paper bag.

"What is it?" she said reaching for it. "A bottle?"

"No," he said. "The gloves."

She heard them along the curb, then, calling and applauding. In what light there was, she could see him—in a white cap, a white towel around his neck. Then he had the towel in his hands, and he was pushing through them, acknowledging them in a thick voice, until he climbed the steps and saw her.

"Hello, honey," he said, going to her and kissing her quickly.

They walked into the house together, their friends around them. They stood for a minute in the middle of the crowd, Rocky answering Weissman's questions.

Rocky said, finally, "I'm gonna take a hot bath now, if you'll excuse me. I mean I'm all sweaty. You know? I gotta relax."

"Sure. Sure," they said.

She walked out with him, through the dining room and the kitchen and down the hall to the bathroom to run the water into the tub—to be glad again, finally—at two o'clock in the morning—that she is this fighter's wife.

"But don't you want him to retire?" a reporter said to her once. "I mean as soon as you get a little more money?"

She was sitting in a chair in the corner of the room and the reporter was sitting across the room from her.

"No," she said, "I mean, that's not up to me. I think a husband should do whatever work he likes to do. I think if a wife sees her husband happy, that's enough."

Punching Out a Living

Billy Graham, Boxing's Uncrowned Champ

It was three weeks and one day away from the fight when Billy Graham drove out to Long Pond Inn to go into camp. When you are a prizefighter and thirty years old and married and have two small kids, you can't get into shape any more living at home.

"You have too many distractions," Billy was saying, driving out. "My wife understands, but take like this morning. At seven thirty the kids wake me. They wake me at eight thirty. At nine thirty, they wake me again. I said to Lorraine, 'Look, can't you keep these kids away from me? I gotta get my sleep.' She said, 'You slept enough, didn't you?'"

So he got up and drove Lorraine down to the supermarket to load her up with groceries for the three weeks. Then they drove over to Sunrise Highway to buy a red wagon for young Billy's third birthday, two days away, and at three o'clock, he left Long Island and drove to Manhattan and then across town and into the Lincoln Tunnel.

When you're a young fighter and make your first big pay night you buy a big yellow convertible. By the time you go into camp for your 118th fight in twelve years, you know it's a hard dollar and you're paying off the house in Springfield Gardens and you have the kids to think of, and so you drive a small sedan.

Collier's, May 2, 1953.

"With me it's a case of winning every fight now," he was saying, driving. "If you don't have the big punch—you know, the glamour—you have to win for your bargaining power. All you have is your record."

Billy's record, on pages 399–400 of Nat Fleischer's *Ring Record Book*, with a picture taken ten years ago, shows ninety-nine wins going into this one, but only twenty-five by K.O., eight draws, and ten losses, eight of them of split decisions.

"A punch is something you're born with," he was saying. "Either you have it or you don't. I gave it a try. I thought punching the heavy bag would do it. In 1946 I knocked out Pat Scanlon in five. I knocked out Frankie Carto in nine and sent him to the hospital. When I fought Tony Pellone he just managed to keep his balance, and I had Ruby Kessler on the deck. The papers were starting to write I was becoming a puncher."

It was a gray afternoon and he was driving out Route 3. It is a wide, flat concrete highway with here and there a gas station or a roadside restaurant or a place that sells outdoor furniture and pottery.

"Then I boxed Tippy Larkin in the Garden, and I was looking to K.O. him, too," Billy said. "He won it big. After that, I forgot about the big punch."

After the Larkin fight they talked about it one day in Stillman's—Billy and Irving Cohen, who manages him with Jack Reilly. Jack is the one who discovered him in the boys' clubs about fifteen years ago, and Irving does the front work.

"Billy," Irving said, in that soft way of his, "you're trying to put everybody away with two punches. When you try that, you tighten up, so let's get back to boxing. That's what you do best. You'll make money that way."

How much money do you make? In 1949, and always rated in the first half dozen welterweights, you clear about $7,500. In 1950, you split two fights with Kid Gavilan and clear a little better than $10,000. In 1951, you make about the same, and in 1952 you have your best year and your end comes to about $20,000.

"Every once in a while," he was saying, "Lorraine talks about me giving it up. It's tough on a wife. At first there's some glamour to it. You go out and you're recognized, but you're keeping in shape so you can't go out a lot. She's alone—like now, for three weeks—and it's rough. So I tell her, 'Sure, I'll quit, but what else am I gonna do? Do you want to live on sixty a week? Let me work something out.'"

Greenwood Lake extends north across the line from New Jersey into New York State. The camp is on the highway that runs along the west shore of the lake, a long, low concrete building painted white with green trim, built between the highway and the lake where the shore drops down to the water. At the south end, the steps lead down from the parking space to the bar and dining room and kitchen under the gym and the dressing rooms and the rooms where the fighters sleep.

"Johnny Dee," Billy said to the bartender.

"Billy Graham," Johnny said. "How's Billy Graham?"

Johnny was behind the bar, leaning on it and talking to a customer. In the back of the dining room, Rollie LaStarza was sitting at the end of the table, eating with Nick Florio, who trains him, and with James J. Parker, the heavyweight out of Canada. Eddie McDonald, who owns the place with his wife, Catherine, and Ollie Cromwell, was standing there, a cigarette hanging out of his mouth, watching them eat their steaks and talk.

"How's Billy Graham?" LaStarza said.

"Good," Billy said, shaking hands all the way around. "How are you?"

"He's in great shape," Eddie McDonald said. "He'll lick this guy, take it from me. Rollie will put lumps on Mr. Rex Layne. He'll play football with him."

"How long you been here?" Billy said, sitting down at the other end of the table.

"Five weeks," LaStarza said.

"When you leavin'?"

"Tomorrow morning. When's your fight?"

"Three weeks," Billy said.

There are always fighters coming and going through Long Pond Inn. On the next morning Rollie LaStarza would go into New York to beat Rex Layne in Madison Square Garden, and James J. Parker would knock out Jack Nelson in the semifinal. The following Friday, Paddy DeMarco, who trained here before leaving to finish up in Brooklyn, would lose to George Araujo in the Garden. Two weeks after that, Billy Graham would check out to go into the Garden against Joe Giardello, who held two decisions over him.

"And I'll tell you something else," Eddie McDonald said, still standing, the cigarette still hanging from his lips, the ash on it long now. "Mr. Bill Graham will give Mr. Giardello a real good lickin' this time. He'll win."

"Yeah, I'll win," Billy said, giving a short laugh, "but will I get it?"

The question is what made this fight important. On December 19, Billy Graham had boxed Joey Giardello, a middleweight out of Philadelphia, in the Garden, and when Johnny Addie had announced the decision there had been a near riot. The referee and one of the judges had given it to Giardello, and there was Billy walking up and down in the ring holding out his hands in appeal and the crowd booing and hollering.

A few minutes later Robert K. Christenberry, chairman of the New York State Athletic Commission, and Dr. Clilan B. Powell, one of the two other commissioners, had changed the card of one of the judges, Joe Agnello, to give Billy the fight. The switch in decision had made headlines, and a week after Billy got into camp it was to make headlines again when a Supreme Court justice named Bernard Botein reversed Christenberry and Powell.

"You'll get it," Eddie McDonald said. "You'll get into great shape up here. Skipper will help you. Skipper!"

Skipper is a brown and white dog, part beagle. Whenever Eddie cannot think of anything else to do he calls the dog and he keeps at him until the dog yawns and makes a guttural sound in his throat that Eddie says is talking.

"Here, Skipper!" Eddie said. "Say hello to Billy. Say 'Mama.'"

The dog was sitting at Eddie's feet. He was just sitting there, looking up at Eddie and not doing a thing.

"This is a real smart dog," Eddie said. "He likes Billy."

Billy put away a steak and some vegetables and a green salad and a cup of tea. Eddie told him to take the back room, and he went up and lugged in his bag and then his road shoes and the black footlocker with his boxing things—gloves, headgear, white terry-cloth robe, long underwear, sweatshirts, windbreaker, and the gray-green Marine trousers he wears on the road. Then he went to the movies.

"You get older," he was saying the next morning, "and you find it takes about three weeks to get ready. The first couple of days I just like to rest—sleep long and eat good and walk."

On Saturday, two days after Billy got there, Irving Cohen and Jack Reilly sent up Frank Percoco, the trainer. Billy went on the road for the first time that morning with Walter Cartier, the middleweight who came up to train for a bout with Randy Turpin in England. In the afternoon Billy went into the gym for the first time.

The gym is a nice, clean place with knotty-pine planking on the walls and the ring set over by the windows that look down and out into the lake. The first dressing room off the showers is for the sparring partners, and the room beyond that is for the fighters; inside is a rubbing table with clean sheets always on it.

The first four days Billy just loosened up. He shadowboxed and did sit-ups on the mat and rolled on the medicine ball to get the weight off his middle. Then he would skip rope and punch the light bag. Frank Percoco left after the fourth day and Whitey Bimstein came up to take over, bringing Johnny Noel, a sparring partner, with him. That afternoon Billy boxed.

At first you go three rounds. After a while, you work it up to six. Irving Cohen earned an edge for Billy by arranging to have the fight go twelve rounds. Cohen figured Giardello is just a twenty-two-year-old kid who never went more than ten and Billy went fifteen twice with

Gavilan and knows how to pace himself. Still, you never box more than six in the gym, and you build up your wind and your legs on the road.

Every morning at 8:30, Whitey would get Billy up, and Billy would wake Walter Cartier, and they'd go out on the road. Different fighters do it in different ways, but Billy and Walter would just start out from the camp, running easy along the left side of the concrete highway north and into the town of Greenwood Lake, then off to the right along the shore of the lake by the white cottages with the rowboats turned bottoms up on the lawns. Then they'd make the circuit back through the town again and down the highway to the camp, a full distance of 3.3 miles.

When they'd come off the road they'd go to Billy's room. Whitey would bring up hot tea and lemon and they'd sit there with towels around their necks, sipping the tea and sweating and talking. Then Walter would go into his room to lie down and listen to some disc jockey on the radio, and Billy would lie down on his bed and cool out and hear the radio through the wall.

"I used to think a training camp was wonderful," he said, lying there one morning. "The first time I ever went to one I was boxing Pat Scanlon and they sent me out to Ehsan's at Summit as a sparring partner for Dorsey Lay. It cost me nothing, and I thought it was great. It was new. I liked it, you know? It was like I used to read about as a kid, getting up and doing roadwork, eating with the other fighters."

Whitey came in while Billy was talking. Billy got up and started to undress, taking off the layers of sweatshirts and long underwear so Whitey could rub him down with alcohol.

"Gus Lesnevich was there," he said, "training for a fight in England. Bernie Reynolds was there, but you're not in a camp for pleasure. You got to drive yourself. People say you eat steak every day, but after a while it's not gonna taste so good. A camp is a place for work. A camp costs money."

The camp costs about $700 to get ready for a main-event fight. It's $10 a day each for you and Whitey and the sparring partner, and you pay the sparring partner $5 a round. All in all, with publicity, you've paid out about $1,000 by the time you climb into the ring.

"At first I'm glad to get here," Billy said. "I got quiet. I can sleep. The food is good. Then you start missing the wife and kids."

One of Billy's brothers, Jackie or Robbie, would drive up with Lorraine and the kids—little Billy and Ellen, who is two—on Sundays. They'd be there a couple of hours, watching Billy work in the gym. Then they'd leave and the rest of the time it would just be the running on the road every morning and the work, sweating, in the gym in the afternoon. Once, some of Billy's pals drove out—Ray O'Connell and Joe De Chara and George Papageorge and a couple of others—and they sat around and amused Billy, but the rest of the time he would just shoot a few games of pool with Ollie Cromwell or listen to Eddie McDonald argue fights or talk to the dog.

"Watch this, Billy," McDonald would say. "Watch Skipper. Skipper is a real smart dog."

There would be the same songs, time and again, on the jukebox, too. A guy and a gal would drop in for a drink at the bar, and the guy would plunk a coin into the jukebox, and out would come "Don't Let the Stars Get in Your Eyes" or "Blues in the Night" or "Glow-Worm," over and over.

"Billy can go with any style," Whitey was saying one evening while the jukebox was going and Billy was out taking his walk with Walter Cartier. "Billy don't have to train a certain way for a certain style."

"That's right," Eddie McDonald said, sitting down next to Whitey.

"This fight depends on condition," Whitey said. "Billy's got to set the pace with more infighting. The other guy don't fight inside, and Billy is one of the best infighters in boxing today. The last couple of years he picked up them inside punches."

"Billy can take a punch," Eddie said.

"Nobody in boxing takes a punch like Billy Graham," Whitey said. "All the fights he's been in, and he's never even been staggered. All the tough fights he's in, and I never seen him blow his top."

"Billy will lick this guy," Eddie said. "Billy will lick him, but good. He will make mincemeat of Mr. Giardello."

Billy licked Kid Gavilan for the title, in the Garden on August 29, 1951, but he didn't get it. All the newspapers said he won it, and the writers called him "the uncrowned welterweight champion of the world." But the only title that counts, the only one you can make any money with, is the one you get in the ring.

In the gym, Whitey would stand on the ring apron while Billy was boxing, leaning on the ropes and never taking his eyes off Billy. Every now and then he'd holler at Billy, getting him to throw his punches in combinations and making him move in under Johnny Nocl's leads to punch more to the body.

"Stick!" Whitey would call, just loud enough for Billy to hear. "Now inside. Under and over."

It all started when Billy was a kid, growing up around Second Avenue and Thirty-sixth Street, on New York's East Side. There was Robbie, a year and a half older than Billy, and then Billy and then Jackie, five years younger, and then Jimmy, who was three years younger than that.

Billy's old man ran a candy store between Thirty-fifth and Thirty-sixth on Second, where he sold school notebooks and pencils and pens and a little sporting goods, too. At this time, Billy's old man was crazy about Jimmy McLarnin, and he gave Robbie and Billy boxing gloves and they used to square off in the room in the back of the store. When Prohibition went out, the candy store became a bar, and then it moved up to the corner of Thirty-sixth and Second, but Billy still calls it "the store."

When Billy was ten, his old man took him up to the Catholic Boys' Club on Thirty-seventh Street between First and Second. It was in an old tenement, and they'd ripped out the walls to make one big room on each floor. The top floor was the gym, with a mat for a ring and a big sandbag.

Every night Billy would go up there from 7:00 P.M. until 9:00 P.M. and Ed Tirnan—a nicely built guy with reddish hair and a little bit of a fighter's nose—would line the kids up and show them how to box. He was the one who taught Billy how to jab—straight out all the way from the shoulder, turning your fist down.

Billy weighed sixty-five pounds and he started to box for the Catholic Boys' Club and later for the Madison Square Boys' Club. He got so good that the other clubs were trying to steer their best kids out of Billy's weight class. In about eighty of those fights Billy won all but two or three.

"School was murder," Billy was saying once. "I went two years to high school, but I couldn't get over that Latin. I didn't study at all. I had my mind set on being a fighter."

Popeye Woods was fighting out of Billy's neighborhood then. This was in the late thirties, and if Popeye had worked at it and lived right he might have been the middleweight champion of the world.

"I'd see him hanging around on the corner or at the Boys' Club," Billy was saying. "I'd say, 'What round you gonna knock him out in?' When he fought at one of the clubs in town I'd save up. A seat was seventy-five cents upstairs, and to get there I'd sneak on the subway or hitch on a bus or a taxi or any car that stopped for a light."

Billy was walking on the road, walking his breakfast down one morning. There is a place near the camp where a little trickle of a stream comes down the hillside to the highway, and Billy would never walk by it without bending down to get a drink. He'd say it was the best water he ever tasted.

"Popeye used to bust guys up just with his jab," Billy said. "He once told me, 'You can watch a bum, and he may do one thing you can use.'"

Any fighter has a little bit of every fighter he ever saw and admired. Even now, Billy still loops a right hand once in a while instead of shooting it straight because when Billy was a small kid Max Baer had a looping right hand and it made Max the heavyweight champion of the world.

Four times Billy tried to get into the Golden Gloves and each time they turned him down for what they called a heart murmur. It got to be a joke around the neighborhood.

"What's your old man doin'?" the guys would say. "Payin' the doctors so you won't get your brains knocked out?"

Billy went to work as a stock boy, six days a week, at the Lord & Taylor department store in Manhattan. He worked at it for three months. It's the only job he ever had, because one Sunday Jack Reilly came to the family bar and made a suggestion. The way he had it figured, Billy could take out an application for the pros and, if he passed the physical, he could have five or six fights to see how he liked it.

Billy passed. That was early in 1941. Then Jack took him to meet Irving Cohen. They went to a luncheonette and soda fountain at Twenty-ninth Street and Second Avenue.

"Irving came in and he was sitting there," Billy was saying, "and he had a pencil and a piece of paper. He wrote on the paper, and then he said, 'Willie Graham, William Graham, Bill Graham, Billy Graham. I like Billy Graham best. It'll look better in an ad.'"

You do a lot of talking in camp. There isn't much else to do, just working and sleeping and eating and talking, but the one thing Billy never talked about unless somebody else brought it up in a question was Giardello and the coming fight.

"Joey's a good fighter," he'd say. "I have nothing against him. It was the officials who couldn't see it."

For the last day of work, two days before the fight, they brought Jimmy Herring, the middleweight, up from New York to sneak right hands over Billy's left, like Giardello. Just a year before, Billy had outboxed Herring in the Garden and he could handle him again, but that afternoon Billy didn't look good and Herring was dropping that right hand in there almost every time he let it go.

"Don't worry about it," Billy said later. "It'll be all right."

Billy's brother Jackie came up for the last workout and to take Billy's car back. That same day Paddy Young came in to get in shape for Ernie Durando in the Garden. The last night, Paddy drove Billy to a movie in Warwick and by ten o'clock Billy was in bed.

The morning of the fight, he got up at 9:45, and he was shaving when Whitey went in at 10:00 to wake him. Whitey helped him pack, and then Whitey and Johnny Dee loaded the stuff into the trunk of Johnny Dee's car.

Johnny drove, with Billy in the front on the outside and Whitey in the back along with Eddie McDonald and his wife. On the way down Whitey fell asleep, and when they got into town they dropped Eddie and his wife off at Eighth Avenue and Forty-eighth Street. Then Johnny drove around to the Athletic Commission offices on West Forty-seventh Street. By the time Billy got upstairs there was a crowd in the big room, with Giardello there in a light gray suit and sitting on a bench talking with Tony Ferrante, one of his managers, and a couple of others.

"Inside, Billy," somebody said.

In the back room Dr. Alexander Schiff was examining a preliminary boy and he nodded to Billy, who walked over to where Dr. Vincent Nardiello, the ringside physician for most Garden fights, was waiting for him. Billy stripped to the waist and the doctor took his blood pressure and put the stethoscope on him and then examined his eyes and mouth.

"Very good," Nardiello said, finally. "Good luck to you."

For his first pro fight, four rounds with Connie Savoie in St. Nick's Arena on April 14, 1941, Billy personally sold $160 worth of tickets around the neighborhood. When Dr. Schiff had started to examine him that day, Billy was so nervous the doctor made him sit down for a while to relax. This day Billy was completely calm.

On the scales Giardello weighed 155½ and Billy 149¼; when Irving made the match he gave Giardello all the weight he wanted just to get the two extra rounds. Irving figured the weight wouldn't help Giardello much and the distance would help Billy.

Whitey got Billy to try on the gloves and then put on the black trunks with white stripes. Then the newspaper photographers asked Billy to take a fighting pose with Giardello; the two of them stood on a bench with the photographers shooting up from below.

"You watch them take that picture?" Billy said to Jack while Jack was helping him dress.

"Yeah," Jack said.

"Did you see his right hand?" Billy said. He made a fist and shook it to show Jack how nervous Giardello was, and that was the way he himself had been, weighing in twelve years ago for that first fight.

"Are you sure I can handle him?" he had asked Jack after looking at Savoie. "Look how tough he looks."

"He's the walk-in type," Jack told him. "You'll jab his head off."

Billy was so nervous he didn't wait to find out. He walked right out and started throwing punches and flattened Savoie in the first round.

Now, after the weigh-in with Giardello, Johnny Dee drove Billy and Whitey up to the Shelton Hotel on Lexington Avenue and they checked into a room there. Then they went into the dining room, and Billy had his breakfast. It was 1:30.

"Take good care of Mr. Graham," the headwaiter was telling the waiter. "He fights tonight."

"Orange juice," Billy said, "two soft-boiled eggs, tea, and toast."

While Billy was eating, his mother came in, and he got up and kissed her, and she sat down. She is a little woman—four feet ten—with wide blue eyes, and she didn't say much; she just sat there and watched Billy until he finished eating and got up to go upstairs.

"Good luck, chicken," she said when he bent down to kiss her again, and then she turned to Whitey and said, "I hate to think of it. I don't even watch TV."

Billy bought the papers at the newsstand in the lobby, and then went up to lie down on the bed. He went through the papers quickly, just reading the stories on the fight, spotting the odds. They all had him 8½ to 5.

"They all pick me," he said finally, putting the papers down. "I guess it proves I won the last one. If I didn't, why would they be picking me now?"

"You're right," Whitey said.

At three o'clock they walked to the Scribes Restaurant, not far from the hotel, where Billy knows the bartender. He put in his order—steak and green vegetable and tea—and then he and Whitey went for a long walk.

For that first fight, twelve years ago, he had the steak at home. Then after he took his walk he was thirsty. Jack and Irving had told him not to drink much water, so he had two glasses of milk instead. When he started throwing punches he almost lost everything he'd eaten.

"That shows you how much I knew," Billy said, telling it once. "I was a real green kid."

They walked back toward the hotel and then up fourteen blocks and across one block and then back. All the way along, people kept popping out of the crowd to wish him luck, and at one place a guy came out of a bar and dragged him in to meet a couple of others.

"It's television," Billy said when he came out. "The last couple of years everybody recognizes you."

"Excuse me," a man said, on the sidewalk. "I been thinking of you for three months."

He was a little man, in a camel's hair coat and wearing a gray fedora. He had a small blond mustache, the ends pulled to points.

"I was gonna write you," he said, holding the lapel of Billy's camel's hair. "When you throw that right hand, step in with the right foot. You gotta do that. You see, I used to fight. I fought Young Corbett, Frankie Neil. I fought champions. I was no good, but I had Young Corbett on the deck and not many did that. Like I said, when you throw the right, step in with it. I'd have written you, but you might never have read it. All right?"

"All right," Billy said, nodding.

"So good luck," the man said.

The guy was right, but what they don't understand is that if it's not part of you after all these years it never will be. Try to step in and you're in trouble, because it's against your style and there's no way for you to get out.

When they got back to the hotel it was six o'clock. Whitey went down to the lobby and left Billy alone, lying in the bed with his clothes off for an hour, and at seven he went up again and Billy got up. They were packing the ring clothes into Billy's bag when Robbie came in with another bag, and in it was the blue satin robe with the white trim and the name on the back in white. For his first four or five fights, Billy wore an old flannel, Indian-design bathrobe he used to wear around the house. Then Robbie and Jackie and Jimmy chipped in and they bought him this one. It meant a lot to Billy and he has had it ever since.

"I just spoke to Lorraine," Robbie said. "She's fine."

"I know," Billy said. "I was just talking with her on the phone. She's gonna stay with her mother."

They were married on October 2, 1948, in the rectory of St. Patrick's Cathedral. It was a beautiful day, warm and with the sun shining so that you didn't even need a topcoat. He had seen her the first time a year before when his brother Jackie and Pete Cassidy took him up to her folks' place across the street from the bar. She has blue eyes and long wavy brown hair, and that time she had on a pair of black lounging pajamas with gold on the jacket, and Billy tried to make a date.

"I've made plans to go to the hockey game in the Garden tonight," she said.

"What do you want to watch that nonsense for?" he said.

They used to go to dinner and to dance at the Century Room of the Commodore and the Café Rouge at the Statler. At first she couldn't understand how you can go into a ring and punch someone. A few times she watched it, and then she gave up.

It was eight o'clock when they got to the Garden and went into the Fiftieth Street entrance. They had the big dressing room on that side. After a while Jack and Irving came in, and they stood around Billy, who was sitting on the bench against the wall, talking the fight.

"There are three things you got to remember," Jack was telling Billy, and Irving was nodding. "On the break you have to get off fast, because he likes to sneak you there. Second, he's gonna look to throw the right hand over your jab, so after you jab you gotta weave. Third, you must go to his body, and slow him down. He don't like it in the body. Will you remember that?"

"Sure," Billy said. "Don't worry, Jack." Billy was the coolest of them all.

He always bandages and tapes his own hands. When Ferrante and one of Giardello's other seconds came in to watch it and got into an argument with the boxing inspector working Billy's room, Billy just went on taping.

"What's this, a new rule that two of us can't watch?" Ferrante said.

"Yeah," the other guy said, nodding toward the inspector, "and this guy just made it."

"Never mind," the inspector said. "One of you get out."

"Is this okay?" Billy said, showing Ferrante the left hand.

"Okay," Ferrante said.

He was as cool as that going out. "The Star-Spangled Banner" caught him just starting down the aisle, and he stood there at ease.

"You're a little nervous," he had explained once at Stillman's Gym, sitting on one of the benches behind the ring, "but not afraid. You know you can smother the other guy's leads and handle anything he can do. You're just a little nervous about fighting your best fight."

It was the best house in the Garden in a year, and you could feel it when Billy got into the ring. The wrangle over the last fight made it a natural rematch, and then Giardello said in the papers he was going to knock Billy out.

Joey started out like he meant it. Billy stuck out the left, and Giardello dropped the right over it, and a shout went up. He did it again, and then Billy tried to weave under as they planned and his nose banged into Giardello's head, and when he came up, there was the cut, right across the bridge, and the blood coming out of it and smearing on his nose and cheeks.

Blood always looks bad to the crowd, and when Billy lost the first two rounds they probably thought he was in for it. In the corner, Whitey did a real good job, closing the cut while Irving and Freddie Brown, who was the other corner man, kept talking.

"Stop fighting this guy and box him," they kept telling Billy. "Get your jab moving and back him up with it and then move inside."

From the third round on, Billy started forcing it. He'd jab real stiff, turn in behind it to make Giardello miss the right, and then he'd bang to the body. By the middle of the fight it was a pro working on a kid.

"Young fighters don't hold their class," Billy said once, "because you have to build up to it. Over the years you build up your stamina, and you go ten rounds over and over and you learn pace."

Sure, Giardello made a fight of it. He's a strong kid and he'd land. In the fourth round he shifted to his left and caught Billy with a right-hand uppercut, and when he came on to take the tenth it was still close.

"Now forget the first ten rounds," Irving said to Billy in the corner. "You must win these next two."

"Sure, Irving," Billy said, looking at him. "Don't worry about it."

Billy just turned it on in the last two. Giardello was swinging instead of punching now, his arms pulling his body after them. And all the time Billy was fighting well, still on a straight line, making Giardello miss and hitting him inside and then rocking his head back. Now he could do the things they had worked on in camp because the pace and the distance were too much for Giardello, a kid who was just in there now on heart.

"And the winner by unanimous decision," Johnny Addie, the announcer, said, "Billy Graham!"

"Don't let anybody tell you otherwise," Billy said in the dressing room. "The kid's a real good fighter."

Dr. Nardiello put five stitches across his nose. Billy just lay down on the rubbing table with a couple of towels doubled under his head and the doctor trimmed the edges of the cut and put in the thread and Billy never moved.

"You don't need an anesthetic," Billy was explaining to them later. "You're still worked up from the fight, and you don't even feel it. You didn't see me move, did you? I'd move if it hurt."

"How Billy came down that stretch," one of the sportswriters said, as Billy was lying there and the doctor was stitching him, "like a thoroughbred."

With the newspapermen asking questions and the guys coming in to shake his hand, it was an hour before he got out of the Garden. Then Robbie drove him down to his dad's place, where there was a big mob and some of them had overflowed to the street.

He was standing there on the sidewalk. They were shaking his hand and clapping him on the back when Lorraine came out. He threw his arms around her and kissed her and together they walked into the crowded, smoky bar. When he came in, they let out a cheer.

"These," his brother Robbie said, "are his fans. These are the guys who bought the tickets for the four-rounders and the six-rounders and the eight rounds at the Broadway and the Ridgewood and the St. Nick's, and they've been with him ever since. These are the most important guys in the world."

He and Lorraine didn't get back to the hotel until 5:30 that morning, and around noon he and Irving went over to the Garden and picked up the check for $9,400. You take out the dough for the training camp and pay Whitey and take out the dough for Irving and Jack and it leaves you about half. Three weeks later, if the nose heals all right and Irving can make another match, you take off again for camp.

Young Fighter

The Trouble with McNeece Is That He Fears Nothing

IT WAS ABOUT AN HOUR before the fight, and we were alone in the dressing room. It was warm in the room, and the fighter had stripped and then put on just his ring socks and shoes, and now he was lying on his back on the rubbing table with just a towel across his middle, staring up at the ceiling.

"You know something?" he said after a while.

His voice startled me. I had been sitting there listening to the sounds and the small talk of the preliminary fighters, and occasionally turning my head to watch them beyond the opening at the end of the black shower curtain with the pink flowers on it that hung between them and us.

"What?" I said.

"I feel different tonight," he said slowly, still looking up at the ceiling. "I don't know why, but I do."

"That's sometimes a good sign," I said. "You may fight your best fight."

It was his youth and his lack of experience talking. After he has fought a lot of fights he won't talk like that any more.

"I don't know," he said. "I never felt like this before."

Why do they do it? In this country last year there were about three thousand professional prizefighters. By the end of the year two of them had lost their lives in the ring, and only about two dozen had profited by as much as $10,000. The rest fought in the small clubs or populated the preliminaries in the bigger clubs, and Billy McNeece, now lying

---

Esquire, July 1955.

on his back in the small, musty dressing room at the Eastern Parkway in Brooklyn, is one of these.

"Just before they go into the ring," I said, "most fighters feel tired."

I had been watching beyond the curtain, a preliminary boy named Andy Viserto. He had been moving around with his robe on, shadow-boxing and trying to loosen his shoulders, and while he had been doing this he had been yawning. He must have yawned five or six times in the thirty seconds or so that I watched him.

"I don't feel tired," McNeece said now. "I don't know how I feel."

I came to know McNeece through Jimmy August. We were standing together one day in Stillman's, watching the sparring in the two rings, when Jimmy said, "I've got a kid for you. If you're looking for a kid that's typical of the kind that comes into boxing, I've got one—wild, absolutely fearless, makes every fight a war, but a real nice kid with it all."

I have known Jimmy now for close to ten years and respect him as one of the few capable trainers, teachers, and handlers of fighters still in the business. He is a short, stocky, bald man with brown eyes, who quit studying pharmaceutical chemistry at Columbia University thirty years ago to work with fighters, and he is particularly good with the young ones, since he is patient and painstaking and somewhat of an amateur psychologist.

"This kid was sent to me about six years ago," Jimmy said, "by a fighter I used to have, Dennis Deegan, who was a welter, back around 1936 or '38. You may remember him. He had about forty pro fights and topped the Ridgewood and the Jamaica Arena."

"Deegan?" I said. "What did he look like?"

"A good left hand," Jimmy said.

"I don't recall him," I said.

"He works as a track foreman on the Independent Subway and he's friendly with the family of this kid," Jimmy said. "One day he come up to me here and told me he had a kid he wanted me to make a fighter of. Then he brings the kid up, and when I got through working with the other kids I started to teach him, believe me, from A to Z."

"Was there anything that impressed you about him from the start?" I said.

"All heart, that's all," Jimmy said. "A big gangling kid, about a hundred forty, like what you call an ostrich, but all fighter."

"I'd like to meet him," I said.

I met him a few days later. It was the middle of the afternoon and raining, and we walked up from Stillman's to the Neutral Corner and sat across from each other in one of the booths in the back room.

The Neutral Corner is a bar and grill on the southwest corner of Eighth Avenue and Fifty-fifth Street, in New York City, half a block north of Stillman's. It is owned and operated by Frankie Jay, Chicky Bogad, and Nick Masuras. Frankie used to manage fighters, including Tony Janiro, a good-looking welterweight of a half-dozen years ago who almost broke Frankie's heart; Chicky grew up with the good Jewish fighters who came out of the Lower East Side about thirty-five years ago, and once, for a few months, he was matchmaker for Madison Square Garden; Nick used to be a fighter himself, a middleweight.

"That scar under your right eye," I said to McNeece, after we had talked a few minutes. "Where did you get it?"

McNeece is twenty-three years old and stands six feet and weighs about 165. He has pale, freckled skin, red-blond, wavy hair, and pale blue eyes.

"Scar?" he said, feeling with the fingers of his right hand across the scar and then around it. "I haven't got any scar."

"It looks like a scar," I said, and reached across the table and placed my fingers on the little crescent of tightened skin on his right cheekbone. "It's an old one, but it's there."

"I don't think so," he said, puzzled. "I was never cut there."

In the bar and in the back room at the Neutral Corner the walls are hung with black-framed photographs of prizefights and prizefighters, managers and handlers. In each of the half-dozen booths, centered on the wall between the pictures, there is a small, narrow mirror.

"Take a look in that mirror," I said. "You'll see it."

The fighter turned to the mirror, and then he moved his head to get the light right. Then, with his fingers, he went over the small scar twice and turned back with a half-smile on his face.

"You're right," he said. "I didn't even remember it. I got it in a kid fight so long ago I forgot it."

"What about the fight?"

"I don't remember it. I just vaguely remember that I got cut there once in a kid fight. I don't remember anything about the fight, and I didn't even remember that I had the cut."

"The bridge of your nose," I said. "It's starting to broaden. Was it ever broken in a fight?"

"No," he said, feeling his nose. "It's just from my amateur fights and my fights as a pro."

"Does it bother you that your face is getting marked?"

"No."

"When Billy Graham was a kid in school," I said, speaking of the fighter and not the preacher, "he used to box in the boys' clubs. After a fight he'd wear a patch over his eye to school. There wasn't any cut under the patch; he just wanted to look like a fighter. Did you ever do that?"

"No," McNeece said. "I never did that, but I was never ashamed of anything for sure. When I get banged, I get banged."

I would say that tells a lot about what makes a fighter right there. I go along with the poet who said my body is the mansion of my soul. I can tell you exactly how I got the scar on my lower lip and the one on the index finger of my left hand and the one on my right knee. That's one of the reasons why I was never a fighter, and why McNeece is.

McNeece grew up in Central Islip, Long Island. There were three kids in the family—his sister Mary, who is a year older than the fighter, and his brother Jimmy, who is a year younger.

"Have you had a hard time around your home?" I said.

"Sure," McNeece said. "My father's a laborer, a construction worker."

"Was he ever out of work?"

"Sure. When the weather is bad or you're sick, you can't work. Ever since we were little kids my mother worked in the state hospital, too. We never had much money."

I will admit that not all fighters are impelled by financial poverty. I have known a few who attended college, but they were less as fighters because of it. There was always the knowledge within them that they could make a living in another way, and so it has always been that most fighters, and the best fighters, are those who know that fighting will give them their only chance to make a real pile.

"I never wanted to be anything else but a fighter," McNeece said. "Me and my brother—he's in the Navy now—I guess the first thing we ever got was boxing gloves. They threatened to burn the gloves a million times, the fights we used to have."

He was sitting there, friendly and alert to my questions. He had on a pair of gray slacks and a soft yellow sports shirt, open at the neck, and a light tan wind jacket. He is big-boned and, although considered to be a middleweight, he will probably build up with proper training and with proteins to add about ten pounds of good weight and become a light heavyweight.

"From a little kid on," he said, "I got all the record books and I know every fighter from away back. My mother used to wake me up at ten o'clock so I could listen to the fights."

I think that's important in this, too. Some fighters have to go against their families to do it, but in the majority of cases the resistance is what the Army used to call sporadic, at best. That is why I decided to drive out to Central Islip to try to find out what forces, outside of himself, impelled this fighter toward the ring, and why, at home, the climate, as they say, was right.

Central Islip is a crossroads town about fifty miles from New York City and in about the geographical center of Long Island. Robert Ripley once ascertained, after what could have been some very pleasant research, that there were more bars per capita in Central Islip than in any other town or city in the United States. Its population has been about 90 percent Irish Catholic, and most of its residents work in the three nearby state mental hospitals and in the Grumman and Republic aircraft plants.

"This is a fighting town," Joe Barlin, the physical education instructor and coach of Central Islip High School, told me. "Kids around here fight more than in any other town I've ever known."

Barlin, McNeece, and I were in the small faculty room off the stage in the gymnasium. Barlin, still a young man, was smoking a pipe.

"I was quite aghast when I first came here," he said, "but I've come to let the kids throw a few punches. You see, it's a hospital town. The parents work around the clock, and the kids are left to shift for themselves more than in most places."

I suppose McNeece was amused by the efforts I was making to reconstruct the background that propelled him into professional fighting. In his own mind it is all very simple. He always wanted to be a fighter.

"If you ask me why he became a fighter," Barlin said, "I'll give you three reasons. One, he's Irish. Two, he's got a younger brother. Three, he was always a fierce competitor."

"My brother and I, we'd be mad at one another about almost everything," McNeece said, smiling. "We fought all the time. When we played on the same teams here they would never put us both into the game at the same time."

While in high school, he had played varsity basketball, soccer, and baseball. He had never failed a subject, but after his third year and at the age of seventeen he quit to enlist in the paratroops.

"Whatever he played here," Barlin said, "he fought like hell all the way. I wish we had more like him. He'd just as soon tell you to go to hell as not, but he'd always tell the truth. He has what I'd call an open personality."

A slim, neatly dressed man in his thirties came in carrying a book and some papers. Barlin introduced him as Ted Jamison, the assistant principal, and after he had shaken hands with me and greeted McNeece warmly, he sat down and I explained my interest in McNeece.

"Would you," I asked him, "say that there is something in the general environment here that Billy has been trying to escape?"

That is, really, the way we regard fighting in our time. We examine the exponents of it, and their origins, as if they were confirmed criminals.

"Definitely," Jamison said. "We have that problem here constantly, and I've even held up Billy, here, as an example of what one individual can do about it. A lot of kids here have a defeatist complex. They say, 'What have I got to look forward to? To work in the hospital or the aircraft plant all my life?'"

"I always said I wouldn't be working in the hospital," McNeece said.

"Exactly," Jamison said. "I just couldn't see Billy doing that. I think he'd go crazy in a factory, too. I think he'd walk out and tell the boss what to do."

"I think I would," McNeece said, smiling.

While the McNeece children were small, the family lived in an aging gray frame house behind a lumberyard near the center of town. Six years ago they moved into a home of their own, a new ranch-type bungalow in a development of small houses on the northeast edge of the town.

When we arrived at the house the fighter's older sister Mary was there with her two-year-old son. As I talked with her it was apparent that she sees nothing surprising about the fact that her brother has become a fighter and, as a result, has never attempted to analyze the reasons for his choice of this profession.

"But when you and your brother were small," I said, "I'm sure there were occasions when your parents punished you. Do you recall how your brother reacted to punishment?"

"Oh, yes," she said. "I remember that when my mother would smack him, he'd just stand there. I remember he'd never cry or anything."

The fighter's mother is a small, auburn-haired woman, now forty-four years old, who came to this country alone from Ireland when she was sixteen to live with relatives. On this particular day she got home early from the hospital.

"He wasn't difficult as a child," she said. "I would say he was just adventurous. They used to have the Tarzan movies then, and I'd come home and find rope strung from tree to tree. I did worry a little, but he always seemed to come out all right, and I got over that."

Mrs. McNeice—the fighter changed the spelling of the name when he began to box—said it was much the same when her son started fighting. At first she was nervous, but when she saw that he was not being hurt she ceased to worry deeply, and she has attended each of his fights in and around New York.

"I went to his first one here, at the Eastern Parkway," she said. "He won, and then I felt that I never wanted to change anything, so I still go."

"The chance to make a lot of money draws all fighters to the ring," I said. "Would you say that your son has always been conscious of how difficult it is for many people to make a good living?"

"Often," she said, "he would say to me, 'Someday I want to make a lot of money.'"

"When I was in the Army," the fighter said, "I used to read about guys I boxed in the amateurs moving ahead. I'd tell my mother, 'Wait till I get out of the Army, and then we'll have some of the nice things.'"

"Billy worked after school, too," Mrs. McNeice said.

"Once I worked in the ravioli factory here," the fighter said. "I labeled jars from five in the afternoon to ten. I was about twelve years old, and one day the inspector came in and found me."

When the fighter was thirteen he piled lumber for the Central Islip Lumber Company. When he was fifteen he worked at Camp Upton, Long Island, on a construction job with his father.

"He always brought home the money," Mrs. McNeice said, "and waited for his cut."

Shortly after four o'clock, William McNeice, Sr., came home. He is a thin, ruddy-faced, sandy-haired, blue-eyed man, now fifty years old.

He was born in the Williamsburg section of Brooklyn and left school in the eighth grade at the age of fourteen to work as a truck helper. Then he became a brick handler and finally a construction laborer.

"Coming from the Williamsburg section," he said, when I began to question him about fighting, "I followed fighters since I was a kid. I thought there was nobody like Mike O'Dowd."

This reminded me of the one question I had saved. I wanted to ask it of the mother and father together.

"All of the motion pictures and all of the fiction that are written about boxing," I said, "depict the seamy side. They're concerned with death in the ring or dishonest fights or dishonest managers or gangsters. Were either of you worried about your son getting into a business that is always portrayed in that manner?"

"I never believed that stuff about the cheating managers or the fixed fights," the father said. "I never worry about the boy getting hurt, either. I've seen many fights in my line of work, and I saw many a fight in the Ridgewood or the armories or Ebbets Field. I saw the boy in all his Golden Gloves bouts, and from the way he handled himself I figured he wasn't being hurt."

"But didn't what you had seen in the movies or read about boxing concern you?" I asked the mother.

"Billy used to talk so much about boxing that it never bothered me," Mrs. McNeice said. "I never believed the other things, and I met Jimmy August and Billy's manager and they're nice men."

When McNeece finished his four years in the Army early last year and resumed professional fighting, August turned over the management of him to Irving Cohen. Cohen, a short, semistout, round-faced, blue-eyed, soft-spoken man, manages Billy Graham and managed Rocky Graziano to the middleweight championship. He is completely honest in his dealings with his fighters, and is so cautious that seldom does he put one of them into a ring unless he is reasonably certain that the fighter has better than an even chance to beat the other man.

"Out here," the fighter said now, "I guess the guys that follow boxing were surprised that I got Irving Cohen for a manager."

I did not see the fighter again until the evening of the fight. He had been at Greenwood Lake, New York, for twelve days training to fight Jackie La Bua, another young middleweight, at the Eastern Parkway, and he and August had taken a room at a hotel just off Times Square for the night before the fight.

La Bua had had twenty-five fights and had won twenty-two—McNeece had won ten of twelve—and was working on a winning streak of eleven. Although the New York newspapers had not given much space to the fight, they had been unanimous in the opinion that La Bua was the logical favorite to lick McNeece.

"How is he?" I said to August when I met him in the hotel lobby.

"He's resting," August said. "He'll be down in a few minutes."

"How will he do?"

"Who knows?" August said. "He can lick this guy, but it depends on him. The trouble with him is that he fears nothing."

"I know," I said.

"It's a tough job for a conscientious trainer and manager to put fear and respect in a guy like this," August said. "He takes chances he shouldn't take. He can box like hell, but he gets hit on the chin and then he's a sensational fighter for no reason at all.

"A guy with too much guts is hard to teach. A guy with a little geezer in him is the greatest fighter in the world. You teach him a trick and he'll learn it. This guy, he says, 'Aw, I'll run him out of the ring.'

"So the other trainers," August said, "they say to me, 'Why must he go wild? Why can't you cool him down?' How am I going to cool him down? In one fight he went wild altogether, and he came to me and he said, 'Why can't you control me?'

"He's asking me? I've tried everything. I've conned him and I've abused him, because let's face it. You know what an Irishman or a Jew who can fight can mean at the gate."

"I know," I said.

"Even managers get excited when they think about it," August said. "If I can cool him off and let him use the ability God gave him, good. If I can't, he'll have a short career, and that's what it'll be tonight. If he loses his head, he's gone. If he fights his fight, he'll lick the guy without too much trouble."

The fighter came down and went out and got into his secondhand Dodge convertible. With Jimmy Moulton, a young lightweight who was to box a four-rounder on the card, driving, and with McNeece sitting up front with him, we started for the Arena.

"How are your folks?" I said to McNeece after a while.

"They're fine, thanks," he said. "That is, my mother's fine, but my father's sick. He can't move."

"He can't move?" I said.

"They brought him home from work," McNeece said, "and he couldn't move. He's lying there in the house and he can just move one hand."

"Did he have a stroke?" I said to August, who was riding next to me in the back.

"It must be," August said, shrugging. "They didn't want Billy to know before the fight."

"They tried to keep it from me," the fighter said. "I heard about it and I went out there yesterday."

"The dough you'll get for tonight," August said, "will come in handy."

In the preceding twelve months McNeece had earned $900 in purses in five fights. For this one, however, he would clear about $1,000 after expenses for his end.

"I'll say," he said. "I'll go out there tomorrow, and we'll take him to the hospital. I'll have the money to put right down."

The Arena's dressing rooms are to the left of the lobby; half of the preliminary fighters are in one room and the men they are going to fight in another, and because McNeece was boxing the ten-round main event, he had a private cubicle, about ten feet by eight, with the shower curtain separating him from the preliminary boys.

In the two and a half hours that we waited there he was more quiet than he had been on the other occasions when I had been with him. If he heard the talk of the preliminary boys he paid no attention to it, resting on his back on the rubbing table and then later he sat up while August bandaged and taped first one hand and then the other, and I thought of what he had told me about his feelings before a fight.

"When you enlisted in the Army," I had asked that afternoon in the Neutral Corner, "why did you pick the paratroops?"

"For the extra pay," he said.

"Had you ever been up in a plane before?"

"Not until I jumped."

"Were you scared?"

"I was as nervous as anybody else, but I think you do it because it's just follow the leader. I always had pride, and if anybody said I couldn't do something I'd do it."

"Did you know any men who wouldn't jump?"

"Sure. They have a heck of a lot of quitters. Maybe almost half the class were quitters, but I never thought about them one way or the other. Some of the guys laughed at them, but at times even I myself felt like saying, 'The hell with this stuff.' That's the reason I wouldn't quit. If the other guy could do it, so could I."

"Did you pray before your jumps?" I said, remembering that he had told me that he and his brother had been altar boys and had attended parochial school.

"I went to church the night before my first jump. I always make a visit to church just before a fight, too."

"For what do you pray?"

"I ask for a real good fight, and that I don't get my eyes busted up."

"Do you pray to win?"

"No. If I ask to win, I still might get beat, and I don't want to be disappointed."

There were about five hundred spectators in the Arena, which will hold four times as many, when McNeece, with August and Cohen and Whitey Bimstein behind him, came down the aisle. When he was introduced from the ring, about half of them sent up a noise, and when La Bua, who lives in East Meadow, Long Island, took his bow the effect was about the same.

As the bell rang, McNeece came out fast and he was three quarters of the way across the ring when he and La Bua joined. Immediately it was apparent that La Bua was the calmer of the two, and he met McNeece's rush with two jabs that brought the color to McNeece's face.

"Easy, Irish!" Bimstein hollered up. "Hold it, Irish!"

It was that way through the first minute of the first round, with McNeece's anxiety showing in the punches he was missing and with La Bua pacing himself nicely. Then, suddenly, halfway through the round, McNeece landed a right hand to the body that hurt La Bua and backed him up. The moment he felt La Bua give under the punch, McNeece moved in after it, forcing, and it was apparent now that this, unless La Bua could do something to change it or McNeece lost his head, would be the pattern of the fight.

It was the same in the second round, with McNeece pressing, keeping La Bua from getting set. La Bua's corner must have noticed this, because in the third round La Bua came out and tried to take the lead. He was putting more authority into his jabs, snapping McNeece's head back. For a moment he backed McNeece up, but then McNeece started to drop inside the arcs of La Bua's follow-up punches and hook to La Bua's body, and when he did that it was the same as it had been in the first two rounds.

It would in all probability have been the same for ten rounds except that, in the fifth, a cut opened over La Bua's left eye from one of McNeece's overhand rights. It opened again the sixth, and at the end of the round Dr. Samuel Swetnick, of the New York State Athletic Commission, climbed into the ring. He looked at the eye and then spoke to the referee, and the referee threw his hands out flat to signal the end.

All the way from the ring to the dressing room McNeece, grinning now, his face and hair wet, was accepting the congratulations of his friends. A few minutes later, his green robe over him, he was sitting on the dressing table, holding an ice pack to his left eye, which had purplish welts above and below it.

"You see?" August was saying, bending over MeNeece. "When you jabbed and moved under, his right went over your head."

"I know," McNeece said. "It was good."

"You looked very good tonight," Joe Lee, a sportswriter, was saying. He was standing by the table with pencil and paper in hand.

"He was a very tough guy, a very tough guy," McNeece said, and I could see he was starting to unwind now. "He takes a good rap. I'd just wait for him to start, and then I'd shoot inside to the belly."

"Who'd you like to fight now?" Lee said.

"Anybody my manager says," McNeece said.

"You see?" Bimstein said.

"I know," McNeece said.

"You got a little Jew sense in your head tonight," Bimstein said. "Let the Irish out later."

"He means be more deliberate," McNeece said, smiling and explaining the reference to Lee.

"Let me tell you something," Izzy Grove, who had just come in, said. "You got a lot of ability. You can make a lot of money."

"Thank you," McNeece said, smiling and removing the ice pack. During the middle and late twenties, Izzy Grove was a good middleweight who fought most of the best in and around New York, several champions among them. Now he books dance bands for a living.

"Don't thank me," he said. "Thank yourself. I don't want to tell you how to fight. You got a manager and a trainer to tell you that. Just behave yourself. Don't abuse this body. You got only one."

"I know," McNeece said.

"Have a good time, sure," Grove said, "but not tonight. Wait a couple of days. Don't get drunk."

"Sure," McNeece said.

"Let these words become embedded in your brain," Grove said, tapping his own forehead. "I know. I been through it. There's no business in the world where you can make more money if you take care of yourself."

"I know," McNeece said.

"Remember this," Grove said. "The whole world loves a winner and the losers are on *Strike It Rich*."

"Thanks, Mr. Grove," McNeece said.

In the lobby, fifteen minutes later, there were still several dozen men and women waiting near the door to the dressing rooms. They were talking loudly and kidding one another and laughing, and every now and then one of the men would slap another on the back. They were waiting for a young man who, for many reasons, all of them interwoven, always wanted to be a fighter. They were waiting for Billy McNeece.

Brockton's Boy

A Rising Marciano Lifts All Boats

On September 23, 1927, in Brockton, Massachusetts, Mr. Fred Denly, of 18 Everett Street, succeeded in bringing to bloom a two-headed dahlia. Twenty-five years later, to the very day, Mr. Rocco Marchegiano, of 168 Dover Street, same city, distinguished himself in still another field. In Philadelphia he hit Mr. Arnold Cream, of 1020 Cooper Street, Camden, New Jersey, on the chin and won the heavyweight championship of the world.

Whatever the implications of Mr. Denly's botanical accomplishment held for Brockton, they have been lost in the years. It is safe to say, however, that as long as there is boxing and a Brockton twenty miles due south of Boston, the impact of the punch with which Rocky Marciano (né Marchegiano) knocked out Jersey Joe Walcott (né Cream) will be felt.

In Brockton today, for example, there is a young man named Nicholas Rando, who lives at 69 Bartlett Street—the street, incidentally, where Rocky delivered the *Brockton Enterprise-Times* as a boy—who will forever be lacking the first joint of two fingers of his right hand. When Marciano, with his own right hand, flattened Walcott, the excitement that raged through Brockton's Ward Two Memorial Club reached such a pitch that Rando, then fourteen years old, fed his hand into a ventilating fan.

In the state of Virginia lives Mrs. Dorothy Brown Therrien, widowed nine days after the victory over Walcott. Her husband,

---

Cosmopolitan, June 1954.

fifty-four-year-old Frederick J. Therrien, manager of the Brockton office, State Division of Employment Security, and former drum major of Brockton Post 35, American Legion, had been warned by doctors not to overexert himself. When it was announced there would be a parade to welcome home the new champion, however, he couldn't resist and dropped dead in front of the YMHA on Legion Parkway, Brockton, while marching as a marshal's aide.

At St. Colman's imposing fieldstone Roman Catholic Church, Wendell Avenue at Lyman Street, Brockton, the Very Reverend LeRoy V. Cooney, who married Marciano and Barbara May Cousins there on December 30, 1950, will not forget Marciano, either. Just before the second Marciano–Walcott fight, televised from Chicago on May 15 of that year, he was directing the uncrating of a thirty-inch television set, a gift to the church by the fighter and friend, when he stumbled off the stage in the recreation hall and fractured his right leg.

Despite such occurrences, however, the impact on Brockton of Marciano's rise to the most coveted, most romanticized throne in the world of sport is hardly a tragic one. A manufacturing city of 62,862 residents, many of whom, or their progenitors, came from Italy, Ireland, Lithuania, Poland, Sweden, and French Canada to work in its shoe shops, Brockton has benefited by what has happened to Marciano in ways that can hardly be measured.

Last year Brockton exported 12,384,378 pairs of shoes as well as unrecorded tonnages of carpet tacks, storage batteries, sausages, and burial vaults. It is the unchallenged opinion of the manufacturers that no matter what the product, sales were helped immeasurably by the fame that has accrued to the city through the fistic prowess of the thirty-year-old son of Pierino Marchegiano, ex-shoe worker.

"Why, Rocky Marciano has done more to make this city famous than all the shoes ever made here," says Perley Flint, president of Field & Flint, shoe manufacturers. "Now they've heard of Brockton in places they don't even wear shoes."

"Anybody who travels out of Brockton and only carries one line," says J. W. Mahoney, assistant sales manager of the same firm, "also carries Rocky. In Chicago, at the National Shoe Fair last year, they expected anybody from Brockton to be able to predict not only Rocky's next opponent but who would win."

Brockton's delegates to the 1952 political conventions in Chicago found themselves faced with the same questions and so did the thirty-seven Boy Scouts from the Brockton area who attended the National Jamboree near Santa Ana, California, last July. And the *Brockton Enterprise-Times* reported that Brocktonians visiting New York TV studios found themselves plucked for audience-participation shows as soon as they revealed their hometown.

"I've talked to customers on the West Coast," says George Stone, head of the Independent Nail and Packing Company, "and they say, 'Oh, yeah? That's Marciano's hometown.' There's one machine-tool manufacturer in Milan, Italy, who exports to this country, and do you know what he wanted? An autographed photo of Rocky."

"In Birmingham, Alabama, last year," says Dick Stevens, a salesman for Field & Flint, "I wasn't having much luck getting into one of the stores. There were some hard feelings, so I just dropped in and didn't talk business at all. We just talked Rocky. I never said a word about shoes, but now the orders are coming in."

As a matter of fact, the Brockton boy is also an instrument of shoe research. Each year the Doyle Shoe Company presents Marciano with ten pairs of black Vici kid road shoes, size 10½-EE. Even when he isn't in training for a fight, the champion does daily roadwork, and recently he returned one pair that, worn through on both soles, had carried him seven hundred miles.

Marciano's ring shoes, size 10-E, are made, two pairs for each fight, by the Howard & Foster Shoe Company, of black yellow-back kangaroo uppers applied to a lightweight sole manufactured by the Potvin Shoe Company, also of Brockton. They are probably the lightest boxing shoes ever made.

Last year Charles R. Armey, vice president of Howard & Foster, decided to put a lightweight street shoe on the market. The first lot went to a fashionable men's store on South Michigan Avenue in Chicago. Some time later the factory received a letter from the retailer stating that the first pair had been bought by Ezzard Charles, former heavyweight champion of the world, who is now challenging Marciano.

"It's a small world," says Armey, "but the important thing is that our employees feel as though they're helping Rocky in the ring. Just last week the women in the stitching room came out and asked if they could sign their names in Rocky's shoes. We decided they could sign one pair."

The economic influence of Marciano on Brockton industry is confused, of course, by many other factors governing business profit and loss. A clearer index is afforded by the effect of his success—forty-five wins, forty knockouts, and no losses—on the finances of various individuals.

"A lot of working people in this town are a lot better off because of Marciano," says one Brocktonian. "There are families that have suddenly moved into brand-new homes. The man is a factory worker and everybody knows what he makes. They say, 'Where does he get the money to buy a house like that?' It's obvious. He's been betting on Rocky.

"And these guys who have pyramided their cars. They started out with old rattletraps when Rocky started fighting in Providence in 1948. They borrowed what they could on the cars. They won and bought better cars and borrowed again. Today they're driving high-priced automobiles that are paid for."

Before Marciano fought Rex Layne in Madison Square Garden on July 12, 1951, one old Italian woman pulled out of a kitchen coffee tin $500 she had saved in her lifetime without her husband's knowledge. Through a relative, she placed it with a local bookmaker, and when Marciano knocked out Layne in the sixth round, she got back her $500 plus another $1,000.

"When Rocky was getting ready to fight Louis," says Ed Lalli, a Brockton auto dealer, "a guy I never saw before comes in here. He says he wants to sell his car to bet on Rocky. I say to him, 'Look, friend, don't do it. We all think Rocky is gonna win, but suppose something goes wrong? Be smart. Go to a finance company and borrow two hundred bucks on your car and twelve months to pay off the loan.'

"So he did it, and after the fight he comes back. You know what he says? He says, 'You make me lose a lot of money. Look at all the money I could have today if I don't listen to you.'"

It was two weeks before the Louis fight, the most important in Marciano's career up to that point and the second Marciano fight to be televised, that the avalanche struck Brockton's twenty-seven television dealers and twelve TV-service firms. By the day of the fight, it was impossible to buy a new receiver in Brockton or to get immediate repair service.

"People who never had trouble with their sets before," says Joe Nesti, of Corola, Inc., "wanted us to go and check them. They wanted us to guarantee they wouldn't have trouble during the fight. Who can guarantee a thing like that?"

A Marciano fight also exerts a marked influence on Brockton's social life. On such an occasion, it is *de rigueur* on the well-to-do West Side for Brockton's matrons to hold cocktail and supper parties in the stately white colonials and imposing fieldstone mansions where live the city's industrial magnates and more successful doctors and lawyers. Elsewhere in town, bars are crowded and so are Brockton's fifteen fraternal and social clubs that own television receivers.

In factories that employ night shifts, power is shut down between 9:45 and 11:00 P.M. and employees gather before TV screens. Brockton's three motion-picture theaters are almost empty.

On the evening of May 15 of last year, for example, when Marciano fought Walcott the return bout that was televised from the Chicago Stadium, the Center Theater, with 1,034-seat capacity, had sixteen adults and ten children in the house. At the other two theaters, the Brockton and the Colonial, business was equally bad.

"When Rocky fights on TV," says Bob Riordan, city editor of the *Brockton Enterprise-Times*, "the streets are deserted. You can look the length of Main Street and not see a soul. Then between rounds, you see a couple of people hurrying across the street. They're changing bars, looking for better reception or a better look at the screen. The moment the fight ends, everything busts right open."

Cars, their occupants and their horns sounding, tour Brockton streets until 2:00 A.M. Most of these finally descend upon Ward Two, where Marciano was born and grew up and where the Ward Two Memorial Club, of which Marciano is a charter member, is the nerve center of the celebration. The club, which started nineteen years ago in a garage on Winthrop Street, now owns, a hundred yards from Marciano's parental home, a single-story, brown-shingled clubhouse on which a $4,000 mortgage has been lifted, thanks to Marciano's fighting ability.

When Marciano's fights are neither telecast nor broadcast, crowds gather before the red brick front of the *Brockton Enterprise-Times* at 60 Main Street, where two loudspeakers are hung from windowsills of the third-floor editorial rooms. For the first Walcott fight, anxious residents began collecting an hour and a half before fight time, and when the first succinct announcement was made—even round-end blow-by-blow reconstructions of the fight were banned by the International Boxing Club—there were ten thousand waiting before the windows.

"The first round was a bad one for Rocky," came the announcement, edited from the copy received by direct wire from ringside in Philadelphia. "He was down."

Considering that this was the first time Marciano had ever been knocked off his feet in a ring, it can be imagined with what trepidation the almost silent crowd received, at three-minute intervals, the cryptic comments, which varied from that extreme to the occasional opinion that Marciano seemed to be doing a little better but still had a hard fight on his hands. Suddenly, at 11:34 P.M. there came the word.

"The new heavyweight champion of the world," said the voice of staff man Ken Wheeler, "is Rocky Marciano!"

That started it. Four Marines were arrested for street fighting. Three additional police cruiser cars were dispatched to Ward Two, where young Rando was to lose part of his right hand and a man named

Francis C. Reed of 55 Indian Head Street, Hanson, was to lose his wallet and $260.

At police headquarters the members of the night shift assigned to house duty sat back satisfied. They had managed to pick up, on the shortwave radio, a blow-by-blow description from a Canadian station. When it had started to come over in French, they had moved the radio back to the cell block where a Bridgewater prisoner of French extraction had provided them with a translation. The next day in court, the bilingual benefactor was fined five dollars for drunkenness.

Marciano has, naturally, complicated the ordinary routine of the Brockton Police Department. Following his knockout of Louis, the department, the *Brockton Enterprise-Times*, and Rocky's mother, Mrs. Pasqualina Marchegiano, all got postcards threatening Marciano's life. The calls were traced to two teenagers.

On the night of the first Walcott fight, all police leaves were canceled and twenty men were assigned posts on the block of Main Street from Green Street to Legion Parkway, which includes the newspaper's offices. When Marciano returned home after that fight to be paraded before a crowd of fifty thousand, all leaves were again canceled and sixty policemen were requisitioned from the nearby towns of Randolph, Abington, Whitman, Avon, Easton, and the three Bridgewaters. These, plus the hundred men on the Brockton force, were supplemented by a hundred civil-defense volunteers and six motorcycle men of the Massachusetts State Police.

Marciano, of course, could exert tremendous political influence on his city. So great was his appeal after he knocked out Louis on October 26, 1951, that he was exiled from his hometown for three weeks during the close battle being waged for the mayoralty by the Republican incumbent, Melvin B. Clifford, and the present mayor, Democrat C. Gerald Lucey, who ultimately won by a margin of 343 votes out of 29,094.

"I was advised right after the Louis fight," says Marciano, "that if I wanted to stay clear of politics, I'd better wait until after the election before I went home. So Barbara and I went to all the shows on Broadway and lounged around for three weeks."

In 1952, during the presidential campaign, Mayor Lucey discovered the heavyweight champion had more than local political significance. He received a request from Washington to arrange for Marciano to ride on the Adlai Stevenson campaign train between Providence and Boston. Although past heavyweight champions had received thousands of dollars for backing presidential candidates, Rocky turned down the request in order to maintain outward political neutrality.

"Then last year," he says, "Paul Keith, who was running against Lucey, came to my house. He said, 'I just want to meet you because people ask me if I know Rocky Marciano and I want to tell the truth.' So we shook hands and then he left."

Brockton Republican leaders claim, of course, it was Mayor Lucey's many public appearances with Marciano that helped swing the last election for the Democrats. The latter, as naturally, assert it was the usual issues—streets, sewers, and schools.

Brockton has 272.36 miles of streets and roads, 123.78 miles of sewers, and twenty-seven schools. Where Marciano, as a manual laborer for the Brockton Gas Company and the Brockton Department of Public Works, once made a pick-and-shovel imprint on the first two, he now exerts another influence on the last.

Before Marciano's first fight with Walcott, the pupils of the first three grades of the Belmont Elementary School sent him a scroll they had signed. In Brockton High School, where Marciano played one year of varsity football before leaving school to work, the champion is a constant subject of class discussion and a constant inspiration to the athletic teams.

Every coach in the school, according to Charley Holden, athletic director, has used the example of Marciano's climb at some time before or during an important game. Between halves of the Brockton–Quincy football game in 1952, with Brockton trailing 14–0, Marciano himself strode into the dressing room. He spoke to the team about Brockton's fine football tradition, about its fine coach, Frank Saba, and about the responsibility that rested with the players. Brockton won 19–14.

Of all Brocktonians, however, those who have been the most deeply affected by the Marciano ascension are, besides the man himself, the members of his family, his childhood friends, and others who, in one way or another, played a part in his life. One of these is Dr. Josephat Phaneuf, who is now sixty-six years old and head of the red brick ninety-four-bed Phaneuf Hospital, at 688 North Main Street. At 1:00 A.M. on September 1, 1923, however, he was still a young, hardworking general practitioner who was to go on to deliver, in all, 7,235 babies in and around Brockton.

"I remember a delivery at that time at 80 Brook Street," he says. "I recall it was fairly difficult because of the size of the head."

The previous year Pasqualina Marchegiano had lost, in birth, a thirteen-pound boy. When Rocco, the first of six living children—three sons and three daughters—arrived, he weighed twelve and a half pounds.

"I say to the doctor," says Mrs. Marchegiano, "I ask him, 'How much this cost?' He say, 'Forty dollar.' I say, 'Well, Doctor, I give you cash.' He say, 'Well, thirty-five dollar.'"

"Strangely," Dr. Phaneuf says, "I have never seen him fight. A great many of my patients talk about him, though, and when they do I say, 'I was the first one ever to hit him.'"

In Brockton now, Red Gormley is a letter carrier. Less than ten years ago, however, he, like Marciano, was a good amateur baseball player, and they shared their dreams of making the big leagues together, Gormley as a shortstop and Marciano as a catcher. In the spring of 1947 they reported together in an old car to the Fayetteville, North Carolina, farm club of the Chicago Cubs.

"In April," Gormley says, "they released us. We went to Goldsboro, and they didn't want us, either. Our arms were gone. We couldn't throw. We were broke, and I guess we looked like a couple of bums, so we decided to come home."

Gormley's territory is in Ward Two. Standing in front of 168 Dover Street, his mail sack over his shoulder, he looks across at the five-and-a-half-acre James Edgar Playground, where he and Marciano, day after day, year after year, played ball.

"We were driving back in the old car," he says. "Finally Rocky said, 'The heck with it. I'm through with baseball. I'm gonna get some fights, and you're gonna handle me.' There I was, sitting right next to half the money in the world, and I didn't even know it."

He hitches his sack higher on his shoulder and starts up the steps to 168. It is the two-family, green-shingled house where Marciano lived from the time he was eleven years old until last year and where the Marchegianos still live. To this address it has now become part of Gormley's job to deliver some of the mail that comes to the heavyweight champion from all over the world.

"So what's the sense of talking about it?" he says, turning back. "I've got a wife and three kids now."

The bulk of Marciano's mail is a burden on the backs of Norman Fenn and Bill Riley, who deliver it to the cottage at 54 Woodland Avenue, where live Mr. and Mrs. Arthur Bellao. Bellao, a short, intense, brown-eyed young man who sells cars for a living, is an old friend of the Marchegianos and owns a typewriter. When the mail begins to submerge 168 Dover Street, he volunteers to answer it.

"It picks up just before and after a fight," he says. "When Rocky became champ, there were a hundred letters a day, some of them from Saudi Arabia and the British West Indies, asking for autographs or pictures or pieces of equipment to be used for raffles. My wife and I were working from six A.M. until eight thirty A.M. and then from eight P.M. to one thirty A.M. to handle it."

It is in the five immaculate rooms on the first floor of 168 Dover Street, of course, that Rocky's impact is strongest. For more than thirty years Pierino Marchegiano, born sixty years ago in Abruzzi, Italy, and gassed and wounded fighting with the Second Marines on the Marne and in the Argonne, left at seven every workday morning with his lunchbox under his arm to work as a No. 7 bedlaster in the shoe factories. The machine he ran forms toes and heels of shoes, and shoe workers say it takes more out of a man than any other machine in the shop. Two years ago he retired.

"Now I go back," he says, "and I see my old friends and everybody says, 'What a difference, Pete. Years ago you couldn't talk with the super, and now he takes you around the shop.'"

Pasqualina Marchegiano, now fifty-two, was born near Benevento, Italy. She, too, worked in the shoe shops before the children came—Rocco, now thirty years old; Alice, twenty-eight; Connie, twenty-six; Elizabeth, twenty-two; Louis, twenty; and Peter, thirteen.

"I lose my first baby," she says. "The doctor say, 'You gonna have no more baby.' I cry. After a while I say, 'If God want me to have baby, and if God give me children, I gonna do the best I can.'

"All I want is to keep my house clean. I keep my children clean, I make my supper. Always at breakfast I tell my children, 'Now try your best in the school.' I tell them the same like when they go to church.

"Now it's just sit in my heart. It's hard to say the beautiful thing that happen with Rocky. You feel happy, and you feel like crying when you think."

Pierino and Pasqualina do not move as freely in Brockton now as they once did. They are quiet people, and unexpected attention embarrasses them.

"I don't go downtown," Pierino says. "Too much talk."

"I don't go but one day a week," says his wife. "Last week I went to post office and there is a big line and I wait and a man I don't know says to me, 'How is our boy?' I say, 'Fine.' He say, 'You know, we're very proud of him down at the Cape.' Then he introduce his wife and his sister. Who is this man?

"I walk on the street and a woman come up to me. She say, 'God bless you, Mrs. Marchegiano. My son and my son-in-law, they make a fortune on your boy. I tell no one, but I tell you because I want to thank you.' Who is this woman?

"I go in a store. In the store the man say, 'If you need credit, Mrs. Marchegiano, you get credit. Your son make me a lot of money for us.' I go to Rocky's house and I see a letter there from someone who wants his picture. I bring it home and I look at the letter and I say that God been so good to my son to give this beautiful luck, why can't I give to people who like my son? So I sent these poor people the picture. Sometimes I cry."

In Goddard Junior High School, where the Marchegianos' youngest child, Peter, is a pupil, he, too, finds he is different. On the day of the second Walcott fight, John Zoino, the science teacher, announced a test.

"Then he asked me," says Peter, "if I thought I could take it. I said, 'I'm afraid I can't today.' Then he let me take it the next day."

When it was revealed in the *Brockton Enterprise-Times* last year that Marciano and his wife had bought a new home at 46 Harlan Drive, a neighbor counted five hundred cars that stopped there on the following weekend so the occupants could examine from the outside the as yet unfurnished $35,000, nine-room brick, fieldstone, and clapboard ranch house. Marciano, most of whose time is spent in training camps, on personal-appearance tours, or relaxing with his wife and their eighteen-month-old daughter, Mary Anne, at Grossinger's in the Catskill Mountains of New York State, has been home only a total of two months since he won the title, and then he found little privacy.

"When Rocky got home from that tour of the Pacific last December," says Al Columbo, his closest friend since childhood and the man who has helped train Marciano for all his fights, "he got into town late and nobody knew he was here. I went around to his house the next morning to walk with him before breakfast. While we were walking he said, 'You know, it was great to come back to my own home and to wake up and find my wife and the baby there and to have nobody else around.' We walked about five or six miles, and when we got back, there they were—five cars in front of the house."

Vic Dubois, *Brockton Enterprise-Times* sports editor, has appealed to his readers to allow Marciano some privacy. The champion and his wife, however, are reconciled to the inevitable attention focused on the heavyweight champion of the world. What disturbs them more is the change that has come over their old Brockton friends.

"They don't drop in like they used to," Marciano says. "When they do come around, they act different. They even talk different. I know what's bothering them. They think they're bothering me and they're not and I can't convince them."

"It's the same with my old girlfriends," his wife says. "When I'm home alone it's fine, but the minute they come in and see Rocky, something comes over them. It's a shame."

As Brockton generally, however, basks in reflected glory, there is but one dark cloud on the horizon. That is the possibility of a Marciano defeat. Neither Brocktonians nor boxing experts envision that in the near future, but the hope is everywhere in Brockton that when their hero starts to slip, he will retire before succumbing to an opponent.

"God help this town if he ever gets licked," says one taxi driver. "There's one old Italian couple here I pick up before every fight and take up to a loan office. The last time they borrowed three thousand dollars on their house. Can you imagine what it will be like if he ever gets beat?"

Scouting for the Yankees

Between Phone Calls with Paul Krichell

WHERE DOES THE GREATNESS of the New York Yankees begin? It begins in a car passing through the Lincoln Tunnel under the Hudson River and then heading south on the broad, almost flat, black reaches of the New Jersey Turnpike. In the car are Harry Hesse, who has been scouting for the Yankees for nine years, and Paul Krichell, who has been chief scout of the Yankees since December of 1920, and who is generally regarded as the greatest in the business.

"Scouting," Krichell was saying, "ain't what it used to be. In the old days you'd travel around the country and if you saw a young ballplayer you liked, you had a chance. Today, the country is crawling with bootblacks and insurance salesmen and hardware clerks with contracts in their pockets, looking to sign some kid.

"Why," he said, "Hesse, here, was up to a sandlot dinner last winter and they introduced the scouts. There were a hundred seventy-five people at the dinner, and a hundred fifty of them called themselves scouts."

"That's right," Hesse said.

"Bird dogs," Krichell said, thinking about it. "Commission scouts. They only get you into trouble. They recommend everybody."

The success of the Yankees—they have won nineteen American League pennants and fifteen World Series since 1921—is not an accident. It is not predicated upon the amount of money they spend for

---

Collier's, July 11, 1953.

ballplayers—as other clubs that have outbid them have found out—but upon how they spend it. When the Yankee front office signs a young ballplayer or buys an old one, it does so because it has faith in the knowledge and ability of its scouts. "But our scouts die like anybody else's," Krichell was saying. "So we hire new scouts, and the Yankees still keep getting ballplayers. You explain it."

In 1951, Joe Devine and Bill Essick passed away. Devine was the one who discovered Gil McDougald and Jerry Coleman, Charlie Silvera and Andy Carey, and Essick signed Joe DiMaggio and Joe Gordon. In recent years, however, the Yankees have added to their scouting staff Tom Greenwade, from the Brooklyn Dodgers; Pat Patterson, from the Cincinnati Reds; Babe Herman, from the Pittsburgh Pirates; Jake Flowers, who coached at Cleveland; and Bill Harris, who had been scouting for the Giants. It was Greenwade who signed Mickey Mantle two days after Mickey got his high-school diploma.

"The trouble with a lot of scouts, especially young ones," Krichell said, "is they get desperate. They figure they have to pick up a ballplayer, and anxiety leads to mistakes. You look at a ballplayer, and you're trying to force something on yourself that isn't there."

When you scout for the Yankees they do not expect you to come up with a good ballplayer every week. It is part accident even when it happens for the best of scouts. The Yankees want only ballplayers who may someday become Yankees, and so they respect your ability to turn down an inferior kid because by so doing you prove your ability to recognize a good prospect.

"You can't be too conservative, either," Krichell said. "You have to figure that now and then you'll make a mistake. If you don't make mistakes, you haven't got the nerve to pick up a ballplayer."

Scouting for a big-league ball club does not mean simply stepping into a car or boarding a train or plane and going out to look over players. For Krichell the search for talent begins in an office in the Yankee Stadium, ten feet by twelve feet, and in the office are a big glass-topped desk, four chairs, three big, olive-drab steel filing cabinets, and six card-index files. Locked in those files are the records of more than seven thousand ballplayers—sandlot, college, semi-pro, and professional—and Krichell carries the only keys.

"And nobody looks in those files," Krichell was saying once, "unless I say so."

Baseball scouting is the most secret of all operations in the field of sports, and thus the least publicized. Krichell can pull out of his files, however, the report on any one of a thousand kids who tried out at the Yankee Stadium during the summer of 1947 and give you a complete run-down on the kid's strong points and his weaknesses.

"So the kid was, say, sixteen years old at the time," he was saying. "That makes him only twenty-two now, doesn't it? If he's improved enough, he could still make it, couldn't he? That's why you save his card for six years."

It is a long shot, at best. Each year Krichell and Hesse look at that thousand at the stadium, and if they find two dozen that they can consider for even the lowest classification in organized baseball, it is a bumper crop. When Krichell finds a Phil Rizzuto and a Whitey Ford in the stadium tryouts, however, and Greenwade spots Mickey Mantle in high school, it is not, as some call it, "Yankee luck."

"You have to answer a thousand letters a year," Krichell said. "A father writes in and says his kid would like to become a Yankee. The kid is twelve years old. You could throw it in the wastebasket, but you don't. You have to sit down and write him back and tell him to send the kid around in four years."

When the kids make the Yankee chain they also become a part of the file at the Yankee general offices at Fifth Avenue and Fifty-seventh Street. To these offices every night each of the eleven minor-league managers in the Yankee chain wires a report of that day's game. That same night he writes out on a mimeographed form, for mailing, a more detailed report of three hundred to five hundred words, and to this he appends the box score.

"Then you scout your own players," Krichell said. "Every ballplayer of ours is looked at not once but several times every year, and by two or three scouts."

It is still mostly paperwork. There are ten days that Krichell spends in his office for every one he is on the road, like today.

"Next exit, New Brunswick," Hesse said, spotting the sign ahead. "You ever been there, Paul?"

He said it as a gag. Krichell is seventy years old now and has looked at tens of thousands of ballplayers and signed dozens, but the one he first saw on a spring afternoon in New Brunswick, New Jersey, thirty years ago was maybe his greatest find.

"I was starting to scout the colleges then," he said, "waiting for the minors to get leveled off for the season. I got up this morning and looked at the paper, and the only teams playing around New York were Columbia and Rutgers at New Brunswick. I didn't have anything else to do so I got on the train." He knew nothing about anyone on Columbia or Rutgers, but before the game the big Columbia first baseman hit a couple into the trees. Krichell rode back on the train with Andy Coakley, the Columbia coach.

"Who the hell is that big guy you had playing on first base today?" he said to Coakley.

"He's a left-handed pitcher," Coakley said. "His name is Gehrig."

"When you gonna pitch him?" Krichell said.

"Saturday," Coakley said. "Against the University of Pennsylvania."

On Saturday Krichell was at South Field, at Columbia. It was 2–2 in the ninth inning when Gehrig hit one all the way up onto the library steps, and on Monday Krichell brought him down to the Yankee offices and that is where the Yankees signed Lou Gehrig for a $1,500 bonus.

Krichell is a heavy-set man who broke into baseball with Ossining in the Hudson River League in 1902. In 1911 and 1912 he caught for the St. Louis Browns. Later he managed Bridgeport, and he was coaching for the Boston Red Sox under Ed Barrow in 1920 when Barrow moved to New York to become business manager of the Yankees and brought Krichell with him.

As the car sped along, Hesse said, "A lot of this land over here belongs to Princeton."

"Charlie Caldwell," Krichell remembered. "I signed Caldwell out of Princeton."

"The football coach?"

"That's right," Krichell said. "He was a side-arm right-hander. He threw his arm out, but he was pitching batting practice in the Stadium one day, and he hit Wally Pipp on the head. They carried Pipp off, and Gehrig, who had appeared in only a few games, played first base in place of Pipp that day and they never did get him off there."

On June 1, 1925, Lou Gehrig played his first game for the Yankees. On May 2, 1939, he played his last, and in between he played 2,130 consecutive games, setting a major-league record that has never been approached.

"Gehrig scared Hank Greenberg away," Krichell went on. "I was the first one after Greenberg. He was playing for James Monroe High School in New York, and then the opposition got wise to him and started talking along the lines of what chance did he have with the Yankees with that iron horse on first base."

The Yankees face the same problem now. Today the scouts of the other major-league teams are still telling young ballplayers that they have small chance to shoulder their way through the Yankee farm talent to the big time. The Yankee scouts fight this canard by telling them how Mantle made it after only two years and McDougald after three.

"And a kid who thinks along the lines that it's too hard to make it couldn't make it anyway," Krichell said, as they left the turnpike.

They crossed the high arch of the new Delaware Memorial Bridge, and then they turned left on Route 13 and drove south through Delaware. At Smyrna they turned right, off the concrete and onto a narrow, winding blacktop road.

"The next spring after I saw Gehrig," Krichell said, "I was down here looking at the Eastern Shore League, and there are two kids I'm watching. The one kid's name is Jimmie Foxx, and the other kid's name, someone told me, is King."

For years Krichell scouted from Florida to Canada and from coast to coast. There is almost no populated section of the United States that cannot bring back memories to him, and sometimes they are the memories of great ballplayers he didn't get.

"After a ball game in Easton," he said, "I get over to the hotel in Dover, and the clerk at the desk says, 'You must be the most important man in baseball. There's four telegrams for you and four long-distance calls from New York.'"

The wires and calls were from Barrow, and the next morning Krichell called him. The Yankees had sold Cliff Markle, the pitcher, to St. Paul and Markle had refused to report. "You better get out there," Barrow said, "and head him off."

"How the heck do I know where he's going?" Krichell said. "Besides, I'm looking at a couple of kids down here named Foxx and King."

"Never mind those kids," Barrow shouted into the phone. "We don't want to lose that ten thousand dollars St. Paul gave us for Markle. Get him."

Krichell found Markle and got him to report to St. Paul. By the time he got back to the Eastern Shore League, the Philadelphia Athletics had bought Foxx and King, and both of them became great ballplayers and made the Hall of Fame.

Lost in memories, Krichell paid no attention to the countryside as the car moved along at a steady fifty. "The boy somebody told me was named King," he said, "is Mickey Cochrane."

When they got into the town, it was late in the afternoon. It is a town of quiet, almost empty tree-lined streets, and they skirted the business section and drove toward the outskirts until they found the hotel.

"It don't look like much," Krichell said, "but the food is good."

It is an old, square, summer hotel, converted to year-round use. The shingles on its sides are graying, and there is a big porch across the front. There is a small lobby on the ground floor, and off that are two parlors and a dining room.

"You have the rooms for us?" Krichell said to the man at the desk. "We wired down."

"What's the name?" the man said.

"Krichell."

There were a half-dozen young ballplayers standing near the desk. When they heard the name they looked at one another and then looked quickly back at Krichell.

"Young ballplayers," Krichell said once, "are dying for you to look at them and see something. If you do see something and try to sign them, you find they've been reading about those big bonuses and they're your enemy."

"Oh, yes, Mr. Krichell," the man at the desk said now. "I got a nice double room and a single on the next floor."

He came out from behind the desk. He was a bald, sallow-faced man, wearing rimless glasses, and he was chewing on a cigar. He had on house slippers and old brown trousers and a T-shirt.

"Haven't you got anything on the first floor?" Krichell said. "If a place like this catches fire it goes up in a minute."

"I have a nice double room in the back here," the man said.

It was a large corner room with a small screened-in porch. After the ball game that day, Krichell and Hesse came back there, and the manager of the ball club came in and they told stories and listened to the manager's troubles.

"The other night," the manager said, "we had a thunderstorm. The next day we went to the clubhouse and eight uniforms hanging up there were soaking wet. There's a hole in the roof."

"Well, somebody can fix the hole, can't they?" Krichell said.

Krichell has seen hundreds of run-down ball parks since the long-ago time when he started scouting late in the summer of 1920 for the Boston Red Sox.

Krichell and Hesse stayed in town for the series, and each day, a couple of hours before the ball game, Hesse would go out to the ball park and get into a Yankee road uniform and he'd hit to the infielders and outfielders. About a half hour before the game Krichell would get there and find a seat up in the planked stands, sometimes behind home plate and sometimes off one baseline or the other. When the game started, he would mark down the lineups on white, lined cards.

The cards are about five inches by four inches, and Krichell designed them when he started scouting so that he could slip them in and out of his pockets easily. Across the top line of the cards are printed the symbols for Position, Name, Number, Bats, Throws, Remarks.

"No power," he'd write down on the card, watching a hitter take a cut at the ball and lift a fly to short center field. "Can't pull."

On any one play during a game he would watch the delivery of the pitcher and make a mental note of the batter's swing and what kind of a pitch he hit and where he hit it. He would gauge the batter's speed going down to first, and watch the manner in which the infielder fielded the ball and how he got it away.

"Can't run," he would write on his card on the line pertaining to the batter, and then he'd find the infielder on the other card and he'd write: "Fair arm."

There is nothing final about this notation. You do not dismiss a ballplayer with one look, but what goes down on these cards is entered into the records in the steel filing cabinets in the Stadium and at the Yankees' Fifth Avenue office. When another of the Yankees' nineteen scouts looks at the ballplayer again, that goes into the records, too.

"In 1946, about the middle of the season," Krichell said one day as he watched the pitcher run the count up on the hitter, "I was moving around the Eastern League. Jerry Coleman was playing shortstop for Binghamton in a game at Williamsport. He made seven errors—they gave him four but he made seven. You can't tell. Anybody can have a bad day."

In 1949, Coleman came up to play second base for the Yankees. He held it down until, last year, he went back into the Marine Corps.

Krichell recalled a time in 1925, when he was in Pittsfield, Massachusetts. On his way down to dinner in the hotel he happened to meet

Kitty Bransfield, who was managing the Waterbury club, and they sat down to eat together.

"If I was scouting this league," Bransfield said after a while, "do you know who I'd take?"

"No," Krichell said.

"That shortstop at Hartford," Bransfield said.

"But he can't hit," Krichell said.

"I'd still take him," Bransfield said.

When a scout is on the road he does a lot of thinking alone in his hotel room at night. That night Krichell lay in bed, and he kept thinking of the great shortstops he knew who couldn't hit—Bobby Wallace with the Browns and George McBride with Washington, and the others.

"So I went to Hartford," he said, "and I bought the shortstop—Leo Durocher."

As Krichell sat now, watching in the weathered stands, the cries of the infielders came up clearly, but the ball game itself was foreign to him. He was not there to see if one team could beat the other, but to look at ballplayers, and every now and then he would turn around and ask someone the inning or the score.

"Anybody can pick up a perfect ballplayer," he said once, "but we don't get Tony Lazzeri if he don't have something wrong with him and if we don't gamble."

Lazzeri was with Salt Lake City, and the Chicago Cubs had a three-year working agreement with the team. Krichell had been scouting him for three weeks before he called Barrow.

"This Lazzeri," he told Barrow, "takes fits."

"What do you mean?" Barrow asked.

"He gets epileptic fits," Krichell said, "but he don't get them between two o'clock and six o'clock in the afternoon when you play ball."

So the Yankees paid $50,000 and five ballplayers for Lazzeri. They bought Mark Koenig that same year—1925—for the same price. They were in seventh place, and the next three years they won the pennant.

Krichell finished the story of the Lazzeri deal as he and Hesse entered the small lobby of the hotel. He walked up to the desk, and there was an old woman behind it, looking closely at a newspaper.

"If I get any mail or telegrams or phone messages," Krichell said, "where will they be?"

"I don't know," the old woman said.

"Well, what do you do with the telegrams?" Krichell said.

"I don't know," the woman said. "They usually phone them."

"Where?" Krichell said.

"There's the phone booth there," the woman said, pointing.

"This is a fine thing," Krichell said.

When you are on the road you live between phone calls and telegrams. One night Krichell was sitting in his hotel room in Buffalo, trying to sign Emerson Dickman, who later pitched for the Boston Red Sox, when a call came through from Barrow telling him not to lose Charlie Keller, who was still a student at the University of Maryland but who was playing summer ball in Kinston, North Carolina.

Krichell caught a train that night, and next day was at College Park, where he picked up the Maryland baseball coach. In the coach's car they drove to Keller's home outside of Frederick, Maryland, and on the way Krichell rehearsed the coach.

"I told him the highest I wanted to go, with so-much-a-month salary," Krichell said. "I said, 'When we start to argue with the folks we'll start low, and you say, "Mr. Krichell, that's not enough." I'll say, "It's the best I can do." Then you say, "Do you mind if I talk to these people alone?" Then I'll step outside and you raise the figure up to my price and then I come in and we agree.'

"So what does he do when I step outside?" Krichell said. "He raises the salary and the bonus more than I'd told him to, but anyway, I get the father's signature and a note to Charlie and I take the train to Kinston."

He got into the hotel in Kinston at 7:00 A.M. There were four other scouts in the house, so he talked to the desk clerk and found out that

Keller was staying in a boardinghouse about five blocks away. He went there and got Keller out of bed, and it was a hot July morning, and they started walking around the block.

"I sign him against the wall of a building," Krichell said. "I think it was a warehouse or a factory, and that's where I signed Charlie Keller."

He signed Johnny Broaca, the Yale pitcher, in the writing room of the Hotel Garde in New Haven, and Broaca had the pen in his hand four times before he put his name down. He signed Hank Borowy, the Fordham pitcher, in the football coach's office in the Fordham gym.

"He agreed to eight thousand," Krichell said, "and I've got no fountain pen. It's the off-season, and the inkwells are dry. So I go out and borrow a pen from the freshman football coach. When I come back Borowy wants five hundred more. It cost us five hundred dollars because I don't have a fountain pen."

Krichell was laughing at the memory as he packed his bags in the hotel. He and Hesse left the town on the morning of the fourth day and headed back to New York. Scouting for a major-league ball club is a lot like game fishing. You never know where you are going to get one or if you are going to land it or how big it is going to be.

Fifteen years ago, Krichell was in Elizabeth, New Jersey, watching an American Legion game between Springfield, Massachusetts, and Elizabeth. There was a kid pitcher on the Springfield team who had a good fastball, and when Krichell talked with him the kid said he wanted a college education.

"He planned to go to Manhattan College," Krichell was saying on the ride back to New York, "but he failed to make out certain papers, and when he got to the college the classes were all filled up. So he went to William and Mary, and he got himself a good education.

"That," Krichell was saying as the car reached the outskirts of New York City, "is exactly what Vic Raschi cost the Yankees—two-hundred-fifty-a-year spending money while he was in college."

Five days later, Krichell and Hesse were on the field at the Yankee Stadium. It was nine o'clock in the morning, and already the sun was beating down warmly on the close-cropped grass and the exact, raked base paths. The empty light blue stands made a towering arc behind them, and around them moved about five dozen kids, some tall, some small, most of them in ill-fitting uniforms or parts of uniforms with letters spelling out titles like Monarchs and Superbas across the fronts of their shirts. On their backs were pinned square black numbered cloths.

"C'mon," Krichell was saying. "Who's the next hitter?"

He was wearing a dark blue Yankee cap and one of those dark blue nylon jackets the pitchers wear on base, brown trousers, and brown shoes. In one hand he held a clipboard with white sheets of mimeographed paper snapped onto it.

You can never tell. A lot of it is luck, and on a day like this in 1946 there was a little blond kid trying out for first base. Krichell told him he was too small for a first baseman. There are some scouts who would never have bothered to look at the kid again, but when he came back a year later, he had a big, old-fashioned curve and that is how the Yankees got Whitey Ford.

Krichell turned from memories to business.

"All right," he said. "Let's run down these lists and get it over with. Did anybody like any of the catchers?"

The scouts were in the umpires' room under the stands. Krichell and Hesse were sitting in the armchairs, and the others were sitting on stools in front of the dressing stalls—Roy Tarr, who is a veteran of the minor leagues; Tony DePhillips, who caught a few games with the Cincinnati Reds in 1943; and Al Cuccinello, who played a few games at infield for the Giants in 1935.

"No catchers," Tarr said. "Nobody wants to catch any more."

They had timed the kids running. They had watched them hitting and throwing and fielding. They had warmed up the pitchers and then they had had them throw to the batters.

"Pitchers?" Krichell said. "Do we want to ask those two to come back?"

"I've got 'See again' for both of them," Hesse replied.

Paul Krichell started holding schoolboy tryouts at the Yankee Stadium in 1936. After the first tryout he was sitting with several others at a meeting just like this.

"I'd like to see a little more of that Italian kid," Krichell had said then. "He has a sore leg now, but he looks good."

The Dodgers and the Giants had chased the kid away. They had told him he was too small and there are some scouts who would have dismissed the sore leg as an excuse, but Krichell had seen that the kid was great on a ground ball and could throw. At batting practice he had just managed to put one into the front row of the left-field stands, and so the Yankees had looked at him again and signed Phil Rizzuto.

"Of all of them," one of them was asking Krichell upstairs in his office later, "which one gave you the biggest thrill?"

"You must have got a tremendous kick out of Rizzuto," Hesse said.

"Certainly," Krichell said, "but I guess Gehrig was the biggest. Here was a kid playing in a New York college and nobody looking at him and I see him by accident."

"Do any of them," one of the others said, "ever thank you for it? You see something in them and sign them and maybe without you they'd be coal miners or garage mechanics or carpenters."

"No," Krichell said. "Only Durocher. Whenever I see Leo anywhere he says, 'Here's the guy I owe everything to. He saw something in me when nobody else would give me a tumble.'"

He was sitting at his desk by the window. On the walls are black-framed pictures of the ones he found and signed—Gehrig, Lazzeri, Keller, Rizzuto, Ford, Raschi, Borowy, Red Rolfe, George Stirnweiss, Johnny Murphy, and the others.

"Most of them," he said, "say nothing."

The phone rang. He picked it up and talked into it, and then he listened.

"How old did you say he is?" he said. "When does he get out of school?"

The Rocky Road of Pistol Pete

The Dodger They Padded the Walls For

"DOWN IN LOS ANGELES," says Garry Schumacher, who was a New York baseball writer for thirty years and is now assistant to Horace Stoneham, president of the San Francisco Giants, "they think Duke Snider is the best center fielder the Dodgers ever had. They forget Pete Reiser. The Yankees think Mickey Mantle is something new. They forget Reiser, too."

Maybe Pete Reiser was the purest ballplayer of all time. I don't know. There is no exact way of measuring such a thing, but when a man of incomparable skills, with full knowledge of what he is doing, destroys those skills and puts his life on the line in the pursuit of his endeavor as no other man in his game ever has, perhaps he is the truest of them all.

"Is Pete Reiser there?" I said on the phone.

This was last season, in Kokomo. Kokomo has a population of about fifty thousand and a ball club, now affiliated with Los Angeles and called the Dodgers, in the Class D Midwest League. Class D is the bottom of the barrel of organized baseball, and this was the second season that Pete Reiser had managed Kokomo.

"He's not here right now," the woman's voice on the phone said. "The team played a double-header yesterday in Dubuque, and they didn't get in on the bus until four thirty this morning. Pete just got up a few minutes ago and he had to go to the doctor's."

True, March 1958.

"Oh?" I said. "What has he done now?"

In two and a half years in the minors, three seasons of Army ball, and ten years in the majors, Pete Reiser was carried off the field eleven times. Nine times he regained consciousness either in the clubhouse or in the hospital. He broke a bone in his right elbow, throwing. He broke both ankles, tore a cartilage in his left knee, ripped the muscles in his left leg, sliding. Seven times he crashed into outfield walls, dislocating his left shoulder, breaking his right collarbone, and, five times, ending up in an unconscious heap on the ground. Twice he was beaned, and the few who remember still wonder today how great he might have been.

"I didn't see the old-timers," Bob Cooke, who is sports editor of the *New York Herald Tribune*, was saying recently, "but Pete Reiser was the best ballplayer I ever saw."

"We don't know what's wrong with him," the woman's voice on the phone said now. "He has a pain in his chest and he feels tired all the time, so we sent him to the doctor. There's a game tonight, so he'll be at the ball park about five o'clock."

Pete Reiser is thirty-nine years old now. The Cardinals signed him out of the St. Louis Municipal League when he was fifteen. For two years, because he was so young, he chauffeured for Charley Barrett, who was scouting the Midwest. They had a Cardinal uniform in the car for Pete, and he used to work out with the Class C and D clubs, and one day Branch Rickey, who was general manager of the Cardinals then, called Pete into his office in Sportsman's Park.

"Young man," he said, "you're the greatest young ballplayer I've ever seen, but there is one thing you must remember. Now that you're a professional ballplayer you're in show business. You will perform on the biggest stage in the world, the baseball diamond. Like the actors on Broadway, you'll be expected to put on a great performance every day, no matter how you feel, no matter whether it's too hot or too cold. Never forget that."

Rickey didn't know it at the time, but this was like telling Horatius that, as a professional soldier, he'd be expected someday to stand his ground. Three times Pete sneaked out of hospitals to play. Once he went back into the lineup after doctors warned him that any blow on the head would kill him. For four years he swung the bat and made the throws when it was painful for him just to shave and to comb his hair. In the 1947 World Series he stood on a broken ankle to pinch hit, and it ended with Rickey, then president of the Dodgers, begging him not to play and guaranteeing Pete his 1948 salary if he would just sit that season out.

"That might be the one mistake I made," Pete says now. "Maybe I should have rested that year."

"Pete Reiser?" Leo Durocher, who managed Pete at Brooklyn, was saying recently. "What's he doing now?"

"He's managing Kokomo," Lindsey Nelson, the TV sportscaster, said.

"Kokomo?" Leo said.

"That's right," Lindsey said. "He's riding the buses to places like Lafayette and Michigan City and Mattoon."

"On the buses," Leo said, shaking his head and then smiling at the thought of Pete.

"And some people say," Lindsey said, "that he was the greatest young ballplayer they ever saw."

"No doubt about it," Leo said. "He was the best I ever had, with the possible exception of Mays. At that, he was even faster than Willie." He paused. "So now he's on the buses."

The first time that Leo ever saw Pete on a ball field was in Clearwater that spring of '39. Pete had played one year of Class D in the Cardinal chain and one season of Class D for Brooklyn. Judge Kenesaw Mountain Landis, who was then baseball commissioner, had sprung Pete and seventy-two others from what they called the "Cardinal Chain Gang," and Pete had signed with Brooklyn for $100.

"I didn't care about money then," Pete says, "I just wanted to play."

Pete had never been in a major-league camp before, and he didn't know that at batting practice you hit in rotation. At Clearwater he was grabbing any bat that was handy and cutting in ahead of Ernie Koy or Dolph Camilli or one of the others, and Leo liked that.

One day Leo had a chest cold, so he told Pete to start at shortstop. His first time up he hit a homer off the Cards' Ken Raffensberger, and that was the beginning. He was on base his first twelve times at bat that spring, with three homers, five singles, and four walks. His first time against Detroit he homered off Tommy Bridges. His first time against the Yankees he put one over the fence off Lefty Gomez.

Durocher played Pete at shortstop in thirty-three games that spring. The Dodgers barnstormed north with the Yankees, and one night Joe McCarthy, who was managing the Yankees, sat down next to Pete on the train.

"Reiser," he said, "you're going to play for me."

"How can I play for you?" Pete said. "I'm with the Dodgers."

"We'll get you," McCarthy said. "I'll tell Ed Barrow, and you'll be a Yankee."

The Yankees offered $100,000 and five ballplayers for Pete. The Dodgers turned it down, and the day the season opened at Ebbets Field, Larry MacPhail, who was running things in Brooklyn, called Pete on the clubhouse phone and told him to report to Elmira.

"It was an hour before game time," Pete says, "and I started to take off my uniform and I was shaking all over. Leo came in and said, 'What's the matter? You scared?' I said, 'No. MacPhail is sending me to Elmira.' Leo got on the phone and they had a hell of a fight. Leo said he'd quit, and MacPhail said he'd fire him—and I went to Elmira.

"One day I'm making a throw and I heard something pop. Every day my arm got weaker and they sent me to Johns Hopkins and took X-rays. Dr. George Bennett told me, 'Your arm's broken.' When I came to after the operation, my throat was sore and there was an ice pack on it. I said, 'What happened? Your knife slip?' They said, 'We took your tonsils out while we were operating on your arm.'"

Pete's arm was in a cast from the first of May until the end of July. His first two weeks out of the cast he still couldn't straighten the arm, but a month later he played ten games as a left-handed outfielder until Dr. Bennett stopped him.

"But I can't straighten my right arm," Pete said.

"Take up bowling," the doctor said.

When he bowled, though, Pete used first one arm and then the other. Every day that the weather allowed he went out into the backyard and practiced throwing a rubber ball left-handed against a wall. Then he went to Fairgrounds Park and worked on the long throw, left-handed, with a baseball.

"At Clearwater that next spring," he said, "Leo saw me in the outfield throwing left-handed, and he said, 'What do you think you're doin'?' I said, 'Hell, I had to be ready. Now I can throw as good with my left arm as I could with my right.' He said, 'You can do more things as a right-handed ballplayer. I can bring you into the infield. Go out there and cut loose with that right arm.' I did and it was okay, but I had that insurance."

So at five o'clock I took a cab from the hotel in Kokomo to the ball park on the edge of town. It seats about 2,200—1,500 in the white-painted fairgrounds grandstand along the first baseline, and the rest in chairs behind the screen and in bleachers along the other line.

I watched them take batting practice—trim, strong young kids with their dreams, I knew, of someday getting up there where Pete once was—and I listened to their kidding. I watched the grounds-keeper open the concession booth and clean out the electric pop-corn machine. I read the signs on the outfield walls, advertising the Mid-West Towel and Linen Service, Basil's Nite Club, the Hoosier Iron Works, UAW Local 292, and the Around the Clock Pizza Café. I watched the Dubuque kids climbing out of their bus, carrying their uniforms on wire coat hangers.

"Here comes Pete now," I heard the old guy setting up the ticket box at the gate say.

When Pete came through the gate he was walking like an old man. In 1941, the Dodgers trained in Havana, and one day they clocked him, in his baseball uniform and regular spikes, at 9.8 for a hundred yards. Five years later the Cleveland Indians were bragging about George Case and the Washington Senators had Gil Coan. The Dodgers offered to bet $1,000 that Reiser was the fastest man in baseball, and now it was taking him forever to walk to me, his shoulders stooped, his whole body heavier now, and Pete just slowly moving one foot ahead of the other.

"Hello," he said, shaking hands but his face solemn. "How are you?"

"Fine," I said, "but what's the matter with you?"

"I guess it's my heart," he said.

"When did you first notice this?"

"About eleven days ago. I guess I was working out too hard. All of a sudden I felt this pain in my chest and I got weak. I went into the clubhouse and lay down on the bench, but I've had the same pain and I'm weak ever since."

"What did the doctor say?"

"He says it's lucky I stopped that day when I did. He says I should be in a hospital right now, because if I exert myself or even make a quick motion I might go—just like that."

He snapped his fingers. "He scared me," he said. "I'll admit it. I'm scared."

"What are you planning to do?"

"I'm going home to St. Louis. My wife works for a doctor there, and he'll know a good heart specialist."

"When will you leave?"

"Well, I can't just leave the ball club. I called Brooklyn, and they're sending a replacement for me, but he won't be here until tomorrow."

"How will you get to St. Louis?"

"It's about three hundred miles," Pete says. "The doctor says I shouldn't fly or go by train, because if anything happens to me they can't stop and help me. I guess I'll have to drive."

"I'll drive you," I said.

Trying to get to sleep in the hotel that night I was thinking that maybe, standing there in that little ball park, Pete Reiser had admitted out loud for the first time in his life that he was scared. I was thinking of 1941, his first full year with the Dodgers. He was beaned twice and crashed his first wall and still hit .343 to be the first rookie and the youngest ballplayer to win the National League batting title. He tied

Johnny Mize with thirty-nine doubles, led in triples, runs scored, total bases, and slugging average, and they were writing on the sports pages that he might be the new Ty Cobb.

"Dodgers Win On Reiser HR," the headlines used to say. "Reiser Stars as Brooklyn Lengthens Lead."

"Any manager in the National League," Arthur Patterson wrote one day in the *New York Herald Tribune*, "would give up his best man to obtain Pete Reiser. On every bench they're talking about him. Rival players watch him take his cuts during batting practice, announce when he's going to make a throw to the plate or third base during outfield drill. They just whistle their amazement when he scoots down the first baseline on an infield dribbler or a well-placed bunt."

He was beaned the first time at Ebbets Field five days after the season started. A sidearm fastball got away from Ike Pearson of the Phillies, and Pete came to at 11:30 that night in Peck Memorial Hospital.

"I was lying in bed with my uniform on," he told me once, "and I couldn't figure it out. The room was dark, with just a little night-light, and then I saw a mirror and I walked over to it and lit the light and I had a black eye and a black streak down the side of my nose. I said to myself, 'What happened to me?' Then I remembered.

"I took a shower and walked around the room, and the next morning the doctor came in. He looked me over, and he said, 'We'll keep you here for five or six more days under observation.' I said, 'Why?' He said, 'You've had a serious head injury. If you tried to get out of bed right now, you'd fall down.' I said, 'If I can get up and walk around this room, can I get out?' The doc said, 'All right, but you won't be able to do it.'"

Pete got out of bed, the doctor standing ready to catch him. He walked around the room. "I've been walkin' the floor all night," Pete said.

The doctor made Pete promise that he wouldn't play ball for a week, but Pete went right to the ball park. He got a seat behind the Brooklyn dugout, and Durocher spotted him.

"How do you feel?" Leo said.

"Not bad," Pete said.

"Get your uniform on," Leo said.

"I'm not supposed to play," Pete said.

"I'm not gonna play you," Leo said. "Just sit on the bench. It'll make our guys feel better to see that you're not hurt."

Pete suited up and went out and sat on the bench. In the eighth inning it was tied 7–7. The Dodgers had the bases loaded, and there was Ike Pearson again, coming in to relieve.

"Pistol," Leo said to Pete, "get the bat."

In the press box the baseball writers watched Pete. They wanted to see if he'd stand right in there. After a beaning they are all entitled to shy, and many of them do. Pete hit the first pitch into the center field stands, and Brooklyn won, 11–7.

"I could just barely trot around the bases," Pete said when I asked him about it. "I was sure dizzy."

Two weeks later they were playing the Cardinals, and Enos Slaughter hit one and Pete turned in center field and started to run. He made the catch, but he hit his head and his tailbone on that corner near the exit gate.

His head was cut, and when he came back to the bench they also saw blood coming through the seat of his pants. They took him into the clubhouse and pulled his pants down and the doctor put a metal clamp on the cut.

"Just don't slide," he told Pete. "You can get it sewed up after the game."

In August of that year big Paul Erickson was pitching for the Cubs and Pete took another one. Again he woke up in a hospital. The Dodgers were having some pretty good bean-ball contests with the Cubs that season, and Judge Landis came to see Pete the next day.

"Do you think that man tried to bean you?" he asked Pete.

"No sir," Pete said. "I lost the pitch."

"I was there," Landis said, "and I heard them holler, 'Stick it in his ear!' "

"That was just bench talk," Pete said. "I lost the pitch."

He left the hospital the next morning. The Dodgers were going to St. Louis after the game, and Pete didn't want to be left in Chicago.

Pete always says that the next year, 1942, was the year of his downfall, and the worst of it happened on one play. It was early July and Pete and the Dodgers were tearing the league apart. Starting in Cincinnati he got 19 for 21. In a Sunday double-header in Chicago he went 5 for 5 in the first game, walked three times in the second game, and got a hit the one time they pitched to him. He was hitting .391, and they were writing in the papers that he might end up hitting .400.

When they came into St. Louis the Dodgers were leading by ten and a half games. When they took off for Pittsburgh they left three games of that lead and Pete Reiser behind them.

"We were in the twelfth inning, no score, two outs, and Slaughter hit it off Whit Wyatt," Pete says. "It was over my head and I took off. I caught it and missed that flagpole by two inches and hit the wall and dropped the ball. I had the instinct to throw it to Pee Wee Reese, and we just missed gettin' Slaughter at the plate, and they won, 1–0.

"I made one step to start off the field and I woke up the next morning in St. John's Hospital. My head was bandaged, and I had an awful headache."

Dr. Robert Hyland, who was Pete's personal physician, announced to the newspapers that Pete would be out for the rest of the season. "Look, Pete," Hyland told him, "I'm your personal friend. I'm advising you not to play any more baseball this year."

"I don't like hospitals, though," Pete was telling me once, "so after two days I took the bandage off and got up. The room started to spin, but I got dressed and I took off. I snuck out, and I took a train to Pittsburgh and I went to the park.

"Leo saw me and he said, 'Go get your uniform on, Pistol.' I said, 'Not tonight, Skipper.' Leo said, 'Aw, I'm not gonna let you hit. I want these guys to see you. It'll give 'em that little spark they need. Besides, it'll change the pitching plans on that other bench when they see you sittin' here in uniform.'"

In the fourteenth inning the Dodgers had a runner on second and Ken Heintzelman, the left-hander, came in for the Pirates. He walked Johnny Rizzo, and Durocher had run out of pinch hitters.

"Damn," Leo was saying, walking up and down. "I want to win this one. Who can I use? Anybody here who can hit?"

Pete walked up to the bat rack. He pulled out his stick. "You got yourself a hitter," he said to Leo.

He walked up there and hit a line drive over the second baseman's head that was good for three bases. The two runs scored, and Pete rounded first base and collapsed.

"When I woke up I was in a hospital again," he says. "I could just make out that somebody was standin' there and then I saw it was Leo. He said, 'You awake?' I said, 'Yep.' He said, 'By God, we beat 'em! How do you feel?' I said, 'How do you think I feel?' He said, 'Aw, you're better with one leg and one eye than anybody else I've got.' I said, 'Yeah, and that's the way I'll end up—on one leg and with one eye.'

"I'd say I lost the pennant for us that year," Pete says now, although he still hit .310 for the season. "I was dizzy most of the time and I couldn't see fly balls. I mean balls I could have put in my pocket, I couldn't get near. Once in Brooklyn when Mort Cooper was pitching for the Cards I was seeing two baseballs coming up there. Babe Pinelli was umpiring behind the plate, and a couple of times he stopped the game and asked me if I was all right. So the Cards beat us out the last two days of the season."

The business office of the Kokomo ball club is the dining room of a man named Jim Deets, who sells insurance and is also the business manager of the club. His wife, in addition to keeping house, mothering six small kids, boarding Pete, an outfielder from Venezuela, and a shortstop from the Dominican Republic, is also the club secretary.

"How do you feel this morning?" I asked Pete. He was sitting at the dining-room table, in a sweatshirt and a pair of light brown slacks, typing the game report of the night before to send it to Brooklyn.

"A little better," he said.

Pete has a worn, green, seven-year-old Chevy, and it took us eight and a half hours to get to St. Louis. I'd ask him how the pain in his chest was and he'd say that it wasn't bad or it wasn't so good and I'd get him to talking again about Durocher or about his time in the Army. Pete played under five managers at Brooklyn, Boston, Pittsburgh, and Cleveland, and Durocher is his favorite.

"He has a great mind, and not just for baseball," Pete said. "Once he sat down to play gin with Jack Benny, and after they'd played four cards Leo read Benny's whole hand to him. Benny said, 'How can you do that?' Leo said, 'If you're playin' your cards right, and I give you credit for that, you have to be holding those others.' Benny said, 'I don't want to play with this guy.'

"One spring at Clearwater there was a pool table in a room off the lobby. One night Hugh Casey and a couple of other guys and I were talking with Leo. We said, 'Gee, there's a guy in there and we've been playin' pool with him for a couple of nights, but last night he had a real hot streak.' Leo said, 'How much he take you for?' We figured it out and it was two thousand dollars. Leo said, 'Point him out to me.'

"We went in and pointed the guy out and Leo walked up to him and said, 'Put all your money on the table. We're gonna shoot for it.' The guy said, 'I never play like that.' Leo said, 'You will tonight. Pick your own game.' Leo took him for four thousand dollars, and then he threw him out. Then he paid us back what we'd gone for, and he said, 'Now, let that be a lesson. That guy is a hustler from New York. The next time it happens I won't bail you out.' Leo hadn't had a cue in his hands for years."

It was amazing that they took Pete into the Army. He had wanted to enlist in the Navy, but the doctors looked him over and told him none of the services could accept him. Then his draft board sent him to Jefferson Barracks in the winter of 1943, and the doctors there turned him down.

"I'm sittin' on a bench with the other guys who've been rejected," he was telling me, "and a captain comes in and says, 'Which one of you is Reiser?' I stood up and I said, 'I am.' In front of everybody he said, 'So you're trying to pull a fast one, are you? At a time like this, with a war going on, you came in here under a false name. What do you mean, giving your name as Harold Patrick Reiser? Your name's Pete Reiser, and you're the ballplayer, aren't you?' I said, 'I'm the ballplayer and they call me Pete, but my right name is Harold Patrick Reiser.' The captain says, 'I apologize. Sergeant, fingerprint him. This man is in.'"

They sent him to Fort Riley, Kansas. It was early April and raining and they were on bivouac, and Pete woke up in a hospital. "What happened?" he said.

"You've got pneumonia," the doctor said. "You've been a pretty sick boy for six days. You'll be all right, but we've been looking you over. How did you ever get into this Army?"

"When I get out of the hospital," Pete was telling me, "I'm on the board for a discharge and I'm waitin' around for about a week, and still nobody there knows who I am. All of a sudden one morning a voice comes over the bitch box in the barracks. It says, 'Private Reiser, report to headquarters immediately.' I think, 'Well, I'm out now.'

"I go over there and the colonel wants to see me. I walk in and give my good salute and he says, 'Sit down, Harold.' I sit down and he says, 'Your name really isn't Harold, is it?' I say, 'Yes it is, sir.' He says, 'But that isn't what they call you when you're well-known, is it? You're Pete Reiser the ballplayer, aren't you?' I say, 'Yes, sir.' He says, 'I thought so. Now, I've got your discharge papers right there, but we've got a pretty good ball club and we'd like you on it. We'll make a deal. You say nothing, and you won't have to do anything but play ball. How about it?' I said, 'Suppose I don't want to stay in?' He picked my papers up off his desk, and he tore 'em right up in my face. I can still hear that 'zip' when he tore 'em. He said, 'You see, you have no choice.'

"Then he picked up the phone and said something and in a minute a general came in. I jumped up and the colonel said, 'Don't bother to salute, Pete.' Then he said to the general, 'Major, this is Pete Reiser, the great Dodger ballplayer. He was up for a medical discharge, but he's decided to stay here and play ball for us.'

"So the general says, 'My, what a patriotic thing for you to do, young man. That's wonderful. Wonderful.' I'm sittin' there, and when the general goes out the colonel says, 'That major, he's all right.' I said, 'But he's a general. How come you call him a major?' The colonel says, 'Well, in the regular Army he's a major and I'm a full colonel. The only reason I don't outrank him now is that I've got heart trouble. He knows it, but I never let him forget it. I always call him major.' I thought, 'What kind of an Army am I in?'"

Joe Gantenbein, the Athletics' outfielder, and George Scharein, the Phillies' infielder, were on that team with Pete, and they won the state and national semi-pro titles. By the time the season was over, however, the order came down to hold up all discharges.

The next season there were seventeen major-league ballplayers on the Fort Riley club, and they played four nights a week for the war workers in Wichita. Pete hit a couple of walls, and the team made such a joke of the national semi-pro tournament that an order came down from Washington to break up the club.

"Considering what a lot of guys did in the war," Pete says, "I had no complaints, but five times I was up for discharge, and each time something happened. From Riley they sent me to Camp Livingston. From there they sent me to New York Special Services for twelve hours and I end up in Camp Lee, Virginia, in May 1945.

"The first one I meet there is the general. He says, 'Reiser, I saw you on the list and I just couldn't pass you up.' I said, 'What about my discharge?' He says, 'That will have to wait. I have a lot of celebrities down here, but I want a good baseball team.'"

Johnny Lindell, of the Yankees, and Dave Philley, of the White Sox, were on the club and Pete played left field. Near the end of the season he went after a foul fly for the third out of the last inning, and he went right through a temporary wooden fence and rolled down a twenty-five-foot embankment.

"I came to in the hospital with a dislocated right shoulder," he says, "and the general came over to see me and he said, 'That was one of the greatest displays of courage I've ever seen, to ignore your future in baseball just to win a ball game for Camp Lee.' I said, 'Thanks.'

"Now it's November and the war is over, but they're still shippin' guys out, and I'm on the list to go. I report to the overseas major, and he looks at my papers and says, 'I can't send you overseas. With everything that's wrong with you, you shouldn't even be in this Army. I'll have you out in three hours.' In three hours, sure enough, I've got those papers in my hand, stamped, and I'm startin' out the door. Runnin' up to me comes a Red Cross guy. He says, 'I can get you some pretty good pension benefits for the physical and mental injuries you've sustained.' I said, 'You can?' He said, 'Yes, you're entitled to them.' I said, 'Good. You get 'em. You keep 'em. I'm goin' home.'"

When we got to St. Louis that night I drove Pete to his house and the next morning I picked him up and drove him to see the heart specialist. He was in there for two hours, and when he came out he was walking slower than ever.

"No good," he said. "I have to go to the hospital for five days for observation."

"What does he think?"

"He says I'm done puttin' on that uniform, I'll have to get a desk job."

Riding to the hospital I wondered if that heart specialist knew who he was tying to that desk job. In 1946, the year he came out of the Army, Pete led the league when he stole thirty-four bases, thirteen more than the runner-up, Johnny Hopp of the Braves. He also set a major-league record that still stands, when he stole home seven times.

"Eight times," he said once. "In Chicago I stole home and Magerkurth hollered, 'You're out!' Then he dropped his voice and he said, 'Sonofabitch! I missed it.' He'd already had his thumb in the air. I had eight out of eight."

I suppose somebody will beat that someday, but he'll never top the way Pete did it. That was the year he knocked himself out again making a diving catch, dislocated his left shoulder, ripped the muscles in his left leg, and broke his left ankle.

"Whitey Kurowski hit one in the seventh inning at Ebbets Field," he was telling me. "I dove for it and woke up in the clubhouse. I was in Peck Memorial for four days. It really didn't take much to knock me out in those days. I was comin' apart all over. When I dislocated my shoulder they popped it back in, and Leo said, 'Hell, you'll be all right. You don't throw with it anyway.'"

That was the year the Dodgers tied with the Cardinals for the pennant and dropped the playoff. Pete wasn't there for those two games. He was in Peck Memorial again.

"I'd pulled a charley horse in my left leg," Pete was saying. "It's the last two weeks of the season, and I'm out for four days. We've got the winning run on third, two outs in the ninth, and Leo sends me up. He says, 'If you don't hit it good, don't run and hurt your leg.'

"The first pitch was a knockdown and, when I ducked, the ball hit the bat and went down the third baseline, as beautiful a bunt as you've ever seen. Well, Ebbets Field is jammed. Leo has said, 'Don't run.' But this is a big game. I take off for first, and we win and I've ripped the muscles from my ankle to my hip. Leo says, 'You shouldn't have done it.'

"Now it's the last three days of the season and we're a game ahead of the Cards and we're playin' the Phillies in Brooklyn. Leo says to me, 'It's now or never. I don't think we can win it without you.' The first two up are outs and I single to right. There's Charley Dressen, coachin' on third, with the steal sign. I start to get my lead, and a pitcher named Charley Schanz is workin' and he throws an ordinary lob over to first. My leg is stiff and I slide and my heel spike catches the bag and I hear it snap.

"Leo comes runnin' out. He says, 'Come on. You're all right.' I said, 'I think it's broken.' He says, 'It ain't stickin' out.' They took me to Peck Memorial, and it was broken."

We went to St. Luke's Hospital in St. Louis. In the main office they told Pete to go over to a desk where a gray-haired, semistout woman was sitting at a typewriter. She started to book Pete in, typing his answer on the form. "What is your occupation, Mr. Reiser?" she said.

"Baseball," Pete said.

"Have you ever been hospitalized before?"

"Yes," Pete said.

In 1946, the Dodgers played an exhibition game in Springfield, Missouri. When the players got off the train there was a young radio announcer there, and he was grabbing them one at a time and asking them where they thought they'd finish that year.

"In first place," Reese and Casey and Dixie Walker and the rest were saying. "On top." "We'll win it."

"And here comes Pistol Pete Reiser!" the announcer said. "Where do you think you'll finish this season, Pete?"

"In Peck Memorial Hospital," Pete said.

After the 1946 season Brooklyn changed the walls at Ebbets Field. They added boxes, cutting forty feet off left field and dropping center field from 420 to 390 feet. Pete had made a real good start that season in center, and on June 5 the Dodgers were leading the Pirates by three runs in the sixth inning when Culley Rikard hit one.

"I made my turn and ran," Pete says, "and, where I thought I still had that thirty feet, I didn't."

"The crowd," Al Laney wrote the next day in the *New York Herald Tribune*, "which watched silently while Reiser was being carried away, did not know that he had held on to the ball. . . . Rikard circled the bases, but Butch Henline, the umpire, who ran to Reiser, found the ball still in Reiser's glove. . . . Two outs were posted on the scoreboard after play was resumed. Then the crowd let out a tremendous roar."

In the Brooklyn clubhouse the doctor called for a priest, and the last rites of the Church were administered to Pete. He came to, but lapsed into unconsciousness again and woke up at 3:00 A.M. in Peck Memorial.

For eight days he couldn't move. After three weeks they let him out, and he made the next western trip with the Dodgers. In Pittsburgh he was working out in the outfield before the game when Clyde King, chasing a fungo, ran into him and Pete woke up in the clubhouse.

"I went back to the Hotel Schenley and lay down," he says. "After the game I got up and had dinner with Pee Wee. We were sittin' on the porch, and I scratched my head and I felt a lump there about as big as half a golf ball. I told Pee Wee to feel it and he said 'Gosh!' I said, 'I don't think that's supposed to be like that.' He said, 'Hell, no.'"

Pete went up to Rickey's room and Rickey called his pilot and had Pete flown to Johns Hopkins in Baltimore. They operated on him for a blood clot.

"You're lucky," the doctor told him. "If it had moved just a little more you'd have been gone."

Pete was unable to hold even a pencil. He had double vision and when he tried to take a single step, he became dizzy. He stayed for three weeks and then went home for almost a month.

"It was August," he said, "and Brooklyn was fightin' for another pennant. I thought if I could play the last two months it might make the difference, so I went back to Johns Hopkins. The doctor said, 'You've made a remarkable recovery.' I said, 'I want to play.' He said, 'I can't okay that. The slightest blow on the head can kill you.'"

Pete played. He worked out for four days, pinch hit a couple of times, and then, in the Polo Grounds, made a diving catch in left field. They carried him off, and in the clubhouse he was unable to recognize anyone.

Pete was still having dizzy spells when the Dodgers went into the 1947 Series against the Yankees. In the third game he walked in the first inning, got the steal sign, and, when he went into second, felt his right ankle snap. At the hospital they found it was broken.

"Just tape it, will you?" Pete said.

"I want to put a cast on it," the doctor said.

"If you do," Pete said, "they'll give me a dollar-a-year contract next season."

The next day he was back on the bench. Bill Bevens was pitching for the Yankees and, with two out in the ninth, it looked like he was going to pitch the first no-hitter in World Series history.

"Aren't you going to volunteer to hit?" Burt Shotton, who was managing Brooklyn, said to Pete.

Al Gionfriddo was on second and Bucky Harris, who was managing the Yankees, ordered Pete walked. Eddie Miksis ran for him, and when Cookie Lavagetto hit that double, the two runners scored and Brooklyn won, 3–2.

"The next day," Pete says, "the sportswriters were second-guessing Harris for putting me on when I represented the winning run. Can you imagine what they'd have said if they knew I had a broken ankle?"

At the end of that season Rickey had the outfield walls at Ebbets Field padded with one-inch foam rubber for Pete, but he never hit them again. He had headaches most of the time and played little. Then he was traded to Boston, and in two seasons there he hit the wall a couple of times. Twice his left shoulder came out while he was making diving catches. Pittsburgh picked Pete up in 1951, and the next year he played into July with Cleveland and that was the end of it.

Between January and September 1953, Pete dropped $40,000 in the used-car business in St. Louis, and then he got a job in a lumber mill for $100 a week. In the winter of 1955, he wrote Brooklyn asking for a part-time job as a scout, and on March 1, Buzzy Bavasi, the Dodger vice president, called him on the phone.

"How would you like a manager's job?" Buzzy said.

"I'll take it," Pete said.

"I haven't even told you where it is. It's Thomasville, Georgia, in Class D."

"I don't care," Pete said. "I'll take it."

At Vero Beach that spring, Mike Gaven wrote a piece about Pete in the *New York Journal-American*.

"Even in the worn gray uniform of the Class D Thomasville, Georgia, club," Mike wrote, "Pete Reiser looks, acts, and talks like a big leaguer. The Dodgers pitied Pete when they saw him starting his comeback effort after not having handled a ball for two and a half years. They lowered their heads when they saw him in a chow line with a lot of other bushers, but the old Pistol held his head high . . ."

The next spring, Sid Friedlander, of the *New York Post*, saw Pete at Vero and wrote a column about him managing Kokomo. The last thing I saw about him in the New York papers was a small item out of Tipton, Indiana, saying that the bus carrying the Kokomo team had collided with a car and Pete was in a hospital in Kokomo with a back injury.

"Managing," Pete was saying in that St. Louis hospital, "you try to find out how your players are thinking. At Thomasville one night one of my kids made a bad throw. After the game I said to him, 'What were you thinking while that ball was coming to you?' He said, 'I was saying to myself that I hoped I could make a good throw.' I said, 'Sit down.' I tried to explain to him the way you have to think. You know how I used to think?"

"Yes," I said, "but you tell me."

"I was always sayin', 'Hit it to me. Just hit it to me. I'll make the catch. I'll make the throw.' When I was on base I was always lookin' over and sayin', 'Give me the steal sign. Give me the sign. Let me go.' That's the way you have to think."

"Pete," I said, "now that it's all over, do you ever think that if you hadn't played it as hard as you did, there's no telling how great you might have been or how much money you might have made?"

"Never," Pete said. "It was my way of playin'. If I hadn't played that way I wouldn't even have been whatever I was. God gave me those legs and the speed, and when they took me into the walls that's the way it had to be. I couldn't play any other way."

A technician came in with an electrocardiograph. She was a thin, dark-haired woman and she set it up by the bed and attached one of the round metal disks to Pete's left wrist and started to attach another to his left ankle.

"Aren't you kind of young to be having pains in your chest?" she said.

"I've led a fast life," Pete said.

On the way back to New York I kept thinking how right Pete was. To tell a man who is this true that there is another way for him to do it is to speak a lie. You cannot ask him to change his way of going, because it makes him what he is.

Three days after I got home I had a message to call St. Louis. I heard the phone ring at the other end and Pete answered. "I'm out!" he said.

"Did they let you out, or did you sneak out again?" I said.

"They let me out," he said. "It's just a strained heart muscle, I guess. My heart itself is all right."

"That's wonderful."

"I can manage again. In a couple of days I can go back to Kokomo."

If his voice had been higher he would have sounded like a kid at Christmas.

"What else did they say?" I said.

"Well, they say I have to take it easy."

"Do me a favor," I said.

"What?"

"Take their advice. This time, please take it easy."

"I will," he said. "I'll take it easy."

If he does it will be the first time.

The Ghost of the Gridiron

Red Grange Could Carry the Ball

WHEN I WAS TEN YEARS OLD I paid ten cents to see Red Grange run with a football. That was the year when, one afternoon a week, after school was out for the day, they used to show us movies in the auditorium, and we would all troop up there clutching our dimes, nickels, or pennies in our fists.

The movies were, I suppose, carefully selected for their educational value. They must have shown us, as the weeks went by, films of the Everglades, of Yosemite, of the Gettysburg battlefield, of Washington, D.C., but I remember only the one about Grange.

I remember, in fact, only one shot. Grange, the football cradled in one arm, started down the field toward us. As we sat there in the dim, flickering light of the movie projector, he grew larger and larger. I can still see the rows and rows of us, with our thin little necks and bony heads, all looking up at the screen and Grange, enormous now, rushing right at us, and I shall never forget it. That was thirty-three years ago.

"I haven't any idea what film that might have been," Grange was saying now. "My last year at Illinois was all confusion. I had no privacy. Newsreel men were staying at the fraternity house for two or three days at a time."

He paused. The thought of it seemed to bring pain to his face, even at this late date.

True, November 1958.

"I wasn't able to study or anything," he said. "I thought, and I still do, that they built me up out of all proportion."

Red Grange was the most sensational, the most publicized, and, possibly, the most gifted football player and greatest broken field runner of all time. In high school, at Wheaton, Illinois, he averaged five touchdowns a game. In twenty games for the University of Illinois, he scored thirty-one touchdowns and ran for 3,637 yards, or, as it was translated at the time, two miles and 117 yards. His name and his pseudonyms—The Galloping Ghost and The Wheaton Iceman—became household words, and what he was may have been summarized best by Paul Sann in his book *The Lawless Decade*.

"Red Grange, No. 77, made Jack Dempsey move over," Sann wrote. "He put college football ahead of boxing as the Golden Age picked up momentum. He also made the ball yards obsolete; they couldn't handle the crowds. He made people buy more radios: how could you wait until Sunday morning to find out what deeds Red Grange had performed on Saturday? He was 'The Galloping Ghost' and he made the sports historians torture their portables without mercy."

Grange is now fifty-five years old, his reddish brown hair marked with gray, but he was one with Babe Ruth, Jack Dempsey, Bobby Jones, and Bill Tilden.

"I could carry a football well," Grange was saying now, "but I've met hundreds of people who could do their thing better than I. I mean engineers, and writers, scientists, doctors—whatever.

"I can't take much credit for what I did, running with a football, because I don't know what I did. Nobody ever taught me, and I can't teach anybody. You can teach a man how to block or tackle or kick or pass. The ability to run with a ball is something you have or you haven't. If you can't explain it, how can you take credit for it?"

This was last year, and we were sitting in a restaurant in Syracuse, New York. Grange was in town to do a telecast with Lindsey Nelson of the Syracuse–Penn State game. He lives now in Miami, Florida, coming out of there on weekends during the football season to handle telecasts of college games on Saturdays and the Chicago Bears' games on Sundays. He approaches this job as he has approached every job, with honesty and dedication, and, as could be expected, he is good at it. As befits a man who put the pro game on the map and made the whole nation football conscious, he has been making fans out of people who never followed the game before. Never, perhaps, has any one man done more for the game. And it, of course, has been good to him.

"Football did everything for me," he was saying now, "but what people don't understand is that it hasn't been my whole life. When I was a freshman at Illinois, I wasn't even going to go out for football. My fraternity brothers made me do it."

He was three times All-American. Once the Illinois students carried him two miles on their backs. A football jersey, with the number 77 that he made famous and that was retired after him, is enshrined at Champaign. His fellow students wanted him to run for Congress. A senator from Illinois led him into the White House to shake hands with Calvin Coolidge. Here, in its entirety, is what was said.

"Howdy," Coolidge said. "Where do you live?"

"In Wheaton, Illinois," Grange said.

"Well, young man," Coolidge said, "I wish you luck."

Grange had his luck, but it was coming to him because he did more to popularize professional football than any other player before or since. In his first three years out of school he grossed almost $1,000,000 from football, motion pictures, vaudeville appearances, and endorsements, and he could afford to turn down a Florida real-estate firm that wanted to pay him $120,000 a year. Seven years ago the Associated Press, in selecting an All-Time All-American team in conjunction with the National Football Hall of Fame, polled one hundred leading sportswriters and Grange received more votes than any other player.

"They talk about the runs I made," he was saying, "but I can't tell you one thing I did on any run. That's the truth. During the Depression, though, I took a licking. Finally I got into the insurance business. I almost starved to death for three years, but I never once tried to use my football reputation. I never once opened a University of Illinois yearbook and knowingly called on an alumnus. I think I was as good an insurance man as there was in Chicago. On the football field I had ten other men blocking for me, but I'm more proud of what I did in the insurance business, because I did it alone."

Recently I went down to Miami and visited Grange in the white colonial duplex house where he lives with his wife. They met eighteen years ago on a plane, flying between Chicago and Omaha, on which she was a stewardess, and they were married the following year.

"Without sounding like an amateur psychologist," I said, "I believe you derive more satisfaction from what you did in the insurance business, not only because you did it alone, but also because you know how you did it, and, if you had to, you could do it again. You could never find any security in what you did when you ran with a football because it was inspirational and creative, rather than calculated."

"Yes," Grange said, "you could call it that. The sportswriters used to try to explain it, and they used to ask me. I couldn't tell them anything."

I have read what many of those sportswriters wrote, and they had as much trouble trying to corner Grange on paper as his opponents had trying to tackle him on the field.

Grange had blinding speed, amazing lateral mobility, an exceptional change of pace, and a powerful straight-arm. He moved with high knee action, but seemed to glide, rather than run, and he was a master at using his blockers. What made him great, however, was his instinctive ability to size up a field and plot a run the way a great general can map not only a battle but a whole campaign.

"The sportswriters wrote that I had peripheral vision," Grange was saying. "I didn't even know what the word meant. I had to look it up. They asked me about my change of pace, and I didn't even know that I ran at different speeds. I had a crossover step, but I couldn't spin. Some ball carriers can spin but if I ever tried that, I would have broken a leg."

Harold Edward Grange was born on June 13, 1903, in Forksville, Pennsylvania, the third of four children. His mother died when he was five, and his sister Norma died in her teens. The other sister, Mildred, lives in Binghamton, New York. His brother, Garland, two and a half years younger than Red, was a 165-pound freshman end at Illinois and was later with the Chicago Bears and is now a credit manager for a Florida department store chain. Their father died at the age of eighty-six.

"My father," Grange said, "was the foreman of three lumber camps near Forksville, and if you had known him, you'd know why I could never get a swelled head. He stood six one and weighed two hundred ten pounds, and he was quick as a cat. He had three hundred men under him and he had to be able to lick any one of them. One day he had a fight that lasted four hours."

Grange's father, after the death of his wife, moved to Wheaton, Illinois, where he had relatives. Then he sent the two girls back to Pennsylvania to live with their maternal grandparents. With his sons, he moved into a five-room apartment over a store where they took turns cooking and keeping house.

"Can you recall," I said, "the first time you ever ran with a football?"

"I think it started," Grange said, "with a game we used to play without a football. Ten or twelve of us would line up in the street, along one curb. One guy would be in the middle of the road and the rest of us would run across the street to the curb on the other side. When the kid in the middle of the street tackled one of the runners, the one who was tackled had to stay in the middle of the street with the tackler. Finally, all of us, except one last runner, would be in the middle of the street. We only had about thirty yards to maneuver in and dodge the tackler. I got to be pretty good at that. Then somebody got a football and we played games with it on vacant lots."

In high school Grange won sixteen letters in football, basketball, track, and baseball. In track he competed in the 100- and 220-yard dashes, low and high hurdles, broad jump and high jump, and often won all six events. In his sophomore year on the football team, he scored fifteen touchdowns, in his junior year thirty-six—eight in one game—and in his senior year twenty-three. Once he was kicked in the head and was incoherent for forty-eight hours.

"I went to Illinois," he was saying, "because some of my friends from Wheaton went there and all the kids in the state wanted to play football for Bob Zuppke and because there weren't any athletic scholarships in those days and that was the cheapest place for me to go to. In May of my senior year in high school I was there for the Interscholastic track meet, and I just got through broad jumping when Zup came over. He said, 'Is your name Grainche?' That's the way he always pronounced my name. I said, 'Yes.' He said, 'Where are you going to college?' I said, 'I don't know.' He put his arm around my shoulders and he said, 'I hope here. You may have a chance to make the team here.' That was the greatest moment I'd known."

That September, Grange arrived at Champaign with a battered secondhand trunk, one suit, a couple of pairs of trousers, and a sweater. He had been working for four summers on an ice wagon in Wheaton and saving some money, and his one luxury now that he was entering college was to pledge Zeta Phi fraternity.

"One day," he was saying, "they lined us pledges up in the living room of the fraternity house. I had wanted to go out for basketball and track—I thought there would be too much competition in football—but they started to point to each one of us and tell us what to go out for: 'You go out for cheerleader.' 'You go out for football manager.' 'You go out for the band.' When they came to me, they said, 'You go out for football.'

"That afternoon I went over to the gym. I looked out the window at the football practice field and they had about three hundred freshman candidates out there. I went back to the house and I said to one of the seniors, 'I can't go out for football. I'll never make that team.'

"So he lined me up near the wall, with my head down, and he hit me with this paddle. I could show you the dent in that wall where my head took a piece of plaster out—this big."

With the thumb and forefinger of his right hand, he made a circle the size of a half dollar.

"Do you remember the name of that senior?" I said.

"Johnny Hawks," Grange said. "He was from Goshen, Indiana, and I see him now and then. I say to him, 'Damn you. If it wasn't for you, I'd never have gone out for football.' He gets a great boot out of that."

"So what happened when you went out the next day?"

"We had all these athletes from Chicago I'd been reading about. What chance did I have, from a little farm town and a high school with three hundred students? I think they cut about forty that first night, but I happened to win the wind sprints and that got them at least to know my name."

It was a great freshman team. On it with Grange was Earl Britton, who blocked for Grange and did the kicking throughout their college careers, and Moon Baker and Frank Wickhorst, who transferred to Northwestern and Annapolis, respectively, where they both made All-American. After one week of practice, the freshman team played the varsity and were barely nosed out, 21–19, as Grange scored two touchdowns, one on a sixty-yard punt return. From then on, the freshmen trimmed the varsity regularly and Zuppke began to give most of his time to the freshmen.

"That number 77," I said to Grange, "became the most famous number in football. Do you remember when you first got it?"

"It was just handed to me in my sophomore year," he said. "I guess anybody who has a number and does well with it gets a little superstitious about it, and I guess that began against Nebraska in my first varsity game."

That game started Grange to national fame. This was 1923, and the previous year Nebraska had beaten Notre Dame and they were to beat "The Four Horsemen" later this same season. In the first quarter Grange sprinted thirty-five yards for a touchdown. In the second quarter he ran sixty yards for another. In the third period he scored again on a twelve-yard burst, and Illinois won, 24–7. The next day, over Walter Eckersall's story in the *Chicago Tribune*, the headline said "Grange Sprints to Fame."

From the Nebraska game, Illinois went on to an undefeated season. Against Butler, Grange scored twice. Against Iowa, he scored the only touchdown as Illinois won, 9–6. In the first quarter against Northwestern, he intercepted a pass and ran ninety yards to score the first of his three touchdowns. He made the only touchdown in the game with the University of Chicago and the only one in the Ohio State game, this time on a thirty-four-yard run.

"All Grange can do is run," Fielding Yost, the coach at Michigan, was quoted as saying.

"All Galli-Curci can do is sing," Zuppke said.

Grange had his greatest day in his first game against Michigan during his junior year. On that day Michigan came to the dedication of the new $1,700,000 Illinois Memorial Stadium. The Wolverines had been undefeated in twenty games and for months the nation's football fans had been waiting for this meeting. There were sixty-seven thousand spectators in the stands, then the largest crowd ever to see a football game in the Midwest.

Michigan kicked off. Grange was standing on his goal line, with Wally McIlwain, whom Zuppke was to call "the greatest open field blocker of all time," on his right, Harry Hall, the Illinois quarterback, on his left, and Earl Britton in front of him. Michigan attempted to aim the kickoff to McIlwain, but as the ball descended, Grange moved over under it.

"I've got it," he said to McIlwain.

He caught it on the 5-yard line. McIlwain turned and took out the first Michigan man to get near him. Britton cut down the next one, and Grange started under way. He ran to his left, reversed his field to avoid one would-be tackler, and, then, cutting back again to the left, ran diagonally across the field through the oncoming Michigan players. At the Michigan 40-yard line he was in the open and on the 20-yard line, Tod Rockwell, the Michigan safety man, made a futile dive for him. Grange scored standing up. Michigan never recovered.

In less than twelve minutes, Grange scored three more touchdowns on runs of sixty-seven, fifty-six, and forty-four yards. Zuppke took him out to rest him. In the third period, he re-entered the game, and circled right end for fifteen yards and another touchdown. In the final quarter, he threw a pass for another score. Illinois won, 39–14. Against a powerful, seasoned, and favored team, Grange had handled the ball twenty-one times, gained 402 yards running, scored five touchdowns, and collaborated, as a passer, in a sixth.

"This was," Coach Amos Alonzo Stagg, the famous Chicago mentor, later wrote, "the most spectacular singlehanded performance ever made in a major game."

"Did Zuppke tell you that you should have scored another touchdown?" I asked Grange.

"That's right," Grange said. "After the fourth touchdown we called a time-out, and when Matt Bullock, our trainer, came with the water, I said to him, 'I'm dog tired. You'd better tell Zup to get me out of here.' When I got to the bench Zup said to me, 'You should have had five touchdowns. You didn't cut right on one play.' Nobody could get a swelled head around him."

"And you don't recall," I said, "one feint or cut that you made during any one of those runs?"

"I don't remember one thing I ever did on any run I made. I just remember one vision from that Michigan game. On that opening kickoff runback, as I got downfield I saw that the only man still in front of me was the safety man, Tod Rockwell. I remember thinking then, 'I'd better get by this guy, because after coming all this way, I'll sure look like a bum if he tackles me.' I can't tell you, though, how I did get by him."

When Grange started his senior year, Illinois had lost seven regulars by graduation and Harry Hall, its quarterback, who had a broken collarbone. Zuppke shifted Grange to quarterback. Illinois lost to Nebraska, Iowa, and Michigan and barely beat Butler before they came to Franklin Field in Philadelphia on October 31, 1925, to play Pennsylvania.

The previous year Penn had been considered the champion of the East. They had now beaten Brown, Yale, and Chicago, among others. Although Grange's exploits in the Midwest had been widely reported in Eastern papers, most of the sixty-five thousand spectators and the

Eastern sportswriters—Grantland Rice, Damon Runyon, and Ford Frick among them—came to be convinced.

It had rained and snowed for twenty-four hours, with only straw covering the field. At the kickoff, the players stood in mud. On the third play of the game, the first time he carried the ball, Grange went fifty-five yards for his first touchdown. On the next kickoff he ran fifty-five yards again, to the Penn 25-yard line, and Illinois worked it over the goal line from there. In the second period, Grange twisted twelve yards for another score and in the third period he ran twenty yards to a touchdown. Illinois won, 24–2, with Grange carrying the ball 363 yards, and scoring three touchdowns and setting up another one, in thirty-six rushes.

Two days later when the train carrying the Illinois team arrived in Champaign, there were twenty thousand students, faculty members, and townspeople waiting at the station. Grange tried to sneak out of the last car but he was recognized and carried two miles to his fraternity house.

"Do you remember your feelings during those two miles?" I asked him.

"I remember that I was embarrassed," he said. "You wish people would understand that it takes eleven men to make a football team. Unless they've played it, I guess they'll never understand it, but I've never been impressed by individual performances in football, my own or anyone else's."

"Do you remember the last touchdown you scored in college?"

"To tell you the truth, I don't," he said. "It must have been against Ohio State. I can't tell you the score. I can't tell you the score of more than three or four games I ever played in."

I looked it up. Grange's last college appearance, against Ohio State, attracted 85,500 spectators at Columbus. He was held to 153 yards on the ground but threw one touchdown pass as Illinois won, 14–9. The following afternoon, in the Morrison Hotel in Chicago, he signed with Charles C. (Cash and Carry) Pyle to play professional football with the Chicago Bears, starting immediately, and he quit college. Twenty-five years later, however, he was elected to the University of Illinois Board of Trustees for a six-year term.

"I had a half year to finish when I quit," he said. "I had this chance to make a lot of money and I couldn't figure where having a sheepskin would pull any more people into football games."

"How were your marks in college?"

"I was an average student. I got B's and C's. I flunked one course, economics, and I made that up in the summer at Wheaton College. I'd leave the ice wagon at eleven o'clock in the morning and come back to it at one o'clock. There was so much written about my job on the ice wagon, and so many pictures of me lugging ice, that people thought it was a publicity stunt. It wasn't. I did it for eight summers, starting at five o'clock every morning, for two reasons. The pay was good—$37.50 a week—and I needed money. I didn't even have any decent clothes until my junior year. Also, it kept me in shape. After carrying those blocks of ice up and down stairs six days a week, my legs were always in shape when the football season started. Too many football players have to play their legs into shape in the first four or five games."

Grange played professional football from 1925 through the 1934 season, first with the Bears, then with the New York Yankees in a rival pro league that Pyle and he started, and then back with the Bears again. He was immobilized during the 1928 season with arm and knee injuries, and after that he was never able to cut sharply while carrying the ball. He did, however, score 162 touchdowns as a professional and kicked 86 conversion points, for a total of 1,058 points.

What the statistics do not show, however, is what Grange, more than any other player, did to focus public attention and approval on the professional game. In 1925, when he signed with the Bears, professional football attracted little notice on the sports pages and few paying customers. There was so little interest that the National Professional Football League did not even hold a championship playoff at the end of the season.

In ten days after he left college Grange played five games as a pro and changed all that. After only three practice sessions with the Bears, he made his pro debut against the Chicago Cardinals on Thanksgiving Day, November 26. The game ended 0–0 but thirty-six thousand people crowded into Wrigley Field to see Grange. Three days later, on a Sunday, twenty-eight thousand defied a snowstorm to watch him perform at the same field. On the next Wednesday, freezing weather in St. Louis held the attendance down to eight thousand but on Saturday forty thousand Philadelphians watched him in the rain at Shibe Park. The next day the Bears played in the Polo Grounds against the New York Giants.

It had been raining for almost a week, and, although advance sales were almost unknown in pro football in those days, the Giants sold almost sixty thousand before Sunday dawned. It turned out to be a beautiful day. Cautious fans who had not bought seats in advance stormed the ticket booths. Thousands of people were turned away but 73,651 crammed into the park. Grange did not score but the Bears won, 19–7.

That was the beginning of professional football's rise to its present popularity. At the end of those first ten days, Grange picked up a check for $50,000. He got another $50,000 when the season ended a month later.

"Can you remember," I asked him now, "the last time you ever carried a football?"

"It was in a game against the Giants in Gilmore Stadium in Hollywood in January of 1935. It was the last period, and we had a safe lead and I was sitting on the bench. George Halas said to me, 'Would you like to go in, Red?' I said, 'No, thanks.' Everybody knew this was my last year. He said, 'Go ahead. Why don't you run it just once more?'

"So I went in, and we lined up and they called a play for me. As soon as I got the ball and started to go I knew that they had it framed with the Giants to let me run. The line just opened up for me and I went through and started down the field. The farther I ran, the heavier my legs got and the farther those goal posts seemed to move away. I was thinking, 'When I make that end zone, I'm going to take off these shoes and shoulder pads for the last time.' With that something hit me from behind and down I went on about the 10-yard line. It was Cecil Irvin, a 230-pound tackle. He was so slow that, I guess, they never bothered to let him in on the plan. But when he caught me from behind, I knew I was finished."

Grange, who is five feet eleven and three-quarter inches, weighed 180 in college and 185 in his last game with the Bears. Now he weighs 200. On December 15, 1951, he suffered a heart attack. This motivated him to give up his insurance business and to move to Florida, where he and his wife own, in addition to their own home in Miami, land in Orlando and Melbourne and property at Indian Lake.

"Red," I said, "I'll bet there are some men still around whose greatest claim to fame is that they played football with you or against you. I imagine there are guys whose proudest boast is that they once tackled you. Have you ever run into a guy who thought he knew everything about football and didn't know he was talking with Red Grange?"

"Yes," he said. "Once about fifteen years ago, on my way home from work, I dropped into a tavern in Chicago for a beer. Two guys next to me and the bartender were arguing about Bronko Nagurski and Carl Brumbaugh. On the Bears, of course, I played in the backfield with both of them. One guy doesn't like Nagurski and he's talking against him. I happen to think Nagurski was the greatest football player I ever saw, and a wonderful guy. This fellow who is knocking him says to me, 'Do you know anything about football? Did you ever see Nagurski play?' I said, 'Yes, and I think he was great.' The guy gets mad and says, 'What was so great about him? What do you know about it?' I could see it was time to leave, but the guy kept at me. He said, 'Now wait a minute. What makes you think you know something about it? Who are you, anyway?' I reached into my wallet and took out my business card and handed it to him and started for the door. When I got to the door, I looked back at him. You should have seen his face."

Mrs. Grange, who had been listening to our talk, left the room and came back with a small, gold-plated medal that Grange had won in the broad jump at the Interscholastic track meet on the day when he first met Zuppke.

"A friend of mine just sent that to me," Grange said. "He wrote: 'You gave me this away back in 1921. I thought you might want it.' Just the other day I got a letter from a man in the Midwest who told me that his son just found a gold football inscribed, 'University of Illinois, 1924' with the initials H. G. on it. I was the only H. G. on that squad so it must have been mine. I guess I gave it to somebody and he lost it. I wrote the man back and said, 'If your son would like it, I'd be happy to have him keep it.'"

Mrs. Grange said, "We have a friend who can't understand why Red doesn't keep his souvenirs. He has his trophies in another friend's storage locker in Chicago. The clipping books are nailed up in a box in the garage here and Red hasn't looked at them in years."

"I don't like to look back," Grange said. "You have to look ahead."

I remembered that night when we ate in the restaurant in Syracuse. As we stood in line to get our hats and coats, Grange nudged me and showed me his hat check. In the middle of the yellow cardboard disk was the number 77.

"Has this ever happened to you before?" I said.

"Never," he said, "as far as I know."

We walked out into the cold night air. A few flakes of snow were falling.

"That jersey with the 77 on it that's preserved at Illinois," I said, "is that your last game jersey?"

"I don't know," Grange said. "It was probably a new jersey."

"Do you have any piece of equipment that you wore on the football field?"

"No," he said. "I don't have anything."

The traffic light changed, and we started across the street. "I don't even have an I-sweater," he said.

We walked about three paces.

"You know," Grange said, "I'd kind of like to have an I-sweater now."

Work Horse on Ice

Gordie Howe of the Detroit Red Wings

IN FIVE HOURS Gordie Howe would play hockey with the Detroit Red Wings against the New York Rangers. Now it was 3:30 in the afternoon, and he was sitting at the kitchen table in his new home in Lathrup Village, a residential suburb fourteen miles northwest of downtown Detroit. He was eating the meal on which he would play—steak, peas, lettuce, fruit Jell-O, and tea.

"When we play those Saturday afternoon TV games," he was saying, "I just play on my breakfast eggs. Once, when I was with Omaha, I played on a milk shake."

There is a radio built into one of the kitchen walls. It is the center of a communications system that reaches upstairs to the three bedrooms and downstairs to the oak-paneled recreation room, and now the voice of Perry Como was coming over it.

"Don't let the moon get in your eyes," Como was singing. "Don't let—"

"I was seventeen years old," Howe said, "and it was our first swing around the league. We were in Minneapolis, and about four thirty I went downstairs in the hotel to eat. Some of the guys were eating there, but I looked at that big dining room and it looked so nice that I didn't want to go in. I went around the corner to a drugstore and I had the milk shake."

He is six feet and 201 pounds and has brown hair that is beginning to recede at the temples. His face has been cut by pucks and sticks

---

The Saturday Evening Post, January 10, 1959.

more times than he remembers, but the only scar that is obvious is in the form of a small crescent on his left cheekbone.

"Don't you still sometimes feel that way," he said, "when you start to go into a dining room or a restaurant that looks extra nice?"

"Yes," I said.

"I got two goals on that milk shake," he said, "and we beat them, three to one."

Gordie Howe will be thirty-one on March 31, and many observers maintain he is the greatest hockey player of all time. Jack Adams, the general manager of the Red Wings, and Muzz Patrick, who holds the same position with the Rangers, have called him that, and certainly he is the best in the game today. Six times he has been named to the All-Star team. Last year, for the fourth time, he was voted the most valuable player in the league, tying the record set twenty-one years ago by Eddie Shore of the Boston Bruins.

"Back home when we'd skate," he was saying, "we'd have our oatmeal in the morning. That would last you practically all day, if you didn't want to take time out to eat."

All of those who play in the National Hockey League come up the same way, and only the names and the places and the dates are different. This one was born in Floral, Saskatchewan, on the outskirts of Saskatoon, in the heart of western Canada's wheat prairies. He was the fifth of nine children. His father, Ab, tried farming and then moved the family into Saskatoon, where he ran a garage and is now a maintenance superintendent for the city.

"After breakfast," he said now, "we'd put on our skates at home and skate down the ruts in the road to the rink. If we came home for lunch, my mother would have newspapers down on the floor in the kitchen so we could keep our skates on. Sometimes there'd be a whole flock of guys, and she'd give us a stew or a thick soup. We'd do that again for supper if we were gonna skate again at night."

"Do you remember," I asked, "the first time you were ever on skates?"

"My brother Vern had a pair," he said. "He's about eight years older than I am, and he was about thirteen at the time. My sister Edna took one skate and I took the other, and I was so small that I put it on right over my shoe. We went out on the rink in the yard and pushed around on one foot. That was the first time."

"You had a rink in your own yard?"

"A lot of people did. The first few snowfalls you build up your banks, and then when the snow melts it runs off the banks and freezes. Every school and playground had a rink, too. There were rinks all over town. Then when the warm wind—the Chinook—would come, the water would run into the low areas, too, like the Bay Slew, and we'd skate for about seven miles. We'd skate and walk over the Mile Road and skate and walk over the railroad and skate some more. We'd skate four or five miles up the Sasketchewan River, and play a game between the piers of the Grand Trunk."

"How cold would it get?"

"I guess the coldest would be fifty below. A lot of times it would be twenty-five below. It would be so cold that, if you stuck your head out of the door at night, you could hear a guy walking two blocks away. You know? When I played goalie I remember I used to skate a mile from my house to the rink, holding the pads up in front of me to cut the wind. At the Avenue F rink they had a heated shack, and a guy would ring a cowbell and the forward lines and the defense for both teams would go off and sit in the shack by the pot-bellied stove. After a while he'd ring the bell again and the other guys would come in and somebody'd say, 'Who's winnin'?'"

"Didn't you ever freeze your face or your feet or your hands?"

"Sure, but you'd put snow on it. You'd put a scarf across your nose and mouth and when you breathed through it, it would get all white with frost. You'd take a stocking and cut a hole for your eyes and wear it over your head. A lot of kids froze their toes and used to cry."

"How old were you when you got the first pair of skates of your own?"

"I was about five, and we were on relief at the time. A woman came to the door one night with a whole potato sack full of things, and my mother paid her a dollar and a quarter for it. I remember diving into that bag, and there were four or five old pairs of skates in there and I grabbed a pair. They were so big I had to wear a couple of pairs of extra socks."

As he had been telling this there had come a knock on the door leading to the garage. His wife, Colleen, had been rinsing plates at the sink and putting them in the dishwasher. Now she dried her hands and went to the door.

"Is Gordie Howe home now?" a small voice said.

"Yes," his wife said, "but he's eating."

"Oh," the voice said.

"Did you boys want to ask him some questions?" his wife said.

"Yes," the voice said.

"You can come in," she said.

They walked in, three boys about ten years old. They stood awkwardly, looking at him and then looking around the kitchen.

"Hi, fellas," Howe said.

"Hello," they said, staring at him now.

"What are your names?" Howe said.

"Mine's Bill Little," one of them said, "and this is Chuck Watson and his is Miles."

"Do you boys know any babysitters?" Mrs. Howe said.

"Oh, sure," one of them said. "My sister sits, and so does his. They'd like to sit for you."

The Howes have two sons, Marty, who will be five in February, and Mark, who will be four in May. They had come up from playing downstairs when they had heard the strange voices, and now they were eyeing the older boys.

"I don't want no sitter," Mark said.

"Sure you do," Howe said.

"No I don't."

Mrs. Howe had written down the names and phone numbers of the sisters of the boys. Now the boys were just standing at the end of the table and watching Howe finish his dessert.

"Do you fellas have a rink around here?" Howe asked.

"Nope," one said, "but my dad and Mr. Cranbrook were thinkin' to put one up."

"I don't want no sitter," Mark said.

"We have to go now," another said. "Thanks a lot."

"It was nice to meet you fellas," Howe said.

They walked to the door, took a last look at him, and then went out. Mrs. Howe closed the door behind them.

"They were here yesterday," she said, "and they said they wanted to ask Gordie some questions. Then they come in and they're afraid to ask anything."

"It'll wear off," Howe said. "When we first moved into the other district you never saw so many kids coming around in your life, but they get used to you."

"Remember," a voice on the radio was saying, "you can hear the game between the Detroit Red Wings and the New York Rangers over WXYZ tonight at eight thirty."

"Did you have hockey heroes when you were a kid?" I said.

"Ab Welsh, who was a forward with the Saskatoon Quakers, was the first one," Howe said. "I used to hang around the arena and watch them practice, and he'd give me a stick that had lost its life, that was a little loggy. He used a Number 7 lie, and I still use a Number 7 lie today. Once, on the last day of the season, a redheaded defenseman for the Flin Flon Bombers gave me his old elbow pads."

"Who were your idols in the National Hockey League?"

"When I played Pee Wee Hockey they called our team the Red Wings. They'd give you a stick and your socks and a sweater, and the name and number of a Detroit player. I was Syd Howe, so I wrote him for an autographed picture. Later, when I came up to the Red Wings, he was still here, and Jack Adams asked me my name and I said, 'Howe, but I'm not related to him.'"

"Marty!" his wife was saying now. "Get out of there!"

That day she had bought three plastic wastebaskets for the new home and they were standing on the kitchen floor. The boy had his head and upper body submerged in the largest one as he tried to reach something at the bottom.

"What?" he said, straightening. "Why?"

"He gets that from me," Howe said. "When I was a kid, if you sent a Bee Hive Corn Syrup label to Toronto you'd get a picture of a hockey player. All of us kids would be up and down the alleys looking in the ash cans for the labels. I was the champion. I had about a hundred pictures.

"I had this notebook. I remember it had 'Scrap Book' printed across the cover on a slant. It starts out thin, and by the time you get all the hockey pictures and autographs and everything in, it's bustin' the seams."

He looked at his watch. It was 3:55 and he went upstairs and got into his pajamas and lay down and slept for two hours.

"The first time I remember hearing Gordie's name," his wife was saying, clearing the table, "was when he was almost killed in that game here and they had to drill into his head to relieve the pressure on the brain."

That was in the Stanley Cup playoffs in 1950. Ted Kennedy, of the Toronto Maple Leafs, had checked Howe, and he had gone down in a heap against the boards in front of the Red Wings bench. They had carried him, unconscious, off the ice to an ambulance at the back door of Olympia Stadium, and from there to Harper Hospital where Dr. Frederic Schreiber had saved his life.

"Carl!" he had been calling, as he came out of it, calling for Carl Mattson, who was the Red Wing trainer. "Help me, Carl!"

"I didn't know anything about hockey," his wife was saying, "and I'd never heard of Gordie Howe. I was in my senior year in high school here, and that morning after he was hurt, when I came down to breakfast, my dad was storming around. He was a Red Wings fan and he was mad. Of course, I didn't know then that Gordie Howe was the man I was going to marry three years later."

They met the following year at Joe Evans's Lucky Strike Alleys on Grand River Avenue, across from Northwestern High School and three blocks from the Olympia. She was bowling in a league, and Howe was there with Vic Stasiuk, who was a left wing with Detroit then, but is now with the Boston Bruins.

"How did you like meeting a celebrity?" Joe Evans, who introduced them, asked her a few minutes later.

"Is that a celebrity?" she said.

"Are you kidding?" he asked. "That's Gordie Howe of the Red Wings."

They were married at 4:00 P.M. on April 15, 1953, in the Calvary Presbyterian Church on Grand River. Ted Lindsay, Reggie Sinclair, and Marty Pavelich, of the Red Wings, were ushers, and Ted's wife, Pat, was matron of honor. Since then Colleen Howe hasn't missed more than four or five home games.

"I get excited," she said, "but you have to learn to bite your lip."

"Are you ever nervous," I said, "about Gordie being injured?"

In 1946, his first season in the league, he lost his upper two front teeth in Toronto. Against Montreal at Detroit a stick drove his left lateral incisor and cuspid up into his gum and, although Dr. Florian Muske, the team dentist, pulled them down right after the game they are still a little higher than the rest.

He has had operations on both knees, and they had to put him under anesthesia to clean a long gash in his left thigh. Six years ago he played fifteen games with his broken right wrist in a cast, and led the league in goals and assists while setting an all-time season record of ninety-five points. Last year his left shoulder was dislocated, and a week later he was hospitalized for ten days with torn rib cartilages.

His nose has been broken several times, and the skin over the bridge has been sewed so often that it is now difficult to get a needle through it. Like most professional hockey players, however, he is unable to tell you how many stitches have been taken in his face or to recall when or how the cuts resulted. He remembers that one cut under his lower lip had to be reopened, because of a bad sewing job, and that the one in his left cheekbone pained him because they wired it.

"Never," his wife said, "do I go to a game thinking that Gordie might be hurt. Sometimes, when he's already playing with an injury, and I can see somebody on the other team getting mad and banging around, I hope they get him off the ice before he does hit Gordie.

"What you think about more is whether he's getting his goals and assists and whether the team is winning. If he goes five or six games without a goal it begins to bother him. He doesn't say anything, but he gets very quiet. I save up the crossword puzzles for him, because at a time like that he likes to work them to take his mind off it."

When he came downstairs at 6:20 he had shaved and he was wearing a brown suit, white shirt, and brown tie and carrying a brown topcoat over his left arm. The cleaning woman, who comes out from Detroit on Thursdays, was standing in the kitchen with her coat and hat on.

"They tell me the buses don't run here after four thirty," Colleen said to him. "Can you drop Bea off on your way?"

"Sure," he said.

"I don't want to be any trouble," the woman said.

"I wanna go, too," Mark said.

"They're going to pick me up about seven," his wife said. "I'll wait for you afterwards."

"I wanna go too," Mark said.

The blue-and-white station wagon was in the driveway, and when he got in behind the wheel Mark was still with him. He was standing so that his father could not close the door.

"I don't want you to go," he was saying.

"Your daddy has to go," the cleaning woman said from the back seat.

"Why?" the boy said.

"He has to play hockey," she said.

"Here," the boy said, holding something out to his father. It was a yo-yo.

"You give that to Mommie," Howe said.

"Why?"

"I think Mommie might want to play with it."

As he drove through the headlight-broken darkness now, other cars passed him bringing other men home from other jobs. This started with him when he was fifteen and sat in the parlor of the two-story shingled house on Avenue L North in Saskatoon and listened while Russ McCrorry, the Rangers scout, talked to his mother and father.

One night late that summer they put him aboard the sleeper for Winnipeg, and when he got off he asked for the Marlborough Hotel. He roomed there with another kid, a goalie, and all they did was walk to the old Amphitheatre for practice and back again. Only once did he stray far enough to buy his mother a pillowcase with "Winnipeg" on it.

After three days they let the goalie go. Two days later, when Lester Patrick and Frank Boucher called him up to their room to sign him, he just shook his head. He wanted to go home.

A couple of years ago he was signing autographs for three hours in Fort William, Ontario. One of the men in the line asked him if he remembered him. He had been that kid goalie at Winnipeg.

"And now the Kingston Trio," the voice was saying on the car radio, "and the sad story of Tom Dooley."

The next year he sat in the parlor and listened again while Fred Pinckney, the Detroit scout, talked. The Red Wings practiced in the Windsor Arena that August and September, and Jack Adams signed him to a Galt contract.

At sixteen he was too young to play, but he practiced with the farm club and played exhibitions. They enrolled him in the high school, but when he got near that big brick building that first day and saw all the kids outside he walked down the railroad track instead and got a job as a spot welder with Galt Metal Industries.

"This is the street, isn't it?" he said now to the woman in the back seat.

"That's right," she said. "You let me off right here by the corner, and thank you and good luck tonight."

"Thanks," he said.

He left the car at a gas station a block from the Olympia, and it was 6:55 when he walked into the dressing room. Gus Mortson, the defenseman who played for Toronto and Chicago before he was traded to Detroit last September; Terry Sawchuk, the goalie, and Len Lunde and Charlie Burns, the rookie forwards, were already there. Howe walked through to the trainer's room in the back and took off his topcoat and his jacket and hung them up.

"How do you feel?" Sid Abel, the coach, said to him.

Twenty-one years ago, when Abel played center for the Flin Flon Bombers, Howe was the kid who used to carry their skates into the Saskatoon Arena. Nine years later he joined Abel on one of the Red Wing forward lines.

"All right," he said, "but a little tired."

"When he says that," Lefty Wilson, the trainer, said, "he's liable to get three goals."

"I'd like that all right," Howe said.

He got a deck of cards and straddled one of the rubbing tables. He started to shuffle the cards and Mortson pulled up a chair. It was his elbow that took out Howe's teeth that night in Toronto. Several weeks later it was Howe's stick that broke Mortson's nose, and last year it was Mortson's body check that put Howe into the hospital. Now they played gin rummy for about twenty minutes.

"That's enough for me," Howe said, finally.

Before he started to undress he took the bridge out of his mouth and wrapped it in his handkerchief and put it in a pocket of his jacket. He walked out to where some of the pieces of his uniform were spread on the bench, the rest hanging from a hook on the wall, and he stripped.

He has the slope-shoulders they look for in a prizefighter, and the strong but loose wrists that the power hitter brings to baseball. His body is long-muscled, except that the years of skating have built up his thighs, and now he got into the long underwear and then the white woolen socks. He pulled on the long red-and-white stockings and rolled them down to the ankles. He stood up and fastened on the garter belt, and then sat down and fitted the right shin pad and pulled the stocking up over it and fastened the top of it to the garter. He did the same on the left leg, and then he stepped into the red pants.

It was quiet in the room, the players, all dressing now, serious and saying little and keeping their voices down. Overhead, the circular hot-air blower made a whirring sound, and Howe walked over to the stick rack in the passageway leading to the showers. He looked at the half dozen sticks with his name and his number, 9, printed on them. He selected one and examined the tape on the blade.

Last season he broke more than a hundred sticks, and he tried this one, putting some weight on it. Then he got the fingernails of his right hand under the black tape near the heel and ripped it forward. He made a ball of the old tape and tossed it underhand at Norm Ullman, who centers the line with Howe on the right wing and Alex Delvecchio on the left. He went to the tape well in the table near the center of the room and took out a new roll and sat down at his place and retaped the blade, starting about two inches from the heel and working forward.

When he had finished he found a piece of absorbent cotton on the bench, and he rubbed the tape blade with it, some of the fuzz adhering to the tape. Then he took the roll and, to hold his shin pads steady, he taped bands above both ankles and just below both knees. Next he laced on first the right skate, with a pad of cotton under the tongue, and then the left.

"People here in the States who haven't skated much," he said once, "always ask me if our ankles ever hurt. Believe me, I've never heard of a hockey player's ankles hurting."

"Among other things," I said, "that mystify Americans about hockey players is your ability to stick-handle and pass, usually without looking at the puck or where you're going to pass it."

"If you kept your eyes on the puck," he said, "you'd end up in the rafters. You take glances at it, but you know it's there by the feel. What helps you on stick-handling is when you're a kid you play with a tennis ball. There was a family named Adams in Saskatoon, and they had a rink with boards, between their house and the barn. We'd go all day there with a tennis ball, fifteen guys on a side, and when the ball got frozen we'd go over and knock on the windows and the lady would open the window and we'd throw in the frozen ball and she'd throw out another one.

"On passes off the boards you have to get to know how fast the boards are. In Detroit here, the puck comes off the boards real good. Boston is fast, too, but in New York the boards are slow."

"How much did you work on shooting when you were a kid?"

"When there was no ice," he said, "I used to shoot in the yard off a piece of cardboard. I knocked so many shingles off the house with the puck that my mother made me stop it."

Now he put on the shoulder and elbow pads and pulled on the red-and-white home jersey with the white C on the right front shoulder designating that he is the captain. At eight o'clock the team filed out to warm up, Sawchuk leading, wide-legged in his goalie pads, and Howe last.

"There's Gordie! There's Gordie Howe! Hey, Gordie!"

The fans were lined up, three deep, along the green, rubber-tiled path the players tread from the dressing room to the ramp leading to the ice. One of them who called to him was a girl, round-faced and wearing eyeglasses, who appeared to be in her late teens. She had on a blue boy-coat, and to the right lapel was fastened a three-inch red cloth 9, Howe's number.

"C'mon, Gordie," she called. "Get some goals tonight."

He started this season with 386 goals and a record 440 assists. In the history of the National Hockey League only Maurice Richard, the great, thirty-seven-year-old right wing of the Montreal Canadiens, with 508 goals in sixteen seasons, has outscored him. At the end of last season, the six coaches of the National Hockey League, polled by the *Toronto Star*, selected Richard as having the most accurate shot and as the best man on a breakaway. They named Howe the smartest player, best passer and playmaker, and best puck carrier.

Skating onto the ice on this night, however, he had not scored in six games, although he had set up five goals with assists. For most of this game it appeared that he would be shut out again, for although the Red Wings went ahead, 1–0, in the first period, and led, 3–1, at the end of the second, his chances were few and marked by frustration.

In the third minute of the first period he rode Ed Shack, the Ranger rookie wing, off the puck in front of the New York net, but in doing so he overskated it. In the twelfth minute he knocked a high puck down just inside the Ranger blue line, stick-handled it around John Hanna, the Ranger defenseman, shifted Gump Worsley, the Ranger goalie, with a fake to the right, and then hit the other post with his shot.

"You have to accept those things," he said later. "A couple of years ago I had twenty-two posts by Christmas, and I think I still led the league in goals that year."

In the second minute of the second period his shot off Worsley's pads hit the post again. Six minutes later he stole the puck from Shack just inside the blue line, laid a pass on Ullman's stick, took the return fifteen feet out, and was tripped by Bill Gadsby.

On the Red Wing power play he took a pass off the boards from Delvecchio and slapped a high shot from the side that Worsley picked out of the air as it was about to go into the upper left corner. At 19:25 of the period Worsley saved on him again, when the puck hit his right arm.

Through all of this, however, Howe was, as he always is, the work horse of the Red Wings. He plays between thirty-five and forty minutes of every game, and is on the ice not only with his own line but every time the Red Wings, because of penalties, have a one-man advantage or are one man short. He brings to hockey the same long-striding, seemingly effortless grace that Joe DiMaggio brought to baseball, but each time he came off the ice the sweat was running off his nose and down his cheeks and settling in the creases in his neck.

Then, at six minutes and forty-seven seconds of the third period, that thing happened for which the Detroit hockey fans wait. Marcel Pronovost, the Red Wing defenseman, passed off the left boards to Tom McCarthy, on the left wing and just outside the Ranger blue line. McCarthy skated three strides across the line and slid a lead pass to Howe. Howe took it, split the two Ranger defensemen as they attempted to close on him, and then cut to his left to come in straight on Worsley. When Howe was about ten feet out, Worsley came out to meet him. Howe faked the shot to Worsley's left, and Worsley went down on the ice to that side. Completing the motion, Howe pulled the puck back to his own left and backhanded it hard into the open side of the net.

That was the final score, 4–1, and fifteen minutes later, when he took off his uniform in the hot, humid, body-crowded, voice-filled dressing room, his long underwear was gray and heavy with his sweat and clung to him. After he had showered he stepped on the scale, and he had lost six and a half pounds.

"You get it back overnight," he said. "It's just liquid."

When he had dressed he autographed his way through the crowd outside the dressing-room door and met his wife. They drove out to a restaurant on Eight Mile Road, and he drank two glasses of water, waiting for his roast beef sandwich and tea.

"Once you had Worsley out of position and down," I said, "you still drilled that puck as if you were trying to fire it through the cords."

"The cardinal sin is to slide it easy," he said. "In my first year I had Frank Brimsek beat in Boston, and I just slid it and he came over with his lumber and got a piece of it. Sid Abel was playing then, and he said: 'Any time you see that net, drill it.' I went back and beat Brimsek again and really let it go. I never forgot it."

"I suppose you remember your first goal in the big league."

"It was our opening game here against Toronto," he said. "The puck was lying loose ten feet from the net and I just slapped it in."

"Did you save the puck?"

"I kept it and took it home and gave it to the folks," he said, "but I have no idea where it is now. The trouble with those things is that they lose their importance."

He had his right hand to his face and was absentmindedly rubbing the scar on his left cheekbone. When he realized what he was doing he stopped.

"Rubbing a scar gets to be a habit," he said. "When you get a new one they tell you to put cocoa butter on your fingers and rub it a lot so it won't show so much."

"You were saying that things lose their importance," I said. "What about all the honors you've won? Do you derive a lot of satisfaction from thinking about them?"

"No," he said. "You don't think about what you have, but what you're going to do afterwards."

His hockey skills have earned him his home and the home he bought for his folks in Saskatoon. He and Al Kaline, the outfielder of the Detroit Tigers, are partners in the Howe-Kaline-Carlin Corporation, an engineering firm in Detroit, and he works at that during the off-season.

"A lot of the young ones," he said, "they think that when they make the club the job is done. That's just the beginning. All the honors you get, it's not to achieve honors but to achieve a better living."

"Excuse me, Mr. Howe," the waiter said, "but there's someone in at the bar who would like you to autograph this menu."

The Happiest Hooligan of Them All

What a Card This Pepper Martin Is!

It's the same with all of them who know Pepper Martin. When they start talking about him it's as if they want to erect a life-size statue of the man. That goes, too, whether they played with him on the Gashouse Gang or against him or under him in the minors, or whether they're strangers who just talked with him for ten minutes.

To show you what I mean, one afternoon this spring a field sales manager for a firm that makes homogenized topping for desserts checked into a motel here. His name is Joe Tasyn, and while he was standing at the desk, waiting to register, he looked across the lobby.

"I took a double look," he said, telling me about it later. "I said to the clerk, 'Is that Pepper Martin sitting over there?' The clerk said, 'Yep.' I thought, My God! I walked over to Pepper and I introduced myself. I said, 'You don't know me.' Pepper said, 'That's right.' He said, 'I didn't know you were down here, but I recognized that face of yours. I'll never forget watching you play ball, and I'll never forget that 1931 World Series.'"

Of course, no one who ever saw that face or studied a picture of it can help but recognize it. There are those high cheekbones and that beak of a nose, the square jaw and the big, straight mouth that, in a smile, breaks that face right in two. Pepper is fifty-five years old now,

---

True, October 1959.

and manages the Miami Marlins in the International League. He's almost bald and wears glasses when he reads, but there's no more fat on those five feet nine inches today than there was when he started to go in that '31 Series.

When the Series opened Pepper was just a twenty-seven-year-old rookie who'd been kicked around the minors for six years. When it closed he had twelve hits and five stolen bases, and the St. Louis Cardinals had licked Connie Mack's great Philadelphia Athletics. What the sportswriters wrote then is still true today. In all the history of baseball no other ballplayer has ever come out of nowhere as suddenly and as sensationally.

"So Pepper and I got to talking," Tasyn says. "He asked me all about myself, and then he said, 'Have you got a car with you?' I said, 'No. I came in by plane.' Then he said, 'Well, I got a new car and it's standin' right out there. Any time you need a car, Joe, you just take mine.'"

Telling me about it, Tasyn shook his head. "Can you imagine?" he said. "The first time he meets me he offers me his new car. Who am I to someone who has been as famous as Pepper Martin?"

Pepper was famous all right. In 1931 this country was flat. It was at the bottom of the Great Depression, and there were long lines in front of the soup kitchens and guys stood on street corners trying to sell apples for a nickel. They paid Pepper $2,500 a week, though, just to stand up on a vaudeville stage and answer questions.

"Then we have this friend," Pepper's wife, Ruby, says. "His name is Dr. James Parrish and he's a Baptist pastor. A couple of years ago he was in Houston and he saw Pepper's name in the phone book and he called the number. The woman who answered said, 'No. This isn't that Pepper Martin. My husband was born during the 1931 World Series and he was named after the real Pepper Martin.'"

"Heck," Pepper says, "I've had pigs and dogs named after me. One man even gave his race horse my name."

Pepper had hit .300 in the regular season of '31, but when he broke loose in that Series he came as a complete surprise. The Athletics had just won their third pennant in a row and were going for their third straight win in the Series. They had Mickey Cochrane, one of the all-time great catchers, Jimmie Foxx, who ended up second only to Babe Ruth in home runs, and Al Simmons, who led the league in hitting that year with .390. Throwing for them they had George Earnshaw and Lefty Grove, who had led the league for three years, and that season had a record of 31 and 4.

"How do you feel going into your first Series?" Frank Graham, who worked for the New York *Sun* then, said to Pepper just before they opened in St. Louis.

"Like a kid with a little red wagon," Pepper said. He took off his cap and scratched his head. "It seems a shame, though," he said. "Here I am, gettin' into a World Series in my first year as a regular. Think of all the great ballplayers who have been in the majors for years and never get into a World Series."

Think of all the great ballplayers who did get into a World Series, though, and never did what Pepper did. In the first game Grove beat the Cards, 6–2, but he didn't hold Pepper.

"Were you nervous in that first game?" I asked Pepper one day, sitting on the bench at the ball park here.

"When they raised that flag before the game and we stood at attention," Pepper said, "that silence was so strong it was noisy. I don't know how we got 'em out in that first inning, but when I came up there was two men on and two out. I rubbed my hands and resorted to prayer. I said, 'God, be my helper.'"

"I guess He was," I said.

"He was," Pepper said, nodding, "and that fastball of Grove's, if you got ahold of it, it'd ring."

Pepper boomed a double off the right field wall and drove in a run. He also got two singles and stole his first base. When the Cardinals won the second game, 2–0, Pepper got a double, a single, and a walk off Earnshaw, stole second and third, and scored both runs. By the time the Series moved to Philadelphia everyone in Shibe Park who hadn't seen the games in St. Louis wanted to see if Pepper was real.

"Which one," someone would say, "is he?"

"That one there," someone else would say, "with the dirty uniform."

"I must be warm-blooded," Pepper says, "because I'd always sweat a lot playin'. That's why I never wore slidin' pads. After a few minutes my uniform was wet, and then the dirt would stick to it."

Now when Pepper would get on base there'd be a hum in the stands. Then there'd be an eruption at first, the hum would rise in a roar, and Pepper would be streaking for second, the dirt flying behind him. Cochrane would reach for the pitch-out, throw, and there'd be a cloud of dust and Pepper, beak first, would be plowing into second on his belly. Then he'd get up with that big grin on his face, and even the Philadelphia fans would be standing and applauding.

"When I come up in that third game," Pepper says, "Grove said to me, 'You country sonofabitch, I'm gonna throw this right through your head.' I said, 'You country sonofabitch, you do that.' Cochrane had to laugh, and I hit the pitch out to the scoreboard in right center.

"You know, they blamed Cochrane for my stealin', but that wasn't right. It wasn't a question of me studyin' the motion of the pitchers, either. I guess it was the subconscious brain that told me to go. I only got the steal sign once in that Series, but you steal in the first ten steps, and I always knew I had the base stole about the time I got under way. Really, I felt sorry for Cochrane. Once he said to me, 'Don't you ever make an out?'"

Pepper got that double, a single, and another stolen base in that game and the Cardinals won, 5–2. The next day Earnshaw beat them, 3–0, and gave up only two hits. It was Pepper who ruined the no-hitter. He got both hits and stole his fifth base.

"What's he hitting, George?" Connie Mack asked Earnshaw.

"Everything I throw him," Earnshaw said.

"It got so," Pepper's wife says, "that when he'd come up I'd say, 'No. He's not due to get a hit again.' Then he'd get another hit, and finally I just broke down and cried."

That was in the fifth game. Pepper got a homer, two singles, and a sacrifice fly and batted in four runs as the Cardinals won, 5–1. Frank

Frisch was playing second base for the Cardinals then, and he still talks about that one.

"I can see it like it's yesterday," Frisch says. "In the sixth inning Pepper says to me, 'You get on, Frank, and I'll hit one nine miles.' I got a double, and damned if he didn't do it. He lined the first pitch into the left-field seats."

By now Pepper owned Philadelphia like he owned St. Louis. Crowds followed him wherever he went and waited for him in the lobby of the Ben Franklin Hotel and outside on the sidewalk for hours.

"Tell me, son," one old guy said to him. "Where'd you learn to run like that?"

"Well, sir," Pepper said, scratching his head. "I guess I learned it out in Oklahoma. When you get to runnin' out there, there ain't nothin' to stop you."

When the teams left to finish the Series in St. Louis, the crowds mobbed the car Pepper was riding in and jammed traffic on Market Street. At Broad Street Station the cops had to clear a path, and Judge Kenesaw Mountain Landis, who was then baseball commissioner, walked up to Pepper and shook his hand.

"Young man," he said, "I'd give anything to change places with you tonight."

"Well," Pepper said, thinking, "it's agreeable to me, salaries and all."

"I don't believe you," Landis said.

Landis was making $65,000 a year and the Cardinals were paying Pepper $4,500. The A's shut Pepper out after that and won the sixth game, 8–1, but the Cards won the seventh, 4–2, with Pepper catching the last out, and he got $4,467.59 out of the winners' share. Then they paid him that $2,500 a week for the vaudeville tour, but after a month Pepper quit.

"I ain't no actor," Pepper said. "This is takin' money under false pretenses and practicin' deceit."

"It just amazed me," his wife says, "that all those people wanted just to *see* him that much."

When Pepper quit the tour he stopped in at St. Louis to see Branch Rickey. Rickey was the general manager of the Cardinals, then, and he asked Pepper what he'd done with the $10,000.

"Why, I got it right here," Pepper said. "Can't you see all my pockets are bulgin'?"

"Judas Priest!" Rickey said. "Somebody'll rob you."

"No they won't," Pepper said.

Rickey made Pepper buy some bonds, but as soon as he got back to Oklahoma City he unloaded them and paid off the mortgage on his dad's ranch and bought a house for himself and Ruby. Even if he'd carried the cash back in his kick, though, anyone who tried to lift it would have had to kill Pepper or he'd have been killed himself. If you don't believe this you can ask Steve Mizerak.

Mizerak bounced around the minor leagues for years, playing infield and later managing, and now he owns a billiard room in Perth Amboy, New Jersey. Early this season he was down here and he saw Pepper starting to go into the Miami Stadium, where the Marlins play their home games, and he brought a friend up to meet Pepper.

"What a man this Pepper is," he said to his friend, after he had introduced him. "This is some man."

"I know," his friend said. "You told me."

Pepper stood looking down at his shoes, embarrassed. He is five feet nine and still weighs 160 pounds and there's that same big chest and the strength across the back and in the biceps and thighs.

"You remember," Mizerak said to him, "that night I sneaked into that hotel room in Newark?"

"Nope," Pepper said.

"He'll remember," Mizerak said, assuring his friend. "It's 1943 and Pepper is managing Rochester and I'm playin' second base and coachin'. We're roomin' together on the road, and one night I get in late and Pepper's already asleep. I don't want to wake him, so I'm real quiet closin' the door and I don't turn on the light. I'm sneakin' around the room when all of a sudden—*wham!*"

Now, sixteen years later, on the sidewalk, in the sunlight, Mizerak was reliving it. He bent over and threw his arms up as if to protect himself and his voice rose. "In the dark I got Pepper on my back. He's got me by the neck and he's cutting off my wind. He's strong as a bull and finally I get one breath and I scream, 'Pepper! It's me! Steve!' He lets me go, and you know what he says? 'You shouldn't do that. I thought you were a burglar, and I mighta killed ya.'"

"I remember now," Pepper said, nodding. "You should never do that."

"You see?" Mizerak said to his friend. "What a man this is? He's all man."

That's the way they talk about Pepper, too, back where he comes from. In 1952 there was a paragraph in the papers out of Quinton, Oklahoma, saying Pepper had been appointed deputy sheriff. They gave him a gun with his badge, but carrying it made his hip sore, and he says he could never get it out of the holster quick enough anyway, so he always left it at home.

One afternoon Pepper got word that there was a drunk holed up in a cabin and shooting at everything that moved. By the time Pepper got out to the place it was starting to get dark, and he stood around awhile, trying to figure out how to take the guy.

"Finally I decided to just walk in and reason with him," Pepper says. "I walked up to that place and opened the door and I couldn't see nothin'. After a while my eyes got accustomed, and there he was, sittin' and lookin' at me, with the gun right next to him. He come with me, but later I figured how he coulda shot me comin' through that door and I decided I didn't like that job.

"Another time they sent me to get a boy who had run out of the Army in Seattle. It turned out he'd just been married and he'd come home to visit his wife and his mother and dad. They were poor folk, and we got to talkin' and it ended up with all of us sittin' around the kitchen table in that humble abode and drinkin' coffee and cryin'.

"Hell," Pepper says, thinking about it. "Who wants a job like that?"

Then there's Branch Rickey. Rickey put together those great Cardinal teams of the twenties and thirties and those Brooklyn Dodgers that won those pennants in the forties and early fifties, and the Pirates are no longer the joke of the league because of Rickey, too. There is no one, in fact, who has ever known as many ballplayers and understood them as well as this man.

"Pepper Martin," Rickey once told Arthur Daley, of *The New York Times*, "is the most genuine person I've ever met in my life. There never was an ounce of pretense in the man. He was one hundred percent in everything he did. When he fell in love he fell head over heels in love. If he wanted a new bird dog or a shotgun he bought it whether he could afford it or not. He went all out in everything, and that was why he was so great a ballplayer."

"I can't understand that about myself sometimes," Pepper says. "When I was about eighteen I run a motorcycle race with a fella in Oklahoma City. He had high handlebars and wore them glasses, and in those days I thought that was sissy. We started out by the Capitol and he got ahead of me. Then he slowed up, with a car in front of him and another comin' the other way, and I was about a hundred feet behind. I had mine opened up, and I went right between those two cars. It was so close that I had to turn my hands up on the handle grips to keep from gettin' scraped, but I beat him.

"With nothin' at stake but to win the race," Pepper says, thinking about it, "it was a crazy thing to do. I don't know why I'm like that."

When Rickey calls Pepper a great ballplayer, though, he's talking about something that doesn't show in the records. The records say that in thirteen seasons of playing the outfield and third base for the Cardinals, Pepper averaged .298. Three years he led the National League in stolen bases. In addition to hitting .500 and stealing those five bases in that '31 Series, he got eleven hits in the 1934 Series when St. Louis beat Detroit. But statistics are no way to measure Pepper Martin.

"Pepper," Ripper Collins says, "was the kind of a guy who would kill you with a slide just to get to the next base. If you survived he'd stay up all night nursing you back to health. Then, if the same situation came up again the next day, he'd do it again."

Rip played first base for the Cardinals and later for the Cubs and the Pirates. When he first showed up in a Cardinal camp, though, they tried him in left field.

"They warned me," he once told Frank Graham, "to look out for Martin. They told me never to try for a ball on the fringe of his territory and to keep out of his way if he came into mine, because I might be knocked down and trampled. They told me, too, that it wouldn't do any good to yell for a ball, because he wouldn't hear me.

"I played next to him for four days, being careful to keep from under his feet, and this day, after he'd run from center field into my territory and caught a ball, he discovered his shoe was untied. He threw the ball back to the infield, called time and then knelt and tied his shoe. I stood there, looking at him and he looked up and smiled and said, 'Hello, son. What's your name?' I said, 'Collins.' And he said, 'Collins, eh? When did you join us, today?'"

Rip Collins can tell stories about Pepper by the hour. One of them has to do with the time Bill Terry was playing first base and managing the Giants, and he and Rip met on the field.

"Terry," Rip says, "said to me, 'You don't know how lucky you are not having to play against that Martin. When he's running for first I can hear him coming like doom, and it scares me.' So a couple of years later I'm playing first for the Cubs and here comes Pepper running for first, and it scared me, too."

"I used to bring my knees up high," Pepper says. "I liked to get a good piece of the ground."

"A good piece of the ground?" Joe Ryan says, laughing. "Remember that time you went up to the Georgia border and got all that red clay?"

Joe Ryan is the general manager of the Miami Marlins, and he was running the Fort Lauderdale, Florida, club when Pepper managed there in 1954. Now he was sitting at his desk in his office in the Miami

Stadium, and Pepper was sitting on the red leather sofa across the room, smoking his pipe.

"Pepper," Ryan said, "heard about this red clay up above Tallahassee, so he goes up there and shovels a load of it and drives it nine hundred miles back to Lauderdale to make a pitcher's mound."

"But when I got done," Pepper said, "the league had blew up."

"We still had the only red-clay pitcher's mound," Ryan said, laughing again. "We had a beautiful batting cage, too. We had needed a cage and we didn't have the money, so Pepper said, 'You get me the pipes and the tarpaulins and the netting and the wheels and an acetylene welder and I'll make one.'

"So Pepper went to work with a five-foot-two-inch Nicaraguan catcher and a Panamanian right-hander. I don't know what language they spoke, but in three weeks they finished it."

"I put the tractor inside so you couldn't see it," Pepper said. "The cage looked like it was goin' off by itself."

"So the day it was unveiled," Ryan says, laughing again, "the announcer says, 'Ladies and gentlemen, there goes Pepper's batting cage off the field now!'"

"I come out and bowed," Pepper said, "and everybody applauded. Then Joe give me the acetylene welder and I took it home to Oklahoma and messed up my eyes with it making a feeder and squeeze-gates for the cattle."

Since 1941 Pepper has managed, on and off, in nine different minor-league towns. In 1944 he returned to the Cardinals and played forty games in the outfield. In 1948 he scouted for the Dodgers. In 1956 he coached with the Chicago Cubs and last year he coached at Tulsa. In the off-season he and his wife live on their 960-acre ranch twenty-one miles northeast of McAlester. Their two older daughters are married now and the youngest is finishing nurse's training.

"I'll never forget when that third one was born," Rip Collins says. "You know what a sincere, serious guy Pepper is. He had those two daughters and when Ruby was going to have another baby, Pepper simply had to have a son. You can't imagine what it meant to him. He prayed for a boy and he talked about nothing else."

"I wanted a ballplayer," Pepper says. "I wanted a sidekick to go huntin' with me and to help me mend fences and to grow up to be a cultured gentleman."

"Well," Collins says, "it's the seventh inning of a tight ball game in St. Louis and an usher called me over near the dugout. 'Mrs. Martin just had another baby girl,' he said. 'Shall I tell Pepper?' I said, 'Wait'll I talk to Frank Frisch. He's the manager.' I told Frank and he said, "Jeebers! How're we gonna tell Pepper? We gotta win this game."

"I got Pepper aside and I told him. I said, 'Everything's swell, fella. Ruby just had a fine girl, and Ruby feels fine.' He said, 'Oh, no! The good Lord wouldn't do that to me!' Big tears started rolling down his face, and just then it's his turn at bat. He pulled his cap down over his face to hide the tears and stepped up there. The park was full of people and nobody knew he was crying. He hit the first pitch for a double. The next guy singled and Pepper slid home with the winning run. Then he sat on the bench and bawled his heart out."

"But that third one," Pepper says now, "was the cutest of them all."

Pepper was born on a 160-acre cotton farm outside Temple, Oklahoma, the youngest of seven kids. His legal name is Johnny Leonard Roosevelt Martin, and when he was six the family moved to Oklahoma City where his father worked as a carpenter and house painter.

"My folks didn't want me to play baseball," Pepper says, "and I didn't have no glove, anyway. My mother wanted me to grow up to get an education and not smoke cigarettes. I had a newspaper route, though, and I used to read everything I could about the big-league stars and the champions in boxing and I used to memorize their records. There was a kind of a sandlot team, too, and I'd drag a cart full of sody pop to the game and sell it and shag flies in the outfield."

While Pepper was still a student at Irving Junior High he played two seasons of football for Classen High School. But he never actually reached high school. Turtleneck sweaters were popular in those days, and when Pepper couldn't raise the price of one, he quit.

"I was a little bit shy," he said. "I think a fella without a turtleneck sweater couldn't be anything else but shy."

He went to work in a tin shop, and then as a delivery boy for a shoe store. He dug postholes for the Oklahoma Gas and Electric Company, and on Sundays he raked golf balls out of the water hazards at Lincoln Park.

"One day I was rakin' golf balls," he says, "and Cliff Campbell—he'd been a catcher who'd played pro ball—told me about a team up in Guthrie. I took an extra shirt rolled up in a newspaper and I went up there and I played shortstop. I played all season and got two weeks' pay."

The following year Charley Barrett, scouting for the Cardinals, saw Pepper playing for Greenville, Texas, and he signed him. The next season, 1925, they sent him to Fort Smith, Arkansas.

"That's where I got the name," Pepper says. "Blake Harper was the general manager, and when I got into town the newspaper said that Pepper Martin was reportin'. At first I thought there was two Martins. When I found out he was talkin' about me I told Blake Harper I didn't like that name. He said, 'It's a good trade name for baseball.'"

In 1926 the Cardinals sent Pepper twenty-five dollars travel money and told him to report to Greenwood, South Carolina, where the Syracuse club was in spring training under Burt Shotton. Pepper had never been on a train, so he put the money in his pocket and hopped a freight.

"I didn't know too much about hoppin' freights," Pepper says, "but I met people that knew. In those hobo camps I met some real intelligent people. I met one man who could quote Shakespeare by the hour, and I'm damn glad I experienced it.

"When I got into Greenwood it was four A.M. and I'd lost my money somewhere and I was covered with soot. The clerk in the hotel didn't know whether to let me in or not."

That year Pepper hit .308 for Syracuse. The next spring the Cardinals told him to report to them at Avon Park, Florida, and that was where Frank Frisch, who'd just been traded from the Giants to the Cardinals, got his first look at Pepper.

"I was scared," Pepper says. "I walked out on that field with all them big-league players I'd read about, and I was in awe."

"He didn't stay scared long," Frisch says. "He was playin' right field and instead of heavin' that ball to the relay man he threw it right over my head. If it had hit me, it woulda killed me. I couldn't believe he had that kind of an arm."

The Cardinals were loaded with outfielders in 1927, so they sent Pepper to Houston. After the baseball season he'd go up to the Osage Reservation, north of Tulsa, and play football for twenty-five dollars a game.

"I played halfback with the Hominy Indians," he says, "and we had a great team. There was no grandstand, but people would sit in their cars and pay a dollar a head and there'd be two thousand at a game. There were these older Indians that walked along the sideline with braids down the backs of their necks, and they were very dignified and very wealthy. They'd give you five dollars for scorin' a touchdown."

In 1928 Pepper sat on the Cards' bench and pinch-ran and hit .308 in thirteen times at bat. He was at Houston again in 1929, but in 1930 he hit .363 for Rochester. That's where one of the newspapermen named him "The Wild Horse of the Osage," and the Cards brought him up to stay in 1931.

It would be wrong to say that Pepper's success in that Series didn't change him much; it didn't change him at all. One year he arrived in the Cards' camp in St. Petersburg, Florida, in a station wagon with a mattress in the back, his shotgun, a frying pan, and a side of bacon.

When the club would go on the road Pepper would take a trunk. All he'd have in it would be an extra suit and a few accessories, but Pepper always liked tools and machinery and he'd visit the secondhand shops in all the towns on the National League circuit. By the time the trip was a week old, the bellhops could hardly lift the trunk into Pepper's room.

During the hot weather Pepper's room would be a sight, too. He'd pull the mattress off the bed and sleep on it on the floor. If it was real hot he'd pull it out on a fire escape and sleep out there.

"It took you a little while to get used to Pepper," Frisch says. One day in Boston Pepper was playing third, and when he threw to first a stream of bandage followed the ball. Frisch called time, and by now Pepper had picked up the bandage and he was starting to wrap it around his thumb again.

"Wait a minute," Frisch said. "Let me look at that."

There was a cut about an inch long. Out of it the blood was oozing. "Get out of here," Frisch said. "Have Doc Weaver sew that up."

"Aw, Frank," Pepper said. "I can play. Give me a hand with this bandage."

"Beat it," Frisch said.

That night Frisch called Pepper. When he got to Frisch's room, Frisch asked him how he got the cut.

"Well, Frank," Pepper said, "you see, right under my window here some old dolls come out to walk their kiyoodles about ten o'clock every night so I thought I would have some fun. I got a pitcher of water and when a kiyoodle would come in range I'd let him have some. Frank, you'd laugh fit to die to see 'em jump and holler! I swear, I . . ."

"The thumb," Frisch said.

"A bad accident," Pepper said, shaking his head. "I hit the pitcher against the windowsill. It broke the pitcher and it cut my thumb."

"A big-league ballplayer throwin' water on old ladies and their dogs," Frisch said. "Get out of here and go to bed."

"Thanks, Frank," Pepper said.

Pepper and Dizzy Dean used to room together, and one morning in 1936 they were standing in the lobby of the Bellevue-Stratford in Philadelphia without much to do. Finally Pepper remembered a hock shop where he could buy tools cheap.

"Diz said he'd go along," Pepper says, "and when Diz said he'd go, Diz's brother, Paul, said he'd go, too. Then Heinie Schuble said he'd go and we all went. I picked out a pair of union-alls, and because I did, Diz did. Because Diz bought a pair, Paul did, and because Paul did, Heinie did. Then Diz suggested we wear 'em back, over our clothes, to the hotel.

"When we got back to the lobby Rip Collins was there. He always dressed fastidious, and he asked us what we were doin'. We said we thought we'd paint the lobby, so Rip acted like the contractor. We talked it up loud—how we'd change this thing here and paint that wall a different color—and pretty soon a whole crowd of people were gathered around.

"Then there was this barbershop in the basement run by a Greek. We all went down there and started to talk loud about what we'd do to that place. That Greek, he was shavin' some guy, and when we started talkin' about movin' all the bottles and takin' down the mirrors he became angered and he come around from behind that guy, wavin' that razor and—well, we didn't change that barbershop much.

"We went back upstairs instead, and there was a dignified luncheon goin' on. We eased in there and turned over one of the empty tables, but somebody recognized Diz. There was a man speakin' at the time, but he sat down and it ended up with Diz makin' the speech and the guy listenin'."

For a while Pepper helped train and seconded a Chickasaw Indian heavyweight named Junior Munsell. Pepper and Rip Collins and Jack Rothrock once worked out a juggling act that they used to put on between games of doubleheaders.

"Only if we won the first game," Pepper says. "Otherwise Frisch wouldn't let us. It was just entertainment for the people, and I remember one day in St. Louis when the temperature was up over one hundred and it was too hot to take battin' practice. It was Ladies' Day and the ladies were just sittin' there without anything to amuse them and I felt sorry for them. I got some paper and went under the stands and found some wood. Then I got a blanket from the clubhouse and I built a fire in front of the dugout and sat down in front of it with the blanket around me. Then Diz and Rip Collins, they come out with blankets and sat down with me, and that amused the ladies."

Pepper's two big diversions, though, were his midget racer and his Mudcat Band. One winter, when he came into St. Louis to sign his contract, he saw some midget races at the Arena.

"When I seen 'em run," he says, "I wished I had one, and the next year I had one built. It cost me fifteen hundred dollars, and about every other week I had to send it to Milwaukee to get it fixed for fifty or a hundred dollars."

Lou Schneider, who won the Indianapolis 500 in 1931, drove for Pepper. The car was white—with "Martin Special," a ball bat, and two cardinals painted in red on the side—and Schneider won a few races with it.

Once, in the clubhouse before a game, Frisch was giving the club a raking over when suddenly he ran out of words. "Why don't you sons-ofbitches say something?" he said.

"Well, Frank," Pepper said, "what do you think? Should I paint my racin' car red instead of white?"

Another time, the Cards were opening a crucial series with the Pirates in St. Louis and Pepper missed batting practice. When he did come running into the clubhouse there was grease up to his elbows.

"Where you been?" Frisch said, starting on him.

"I'm sorry, Frank," Pepper said, "but I had a bet with a guy I could beat him in a two-mile race and he was late showin' up."

"That's great!" Frisch said. "We're tryin' to win a pennant and you're tryin' to win a racing bet. How much was the bet?"

"Two quarts of ice cream," Pepper said, "and I won, too."

"No," Frisch said, shaking his head. "We're not crazy. We're perfectly sane, all of us."

"The Dutchman," Dizzy Dean said to Pepper, "is goin' out of his mind."

When the club got to Chicago, Pepper and Dizzy and Paul met Paul Russo, the race driver. Russo got to telling them what a good driver his sister was, too, so Dizzy and Paul matched Pepper against her.

"When I took my warm-up spin, though," Pepper says, "I ran through one of those bales of hay on the turn and I circled the track on the outside. When I came back she wouldn't race me. Finally Mr. Rickey made me take the car off the track, and I took it home and a guy gave me four hundred dollars for it."

It was about that time that they had that "Pepper Martin Day" in St. Louis. When they got through presenting the gifts the infield looked like the county fairgrounds. They gave Pepper two Belgian mares, two sets of harness, a Holstein heifer, a sow with seven young, a hen, a rooster, a beagle pup, a pair of rabbits, a plow, a hay rake, two hand rakes, an electric churn, two milk cans, a scythe, and two spades.

"I had to rent a boxcar for four hundred dollars," Pepper says, "and I had to build stalls in it for the animals to get them shipped back home. For a while, though, we had them animals out in the suburbs, where we rented a house in a dignified neighborhood, and those city kids had never seen anything like it. Another time I raised tomatoes where we were livin'. I used to hoe 'em in the morning before I went to the ball park and I made tomatoes that were tremendous. Ruby canned two hundred cans of 'em."

The Mudcat Band started when Ruby gave Pepper a guitar one Christmas. When he left for spring training he took it to St. Petersburg with him.

"I could pick that thing a little," he says, "and Lon Warneke could pick it, too. Max Lanier could pick it and play the harmonica, and Bill McGee could play a violin. Bob Weiland, he could blow on a jug, and Frenchy Bordagaray played on the washboard with thimbles.

"One night in trainin' we were playin' on the veranda of that hotel and one of the newspapermen asked me, 'What kind of an orchestra is that, Pepper?' I said, 'Why, it's a mudcat band.' They started writin' about the band, then, and finally we got cowboy uniforms and we'd get fifty or a hundred or maybe six hundred dollars on a radio program to play.

"We'd play songs like 'Possum Up a Gum Stump' and 'Buffalo Gals,' and once we got fifteen hundred a week for two weeks to play in theaters. Bordagaray and I were drivin' up to Dayton to play and we picked up this hitchhiker. His name was Brown and he could play a harmonica. The best part, though, was his first name was Elmer, so we put him in the band and he played the two weeks with us. I don't know what become of him.

"Finally, we had an exhibition game in Rochester, New York, one year and when we got in town the papers all said, 'Pepper Martin and his Mudcats play tomorrow.' Joe Medwick said, 'What the hell is this, a ball club or an orchestra?' When we got back, Mr. Rickey called me in and he pointed out certain values. Then he said, 'I know what you'll do, Pepper.' I said, 'I know, too. The Mudcats are disbanded, as of now.'"

The first club that Pepper managed was Sacramento, in 1941. Early in the season Doc Weaver, the Cardinals' trainer, got a wire from Pepper.

"Alas, Doc," it read, "no diathermy machine out here and we sure need one. Club overhead terrific. Could you send us one of yours this year? In return, could give you autographed ball, left-handed pitcher, or a couple of fat pigs. Hopefully, Johnny Pepper Martin, manager, player, coach."

"He sent me the machine," Pepper says, "and I got a couple of pigs and crated 'em up and sent 'em to him."

Sacramento finished second that year and Pepper blames himself because they didn't win. One day Ruby was driving the car in Marysville, California, with Pepper riding next to her and the three girls in the back seat. When she stopped at a light a car in back hit the bumper.

"There wasn't any damage," Pepper says, "but the three guys in the car kept drivin' alongside of us, hollerin' vulgar remarks. I finally shouted at them to pull over, and I took the biggest one and hit him a punch on the jaw and knocked him down. Then I jumped on him and I was chokin' him, but Ruby was screamin' at me to stop and the girls were cryin' so I let up. I told the three of them, though, 'That ought to teach you a little courtesy.'

"I shouldn't have done that," Pepper says, shaking his head. "I broke the cap on one of my knuckles and I couldn't play for ten days. We'd have won the pennant, because we won it the next year."

In Lakeland, Florida, in 1951, Pepper hit a fan and was fined twenty-five dollars in Municipal Court and fifty dollars by Phil O'Connell, who was president of the Florida International League. Pepper says the fan had been riding him all through the game, sticking his head over a low fence near the dugout, and when he got personal Pepper jumped the fence.

"I don't like to hurt people," Pepper says, "and I don't believe other people like to hurt people either, but I hit him one and he run. I chased him under the bleachers but I couldn't catch him good. I hit him in the kidneys and once on the back of the neck, but anyway, by God, I bet he kept his mouth shut after that."

When Pepper was playing, you see, he used to be able to work that excitement off. He never had any trouble with fans and very little with umpires. Down in Havana near the end of the season of 1950, though, he really got tied up.

"We still had a chance for the pennant," he says, "and we're leadin' by one run. The umpire had called against us in close plays at first and second and we had this trick play at third base. Knobby Rosa, my third baseman, had tricked the man, but the umpire called him safe and Knobby got mad.

"Then the umpire lectured me about gettin' Rosa off the field and I said somethin' about the best thing would be to get the umpire off the field. Next he pulled his watch on me, and I just grabbed him by the throat before I thought. He wasn't a bad fella, really. The next thing you know the police come out of the stands with their guns on Rosa and me."

Phil O'Connell fined Pepper $100 and suspended him for the rest of the season. Happy Chandler was baseball commissioner then, and the next spring he saw Pepper.

"I asked Pepper," Chandler said, telling it later, "about that matter of the umpire. I said, 'When you had your hands on that umpire's throat, just what were you thinking?'

"So Pepper looked me right in the eye and said, 'Mr. Commissioner, I was thinking I would like to choke the sonofabitch to death.'"

"So," somebody said to Chandler, "what did you say?"

"Say?" Chandler said. "What *could* I say? The man told me the truth."

It's what Fresco Thompson says about Pepper. Fresco is now one of the vice presidents of the Los Angeles Dodgers, and one day, at spring training at Vero Beach, Florida, he was talking about Pepper to Red Smith, who writes the syndicated column for the *New York Herald Tribune*.

"It is not possible," Fresco said, "to conceive of a more honest guy than Pepper Martin. He looks so honest and he talks so honestly and such sincerity oozes out of him that, if you could get him as front man in some crooked con game, why pretty soon you'd have all the money there is in the world."

"I had an idea once," Pepper says, "and it woulda worked. My idea was to get somebody to make a baseball out of pastry, like a piecrust. You could maybe win an important game with it, like the seventh game of a World Series.

"Let's say that the other team has a man on third with the tyin' run, and two out in the ninth inning. You're playin' third and you got the ball, also you got this piecrust ball. You throw the piecrust ball to the pitcher. The runner sees it and steps off the bag. You tag him with the real ball, and meantime the pitcher eats the piecrust so there's no evidence.

"I think that would really work, and I talked about it in St. Louis with Doc Weaver. He was for it, and he knew a guy who could make the piecrust ball. He said he'd better make two of 'em, in case somebody sits on one on the bench.

"Heck," Pepper says, thinking of it. "There's no rule against it and it woulda worked. You see, in the excitement and the confusion, nobody notices the pitcher eatin' the piecrust ball. Diz coulda eaten it easy."

John A. Heydler said it, too. He was president of the National League in 1909 and from 1919 to 1934. He said it after the 1931 Series, and when he died in 1956 it was still true. It's still true today.

"Fellows like Pepper Martin," he said, "come along once in a lifetime."

The Rough and Tumble Life

Jim Tescher, Rodeo Rider

HE HAD DRIVEN into Phoenix the night before with his wife and their four-year-old son in the two-year-old red Chevrolet. The pillow and blankets were in the back seat and his saddle was in the trunk along with dirty laundry stuffed into a pair of his blue jeans. They had been on the road for five weeks, and at Fort Worth and San Antonio, Houston and Baton Rouge, he had picked up $5,753—about $5,000 riding saddle broncs and the rest of it wrestling steers. Now he was standing with a half-dozen others in the shade of the white-painted wooden office set up on the big flatbed trailer in the dusty parking area just outside the contestants' entrance to the State Fairgrounds. It was 1:40 in the afternoon and they were looking over the typed lists of the draws posted on the front of the office.

"What'd you get?" one of the men behind him said. "Anything good?"

He is thirty-five years old now and he has been riding horses since he was four. When he was ten he rode his first steer for one dollar in a Fourth of July rodeo in Medora, North Dakota, twenty miles from where he was born and grew up in the Gumbo Butte country of the Badlands, and now around rodeo they call him "the bronc rider's bronc rider" and "the old pro."

"Good?" he said now. "Yeah, for a cripple or an old man."

True, February 1965.

There is no sport that is more indigenous to this country than rodeo, because it goes back as far as the Spanish land grants in California and to the earliest cattle drives in Colorado and Texas when American cowboys would meet on the trail and at shipping points and the bragging—"we got a guy can ride anything"—and the betting would start. Sometimes those outfits would bet the works, and we have no other sport that grew as naturally out of a way of life.

Last year there were 582 rodeos in this country and Canada and they attracted 9,400,000 spectators and 90,000,000 television viewers and paid out $3,511,247 in prize money. A lot of it is show, even circus, now, but there are still the classic events, like saddle-bronc riding, and there are still rodeo cowboys who grew up on a ranch and still work a ranch and are reminders of that way of life that is almost gone now forever. And this man is one of them.

As soon as he had found his name—Jim Tescher—on the bucking list and then had run his eyes across to the name of the horse—Oley—he had known he would not win on it. In the saddle-bronc riding each of the two judges gives 1 to 25 points for the horse, 1 to 25 points for the rider, and then each totals his points and they add the totals. A perfect score would be 100. What it comes down to is that bronc riding is not only a contest between a man and an animal but also a partnership, and the horse is as important as the rider.

"You ever been on this Oley?" one of the men next to Jim said now.

"No," he said, "but I know him."

He knows them all—all he has ever ridden or even seen. He has studied them all, the way in big-league baseball the pitchers study the hitters and the hitters the pitchers and in pro football the defensive backs keep mental book on every change of pace and fake and move of every receiver they have to face.

In the last sixteen years he has ridden hundreds of horses and won more than $160,000 at rodeos. In 1952, with his rodeo savings, he started to put together his ranch on the west bank of the Little Missouri River in the heart of the Badlands, and now there are 2,320 acres with 240 white-faced Hereford on them and twenty-five registered quarter horses. In 1960 he and his wife, Loretta, and the first three of their four children moved out of the log house they'd started with and into a cement-block basement and one of these days they'll build the new house on top of it.

Now, looking at that saddle-bronc list, Jim Tescher knew this Oley right away as the blaze-faced sorrel he had helped Alvin Nelson on—helped saddle in the chute—at Sidney, Iowa, about seven months before and he had helped others on it before that. He knew it for just an average horse that likes to come out of the gate straight and make a big, sweeping turn to the right. It has rhythm, so you can get in your licks—the spurring strokes front and back—but it never comes up with the big explosion—the big buck or big kick—that you need to score high.

At Sidney that afternoon, in fact, after he had helped saddle Oley, he himself had ridden the kind of horse you always hope to draw, and he could see it now. It was the big sensational strawberry roan named Mountain Dew that Beutler Bros., the livestock contractors, had used first as a bareback horse.

He had ridden it out to the whistle that day at Sidney, but then it had got to bucking so rank, whirling and spinning to the right in such tight turns, that he had known it would lose its footing. For three or four seconds he had known it, but there was nothing anyone could have done and then it had come over on top of him, about fourteen hundred pounds of it, and the last thing he remembered was his head hitting the ground.

"Jim?" he had heard someone saying. "Jim, can you hear me?"

Through the haze he had seen cowboys and then the two doctors standing over him and he had realized he was in the first-aid room and that there was pain in his back. The year before, his neck had been broken at Beach, North Dakota, but this time the doctors had turned him over and had found that it was just a rock, a little bigger than a golf ball, under his belt. For weeks after that, though, his back had been swollen and black and blue, and he had taken pain pills every time he worked.

"It's not that a person can't stand pain," he said later, explaining it to me, "but it changes his reflexes."

Now, in the shade of the office overhang at Phoenix, the others around him talking but their words not registering in his mind, he was checking over the rest of the saddle-bronc list. He was looking for the good riders and the good horses and the pairings that would win money . . . Bill Martinelli on Peaceful, a good rider and a good draw and liable to win with a score in the 70s . . . George Williams on Roly Poly, the horse he had hoped to get because he had never been on it and he had seen Bill Feddersen win with it in Las Vegas and had watched it buck his own brother, Tom, off at the National Finals Rodeo in Dallas in 1959 . . .

He scanned the list further . . . Kenny McLean, one of the toughest going down the road if he'd just go down the road more, but on Pretty One, that you'd have to call a dirty draw because even if you do ride him well you don't win . . . Marty Wood . . . Winston Bruce . . . both tough riders but both on bad draws . . . Ronnie Raymond, who could get high in the 60s and maybe win on Knott Inn . . . Guy Weeks, the '63 champion, on Revenue, no better than his own Oley . . .

The big-league ballplayer is on salary and the professional fighter knows that he will be paid whether he wins or loses. In tournament golf they pay off to thirty and sometimes to fifty places, but here there were forty-seven riders, all paying their own expenses and all putting up the thirty-five-dollar entry fee, going for $1,759.14—$706.06 for first, $526.55 for second, $351.03 for third, and $175.50 for fourth. In this draw on this horse, he was reasoning now, walking down the steps of the trailer and into the warm sunlight, the best he could hope to score would be something in the middle 50s. That didn't figure to get him even fourth money, but at least it wouldn't kill him in the average. There would be a second draw—a second go-round—with the same amount of money up again, and they would pay off to four places in that and then to four places in the average—the total of the two go-rounds.

"Hey, Jim!" he heard someone calling, and he saw Russ Taylor, the chaps maker from Moorcroft, Wyoming, standing by the tailgate of a white station wagon, and motioning to him. He walked over to him and they shook hands and Taylor reached into the wagon and came out with a new pair of Tescher Bronc Chaps and handed them to him and he tried them on.

They are dark brown cowhide, with the trim and leather fringe dyed green, and they sell for $35 and were named after him when he won the saddle-bronc riding at the National Finals—the World Series of rodeo—for the first time in Dallas in 1959.

"I don't know," Tescher said, looking down at the fringe breaking over the fronts of his boots. "I think they're a little long."

In bronc riding one of the things they judge you on is your lick—the spurring stroke with the first punch in front of the points of the horses' shoulders and the second back on the flanks. When the chaps are too long they may hide the spurs on that first punch.

"Suppose I take an inch off?" Taylor said.

"That'd be fine," he said.

"Anything you say," Taylor said. "You're the boss."

When Jim started to rodeo seriously, back in 1948 and long before he became a name cowboy himself, his hero was Bill Linderman, who twice won the saddle-bronc title and in twenty years won $426,669 in prize money. In those days Tescher used to travel with his brother Tom, who is four years older, in Tom's 1936 Ford with wood and cardboard in place of the broken glass in the windows and no starter and almost no brakes but with a good motor and good tires. The first Rodeo Cowboys Association rodeo they went to was in Sheridan, Wyoming.

"When we got there," he was telling me one night when I came out to see how he and his wife and their kids live in the Badlands, "we saw in the paper that Bill Linderman and some other name cowboys would contest, and it just sickened us. We thought of comin' back home and then we waited until a few minutes after the entries closed, hopin' they wouldn't let us in, but they did. Tom won a third in the bareback and

I won the saddle-bronc and it paid a hundred ninety-two dollars and I thought I'd never see another poor day."

That money was big money in those days because he was one of fifteen children and, although his dad had fifteen hundred acres outside of Sentinel Butte and raised commercial cattle and wheat, it was always a struggle. Then, when he was in the fifth grade the house burned down. When the rest of the family moved into town, he and his brother Alvin, who is eight years older, stayed on the ranch. They lived together in the two-room bunkhouse for six years and he went through the eighth grade in the one-room school where there were just six other boys.

"I thought of goin' to high school," he said, "but I also thought it was a disgrace for a ranch boy to live in town. The people I admired most were ranchers, and they still are. I still think more of bein' a ranch hand than a rodeo cowboy."

When he was still small, and his dad wasn't around, he'd ride milk cows, and when he and Alvin lived together Alvin was sort of a model for him and taught him by letting him get up on anything. Every once in a while, somebody would leave a horse with them to be broken and in three weeks to a month they'd have it roughed out and ready to handle and they'd take it back to the owner. That was how he got the $13 for his first pair of boots when he was twelve, and it ended his shoe wearing right there.

"We used to run wild horses, too," he explained. "In those days these Badlands were full of 'em, and when I was seventeen I had forty-three head."

"In other words, when you wear those jeans and boots and that hat it's not just a costume and you're not acting."

"I guess that's right," he said.

"I understand that some people don't know that. They tell me that when you and Tom were rodeoing together and somebody, in a bar, would start the abuse with 'Where'd you park your horse, Tex?' it was a delight to see. They say that you two, wreathed in smiles, would just clean out the place."

Tescher is only five feet eight and a half inches, but he weighs 187 pounds. He measures only thirty inches around the waist, so it's up there in his chest and shoulders and arms and down in his thighs and calves.

"They told you that, did they?" he said.

"That's right. I understand that you're on the Board of Directors of the Rodeo Cowboys Association and last summer at Cheyenne this cowboy came up and shook his finger in your face and said, 'You R.C.A. directors are all a lot of fat-headed sonsabitches.' They say you just knocked him on his tail and he was still out five minutes later."

"I guess that's about right," he said, and it was.

He could remember another night when he and his wife Loretta were going to Fort Madison, Iowa, and they had stopped in a café over in Dickinson to wait for Pete Fredericks, from Halliday, who was going with them. While they were eating, there were three or four fellas in the next booth who got to arguing and cussing and finally the big guy challenged the little fella to go out in the street and Jim followed them out and watched the big guy bloody the little fella up and finally knock him out.

The trouble was that it didn't end there. The big guy was feeling good now, back in the booth with the others, and he was using some pretty rank language and Loretta could hear it and finally Jim said to the big guy that there was a lady present and he should shut up. With that the big guy jumped up and said, "I'd like to have you shut me up!" There was the back of the booth between them but, using his right hand on the top of the booth as a pivot, Jim let a hook go and the big guy went sprawling over the table.

Then Jim was out of the booth. As the big guy came bounding off that table, he let another one go and flattened the big guy on the floor, and then he just picked him up and threw him out.

By this time the manager had called the law and when they got there the manager said, "It's all right now, officers. This gentleman has already handled it." And one of the cops said, "Was that you, threw him out in the street?" And Jim said, "That's right." And the cop said, “You know, as we come along in the dark, we thought you were throwin’ out a saddle.” Then the manager wouldn’t let him pay for the two dinners.

“So what about that time in Dallas?” I said next.

“They told you about that, too?” Jim said, then deciding that he might as well tell about it. “Well, we got paid off kinda late that year and it was about two A.M. when I went to eat in this café right across from the hotel. There were about a dozen cowboys and a lot of others there but there was only one waitress and we had to wait. There was this fella there and he started that ‘Tex’ stuff. The longer nobody said anything the worse he got and finally I’d finished eatin’ and George Williams just kinda nudged me.

“So I said to this fella, ‘Why don’t you just get out?’ He said, ‘Maybe you’d like to try to put me out.’ Then we went to it, and as soon as we did I knew he could fight. I guess we must have gone for about three or four minutes until finally I hit him a good right and he went down and just lay there by some chairs. The other fellas got me out then, because they figured the law was comin’.”

When he went back later, though, to pay for his meal, he found out he had been right. The manager said one of the other cowboys had paid his bill and then he said, “Do you know who that fella is that you knocked out?” And he said, “No.” And the manager said, “He’s the light-heavyweight champion of Texas.” He had known from the way that fella had moved and slipped punches and didn’t waste any of his own that he could fight.

Jim walked now in the Phoenix sun to his own car and opened the trunk. He took out the bronc saddle that he paid $185 for in 1949 and has been using ever since and he placed it on the ground. The leather is scarred and dry now, and when I saw it I asked what he treats it with.

“Just with abuse,” he said with a smile.

Now he took out his own worn Tescher chaps, folded, and the rein—the six-foot length of four-plait braided manila rope. He slammed the trunk shut, and then he heard someone behind him.

"Excuse me," the man said. He was middle-aged, thin and wearing glasses, and in a white short-sleeved sports shirt and tan slacks.

"What can I do for you?" Jim said.

"Excuse me," the man said, "but are you a bronc rider?"

"That's right."

"I've always wanted to ask something," the man said. "I mean, how do you fellas get the courage?"

"Oh," Jim said, "I don't imagine it's courage."

"I've watched you fellas get hurt," the man said. "You ever been hurt?"

"Yes, sir."

"Then how can you fellas do that?"

"I guess 'cause it's our job," he said. "I don't know."

"Well, thanks anyway," the man said. "And good luck to you."

"Thanks," Jim said.

It's not something you can ever explain. It's just something you grow up with, never thinking you're going to be hurt, and when you are you never give it much thought. Except that I did get him to go over all his injuries and it made quite a list.

When he was fourteen, he was hunting deer and riding down off one of those almost mustard-colored buttes into a draw when the horse turned a somersault and his right arm was broken. When he was sixteen his left ankle was broken while he was rodeoing at Dickinson, North Dakota, and a bareback horse ran away with him. For a week he didn't bother to go to the doctor and then, after the doctor put the cast on, he rode bareback at Glendive, Montana, for the three dollars mount money.

When he was twenty he had three vertebrae broken in the small of his back in a car wreck. They told him he shouldn't do any work for three months, so he went to Florida and started rodeoing in Miami and Orlando and Davie and Miami Springs and Kissimmee and came home with $1,000 more than he had left with. Then at Spencer, Iowa, one year he broke his left thigh bone when the horse reared in the chute, but they poured a couple of drinks of whiskey into him and he got back on the horse.

In 1959 his collarbone was broken when he was thrown in Madison Square Garden in New York. Two years later he broke the third and fifth vertebrae in his neck at Beach, North Dakota, just playing around after the rodeo with Alvin Nelson—betting on riding and using each other's saddle—and he was in a brace for two months. He has had calcium deposits removed from his left shinbone.

In many rodeos, he also wrestles steers. He has had horns tear the left side of his nose loose, rip his left upper lip and his right upper lip, but he couldn't tell me how many stitches have been put in his mouth and face. In fact, he forgot then that he also had a cast on his left ankle when his brother Tom was married. That was from the chute at Grand Forks, North Dakota, when he got back on the horse and won money anyway.

"But don't you ever have any pain from any of this?" I asked him.

"Most all the time," he said. "I can feel it now, sittin' here, and it bothers me lyin' in bed. It doesn't bother me when I work, though, or when I ride, just afterwards. When it gets real bad I know those vertebrae in my back have slipped, so I get Benny Reynolds to put 'em back in place."

Benny Reynolds is a six-foot three-inch, 195-pound, easy-going, four-event cowboy out of Melrose, Montana. In 1961 he won $31,309 and the All-Around Championship.

"Benny remembers what twist to give 'em," he explained, "so why pay one of them fellas three dollars?"

Jim had the rope rein around his neck now and the folded chaps in one hand. With the other hand he was carrying the thirty-four-pound saddle and he walked between the parked cars and through the contestants' entrance, and then he stopped and he put the saddle down. To his right was the back of the temporary grandstand, to his left was the refreshment booth with cowboys standing in the sunlight in front of it and drinking their Cokes, and suddenly it all started to come back to him.

I remember this part of it right here, he was thinking, *but it's like something in a dream.*

In 1957 he had had his best year here in Phoenix when he won $2,700, but last year here a horse named Thunderbolt had bucked him off. Now, back again for the first time since then, he was trying to recapture the fall—waiting for it to return, if it would—because it is a part of his life that he knows he lived but of which he has absolutely no memory.

At Sidney, Iowa, before he blacked out, he could remember his head hitting the ground. The time he hung up in the stirrup at that little Sunday-afternoon rodeo at Burns Creek, Montana, he could remember his head a foot from the rail fence before the horse swung him against it. Even the time that he went through the windshield of his car and landed fifty feet away with his head down in the ditch he could remember everything up to the last second.

Here in Phoenix, though, he could not remember getting on the horse or the ride. For twenty-four hours he couldn't even remember who he was or where he was and they told him later he kept asking over and over. He must have asked Duane Bruce, who had helped him in the chute, twenty times what rein he had given the horse and what side he'd bucked off on. He just couldn't get it back, and the doctor had given it some name and explained that you can lose out of your life a period of time and just never recover it.

He could hear now, coming through the open stands and over and around them, the voice of Mel Lambert, the public-address announcer—". . . and here's a cowboy who last year . . ." It was the steer wrestling, and then they'd have the calf roping and then the Hollywood cowboy and then the saddle-bronc riding. The more than $5,000 he had won in the last five weeks had put him first among the money winners in the bronc riding, and in rodeo the top money winner at the end of the season in each of the seven events is called the world champion and the biggest earner in two or more events is the all-around champion. In 1959, his best money year, he made $22,223 and finished fourth in the saddle-bronc standings with $12,157. In 1963 he won $20,904 and with $15,099 of it for getting up on bucking stock, he was third.

"But how come you've never been world champion?" his oldest boy, Gary, who is thirteen now, had said to him one night. Jim was showing him the gold-and-silver belt buckle set with diamonds that he had just won at the National Finals in Los Angeles. They were standing by the washing machine and dryer just off the kitchen in the basement and he had tried to explain it to his son—that being with his family and building up the ranch had always seemed more important to him than going halfway across the United States to some little rodeo just to win $100. When you make only thirty or forty rodeos a year you can't expect to finish as high in the final standings as somebody who makes eighty or ninety, and when he and Tom were competing together Casey Tibbs, a nine-time world champion, said it for them.

"There's no tellin' how far those Teschers could go," Casey said, "if they weren't plagued with common sense."

It's what Gene Pruett says, too. Gene rode saddle broncs for twenty-one years and won the world title in 1948 and quit in 1955. Now he's the editor of *Rodeo Sports News*, the biweekly published by the Rodeo Cowboys Association in Denver, and no one knows rodeo better.

"It'd be real hard," Gene Pruett says, "to pick out even two guys who can ride as good as Jim Tescher—maybe not even one—because he's just about as good a bronc rider today as there is. If Jim and Tom had just rodeoed and rodeoed they'd been champions, and besides, the National Finals are the real test as far as I'm concerned."

"So I'll tell you what I might do this year," Jim had told his star-gazing son that night when the boy had brought it up. "If you'd really like me to be world champion I might give it a try. If I start out winnin' pretty good and everything's all right here at the ranch I might just stay with it more." He said this mostly for the boy, because the one event he really cares about winning—and did win last year—is the annual match riding he and Tom put on for the benefit of the Diocese of Bismarck's Home on the Range for Boys. (Last December, in Los Angeles, Jim finished second in the National Finals with a total of $21,577—just about $600 short of a world championship.)

Jim's son is a fine boy. Young as he is he's about as useful as any hired hand and a good student, too. That one-room school he goes to with Les Connell's boy and George Wolf's boy and the three Mossers and the two Meyers is across the river, so to get there he walks out to the bank above the river where that railroad tie is buried upright with just the top sticking out of the ground. Attached to the top of the tie is the three-quarter-inch steel cable that runs 320 feet across the river to a cottonwood tree on the other bank. Tied to the tie is that weathered wood platform, about five feet long and three feet wide, suspended by two iron frames from two pulleys that ride the cable.

The boy has his lunch in a Karo syrup pail and he puts that in first and then he kneels on the platform and pushes off. The platform slides down the cable to the midpoint, about eight feet above the water—or ice in winter—and then the boy grabs the cable over his head and pulls the platform over to the cottonwood tree. He climbs down the seven boards nailed to the trunk of the tree and gets into the Jeep, which he left there the afternoon before, and he drives the four and a half miles to the school.

It's hard country, all right. They say that in the wheat lands of North Dakota the topsoil is from six to eight feet deep, but out on those buttes there's no more than six to eight inches of it on top of that yellow gumbo. The nearest bridge crossing is thirty-eight miles upriver and the nearest telephone is thirty-five miles away in Sentinel Butte where, according to Matt Tescher, the boy's grandfather, there are also 175 people. Matt Tescher should know because he is serving his fourth term in the State Legislature and they call him "Landslide" Tescher since he won his next-to-last election by one vote.

"A lot of people thought Jim wouldn't make it out in the Badlands," his brother-in-law, Roy Kittelson, likes to say, "but Jim mined his own coal, smoked Bull Durham, and saved every penny he could."

The time was drawing near for the saddle-bronc competition. "Jim Tescher?" he heard someone say, and he turned and saw a cowboy in a white shirt and black hat. "Bud Martin's my name."

"How are you?"

"Can you tell me somethin' about Blue?"

"Yes," Jim said, and held out his two fists, but with the thumbs extended and touching, to indicate how much rein to give the horse. "I'd say he takes about four or five inches over average."

When they don't kick high with their back legs but buck hunched up high in the middle, they drop their heads and take a long rein. When they kick high they throw their heads back and take a short rein. If you figure a horse wrong, though, a long hold may leave you lying back over the rump or a short hold may send you over the head, and it is a tradition in rodeo that what you know about a horse you share.

"Thanks a lot," Bud Martin said.

"He's a little touchy in the chute, too, but that's all right if you just handle him. At El Paso he turned back to the right real short with me right out of the gate. Then he really bucks the first four or five seconds and he's another one that has a tendency to duck to the left and stand you in the right stirrup."

"Thanks a lot."

"That's all right," Jim said.

Now they had finished with the calf roping and he could hear, over the P.A. system, the voice of the Hollywood TV cowboy telling gags . . . "so you just think about it, and you'll holler later . . ." and he bent down and picked up the chaps. He unfolded them and put them on, fastening the buckle of the waist strap and the three buckles at the back of each leg. Then he picked up the saddle.

"Well," he said. "Time to go to work."

"Good luck," Kenny McLean said.

"That's right," Jim Clifford said.

"I'll need it," he said.

This was one of those times, he knew, when he would have to give the horse all the best of it. This Oley is a little light-headed so that, if he wanted to, he could take a short rein on it, but he was reasoning now that if he gave it, instead, a little over the average rein he might encourage it into the real big try he needed from it to mark anywhere in the mid-50s.

When he got to the gate one of the cowboys standing there and listening to the TV cowboy singing now opened it for him and he walked through. Across the arena he could see the faces of the crowd filling the permanent covered grandstand. In the middle of the arena the TV cowboy was standing with a guitar player on the big, rubber-tired trailer, next to a piano.

"Gonna build a mountain," he was singing, "from a little hill . . ."

"Hey, Tescher!" he heard someone calling, and it was Sonny Linger, the chute boss. "Over here!"

He put the saddle down outside the chute and took the leather halter from Winston Bruce. He climbed up onto the gate and, bending over the top, saw the horse below him, parallel to the gate, his head to the left and filling the chute but quiet in it. He slipped the halter on, pulling it up over the nose and buckling the cheek piece. Then he took the rope rein and passed the spliced loop on the one end behind the noseband on the left side of the horse's head and he brought the other end up through the loop and snugged it.

"Tell me this," the guitar player was asking the TV cowboy in the arena. "How many head of cattle do you have on your ranch?"

"I don't know," the TV cowboy was saying. "They're always facin' the wrong way."

On the ground in front of the gate Jim picked up the saddle and climbed back up the gate. Swinging the saddle so that the stirrups would clear the gate he let the saddle down gently across the horse's withers. The horse was still standing steady, and with his left hand he felt for the back of the left shoulder blade and then, remembering the horse's tendency to throw a saddle forward, he moved it back about an inch. When he did this the horse snorted and shifted and then whistled once, the way the wild ones will whistle when they see you on the range.

"Easy, partner," George Williams, helping on the backside of the chute and holding the halter, said. "Easy now."

Bob Robinson, the Canadian saddle-bronc and bull rider, on the ground below him, reached through the gate with the long wire hook and brought the cinch ring up and threaded the end of the latigo through it. Then he made his two turns through the cinch ring and the D-ring of the saddle and pulled it snug.

"It looks like this old pony's gonna stand," Jim said to Bob Robinson. "You might get the back one now."

Out in the middle of the arena the TV cowboy and the guitar player had finished. A tractor was pulling the trailer off and he waited, on the gate, while Bob Robinson, using the wire hook again, got the buckle of the saddle flank and buckled it loosely.

"So let's go to the chutes!" Mel Lambert was announcing. "The next event is saddle-bronc riding, and we've got the best . . ."

Bending over the top of the gate now Jim picked up the rein with his right hand and brought it back. Making a fist with his left hand he placed the heel of the hand against the swell at the front of the saddle and he extended his thumb. Measuring the length of the rein against this and going an inch beyond, because the others he had seen on this horse had given it this average rein, he grabbed the rein there between his left forefinger and thumb. Then, with his right hand, he pulled a small clump of the reddish brown hair out of the horse's mane and, spreading the plaits of the yellow manila hemp at the spot where he held the rein, he threaded the hair through and tied it once.

"The first cowboy up," Mel Lambert was announcing, "is . . ."

"Tescher!" Sonny Linger was calling. "You're third!"

"All right, Son," he said.

He had climbed across to the backside of the chute and he had taken the end of the latigo from Bob Robinson. As he tried to put the end under the skirt of the saddle to keep it from whipping around he was aware that the saddle felt too tight.

"He's squattin' a little," he said to Robinson, "but I think you better slack it off some, anyway."

". . . and our judges," Mel Lambert was announcing, "mark our first horse and rider 48! Now, here's Don Sievertson from Phoenix, Arizona, on . . ."

"You got that rope there?" Sonny Linger said.

"What do you want us to do with it?"

"Put it under his neck and hold it on the backside."

"You got it, George?"

He watched George Williams slip the five-foot length of rope around the horse's neck and around the top plank of the chute to keep the horse's head up. He saw that Charley Metrose, the chute helper, had placed the flank strap, three inches wide and sheepskin-covered and designed to make the horse kick high behind, just in front of the hips and around the horse's barrel, and when he heard the crowd, almost in one voice, make that ooh-sound he knew that Don Sievertson had been thrown.

"So let's give Don Sievertson a hand, anyway!" Mel Lambert was saying.

He had climbed now to where he was standing with one foot on the inside of the gate, the other on the inside of the chute, straddling the horse. He spit on his hands and rubbed the inside of his chaps. He bent over and picked up the rein lying across the horse's neck and took it in his left hand between his third and little fingers and tightened his fist on it about two inches from where he had marked with the hairs from the mane. He would give the horse that much more head, that much more freedom, in his hope to get the best out of him, and he saw that the pickup men had caught Sievertson's loose horse.

With the rein still in his left hand and using the heel of that fist on the plank of the gate level with the saddle, his right hand on the top plank of the back of the chute, he lowered himself carefully down into the saddle. The horse was steady under him, not moving, and, as he slid his feet deep into the wood-and-metal stirrups he felt now the nervousness that he always feels at this moment. He was not afraid of being hurt, not nervous about his ability to ride the horse, only concerned that he would not be able to ride it the way he wanted to.

"Our next rider," Lambert announced, "is Jim Tescher of Medora, North Dakota, currently leading for the championship of the world!" And it was time.

He knew that behind him Goldie Carlton, the flank man, was holding the end of the flank strap and that, before dropping the end, he would allow the horse's momentum, as it started out of the gate, to pull it tight. He saw that outside the gate Charley Metrose had the end of the gate rope in his hand, waiting. Beyond him he saw that the arena was empty and he moved his feet and the stirrups forward so that both his spurs were in front of the points of the horse's shoulders. Here, by rule, they would have to remain until the horse's front feet hit the ground on the first jump out of the chute. He leaned back now, bringing his left hand grasping the rein up high and, with his right hand and careful not to make any sudden movement, he dropped the loose end of the rein over his left shoulder. Then, carefully, he squirmed deeper in the saddle and he was concentrating now and the nervousness was gone.

"All right," he said, "let's try the horse."

When he said this Charley Metrose jerked the gate open and George Williams dropped the neck rope and the horse wheeled to the left and out into the arena, its head down and its muscles bunching. He still had his spurs pressing against the horse's neck, concentrating on the right one from which the horse was turning, when the horse, snorting and breaking wind, made the first jump. As it hit on its front feet, the spurs still up there, he felt the saddle give. In that small part of a second he had the thought that he and the saddle were going over the horse's head, as he had gone over the head of that King Tut—he and the saddle and the halter, too—at Tulsa a couple of years before.

At that moment the hind feet hit and he had his spurs back and he was all right. He was in good shape again, the rein taut in his left hand, his right arm out for balance, his spurs forward again. The horse was ducking to the right now, instead of making the wide circle he had expected, and he knew his lick wasn't as full-stroking as it should be but at least he was in time with the horse. He sensed that his rein was correct, his left hand almost thinking for itself, neither throwing the horse's head away nor snubbing it. As he moved with the rise and fall of the horse, keeping his upper body parallel to the front legs, keeping his spurring strokes going, he was aware that it was almost as if he were trying to lift the horse under him into a bigger try. Then he was anticipating the ten-second klaxon, then expecting it, still spurring in rhythm, still hoping that the horse would just erupt under him, when he felt the horse make his first big turn to the left, and he heard the klaxon.

With the horse still bucking, he looked now for one of the pickup men. As he did he realized the horse was going for the wire fence. There it was—the eight-foot wire fence—right in front of him, when the horse turned left again and he shifted all of his weight into the right stirrup, kicked his left foot free, and, dropping the rein and reaching, grabbed with both hands the pipe along the top of the fence. The horse bucked away from him and, as he released his grip and dropped to the ground, he could hear the applause of ten thousand people cascading down around him from the stands.

"And here's a good score!" he heard Mel Lambert announcing. "The score on Jim Tescher is 52!"

He was walking along the fence line, to circle back around the end of the arena, and he knew it was not good enough. It was to turn out that he was right because, as he had figured, Bill Martinelli was to win it with a 74 on Peaceful, Ronnie Raymond would score 64 on Knott Inn, Floyd Baze would mark 63 on Sandhills, and three others would split fourth money with 58, but there would be other draws.

"You think your rein was all right?" George Williams was saying now.

"I sure do," he said, "but we shouldn't have slacked off on the cinch. On that first jump I thought I was goin' over his head."

On Sunday he would have to call his oldest boy. The boy would go into town to church and then have dinner with his grandparents and he could call him there.

"That's the best I ever saw him buck," George Williams said.

The boy would be disappointed, but maybe, if he should find that everything is all right at the ranch, and if his wife agreed, they might make Lubbock, Texas. And if they had to get back to the ranch there would still be another day. Maybe he could make Edmonton, up in Alberta, the next week.

"Will you tell me somethin'?" he said now, taking off his hat. "How can I get so sweated up in just ten seconds?"

The Twilight of Boxing

They're Dimming the Lights at Stillman's Gym

IT WAS A TYPICAL DAY at Stillman's Gym, on the west side of New York's Eighth Avenue between Fifty-fourth and Fifty-fifth streets. The place was crowded with fighters and managers and trainers—for this was a dozen years ago—and listening to them was like living something Damon Runyon had written.

Dumb Dan Morgan was talking with Francis Albertanti. Dan Morgan in his more than seventy years managed 150 prizefighters, including three world champions; Francis Albertanti was a sportswriter and later a boxing press agent.

Morgan was saying, "Let us talk about the old-timers, Napoleon and Brian Boru and—"

"Pete the Goat," Albertanti said.

Morgan kept on. "And what was the name of that guy at the bridge?"

"What guy?"

"The big gossoon who stood at the bridge and fought off the mob."

"Horatius," Albertanti said.

"That's right, and he ended up takin' a dive, didn't he?"

"Into the river," Francis Albertanti said. "But one day Pete the Goat . . ."

Now Morgan and Albertanti have passed on, and soon wreckers are going to tear down what is left of the Stillman's Gym I knew. A

The Saturday Evening Post, January 7, 1961.

year ago last July proprietor Lou Stillman sold it to Walter Scott & Company, New York real-estate agents, and in the near future the gym and adjoining property will be replaced by a twenty-story apartment house. Meanwhile, renamed "The Eighth Avenue Gym," it is being operated on a month-to-month basis by Irving Cohen, who managed Rocky Graziano to the middleweight title and is now the matchmaker for the St. Nicholas Arena in New York.

"I'm losing a hundred dollars a month," Cohen says, "not counting my time. I've offered it to every manager in the business, but nobody will take it."

Thus, unwanted if not unmourned, the most famous gymnasium in the world is passing from existence. To Stillman's came thousands of fighters from every continent but Antarctica, among them every heavyweight champion from Jack Dempsey through Floyd Patterson. Along with the fighters came some of the most ruthless and venal men I have ever known—and some of the kindest and most sincere. Stillman's was a circus of slapstick comedy and also a stage on which at any moment tragedy might appear. It was never a hangout for gangsters in the sense that they congregated there, although Jack (Legs) Diamond and Owney Madden and, in later years, Frankie Carbo occasionally were visitors.

The decline of boxing and the passing of its foremost atelier cannot be blamed, however, on gangsters. They plagued the fight game for more than thirty years, but boxing is dying of natural causes.

Once there were more than four hundred fight clubs in this country; last year there were fewer than forty that ran one boxing show or more. In 1946 the gross gate receipts from boxing in the United States were approximately $14,000,000, and in 1959 the figure was $4,100,500. In 1945 exactly 547,136 persons paid $2,263,259 to attend forty-three boxing shows in Madison Square Garden, and in 1959 there was a total of only 59,558 persons paying $123,699 at twenty-four shows.

Many other equally dismal comparisons can be made. Ten years ago the files of *The Ring*, boxing's leading publication, held the cards of

12,000 active professional boxers, 9,000 of them in this country. Presently there are cards for only 4,200 boxers, 3,000 of them Americans. Finally, where 350 fighters at a time once used Stillman's Gym, now there are just thirty-three who have paid the fifteen-dollars-a-month fee for a dressing room or the eight dollars for a locker.

The causes are three—economic, sociologic, and electronic. Boxing has always been a refuge for underprivileged minority groups, as is clear from the names and backgrounds of the great fighters over the years. First there were the great Irish boxers, and then came the Jewish, the Italian, and the Negro fighters. These have been times, however, of broader job opportunities and advancing social equality, and this has also been the era of free TV fight shows in the living room.

"There's too much work around," says Jersey Jones, assistant editor of *The Ring*. "A kid doesn't have to become a fighter. And in the old days, what did the average kid in the street have to look forward to? Baseball, if he lived near a vacant lot, or boxing. Golf was for old men, tennis for sissies, football was for college, and basketball was a YMCA and settlement house game. Now a kid says, 'Pop, how about the car tonight and ten bucks?'"

Says Nat Fleischer, editor of *The Ring*, who has been observing boxing for fifty-five years, "At the Olympics in Rome I watched two hundred and eighty fights from beginning to end. All ten members of the Italian team are going to turn pro, and they had five damned good boys and won three gold medals. France, however, had nobody worth a row of pins, and they must stay in the amateurs anyway until they've served in the military. In England only two are going to turn pro, and it's the same with the Americans, three of whom won gold medals. One boy wants to take a law course, another is making the Army his career.

"Ten years from now I expect to see only studio competition, with the public looking in on television. You can't give something away free and sell it too. What you'll have eventually will be mostly amateur boxing, with an occasional professional title fight. Boxing, as we have known it, is finished."

There is no place where the passing of boxing is as apparent or pathetic as at what used to be Stillman's. It is open daily except Sunday from noon until 3:00 P.M., but usually closes an hour earlier for lack of business. Monday through Friday it reopens from 4:30 until 8:00 in the evening to accommodate fighters who must hold other jobs to make a living.

Once it was open every day of the year from 11:30 A.M. until 5:00 P.M. "Yom Kippur and Christmas included," says Lou Stillman, who in forty-three years never took a vacation and one New Year's Day unlocked the folding iron grille across the entrance on Eighth Avenue while still wearing white tie and tails.

Although Stillman's was a New York landmark, it had a mobility that, say, the Empire State Building and Rockefeller Center lack. It started in 1917 on 125th Street in Harlem, moved four years later to its present address, then was transported successively to Seventh Avenue and Thirty-eighth Street and to Eighth Avenue and Fifty-seventh Street. In 1936 it came back to the second-floor loft where it is now expiring.

The gym and its longtime proprietor took their names from Marshall Stillman, a millionaire philanthropist. It was the original Stillman's idea to open a boxing center for criminals and teach them to use their fists instead of guns and knives. The possibility that the gym might simply teach them to use their fists in addition to their hardware was dismissed.

A private detective named Lou Ingber was hired as overseer. The clientele, most of whom had as little respect for surnames as they did for almost everything else, took to calling Ingber by the name of the establishment. Thus Lou Ingber became Lou Stillman.

Some years later he hired an assistant named Herman Salzman—now dead—whose identity went through an even stranger metamorphosis. This was the man who became known as Jack Curley. "My hair is curly since I'm seven years old," he once explained to me, "so they called me Curley. When I went to work for Lou Stillman, the guy who worked for him before me was called Jack. So they called me Jack for him and Curley for my hair. Jack Curley. Get it?"

The Marshall Stillman experiment, noble in concept, was short-lived, and Lou Stillman took over on a business basis. It is his opinion that the founder had aimed too high. "To get in," he says, "you couldn't be just any kind of a criminal. You had to serve time in a state prison. Those guys stole everything but my ears."

Having already sacrificed his name, but determined to preserve his auricles, Lou Stillman forsook idealism and adopted the fight mob. The mob, in search of suitable surroundings where fighters could exercise their muscles and managers their wiles, poured in. Stillman's became a center for fighters, managers, trainers, promoters, matchmakers, sportswriters, hangers-on, and the merely curious, the latter at 25 cents—later 50 cents—a head.

On the wall in the locker room Stillman posted two signs laying down the house rules. The first seemed to impose a penalty primarily on ineptitude.

ANYONE CAUGHT STEALING
WILL BE BARRED FOR LIFE

The second invoked legal authority.

WASH YOUR
DIRTY CLOTHES
BY ORDER OF THE
BOXING COMMISSION

"Big or small, champ or bum," Stillman explained at retirement, "I treated them all the same—bad. If you treat them like humans, they'll eat you alive."

The main room of the gym measures fifty feet by sixty-five feet and contains two rings, a half dozen rows of folding chairs, a bank of four phone booths, and a lunch counter. Two doors lead to the dressing room and lockers. An iron stairway rises to a balcony and a room used for bag punching and rope skipping and which has additional lockers.

The walls were once painted a dark gray, but they are darker now—where they are not chipped or peeling—after years of subjection to dust, steam, and tobacco smoke. Today they echo to the talk of perhaps a dozen trainers and their fighters and a dozen hangers-on, where once they reverberated to the cacophony of the greatest marketplace in sports, and to the applause of several hundred spectators if Primo Carnera or Rocky Graziano—the two all-time top attractions—was working out.

Over all this activity Stillman presided from a high stool placed near the rings and under the wall clock that timed the rounds. On a shelf by his shoulder stood a microphone—although there were those who held that the mike was just for show, that Stillman could be heard unamplified out on Eighth Avenue.

Stillman once said to me concerning a writer, "Where did he get off saying I got a garbage-can voice? Don't he know I put my son and my daughter through college and they got degrees?"

If one knew Stillman only in his métier as a volatile, quick-eyed, dagger-tongued dogmatist who could quickly force a main-bout heavyweight into servile submission, there is much one would not know about him. He is a different man in the comfort and quietude he shares with his wife in their Central Park West apartment. He doesn't drink and gave up smoking some years ago. For years his hobby was painting in oils.

These facets of his personality were never apparent when he was on the job. "Now boxing in Ring Number One," he announced into the microphone one afternoon, "Benito Mussolini."

"What's that fighter's real name?" I asked.

"Who cares?" Stillman said, possibly still suffering a traumatic aftermath of his experience with his own name. "Yesterday I introduced him as Hermann Göring. What difference does it make?"

"It might make a difference to the fighter," I suggested.

"Nah," Stillman said. "He's from Italy and he can't understand English. You know what they taught him to say in English?"

"I'd rather not hear it," I said.

"They taught him to say, 'You too.' That's all he can say. The other day I looked at him and I said, 'You know, you're a stupid-lookin' dope.' He smiled and said, 'You too.' The next time I saw him I said, 'You're all right. You're a nice guy.' Again he smiles and says, 'You too.'"

"That's pretty good," I said.

"I like it," Stillman said. "I don't know why, but I like it."

For a period of about five years I visited Stillman's on an average, I guess, of once a week. I went at first primarily to watch the fighters spar. Once you know a fighter's style, though, there isn't a great deal you can learn from his workouts. As much as anything, I kept going to the gym to listen to the talk and to witness the whole spectacle.

One of the most popular personalities ever to entertain the crowd there was Jimmy Grippo, the professional hypnotist and sleight-of-hand man. Grippo managed Melio Bettina to the New York State version of the light-heavyweight title. He was chiefly celebrated at Stillman's, however, as the only man who ever victimized the proprietor. One day, in the course of a handshake, he lifted Stillman's wristwatch. He apologized and then relieved him of his wallet.

"What's so great about that?" Stillman said afterward. "He once picked Herbert Hoover's pocket in the White House."

The house patsy was Battling Norfolk, a former heavyweight who made a living by rubbing down fighters after their workouts.

"You should have been here earlier," Stillman said to me one day. "They set up a tiger rug, head and all, in my office, and then they sent Norfolk in."

"I weren't scared," Norfolk said. "It just make me sick to my stomach."

Somebody else said, "How about the day when they called Norfolk on one of the phones and then put a rabbit in the booth with him and held the door? When Norfolk came out, his eyes were as big as cups, and he said, 'They put me in there with a monster.'"

"That make me sick to my stomach too," Norfolk said.

Norfolk's playmate for many years was Beezy Thomas, a diminutive escapee from the Congo who had jumped ship in New York. While Tony Canzoneri was lightweight champion of the world, Beezy was his court jester. Then he took to shining shoes at Stillman's and buddying with Norfolk until, for some reason, they had a falling out.

For two years neither spoke to the other. Finally agents of the United States Immigration and Naturalization Service caught up with Beezy. They took him to Ellis Island, but the day before they placed him aboard ship for his return home, they heeded his pleas and escorted him back to Stillman's for one last visit.

"You should go over and speak to Beezy and be nice to him," someone said to Norfolk. "You'll never see him again."

Beezy, flanked by two escorts, was standing at the lunch counter, his friends buying him all the coffee he could hold. Tears were running down his cheeks. Norfolk walked over to him and stood there for a moment, scratching his head.

"Beezy," he said finally, "why you cryin'?"

"Because they gonna deport me."

"Where they gonna deport you?"

"Back to the jungle," Beezy said, wiping the tears with his sleeve.

"What you gonna do there?" Norfolk said, apparently moved now.

"I don't know," Beezy said.

"I know," Norfolk said, shaking his head. "You ain't gonna do nothin'. All them old monkeys in the jungle, they forgot you. All them new ones, they never heard of you at all."

The scene, blending as it did the two basic ingredients of great theater—comedy and tragedy—still lives in the memories of witnesses after almost twenty years. In my own memory there are many unforgettable scenes, for I met at Stillman's greater teachers than I met in eighteen years of formal education. I came to know philosophers who never heard of Plato, Aristotle, Voltaire, or Kant, but found their own truths of life, and artists as dedicated to their own form of expression—boxing—as a man can be to any form.

No fighter I ever knew belonged more completely to boxing than Sidney Walker, whose ring name was Beau Jack. An illiterate Augusta, Georgia, shoeshine boy, he rose to New York State recognition as lightweight champion of the world. In twenty fights in Madison Square Garden he brought in $1,578,069.

Beau would be at Stillman's when it opened and he would be there when it closed. When he was not bag punching or rope skipping or boxing, his eyes would be fixed on those who were. After a fight, win or lose, he always would have the same question. "Were it a good fight?" he would ask. "Did the people like it?"

I once said to Beau in his dressing room at Stillman's, "I understand that you pray before every fight."

"That's right," he said, grinning.

"For what do you pray?"

"I pray that nobody get hurt. Then I pray it be a good fight."

"Don't you ever pray to win?"

"No," he said, shaking his head. "I would never do that."

"Why not?"

"Suppose I pray to win," he said. "The other boy, he pray to win too. Then what God gonna do?"

Beau retired five years ago after 112 fights. Now he is shining shoes again, at a Florida hotel. Recently I saw Chick Wergeles, who was one of Beau's managers, and I asked him about Beau.

"He's doin' fine," Chick said.

"How fine can he be doing?" I said. "He started as a shoeshine boy and he's a shoeshine boy again."

"But now when he shines shoes, he gets twenty bucks," Chick said. "Them guys with money, they want a former world's champion to shine their shoes, so they ask for Beau."

Then there is Harry Lenny. He and his brother Eddie were lightweights during the early years of this century. Later Harry became one of the truly fine teachers of boxing, a manager of fighters and the first white man to work in Joe Louis's corner. No longer active at Stillman's, he is also a faith healer and a masseur—he gave Franklin D.

Roosevelt sixteen massage treatments at Hyde Park and in the White House.

Roosevelt, of course, was his favorite president. His favorite fighter was Joe Gans, the old Negro lightweight champion who was, perhaps, the greatest boxer, pound for pound, of all time.

"I once had an operation," Harry was telling me one day, walking down the stairs from Stillman's. "I was lyin' there in the hospital, coming out of the ether, and do you know what I saw?"

"No," I said.

"It was the most beautiful sight I ever saw in my life," Harry said. "There was this pure blue sky, and I could see right up into it. In the middle of the sky was a circle of white lights, and in the middle of that light I was boxin' with Gans."

Also prominent at Stillman's has been Charley Goldman, who had more than four hundred fights as a bantamweight. He stands five feet one inch and has two broken hands and a broken nose. He has trained four world champions.

"How are you making out with that fighter from Massachusetts?" I asked him on one occasion at Stillman's.

"He's just a beginner," Charley said. "I had him here one Sunday because the C.Y.O. gym was closed, but I keep him down there because he looks so crude that, around here, somebody might laugh.

"He scares me, though," Charley reflected, thinking about it. "I mean, he does so many things wrong, but I'm scared to change him much because, trying to give him something else, I might take away what he's got."

Charley Goldman, who is now the athletic director of a Florida hotel, never took away from what the fighter had. Carefully he molded him into the only undefeated heavyweight champion of the world, for the fighter was, of course, Rocky Marciano.

Another perceptive figure on the Stillman scene was Ray Arcel, who has worked with thousands of fighters—sixteen of them champions—over a period of forty years.

"The one place I don't want a boy to get hurt," he told me once, tapping himself over the heart, "is here. You can close a cut. You can set a broken nose or a broken hand. But you can't repair a boy's spirit—and when he's through with boxing and walks out of this place for the last time, he's going to need it."

For the past five years Ray Arcel has been the purchasing agent for a manufacturing plant in New Brunswick, New Jersey. In the mid-thirties, when he and Whitey Bimstein worked as a team, they trained as many as forty fighters at a time. Whitey is still in boxing, but he and his present associate, Freddie Brown, are handling only ten men.

"Today there's nothin' around," Freddie Brown was saying on a recent day at Stillman's. "I mean, if a fighter's got a title, he can get, maybe, a hundred thousand from the television sponsor. The guy who fights him gets a good purse, but what about the rest of the fighters? For a regular fight, if a guy's lucky to be on TV, he gets four thousand and a few bucks from the gate. But with no small clubs runnin', where are you gonna take a kid so he can make some money and so he can learn?"

"Learn?" said Doc Moore, who has been around boxing since 1905. "Today most of them managers and trainers sic a fighter like he was a dog. You go in each corner, and they're sayin', 'Go in there and get him.' They destroy fighters."

It was 5:30 in the afternoon. Upstairs, in front of his locker, a twenty-two-year-old welterweight named Bobby Bartels was getting out of his street clothes and into his ring gear. He was born in Queens, a borough of New York City, and still lives there. Since he turned professional in June of 1958 he has had sixteen fights, winning eleven, losing four, and boxing one draw. During the past year he had four fights, winning two and losing two. His purses totaled $2,835.

"For one fight," his manager, Al Serra, said, "he got a hundred and fifty-six dollars, so I let him keep it all. His last two fights he got more, but he didn't have a fight in eight months, so I only took a small cut.

"Then you got expenses. The gym costs eight dollars a month. He uses fifty cents' worth of bandages and tape every night for his hands. A pair of big gloves every year costs twenty-five dollars. Two pairs of shoes a year cost fifteen dollars a pair. The headgear costs twenty-five dollars. The speed bag costs fifteen dollars and the swivel nine dollars, and he's had three bags since 1958. Then you got trunks and sweatsuits, and we give twenty-five dollars to a sparring partner for the last week and a half before a fight."

"How can you live on that?" I asked the fighter.

"I work," he said. "That's why I train at night. That's why they got the gym open nights now, because so many fighters have to work."

A high-school graduate, Bartels works on one of the Hudson River piers as an office clerk. Each morning he gets up at 5:30 and does his roadwork in Astoria Park, under the Triborough Bridge. After he has showered and had breakfast, he takes the subway to the pier, where he works from 9:00 until 4:30. Then he takes the subway to the gym, where he works out for two hours. At 10:30 he is asleep.

"Why did you want to be a fighter?" I asked him as I have asked dozens in Stillman's.

"My father fought in the amateurs," he said, "and my uncle was a sparring partner for Harry Greb. I wasn't a tough guy, but somehow I used to get into fights, so my father said, 'Try it. Make some money.'"

"When you were growing up, did you have any heroes among the fighters?" I asked.

"Sure," he said. "Tony Pellone. Did you ever know him?"

"I remember Tony," I said.

Tony Pellone was a welterweight who was not overly gifted, but who tried hard and made good fights. He grew up in New York's Greenwich Village, one of eleven brothers and two sisters. One of the girls was killed by a bus when she was three years old.

"My mother wants to adopt another little girl," Pellone told me one day at Stillman's.

"With twelve children," I said, "she wants to adopt another?"

"I got a good mother," Pellone said.

"What do you do with your money?" I asked him.

"Whatever money I make I always take home to my old man. At first I didn't make much, but I'd give it to my old man, and he'd give me five dollars out of it. Then the time I fought Bob Montgomery in the Garden I got eight thousand five hundred and thirteen bucks for my end. So I took it home and I give it to my old man, and he said to me in Italian, 'How you fixed?' and I said, 'I'm broke.' 'All right,' he said, 'here.' He gives me the thirteen dollars. I said, 'Hey, thirteen is unlucky. Give me fourteen dollars instead.' Then my old man said, 'No, give me one dollar back. That makes twelve.'"

I didn't tell these stories about Pellone to Bobby Bartels, the new fighter who used to admire him. "What other heroes did you have among fighters?" I asked Bartels.

"I didn't know much about Rocky Graziano when he was fighting," he said, "but I saw that movie they made of his life—*Somebody Up There Likes Me*. I think that made me want to be a fighter too. It made me feel good—that you could come up from nothing, like he did."

Graziano, of course, was one of the top personalities at Stillman's. His dressing room was always crowded with courtiers from the Lower East Side. One of them was a bespectacled little man named Barney, who wore a cap and played the harmonica.

"Wait'll you hear this guy," Graziano would say. "This guy's terrific."

Barney always played the same three numbers—"Beer Barrel Polka," "Darktown Strutters' Ball," and "Bugle Call Rag." The last he would play while standing at attention, saluting with his left hand and blowing on the harmonica through his nostrils.

"Ain't he great?" Graziano would ask. "Why can't you get this guy a job?"

"Doing what?" I asked once.

"In a nightclub," Graziano said. "Wouldn't they like him?"

Things are different now for present-day fighters such as Bobby Bartels. "Maybe there isn't much money to be made any more," Bartels told me, "but I figured I'd give it a try anyway. After all, I still got my regular job."

"Listen," his manager said. "This kid, if he don't lose his head and boxes like I show him, might go all the way."

"I hope so," I said.

I walked down the stairs to the main gym. In the big, quiet room two lightweights were sparring under the two naked lightbulbs over the first ring. Another fighter was doing sit-ups on the table behind the rings, and Frank Percoco was standing behind the empty rows of chairs and talking with the current proprietor, Irving Cohen. It was Percoco who used the hard edge of a quarter to open a swelling over Rocky Graziano's eye when Rocky was virtually blinded during his middleweight-title fight with Tony Zale in Chicago in 1947. Graziano went on from there to win sensationally by a knockout. He fought profitably for five more years, sold his life story to Hollywood for $240,000, and became a television performer.

"Have you still got that quarter from Chicago?" I asked Percoco.

"Sure," he said. "You don't think I'd let go of that, do you?"

"I never knew of twenty-five cents that paid off at such a price," I said.

"The way things are going," Percoco said, "I may have to blow it on a hamburger yet."

"Listen," Irving Cohen said. "We had a good prospect came in here the other day. I swear he must have been sixty years old. He said he wanted to train, and I asked him, 'For what?' He said he feels that if he gets in shape, he can lick Floyd Patterson. I had to think quick and I told him that we have an age limit. I told him no one over thirty-five can train here, and since he looked at least thirty-seven, he was out."

"You should have held on to him," Percoco said. "We may have to use that kind yet."

When I left them and walked out through the dimly lit hall and down the dark stairs to Eighth Avenue, I wondered if I would ever again come back to what remains of Stillman's Gym.

★ AMONG THE MONUMENTS ★

The Shy One

The Quiet Power of Floyd Patterson

"Floyd is a kind of a stranger."

Cus D'Amato, 1954

ON THE TELEPHONE two nights before, he had told me to turn off the New York Thruway at the New Paltz exit and then left on Route 299. He has said that I should follow that through the town, across a railroad track and over a bridge, and then take the first road on the right.

"What's the name of the road?" I had asked.

"Springtown Road," he had said. "You go half a mile to a fork and then take the right. Two-tenths of a mile after that it's the first house on the left."

"And what time do you want me to show up?"

"Three o'clock," he had said. "I'm looking at my schedule. I may have an appointment, something to do, for a half hour at three thirty, but three o'clock is all right."

It was just after 2:00 when I turned off the Thruway. There was a motel off to the left, but I decided to drive into the town and, perhaps, find one that would be closer and more a part of the town.

The terrain there, west of the Hudson and just south of the Catskill Mountains, is hilly, and the town, with Route 299 as its main street, spreads down over the western slope of a ridge. The stores, restaurants, and other places of business are close-packed on both sides of

---

Chapter 1 of *Once They Heard the Cheers*, 1979.

the steeply slanting street that was congested now with traffic, and off to the south and on the crest of the ridge there is a multistoried high-rise, an architectural aberration erected without regard for the still-rural nature of the countryside. Seeing it towering alone there on the ridge like the beginning in New Paltz of a new Bronx, I surmised that it would turn out to be a part of the college, a branch of the State University of New York.

Coming down off the ridge, the road crosses the railroad tracks with the old wooden station on the right, and there was a sign on the station offering it for rent. Beyond the tracks I drove over the bridge and out onto the flat of a valley with farming lands on both sides of the blacktop road. Ahead I could see another blacktop to the right, and when I reached it and saw the Springtown Road sign I backed around and drove the way I had come and back up the hill through the town.

There was a small motel on the left, and when I got to the top of the hill I pulled off and into a gas station. The attendant came out, a young man with red hair and wiping his hands on a rag.

"Fill it up?" he said.

"Please," I said, "and maybe you can tell me something. Do you know where Floyd Patterson lives?"

I wanted to get an idea of how well a former heavyweight champion of the world, this former heavyweight champion of the world, might be known in his adopted town. He had always run from renown, and even as champion had sought seclusion. The fame that came with his title seemed to embarrass him, as if he could never forget that he was a refugee from the black ghetto of the Bedford-Stuyvesant section of Brooklyn. As a child, he had been so shy that he could never look others in the eye and so maladjusted that only special schooling saved him. I liked him very much because, although he was always so serious—even appearing troubled—that I never heard him laugh, his observations were perceptive and reflected a supreme sensitivity, and his answers were honest. He always seemed to me, though, to be the most miscast of fighters, for while he had the physical attributes to be a fighter—always excepting his inability to absorb a heavyweight's big punch—he also had the compassion of a priest, and I never knew anyone else in sports whose antennae were so attuned to the suffering of others.

"Are you bothered by the sight of blood?" I asked him once.

"How do you mean?" Patterson said.

"Have you ever been scared, as a child or since, when you've been cut?"

I asked this question because a fighter must regard lightly the changes his profession makes upon his physical person. He must also be relatively unaffected by the hurt he inflicts upon others.

"No," he said. "I've seen my blood flow from me when I was younger. One time I got a nail stuck in my foot, and I kept it there for three hours, until my mother came home from work. You see, there was this lady babysitting for us, and I was scared to tell her about the nail because she was very mean and she would beat you. So when I got this nail in my foot I kept it there and stayed in the front room for three hours until my mother came home and I told her about it."

"What about seeing blood on others?" I said.

"On somebody else?" he said. "Well, this hasn't happened lately, but in the wintertime, when it's cold and my nose feels cold, I'd sometimes see two people fighting in the street. I'd actually see a guy with a big fist hit another guy square on the nose or face. You know?"

"Yes."

"Well," he had said, "when I'd see that, I'd feel it myself. It really seemed that I could actually feel it, and I would rather be fighting the one guy and taking the punishment than to see the other guy taking it, because I could just imagine how it feels to get hit when you're cold like that."

He was that way in the ring, staying away from a cut when he opened one on an opponent. The day of his second fight with Ingemar Johansson they weighed in at noon at the Commodore Hotel. The big room was crowded with sportswriters and photographers and members of the fight mob, and I was talking with Johnny Attell, who had been matchmaker around New York for many years, when Billy Conn, who had been one of the best of the all-time light heavyweights and enough of a heavyweight to give Joe Louis one of his toughest fights, walked over.

"Who do you like tonight, Bill?" Attell said to him.

"Me?" Conn said. "I like the Swede for his punch."

"I don't know," Attell said, shrugging. "Patterson's got the equipment to take him if he fights him right."

"You hear what somebody had Patterson say?" Conn said.

"What?" Attell said.

"Patterson said that when he gets a guy cut he lays off the eye and hits him in the belly," Conn said. "You know somebody told him to say that, because he'd pour salt in a cut if he could."

"No he wouldn't," Attell said.

"Are you kidding?" Conn said.

"No," Attell said. "This guy Patterson is really that way."

"Then he's got no business being a fighter," Conn said.

But he was a fighter, an Olympic champion, and then the youngest ever to win the heavyweight championship of the world and the first ever to regain it. I hadn't seen him to talk to since 1963, before the second of his two fights with Sonny Liston, in which he never got by the first round. Liston, I knew beforehand, would out-body and bully him, and I had given Patterson no chance, and then on television I had watched Muhammad Ali humiliate him twice. Howard Cosell, who knew him well and had seen much of him while Patterson's career was running down, had written in his own autobiography that Patterson had come to live off martyrization and sympathy. Then I had heard that he had been appointed to the New York State Athletic Commission and was living in New Paltz, and I wondered how he was totaling the wins and losses of his life.

"Floyd Patterson?" the attendant said now. "Sure."

"You know where he lives?"

"Sure," he said, pointing. "You go down through town here and across the steel bridge and you take the first right. That's Springtown

Road. At the fork you take a right, and I think it's the second house on the left."

I was thinking that no, Floyd said it was the first house on the left, and the young man's earnestness and sincerity made me a little ashamed of my deceit.

"Fine," I said, "and tell me something else. Is that motel beyond the top of the hill the best around here?"

"Right," he said. "That's a good one."

I checked into the "good one" that would have been better if someone had washed the woodwork in recent time. When I turned the thermostat on the air conditioner-heater the sound that came from behind the bent vanes of the grill low on the wall was of a spin-dry washer gurging a load of nuts, bolts, and aluminum pie pans. The bathroom had been scrubbed clean, however, and overall, it was an improvement over some of the places where I had known Patterson while he was a fighter.

First there was the Gramercy Gym, on East Fourteenth Street in Manhattan, with the two flights of stairs that groaned and gave underfoot and led up between the mustard-colored walls that were dusty with soot and stained with grime. At the top of the stairs, and low in the door into the gym, there was a jagged hole covered with heavy wire mesh, and behind the door and snarling through the mesh there was a German shepherd that Patterson or Cus D'Amato, who managed him, would chain in a back room before they would let a visitor in. D'Amato reasoned that this approach would weed out the faint-hearted who just thought they might like to be fighters.

Then there was La Ronda, in the woods outside of Newtown, Connecticut, where Patterson lived and where he trained almost as a recluse most of the time, for nine months through the autumn of 1959 and the following winter and spring, to get his title back from Ingemar Johansson. It was an otherwise abandoned roadhouse that was owned and had been operated by Enrique Madriguera, who had finished second to Xavier Cugat in the battle of the big Latin dance bands. Set into the wall beneath the stairway to the second floor there was a cracked ornamental tile of a young boy playing a violin, and that had been Madriguera when he had been a child prodigy, and once, scattered amid the debris in the backyard, I had found pages of sheet music, blowing in the wind. The place was infested with rats that Patterson shot with a .22. While Johansson lived in a private cottage at Grossinger's, the luxury resort in the Catskills, and had his meals served in style, Patterson and Dan Florio, his trainer, cooked for themselves and the sparring partners in the vast kitchen and on the big ranges and in the oversized pots and pans that had been intended to hold the Iberian edibles for the multitudes of music lovers and conga dancers who never came.

When I turned onto Springtown Road now for the second time, I went to the fork and took the road to the right. I watched the odometer, and after two-tenths of a mile, as Patterson had said, on the left on a rise beyond a field of golden-brown stubble, I saw the two-storied, white-shingled house. The blacktop driveway rises for almost a hundred yards between tall pines, and as I drove up it I saw the two gray metal boxes, one on either side of the driveway amid the trees. At the top I turned left and parked by a stone wall in front of the garage doors under the house, and got out. There was an off-white dog of good size and indefinite breeding confronting me and barking at me as I got out of the car, and I could hear a male voice calling.

"Cotton! Cotton! C'mere, Cotton!"

It was Patterson's voice, and as the dog turned from me and started up the steps toward the back of the house, I followed it. Patterson was holding an aluminum combination storm and screen door open, and when the dog disappeared inside, he came out and we shook hands. He was wearing freshly laundered blue jeans and an immaculate white T-shirt, and he didn't look much heavier at age forty-one than he had at age twenty-five when, that night in the Polo Grounds, he landed that wide left hook on Johansson's jaw and became the first fighter ever to regain the heavyweight title.

"Nobody can sneak up on you here," I said.

"That's right," he said.

"I mean with the dog and those boxes down on the driveway. Is that a warning device?"

"It rings a bell in our bedroom," he said. "It's mostly for at night."

He was the third oldest of eleven children, born into poverty and an overcrowded world that he found frightening and from which, from his earliest years on, he tried to escape. Once he told me that when he was six he used to hide all day in the basement of P.S. 25, the school he was supposed to be attending. As he became older, and when he had the eighteen cents for admission, he hid in the Regent and Apollo and Banko movie theaters, and some nights he slept in Prospect Park and others in subway stations.

"You have a lovely home here," I said.

He had led me through the kitchen and the dining room and, off the entry hall, into a family room. There was a twenty-foot fieldstone, mahogany-topped bar curving in front of the far wall, the mounted heads of two mountain goats above it, the windows behind it looking out onto the driveway. Across the entry hall I could see the living room, with a baby grand piano, and I was impressed by the orderliness of everything, the furniture precisely placed and none of the incidental leavings of daily living lying about.

"It's nice," he said.

"How many rooms are there?" I said.

"Well," he said, "there's four bedrooms, one play room, the living room, the kitchen, the dining room, the bar room, and four baths."

"Does your wife have help?"

"Help?" he said.

"Someone who comes in to clean?" I said, and his own mother, whom I remember as a serene, soft-spoken, and sensitive woman, had been a domestic before she found a job in a Brooklyn bottling factory.

"Nope," Patterson said. "I help her."

"How much land do you have?"

"Forty acres," he said, and he walked to a window and pointed down at the field between the house and the road, the grass stubble in it that golden brown in the sunlight. "You see that field? I did it with a hand scythe and with a handsaw, all summer long."

"That's good," I said, "but what's that monstrosity over there on the ridge?"

"The what?" he said.

"That tower," I said.

"Oh, that's the college."

"That figures," I said. "We're trying to teach people to live with the environment and not abuse it, and a college does that."

A yellow school bus had stopped at the foot of the driveway. Two small girls had got out and were starting to walk up the drive.

"That's my daughters," he said. "They go to the Duzine School. That's the public school, what they call the Duzine School, but next year they'll go to the Catholic school in Rosendale, and I'll have to drive them over."

"You don't like the public school?"

We had walked back from the window. He was sitting on one of the bar stools, and I was sitting on another.

"The public school's all right here," he said, "but New Paltz was number two in the nation for drugs. Los Angeles was number one."

"Can that be correct?" I said.

"That's right," he said. "Three or four years ago I read it in the *Daily News*. That's why I started my boxing club. The Huguenot Boxing Club."

I had read somewhere that he was training young amateur fighters. As a fighter himself he was prone to errors, as the naturally gifted in anything often are. In most of his fights, however, his great hand speed and mobility covered his mistakes and let him get away with them although, of course, they were still there.

"There's this Father Daniel O'Hare," he said, "and he's the founder. It's called AMEN—Americans Mobilized to End Narcotics—and he founded it. He used to be in the rectory here, and about three years ago I got to know him. He's now in the rectory in Newburgh, and he's a very down-to-earth priest. I've gotten to know him so close that sometimes I say a word you don't say to a priest."

"I know what you mean."

"I joined up two years ago, and he takes care of the educational parts, and I take the physical."

"About this drug problem," I said. "I keep reading that it's been with us always. Were there drugs around when you were growing up?"

"No," he said, "the only thing was cigarettes."

"Not even in Bedford-Stuyvesant?"

"Nope," he said. "There were no drugs around in the fifties, but I remember as a youngster I was always getting in trouble, stealing fruit and, from the five-and-ten, small stuff. Who knows what I'd be now if it wasn't for boxing."

"You're not the only one," I said.

"So I opened the boxing club," he said. "If you give a youngster something to do that he enjoys, he won't hang around on corners."

"That's right."

"About a year and a half ago," he said, "I opened the gym in this building right out here. It was a barn and a chicken hatchery, and I took young and old. Then I said I was going to close it because they were abusing the equipment, but my wife told me things I didn't know."

In 1956 Patterson had married Sandra Hicks, when he was twenty-one and she was eighteen, and they had three children. I had heard that they had been divorced, and that Patterson had married a white woman, and that they had two daughters, the two girls I had seen starting up the driveway.

"My wife is very personable," he was saying now. "She talks to all, and they tell her things they wouldn't tell me. She told me about this Thruway attendant who had a couple of kids, and every night he used to stop at a bar on the way home. Since he got into the boxing here, he hadn't done that, and I kept the gym open."

"How old are these fighters?"

"The one I told you about is twenty-one. He was about nineteen then, and I have several fifteen-year-olds. I have one—Andrew Schott—who feels as I did. It's like a religion. The kid is here every day. He has had twenty-five fights, and he can recall every fight he's had. There's no chance of him ever getting involved in drugs."

"How many of them," I said, "do you take to tournaments and get fights for?"

"There are fifteen actual fighters," he said. "Then there are two firemen from Poughkeepsie and a councilman from Rosendale that work out and spar to keep in shape. The councilman lost forty-five pounds, and he's been coming here a year and a half, and the gym is open seven days a week, except when we have fights."

"I would think that the town would appreciate what you're doing," I said.

"I like the town," he said, "and I like the people. I have no trouble whatsoever with the people in general, the old as well as the young, as long as I keep away from politics."

"You have a right to be interested in politics," I said.

"It would cause a lot of flak," he said. "Everybody knows me as just plain Floyd. I'm liked by most people, but not by all. No one has done anything to harm me, but I know, given the opportunity, the ones who don't like me would hurt me. I don't know how to say it, and I don't want to say it."

"But you went down to Alabama with Jackie Robinson at the time of all the trouble in Birmingham and Selma," I said.

"Jackie asked me," he said. "A lot of name people went, and I remember landing at the airport and for the first time in my life I saw different restrooms for blacks and whites. I took movie pictures of the signs—actually there was no film in the camera—so the people would know it was unusual to me, and I was taking it back."

His two daughters were standing in the doorway, and he called them in and introduced them—Janene, who was nine, and Jennifer, seven. We shook hands, the older one looking right at me, and the younger, her head down, examining me out of the tops of her eyes.

"How is school?" I said.

"Fine," the older one said.

"Excuse us a minute," Patterson said. "I have to ask my wife something."

He left, with the girls following him, and I walked around the room, looking at his two championship belts, the plaques and trophies he had been awarded, and the framed photographs. There were pictures of him with Eartha Kitt, Jimmy Durante, Harry Belafonte, Jack Palance, Bob Hope, Jackie Gleason, Lauren Bacall, one with James Cagney and Roland Winters that I remembered being taken at Newtown, and another, taken in the White House, with Patterson, his wife, and their two girls standing with Richard Nixon. There was, also framed, the gatefold I had put together for *The Fireside Book of Boxing* in 1961 of pictures of all the heavyweight champions in succession from John L. Sullivan through Patterson. I had discovered three photographs that, when placed together, showed the crowd of eighty thousand crammed into Boyle's Thirty Acres in Jersey City on July 2, 1921, for the Dempsey–Carpentier fight, the first million-dollar gate. I needed something for the other side of the fold, and lined up photographs of all the twenty champions in their fighting poses, Patterson twice and on either side of Johansson.

On a shelf at the right of the bar were record albums of Percy Faith, Johnny Mathis, Roger Williams, Jackie Gleason, André Kostelanetz, Hank Williams, and Jo Stafford, the music I remember Patterson listening to in his training camps. Behind the bar the glasses were neatly aligned, the only bottles being two fifths of Seagram's Crown Royal, the tax seals on them unbroken.

"Do you do much business at this bar?" I asked, when Patterson came back.

"It was here when we bought the house," he said. "Like those animal heads up there. My wife takes a drink now and then, but I can't stand the smell of the stuff."

"Don't fight it," I said.

"I was going to have an appointment, like at three thirty," he said, "but the man didn't come. He's the piano teacher, and I told him, 'I'll call you if I'm not going to be here today.' I just called him now to see where he was, and he assumed I would call if I wanted him to come."

"Who's taking the lessons?"

"My daughters and I. I take them because Jennifer is a perfectionist, and she hates to make a mistake and she won't play in front of the teacher. She has taken one lesson and Janene has taken three and I've taken three, and Jennifer plays better than both of us. She's the only one who doesn't have to look at the keys, so I reasoned I should take lessons with her and maybe that would help her.

"She's a natural athlete, too," he said. "She has tremendous coordination, but she hates to be the center of attraction. I remember when she was small and her birthday came and we got her a cake. My wife and I and my older daughter started to sing and she was crying, 'Don't! Don't!'

"In the school she'll play all the games with team participation, but when it comes to her doing it alone, she won't do it. She took ballet. The teacher, he told me she was fantastic, the best of all, and he had about fifty between the ages of six and twelve, but we took her out because she wouldn't do it alone in front of the others."

"I think I can understand that," I said.

"It's understandable to a certain degree," he said.

"I mean," I said, "that I remember a fella who was very shy."

"Yes," he said. "I know."

It was only three weeks after he had knocked out Archie Moore to win the heavyweight championship and it was just before Christmas, but he was back in training at the Long Pond Inn at Greenwood Lake, New York. The inn burned to the ground some years ago, but there used to be a bar and restaurant on the first floor with the living quarters and the gymnasium over it. When I checked with Ollie Cromwell, who was one of the owners and tended bar, he said that Patterson was up in his room, and I went up there where he was lying on the bed and listening to that music, and we shook hands.

"What time is it?" he said.

"One o'clock," I said.

"I'll be down in the dining room in a half hour," he said.

I waited in the dining room for three and a half hours. As I sat there, the place came alive with teenagers who had been ice skating on the lake, and who had come in to play the jukebox and dance. Finally, at 4:30, one of Patterson's sparring partners came in and walked over to the table where I was sitting.

"Floyd says he'll meet you in the gym in five minutes," the sparring partner said. "He apologizes."

"That's fine," I said, annoyed. "Where has he been?"

"Up in the room," the sparring partner said. "He came down a couple of times, but when he saw all these kids here, he went back. He was embarrassed to come in."

I said nothing about it when I met him in the gym, but two nights later we were standing and talking by the pool table beyond the bar. A couple of sparring partners were shooting pool, and I was working Patterson around slowly when I mentioned it, trying to get him to elaborate on the feelings he had had when he saw the dining room jumping with those kids.

"You're heavyweight champion of the world now," I said. "Doesn't that give you the security to walk through a room of teenagers?"

"No," he said. "I still don't like to be stared at."

I thought of John L. Sullivan, this country's first sports hero, who used to stride into saloons and announce, "I can lick any man in the world!" The next morning we were standing in front of the Long Pond Inn, waiting for one of the sparring partners who had been sent to town to buy the morning newspapers, when I came back to it.

"But you're going to be stared at a lot," I said.

"I know," Patterson said.

"When did you first realize that this was going to be a problem?"

"The day after I won the title," he said. "Just before the fight my wife gave birth to our daughter, so right after the fight, these friends and I, we got in the car to drive back from Chicago. The next day we stopped at one of those roadside restaurants and went in. By then the fight was all over the pages of the newspapers, pictures and all, and I could see the people around the place recognizing me and starting to whisper. I figured we better get out of there quick, so we didn't even finish our meal."

Just before he won the title, Patterson had bought a ten-room house in Mount Vernon, New York, for his mother and the eight youngest of her eleven children. After Patterson beat Moore, the mayor of the city, who was an ex-fighter, staged a torchlight parade for him, and I asked Patterson what that was like.

"I was ashamed," he said.

"Why?" I said.

"Me sitting in an open car and waving to people," he said. "Those are things you only see kings and presidents doing."

A heavyweight champion has to spend some of his time banquet hopping, and Cus D'Amato made Patterson buy a tuxedo. He said it embarrassed him to wear it because, in his view, formal clothes were for those who had been born and raised to them, and he was not. When he was not in camp he lived with his wife and daughter in St. Albans, on Long Island, and he would do roadwork in a park there a couple of days a week.

"What time do you run?" I asked him once.

"I get up at five thirty, so I finish before the people start to work and see me," he said.

"Doesn't anybody ever see you?" I said.

"Usually I run on Saturday and Sunday when everybody don't get up so early," he said, "but one day I ran during the week. It was a Thursday, and after I finished in the park the fella who was supposed to pick me up was late. About an hour passed before he came, and there I was sitting on the park bench with my heavy clothes on and all sweaty and a towel around my neck. All these people were going to work by then, and they were looking at me like I was crazy."

"Didn't anyone recognize you?" I said.

"No," he said. "I was the champion, so I hid my face."

"Shyness is so deeply ingrained in you," I said to him another night at the Long Pond, "that I suppose one of your earliest memories is of being embarrassed in public."

"I guess that's right," he said. "I remember when I was just a little kid. I used to have long hair and my father would comb it. Then he'd send me around the corner for cigarettes, and I remember one day a lady stopping me and running her fingers through my hair. I was so embarrassed that I wanted to cry, and I ran."

He thought about it. It was after dinner and we were still sitting at the table.

"I had to be just a tiny kid for a lady to do that," he said, "but I never forgot it."

So all of that was twenty years before, and now he was supplying a gym and running a boxing club to provide a port for the young of the area who need it. At forty-one he was starting to take piano lessons to help a daughter in whom he saw himself.

"I hope she can come out of it by herself," he said now. "The first time somebody asked me for my autograph there were like twenty people waiting, and the guy gave me the piece of paper and I forgot how to spell my own name. I got a mental block."

"I remember you saying how long it took you to be able to look people in the eye."

"It took years," he said, "and I don't want her to have to go through what I went through. When I came back from the Olympics—and I won the Olympics when I was seventeen—I went to a dinner and they handed me a microphone. I panicked. Fortunately the gentleman before me had said something, and I stopped to think about that and I commented. Thousands of microphones have been handed to me since then, and it's easier, but it's never easy."

"I recall," I said, "how you used to say that someday you wanted to own a place in the country and have horses. Do you own horses?"

"No," he said. "We've got three dogs and a cat and we travel. I take the family wherever I go, to England, to Sweden, to Portugal, to Spain, and to get somebody to take care of horses, too, would be too difficult.

Even for me it would be difficult, because I devote so much time to my family. I get up with the kids, and I put them to bed at night. I try to do as much with them as I can, because in my first marriage that was lacking. I was in camp all the time."

"How are your other children?"

"My son spent three weeks with me this summer, and he's thirteen now. The two daughters I see occasionally, but they live in Springfield, Massachusetts, and I don't see them as much as I'd like."

"How did you meet your present wife?" I asked.

"Janet?" he said. "It's strange how I met her. After I had re-won the title—not right then but in 1962—the secretary I had got married. I used to get thousands of letters, and I needed someone to answer the mail. I have this friend, Mickey Allen . . ."

"I remember him. He wanted to be a singer, and once you arranged for him to sing the National Anthem at one of your fights."

I remember how pleased and excited about it Allen was. He reasoned that the exposure on national television would launch him on his vocal career.

"That's right," Patterson said. "He owns a discothèque and a catering service now, and he said, 'My wife's sister can type. She was secretary to the vice president of the New York Stock Exchange.' So she worked for me once a week, and that's how I met her. She was born in Rosedale, New York, but her parents moved to Greenwood Lake. I have a house right here for her parents when they come here, and they may stay a week or a month."

"I'd like to meet your wife," I said, "and I'm wondering if I might take you both to dinner tonight?"

"That would be nice," he said, "but I'm not sure. There's this seventy-five-year-old woman my wife got to know, and she just lost her husband. She's lonely, and I know it's on the calendar that we're supposed to visit her tonight. Maybe she can change it to tomorrow night, and I'll ask her."

He went out and I walked around the room again reading the inscriptions on the plaques, and there was a framed hand-lettered quotation from Vince Lombardi that had been presented to Patterson by the 501st Replacement Detachment of the First Armored Division. It was about making winning a habit, even as losing can be, and about doing things right not once in a while but all of the time.

"I'm sorry," Patterson said when he came back. "My wife says the lady is expecting us, and she's very lonely and she doesn't want to disappoint her. She's sorry."

"I understand," I said.

"It's time I went over to the gym," he said. "You want to come along?"

"Yes, indeed," I said.

We walked out through the entry hall and the dining room and into the kitchen. The two girls were in the kitchen.

"I'm going over to the gym now," Patterson said to them, "and you lock the storm door after us. All right?"

Outside he turned and waited while one of them locked the door. We walked across the parking area at the top of the driveway to the white-painted two-story barn. The ring is on the first floor, with stairs leading up to the loft, like a balcony, overhanging the first floor. In the loft were a couple of heavy punching bags and one light bag and two full-length mirrors. At the back of the loft is the dressing room with steel lockers, and there was a hand-printed notice on the wall:

TO ALL CLUB MEMBERS
Do Not Invite Anyone To The Gym Without
First Telling Me—I Do Not Want Strangers
Wandering Around My House—Casing the
Place—Should Anyone Violate This I Will
Have To Ask Them To Leave.

There were four young fighters, who seemed to be in their teens, undressing in front of the lockers and getting into their ring trunks and boxing shoes. It had been chilly all day and it was cold in the locker room and, after he had stripped, Patterson put on thermal underwear and a sweat suit.

"You see," he was saying, sitting and lacing one of his ring shoes and looking up at one of the young fighters, "if anybody quits, they can't come back. I take the time. I take the punches, so they can't come back."

"I know," the fighter was saying, nodding. "I know."

Two more young fighters came in, and when Patterson finished lacing his shoes and got up, the ones who were ready followed him down the stairs to the gym. It was 5:15, and it was 7:15 when Patterson called it quits. Others came in, the two firemen from Poughkeepsie among them, and Patterson took them on one after the other, moving around on the worn canvas patched with green plastic tape, blocking and picking off their punches, occasionally countering, and the sweat beading on his neck and face so that between rounds he had to towel. For two unbroken hours there was the thwack sound of gloves against gloves and the thup sound of gloves landing to the body, the shuffle sound of the shoes on canvas, the rhythmic sound of heavy breathing, and over it, Patterson's comments.

"You're not bringing your second jab back. Bring it all the way back," he was telling one. To another, "The moment you get close you tend to rear back. Keep your distance. That's it, but don't pull your shoulder back. Keep it relaxed, and when you throw the right hand, throw it from there. If you hold the shoulder up you force the right hand down." To another, "When are you gonna get your hair cut? Every time you lower your head your hair covers your eyes and you have to raise your head." To another, "Why move in? You're smothering your own punches. You have to keep your distance, and you know why you're missing so much? I know what punches you're gonna throw before you throw them. You have to mix them up." To another, "Keep your head down. Every now and then touch your chin to your shoulder." To another, "Throw the right. No good. You're just putting it there. Throw it. That's better. Again. Good."

When we judge professional performers we tend to take for granted, and forget, some of the things that they do well. During the years when I had watched Patterson fight I had fastened on his flaws, and I was impressed now by his boxing knowledge and his ability to spot the errors of the others, even though they were just beginners.

"You see," he was saying to one of them, after I had followed him and the others back upstairs, "as much as I know about boxing, if I was going to fight again I'd need a trainer, because I can't see what I'm doing wrong. I don't know. That's why I tell you these things, because I can see."

He started to undress, then, to take his shower, and I told him that I thought the boxing lessons had gone very well. I said I wanted to see him again the next morning.

"That's all right," he said. "How about ten thirty?"

"Fine," I said.

At 10:30 the next morning, when I drove into the parking area at the top of the driveway, Patterson was washing a car. It was a golden-tan Lincoln Continental with the New York license plate FP 1, and Patterson was in the jeans and T-shirt. He turned off the hose and we shook hands.

"Here's something that might interest you," I said.

I had brought along a copy of the February 28, 1959, issue of *The Saturday Evening Post*. In those days the magazine ran long interview pieces they called "visits" with celebrities, and they used to give me the fighters. I did Patterson and Johansson and Jack Dempsey, always with Jacob Lofman photographing it and with my friend Jim Cleary taping it because, although I had been taking accurate notes for twenty years by then, the magazine insisted that everything be recorded and then transcribed onto some sixty pages of typescript from which I had to work.

The Patterson piece led the issue, and on the opening page there was a picture of him in the ring after he had knocked out Hurricane Jackson. At the bottom of the page was a shot of the two of us sitting and talking by the ring in the Gramercy Gym. Patterson, gesticulating, was wearing a sand-colored, medium-weight cardigan.

"You haven't changed much," I said, showing him the picture, "but I have."

"Look at the sweater," Patterson said. "I still have that sweater."

"I remember it as a particularly fine one."

"Is it all right if I show this to my wife?" he said. "My wife would be interested to read it."

"Of course," I said.

He took the magazine, and I followed him around the front of the house and into the entry hall. He motioned me into the bar room and then excused himself and disappeared with the magazine.

"I'm always interested," I said when he came back, "in the relationships, years later, between fighters who fought each other. In your travels do you ever see Johansson?"

"I've been to Sweden a few times," he said, "but I and Johansson never showed any friendship until lately. He said so many derogatory things. In 1964, when I beat Eddie Machen in Stockholm, he said that Machen would knock me out and that Floyd was over the hill. It was an afternoon fight, and just as I walked out to get in the ring, Ingemar was in the first row. Our eyes met and I went over and shook hands and everybody booed. I don't know why."

"Probably," I said, "because he'd taken himself and his money to Switzerland."

"Then in 1974, after I hadn't fought in two years, I was in a restaurant in Stockholm, and who walked over but Ingemar Johansson. He was very nice then, and I've seen him a few times since."

"What about some of the other fighters you fought?"

"There were some of the guys, coming up in my career, like Hurricane Jackson and Jimmy Slade who were in the same camp until we fought. In camp, Jimmy Slade and I would play cards, and he'd get angry when I won. He'd throw the cards in my face, and in camp he'd be in charge.

"Then one day Cus asked me would I fight Jimmy Slade. I said, 'Of course not. We're friends.' Cus said, 'There comes a time in a fighter's career when he has to forget friendship.' I said, 'Ask Jimmy.' Jimmy said, 'Sure.' I was hurt, it came so easy to him.

"The guys I fought I don't dislike," he said, "and I'd like to stay in communication with them. I tried to call Jimmy Slade for days and days after I beat him, but I never got an answer. Dick Wagner, though, my first fight with him was difficult, and in the second I stopped him, but I made it known to the press that I respected him. He's out in Portland, Oregon, where he works on the railroad, and he's married to a schoolteacher. I had dinner at his house and his family met my family and I sent him cards from Sweden.

"A lot of guys I fought, though, have nothing but derogatory things to say. I saw Roy Harris when Joe Frazier fought Bob Foster. I met him in the lobby of the hotel and we talked a while, and the following day there was an article in the press where he said some derogatory things. Brian London said derogatory things. Why do they do this?"

"I guess they're still trying to win fights they lost to you years ago."

"It tends to bring them down," Patterson said. "They should carry themselves like Joe Louis."

When Patterson was small Louis was his idol. He kept scrapbooks filled with clippings and pictures of Joe, and after Patterson won the title the two met for the first time at a dinner.

"What was it like finally meeting him?" I asked Patterson, shortly after that.

"Well," Patterson had said, "I said to myself, 'Is this really Joe Louis? Am I finally meeting the man who is my idol?' I almost couldn't believe it."

"But you were the heavyweight champion of the world," I had said. "You have his old title."

"It seemed to me," Patterson had said, "like Joe Louis was still the champion, and I wasn't."

"Do you ever see Joe?" I asked him now.

"I see Joe often," he said, "and I'll still flash back to when I was nine, ten, and eleven and how I admired him, the way he carried himself. Here it is thirty years later, and I try to carry myself so that they might say the same thing about me."

"You picked a good model," I said.

"I know who I am," he said, "and what I believe in, but today you must be militant—down with Whitey—to be accepted. If that's what it takes, then I'll be the white man's black man, because I won't accept it the other way. I'd leave the country first. In my gym there are whites and colored and Puerto Ricans. I believe in an equal society. I see no colors. Everybody is the same in my gym—but the militants don't like me."

"You know that?"

"I go over to the college here," he said. "This black group—the black something—asked me to give a speech. I knew they'd harass me. This one guy said, 'How come you call him Cassius Clay? Why not Muhammad Ali?' I said, 'First of all, I think Cassius is a beautiful name, and I can't pronounce Muhammad. My tongue won't pronounce it. Then you give him rights you don't give me. I believe Clay believes in a separate society. You believe the same, or you wouldn't be all blacks here. He called Liston "The Ugly Bear." He called George Foreman "The Mummy." He called me "The Rabbit." You must give me the right to call him "Clay."'"

"But what did you say in your speech?" I said.

"I'll get it," he said. "I'll be right back."

What I had really wanted to say was that he should be done with the name-calling, that the beauty he ascribes to the name Cassius and his problem in pronouncing Muhammad are pretexts and have nothing to do with it. Louis would have pronounced it as best he could. When he came back now he handed me the typewritten speech and I read:

"To all you young people, I would like to see you go out in the world and have all your dreams come true, and they can if you work hard at your God-given talents. Our people have come a long way, and we have had to struggle to get where we are today.

"You young people are our hopes and pride. It is you who must continue to struggle. This world is not all black, and we can't make it so. We must live with all people. The sooner we realize that, the happier we'll be. You're young and you're beautiful and have a whole lifetime of living to do. Be conscious of your dreams and pride. Leave color at the end of the list—not the beginning.

"Black power is not a true power. White power is not a true power. What I ask you to look for is the power of right, not the power of might. My career has shaped my life, and I have learned much. I have met people from all over the world, the highest to the most humble. The finest of these people accept a man for what he is. Be men, and other men will know you at a glance. Remember Jesus said 'Love.' Racists say 'Hate.' One of the most renowned Americans who died for what he believed in preached love. He was a black man. Some of our people did not agree with him, but in the annals of history his name will be at the top. I speak of Martin Luther King."

At the age of ten Patterson was unable to read, and he refused to talk. His family had moved seven times, and he had attended irregularly seven schools before they sent him to Wiltwyck, a school for emotionally disturbed boys, at Esopus, New York, and later to P.S. 614, one of New York City's five schools for maladjusted children.

"That's a good speech," I said now.

"My wife helped me with it," he said. "She helps me with all my speeches."

"What kind of a reception did it get? Did they applaud?"

"Yes," he said. "About two thirds did. One third, I guess they couldn't be broke. If I reach one, though, I think it's fine."

"If I may say so," I said, "you should shut your mind to Ali. To begin with, you were in no shape to fight him the first time, and . . ."

"I had a slipped disc," Patterson said. "It started in 1956, before the fight with Archie Moore, and I took three or four days off. Before the fight with Clay it went out. I took some days off, and it was all right. Then in the first round it went out, and there was a knot in my back as big as a fist. The pain was so bad that it was the first time in a fight I was begging to be knocked out."

Between rounds, as I had watched on television, Al Silvani, who trained Patterson for the fight, would stand behind Patterson and put his arms around him, under the armpits and across the chest. He would lift Patterson, Patterson's feet dangling above the canvas, as Silvani tried to slip the disc back in. Then, during the rounds, until they stopped it in the twelfth, Ali would taunt and torture him.

"In the eighth and ninth rounds," Patterson was saying now, "I was saying to myself, 'The first good punch he catches me with, I'm going to go down.' He hit me good punches. I was down. I was dizzy, but when I opened my eyes I was up again. I could not take a dive."

"I believe that," I said, "and you should be proud of it."

"There are things I like about myself," he said. "I could not stay down. In boxing you learn about yourself. The feeling of shame I will never lose, because I let people down, but I will never again feel ashamed of being ashamed."

"And you shouldn't," I said.

"It's me," he said. "I can't change it."

"I was impressed yesterday," I said, "watching you teach those kids. When it was over you were telling one of them that, if you were to fight again, you'd need a trainer because you wouldn't be able to see what you were doing wrong."

"That's right," he said.

"I know," I said, "and I remember something you used to do wrong, and I begged you not to do it against Johansson in that second fight."

"You did?" he said.

In their first fight, Johansson, firing the big right hand, had had him down seven times in the third round before they had stopped it. Before the second fight, Alvin Boretz, the television writer, and I wrote a half-hour special that was to be aired on the ABC network the night before the fight. With Manny Spiro, the producer, and a camera crew, I had gone to both camps, first to interview Johansson late one afternoon in the octagonal ski hut at Grossinger's, and then Patterson early the next afternoon in the main dining room of the dilapidated roadhouse in Newtown.

We shot them both the same way, from the waist up and full face to the camera and, off camera myself, I asked both of them the same questions, about how they started as fighters, about their previous fights, in particular about what feelings they had had about the men they had fought, before and after those fights. Johansson was excellent, confident and even haughty—the way, if you are handling a fighter, you want him to be.

"After you had knocked Patterson down seven times and were now heavyweight champion of the world," I said, "did you have any feeling, looking across the ring at him, of sympathy for him?"

"No," Johansson said, "I did not. He'd gladly like to have me in the same situation."

"How about in the days after the fight when you thought about him?"

"I know my sister," he said, "she walk over when Patterson went from ring. My sister walked to him and raised her hand, and did like this on his chin. She feel sorry for him. But not me."

"This guy was great," Leonard Anderson, the director, said, as we walked back to the main building at Grossinger's.

"Terrific," Manny Spiro said, and he was obviously excited. "Just terrific, but what is poor Patterson going to do compared to that?"

"Just wait," I said.

The next morning we drove down to Newtown and, coming right out of Grossinger's, the others were appalled by the place. When Patterson came out to greet us he was in his road clothes, and he shook hands humbly, in that small-boy manner, and then he went back inside while they set up.

"This is unbelievable," Leonard Anderson said. "Looking at the two camps and the two fighters, I can't give this guy a chance."

"I feel sorry for him," Manny Spiro said, and then to me, "After Johansson, what can this poor nebbish say?"

"Relax," I said. "In fact, I'll guarantee you one thing right now. I don't know how he'll do in the fight, but I'll bet you he boxes rings around Johansson and flattens him in the interview segment."

I went inside then, and I found Patterson. I explained to him how we were going to film him, just sitting on a stool and facing the camera.

"But I don't know what you want me to say," he said.

"It's going to be easy," I said. "I'll just ask you questions I've asked you before, about your first fight on the street, and about your feelings for other fighters. I'll ask you about how you felt about Archie Moore after you won the title, and then I'll ask you about how you went into seclusion after the Johansson fight, and then about the little girl in the hospital in Atlantic City. All you have to do is tell me what you've told me before."

"All right," he said.

Sitting there on that stool and looking right at the camera, he told it as he had told it to me before, the voice low-level and neither rising nor falling, but the answers direct and explicit. He told about knocking out Moore, and then looking across the ring and, realizing that Moore had wanted the heavyweight championship as much as he and was now so old that he would never get another chance, feeling sorry for him. Then I asked him about the month he had spent in seclusion at home after Johansson had knocked him out, and he explained how he had felt that he had let all of his friends and the United States down, and that late one night he was sitting in the game room in the basement, still feeling sorry for himself.

"I was just sitting there, thinking," he said. "You know, when your mind just wanders. I was thinking about some things that had happened in some of the places that I had been to, and I thought about being in Atlantic City one time and going through a hospital for leukemia and blood diseases and cancer, and I specifically remember a girl in the hospital.

"She had leukemia," he said, and he gave a pause that you would celebrate a professional actor for timing. "Cancer. The doctor was showing me through the wards, and he brought me into this little girl's room and she had a tube running through her arms and whatnot, and said she was about four and she was small for a four-year-old girl and you'd think she was just born. She was just nothing but bones, and as I walked out of the room and upon viewing this, I remember the doctor saying to me it would be a miracle if she should live past tonight or tomorrow.

"So," he said, "after thinking about this, I thought, 'Who am I to feel sorry for myself? I should get down on my knees and thank God for the things I do have, and actually all I did was lose a fight, and I got paid for the fight and I have a beautiful home, and all the things the average man would want and even more. So, why should I feel sorry for myself?' I began to come out of it then, and I started going out the very next day, and that night was the first night that I think I got a good night's sleep."

"Cut!" Leonard Anderson said. "Great!"

"Thank you, Floyd," I said.

"You're welcome," he said.

"Floyd, you were terrific," Manny Spiro was saying. "That was absolutely terrific."

The whole thing had taken no more than fifteen minutes, but I was spent. I walked out into the sunlight and onto the terrace, with the weeds starting to grow between the cracked and uneven slates. Bill Mason, the sound engineer, had set up his recording equipment out there, with the cord to the microphone running through an open window, and he was still sitting there in front of his gear on a wooden folding chair.

"Wow!" he said. "What an interview!"

"It was all right," I said.

"All right?" he said. "Let me tell you something. I've been in this business for twenty years, and I've recorded everybody, including presidents in the White House. I never recorded anything like that."

"That's Patterson," I said.

"When he told that story about the little girl dying in the hospital," Mason said, "I couldn't see him, but just sitting here with the headset on and listening—I'm telling you—the tears were running down my cheeks."

They had signed up James Cagney to host the program, and I could remember him dying on the church steps in *The Roaring Twenties*, his body riddled with the submachine-gun bullets that had spewed out of the black limousine as it came around the corner, sliding and careening across the screen, while I sat, a teenager, in the Proctor's theater, gripped and hollow-sad. I could remember him, dead and bound like a mummy and propped against his mother's front door, falling forward onto the floor in *Public Enemy*, and now the teenager still in me found it almost absurd that he should be reading lines I had written.

"Patterson's great in the interview," he had said, after we had shown him and Robert Montgomery in a screening room on Broadway the rushes of what we had shot in the camps, "but can he lick the other guy?"

Between reels, while we waited for the projectionist to change over, we had talked about fights and fighters he remembered, and I had found that he has what I call the ability to read fights. It is like the ability to read writing, when the writing is worthy of it—not just what a writer says, but what he doesn't say and what he implies. Reading fights is not just reading the punches, which are obvious, but it is reading between the punches, the styles and the thinking, or what each fighter should be thinking, to set up what he has to say while silencing the other.

"He can lick him if he fights him right," I had said. "All he has to worry about is that one punch, the right hand."

"It's some right hand," Cagney had said, "and the way Patterson comes up out of his crouch he bobs right up into it."

Alvin Boretz had shown me how, filming Cagney in the studio, we could interpolate him into the interviews, and then I had had to convince Jack Dempsey to give Patterson a chance. For the last segment of the program I had wanted Dempsey and Joe Louis, the dream match, with Dempsey picking Johansson and Louis explaining how Patterson could beat him. Someone at the advertising agency, or perhaps the sponsor, had discovered, however, that Louis was associated with an advertising firm that represented an account in Castro's Cuba, and so they had turned down Joe, who had defended his title without pay for Army and Navy relief and is one of the noblest of men any of us has known in sports, and they picked Gene Tunney.

"I like Johansson," Dempsey had said, when I had gone to see him in his Broadway restaurant about the segment on the show. We were sitting in one of the booths.

"I know," I said, "but Tunney picks Johansson. Let me tell you what I'd like you to say."

It was another absurdity. A small boy, his hair freshly shampooed and his mother insisting that he not go to bed before it had thoroughly dried, would come down the stairs to listen on the radio to the Clicquot Club Eskimos, the A & P Gypsies, or Billy Jones and Ernie Hare, who called themselves "The Happiness Boys" when they broadcast from the Happiness Restaurant in New York, and later "The Interwoven Pair" when they advertised men's hose. The small boy, outpunched in the playground and scared in the street scrambles, would be wearing a heavy flannel bathrobe with an Indian blanket design on it, as he walked into the living room.

"Here he comes now!" his father would inevitably announce, and the boy would inevitably cringe inside. "Jack Dempsey!"

So I told Dempsey how I thought Patterson should fight it. If he worked inside Johansson's left jab, which in the first fight had set him up for Johansson's right, and if he kept firing left hooks while he turned it into a street fight and backed Johansson up, he could win it.

"That's right," Dempsey said. "If he does that, he could lick the Swede. I can say that."

After we had filmed Cagney in the studio, leading into the interviews and then with Dempsey and Tunney, someone had asked him to visit the two camps for some publicity still photos with the fighters. The next day, he and his friend Roland Winters drove into Patterson's camp where a half-dozen of us were waiting.

"You have a picture over there on the wall," I said to Patterson now, sixteen years later, "of you with James Cagney and Roland Winters. That was taken for that TV program before the second Johansson fight when I interviewed you and Ingemar."

"That's right," he said. "I remember."

"After the picture taking," I said, "the rest of us went to lunch at the inn in Newtown. You weren't having your meal then, but you came along and sat with us. You were at the end of the table, with Cagney on your right and me on your left. We talked awhile, and you were about to leave to work out, and that's when I asked you not to make the same mistake again."

"You did?" Patterson said.

"Sure," I said, thinking that he should remember this. "I said, 'Floyd, do yourself and me a favor. This guy has only one punch, the right hand. His jab isn't much, but it's just heavy enough to keep you in range for the right, so you've got to slip the jab, work on the inside, back him up, and turn it into a street fight. None of these fellas from Europe, who have that stand-up continental style, can handle it when it's a street fight.'

"Then," I was saying now, and I was up and demonstrating again as I had in that dining room at the inn, "I told you to finish every one of your combinations, every sequence of punches, with the left hook. I said, 'This is the most important point of all. When you finish with a right hand, and if you hurt him with it or back him up, it still leaves you over here on your left, and in line for his right. You've got to finish with the hook, every time, and I don't care if you don't even hit him with it. Even if you miss it, it will carry you over to your right and out of line of his right.'"

"That's correct," Patterson said now, sitting there and nodding. "That's right."

"So you said, 'But I'm not sure I can learn that, to always finish with the left.' I said, 'Of course you can. When you're shadowboxing, when you're sparring in the ring, finish with the hook. When you're running on the road, throw half-punches and finish with the hook. Keep telling yourself, "Left hook. Left hook." You've got to do that, because you'll be taking away his only punch and throwing your best one. You can learn it.' Then you said, 'I'll try.'"

He had shaken hands with us then, to go back to camp. I didn't tell him now what Cagney had said as soon as he had left.

"Tell me something," Cagney said to me. "Who's been teaching this guy?"

"I remember," Patterson said now, "somebody telling me that about the left hook, but I forgot that it was you. Then I remember I also got a letter from a man—I don't know who he was—and he told me to always double-jab."

"That was good advice," I said, "because Johansson liked to throw the right hand over your single jab. That was very good advice."

"And that was some hook I hit him with," Patterson said, a small smile of satisfaction crossing his face.

That night at the Polo Grounds, left hooks and the only anger he ever carried into a ring won the fight for Patterson. He had backed Johansson up from the start, working inside the jab, but he had been in and out of trouble a half-dozen times when he had forgotten to finish his combinations with a hook. Only Johansson's inability to spot this and time him had saved Patterson, and then in the fifth round, with Johansson backing up again, he had let go a wide hook, that was more a leaping swing. Johansson's back was to his own corner, and when he went down he landed on his rump and then his head hit the canvas and he lay there, his right leg twitching and the blood coming out of his mouth, for what seemed like ten minutes, while I feared for him, and before they dared move him back to his corner and prop him up on the stool.

When I next saw Patterson he was going into training for the third Johansson fight the following March in Miami. I asked him how he had felt after he had won the title back.

"When I left the Polo Grounds," he said, "the promoters had a car and chauffeur waiting for me. I was sitting in the back seat alone, and when we drove through Harlem and I saw all the people celebrating in the streets, I felt good."

"You should have," I said. "There'd been nothing like it since Louis knocked out Billy Conn."

I meant there had been nothing like it for the Negro race in this country, and this will show you how far we have come. In the summer of 1936 I worked with a mixed gang on the railroad tracks that run through the Bronx and into Manhattan, and the day after Max Schmeling knocked out Joe Louis, Joe's people, so expectant and exuberant the day before, worked all day in saddened silence. Then, after Louis had knocked out Schmeling in two minutes and four seconds in their second fight, I had read about the all-night celebration in Harlem, and I had seen some of it after the second Conn fight and after Patterson had knocked out Johansson, and we have all come so far that there has been nothing like it since.

"Then I thought about Johansson," Patterson had said, describing that ride through Harlem. "I thought how he would have to drive through here, too, and then he would have to go through what I went through after the first fight. I thought that he would be even more ashamed than I was, because he'd knocked me out the first time. Then I felt sorry for him."

"Do you think," I had asked him, "that you can call up the same kind of anger and viciousness the next time you fight Johansson?"

"Why should I?" he had said. "In all my other fights I was never vicious, and I won out in almost all of them."

"But you had to be vicious against this guy," I had said. "You had to turn a boxing contest into a kind of street fight to destroy this guy's classic style. When you did that, he came apart. This was your greatest fight, because for the first time you expressed emotion. A fight, a piece of writing, a painting, or a passage of music is nothing without emotion."

"I just hope," Patterson had said, "that I'll never be as vicious again."

He never was, in his third fight with Johansson, when he was on the floor himself before he knocked Johansson out, or in the two each with Liston and Ali, when anger translated into viciousness might have given him the only chance he had. In what is the most totally expressive of the arts, for it permits man to vent and divest himself of his hatred and his anger, deplorable though they may be, he had delivered his finest performance when he held himself to be out of character, or at least the character he has tried always to assume.

"You earned a good deal of money," I said now. "Did you get good advice as to how to handle it? Did you have good investment help?"

"I helped myself," he said, "after experiencing losing tremendous amounts of money through people who were handling my finances. I supposedly made nine million dollars in the ring. I don't know who got most of it, Uncle Sam or the persons handling it. All the money went to the office. Like a hundred thousand at one time would go to the office, and I would call and say, 'Send me a thousand to run the camp.' Then I would go back and look at the account and there would be twelve thousand dollars in it. I'd say, 'Where's the rest?'"

"But you'd had no training in investments," I said.

"I started learning about various things," he said. "I had some stocks that were very successful. With stocks, if it was not too much of a gamble, I would chance it."

"So you won't ever have to work again?"

"I hope not," he said. "I sure hope not. When you retire and leave the limelight, you do what you really want to do. The days go slower. It's healthier, and you live longer. I think all the time. I do most of my thinking while I'm working, and before I realize it, it will be four or five hours later. It's the same thing when I go to sleep. I think a lot."

"And what are the thoughts that go through your mind?"

"I think about life now, as opposed to the way it used to be, and about my peace of mind."

"And the life you have now," I said, "is it what you wanted, and hoped that someday it might be?"

"Let me put it this way," he said. "Being raised in Brooklyn and coming up through the slums, life is very different. I don't think anyone knows what they want in life. They know what they don't want. It's a process of elimination. I knew what I didn't want. I didn't want the slums.

"Living here," he said, "married, with a couple of kids—I didn't know I wanted this, but I am perfectly contented. I have to remember, though, and that makes me appreciate more what I have today. I wouldn't change one thing in the past because it helped me to this."

"That's the proper way to look at it," I said. "If we could all look at our lives that way, realizing that there's nothing we can do about the past, we'd all be the better for it. I'm happy for you."

"Thank you," he said.

We talked for a few minutes more, about other fighters I would be seeing for the book and about the decline of boxing. Then I stood up to leave.

"If your wife has read that piece," I said, "I'd like the magazine back. It's the only copy I have."

"Oh, yes," he said, and then, after he had come back with the magazine, "My wife enjoyed it."

"I'm glad," I said.

He walked me out to the car and we shook hands. I backed out and drove out to Route 299 and back up the hill through the center of the town. I had checked out of the motel, so I turned onto the Thruway, and I was sorry that, for whatever reasons, I had not met his wife. Perhaps, if they had gone to dinner with me, and if she had trusted me, I could have led them to tell me what it is like, a mixed marriage, an island in the sea of our still-social segregation. Perhaps they would have told me, if they had known that I have believed for a long time that fifty or a hundred years from now, if this planet survives that long, it will be accepted that the ultimate and only rational solution will be miscegenation.

The Man Who Belongs in Blue Jeans

Jim Tescher Revisited

Levi Strauss ended last year looking robust as ever, with sales up 20 percent to $1.2 billion and profits up 62 percent to $105 million.

Newsweek, July 5, 1977

THE INTERSTATE HIGHWAYS in this country are a monument to the surveyor's calling, the engineer's profession, and the cement and asphalt industries, but traveling them is like reading those summer novels the critics suggest you pack along with your bathing apparel, the tennis gear, the suntan lotion, and the Maalox. Surviving them, you have the feeling that you haven't seen anything, come to know anyone, or been anywhere.

This country comes alive between the highways and not on them, and we had driven halfway across it to the midline of America. Medora, North Dakota, dates back only to 1883 and has a year-round population of only 129, but in 1962 they started restoring it, and it has its history. In 1876, George Armstrong Custer, on his way to his unannounced retirement at Little Big Horn, camped with his Seventh Cavalry just five miles south of where the town was shortly to be built. After the Sioux were chased out and the Northern Pacific pushed past on its way

Chapter 3 of *Once They Heard the Cheers*, 1979. The text has been slightly abridged for its appearance here.

west, the town grew up as a railhead and terminus for the cattle drives that started twelve hundred miles south on the Oklahoma–Texas border. Cattlemen fattened their stock in the grasslands bordering the town and in the Badlands to the north. From 1883 until 1898, Theodore Roosevelt owned two ranches here, one five miles south of the town and another thirty miles to the north, and there is a National Memorial Park, in three units, named for him. Medora, itself and in season, sells Teddy to the tourists with a board-sided Rough Riders Hotel and a museum, an amphitheater, a trout pond, gift shops, and a zoo offering "all animals native to North Dakota in Teddy Roosevelt's time."

It was mid-September and the tourists were gone, leaving what were left of the trout, I presumed, to their peaceful pursuits and zoo animals to their privacy. The hotel was closed, but at the smaller of the two motels—the one that had answered my wife, Betty's, postal enquiry addressed to "Chamber of Commerce"—the middle-aged, motherly woman who runs it with her husband had pointed us, the first evening, to the Little Missouri Saloon and Dining Room for dinner, and the next morning, to Bud's Coffee and Gift Shop for breakfast. Now she brought out a large-scale map of the land sections, and spread it on the counter in the motel office.

"You'll have to go down here and onto the Interstate," she said. "Then it's about fourteen miles to Sentinel Butte."

"Good," I said. "I spent a night there in '64."

"Then the road goes north, right here."

"I remember that," I said, "and I think it's right about on this bend of the Little Missouri."

"I wouldn't know for sure," she said, "but I know it's out there somewhere."

"At Bud's they said the road would probably be all right."

"I would think so," she said. "We haven't had much rain."

"Do you know where I might get a map like this?"

"You can have this one."

"Thank you," I said.

"That's all right," she said. "I hope you find it."

At Sentinel Butte the road that leads off the Interstate curves down a gentle hill into the town. The population of Sentinel Butte is 125, and at the corner there is a white-stuccoed general store with two gas pumps under the overhang in front.

"Do you have any high-test?" I said.

"No," he said, middle-aged, tanned, and looking healthy, as you're supposed to look if you live in Sentinel Butte.

He put in ten gallons of the regular, and when I handed him the ten-dollar bill and he went inside to make change, I followed him.

"I want to go out to Jim Tescher's ranch," I said. "Do you know how I can get there?"

"Jim Tescher's?" he said. "Sure."

"Wait till I call my wife in," I said. "She's the navigator."

I introduced Betty, and myself, and he said his name was Ward Cook. He marked the route on the map for us, and then, on the back of a letter I was carrying, he drew the route with the landmarks on it.

"You go across I-94," he said, "and take a left with Camel's Hump Butte on the right. You follow the main road for ten or twelve miles to some old run-down farm buildings here on the left. You go straight about eight or nine miles to a deserted schoolhouse here on the right, and about a half mile past that you turn off left across a cattle guard. You follow that, and after maybe about twelve miles or so there'll be some signs of Jim's, I'm sure."

"How far is it?"

"About thirty-six miles," he said. "I haven't been all the way out there in twenty years."

"You think that car of mine will make it? It's kind of low-slung."

"You can make it at this time of year," he said. "You know Jim Tescher?"

"Yes. I met him twelve years ago in Phoenix, while he was riding saddle broncs."

"Jim and his brother Tom were great riders," he said, "but nobody knows it."

"They knew it once in rodeo," I said.

When Betty and our daughter and I had got off the plane in Phoenix on that day, in '64, Skipper Lofting had come walking with that slow rolling gait down the ramp to meet us. He used to write short stories for *The Saturday Evening Post* and the other magazines that ran fiction in those days. He had ridden some in rodeo, and his father wrote the first book that captured me. In the first grade, each day after lunch, Miss Kessler, in a black dress and her black hair done up with a bun in the back, would stand up in front of the class and read us another chapter of Hugh Lofting's *The Voyages of Doctor Dolittle*, and each day I could hardly wait to hear what the doctor who talked with the animals, and the duck and the monkey, were going to do next.

"I'll tell you what we'd better do," Skipper had said that first night, sitting in the bar of the motel. "I'd sure hate to steer you wrong, hang you up on somebody who just wouldn't be right for everything you want. Maybe we should go up and see Stiffy."

It was early March, and the rodeo was on for four days. The bar was filled with big hats and broad shoulders, western shirts and big belt buckles, and jeans that tapered down into the boots with the slanted heels and pointed toes. Stiffy, after a western cartoon character, is what Skipper calls Gene Pruett. For twenty-one years Gene Pruett rode saddle broncs. In 1948 he won the world title, and he quit in 1955 and now he was editing *Rodeo Sports News*, the biweekly published by the Rodeo Cowboys Association.

"What I want to do, or try to do," I said, after Skipper had telephoned and we had gone up to Pruett's room, "is write the definitive magazine piece about rodeo through the life of one cowboy who still ranches. I want a bronc rider or a bull rider, because they put their bodies and sometimes their lives on the line. I want him to be able to tell me how he got into rodeo and why he's in it, and I want to follow him around and into the chutes and find out not only what he does but how he does it."

"That'd be right fine," Pruett said. He goes to well over six feet and he's thin and bony, and he was sitting sprawled, his back to the desk, with his legs stretched out and his feet on the bed. "I'd admire that."

"But I need the right man," I said. "He doesn't have to be a champion—I don't care about that—but he does have to be the cowboy the others look up to, so that when the piece runs and they read it, they'll say, 'Yeah. That's it.'"

"Well," Pruett said, "I'm thinkin', and there's several, but I've been thinkin' about Jim Tescher. How about Tescher, Skip?"

"Well," Skipper said, "I've thought of Jim Tescher. Everybody respects him, and he sure can ride and he ranches, but I'm not sure how much he'll talk."

"He's not big on the brag," Pruett said, "but I'll tell you something. It'd be real hard to pick out even two guys who can ride as good as Jim Tescher—maybe not even one—because he's just about as good a bronc rider as there is today. If Jim and his brother Tom had just rodeoed and rodeoed they'd a been champions."

"That's what Casey Tibbs said," Skipper said, and Casey Tibbs was a nine-time world champion. "Casey said, 'There's no tellin' how far those Teschers could go, if they weren't plagued with common sense.'"

"I like that," I said.

"That's the truth," Pruett said. "Tescher has that ranch he owns north of Medora, North Dakota, and he just doesn't get to enough rodeos."

In rodeo the champion in each event is the one who has earned the most prize money during the year, and the world champion is the one who has earned the most in two or more events. That is like giving the Nobel Prize for medicine to some Park Avenue specialist, and I wanted a cowboy off a ranch and not one of the new school, living in a condominium somewhere, flying his own Cessna 182 or 206 and making two and sometimes three rodeos a day. I wanted that, because rodeo is a reminder of a way of life that is almost gone now forever, and there is no other sport that is as indigenous to this country alone.

"Heck," Skipper Lofting said, "I think Jim will talk."

Skipper introduced us the next morning, and Tescher and I walked across the street to the Pancake House, where we ate and talked. He had driven in the night before with his wife, Loretta, and their then four-year-old son, Barry—the third of their then four children—in the two-year-old red Chevrolet. The pillow and blankets were in the back seat, and his saddle was in the trunk along with the soiled laundry stuffed into a pair of his blue jeans. He had managed to get away from the ranch for the five weeks they had been on the road, and at Fort Worth and San Antonio, Houston and Baton Rouge, he had won $5,753—about $5,000 riding saddle broncs and the rest of it wrestling steers.

He was thirty-five years old then, and had been riding horses since he was four. When he was ten he rode his first steer for one dollar in a Fourth of July rodeo in Medora. Although he had never made enough rodeos to win enough to be the world champion in the saddle-bronc riding, he had won the event at the National Finals rodeo, where only the fifteen top contestants in each event compete, in 1959 and 1963.

"Besides," Gene Pruett had said, talking about him, "the National Finals are the real test as far as I'm concerned."

He is five feet eight and a half inches, and while he was riding he weighed 187 pounds but had a thirty-inch waist. It was all up in his chest and shoulders and arms and down in his thighs and calves. His build was like that of a middleweight fighter, but on a larger frame. He talked easily, although not expansively, and I followed him around for the four days, climbing up onto the back of the chute when he mounted to ride, watching how he measured the length of rein he would give the horse and how he took his hold on the rosined rope before he nodded for them to swing the gate open. Being with him I had the same comfortable, secure feeling I used to have being around one of those quiet, competent front-line lieutenants and captains who never raised their voices and whose kids were always telling me they wished they could get them a medal.

In rodeo the riding events are not only a contest between the man and the animal but also a partnership. The judges give points for how well the animal bucks as well as for how well the contestant rides, and Tescher drew poor horses and finished out of the money. He had put up the thirty-five-dollar entry fee twice, had the travel expenses for himself, his wife, and their son, and now they would be driving the sixteen hundred miles back to the ranch where, he had told me, they were living in a basement—the upper story of the house to be built when he had earned the money.

"I'd like to see how you live and ranch," I had said to him.

"You'd be welcome to come any time," he had said.

"Is there a motel near there?"

"Not really," he had said. "We live quite a way out, but we've got room, and you're welcome to stay with us."

So I had given him a day and a half's head start and, after my wife and our daughter had taken the plane back east, I had flown up to Billings and from there to Miles City and then to Glendive, Montana, where Tescher's brother-in-law, Roy Kittelson, had met me at about ten o'clock at night. In a pickup he had driven me the thirty miles east across the state line to Sentinel Butte.

"A lot of people thought Jim wouldn't make it out in the Badlands," Kittelson said, driving through the night. "In the wheat lands they say the topsoil is from six to eight feet deep, and out on those buttes there's no more than six to eight inches, but Jim mined his own coal, smoked Bull Durham, and saved every penny he could."

In Sentinel Butte he drove me up to Jim's father's house. Matt Tescher had once raised cattle and wheat on fifteen hundred acres outside of Sentinel Butte, and had fathered fifteen children. When Jim was in the fifth grade, the house had burned down, so Matt Tescher had moved the rest of the family into town, while Jim and his brother Alvin, who was eight years older, stayed on the ranch. For six years they lived together in the two-room bunkhouse while Jim went through the eighth grade as one of seven pupils in the one-room school, and then started making a living breaking horses and hiring out to ranchers.

The house, as we got out of the pickup, seemed completely darkened, but Kittelson led me up a lighted back stairway to the third-floor finished attic where there was a double bed and where, he said, rodeo cowboys on their way through regularly slept. The next morning, after breakfast and after I had talked with Matt Tescher about Jim, asking him every question I could think of, Kittelson had picked me up again and driven me out to the ranch on the road we were now trying to find once more.

"In 1964," I was saying now in the general store, "I spent a night in Jim's father's house, but I have no idea where it was."

"Jim's father just passed away," Ward Cook said.

"I'm sorry to hear that."

"The house is right up here," he said. "You passed it on your way in. When you go out and start up the curve to the left, it's the last house on the left."

We drove back on the blacktop leading out of town, with the square, three-story gray-painted clapboard house the last one on the left, and across the Interstate. We turned left onto the dirt and gravel road, with Camel's Hump Butte like a fortress on the right, and we drove north through the grasslands, some of it mowed, some with white-faced Herefords grazing on it, all of it dry and golden-yellow in the morning sun.

We followed the road for more than an hour, the grasslands giving way to the Badlands, the road narrower now, rising and falling and curving around the mustard-sided, stratified, flat-topped buttes. A coyote, like a small gray-white collie, streaked across the road about fifty feet ahead of us, and a chicken hawk on its hunting glide was low enough to pass through the windows of the car.

This is land that waters flowing eastward from the Rocky Mountains laid down some sixty million years ago. Many centuries of warm rains that followed turned it into a jungle, and new layers of sediment compressed the swamp vegetation into layers of lignite, a soft coal. Clouds of ash from the volcanoes that formed the mountains of the West drifted down and decomposed into strata of blue bentonite clay. After the plains had developed, the streams that drained this land started the erosion that still goes on, cutting down through the soft strata and sculpting the Badlands into the buttes, the plateaus, and between them the valleys and gorges.

When you drive through here you drive through eons, the horizontal strata on the sides of the buttes the visible evidence of what were the horizons of their time. Once, off to the left and coming down off a tableland, we saw a black-hatted horseman riding after a stray Hereford. Once a Jeep, red and with the dust rising after it, passed us going the other way, and once, unable to find the landmarks—the deserted farm buildings and the vacant one-room school—I drove into the only ranch we saw along the road. My wife got out with the section map in her hand.

"I guess they were startled to see me drop in out of nowhere," she said when she came back. "There were two men working on some machinery, and I said, 'Are we on the right road for Jim Tescher's?' One of them said, 'That's right.' Then the other one, kind of laughing, said, 'But do you know the way the rest of the way?'"

"Did they say how much farther it is?"

"I didn't ask," she said. "We're on the right road."

We drove, slowly and with the car nodding up and down, over cattle guards—a dozen or so four-inch pipes set six inches apart between the wire fencing—and at some of them the cattle, unable to cross the guards, lay in the road and, protesting with their mooing, moved only when I advanced on them sounding the horn. Beyond the landmarks, and after turn-offs to other ranches, the road in places was no more than wheel tracks and then, where it widened again and climbed up onto a plateau, we saw the first of the signs—Tescher's name among four others, and then another pointing to the right and finally, with the letters cut into a plank supported on two posts: "Tescher Ranch." Between the words was the brand, the inverted V with the single rocker through it, and below, in smaller letters: "Quarter Horses. Herefords."

In the dozen years that had passed so quickly I had wanted many times to return here, just to be reassured that America can still make it. When a national poll reveals that more than half of all workers are dissatisfied with their jobs, and the products they turn out and the services they perform prove it, when exaggerated advertising creates artificial appetites for those products and our economy is based on the waste of the natural resources we should be preserving for generations to come, when the founders' dreams of equality for all go up in ghetto flames and are dissipated in looting, and when, among our highest elective officials and their appointees, integrity becomes, for so many, no more than a word, one should have some place to go to find that a man and his family, not afraid of the hard way and rejecting the superficialities and the deceits of our society, can still more than survive.

"Yes, we are still ranching," Loretta Tescher had written some four months before, "although cattle prices aren't anything to brag about. We built our new home and also have a modern bunkhouse that you and Mrs. Heinz are very welcome to stay in instead of Medora, if you wish.

"Our family is growing up. Gary is rodeoing and is setting twelfth in the standings. He rides broncs and bulls. Bonnie, our youngest, is eight and she is nursing a collarbone she broke while riding horseback. Here's hoping to see you this fall."

The top of the plateau was planted in alfalfa, the road across it straight between the ankle-high deep green. Off to the right, and below, we could see the almost dry bed of the Little Missouri, cottonwoods clumped along its banks, and as we started down the curve toward the river we could see, amid the trees, some buildings.

"That must be it down there," my wife said.

"It has to be," I said. "There's no one else out here."

Where the road flattened just above the riverbed we came around a curve, and we drove into the ranch yard and up to the house of stained-cedar siding now standing atop the cement-block foundation and basement where they had been living and I had stayed that night twelve years before. I walked up the three steps and opened the door into the boot room and walked in.

"Hello?" I said. "Anybody here?"

"You made it," his wife said, coming out of the kitchen and shaking hands. She is slim and dark-haired and was wearing slacks and a blouse. "You look just the same."

"I doubt that," I said.

She had grown up on a ranch at the edge of the Badlands. After she was graduated from high school at sixteen, she had taken summer courses at North Dakota State Teachers College at Dickinson and for five years had taught in a one-room school.

"You have any trouble finding it again?" she said.

"A little," I said. "My wife had to ask at one ranch, and we had our doubts a half-dozen times."

"Bring your wife in," she said. "Jim's on the phone, but he'll be off in a minute, and Gary's here. He has to be in Abilene tomorrow night, but he said he wouldn't leave till you got here and he saw you again."

He was not quite thirteen then, and he had been a part of my story. In December of 1963 Jim Tescher had won the saddle-bronc riding at the National Finals at Los Angeles, and three months later, during the night I spent with them in that basement, he had told me about coming upon the boy admiring the gold-and-silver belt buckle set with diamonds.

"He said to me," Jim had said, "'But how come you've never been world champion?' I tried to explain it to him—that I feel it's more important for me to be with the family and build up the ranch than to be going halfway across the United States to some little rodeo just to win a hundred dollars and build up my standing. I told him, though, what I might do this year. I said, 'If you'd really like me to be world champion, I might give it a try. If I start out winning pretty good and everything's all right here, I might just stay with it more.' I'll have to see how it goes."

Jim and Loretta had moved out of their bedroom that night and into the other room with the three smaller children. Gary and I had shared the double bed, and it seemed to me that most of the night he was riding broncs or bulls. The next morning, when he started for school, I had followed him out into the damp, gray chill of mid-March and across the yard to the bank above the river. Fastened to two posts in the ground was a three-quarter-inch cable that ran the 320 feet across the river to a cottonwood tree on the far bank. Tied to the forward post, and suspended from two pulleys that rode the cable, was a weathered wood platform, about five feet long and half as wide and with eight-inch sides.

The boy had his lunch in a Karo syrup pail. He put that on the platform and then he climbed on. Kneeling, he loosened the tie and he pushed off, the platform sliding down the sag of the cable to the midpoint about eight feet above the water that would be ice during the winter. Then the boy grabbed the cable over his head, and he pulled the platform across the river over to the cottonwood tree where he climbed down the seven slats nailed to the trunk of the tree. He got into the Jeep, which he had left there the afternoon before, and he drove the four and a half miles to the one-room school he attended with seven others.

In 1964 it would go well for Jim Tescher. Going into the National Finals he had won $20,041, and he was second to Marty Wood by $1,206. With Loretta and the boy watching that week in Los Angeles, he won $1,516, gaining $635 on Marty Wood, but with $21,557 for the year he finished second. He was short by $571, and someone told me later that, sitting in the stands that last night, the boy had cried.

"And you're built like your dad," I said to Gary now. "How are you doing?"

He was twenty-five, and although slimmer than his father, he too had it up in the chest and shoulders and arms. He was wearing jeans and a dark green shirt, and he had greeted us in the kitchen and I had introduced my wife. His father was sitting just inside the living room, the phone cord running from the kitchen, and he had waved to us, with some papers in his hand, as we walked by.

"I guess I'm not doin' too good," Gary said. "I'm not in the top twenty. I was a thousand dollars out of the top fifteen, I saw in the *Billings Gazette*."

"Are you making a lot of rodeos?"

"I'm trying to," he said, "but I got hurt in August. A horse threw me down over its head, and stepped on my arm. It didn't break nothing, but it laid me up."

I remember his father's hurts. When he was fourteen, he was hunting deer and riding down off one of those buttes into a draw when the horse turned a somersault and his right arm was broken. When he was sixteen his left ankle was broken while he was rodeoing in Dickinson, North Dakota, and a bareback horse ran away with him. For a week he didn't bother to go to a doctor, and then, with a cast on, he rode bareback at Glendive, Montana, for the three dollars mount money. When he was twenty he had three vertebrae broken in the small of his back in a car wreck coming away from a rodeo in Forsyth, Montana. At Spencer, Iowa, one year he broke his left thigh bone when the horse reared in the chute, but they poured a couple of drinks of whiskey into him and he got back on the horse. In 1959 his collarbone was broken when he was thrown in Madison Square Garden, and two years later he broke two vertebrae in his neck at Beach, North Dakota, just playing around after the rodeo with Alvin Nelson—using each other's saddles and betting on riding—and he was in a brace for two months. His left ankle was broken in the chute at Grand Forks, North Dakota, where he remounted and won money anyway, and he had had calcium deposits removed from his left shinbone. Wrestling steers, he had horns tear the left side of his nose loose and rip his upper lip. And Jerry Izenberg said it well.

"The cowboys," Jerry wrote once in the *Newark Star Ledger*, "represent the last frontier of pure unpampered athletes in an age when basketball players put Ace bandages on acne."

"But don't you ever have any pain from any of this?" I had asked Jim Tescher that night, sitting in the living room in the basement. Just before dusk I had ridden in the pickup with Roy Kittelson driving among the cottonwoods while Tescher, standing in the back, had thrown the seventy-five-pound hay bales to the cattle.

"Most all the time," he said. "I can feel it now, sittin' here, and it bothers me lyin' in bed. It doesn't bother me when I work, though, or when I ride—just afterwards. When it gets real bad I know those vertebrae in my back have slipped, so I get Benny Reynolds to put 'em back in place."

Benny Reynolds was a six-foot three-inch, 195-pound, easygoing, four-event cowboy out of Melrose, Montana. In 1961 he won the All-Around World Championship.

"Benny remembers what twist to give 'em," Tescher said, "so why pay one of them fellas three dollars?"

Now, twelve years later, he came off the phone and walked in to where we were sitting at the dining-room table and we shook hands. He was wearing blue jeans and a checkered shirt, and he appeared the same, perhaps just a little heavier.

"I'm sorry to hear that your dad just passed away," I said. "Ward Cook told us in Sentinel Butte."

"Thank you," he said. "You met Ward?"

"I stopped there for gas and directions," I said. "He also told me that you and Tom were great riders, but nobody knows it."

"Ward said that?" Tescher said, smiling. "Well, I went to high school with him. That is, I guess I shouldn't say that because I only went two days."

"Coming out here again," I said, as we three sat down, "I've naturally been remembering when Gary and I slept together, and he seemed to be rodeoing all night. Then, of course, I remember how much he wanted you to win the world championship."

"Sometimes now," Tescher said, "I wish I had had sense enough to go to a few more rodeos, not for me but for my friends and family. I stayed home for harvest, and at Denver I judged, where Marty won, but I was just so darned tickled to finish second."

"I was the one that hurt," Gary said. "I remember that night I was in tears, and I promised myself I was gonna win it. When things are goin' tough, I guess that keeps me going, because I think that if a guy just rides hard enough, he can win it."

Loretta and Betty were starting to set the table for the noon meal that, where the work is still around the home and the workday starts at 5:30 A.M., is still called dinner, and we moved into the living room. When I asked him about his schooling, Gary said that after he finished high school in Beach, which is forty-four miles to the south, he had a rodeo scholarship for one year at Jasper Junior College, in Wyoming, and then he went for one semester to North Dakota State Teachers College in Dickinson, and for another to North Dakota State in Fargo.

"I was having to sell my cows to go to college," he said, "and I wasn't gettin' any rodeos. Then one year I didn't go anywhere. I got a job in Beach in a cheese plant. I wanted to see what it was like, and to prove to myself that I wouldn't like it."

"And other than rodeo," I said, "what do you hope to do?"

"I've been workin' on a loan to buy a ranch up here," he said. "It's about thirty miles northwest, and Dad owns it. It's a two-hundred-head place, with five sections of land on it, seven miles from Trotters."

"What's Trotters?"

"There's a general store and gas station and a post office and a church."

"We built this basement here in 1960," Tescher said, "and we lived in it for six years. Now the FHA wants you to have the best, the biggest tractor, the biggest house that a young fella don't need. They won't let Gary live in a basement, and it's tough on the young."

"What about the others you went to school with around here?" I said to Gary. "Back East a lot of the younger generation haven't known what to aspire to, and they're lost."

"It's like that here."

"Really?"

"A lot of the guys I went to grade school and high school with were straight and clean-cut, but now some of them have sure strayed. They're long-hair, pot-smoking guys, and some have been alcoholics already."

"A lot aren't willing to work," Tescher said. "They think they need big modern equipment, and to hire other guys."

"Why do you think this has happened to your age group," I said to Gary, "where it didn't happen to your dad's?"

"People get exposed more now," he said. "They see a life that looks easier to them."

"You mean on television, where in the commercials everybody is lolling around at beach parties drinking beer, or if they're not doing that, they're flying off to Hawaii or comparing the riding qualities of a Lincoln Continental with those of a Cadillac?"

"I think that does it," Gary said. "People get an outside look they never had before."

I asked about the rest of the family, and Tescher said that Cindy, the second oldest, is married and living in Beach. Barry, whom I remember as a four-year-old walking around the motel in Phoenix in boots, jeans, and a western shirt and under a Stetson that, Skipper Lofting said, made him look like an ant moving a soda cracker, was living with his sister and her husband and going to high school in Beach.

"Troy's thirteen and Bonnie's eight," Tescher said. "They'll be out of school in a few minutes, and they'll be in for dinner."

"Where is the school?"

"It's in a house trailer out back in the yard here."

"It's right here?" I said. "How does that come about?"

"Well," Tescher said, "there were the two of ours that go and Rodney Burnam, who's an eighth-grader with Troy. He lives across the river and comes over in the cable car, so because we have the two they moved it here."

"In other words, the school moves to the home place of the family with the most pupils?"

"That's right."

"And there's a teacher for just Troy and Bonnie and the other boy? Where does she live?"

"In the teacherage, in the back of the trailer," Tescher said. "We can go out and look at it later, if you care to."

When Troy and Bonnie came in and we were introduced, we sat down to dinner. Tescher said grace, and we had buffalo steaks and prairie hen, homegrown vegetables, home-baked bread, and homemade ice cream. After we had eaten, Gary started to carry some things to his car and I followed him out.

"Do you like this car?" I said. It was a Chevrolet Nova, not quite a year old.

"I like it fine," he said. "The only thing I have against it, it's not paid for."

It reminded me of his father. In Phoenix in 1964 I had watched him take out of the trunk of his car the bronc saddle he had paid $185 for in 1949 and had been using ever since. The leather was scarred and dry, and I had asked him what he treated it with.

"Just abuse," he had said.

"How far have you driven to rodeo this year?" I said to Gary now.

"I'd say about a hundred thousand miles."

"Do you share the driving with others, or do you do most of it alone?"

"Alone," he said. "North Dakota is kind of the armpit of the world as far as rodeo goes now, and there's not too many guys from around here."

"So to get to Abilene by tomorrow evening," I said, "you'll be driving most of the next twenty-eight hours. How do you stay awake?"

"I drink a lot of Coke," he said. "Coffee gives me heartburn. There's a lot of tricks, too. Eat sunflower seeds. Take your boots off. If you've made a good ride, though, you can drive around the world."

When he went back into the house to say good-by, I waited by the car, and when he came out his father was with him. They talked awhile, standing on the walk, and then he came over and I shook hands with him and wished him luck.

"Thanks," he said. "I sure hate to leave."

"I was the same way," his father said. "I always stayed too long."

We watched him drive out the gate for Abilene and then Albuquerque. When the car had disappeared down the slope, we started to walk slowly around the outside of the house.

"He's a fine young man," I said, "and I hope he makes it in rodeo."

"I've talked to two or three bronc riders who said he's goin' good," Tescher said, "but he just hasn't been drawin' good."

"Realizing how much he wants to win the world championship," I said, "and knowing how difficult that is, I've been wondering if I'm partially responsible. I mean, in that piece I wrote about you, I wrote how he wanted you to win it and how, when you just missed out that last night, he cried. I'm wondering if, focusing that attention on it, I may have helped to start him reaching for something he may very well never attain."

It is a responsibility that has concerned me for many years. A writer pries into many lives, and since what he writes and is printed and is read can alter those lives to some degree, he can only hope that, while it is accurate and the truth, it is also for the better.

"I don't think so," Tescher said. "I think he'd have tried anyway. I told him, 'If you're doin' it for me, don't do it.'"

"Do you give him any coaching, or any advice?"

"If I know the horse he's drawn. This one he's on in Albuquerque, I tried him out when Mike Cervi bought him. He's the biggest rodeo producer in the world, and Gary and I and two nephews went down to Spearfish to try out about fifteen horses for him when there was still snow on the ground in the arena. I just told Gary now that he's got to really hustle and keep throwing his feet ahead, because the horse really snapped, and you really have to hurry on him."

In Phoenix he had known them all, all he had ever ridden or just seen. He had studied them all, the way in big-league baseball the pitchers study the hitters and the hitters the pitchers, and in pro football the defensive backs keep mental book on every change of pace and fake and move of every receiver they have to face.

"You know what these are?" he said now.

We had walked around to the far end of the house. There were a half-dozen large animal skulls, bleached an off-white, propped against the foundation.

"Buffalo," he said. "They're a hundred years or more old. We found them buried ten to twenty feet underground. Where the draws wash out you see a horn, and you dig it out. They died in the creek or were washed in, and where Roosevelt lived they found a hairy elk. There are people who pay money for these now."

"Those buffalo steaks we had," I said. "Where do you get those?"

"I bought ten buffalo calves three years ago," he said, "from the fella who restored Medora, and I've still got two left. Two years old is prime, though."

"What about the buffalo in the National Park here?"

"About a dozen years ago," he said, "they began to rebuild the herd. It got to two hundred and twenty head in the south unit, and last year they shipped out over a hundred head to Indian reservations and other parks. There's about a hundred and fifty or sixty in the north unit, and when they're movin' them, we help round 'em up."

"You actually round up buffalo?"

"About eight or ten ranchers and a few rangers that can ride. Some are help, and some are hurt. You've got to be mounted real good, because they're hard to handle. You have to crowd buffalo a lot to get 'em started or to bend 'em, and if you're not mounted good, you don't dare get in there.

"They'll charge you real bad, the cows with the bulls and when the bulls get tired. You just have to outrun 'em, and I think the biggest thrill I ever had in my life was last year. Some other fellas were bringin' some in, and I had to run my horse real hard to help bend 'em, and it stepped in a prairie dog hole. It turned a somersault and skinned up its nose and head, and that takes a lot of drive out of a horse. It hurt my leg, but I remounted and rode in to help. One fella said, 'Look out, or that one cow will really take you.' She was the worst I ever seen. She charged me and she took me two hundred to three hundred yards through sagebrush, and it was thick. I couldn't see downed trees or holes or whatever. She was on my tail, and my hat fell off and she turned with that. We had trouble with her for two days straight.

"They're more vicious than the bulls," he said, "and they're so strong. There was a brand-new semi backed up there, and one took a run at another. Their horns come out straight and up, and they're terrible sharp. The one got its head under the other and threw her and the second one's horns went through the roof of this new semi. I remember the driver was kind of complainin', cryin' about his new semi. The biggest will go to twenty-four hundred pounds and one bull hit the gate eleven times and broke it. They have no reasoning power, and the last half mile from the pens you have to go as fast as you can, hootin' and hollerin' so they can't turn back."

"And how long does one of these round-ups take?"

"About three days."

My wife had come out of the house, and we walked down to the bunkhouse. There was a large main room, with a poured concrete floor and a fieldstone fireplace, and, at one end, two bunkrooms and a bath.

"Who built this?" I said.

"We put in the foundation," he said, "and hunters who come up here regular stayed for five days and put up the shell, and then we finished it. We've had two wedding dances in here, and they have the Christmas pageant in here, too."

"A Christmas pageant?"

"One year we had it back at the house in the living room," he said. "There's another school ten miles from here, and they combined. There were eight to ten kids, and the teacher took a part. All the neighbors will come from up and down the river, maybe thirty or so. Would you like to look in at the school?"

"I don't think we should go in while it's in session," my wife said. "I told Loretta we'll be going back to Medora for tonight, but we'll come out again tomorrow and stay over, if we may, and we'll see the school then."

"Fine," Tescher said. "Whatever you say. We're just pleased to have you."

Driving back out that afternoon, we were almost as hesitant as we had been coming in, afraid of taking a wrong turn, even of being stranded by a mechanical breakdown in this country where we did not see another vehicle or another person for the more than thirty miles. The next morning, after we had eaten breakfast again at Bud's

Coffee and Gift Shop and I had checked out of the motel, we drove the Interstate and turned north once more. Now, knowing where we were going, we were relaxed enough to notice even the smaller bird life, the meadowlarks and magpies, and to appreciate the patterns of sunlight and cloud shadow playing across the grasslands and illuminating the buttes and down into the draws.

We were to sleep that night in the basement room I had shared, that night twelve years before, with Gary, and after I took the bags out of the car, Loretta led us down. There were the two bedrooms, with the bath between, and what had been the kitchen and laundry, and off that, what had been the living room, all of it where they had lived for eight years under the flat roof of six layers of tar and tar paper.

After we had eaten that evening in 1964, Tescher and I had sat in the living room having a couple of drinks, and I had got him to talking about how, when he and his brother Alvin were living alone in the bunkhouse after the family ranch house had burned, someone would leave a horse with them to be broken. It would take them three or four weeks to get it roughed out and ready to handle, and then they'd take it back to the owner. That was how he got the thirteen dollars for his first pair of boots and ended his shoe wearing right then.

"We used to run wild horses, too," he said. "In those days these Badlands were full of 'em, and when I was seventeen I had forty-three head."

"In other words," I said, "when you wear those jeans and boots and that hat, it's not just a costume and you're not just acting."

Levi Strauss, a Bavarian sailmaker, brought blue denim and dungarees to the California gold miners in 1850, and the American cowboy adopted them. In the 1950s the jeans, which when new will almost stand alone, became a prop for the newly pubescent and an excuse to go unwashed for the arrested adolescent. They have since been bleached and bespangled, hijacked, counterfeited, and even corrupted by couturiers into costumes for the chic.

"Just acting?" he said. "I guess that's right."

In the pantry in that basement now, Loretta was showing my wife where she stacks on the shelves each year the three hundred quarts she puts up of tomatoes, peas, beans, carrots, corn, and peaches, along with the thirty or more jars of jellies and honey. At noon we ate buffalo meatballs, and then, with Loretta and my wife in the car, I drove Tescher the seven miles to their nearest neighbors, the Harris Goldsberrys, where Tescher was to pick up the Caterpillar to bulldoze some cattle trails in his winter pastures.

When we got there, Harris Goldsberry, a slim, taciturn man, was working on the Caterpillar, replacing the hydraulic pump. While Betty and Loretta went into the ranch house, where, they said later, they talked gardening with Margaret Goldsberry and had iced tea she had steeped in the sun, I watched the work on the Caterpillar for an hour, and then we left Tescher to drive the machine back while we drove back in the car. By then the school was out for the day. Rodney Burman had taken the wooden-platformed cable car back across the river, and Troy and Bonnie were about their chores when Loretta knocked on the trailer door.

"May we come in?" she said.

The white trailer was set up between the white-painted chicken house and the white-painted privy. There was a basketball backboard and basket off to the right, and there were a couple of dozen white hens and a couple of roosters wandering around. Inside the trailer, after Loretta left us to go back to the house, Sandy Schulz, five years out of North Dakota State Teachers College in Dickinson, and in her fourth year of teaching here, showed us around. Her living quarters were in the back half of the trailer—the sofa bed, a chair, a small television, the gas range and refrigerator, and the sink to which she would bring the water from a spigot outside. In the schoolroom half were her desk and the three others, bookshelves, a blackboard, and a wall rack of rolled maps.

"I suppose Bonnie gets reading and writing and arithmetic," I said. "What subjects do Troy and the Burman boy get?"

"The eighth-graders?" she said. "We have reading, math, spelling, United States history, North Dakota history, and earth science."

"And your books?" my wife asked. "You're able to get whatever books you need?"

"Oh, yes," she said. "The county librarian sends out the boxes of the books you write for, and it's always exciting when we get new books."

It was getting toward six o'clock when we heard the Caterpillar coming up the road and into the yard. Tescher came in and washed up and changed for dinner and we had pheasant. After dinner we sat in the living room with the glass-topped wagon-wheel table, with the award buckles—several dozen of them—set between the spokes under the glass. The two National Finals award saddles were on their stands, and the rodeo trophies were on the mantel of the fieldstone fireplace.

"I gave away about sixty-five buckles," Tescher said. "Some to relatives, some to rodeo fans, some to neighbor kids."

In the ten years he had rodeoed, he had won $160,000, but half of that had gone into expenses. Out of the rest he had built up the ranch, six thousand acres now in three units with 350 head of Hereford and the two dozen registered quarter horses from which he sells three or four colts a year.

"We bought the place in the fall of '52," he said. "I sold a new Packard car to pay the five-thousand-dollar down payment. There was this old log house, sort of stuccoed on the outside. It was out where the school is now, and I remember sitting in the kitchen and tryin' to read the newspaper and having to hold it down so the wind wouldn't blow it away. It was cold. That first winter I trapped bobcats and beaver to buy our groceries, and we lived off that."

"Do you still trap and hunt?"

"That's right. We reload our own shells, and we get coyote and some bobcat and trap beaver and coon. The coon bring two to five dollars and coyotes forty. Their furs sell good over in Europe, and a fella told me a coat sells as high as two thousand dollars over there. Bobcat hide are up to two hundred dollars apiece, and the beaver run twenty-five or thirty-five."

"And you've got your own bees and chickens," I said.

"We've got fifty hens," Loretta said. "We try to give the eggs away, but the neighbors give the children money."

"And the children, I suppose, have their chores?" Betty said.

"Troy gets up at six to milk," Loretta said. "Bonnie takes care of the chickens."

"And they break horses," Tescher said, "and they fill the creep feed."

"What is that?" I said.

"It's a bin in the calf bottom, where only the calves get in. It's oats and hay and they take care of that, every morning and night, from November first until about April twentieth. Then they have their own. Troy has three cows and a couple of yearling steers. When they get out of school, they have something to sell to go on to college if they want to.

"They're beef cows," he said, "and they all have their own brands, simple to put on, just straight irons and not writing all over the critter so they blotch. Barry helped brand this year, heelin' the calves and draggin' them out. There'll be three or four calf-rasslers—neighbors—and one dehorning and some vaccinating. One will do the castrating, and the women and children do the vaccinating."

"And how long does this take?"

"We'll do three hundred a day, usually June twentieth to July fourth. You have to spend two weeks ridin' to bring them in before branding."

"And then you have to bring them all in close to here before winter?"

"In the fall you spend a week gathering your stock for sale. Then the last two weeks of December we're ridin' to get them out of the common pastures and into the private pastures."

"When there was that buyers' strike against beef prices about four years ago," I said, "did that hurt?"

"I actually think the cattle were too high," Tescher said. "Prices went up over the counter, and ours started droppin'. People thought we were reapin' in money, but we'd been losin' money for three years, and I think TV has a lot to do with it. I think it hurts the farmer and rancher, because just as soon as they hear one morning that round steaks went down in New York City, it's plumb across the country and cattle drop that much.

"You take cattle to market now, and you don't know what they'll bring. The next day it may be up, but otherwise supply and demand took care of it. This way it's just talk, and now our fat cattle are bringin' the lowest since 1953, and a lot of people are goin' broke. The land is so high that there's no way of payin' for it, and the wrong people are gonna end up with it, for a sideline and a tax deduction.

"It's sad," he said, "when a young fella who's willing to work can't go out and buy a ranch and make it pay for itself in twenty years. There are people who owned land for thirty years who are goin' broke. I'm sure that the supermarket gets a lot of it. I think, though, that three quarters of the people in the United States are livin' too high off the hog, includin' ourselves, and we've pure had to back off.

"I'll tell you," he continued, "I think it's a lot tougher world to live in now. Things are too easy, and that's why it's tougher to amount to something. Work don't pay all that well now, and there's millions of people who get paid for not working. There's no pride left in work. I think there's more pride left in ranching than in most anything else."

"Well you should be proud of what you and Loretta have done here," I said. "I remember twelve years ago when your back used to hurt you when you'd take some time to sit down."

"It's pretty good now," he said, "if I don't work too hard. Haulin' bales by hand, it hurts all the time."

"And if it goes out, you haven't got Benny Reynolds to snap it in."

"Once in a while the chiropractors could get it back in place, but most couldn't," he said. "Probably they weren't strong enough, but Benny could, and it sounded like snappin' a log chain."

"Speaking of hauling bales by hand," I said, "I remember you telling me that the children, when they were just little tots, would drive the pickup in low gear while you stood in the back throwing off the bales."

"That's right," he said. "They'd go with me feedin', and they'd drive when they were about three. When they wanted to stop, if we came to a tree or whatever, they'd just shut the key off. By the time they were third-graders they knew how to drive."

"That's amazing," my wife said.

"A lot of this amazes me," I said. "When I was out here before, you didn't have a phone. The nearest one was your dad's in Sentinel Butte."

"That's right," he said. "The phone came in in 1971, and it made *The New York Times* and *The Wall Street Journal*. There are a hundred people on the exchange—it's Squaw Gap Exchange and there's an exchange building up here in the middle of nowhere—and everybody else is long distance."

"And what about the mail?" my wife said.

"The mail comes Mondays and Thursdays," Loretta said. "The postman comes to the mailbox across the river, weather permitting. Sometimes we'll go for several weeks without mail, but if somebody goes to town they pick up everybody's mail."

"Do you still mine your own coal?" I said.

"We dynamite in and use coal augers," Tescher said. "It's during Christmas vacation and the kids help. Five families get coal off my vein along the riverbank, and we take out twenty to thirty ton a winter."

"How cold does it get here in winter?" my wife said.

"I've seen it fifty-two below," Tescher said. "In January, three weeks at a time it'll never get up to zero during the day, and it'll be twenty to thirty below most nights."

"How hot does it get at the height of the summer?" I said.

"I've seen it a hundred and ten," he said. "It was a hundred and five one day in early September, and three nights later it froze."

"How much snow do you get?"

"On March twenty-third last year," he said, "everybody was startin' to calve, and on March twenty-fifth it was twenty below, and it snowed."

Loretta had left the room. When she came back she had a leather-bound diary in her hand.

"I have it in here," she said, and she read from it. "Sixth of April, still snowing and raining . . . Eighth, still stormy . . . April tenth was the last time it snowed. There were thirty-four inches."

"A lot of calves smothered in the snow," Tescher said. "Some froze to death and some got pneumonia. Some were three weeks old, and never saw the sun. In weather like that you've got to be right with them. The mother can save the calf at twenty below, but in the wet and chill they can't get dry. You didn't pay any attention to when the day started or ended because you had to be up all night. Everybody lost. Throughout this area we lost twenty percent of the calves, but in a way it done us some good, because everybody was overstocked.

"There was an old-timer lived down here," he said. "He came in 1904, and even guys like that say they'd never seen anything like it. Easter came and we couldn't get in or out, and we called a pilot who flies some around here to round up the horses. He went and got 'em up on top of a plateau about a mile from here, and the Goldsberrys have that Caterpillar and it had a plow on it. For six days that Cat wasn't shut off. We had to plow trails for the cows. It was the only way they could get to the feed."

"Do you ever get angry at the elements at times like that?" I said.

"No," he said. "I'm sure some people do, but I take it in stride, and make the best of it. I get down when the machinery breaks down and repairs are so high-priced."

"I guess the neighbors out here are all pretty special people," my wife said.

"If you don't neighbor," Tescher said, "you're not gonna make it. We had a bad winter in '64–'65 when we were isolated for seven or eight weeks. One winter it was longer than that. That road you came in on, it was closed from Thanksgiving to March. When we had the old roads, the only road we had would be to come up the ice in the winter."

"What about illnesses?" my wife said. "Are you able to get to a doctor?"

"The nearest doctor is in Beach," Tescher said. "That's forty-four miles, but we usually doctor in Dickinson and Williston. The one is ninety-five miles, and the other a hundred and twenty."

"Beach has changed, though," Loretta said. "They have two new doctors."

"Cindy broke her arm while she was in the eighth grade," Tescher said. "She had this horse she was breakin', and it drug her around the corral and hit the feed bunks and hooked on a post. She was kind of out of her head in the barn, and I didn't know if she was hurt internally. It was about four thirty and in February, and we'd never been plowed out. We had to go down the river and it was three to four feet deep and the water would go over the lights. We had her laid out in the back seat, and I'd given her a painkiller. We had to go six miles down the river, north and east, and across Beaver Creek to where the road was partially open, and we got to Beach at about eight o'clock."

"Then once, when we were snowed in," Loretta said, "Bonnie fell and hit her head on the fireplace. If we could have taken her in and she'd had stitches in it, it wouldn't have a scar now, but Jim taped it."

"What if you get, say, the flu, and you can't get out?" my wife said.

"I've given all the children and Loretta and myself penicillin shots for the flu and sore throat," Tescher said.

"How did you learn this doctoring?" I said.

"We have a Red Cross first-aid book," Loretta said.

"It's livestock penicillin," Tescher said. "I asked a doc about it and he said, 'That's all right, but what do you do if you have a reaction?' I said, 'Give 'em some of that stuff we have for the cattle. Epinephrine.' He said, 'Yeah. You're on the right track.'"

The next morning at breakfast we had orange juice, fried eggs, and Canadian bacon, pancakes with whipped cream and buffalo berries, red and tart, on them, and coffee. After breakfast, Tescher and I sat for a few final minutes in the living room, talking.

"As you look back over what you've lived up to now," I said, "are these the best years of your life?"

"The best years of my life," he said, "were the 1930s, my childhood. We were very hard up, with a house full of kids, but I was happiest then, ridin' and breakin' horses, ridin' to other ranches and helping them brand. Then the idea of responsibility started to invade, but when I was Troy's age it was the best years of my life."

"And when you first found out you could win money in rodeo," I said, "those were good years, too."

"That's right," he said.

He was eighteen, and his hero was Bill Linderman, who twice won the saddle-bronc title, and he had told me about it that night, sitting in the basement. In those days he and his brother Tom, who is four years older, used to travel in Tom's twelve-year-old Ford with wood and cardboard in place of the broken glass in the windows and no starter and almost no brakes, but with a good motor and good tires. The first major rodeo they went to was in Sheridan, Wyoming.

"When we got there," he told me, "we saw that Bill Linderman and some other name cowboys would contest, and it just sickened us. We thought of comin' back home, and then we waited until a few minutes before the entries closed, hopin' they wouldn't let us in, but they did. Tom won a third in the bareback and I won the saddle-bronc, and it paid a hundred ninety-two dollars and I thought I'd never see another poor day."

"When I won in New York in 1955," he was saying now, "it was the highest my feet were ever off the ground. A lot of times I felt I was overpaid. I didn't know how it could be happening to me. Will Rogers said that he'd rather be lucky than good, but if you're good you're lucky. A lot of people work real hard and can't make it, but just having the determination to work hard is a stroke of luck, too, because I think a person gets a lot of satisfaction out of working."

"What do you think is going to happen to this country in the years just ahead?" I said.

"I don't know," he said. "I sure don't know, but I think that people have to learn again to have respect for their work."

We had said good-by to the children in the kitchen before they had started across the yard to the trailer school. We said good-by to Loretta and Jim Tescher standing by the car. We said that yes, we would hope that someday we would be able to get out that way again, and they said that, if they could get away from the ranch sometime, they might visit a sister of Jim's in the East, and then we would see them again. As we drove out of the yard and looked back they were waving to us.

"What a reassuring experience," Betty said, "just to know that there are still people like that in this country."

"They're what's left of an America that once was," I said, "and soon won't ever be again."

We drove mostly in silence, until we saw, about a quarter mile off to the right and coming off a rise, about a dozen antelope. When they saw us they turned, their white rump patches showing, and crested the rise. Then, just over the rise, they turned again and peered at us, like small children in a playground who see something of interest passing outside. The last we saw of them they crossed the road about a half mile ahead and disappeared down into a draw.

So Long, Jack

John C. Hurley, 1897–1972

"There are two honest managers in boxing. The one is Jack Hurley, and I can't remember the name of the other."

Damon Runyon

IT WAS WHILE we were still driving West, heading for Medora and then Jim Tescher's. We were crossing the Red River on the wide, many-laned bridge between Moorhead, Minnesota, and Fargo, North Dakota, and it was midmorning.

"Are we going to stop in Fargo?" my wife said.

"Maybe on the way back," I said. "I'm not sure."

I have a friend named Walter Wellesley Smith, whose mother called him Wells, and who is known as Red. He was born and grew up in Green Bay, Wisconsin, and while he was running an elevator in the Northland Hotel summers and going to Notre Dame the rest of the year, he used to dream about sometime seeing a World Series, a heavyweight championship fight, and a Kentucky Derby. He writes a sports column for *The New York Times*, and in close to a half century he has attended forty-four World Series, fifty-four heavyweight championship fights, and thirty-three Kentucky Derbies.

"When we drive out to Jim Tescher's," I was telling him several months before, "we'll be going through Fargo. I'm thinking of stopping there and seeing if anybody remembers Jack."

"Oh, sure," he said. "You've got to do that."

Chapter 4 of *Once They Heard the Cheers*, 1979.

"I'll go to the sports department of the paper," I said, "and ask somebody, 'Can you tell me where Jack Hurley is buried?'"

"Of course," he said, "and you'll get some young noodnik who'll say, 'Jack who?'"

"I'm not much for visiting graves," I said.

"Oh, but you've got to do that," he said. "You've got to get Jack in the book."

About ninety miles west of Fargo I turned off the Interstate where we saw several of those gas-station signs on their high-legged towers, and got gas and drove into the adjacent restaurant for lunch. The waitress led us between two rows of booths, and in one of them a young man in his late teens, blond, blue-eyed, and sturdy, was sitting, looking at the menu. He had on a freshly laundered, blue football jersey with the white numerals 54 and, in orange block letters, the name WASHBURN across the chest, and he was leaning back at ease the way in high school my football heroes used to loll in class.

"Oh, you're from Washburn?" I heard a woman say in a reedy, treble voice. She was one of three, all of them white-haired, that the waitress had started to lead between the booths and, while the others had gone on, she had stopped at the young man's.

"Yes, ma'am," the young man said.

"I used to live in Washburn," she said. "What's your name?"

"Tracy," he said.

"Tracy?" the white-haired woman said. "Tracy? Well, you're a younger generation. I don't remember a Tracy."

"But I'm from Washburn High in Minneapolis," he said, indicating the name on the jersey.

"Tracy?" she said. "It's been such a long time since I lived in Washburn. Tracy?"

The young man started to say something but then, embarrassed, he shrugged and looked away. The woman, still repeating the name, walked on and joined the others in the booth. I looked at my wife and shook my head, and when I glanced over at the other booth again the young man had left.

"She scared him right out of the booth," I said. "Jack Hurley should be here, and it would get him started on the creatures again."

It was Jack Hurley's contention that more fighters are ruined by women, whom he called creatures, than by opponents' punches, alcohol, or whatever. The affliction, as Hurley saw it, was epidemic, affecting not only fighters but all married men, whom he called mules, in all callings, and nothing reaffirmed this for him more convincingly than the sight of women of advanced years enjoying a meal in a public place after, he was certain, they had driven their husbands into early graves.

"On the way back," Betty said, "we'd better stop in Fargo. After all, Jack Hurley meant so much to your life."

Of all those I came to know in sports nobody else ever fascinated me as did Jack Hurley. He seemed to me to be a literary character, as if he had stepped out of the pages of a novel, and I put him in one about a prizefighter and his manager. A novel, of course, should be larger than life but there was no way I could make my Doc Carroll bigger than Jack.

There were the last days I spent with him in Seattle and Boise in September of 1966, and all week I kept telling myself that I had written the book ten years too soon. He was moving his last fighter then, a heavyweight named Boone Kirkman, and when I got off the plane he was at the airport. I hadn't seen him in eight years, but there he was at the edge of the crowd, tall and bony, craning his neck and then waving. He looked a lot older and thinner and paler, and there was dark green glass over the right lens of his bifocals.

"How are you?" I said, as we shook hands.

With Jack I always knew what the answer to that one would be. The moment I would ask the question, I would get the feeling that I was the straight man in an act.

"No good," he said.

That had to be the truth. He was sixty-nine then, and wracked with the rheumatism he said he picked up in France in World War I. In addition to that, the surgical profession had been whittling away at him for years. They had taken his tonsils and his appendix for starters, and then, after he retired Billy Petrolle—his one great fighter—in 1934, they took two thirds of his stomach because of ulcers. While they were still trying to cure sinusitis with surgery, he had twenty-three operations, and recently I had read in *The Ring* that he had had a cataract removed from his right eye.

"Who hit you in the eye?" I said.

"Ah," he said. "Cataracts, so I decided to go for the operation."

"Good," I said. "That's one they've become very proficient at."

"Don't I know that?" he said. "So what happens? When it's over, I say to the doctor, 'Now, Doc, I understand that after ninety percent of these operations, the patient's sight can be corrected with glasses to twenty-twenty. Is that right?' So he says, 'Well, that's about right.' So I say, 'But, Doc, I'm not gonna have twenty-twenty, am I?' He says, 'Well, no.' So I say, 'All right. How good is my sight gonna be?' He says, 'Well, pretty good.'

"Now wouldn't you know that?" Jack said, that pinched look of disgust coming over his face. "Ninety percent are successful, but I have to be in the other ten percent. Why?"

"I don't know," I said.

"Now tell me something else," he said. "What does he mean by 'pretty good'? Just how good is 'pretty good'?"

"I don't know that, either," I said.

"I can't see a damn thing," he said. "Oh, hell. I can see some, but at the hotel I've already fallen down the stairs twice, and now I've gotta have the other eye done. How about that 'pretty good' though?"

Jack had been living in Room 679 of the Olympic Hotel since he had left Chicago seventeen years before to manage a light heavyweight named Harry "Kid" Matthews. He had also left his wife.

"So I'm hustling to make a living in Seattle," he told me once, "when one day these two detectives from Chicago show up. They've got a paper charging me with desertion, and they drag me back. Now I'm in Chicago again, and late one afternoon I come into the lobby of the hotel where we're living. All the creatures are sittin' around there—they've got nothing else to do—and as soon as I walk in I see them start lookin' at one another and their heads start going. One of them says to me, 'Oh, Mr. Hurley. When you get upstairs you won't find your wife there.' I say, 'Is that so?' She says, 'Yes, she's left you.'

"You see?" Jack said. "She can't wait to let me find it out for myself. So I say, 'Is that so?' She says, 'Yes, she's gone to Miami.' I say, 'Thank you.' I turn right around and I go over to the station house. I walk up to the desk sergeant, and I say, 'I want to report that my wife has just left me.' So the desk sergeant says, 'So what?' I say, 'So what? I'll tell you what. You know those two donkeys you sent out to Seattle to bring me back? Now I want you to send them down to Miami to bring my wife back.' You know what he said?"

"No," I said.

"He said, 'Listen, Hurley. You get out of here before I lock you up.' Now, isn't that terrible? What kind of justice is that?"

It was Hurley the teacher and ring strategist, however, who captured me. In boxing I knew three great teachers. Ray Arcel worked with seventeen world champions and, as one of the most gentle, kind, and refined of men, was concerned about the fighter as a person more than anyone else I ever knew. To him I would have entrusted a son. Charley Goldman worked on a fighter like a sculptor working on a block of marble, always trying to bring out all the truth within, and always afraid that if he did not go deep enough, he would leave some of it hidden, but also afraid that if he cut too deep, he would destroy some of it forever. Over a period of several years I watched him as, without destroying the fighters' gifts, he made a great heavyweight champion out of the awkward Rocky Marciano. Jack Hurley, the great ring strategist and perfectionist, as he crouched at ringside, squinting through those thin-rimmed glasses, saw a fight as a contest of the mind in which he was always moving his fighter a move or two ahead.

"I don't know why it is," Jack was telling me once, "but I can look at a fighter and know that he must do this or he must do that to lick the other guy. There are a lot of things I can't do. You can sit me down at a piano and I couldn't play 'Home Sweet Home' if you gave me the rest of my life, but I can just look at fighters and know what's right.

"Some people are just like that. Some years ago out in the Dakotas there was a kid playing third base for the Jamestown club in the Dakota League. Behind first base there was this high fence, and this kid playing third used to field the ball—and he had a terrific arm, and he'd not only throw the ball over the first baseman's reach, but he'd throw it over the fence.

"So one day," Jack said, "the word got around that a scout for the Yankees was in town to look at the kid. Everybody laughed. They said, 'What is this? He's wasting his time with a kid who can't throw any better than that.'

"The scout knew something, though. He had the ability to see something that no one else could. He took that kid and put him in at shortstop. He put him at deep shortstop, where the kid could cover a lot of ground and where he could make the throw. He played shortstop for the Yankees for a number of years. His name was Mark Koenig. I still don't know why it is that somebody can see something when everybody else can't."

Over the years, though, I came to know why Jack could see things in fighters and fights that others couldn't. I never saw his one great fighter, Billy Petrolle, in the ring, but fifteen years after Petrolle retired, Wilbur Wood was still telling me about his fights. Joe Williams, the Scripps Howard sports editor and columnist, once wrote that, in twenty-five years of watching fights in Madison Square Garden, the greatest he ever saw there was the first Petrolle–Jimmy McLarnin fight. As I watched Jack work with other fighters, and listened to him for hours while he talked about Petrolle's fights, it was obvious that he could see what no one else could because he had analyzed and broken down the science that precedes the art.

Jack was born and grew up in Fargo, and he was thirteen when his father, who was a switchman on the Canadian Northern, was killed pulling a coupling between boxcars. As the oldest of five children Jack had to go to work, and he started selling newspapers on Broadway and Northern Pacific Avenue where, to protect his corner, he had to fight.

There was a gym in the basement of Saumweber's Barber Shop across the river in Moorhead, and he started to hang around there, learning what he could by watching the other fighters. When he was fifteen he weighed 120 pounds, and he began boxing at smokers at night.

"I liked the boxing business," he told me once, "but I figured there must be an easier way. Then I got the idea of using the talents of others. I figured that if I could get a half-dozen kids and get them each a fight a month I could make more money than if I was fighting myself."

He was eighteen when he started managing fighters. He would go down to St. Paul and corner Mike and Tom Gibbons. They called Mike "The St. Paul Phantom," and Tom went fifteen rounds with Dempsey, and Jack would ask them questions, and as he watched fights, he would lift a move here and a move there, starting to build up his own library of moves and punches.

When World War I started, Jack got into it. He was in D Company of the Eighteenth Infantry of the First Division that, a generation later, I would come to know in Normandy and the Hürtgen and in Germany on both sides of the Rhine. For a while they were in Heudicourt, in the Saint-Mihiel sector, and the British sent in a sergeant major named Cassidy to teach the Yanks the bayonet manual.

"He was a miserable S.O.B.," Jack used to say, "but he knew his business. He would stand there unarmed with his hands down at his sides, and he'd say, 'Stick me!' You'd have your rifle with the bayonet fixed, and you'd make a lunge at him and you'd miss. Maybe the next time your rifle would go up in the air, or you'd get the butt of it under your chin. He did it all with feinting and footwork. He'd draw you into a lead, and that would be the last you'd have to do with it. You'd have the bayonet, but this Cassidy, without even touching the bayonet, would be controlling it.

"I used to go and see this guy at night," Jack said. "His stuff fascinated me, so one night I said to him, 'This puts me in mind of boxing.' He said, 'The bayonet manual was taken from boxing. If you're standing in the on-guard position, and I take the rifle out of your hands, you're standing like a boxer. Now I put the rifle back in your hands, and at the command of "long point" you make a left jab. Now you move the opponent out of position, and you come up to hit him with the butt. Isn't that the right uppercut?'"

It was the footwork that impressed Jack, though. As Jack told it, this Cassidy would stand right there with his feet spread, and he wouldn't move them more than a couple of inches and still they couldn't reach him with the bayonet.

"If a boxer would master this style," Cassidy told Jack, "he'd save thousands of steps. He'd be just as safe as I am, and he'd save all those fancy steps."

"And can't you see it now?" Jack would say. "As you look back on Billy Petrolle, can't you see where I got that famous shuffle step?"

Jack would forget, of course, that I had never seen Petrolle fight, that I was a high school kid at the time, but I had built up such a book on him, listening to Jack and others talk about him, that it was as if I had been at all those fights. Even now, after watching thousands of fights, I can "see" those Petrolle fights, punch by punch, as I have seen few fights.

There was the first McLarnin fight, that Joe Williams cited as the greatest he ever saw in the Garden. One of the moves that Jack had taught Petrolle was the knack of turning away from a right hand and throwing a right hand back, and just before the fight he sat down with Petrolle to map it out.

"Now remember," he said, "you can't turn away from McLarnin's right because he punches too long and too sharp. You'd be too far away from him to hit him. With this guy you have to resort to an amateur move. He won't expect it from you because he knows you're a good fighter, and he thinks you know too much. What you've got to do is drop the left hand. He'll throw the right, and you lean down under it and counter with the left instead of the right. He won't be looking for it, and you can't miss him with it."

Petrolle started drawing the right and countering with the left, and McLarnin didn't know where those punches were coming from. He knew they weren't coming from Petrolle, because Petrolle wouldn't do a thing like that and, as Joe Williams wrote later, at one point he looked at Patsy Haley, the referee, as if to ask, "Are you hitting me?"

"But McLarnin was some fighter," Jack said, and of course McLarnin went on to win the welterweight title, "and after a while he figured it out. Then I had Petrolle switch. He walked out there and started jabbing and missing, jabbing and missing. McLarnin thought he had him all figured out again, and he tried to anticipate Petrolle and moved in. He came in, right into a right that Petrolle had been building up all the time, and down he went."

Petrolle won that decision, but Jack always said his greatest fight was with Justo Suarez in the Garden seven months after McLarnin. Suarez was out of the Argentine, a bull of a lightweight, and they called him "The Little Firpo." After he came to this country and licked three of the best lightweights around, no one wanted to fight him, but Jack took him for Petrolle.

"After the match was made," Jack used to say, telling about it, "I went up to the gym to get a line on Suarez. He used to box sixteen or eighteen rounds a day without more than breaking a light sweat. The day I was watching him, he fell out of the ring and landed on his head and got up and went right back in. I said, 'Oh-oh, this is going to be it!'

"Well, Petrolle was some hooker, you know, and in the first round he had Suarez down three times. At the end of the round Suarez had Petrolle back on his heels, and when Billy came back to the corner, I said, 'Now don't hit him on the chin again. When you leave this corner you bend over and you punch with both hands to the body.' Petrolle used to follow orders to the letter, and for six rounds it was the most scientific exhibition of body punching anybody ever saw. At the end of the seventh round Petrolle said to me, 'Jack, I think he's ready.' I said, 'Not yet. Stay right down there and punch up.'

"At the end of the eighth round I said, 'All right, now is the time. Start this round the same way, and after three or four punches to the body, raise up and hit him a right hand on the chin. If he don't go, get down again and then raise up and hit him a left hand on the chin. If he don't go, you stay down.'

"Petrolle went out, belted that Suarez three shots in the body, and then came up. He landed the right hand flush on the chin and he shook Suarez. Now, another fighter would have been tempted to throw another right, but Petrolle went back to the body, and the second time he rose it was with the hook, and Suarez went over on his head. Hell, it was easy, if they'll only do what you tell them. The other fella doesn't know what he's doing. He's just guessing, but you know, because you've got it figured."

What Jack meant was that Jack had it figured. Crouched there below the corner he wouldn't be watching his own fighter, because he knew what his own fighter could do. He would be watching the other fighter, and not slipping or ducking any punches, he would be studying the other fighter's moves and analyzing his errors.

"So tell him about the Eddie Ran fight," Wilbur Wood said to him one day. We were in one of the dressing rooms at Stillman's Gym when Jack had Vince Foster, who looked like another Petrolle until Jack lost his grip on him to whiskey and women, and at the age of twenty-one, he died one night in a highway crash near Pipestone, Minnesota.

"Yeah," Jack said, "but the thing about Petrolle was that people never knew how good he was. They thought he was a lucky fighter, but what he did he did because it was planned that way. It wasn't any accident when he won a fight.

"Petrolle, you know, wasn't easy to hit. He gave the impression that he was easy to hit. Sure he did. He invited you to hit him. Do you know why? Because then he could hit you back. Petrolle would go in there and put it up there where you could hit it. He'd take two or three jabs, and then slip under and let go with the heavy artillery. That's a good trade any time you can take three light punches to let go with the heavy stuff. What gave people the impression that Petrolle was easy to hit was that he was always on the edge of danger. That's the place to be. Be in there close where you can work, where you take advantage of it when the other guy makes a mistake, and . . ."

"And don't pull back," Wilbur said. "That's where they get hurt."

"Certainly," Jack said. "For fifteen years I've been schooling myself. If I ever get into a theater fire I'm not gonna get up and rush for the exit. What chance have I got? Like the others, I'm gonna be trampled to death. Do you know what I'm going to do? I'm gonna sit right in my seat for thirty seconds and figure it out. Then I'm going to get up and walk over the others and pick my exit."

"But tell him about the Ran fight," Wilbur said.

"Sure," Jack said, "but, you see, it's like that when you fight. You're safest when you're closest to danger. You're inside where you may get your block knocked off if you don't know what you're doing, but if you know what you're doing it's a cinch. You look so easy that the other guy has to try to hit you. Don't you see? He can't help himself, and then when you've got him coming, you work your stuff, you let the heavy stuff drop. Why, Petrolle used to just sit there in that rocking chair and belt them when they came in."

"The Ran fight," Wilbur said.

"Yeah," Jack said. "In the first round he had Ran down a couple of times with hooks. When he came back to the corner I said, 'You're not going to drop him with a hook again. You've got to get him to throw the right. You've got to slip it like this . . .'"

He had his hands out in front of himself, and he moved his head as if he were slipping a punch.

"Do you know," he said, "that we had to wait until the sixth round for that chance for Petrolle to get that opening for his own right? He went out there, jabbing and jabbing and hooking light and sticking it right out there, and Ran wouldn't do anything. All of a sudden, though, Ran fired that right, and Petrolle slipped it and let his own go. It was really a hook with the right, and Ran went down—like this—like he'd been cut down at the knees with a scythe.

"After the fight, though," Jack said, that pinched look of disgust coming into his face again, "do you know what they said? They said Petrolle was lucky. They said, 'My, what a lucky punch. What a lucky fighter.' It wasn't luck. It was the work of an artist, and after Petrolle got dressed he went into Ran's dressing room. Ran said to him, 'Billy, I'm embarrassed.' Petrolle said, 'Why?' Ran said, 'I'm embarrassed of Eddie Ran. I knew you were gonna do that to me, but I couldn't help myself. You made it look so easy I just had to throw that right.'

"Then when he came out," Jack said, "Petrolle says to me, 'Jack, we'd better not fight them again. They're hep.'"

I wrote that for the next day's paper, the conversation in the dressing room with Jack talking and making the moves and Wilbur Wood cueing him. A couple of days later the old, white-haired receptionist at the paper who, it seemed to me, must have been there when they ran the headline that Lincoln had been shot, came shuffling into the sports department, and he had the name on the slip of paper and he said, "There's a Mr. Eddie Ran here to see you."

"Oh?" I said. "Send him in."

Seventeen years had gone by since the fight. How many times Eddie Ran had refought that one I had no idea, and how does a man react when, suddenly in a newspaper, he reads a description that brings back a night when he was knocked out?

"Mr. Heinz?" he said, walking up to me and putting out his hand. "I'm Eddie Ran."

He had on heavy work clothes, brown pants and a brown windbreaker and heavy work shoes. He was slim, and his face was tanned.

"I'm glad to meet you," I said, shaking his hand and waiting.

"I'm glad to meet *you*," he said, and then he smiled. "Gee, that was some column you had in the paper yesterday. I'm working on the docks over at the river, so I just had to come in and tell you."

"All I did was write what Jack Hurley said."

"Hurley told you the truth," he said. "That was some fight, and like Hurley said, I knew Petrolle wanted me to throw that right, but I just couldn't help myself."

Jack named Petrolle "The Fargo Express," and gave him one of the great trade names of boxing. Petrolle was of Italian descent, but he had high cheekbones to go with his black hair and dark eyes, so Jack gave him one of the great trademarks—an Indian blanket—to wear into the ring. When Petrolle retired after 255 fights and built a home in Duluth, he wanted to hang that blanket on the wall of his den.

"But it has blood on it," his wife said.

"Only some of it is mine," Petrolle said.

All Petrolle and Jack ever had for a contract was a handshake, but after thirteen years Petrolle retired during the Depression with $200,000 and an iron foundry in Duluth. When I met him years later, he owned a religious-goods and gift shop in Duluth, and he was the chairman of the board of directors of the Pioneer National Bank.

After Petrolle retired, after his hook was gone, and after his legs had left him, Jack announced in Duluth that he was looking for somebody to take the place of "The Fargo Express." The story went out over the Associated Press wire, and within the next week six hundred candidates showed up in Duluth.

"I forgot what it cost me to get them out of town," Jack used to say. "The Police Department came to me and said, 'Look, you got Michigan Street loaded with guys stranded here.' I had to pay the fare home for half of them, and there wasn't a fighter in the lot. Most of them should have been arrested for even entertaining the thought that they could be taught to fight."

There were very few people in the fight business then who wouldn't have found a way to make some money out of those six hundred, but not Jack. To Jack a fighter was a tool, and he was always looking for the tool that, when he finished shaping it and honing it over the years, would be the perfect tool to do the perfect work. He put all of himself into it, and when a Hurley fighter went into the ring Jack took every step with him. That fighter was what Jack would have been if he had had the body for it, and that is why it took so much out of Jack when, under pressure, the tool broke.

The best Jack had after Petrolle was Harry "Kid" Matthews, who had had seventy fights in twelve years but was getting nowhere when Jack took him on. Before he was done with him, Jack actually started a congressional investigation into why the International Boxing Club wouldn't give Matthews a fight in the Garden. When they did, they put him with Irish Bob Murphy, who was belting everybody out, and they gave Murphy to Jack because nobody else would take him.

"Well, you're in," somebody said to Jack. "All you have to do is lick this guy and you're in."

A half dozen of us were sitting around in the boxing office on the second floor of the Garden. We had just been making small talk when Jack had come in. He was fifty-three then, and Royal Brougham had written in the *Seattle Post-Intelligencer* that he looked like a stern-faced deacon passing the collection plate at the First Methodist Church.

"Sure, we're in," Jack said, those ice-blue eyes narrowing behind those glasses, and a hurt look coming over his face. "We're in with a murderer. This guy never lets up. He rips you and slashes you and tears you apart inside. He's rough and strong, and you can't hurt him."

Jack turned and started to leave. He got as far as the door, and then he turned back and his eyes were big now behind the glasses and he had fear all over his face.

"That's the kind of guy you have to fight to get in here," he said. "Why, we're liable to get killed."

He left then. Pete Reilly was sitting there, and he had been around for so many years and worked so many a deal that they called him "The Fox."

"Listen to Hurley," Pete said, smiling and shaking his head. "When Jack talks like that you know he's got it figured. You know he's ready to slip one over. You can bet your bundle on that."

The smart money bet the bundle on Murphy, and it was some licking that he and they took. Matthews would draw a lead, and then he would slide with that shuffle step into one of those Hurley moves and he would belt Murphy so that the cops with the duty out on Eighth Avenue must have felt it. It was the greatest exhibition of body punching I have ever seen, and all the time that it was happening to Murphy there wasn't any way that Murphy could avoid it without turning his back and walking out.

The next day, up in the Garden, everybody was crowding Jack. They were slapping him on the back and telling him it had been years since they had seen anyone who could punch like that, and that it had been some fight.

"When I got home last night and went to bed," Irving Rudd was telling Jack, "it was like I had just finished a great book. I kept seeing it over and over, and I couldn't get to sleep."

"Why, in the ninth round," Jesse Abramson said to Jack, and Jesse was writing for the *New York Herald Tribune* then, "your guy hit Murphy seven solid hooks without a return. I counted seven terrific hooks to the body, and Murphy couldn't help himself. It was wonderful."

"Yes, wasn't that wonderful?" Jack said, and now that pained look came into his face again. "Why, that was stupid. After he'd hit that Murphy with three of those solid hooks and turned him around, if he'd just thrown one right-hand uppercut he'd have knocked that stiff out."

"But it was still a great fight," somebody said.

"And he'll do the same with that Marciano," Jack said, "if I can get him the fight."

That was one I never wanted for Jack, and I tried to talk him out of it. Putting Matthews against Marciano was like sending an armored jeep against a tank, but by the time Jack had sold the press and the public on Matthews he had also sold himself.

"I've been watching Charley Goldman working with Marciano," I told Jack. Jack had come into New York and we were having lunch in one of the booths in Muller's across Fiftieth Street from the Garden.

"Oh?" he said.

"Charley's really making a fighter out of him," I said.

"He is, is he?" Jack said.

"That's right," I said. "He's got him moving inside now and punching to the body, and you know he can sock."

"Ah," Jack said. "You know what you do with those body-punchers? You belt them right back in the body, and that puts an end to that."

"But this guy is too strong for your guy," I said. "You can't hurt him."

"Ah," Jack said, and there came that look, as if he had just bitten into another lemon. "Matthews will do to that Marciano just what he did to that Murphy. It'll be the same kind of fight."

Jack really believed it, and he had $10,000 bet on Matthews when they climbed into the ring in Yankee Stadium that night. I had to give Matthews the first round, because there he was, drawing Marciano's leads, moving off them and countering in that Hurley style, but all the time that it was going on, Marciano was backing him up. Matthews was winning the round, but losing the fight, and then, just as the bell sounded, Marciano hit him a right hand under the heart and Matthews bent under it, straightened up, and started for Marciano's corner. Jack hollered at him, and he turned and walked to his own corner and I knew it was over. Early in the next round, and with a left hook, Marciano knocked him out.

"So are we going to stop in Fargo?" my wife was saying now. "We'll be there well before noon."

Driving back now from Jim Tescher's, we had got as far as Bismarck, and had spent the night in a motel on the outskirts. We were having breakfast, and I was looking at the front page of the *Forum*, the Fargo-Moorhead paper. There was a two-column picture of a farmer standing thigh-deep in a fissure in his alfalfa field near Durbin, North Dakota. The farmer's name was Richard Hillborn, and it said in the caption under the picture that he couldn't recall conditions ever being so dry, even in the drought of the 1930s.

"I guess so," I said, "but as it's a Saturday, there may not be anybody in the sports department of the paper. They may all be out covering football games for the Sunday paper."

"But I'm sure there'll be someone there in some department," she said. "You'll probably find someone to ask."

"I'd like to find somebody in sports, though," I said. "I doubt that anybody on the city side will remember Jack, but I'll find out."

When we passed the turnoff to Jamestown, and I saw the high-towered gas station signs on the left now, it reminded me of the white-haired woman who had flushed the high school football player out of his booth. The last we had seen of him he had been having a sandwich across from the cashier's counter when I had stopped to pay the check. The last we had heard of her she was still rasping, as she had been throughout our lunch, about ailments, not only her own but those of what must have been a whole battalion of invalided friends or acquaintances, none of whom, as walking wounded, could compare with Jack.

"Now isn't this something?" Jack was saying outside the Olympic when we got out of the cab that time he met me at the Seattle airport. "I checked in here for a week to manage that Matthews, and I've been here seventeen years. You have to remember, too, that I've got the two worst things in the world for this climate—rheumatism and sinus."

He waited while I checked in, and then we followed the bellhop up to the room. The bellhop went through all the business with the window shades and the closet doors and the bathroom light, and Jack beat me to the tip.

"All right," he said, when the bellhop had left. "Let's go down and get something to eat."

"Eat?" I said. "It's the middle of the afternoon."

"You know me," Jack said. "You know I have to eat every three hours."

Jack hated to eat alone, and that was how Ray Arcel came to call him "The Life-Taker." Jack was still around Chicago at the time, and it was just after they had taken two thirds of his stomach and he had to eat six times a day.

"It was during the Depression," Ray told me once, "and Jack had just retired Petrolle and had money, so he'd take these poor guys who were half-starving to eat with him. Jack would have a bowl of soup, or milk and crackers, but they'd order big steaks. One guy ate so much that Jack had to buy him a new suit of clothes, and another one actually ate himself to death."

They used to say around Seattle that while Jack had Matthews he would spend $1,000 a month feeding sportswriters and cops and press agents and hangers-on. Whenever he had it, he spread it around.

"When Petrolle was fighting," he told me once, "I loaned out sixty thousand dollars. I had it all in a little book. Then, when I had the ulcers and I went into the Mayo Clinic, I sent out eight letters and six telegrams to guys who owed me five hundred dollars and up. I never got one reply, and I've got seventy-five thousand dollars more standing out since."

That first afternoon I walked Jack down Fourth Avenue to his favorite cafeteria, and watched him have a bowl of soup and a sandwich and a cup of tea. Then we walked over to the Eagles Temple at Seventh and Union, where the fighter trained, and all along the way people recognized Jack.

"How are you, Jack?" they'd say.

"No good," he'd say.

"Why, Jack!" they'd say. "How are you feeling?"

"No good," he'd say.

One noon we sat down in the restaurant in the Olympic Hotel. He had been living in that hotel for so long by then that just about everyone on the staff knew him, and when the waitress came over she was smiling.

"Why, Mr. Hurley!" she said.

"Hello, Hilda," Jack said.

"Mr. Hurley," she said, "you won't like what I'm going to say."

"What's that?" Jack said, squinting up at her.

"You're looking much better than the last time I saw you."

"Isn't that terrible?" Jack said to me. "You know I set the world's record for those sinus operations. They found out with me that there's no sense in operating. I was a guinea pig for medical science, just a living sacrifice to make the world safe for guys with bad noses."

That first afternoon at the Eagles Temple, I could see why Jack was high on the fighter. He was a dark-haired, dark-eyed kid who looked right at you, and you could tell that he was not going to be cowed by anybody or anything. He had a good pair of legs, but the best of him was up in the arms, chest, and shoulders, and he was just the right height to carry 195 pounds and still get under tall jabbers who stick out a left hand and think that they're boxing.

"So he was the 1965 National A.A.U. heavyweight champion," Jack was saying while the fighter was getting into the ring, "but he was like all amateurs—awkward and over-anxious, and just a wild right-hand swinger. For six months, every day, we worked on the footwork. His stance was too wide, so I had to tie his feet together with shoelaces and a piece of inner tube that would give about six inches. He'd walk with it, shadowbox with it, and this is a long tedious thing. You get sick and tired of it, but it's balance and leverage that make punching power.

"All right," he said to the fighter. "Move around. Let's see how fast you can move. Now slow it down. Good.

"You see?" he said to me. "He slows the action down to where he wants it—to one punch. I've taught him that speed is detrimental, because if you're moving fast you're also moving your opponent fast. If you're out hunting, would you rather shoot at a slow-moving or a fast-moving target? It's the same thing. He's been taught how to put two thirds of the ring behind him. He doesn't want it, but those jabbers and runners do, and he deprives them of it."

Jack had the fighter box three rounds then, but there was the same shortage of fighters in Seattle as everywhere else, and the light heavyweight he was in with had been around Jack and the fighter too long. As soon as the fighter would start to build up a move the light heavyweight would know what was doing, but you could see one thing. You could see that this was another Hurley fighter, and if you knew anything about boxing you could tell a Hurley fighter from the others as easily as an art expert can tell a Rembrandt from a Harry Grunt. There was that shuffle step, that came out of Heudicourt and the bayonet drill that Jack perfected with Petrolle, and there were those moves, with the hands low and in punching position, inviting you to lead and have your block knocked off with the counter.

"But don't you see?" Jack was saying to the fighter when it was over. "You were jumping in instead of sneaking that right foot up. You gotta sneak it up so they don't know it's coming. They think you're just jabbin', but that's only the camouflage so you can move the artillery up behind the jab. I don't even care if the jab misses."

With Jack eating every three hours and not going to bed until two or three in the morning because he had trouble sleeping, we spent a lot of time sitting around restaurants and cafeterias and the lobby of the Olympic with Jack's cronies, talking about the way things used to be and what the world was coming to. That was Jack's hobby.

"Isn't it terrible, the condition the fight game is in today?" Jack would say. "You wouldn't believe it, would you? A lot of Johnny-come-lately booking agents who call themselves managers and don't know the first thing about it. Amateurs! Why, amateurs just clutter up the world. They louse up everything they put their hands to.

"Look at what that television did, too," he'd say, "and it'll do it to pro football next. Why, you can't give your product away free and have people still respect it. That TV cheapens everything it touches. It would even cheapen the Second Coming."

Late every afternoon, of course, we would be over at the Eagles Temple, with Jack hounding the fighter. No matter what the fighter would be doing—boxing, shadowboxing, punching the bag, or skipping rope—Jack would be after him.

"No, no," Jack would say, the fighter shadowboxing around the ring. "Don't set your feet. Just walk. Now the left hook to the head. You're too tense. Just turn with it. All right. Now you jab, and the guy is a runner, so you're too far away. Now you gotta step again. Now the guy is pulling away, so you gotta throw three punches, but only one is gonna land. Now you're with a guy throws an uppercut. Now turn away so it misses, and throw the right hand up into the body. Good.

"You see?" Jack said to me. "He's like a pool player, practicing those draw shots. He's gotta get that ball back there, so he practices hour after hour until it becomes instinct. Like a pool player, he's also playing position at all times, and you know how long this practice lasts? His entire career. He'll still be practicing it when he quits, and you know something? If he's having trouble hitting a left hook to the body, it's nothing for me to sentence him to two weeks of doing nothing else. He wants to learn it to get rid of me.

"All right now," he'd say to the fighter. "You're in there with one of those runners, so you don't want to scare him or he'll start running again. Easy now. Left hook to the body. No, no! Let him see it. Start it back farther so he'll be sure to see it, because you want him to drop his hands. Good. Do that again.

"You see?" Jack said to me. "Other guys breed fear, but it's like cornering a frightened pig. This guy has been taught to encourage them, to make them feel safe. He'll sometimes miss a jab to give 'em courage, and Petrolle even had the facial expressions to go with it. The first thing you knew, he'd catch those suckers moving in."

The last afternoon, though, Jack was discouraged. We had to be in Boise the next day so Jack could go on TV and radio and talk up the fight. The fighter was going to come in two days later, just in time for the weigh-in, with Marino Guaing, the little Filipino who was training amateur fighters around Seattle and helped Jack.

"No, no," Jack was saying to the fighter, watching him hit the big bag. "The left hook is too tight. It's gotta be looser. Just throw it up there. No good. Your feet were off the floor. No. Bend those knees a little. It's like you're on stilts.

"Isn't that terrible?" Jack said to me, turning away from the fighter and shaking his head. "He never did that before. You gotta watch 'em every damn minute of the day.

"Now start soft," he said to the fighter. "Easy. Now increase the power a little. Now you're stiff-legged again. Start over."

The sweat was dripping off the fighter's chin. The floor under the bag was speckled with it, but Jack was still unhappy walking back to the hotel.

"Now where would he have picked that up?" he said. "You see what I mean? He picks up a bad habit, or he goes on the road and he steps on a pebble and he turns his ankle. He's liable to sleep with the window wide open and catch a cold. He comes to the gym and he may get his eye cut or hurt his hand. That's why, when you manage a fighter, you end up with cancer, heart trouble, or ulcers. I took the least."

"But look at the rewards," I said, hoping to kid Jack out of it. "How about all that fame and fortune?"

"Yeah," Jack said. "You raise him like a baby. That ring is a terrible place to be in if you don't know what you're doing in there, but you teach him how to survive. You teach him how to make his first steps, and you bring him along until he becomes a good fighter and starts to make money.

"Now, when you come into the ring with him you don't do nothin'. He's a professional fighter. He doesn't need people pawing at him and dousing him with water and tiring him out. He needs a little quiet advice, but no one sees that. So they see me up there, and they say to the fighter, 'What's *he* do for you?' Twenty guys say it, and it means nothin'. By the time eighty guys say it, though, the fighter forgets. This one will too.

"I'll tell you," Jack said. "Regardless of the outcome, this is my last fighter."

At 7:30 the next morning I met Jack in the lobby, and a bellhop named Harry carried our bags out and wished Jack luck. In the cab on the way to the airport Jack was looking at the heavy traffic heading into town.

"Look at the mules," he said. "Isn't that terrible? At four thirty they'll all be heading the other way to take those paychecks back to the creatures. When I started out, my mother wanted me to get a steady job. I said, 'Mom, a steady job is a jail. I see these fellas I grew up with here, and they're in prison ten hours a day. I want to see something, go somewhere, and I can make a living doing it.' You care where you sit on the plane?"

"No," I said.

"I like to sit over the wing," Jack said. "It kinda gives you the feeling you've got something under you. Besides, I couldn't sleep last night. I think I slept an hour, so I want to grab a little nap."

We were the first in line and the first on the plane, and I had Jack take the window seat where he wouldn't be bothered by the traffic in the aisle. I reached up and got him a pillow, and he had just settled his head back and closed his eyes when I heard the small voice right behind us.

"Eeee choo-choo, Mommy?" the voice was saying. "Eeee choo-choo?"

"No," the woman's voice said. "Not choo-choo, dear. Airplane."

"Eeee choo-choo?"

Jack opened his eyes. He had that pinched look on his face again, and he sat up.

"Isn't that something?" he said, shaking his head. "With the whole plane to pick from I gotta draw a creature and her kid. Wouldn't you know it? Ninety percent of those eye operations are successful, too, but I gotta be in the other ten percent."

It didn't make any difference, because Jack wasn't going to sleep anyway. We weren't off the ground more than twenty minutes when Jack's rheumatism started to act up, and he had to stand in the aisle, holding on to the arm of my seat, almost all the way to Boise.

"Isn't that terrible?" Jack said, as we were getting off. "A whole plane, and that creature and the kid have to sit behind us."

"But he was a cute kid," I said.

"Yeah, you're right," Jack said. "I took a look at him, and he was."

Then Jack really went to work. After we checked into the hotel we walked down Main Street, with Jack saying he couldn't see a thing in the bright, shimmering sunlight and with me helping him up and down the curbs, to Al Berro's. Al Berro was promoting the fight, but for a living he was running the Bouquet Sportsmen's Center. The Bouquet had one of those long Western bars down the right side, with the meal for the day chalked on a blackboard at the far end, and along the opposite wall a half-dozen tables with faded green baize covers and the nine-card joker rummy games going.

"Am I glad you're here!" Berro said, shaking Jack's hand.

"How's it look?" Jack said.

"Pretty good," Berro said.

"There goes that 'pretty good' again," Jack said to me.

"I think we'll do all right," Berro said, "but I've got you lined up for the radio and TV. You ready to start?"

In the next eight hours, with Berro driving us around town, Jack was on two television and four radio stations, and at nine o'clock that night he was over at the *Idaho Daily Statesman*.

"Now what brings you to Boise?" one of them, interviewing Jack on the TV or the radio, would say, as if he didn't know.

"Well, I've got Boone Kirkman boxing Archie Ray, from Phoenix, at the Fairgrounds Arena on Thursday night," Jack would say. "My best friends in the boxing game tell me I may be making a mistake, though, because my fighter has had only four fights and Archie Ray has had twenty-three, with eighteen wins, ten by knockout."

"What's going to happen at the Fairgrounds Arena on Thursday night?" another would say.

"Well, it's hard to tell," Jack would say. "All the people in the fight game tell me Archie Ray is gonna lick my fighter for sure, but of course I don't think so."

"Jack, is Boone going to shoot for a first-round K.O.," another would say, "or is he going to play with this fella?"

"He doesn't play with anybody," Jack would say. "You see, all my boxing friends tell me Archie Ray is gonna be too much for my guy, but we'll find out Thursday night at the Fairgrounds Arena."

Jack did some job. Knowing how he felt, and that he hadn't slept much the night before, I was amazed that he got through the day.

"Ah, I don't have the enthusiasm for it any more," he said when we got back to the hotel.

"You've got me beat," I said.

"I'm old and I'm sick and I'm tired," he said, "but you can't let the bastards know it. They'd kill you."

On the day of the fight, the fighter and Marino, the trainer, got in about twenty minutes before the one o'clock weigh-in at the State Capitol. The elevator operator who took us up was a middle-aged woman wearing a white uniform blouse and dark skirt. She was sitting on a stool in front of the panel of buttons and, open on her lap, was an instructional volume of the Famous Writers School.

"Do you subscribe to that course?" I asked her on the way down.

"Yes," she said, looking up at me and her face brightening. "Do you?"

"No," I said, "but I've heard about it."

"I think it's just wonderful," she said. "I'm really enjoying it."

"Good," I said.

"What was all that about?" Jack said to me when we got off.

"She's taking a correspondence course in how to be a writer," I said. "It costs over four hundred bucks, and I think that, for the ones like her, it's a lonely hearts club."

"That figures, don't it?" Jack said.

When we got back to the hotel, Jack had the fighter rest until 3:30. Then we took him to the restaurant across the street.

"You'd better bring him two of your top sirloins," Jack said to the waitress, "and a baked potato and hot tea."

"The baked potato doesn't come on the menu until five," the waitress said.

"In Idaho?" the fighter said.

"Isn't that terrible?" Jack said, looking at me. "They want you to eat what they want you to eat when they want you to eat it."

After the fighter finished eating he took a walk with Marino, and Jack and I went down to a café he liked on Main Street, and he had a ham sandwich on whole-wheat bread, sliced bananas, and a cup of tea. At 7:30 Jack was sitting in the hotel lobby when the fighter and Marino came down from their rooms with Marino carrying the fighter's black zipper bag.

"Listen," Jack said to the fighter, "when you finished eating across the street there, did you remember to tip the waitress?"

"Gee, no," the fighter said. "I forgot."

"Here," Jack said, handing him a bill. "Go over and do it now." When the fighter came back we all got in a cab and went out to the Fairgrounds. In the dark the cabbie missed the main entrance, so we rode around between a lot of barns before we got to the arena with the sign SALES PAVILION over the door.

"You see?" Jack said when we got inside, the customers milling around us. "It's like the old Cambria in Philadelphia."

From where the ring was set up in the middle of the floor the solid planking of the wooden stands went back and up like steps on all four sides to where the walls and the ceiling rafters met. The stands were about half full, with more customers climbing up and sliding along the rows and sitting down.

"You gonna fill up?" Jack said to Al Berro.

"I don't know," Berro said. "I've got eleven hundred and fifty bucks in, and I've only collected at the Stagecoach, Hannifin's, and a couple of others. I've got Homedale and Mountain Home coming in yet, so we'll do pretty good."

"There goes that 'pretty good' again," Jack said.

They had the fighter dressing under the stands in a small room with a wash basin and a toilet in it and a shower without a curtain. There was no rubbing table, only a green painted bench, and when the fighter stood up, he had to be careful not to hit his head on the naked lightbulb sticking down from the low ceiling.

It was hot in the room, so the fighter had stripped down and was in his black trunks with white stripes. He had put on his white socks and was lacing his ring shoes. Through the wall you could hear the ring announcer bringing on the first preliminary.

"Marino," Jack said, "tell them I'm gonna start bandaging and to send somebody over here if they want to watch."

"But I was just there," Marino said. "They don't come in yet."

"Then the hell with them," Jack said. "I'm gonna start anyway."

"Oh, excuse me," one of the customers said, looking in. "I thought this was the men's room."

"Next door," the fighter said.

"This will go on all night," Jack said. "They sell a lot of beer here."

With his bad eyes Jack had to squint to see what he was doing, but after bandaging fighters' hands for a half century, he could have done it with his eyes closed. While he was putting it on—the gauze around the wrist, and then across the palm and between the thumb and index finger, and then back around the wrist and around the hand and across the knuckles, and then the tape—we could hear the crowd hollering and then, over our heads, the stamping of feet.

"All right," Jack said to Marino when it was over. "Grease him up."

Marino rubbed the cocoa butter on the fighter's arms and shoulders and chest and neck and face. When he had finished, Jack sent him to watch the other people bandage and put the gloves on. The fighter was sitting on the bench, his bandaged hands in his lap, serious now.

"The hell with them," Jack said after a while. "We might as well get into the gloves. Then you'll have plenty of time to loosen up, because they take that intermission to sell more beer."

"Good," the fighter said.

Jack helped the fighter into the right glove first, the laces down the palm and then around the wrist, then tied the ends and put a strip of tape over it. When he had finished with the left glove, Marino was back.

"They all done now," he said.

"All right," Jack said to the fighter. "Loosen up, but be careful of that light. Now jab . . . hook . . . jab . . . move up behind it. All right, but don't stand there. You gotta move right up behind it. And another thing, if you start to miss punches just settle down and start over again."

"I know," the fighter said.

"We're ready to go, Jack," Al Berro said, sticking his head through the doorway after the fighter had had about five minutes of it. "You ready?"

"Yeah," Jack said, and then to Marino, "You got the mouthpiece?"

They went out and down the aisle, Marino first, carrying the pail, and then the fighter and then Jack. The aisle was crowded, some of the customers still trying to get back to their seats with their containers of beer, and then the calls started from the stands.

"Hey, Jack! How many rounds?" . . . "Good luck, Jack!" . . . "Hey, Kirkman, how about our money's worth tonight?"

When the bell rang, Jack's fighter walked out in that Hurley style, hands low and in punching position, and he walked right to Archie Ray. Archie Ray was a straight-up fighter, with a pretty good jab and a straight right hand, and he started out to make a fight of it. He punched right with Jack's fighter, and I gave him that first round. Jack hadn't said a thing, but now he was up in the corner, bending over the fighter and lecturing him, and when he came down the steps at the start of the second round I could see he was still mad.

"Hey, Kirkman!" some loudmouth was hollering. "You're gonna get yours tonight!"

"His stance was too wide, and his feet are too flat," Jack said. "What's the matter with him?"

"He's tense," I said. "He'll fight out of it."

"Tense, hell," Jack said. "He's never been like this before."

He didn't fight out of it. In the second round you could see he was trying to settle down and put his moves together, but he was still too anxious. The young ones, if they're really fighters, are usually that way. They know what they're supposed to do, but then they are hit with a good punch, and they widen that stance and start swinging because they want to end it with one. Jack's fighter was still throwing punches from too far out, but he was hurting Ray with right hands. You had to give him that second round and the third, too, although he came out of a mix-up he should never have been in with his nose bleeding.

"Hey, Kirkman!" the loudmouth was hollering when he saw the blood. "How do you like it now?"

"Isn't this terrible?" Jack was saying. "All he's got to do is jab and move up before he lets those right hands go. What's the matter with him?"

"He's still trying too hard," I said.

"Hell," Jack said.

In the fourth round he had Ray against the ropes and then through them, but he couldn't finish him, and in the fifth round he dropped him with a nice inside right hand to the body and still couldn't put him away. Ray looked like he was in there just to stay now, and by the sixth round you could see Jack's fighter tiring, the way they all do until they learn pace. He would be all right for the first half of a round, but then he would flatten out and start to flounder. In the eighth round, though, he made one good Hurley move. He drew that right hand of Ray's and, when it came, he turned from it and turned back with his own. It was a little high—on the cheekbone—but it caught Ray following through and moving into it, and Ray's knees started to go as he backed off.

"He's got him now," I said to Jack.

"And everybody in the house knows it but him," Jack said over the roar, and by the time he said it, the chance was past. "Isn't that terrible?"

That was the last round, and it had been enough of a war so that the crowd liked it. Jack's fighter got the unanimous decision, but when we got to the dressing room he was still disgusted, and Jack was, too.

"I swear I can fight better than that," the fighter was saying to two of the local sportswriters. "That's the worst fight I've ever had."

"He was in a trance," Jack said. "He couldn't even follow orders, and he always follows orders to the letter."

"I didn't even feel like I was in a fight," the fighter said. "I can't understand that."

"The hell with it," Jack said finally. "Let's get out of here."

An hour later we were still sitting in the restaurant across the street from the hotel. The fighter had a milk shake, and Jack was nibbling on a ham and cheese sandwich on whole wheat and still going over the fight.

"He comes back at the end of the first round," he said to me, "and he says, 'I'm not sick, but something's the matter with me.'"

"That's right," the fighter said.

"So I said, 'It's too bad, but you're here. You're having a bad night, but you'll fight out of it. You're punchin' from too far back. Jab and move up and then wing those right hands.'

"So you've got him against the ropes," Jack said to the fighter now, "and he's lookin' for the punch, ready to duck it, and you give it to him, instead of the jab. Let him duck the jab and into the right."

"I know," the fighter said, shaking his head.

"Now you know what it takes to be a fighter," Jack said. "You've got to settle down and live it and sleep it and eat it."

"But I do," the fighter said.

"But you've got to do it more," Jack said. "You can't afford bad nights like this."

"I know," the fighter said.

The fighter left then to pick up a couple of the display cards with his picture on them that Al Berro had for him. That is how new he was, and Jack took another bite of the sandwich and then left the rest of it and we walked out onto the street.

"That's the worst I've seen him," Jack said. "He knows how to do those things. Why couldn't he do them? How could he possibly be that bad?"

"Don't get sore," I said. "When you figure it out, he's had six rounds of professional boxing before tonight. You know it takes time."

"But I haven't got too much time," Jack said. "Hell, I think I'll walk down to Berro's and find out how much they took in tonight. Maybe I'll finally find out how good that 'pretty good' is."

"I'll go along with you," I said.

"No," Jack said. "You've got that early plane to grab. You've got to get some sleep."

"I'd rather go with you."

"I can make it alone, " Jack said. "Hell, the way the eyes are now, I can see better at night than I can in that damn sunlight."

"If you say so," I said, and we shook hands, "but take care of yourself."

"Yeah," Jack said, "but wasn't that terrible tonight?"

The last time I ever saw him I watched him then, old and half-blind and aching all over, start slowly down the empty Main Street of Boise, Idaho, at one o'clock in the morning, heading for the Bouquet Sportsmen's Center to find out how much money there had been in the house. Once, after that, I did see him in a way. Four and a half years later, I sat in a theater and watched as George Foreman, too big and too strong for Boone Kirkman, took him apart in two rounds. It was the armored jeep against the tank again, and the old Hurley moves never got started. The old dreamer that was in the old pragmatist had dreamed too much too late, and Jack's forty-year search for another perfect tool like Billy Petrolle was over.

When we turned off the Interstate now, my wife had the Rand McNally road atlas in her lap. There was a two-page spread of the Dakotas, and a street map of Fargo, and the Saturday traffic was light. We found the *Forum*, and I parked in a black-paved lot across the street.

"I don't know how long I'll be," I said. "If there's no one in there who ever heard of Jack, that'll be the end of it, and I'll be right out."

"Take your time," she said. "I'll just wander around."

Off the lobby on the left there was a door identifying the classified advertising department, and I opened that. It was a large room, with a counter along the right and a lot of desks. Behind two of them, and facing the counter, two young women were sitting, and when I walked in they looked up.

"Excuse me," I said, "but can you tell me where your sports department is?"

"The sports department?" one of them said. "That's on the second floor."

"And I go up these stairs out here?" I said. "And then it'll be on the left or the right?"

"The left or the right?" the same young woman said, and then she stood up. While I watched, she turned her back to me and she pointed with one hand one way, and with the other hand she pointed the other, and then she turned around again. "It'll be on the left."

"Thank you," I said. "Thank you very much."

"You're welcome," she said.

Jack should have watched that, I was thinking, walking up the stairs. Out in Seattle that last time, before we flew down to Boise, we were sitting around the lobby of the Olympic with some of Jack's cronies one night, and Jack was expounding again on all the hazards and all the heartbreak in trying to make and move a fighter.

"And how about women?" I said to him, playing the straight man again. "Have you explained women to this fighter?"

"The creatures?" Jack said. "I've explained it all to him. I've told him, 'Look, marriage is for women and kids, and it's expensive. You've got to be able to afford it. Your best chance to make a lot of money is to become a good fighter, and then you'll be able to afford marriage.' He understands that point.

"Did I ever tell you," he said, "about the fighter I had who started looking at the creatures, and one day he went to the movies? When he came back, I said, 'How was the picture?' He said, 'It was good. It was a Western.' I said, 'Any dames in it?' He said, 'Yeah, one.' I said, 'How many guys were after the dame?' He said, 'Three.' I said, 'Anybody get killed?' He said, 'Yeah, two.' I said, 'The dame one of them?' He said, 'No. Just two of the guys.' I said, 'There! Doesn't it figure? Don't you see how the odds are stacked for those creatures?' It didn't do any good.

"Then I had another one," Jack said, "who was starting to think he was in love. You can tell when they don't have their minds on their work, so one day we're walking along the street and the light changes and I said, 'Wait a minute.' Next to us is this creature with a little creature, about three or four years old, and the little creature is all dolled up and has a little pocketbook. I nudge the fighter, and I said to the little one, 'Hello, little girl. That's a very nice pocketbook you have there. Do you have any money in it?' So she says, 'Yes, three pennies.'

"So the light changes again and they go on their way, but I say to the fighter, 'Don't move.' Here comes another creature now with a little boy, and the light changes again, and they stop. I nudge the fighter again, and I say to the little boy, 'Say, son, that's a nice new suit you're wearing. Do you have any money in your pocket?' The little kid looks up at me, and he shakes his head, and he says, 'Nope.'

"So I say to the fighter, 'You see that? That little creature with the pocketbook is being educated in how to handle money. This poor little mule here is being taught nothing. All he'll be taught when he grows up is to bring the paycheck home each week to the creature. Don't you see that?' You know what the fighter said to me?"

"No," I said.

"He said, 'But, Jack, my girl is different.' Now the light changes again, and this time I go *my* way. Isn't that terrible?"

At the top of the stairs now I turned left and walked into the city room, almost somnolent now on a Saturday morning. Across the room, at the far right, a young man, bearded and in a short-sleeved sports shirt, was typing. On the left two others, older, were sitting at their desks and talking, and from the right another was walking toward them.

"Excuse me," I said to him, "but I'm looking for your sports department."

"Over there," he said, pointing, "where you see that young fella."

"Thank you," I said, and I walked over between the desks. I waited until he stopped typing and looked up at me.

"I'm sorry to bother you," I said, "but can you tell me where Jack Hurley is buried?"

"Jack Hurley?" he said. "I don't know, but that man over there can probably tell you."

"The one in the white shirt?" I said, thinking that well, at least he had heard of Jack.

"Right."

"Thank you," I said.

"Okay," he said, and as I turned he went back to his typing.

The one in the white shirt was still talking with the other at the next desk when I walked up. He stopped and turned toward me.

"Excuse me," I said, "but can you tell me where Jack Hurley is buried?"

"Jack?" he said. "Gosh, I don't know. It's in one of the cemeteries around here, but I forget which one."

"There are several?"

"Three," he said, and he reached into a drawer of his desk and brought out a telephone directory. He started to turn through the yellow pages, and then he said, "Wait a minute. His brother Hank is still around town."

"He is?" I said.

I had known that Jack was the oldest of five children, but he had talked little about the others. It had been as if it would have detracted from his pose as an opponent of all domesticity.

"Sure," the one in the white shirt said now. "He's got a religious-goods store. Here it is. It's at 622 Second Avenue, only a few blocks from here."

He gave me the directions and I thanked him and I went out and walked over. At the address he had given me, the store was vacant.

"Excuse me," I said, "but I'm looking for Hurley's religious-goods store."

He was standing in a doorway. He needed a shave, and he looked as if he were coming off a bad night, or several of them.

"It ain't here any more," he said. "They moved around the corner there to Broadway, just up there."

"Thank you," I said.

"Yeah," he said.

The sign outside made clear that it was a gift shop and religious-goods store, and the shelves and the counters displayed dishes and glassware and household ornaments. When I walked in, a woman, smiling, came forward to meet me.

"May I help you?" she said.

"Is Mr. Hank Hurley in?" I said.

"Hank Hurley?" she said. "No, he's not. He doesn't own this store any more. Mr. Donald McAllister owns it now."

"Oh?" I said. "Do you know where I might find Hank Hurley?"

"I don't," she said, "but maybe Mr. McAllister can help you. He's back there in the office."

He was coming out of the office as I walked toward it. I introduced myself, and told him I was trying to find Hank Hurley.

"Hank?" he said. "He lives in the hotel right around the corner here. The college has taken it over, but they're letting him keep his room for a while. Maybe I can get him on the phone."

He picked up the phone and he dialed and he asked for Hank Hurley. He waited, and then he put the phone down.

"He's not in his room," he said. "He's probably at the Elks Club, having his lunch. He always eats early, and we could try him there."

"That's all right," I said. "I can try him at the hotel later, but I'd like to know where his brother Jack is buried."

"Jack?" he said. "I think it's the Holy Cross Cemetery. It'll be right here in the book from the funeral."

From a drawer of the desk he took out the book with its light gray watered-silk cover. He opened it on the desk.

"This is Hank's desk," he said. "A year and a half ago he sold the business to me, but I've still got the desk and Jack's trunk down in the basement. It's full of scrapbooks and I don't know what."

"I can imagine," I said.

I remembered the trunk from Room 679 at the Olympic Hotel. The room was just big enough to contain the bed, the steamer trunk, the footlocker for Jack's files, and the desk where, on the thirty-year-old Corona portable, Jack pounded out the publicity. While he was making Harry "Kid" Matthews into a leading contender and starting that congressional investigation, he was spending $10,000 a year for stationery, stamps, and the newspapers that carried stories about him and the fighter that he used to clip and send to sportswriters throughout this country.

"Don't write about me on Sundays," he used to tell his friends on the sports pages. "Sunday papers cost more, and you're running up my overhead."

"Here it is," McAllister said now, reading from the book, "'Holy Cross Cemetery, West ½, lot 35, block 7, old section. Laid to rest, November 21, 1972, 12:15 P.M.' Say, you almost made it!"

"Made it?" I said. "Made what?"

"You almost made twelve fifteen P.M. It's twelve forty-five now."

"How about that?" I said.

"'Born December 9, 1897,'" he said, reading from the book again.

"'Died November 15, 1972.' Then here's all the relatives and friends who came and signed their names."

"May I look through those?" I said.

"Sure," he said. "I've looked at this before. These two sisters have died since, but here's Billy Petrolle's signature. He was here."

"Good," I said, "and I'm glad to see that so many came."

"Well," he said, "let's count the pages here. There are, let's see, nine pages of signatures. Now let's count how many signatures there are on a page. Eighteen. Just a second."

He reached over to the adding machine. He punched some numbers on it, and looked at the tape. He went back to punching numbers again.

"I'm not doing something right," he said, "but there must have been about a hundred sixty to a hundred seventy-five attended."

"I make it one sixty-two," I said.

"Right," he said. "You know, Hank goes out to the grave twice a week to water and put flowers on it. It's been so dry that he's been doing it every night. In case you don't find Hank, I'll draw you a map of how to get there."

On a page from a desk memo pad, he drew the map showing how we should go north to the airport and then turn left. The page bore the imprint of the Muench-Kreuzer Candle Co., Inc., of 4577 Buckley Road, Liverpool, N.Y. 13088.

"You've really been most kind," I said, as we shook hands, "and I thank you."

"Glad to do it," he said, smiling. "I guess Jack was quite a guy."

"Yes," I said. "He was."

I walked around the corner to the hotel and, when I had the college student at the desk ring the room, Hank Hurley answered. He said he was amazed, and he sounded it, that I should be right there in the lobby. He had been about to take a nap, he said, but he would be down as soon as he dressed. I told him I would walk back to the *Forum*, where my wife would be waiting in the car, and he said he would meet us in the parking space across from the hotel. When we got out of the car he walked up, shorter and with more weight on him than Jack, but with the same look in the eyes and the same mouth. He took us to lunch at the Elks Club, and while we ate, he talked about Jack.

"You know," he said, "Jack used to say to me, 'When the good Lord takes me, I hope he does a clean job.' I told my sister, 'He couldn't have done a cleaner job.' If he'd had all his marbles and been in one of those nursing homes, he would have been oh, so unhappy."

"How did he go?" I said.

"At the Olympic," he said, "Jack was always there at the front desk when the four o'clock mail came in. When he wasn't there, and it got to be four forty-five, somebody got the assistant manager and they found him dead at the foot of his bed in that Room 679."

It was out of that room that, in 1957, Jack also promoted the Floyd Patterson–Pete Rademacher fight for the heavyweight championship of the world. Cus D'Amato was protecting Patterson then, and he accepted Rademacher, who was the Olympic heavyweight champion but had never had a professional fight, as a likely victim and Jack as the logical promoter. Jack forgot for a while that he had no use for amateurs and, out of his pockets and a box under the bed, he sold $74,000 worth of tickets out of the $243,000 they took in, and Rademacher, green as he was, had Patterson down in the second round before Patterson put him down six times and then, in the sixth round, knocked him out.

"Just think," Jack said, after it was over. "An amateur did this for me. I guess it just goes to show there's some good in everybody. Somebody told me that he went to a college, too, and took a course in how to be an animal husband. Now what kind of a college course is that?"

"At the Olympic," Hank Hurley was saying now, "they put a floral display on the door of the room. In the dining room, at the table where Jack always sat, they had a black ribbon and a single rose and a card that said, 'Reserved for Jack Hurley.' At a chair at the counter they had another single rose and another card, and they kept them there for a week."

"They thought a lot of him there," I said, "and I remember he used to tell me, 'You know I've got my plantin' suit. I've had it for years, and every now and then I try it on to see that it still fits.'"

"He had several plantin' suits," Hank Hurley said. "Every now and then he'd buy a new one."

"He said he had sent you an insurance policy and told you, 'When I check out, this is for the burial, but nothing fancy. Just have them sharpen my feet and drive me into the ground, and I hope it's not during the winter.'"

"That's right," Hank said, "he used to tell me, 'Don't make a production of it, and don't open the casket except for you and our sisters and a couple of friends. Nobody else knows me there.' We did open it for our sisters and for Billy Petrolle."

After lunch he drove us out past the airport and then turned left onto a gravel road past two cemeteries on the left and then into the third. He stopped the car about 150 feet inside the gate, and we walked over the sunbaked sod, the dried yellow grass making a sound under our shoes. Backed by two spruce, there was the gray granite headstone with Jack's father's name on it and a cross on top and a red geranium at the base. To the left there were two granite markers, one with Jack's mother's name on it and the other with his sister's. On the right was the marker that said "John C. Hurley." So severe was the drought that there were cracks about an inch wide in the black topsoil and they outlined in a rectangle the shape of the coffin.

"Jack hated that name John," Hank Hurley was saying. "Oh, how many fights he got into in school when somebody called him 'Johnny.' I guess I made the mistake. On the memorial card it said 'Jack C. Hurley,' and I sent it out to the stonecutter. When I saw this I called him and he said, 'But you ran a line through it and wrote "John."' I guess it's my fault."

"Forget it," I said. "It was the name with which he was christened. That makes it right."

"I don't know," he said. "I don't remember doing that, but I guess it was my fault."

After he drove us back to our car and we thanked him and said good-by, I drove back through the city and out to the Interstate once more. I was seeing again that rectangle in the ground.

"I can just hear Jack," I said to my wife. "I can hear him saying, 'Wouldn't you know it, ninety percent of the people get planted and everything goes all right. They plant me, and they have this drought. Why, there's a farmer in Durbin, North Dakota, who says it's worse than it was in the thirties. Isn't that terrible? How can you explain that?'"

The Fireman

Joe Page's Good Days

The Yankees beat the Dodgers in the Series because I had an edge on Burt. I had DiMaggio and Page. Gentlemen, I give you Joe DiMaggio . . . and Joe Page.

Bucky Harris

We drove east out of Texas and across seven states and into western Pennsylvania. It took us three days, and I called him on the phone from South Hapeville, Georgia, and then from Beckley, West Virginia, to let him know where we were and when we might be in.

"How are you tonight?" I said the last night out, and when he answered his voice was flat and tired-sounding again.

"Oh, so-so, Billy," he said. It was what he had said two nights before.

"Only so-so?" I said.

"Yeah, Billy," he said. "When you coming in?"

"I figure we should be there early tomorrow afternoon," I said. "Will you be there then?"

"I'm here all the time," he said, the voice the same.

The address the Yankees had given me was in care of Joe Page's Rocky Lodge, Route 30, Laughlintown, Pennsylvania. Both times that I had called he had answered the phone himself and almost immediately, and so I had pictured him perhaps in a small office or maybe picking up a phone at the end of a bar.

Chapter 8 of *Once They Heard the Cheers*, 1979.

"We'll need a couple of rooms for a night," I said. "What is Joe Page's Rocky Lodge?"

"It's a small inn," he said, "but I don't have any rooms. You won't have any trouble getting rooms in Ligonier, though, and that's only three miles. There's a couple of good motels there."

"Don't worry about it," I said. "I'll be there tomorrow."

"Sure, Billy," he said.

"He's not well," I said to Skipper Lofting after I had hung up. "He's real down, the same as the other night. I'm sure he's in poor health, and that makes me feel like a louse. I should know."

"How would you know?" Skipper said. "How many years is it?"

"It was 1950," I said, "and I said good-by to him in the Yankee clubhouse at the Stadium. The White Sox had just knocked him out of the box. I think it was Aaron Robinson who doubled in the winning run, and he used to catch Joe in the minors and on the Yankees before they traded him to Chicago. Two days later they sent Joe down to Kansas City, which was a Yankee farm club then."

"That was twenty-six years ago," Skipper said.

"That's what's wrong with this business," I said. "We're a lot of hustlers. We latch on to someone because he's in the public eye and we need to make a living. We plumb his background and pick his brain. We search out his motivations and his aspirations, and if he's a good guy, an association, even a friendship, forms. Then we say good-by and good luck, and if his luck runs out where are we? We're long gone, and on to somebody else."

"You can't be everybody's brother," Skipper said, "and besides, I'm getting hungry. When are you figuring to eat?"

When he had it, in '47 and '49, he was one of the great relief pitchers of all time. He was a fastball left-hander who, as the expression used to go, threw aspirins. Baseball, in New York at least, was reaching its peak of post-war popularity, and for the crucial games, and for those two World Series, of course, the Stadium would be packed. I can still see it the way it was in the late innings, the Yankee pitcher faltering with men on the bases, the conference on the mound, then Bucky

Harris in '47 and Casey Stengel in '49 taking the ball from the pitcher and signaling with his left hand. In the stands seventy thousand heads would turn and seventy thousand pairs of eyes would fasten on the bullpen beyond right field.

"Now coming in to pitch for the Yankees," the voice of the public address announcer would sound, echoing, "Joe Page!"

It was like thunder, rolling, and it made a cave of the vast Stadium. They rose as one, all their shouts and screams one great roar, and the gate of the low chain-link fence would open, and he would come out, immaculate in those pinstripes, walking with that sort of slow, shuffling gait, his warm-up jacket over his shoulder, a man on his way to work. In '47 he was in fifty-eight games, of which the Yankees won thirty-seven, including the seventh against the Dodgers in the Series. In '49 he appeared in sixty, forty-two of which the Yankees won, and in the Series he saved two, again against Brooklyn.

He was six feet three, perfectly proportioned at 215 pounds, and he was handsome. He had a smooth oval face, dark hair, blue eyes, and a smile that, in those days, could have sold Ipana toothpaste. Of all the Yankees only Joe DiMaggio, his buddy and roommate on the road, surpassed him in popularity. After the '47 Series, a Mr. and Mrs. Bernard MacDougall, in Inverness, Nova Scotia, named their son Joe Page MacDougall after him.

He was the oldest of seven children, and his father had been a miner in the coalfields along the Allegheny just northeast of Pittsburgh, and he himself had worked in the mines for two years. As a rookie with the Yankees in 1944, he made the All-Stars, but the night of the game his father died. A sister had been killed in an automobile accident earlier that year, and his mother had passed away the year before. He was married then to Katie Carrigan, whom he had known since they were children, and now he became the main support of three sisters and two brothers, the oldest eighteen and the youngest eleven.

"I had written a piece for *Cosmopolitan* called 'Fighter's Wife,'" I was telling Skipper Lofting, "about Rocky Graziano's wife, Norma. The night he fought Charley Fusari, when it started to come over the radio she ran out of the house, and I walked the streets with her and then waited with her until he came home. Then I got an assignment from *Life* to do 'Ballplayer's Wife' with Katie and Joe. When the Yankees would come off the road for a home stand, I'd sit with her in the wives' section, waiting for Joe to come in and save the game.

"I sat there with her for four weeks in all, and it was sad. In would come Joe, and he just didn't have it any more. When a speedball pitcher loses just that little bit off it, those hitters who have been standing there with their bats on their shoulders just love it. They tee off, and it is brutal. Sometimes we'd go to dinner afterwards, and I'd try to console them, but it wasn't any good.

"That last game he pitched for the Yankees, after he lost it, I left Katie and went down to the clubhouse to tell him she'd be waiting in their car. He always had the dressing stall next to DiMaggio, and he was sitting there with his head down. I said, 'Joe, tough luck.' He looked up at me, and he said, 'Billy, you're jinxin' me.'"

"Well," Skipper said, "you know how superstitious ballplayers are, or used to be."

"I know," I said, "but he meant it right then. He was grasping for anything. I said, 'You may be right, Joe, and I'm dropping the story.' I told him he'd probably get it back his next time out, and I wished him luck and shook hands, and I left. End of story."

"I guess you couldn't write about losing in those days," Skipper said.

"Only in literature," I said.

Now, after we had checked into the motel in Ligonier and had lunch, we drove southeast out of town on Route 30, the mid-December sun lowering behind us, and then through Laughlintown. Where the road started to rise toward a ridge, stands of hardwood crowded it on both sides, and then on the right we saw the blue sign with the white letters: JOE PAGE'S ROCKY LODGE. Set among the trees was a three-story building of fieldstone and wood, and the only vehicle in the parking space in front was a light blue pickup.

I got out of the car, and on the gravel of the shaded driveway there were patches of frost and on some of the dry, brown leaves a light sugaring of dry powder snow. Drapes had been drawn across the first-floor windows of the building, and as I reached the door under the overhang, I heard the lock turn. I could hear the sounds of a football game on a television, and I knocked on the door.

"We're closed," a voice said.

"I'm Bill Heinz," I said. "Joe Page is expecting me."

"Oh," the voice said, and then the lock turned again and the door opened, and he said, "I'm his son Joe."

"And you look like him," I said, as we shook hands. He was in his late teens and wearing glasses with narrow steel rims, but it was there in the blue eyes.

"That's what people say," he said, smiling.

"I have a friend with me," I said. "I just want to go back to the car and bring him in."

He waited at the door, and I introduced Skipper to him. The bar room, deserted, was to the right, and he led us to the left into a long, darkened room, the only illumination coming from ceiling lights in the back. To the left, against the front wall, there was a jukebox, and next to it the television. On the right a log fire was going in a fieldstone fireplace, dining-room chairs and small tables were stacked against the other wall, and in an armchair his father was sitting. He got up slowly and walked toward me.

"You look good, Billy," he said, putting out his hand. "A little heavier."

It was Joe Page, all right, but I knew it only by those eyes. That dark hair was gray now, and his mouth was shrunken. The left side of his jaw was hollow behind a gray beard of several days, his neck was thin, and that great left arm hung loosely at his side.

"How are you, Joe?" I said.

"Oh, so-so," he said.

I introduced Skipper to him, and he introduced his younger son Jon, who was seventeen, and two years younger than his brother, and Bryan Miller, a young friend of Jon's who had come in to watch on TV the Washington Redskins and the Minnesota Vikings in their National Football Conference playoff game. We found straight-back chairs, and he sat down slowly again in the armchair, as I tried to find a way to ask the question.

"Cancer of the throat," he said, while I was still groping. "It tears the hell out of you, the muscles all the way down. I can't shave. They took all my teeth, and just left me two, and I can't eat."

"When was that?" I said.

"In 1973," he said. "In August of 1970, I had the heart attack at the Old-Timers Game. I walked up in the stands and started to sweat and couldn't talk. They sent me down to Lenox Hill Hospital, and then I come home and had the open heart at St. Francis in Pittsburgh."

"They've really been beating up on you," I said.

"That's what happened to my arm," he said, reaching across with his right and rubbing his left arm. "These fingers go numb. They want to give me a new jaw, but I don't know if I'll get it. They cut me enough, and I've got a hernia now, too."

I was groping again, but on the TV the announcer's voice and the crowd noise had risen, and his eyes went toward the set. In the backfield Fran Tarkenton was scrambling, with two big Redskin linemen lumbering after him, and then he released the ball and it fell short of a receiver who was coming back for it.

"How long have you had this place?" I said.

"Seventeen years ago I bought it," he said. "First I had one down in Irwin called the Bull Pen. I closed up here about three months ago. I couldn't take that stuff at the bar any more. You ever see any of the guys?"

"No," I said. "I've been writing other things."

"I miss all you guys," he said. "It was a strange life, but once you're out of it there was nothing else like it. DiMag was here, though. They give me a testimonial, and he come in from Frisco. The same old Daig. When was that, Joe?"

"It was two years ago," young Joe said.

"They had Spec Shea here and Tommy Henrich," he said. "It was a nice party. Seven hundred people. The Daig was the same old Daig. He asked me about my back."

"I heard he had trouble with his back," Skipper Lofting said.

"That's right, Skip," he said. "I told him I had jammed up vertebrae and they opened it and straightened it out, and that's been fine ever since. You see him on that TV commercial? What's that thing he's doin'?"

"For the coffee maker?"

"Yeah," he said. "He sent me one. I got the filter, but not the maker."

"When I watch him on those commercials," I said, "I remember a story Frank Graham told. It was a couple of years after Joe came up to the Yankees, and he was still very shy and very quiet. They were at Shor's—Frank and Toots and Joe and a couple of others at a table—and Lefty Gomez stopped by. He told some story, as he can, and made a couple of quips, and when he left, Joe said, 'Gee, I wish I could be like that.'"

"He's some Daig," he said. "When Joe wasn't hittin', you remember that Del Prado where we stayed in Chicago? They had those big mirrors on the doors, and at five o'clock in the morning I'd hear him, and he'd be up there in front of the mirror practicing hittin'."

"One year," I said, "the Giants and the Dodgers opened the season in Brooklyn the same day that you people opened at the Stadium. Joe had the bad heel then, and he wasn't playing, and the next day, when Jimmy Cannon and I walked into the clubhouse, he was taking a treatment. He asked us where we'd been the day before, and we told him we'd been to Ebbets Field. He said, 'Where was the wind?' Jimmy said, 'Behind the hitters.' Joe said, 'The same here. I was coming up here in the taxi and there's a flag on a building about four blocks away and I always look at that to see where the wind is. The wind was just right. It broke my heart.' He was probably the only guy on the ball club to check the wind before he got there, and he did it even when he wasn't playing."

"He's some Daig," Page said, "and Yogi's still goin' all right."

"He was another shy one," I said.

"Yeah," he said. "You're right."

When Yogi Berra came up to the Yankees to stay in 1947, they almost hazed him out of the league, the other Yankees among them.

They mocked his squat, early primate appearance and quoted his malaprops, until Bucky Harris, who was managing them then, put a stop to it. In the seventeen years that Yogi caught for the Yankees, he played in fifteen All-Star games and three times won the American League's Most Valuable Player Award, and in 1972 they elected him to the Hall of Fame.

"It was touch-and-go with Yogi for a while," I said now, "before Bucky straightened you guys out on him."

"Yeah," Page said. "We had a meeting and he told us to lay off. He told a few of the writers, too."

"I remember the day before the '47 Series opened," I said. "You people had worked out at the Stadium and several of us writers were hanging around the clubhouse. They had the table in the middle of the room, with the cartons of balls to be autographed, and Yogi and Spec Shea were sitting there and signing. One of us asked Shea how he felt as a rookie about to pitch, the next day, the opening game of the World Series, and he said something about it being just another ball game where you still just had to get twenty-seven outs."

"Yeah," Page said. "He would have said that. He was like that."

"So Yogi said, 'Yeah, but them shadows come awful early here this time of year.' He was worrying about those hits, with the ball coming out of the sunlight and then into the shadow of those three decks."

"That's the way it is there."

"Then one of the writers said, 'Come on, Yogi, stop worrying about it. You don't figure to get a hit, anyway.' With that, he and the others walked away. Yogi was sitting there with a ball in one hand, a pen in the other, and he said in that low voice, kind of to himself, 'Them writers think I'm kiddin', but they don't have to get up there and hit. They don't have to do nothin'.'"

"Yogi said that?"

"Yes," I said, "and it's a truth I have never forgotten, any time I have interviewed an athlete, or any time I have had to lay a critique on one."

"Yogi was the best receiver I ever pitched to," he said.

"And he could snap that bat," I said. "He had great wrists, so he could wait on the pitch. That's why he could get around on the breaking stuff, and even reach those bad balls."

"And he had a brain," he said.

"Which a lot of people found hard to believe at first," I said. "I remember that night game at the Stadium against the Red Sox—the game that made you. The bases were loaded, and you threw three balls to Rudy York, and Yogi came out from behind the plate and waddled up to you. As you two stood talking, somebody in the press box next to me said, 'This is ridiculous. What can he tell him?'"

It was May 26, 1947, and there were seventy-four thousand in the stands that night, and all that Joe Page became and all that happened to him afterward stemmed from it. The Washington Senators had knocked him out in his first start that season, and several times he had failed in relief. In the third inning, with the Red Sox leading 3–1, two men on base, and nobody out, Bucky Harris brought him in for a last try. He got Ted Williams to ground to George McQuinn, a great glove man, but McQuinn bobbled it. Now the bases were loaded, and he threw those three balls to York and, as Yogi walked to the mound, Bucky Harris had one foot up on the dugout steps, and Joe Page was one pitch away from the minors.

"I forget what Yogi said," he said now.

York took two strikes, and then he swung at that fastball and missed. The count went to 3 and 0 on Bobby Doerr, and again Harris was at the steps and again the future of Joe Page hung on the next pitch. He threw three strikes past Doerr, and got Eddie Pellagrini to lift an easy fly ball up into that rising thunder of sound for the third out. The Yankees won, 9–3, and Joe Page was on his way.

"Yogi knew baseball," he said now.

"I know," I said. "You guys won the opening game of that '47 Series, but Yogi had a terrible day. He went 0 for 4, and Burt Shotton had Pee Wee Reese and Jackie Robinson running. They each stole second, with Yogi bouncing the ball down there, and afterward he was sitting in his dressing stall, with his head down. I said to him, 'Yogi, forget it. You guys won, and you'll have a better day tomorrow.' He said, 'I guess I ain't very smart.' I said, 'Yogi, let me tell you something. I once asked you about last year when the Cardinals were in the Series and you were home in St. Louis. I asked you if you went to the games, and you said, 'No, I don't like to watch games.' I said, 'Why not?' You said, 'It makes me nervous, just to watch.' It makes you nervous to watch because you're always playing the game. Don't ever think that you're not smart enough, because you have a fine baseball brain. And Yogi said, 'I don't know. I don't know if you're right.' "

"Bucky knew it," he said now. "Bucky was the best manager I ever played for, but I was sorry when Stengel died. Rough to work for, you know? I'd come in, and Casey would come out talkin', but I never knew what the hell he was saying."

"You weren't the only one," I said.

"After I had the operation," he said, "I saw Yogi in New York at the Old-Timers Game, and he didn't recognize me with this hollow neck. Jon said to him, 'It's my dad, Joe Page.' "

Young Joe had left the room. As he returned I watched him walk across in front of the television with its screen filled with a close-up of uniformed bodies and the sound voluming, and then sit down.

"He walks like you," I said. "When I watch him walk, I can see you coming in from that bullpen."

"The pup's got it, too," he said, nodding toward Jon. "I hope you get a chance to meet the wife. Mildred, but we call her Mitz. In 1954 I got married with Mitz. I think it was 1954. She's great. She's got her own insurance business, and I think she'll be back soon."

She came in a few minutes later. She is slim and dark-haired, and he introduced us to her. She took off her coat and she was wearing a denim jumpsuit. Skipper pulled up another straight-back chair, and she sat down between him and Joe.

"What have you been talking about?" she said.

"The old days," Joe said.

"I can imagine," she said.

"Do you ever get people dropping in here," I said, "who see the sign outside and wonder if it's the real Joe Page?"

"Oh, yeah," he said. "Quite a few people. A guy would come in and say, 'Are you . . . ?' And I'd say, 'Yeah.'"

"One guy came in," young Joe said, "and he said, 'I'm from New York, and I'd like to take Joe Page to dinner.'"

"Joe was in the hospital then," Mitz said. "I told the boys, 'If anybody comes in, don't tell them your dad's in the hospital.' So he told him, 'He's not in now, but if you want to see my mother, she's at work.' He came to the office, but I was at a restaurant, and when I came back to the office he'd gone.

"He came back here," she said, "and our other son here told him, 'My dad's in the hospital, and you can't see him.' I'd gone to the hospital by then, and this fellow came in. I told him he couldn't see Joe, and he said, 'I have to. When your husband was pitching, I was five years old. I sold newspapers, and one night I fell asleep where I was selling them. Your husband came along and he saw me there, and he woke me up and he said, 'You have to go home and sleep.' I said, 'I can't until I sell these papers.' Your husband bought all my papers, and then he took me in and fed me. That's why I have to see him.'

"By now," she said, "he had the nurses and the doctor and me in tears. So we took him in to see Joe, and when we came out he told me, 'If there's anything you need, money or anything, just let me know.' He's a fine man."

"He must be," I said.

"He does hair replacement," she said, and then to young Joe, "Find that card he gave me."

On the business card was imprinted, "International Transitions Center." Under that, "Orange, Conn." Then, in the lower right corner, "George DeRosa, President."

"Where was it," I said to Page, "that you found him asleep and took him in to eat?"

"Patsy's," he said. "You remember we used to eat there? At 112th Street?"

"I remember," I said.

We went there a couple of times, after those bad ball games, when I was trying to console them. I would be trying to get their minds off the game, and so I would get him to talking about what it had been like growing up playing ball around Springdale. The field had been cleared of rocks and stumps, but it was uphill to first and second base, and downhill from third to home. They traveled in the Lockerman's Meat Market panel truck, but they had no money for tires, so they packed them with sod and wired them to the rims.

"I don't suppose," I said now, "that Lockerman is still in business with his meat market."

"Yeah," he said, "the sons are."

"Sam and Jim and Howard," young Joe said.

"They come up to see Joe once in a while," Mitz said.

"I was telling Skipper," I said now, "about the last time I saw you, in '50, in the clubhouse right after the last time you pitched for the Yankees. I was working on that magazine piece that never came off, and you looked at me and you said, 'Billy, you're jinxin' me.'"

"I didn't mean it," he said now.

"I understood," I said. "You were reaching for anything. As I remember it, it was Aaron Robinson who'd got a double off you."

"I don't think so," he said. "Them left-hand hitters didn't hit me. After this throat, though, I couldn't remember nothin'."

"His memory was bad for a while," Mitz said.

"My back's givin' me hell now, too," he said.

"They took his lymph glands," she said.

She got up. She pushed her chair back and, standing behind his, began to knead his shoulder muscles.

"That feels good," he said.

"I think it was Aaron Robinson, though," I said, "because I was struck by the irony of it. He'd caught you on the way up, in Augusta and Newark and then on the Yankees, and it was his hit that sent you down to the minors."

"He was a hell of a catcher," he said. "He took a bottle of Seagram's to bed with him every night."

"He's dead," Mitz said.

"Yeah," he said, turning his head and touching the left side of his neck again. "Cancer."

"I'm sorry to hear that."

"You read what that Lopat said about me?" he said. Eddie Lopat was a left-hander who threw breaking stuff for the Yankees from 1948 to 1955.

"No," I said.

"That Lopat blasted me," he said. "It was in that book they wrote about Joe. They talked to people about Joe, and that Lopat was never in my apartment and he said I used to drink all night and come out the next day. He said I was lushed up every night, so how could I be ready sixty times a year?"

"I don't know," I said. "I didn't read the book."

There was that time, though, in '46, I was thinking, when Joe McCarthy let you have it out on the team plane two days before he quit managing the club. He figured you couldn't find the plate during the day because you'd touched too many bases the night before.

"Then a couple of days after I left you that last time," I said, "they sent you down to Kansas City."

"Casey never called me in the clubhouse," he said. "He saw me in the dugout, and he said, 'I've got your pink slip.' I said, 'Where am I goin'?' He said, 'Kansas City.'"

"What was that like?"

"Bad," he said. "That was more like a rest home. Johnny Mize was there with something wrong with him. Then I went to Frisco under Lefty O'Doul. That was bad, too. Cold, nobody in the stands, and all that goddamn dampness. I never worked for a ball club like I did here."

He came back up to pitch in seven games for Pittsburgh in 1954. His record that year was 0 and 0, and that was the end of it.

"The Old Man," he said, meaning Branch Rickey, who was trying to rebuild the Pirates then with youth, "had kids. They had kids from all around, and we called them 'Rickey-Dinks.'"

While we had been talking, the game on television had finished, the Vikings winning on their way to the Super Bowl. Jon stood up and said he would be going out for a while, and he and his friend shook hands with Skipper and me and left.

"The buck's a good football player," Joe said. "They call him 'The Monster.'"

"He's got a lot of schools looking at him," young Joe said.

"What does he play?"

"Linebacker and fullback," Page said, and he got up out of the chair. He walked slowly to the front door and opened it and went out.

"Where's he going?" Mitz said.

"To get wood," young Joe said.

"You should get it," she said.

When he came back in he was carrying two splits of log. He bent over and put them on the fire.

"They didn't call him 'The Fireman' for nothing," she said, as he sat down. "You watched him pitch. He was always arrogant, and that's the way our youngest son is."

But that was just the pose, I was thinking. When he used to walk in there, he told me once, with those men on base and the thousands screaming, he could feel his heart pumping, and he said it seemed as if his stomach and all its contents were coming up into his throat.

"There was a fellow here from Bethany College, who was watching Jon," she said. "He said, 'You know, I don't think you'll ever make it in football.' Jon said to me, 'You know, Mom, I told him, "I don't know about football, but I'm gonna make it somewhere."' He's just like his father."

As he walked from that bullpen, Tommy Henrich, in right field, would say to him, "Joe, you stop them, and we'll win it for you." Frank Crosetti, who was coaching then, told him, "If you knew how scared they are of that fastball, Joe, you wouldn't worry about anything." When his control would begin to go and he would start to miss the plate, Snuffy Stirnweiss would come trotting over to the mound from second, and he'd say, "You're not bearing down on the left leg again, Joe." It would get him out of it.

"That was sad about Stirnweiss," I said now.

"Snuff?" he said. "Yeah, I read about it. Sad."

One morning in September 1958, three cars of a commuter train out of New Jersey plunged through an open lift-bridge into Newark Bay, and Stirnweiss was one of the more than two dozen who drowned in the cars. He had been a fine baseball and football player at the University of North Carolina, and he played for the Yankees from 1942 until 1950, once winning the American League batting championship, once setting a major-league fielding record for second baseman, and twice, with his speed, leading the league in stolen bases.

"What struck me when I read about it," I said, "was that the speed that made him such a great athlete cost him his life. Someone who had seen him get on the train said that when he arrived at the station it was pulling out and he ran to catch it."

"You remember," he said, "how the first thing he'd do when he'd get on the train was go to sleep? I thought of that."

"In the last game of the '47 Series," I said, "when you threw that spitter to Gil Hodges, did he pop it up to Stirnweiss?"

"No, I struck him out," he said, "but it wasn't a spitter. That was the oil, the graphite oil. I used to keep it inside my belt."

"You told me it was a spitter," I said. "In the clubhouse, during the celebration, I came over to see you and DiMag, and you said, 'Billy, don't write this, but I threw that Hodges a real hocker.' How could I, alone, write it? If I did, you and Joe would have denied it and clammed up on me forever."

"That Roe was throwin' it for them in '50," he said, meaning Preacher Roe of the Dodgers. "He later wrote about it. I used to load it up during a foul ball, when everybody looks up."

He got up now and walked slowly toward the bar room. When he came back he handed me his glove, still formed as it had been to fit his right hand, the dark brown, almost-black leather cracked now.

"A Diz Trout model," he said.

"You ought to put oil on it," I said, as I handed it back.

"We're going to have it bronzed," Mitz said.

He sat down, and she stood up and began kneading his shoulders again.

"Them were good days in New York," he said. "We had a lot of fun."

"One day," she said, "he told Jon, 'Remember, if you're going to make it, you're going to have to work hard. And stay away from women.' Then we were going through some old things, and found a picture of Joe and Joe DiMaggio in Hawaii with these girls. So Jon took it to him, and said, 'What about this?'"

"I tortured a few in my day," he said.

"So you had your good days," she said, "and you should remember those."

"Yeah," he said, "and the young buck can play ball, too."

"Jon was playing over in Johnstown," she said, "and Joe used to tell this story of one he hit there."

"I hit one out three hundred eighty feet," he said.

"So Jon hit one out four hundred forty feet," she said, "and Joe said, 'I'll never tell that story again.'"

"That was the end of that hit," he said.

"I have to get a loaf of bread," she said, walking out from behind the chair, "and where do I get a headlight? The low beam is out."

"In a garage," he said.

"But what one? The outside of the light is square."

"But the light is round," young Joe said. "Go to Mobil."

"I'll be back in a few minutes," she said.

"She don't know cars," Page said, "but she's got a hell of a brain. She works twelve, fourteen hours a day, Skip."

"She seems to be a fine woman," Skipper said.

"You can say that again," he said. "What beats me is that I can't hunt any more, and I've got them guns."

"What have you got?" Skipper said.

"I got a .320, a .406, and a .373 Magnum, and I can't use them."

"Didn't you once go on a bird-hunting trip to Maine with Enos Slaughter and a couple of others?" I said.

"It was South Dakota," he said. "Huron. A guy had to be blind not to get fifty roosters."

"You were telling about it in the clubhouse one day," I said, "and Yogi was listening. You said, 'We were going after birds, and Slaughter had this cyst on his back, but it didn't make any difference to him. He went climbing through that brush and under those branches like it wasn't there.' And Yogi said, 'What the hell kind of a bird is a cyst?'"

"That's right," he said. "That was Yogi."

"With all you've been through," I said, "I've been thinking about that ballplayers' retirement plan. I've forgotten when that came in."

"We started it in '47," he said, "but it went back to '44. I know on the hospitalization they don't give you all of it, only eighty percent."

"But that's a big help."

"Hell, yes," he said, bringing his hand over to his neck again. "This thing cost nineteen thousand dollars."

Young Joe had turned on the TV again, for the American Football Conference playoff. We talked about the game against Boston on the next to last day of the season in '49. The Red Sox led the Yankees by one game in the standings, and were ahead, 4–1, in the second inning when he came in and held them the rest of the way until Johnny Lindell won it with a home run. Then the Yankees beat them again, to win the pennant on the last day.

"The good old days," he said, as we got up to leave. "I'm glad you came, and that you're looking good."

"And I'll call you now and then," I said, "to hear that you're feeling better."

"I was fifty-nine in October," he said.

"I know," I said.

He walked us out, after we had said good-by to young Joe, and closed the door behind him and stood, watching, under the overhang while we walked to the car. Darkness had come by now, and another car, its lights on, drove in and Mitz got out. We walked over and shook hands.

"I'm really pleased you two came," she said. "It's done a lot for him."

"You've done a lot for him," Skipper said.

"It's been a long time," she said, "since he's talked that much or sounded so well, or moved so well."

"I'm glad," I said.

"So any time you're nearby," she said, "stop in to see him again."

"We'd like to," I said.

As Skipper backed the car around I looked back. He was still standing under the overhang, under the pale overhead light, waving good-by with his right hand.

"You know how pitchers are," Skipper said. "When they're talking, especially about pitching, they'll demonstrate with their pitching arm. He has to use his right arm."

"It was one of the great left arms," I said, "and it's a damn shame."

I had a terrible time trying to get to sleep that night. The Derry Sportsmen's Club was having its annual dinner dance in the ballroom of the motel, and it came up through the ventilating system and through the floor. The band must have played "Rock Around the Clock" a dozen times, but I would have had trouble sleeping anyway.

The Artist Supreme

Dancing with Willie Pep

It is not strength, but art, obtains the prize.

Homer

"How did you get my number?" he said on the phone. I had called him one evening late in January at his home in Wethersfield, Connecticut.

"Come on, Willie," I said. "You're not unheard of."

"I'm a has-been," he said. "Nobody remembers me."

He was the greatest creative artist I ever saw in a ring. When I watched him box, it used to occur to me that, if I could just listen carefully enough, I would hear the music. He turned boxing contests into ballets, performances by a virtuoso in which the opponent, trying to punch him out, became an unwilling partner in a dance, the details of which were so exquisite that they evoked joy, and sometimes even laughter.

In 1940, when Guglielmo Papaleo—Willie Pep—turned professional after winning the Connecticut amateur flyweight and bantamweight championships, he was seventeen, still an adolescent. He won fifty-three fights in a row, and then at age twenty, beat Chalky Wright for the featherweight championship of the world. He won another eight before Sammy Angott, the former lightweight champion, a grabber and smotherer and too big for him, out-pointed him. Then he won

---

Chapter 9 of *Once They Heard the Cheers*, 1979.

another seventy-three before Sandy Saddler knocked him out in the first of their four fights. In other words, of his first 135 fights, he won all but the one in which he was out-muscled and out-wrestled. In our time we never saw another like him.

"I'm on the Boxing Commission," he said. "It's in the State Building, so see me there. I'm there every day from eight until four thirty."

He gave me the directions, rapidly, for he always talked the way he boxed, the words spurting out. He told me what exit to take from the Interstate and what streets and how to get around the park and how to recognize the building. Hartford is a city I once knew and walked, but when I drove down the ramp off the elevated Interstate and got into the noontime traffic, I turned into the parking space of the high-rise motel and checked in. I had lunch, and I took a cab. At my age I wanted to have something left for Willie.

"Excuse me," I said. "I'm looking for Willie Pep."

I had found on the directory in the lobby "Athletic Division," under "Department of Consumer Protection." A middle-aged balding man, his jacket off, was sitting behind a desk on which there was a sign that read MICHAEL BOGUSLAWSKI. On the door it had said that he was the assistant to Mary Heslin, the head of the department.

"Sure," he said. "You go out and take a left. Go down one flight of steps and go through the doors. Go straight ahead down the hall to the end. Take a right. It's the fifth door on the left, 31-A."

"I'm sorry," I said, "but will you give that to me again?"

"I'll give him a call," he said, picking up the phone and dialing, and then, "Sure he's here, and you're there, but come up and lead him down."

He came through the doorway quickly, sticking out his hand. He is five feet five, and he never had any trouble making the 126 pounds, but he was a little heavier now, his fifty-four years in his face, and he was wearing a glen-plaid suit and a striped sports shirt open at the neck. He led me down, walking rapidly with those small, quick steps, thrusting the doors open, talking.

"It's a good job," he said. "Last year we had about thirty-five wrestling shows, twenty-three boxing shows. We supervise. We check to see a guy hasn't been knocked out in thirty days. If one guy's got forty fights and another's got ten, we don't allow. We go in before the fight and see that they bandage properly. Hugh Devlin is the director. A good guy. I'm under him with Sal Giacobbe."

He led me into the office and introduced me to Devlin, a rather short, gray-haired, smiling man behind one of the gray metal desks. There were three desks, filing cabinets, a metal locker, a weigh-in scale, a sofa and armchair, and a coat rack.

"Hughie was the bantamweight champion of Massachusetts," he said, and then to Devlin, "How many fights you have?"

"I had a hundred twenty-one," Devlin said, "and I won a hundred thirteen."

"He was a good fighter," Willie said.

"You weren't bad yourself," I said.

"Thank you," Willie said.

"The greatest I ever saw," Devlin said. "I can still see Willie's fights. I'll never forget them."

"He was a creative genius," I said to Devlin, "and he could do those things because he had the reflexes of a housefly."

"Thank you very much," Willie said, sitting down behind his desk. "That's very kind of you."

"I have to laugh at you, Willie," I said. "All we're doing is telling you the truth, and you think we're doing you a favor. You did us a favor being the fighter you were."

"That's nice of you to say that," he said, and that's the way he always was, slipping compliments the way he slipped punches while sticking out another jab.

"The last time I saw you in a ring," I said, "was in the Fifth Street Gym in Miami, about 1952. It was after the third Saddler fight, and you didn't have the title any more, and you were starting to hit the road."

"That's right," he said. "I fought in a lot of places."

He did, indeed. Once the really big pay nights were gone forever, he took what was left of his inimitable talents into Moncton, New Brunswick; Bennington, Vermont; Athol, Massachusetts; San Antonio,

Texas; Lawton, Oklahoma; Florence, South Carolina; Presque Isle, Maine; Painesville, Georgia; and Caracas, Venezuela, among other places. In 1959 he retired, to come back six years later at the age of forty-two to add nine more wins to a record that reads 241 fights, 229 wins, one draw, and eleven losses.

"Tell Hughie," I said now, "about the time you fought the local boy in the town where the sheriff weighed you in."

"That's right," he said, and then to Devlin, "They didn't have no boxing commission, so the sheriff weighs you in with a gun on his hip. The fight's in the ball park, so when he calls us to the center of the ring . . ."

"Wait a minute, Willie," I said. "Tell him about the kid at the weigh-in."

"Oh, yeah," he said. "So at the weigh-in, the kid I'm gonna box comes up to me and says, 'Mr. Pep, can I have your autograph?' I looked at him, and I said, 'Get away from me, kid. There's people watchin' here. We're boxin' tonight, and what are they gonna think?'"

"You were his hero," I said.

"Yeah," he said. "So at the ball park they got a pretty good crowd, and the referee calls us to the center of the ring to give us the instructions. I look at the kid, and he's white. He's scared stiff. I'm thinking, 'Oh, boy, what kind of a fight can this be?' So the bell rings and we move around, and a lot of guys turn white, but this guy is startin' to turn purple. I figure I have to do something, so I threw a right hand over his shoulder, that would look good to the crowd but that would miss, and I stepped inside and grabbed him under the arms, and I said, 'Look, kid. Just relax. These people here paid their money, and we'll give them a show. We'll just box, and you won't get hurt. We'll have a nice evening, and everybody will like it.' That's exactly what I told him."

"And wait until you hear the ending," I said to Devlin.

"So I take my arms out from under his and let him go," Willie said, "and he falls right on his face and the referee counts him out."

"I love that," Devlin said, laughing. "That's a great story."

"That's the truth," Willie said.

"Then there was the time," I said to Devlin, "that Willie boxed Kid Campeche in Tampa. Frank Graham and Red Smith were covering the baseball training camps, and they were driving out of Tampa one afternoon on the Tamiami Trail starting back to Miami. Over the car radio they heard that Willie was boxing that night in Tampa so, without either of them saying anything, Red just turned the car around and headed back. Willie pitched another shutout, and in Campeche's dressing room afterward, either Red or Frank said, 'Well, what was that like?' And Campeche said, 'What was it like? Fighting Willie Pep is like trying to stamp out a grass fire.'"

"Yeah, Kid Campeche," Willie said, nodding. "I remember him."

"He'll never forget you," I said. "None of them will."

He picked up a pair of black-rimmed glasses from the top of his desk, and put them on. He opened the desk drawer and took out a Photostat of a newspaper column by Don Riley and handed it to me.

"He writes for the paper in Minneapolis," he said, "and it's all in there. It's about when I boxed Jackie Graves there in '46."

Jackie Graves was a pretty good puncher out of Austin, Minnesota. He had had thirty-nine fights before he boxed Willie and had won twenty by knockouts while losing two decisions, and Willie knocked him out in the eighth round.

"It's all in there," he said. "Before the fight I told this Riley, 'In the third round I'm not gonna throw a punch. Watch what happens.' So in the third round I did like I told him. I moved around, feinted, picked off punches, made him miss, and I never threw a punch, and all three officials gave me the round. Riley never forgot it."

"How could he?" I said. "And another fight I'll never forget was your one with Famechon."

Ray Famechon was the European featherweight champion. Lew Burston, of the International Boxing Club, had talked him into coming over to box Willie in the Garden for the championship of the world.

"The afternoon of the fight," I said, "I stopped by the Garden to pick up my ticket, and Lew Burston grabbed me. He said, 'You weren't at the weigh-in. You should have been there.' I said, 'Why?' He said, 'Why? Because Eddie Eagan was explaining our rules. He was telling Famechon that you can't spin a man, and Famechon just reached across in front of him and grabbed Pep by the elbow and spun him and said, '*Comme ça?*'"

"Yeah," Willie said now. "He was kind of fresh at the weigh-in. He grabbed me, so I figured I can't fight him here, so I'll see what I can do in the ring."

"So then," I said, "Burston said to me, 'Why shouldn't he treat Pep like that? Who is Willie Pep to him? Famechon has had hundreds of amateur fights and sixty pro fights. He's boxed all over Europe, and fought every style there is and . . .' And I said, 'Wait a minute, Lew. He's fought every style there is except Willie Pep's style, and unfortunately he has to fight that style tonight.'"

"He was a tough guy, and he boxed everybody in Europe," Willie said now. "If he thought I was gonna stand there and trade punch for punch, maybe that's the way they do it in Europe, but not over here. He'd get set, and I'd jab him and move."

"I remember that fight," Devlin said. "Great."

"I'll never forget it," I said. "I never saw another fighter who was as frustrated as Famechon was that night. He was punching at air, and a couple of times Willie was actually behind him, tapping him on the shoulder to let him know where he was."

"Yeah," Willie said, "the guy wanted to punch me, and I didn't like to get punched."

"But what Willie probably doesn't know," I said, "is that the fight was supposed to have economic implications in France. Coca-Cola was starting to sell big over there, and the winegrowers were up in arms. French kids for centuries had been brought up to drink wine, and now they were drinking Cokes. The agency that had the Coca-Cola account must have figured that Famechon would lick Willie, and they were ready. They had a case of Cokes in Famechon's dressing room, and the idea was that, after he won, there'd be pictures on the front pages of papers all over France of the new world champion celebrating with a Coke."

"I didn't know that," Willie said.

"So in the dressing room later," I said, "there was Famechon sitting with his head down, and saying in French, 'I couldn't hit him because I couldn't find him.' There were the agency guys like mourners at a wake, and there was the case of Cokes over in a corner unopened."

"Is that so?" Willie said. "Well, you know how it was. After the weigh-in, I knew what the guy had in mind, but I didn't have the same idea in my mind."

"That was obvious once the fight started," I said.

"But Willie's greatest was the second Saddler fight," Devlin said. "Great."

Willie's record in *The Ring Record Book and Encyclopedia* is a gallery of great art, from the meticulous miniatures that went only a few rounds to the masterpieces that went the distance. Of the latter, the second Saddler fight in the Garden was the greatest boxing exhibition I ever saw, for Saddler had knocked him out in their first fight and had the height and reach and punch on him. He hurt him the second time, too, cut him under both eyes and over the right, and rocked him time and again, but it was Willie's fight from the first round on when he jabbed Saddler thirty-seven times in succession without a return. There were times when he had Saddler so befuddled that he could stop the dancing and stand right there and rock him back and, though battered and cut and bruised, he won it big on everybody's card to send the sell-out crowd out into the streets still buzzing, still carrying the electrical charge of it.

"Willie sold a lot of TV sets that night," I was saying now. "In those days, you remember, boxing and Milton Berle sold TVs. Guys who didn't have sets gathered in bars or in the homes of others who had sets to watch the fights, and I'll bet Willie sold a lot that night."

"I'll bet you're right," Devlin said.

"Who knows?" Willie said.

"Another one I remember," I said, "was when you defended against Sal Bartolo. There was a loudmouth there who was hollering, 'Walk in on him, Sal! He can't punch! Walk in! He can't hurt ya!' After you flattened Bartolo, the guy was hollering, 'Fake! Fake!' Bartolo's jaw was broken in three places."

"I got lucky," Willie said. "I boxed him twice before and never knocked him down, and in the first fight he knocked me down for the first time. He was a good fighter."

"I was thinking of you a couple of months ago," I said. "I was out in Cut and Shoot, Texas, outside of Houston. You remember. You were training in Houston and . . ."

"Yeah, I remember that fighter fought Patterson. What was his name?"

"Roy Harris."

"Yeah," Willie said, and then to Devlin, "He came from out in the woods there. They used to cut and shoot people, and they wanted me to go out there and I said, 'Look, I don't want to go. They're probably nice people, but I'm a city fella and I don't understand that stuff.' I wouldn't go."

"So Willie was training in Houston," I said to Devlin, "and Bill Gore had just attached Willie's speed bag into the overhead socket. Roy Harris has a brother named Tobe, who'd been a fighter, and he walked up and he teed off and hit the bag a smash with his right . . ."

"Yeah," Willie said, nodding. "That's right."

"Well, that was like some country fiddler grabbing Jascha Heifetz's violin. Bill Gore said to this Tobe, 'Don't do that. That's Willie's bag.' And this Tobe, he squared off against Bill."

"That's right," Willie said. "He wanted to belt old Bill Gore. Somebody stepped between them, but I didn't want nothin' to do with that Cut and Shoot place."

"And last fall I went up to see Carmen Basilio in Syracuse," I said. "He also says you were the greatest boxer he ever saw."

"That's nice of him," Willie said. "What's he doin'?"

"He's teaching in a college there."

"He's teachin' in a college?" Willie said. "How can he be teachin' in a college when he can't even speak English?"

"Come on, Willie," I said, "he speaks as well as we do."

"Yeah, I know," he said, "but, I mean, how can he be teachin' in a college?"

"He teaches physical education."

"Oh," Willie said. "Well, he could do that."

"He told me you wouldn't agree with me."

"He told you what?"

"He told me that you wouldn't agree with me. He says that everything he says, you disagree with."

"He's wrong," Willie said.

"You see?" I said. "That's exactly what he said."

"Every time he sees me," Willie said, "he grabs me in a headlock. Why does he do that?"

"I don't know," I said. "He likes you, I guess."

"That's enough," Devlin said, laughing and standing up. "I could sit around here all afternoon listening to these stories, but I have things to do."

He shook hands with me, and put on his coat and hat and left. Willie was sitting back, his hands clasped behind his head.

"So what do you want to know?" he said.

"How things are with you," I said. "I'm presuming you're presently married."

I had lost track of Willie's marriages. The first was to a girl from around Hartford, the second was to a model, the third to an exotic dancer, the fourth to a hatcheck girl and part-time actress. That's where some of the money went. Some went into a home for his parents, and some went at the race track, and some into Chilean oil wells, two nightclubs, and a tavern.

"This is the fifth time," he said. "I'm happily married nine years to this girl—Geraldine. Her father was an All-American basketball player at Manhattan College—Nat Volpe—and he used to referee games in the Garden. When I first met my wife she didn't know Willie Pep from a hole in the wall. I got a seven-year-old daughter—Melissa—a cat, two dogs, and a fenced-in yard, and that's it."

"I remember a little kid, a boy about knee-high, who used to be around the gym here with you."

"I got a thirty-three-year-old daughter. I got two boys. One guy is thirty-one and the other is twenty-four. I run away the first time. We were both twenty years old, and she said, 'Willie, we ought to get married.' I said, 'I can't, until I'm champion of the world.' So two months later we got married. My first two are dead now, and the third and fourth—I don't know what happened to them once we got divorced. I did well by them, though."

"I recall somebody telling me," I said, "that a father of one of your wives told you before the marriage, 'Willie, don't marry my daughter. She's no good, and you're too nice a guy.' I thought that was quite a noble act by a father."

"But that's not so," he said. "Why would the guy tell me that? I was champion of the world, and his daughter was gonna live in style. The wives and me, we couldn't get along, and if you can't get along, it's no good."

The door had opened, and a man in a windbreaker had walked in. He was standing in front of Willie's desk.

"How are you, Willie?" he said.

"Fine," Willie said, looking up at him.

"You want to buy a TV set?"

"I already got a TV set," Willie said.

"How about a nineteen-inch black and white?"

"I already got a nineteen-inch black and white," Willie said.

"I know," the other said, "I'm the guy who's fixin' it for you."

"Oh, yeah," Willie said, "I forgot. Where is it?"

"I got it out in the car," the other said. "You want to come out, and I'll put it in your car?"

"Good," Willie said, and then to me, "Excuse me a minute. All right?"

With those quick steps he went over to the coat rack and put on a topcoat and he followed the other out. In about five minutes he was back, hanging up his topcoat and hurrying over to his desk.

"You see," he said, "I give the set to one guy to fix, and he gave it to this guy. That's why I didn't recognize this guy. I got to call my wife."

He dialed, and I could hear the ringing sound at the other end. Then the sound stopped.

"Hey!" he said into the phone. "The guy just brought the TV back. I'll bring it home tonight. What? All I know is what the guy said. He said he fixed it. There may be a few lines in it yet, but he did the best he could. What? What do I know about a TV? I don't know nothin'. All I know is the guy . . . Hey, wait a minute!"

He took the phone away from his head and held it out from himself. What I heard sounded like a recording tape being run rapidly through the player, and Willie was looking at me and shaking his head and laughing.

"Wait! Wait!" he was saying into the phone now. "Hold it! Listen to me. Oh, boy. Hey, put Missy on. Let me talk to Missy. Please?"

He waited, looking at me and shaking his head and raising his eyes and laughing.

"Hello, Missy?" he said now. "How was school? What? Yeah, I got it. What? Look, how do I know? All I know is the man said he fixed it the best . . . Hey! You sound just like your mother."

He held the phone away from himself again. This time the pitch was higher, as if the tape was being run even more rapidly through the player, perhaps even backward.

"Missy?" he was saying into the phone again now. "Listen. Hey! Never mind. Look. I got it in the car, and I'll be home with it about five o'clock. All right? Good. Good. I'll see you."

He put the phone back on its cradle. He shook his head, and he was still smiling.

"That was my daughter," he said. "I get a couple weeks' vacation, and this year I'm thinkin' of taking her to Disney World."

"She'll like that," I said, "so you'll enjoy it, too."

"I live within a hundred twenty miles of six race tracks," he said. "We also got dog tracks and jai alai, and I can't go. You lose a hundred, and what are you gonna do?"

"Willie," I said, "I'm going to try something on you again. You were a great artist, and . . ."

"Thank you," he said.

". . . and the rest of us are always yearning to learn how the great artist does it. Can't you recall where you learned this move or that move?"

I had tried it on him many years before, but to no avail. It is what Hans Hofmann, the late Abstract Expressionist painter and teacher, once said, "The painterly instincts are stronger than will. In teaching, it is just the opposite. I must account for every line. One is forced to explain the inexplicable."

"Styles are funny," Willie said. "One's guy's candy is another guy's poison."

"That's why no one else could really box Willie Pep's style."

"I don't know," he said. "My father wasn't athletic. He came from the old country, and he worked on construction in Middletown, but he liked sports. On the East Side I was a little kid, and I used to get whacked around."

"And run," I said.

"Right, and the Old Man said, 'Don't come home cryin', or I'll whack you around, too.' I didn't win any fights on the street, that's for sure. Then one guy, some older kid, said, 'Why don't you go to the gym? You're gettin' beat up, and you can get paid for it.'

"I got three dollars in Danbury, Connecticut, in 1937. I got five dollars altogether, but it was two dollars for the license. In Norwich, Connecticut, I weighed a hundred and seven, and a tall black guy from the Salem A.C. gets on and he's a hundred and twenty-six. I said to the guy who was managing me, 'What about this guy?' He said, 'He ain't no good, or he wouldn't be fightin' you.'"

"Ray Robinson."

"Yeah. He boxed me under the name of Ray Roberts."

"And he says that, after he got the decision, they threw him in jail overnight, because they couldn't believe an amateur could beat Willie Pep."

"But he's wrong," Willie said. "I was a nobody then, so why would they throw him in jail for beatin' me?"

"I don't know," I said, "but did you learn anything in that fight, or any fight?"

"I can't say," he said. "You see, with me, guys were always trying to hit me, and I didn't like to get hit. I didn't like to get punched, and I was very fortunate. I think I won thirty or forty straight rounds without losing a round. It just came to me. The other guy was missing, and I was punching. Instinct. I just did it. I jabbed a guy, and then I made him miss, and then I was behind him. I was blessed with a lot of things.

"Then Bill Gore came along," he said, and Bill Gore was his trainer. "I'd come back to the corner, and Bill would be the most relaxed guy. He'd wipe me off, and give me water. He was calm and he made me calm."

"How nervous were you before a fight, say in the dressing room?"

"I was nervous," he said. "I sat. I walked. I wanted to get in there and get it over with. I was scared in every fight in a way, I guess."

"Can you recall anything that Bill Gore taught you?"

"He told me once, 'You jab, and you push your hand out and you step to the side and you leave your hand there.' I fought a guy in Phoenix—you could look it up—and I kept doin' that, and after the fight he was complainin', 'I don't know what's the matter with my neck. It's stiff, and it hurts.'

"Bill Gore," he said, "he told me, 'The way you talk now, you're gonna talk when you quit.' He wouldn't let me get hurt. Against Saddler, the third time, my left eye was shut tight. Bill Gore said to the referee, 'He can't continue.' I said, 'Thank you.' He died in '75 in Tampa, and they buried him in Providence, Rhode Island, and I went to the wake. He was one of the greatest trainers of all time. If he was around New York he woulda been known as the greatest."

"So how did you finally decide, after two hundred and forty-one fights, to finally call it quits?"

"In January of 1966," he said, "in Richmond, Virginia, they told me, 'Come down here and box an exhibition, four rounds.' The day of the fight, Bill Brennan, the commissioner of Virginia, says, 'You're boxing six rounds.' I said, 'It's supposed to be an exhibition.' He told the other guy, Calvin Woodland, 'If you don't fight, I'll suspend you.' He told me, 'I'll have you suspended everywhere.' I stayed at the John Marshall, in Richmond, a real nice hotel, and I was there three days and I had a big tab, so I fought the guy, and he licked me in six rounds and I packed it in."

"And then what did you do?"

"I worked for a brewery for a while, and for a car radio company for a while. Rocky Marciano was instrumental in gettin' me that job in Brockton. I was a goodwill man, and then I got a job as a tax marshal for Connecticut, but I couldn't stand that."

"Why not?"

"I couldn't make any money, and the stories ruined me. Basically, I'm a very soft guy. I'm a sucker for a touch, and a sob story makes me cry. The job was to collect unpaid taxes, and I got paid only if I collected the taxes—six percent. After the tax marshal says 'No funds,' they leave the guy alone, and I was always saying 'No funds.' No money for me. This one guy had a gas station outside of town here, and he owed three thousand in taxes. I knew the guy, but I hadn't seen him in fifteen years. The guy was married, with a kid, and dead broke, and he couldn't pay his bills, so I ended up loaning him ninety bucks. That was no job for me."

"Do you miss the way it used to be, Willie?"

"They told me I grossed close to a million," he said, "but I used to get cut fifty percent. My father told me, 'Don't ever take anything that don't belong to you.' He couldn't read or write, but he knew right or wrong. I never hurt anybody. Maybe I did—I don't know—but I didn't mean to."

"But do you miss being in the ring?" I said. "You know, being able to box so beautifully and thrilling people and hearing the cheers and the praise."

"I don't think about it too much," he said, "because I'll never have it to do again. I made a lot of mistakes, but I'm very fortunate. I came out of them."

When it was coming up 4:30, I asked him to call a cab for me, but he said he would drive me to where I could cross the street to the motel. We walked out to the parking space, and the TV set was on the passenger's side of the front seat. I got in the back, and Willie seemed small, peering out over the wheel. City-soiled snow, sand mixed into it, was banked along the curb where a half-dozen cars were backed up at the stoplight.

"Now don't cross here," he said to me, as I started to get out. "Cross at the corner. I don't want to see you get hurt."

"I never wanted to see you get hurt, either," I said.

"Thank you," he said. "Good luck."

As I approached the corner, the light changed and the cars began to move. When he passed me he waved quickly, just once, and then turned back to the wheel, and that was the last I saw of the great artist, the like of whom I'm sure I shall never see again.

The Coach, Relived

Willie Davis Talks Vince Lombardi

"In Willie Davis we got a great one."

Vince Lombardi

IT WAS THE FIRST WEEK of July 1962, and we were starting to put a book together in Green Bay. It was to be Vince Lombardi's first, and he had a respect for good books, and so, at the beginning, he was caught up in that romance of being an author. For the two weeks before the Packer training camp opened at St. Norbert College across the Fox River in West De Pere, I was living with him and Marie and young Vincent and Susan in their new ranch house at 667 Sunset Circle. Each morning, after he had come back from eight o'clock Mass at St. Willebrord's and we had had breakfast, we would go down into the rec room, and I would get out the notebook. We would put in three hours, and then after lunch we would get in two or three more.

"How are we doing?" he said, at the end of the third afternoon.

"We're doing all right," I said, because you hoped never to have to tell him that you were doing otherwise.

"Are we almost done?" he said.

"Almost done?" I said. "I'm only on my second notebook."

"The second notebook?" he said. "How many notebooks are there going to be?"

"Oh, I don't know," I said. "That's hard to say."

Chapter 11 of *Once They Heard the Cheers*, 1979.

"Three? Or four?"

"Five or six."

"Six notebooks?" he said, those eyes burning into my head and that voice thrown like a spear. "Six notebooks? How am I gonna do six notebooks? Six notebooks? I've got paperwork to do at the office! I've got players I haven't even signed yet! I've gotta play golf! Once training camp starts I can't play again until the end of the season! Six notebooks? How are we ever gonna do six notebooks?"

"I don't know, coach," I said, "but we'll find a way."

"You guys didn't tell me it was going to be this much work," he said.

"You didn't ask."

"Well, we'll have to do some of it in camp," he said. "We'll be living in the dean's suite, and we can get in an hour or two a day there."

"Relax, coach," I said. "I said we'll find a way."

I meant that *I* would find a way, and in the month I spent in camp the dream of working in the dean's suite dissolved, as I had suspected it would, into a total of an hour and a half. Before we went into camp I rode miles in golf carts, following him and his companions around the eighteen holes of the Oneida Golf Club, and then spent hours at the bar listening to replays of hole after hole. While he drove down to Fond du Lac to watch Susan in a horse show, I made notes in the car. We talked over drinks before dinner at home, and in restaurants, and I wedged my way amid the paperwork at the Packer office that then occupied the old two-story, flat-roofed, red-brick corner building at 349 South Washington Street in downtown Green Bay.

"I think I've found a way to simplify this," I said to him late one morning, sitting across from him at his desk, "and it'll save some time."

"Good," he said.

"I'm going to start naming players," I said. "When I give you a name, you tell me the first thing that comes to your mind about him, not as a player—we'll get to that another time—but as a person. Do you understand what I mean?"

"Of course I understand," he said. "Let's get started."

"Right, coach," I said. "Bart Starr."

"Tense by nature, because he's a perfectionist. I've never seen him display emotion outside of nervousness. Modest. Tends to be self-effacing, which is usually a sign of lack of ego. You never hear him in the locker room telling 'I' stories. He calls me 'sir.' Seems shy, but he's not. He's just a gentleman. You don't criticize him in front of others. When I came here he lacked confidence and support. He still lacks daring, and he's not as creative as I'd like him to be, but a great student of the game."

"Paul Hornung."

"Can take criticism in public or anywhere. You have to whip him a little. He had a hell-with-you attitude, a defensive perimeter he built around himself when he didn't start out well here. As soon as he had success he changed. He's still exuberant, likes to play around, but serious on the field. Always looks you straight in the eye. Great competitor who rises to heights."

"Jerry Kramer."

"Nothing upsets him, so you can bawl him out any time. He's been near death, but he's happy-go-lucky, like a big kid. Takes a loss quite badly, though."

"Ray Nitschke."

"The rowdy on the team. Big, fun-loving, rough, belligerent. Like a child. Never gives you an argument, but he'll turn around and do the same thing over again. He's the whipping boy, but he can take it. Criticism just runs off his back. You don't improve him. He improves himself."

"Forrest Gregg."

"Intelligent and, like Marie says, a picture-perfect player. Gives you a hundred percent effort, a team player. Quick temper. I've seen him go at teammates in practice. Has all the emotions, from laughter to tears. Can take criticism anywhere, if it's constructive."

"Jimmy Taylor."

"Uses jive talk that I can't understand. Has a lot of desire, because he wants to be the best football player the NFL has ever seen. He likes to knock people down, and he'll go out of his way to do it. You have to keep after him, though."

"Henry Jordan."

"All-Pro, all-everything, but don't ever flatter him. He needs public criticism. He thinks he's the greatest and tends to be satisfied. Strangely, he's easily upset, but he needs to be upset to perform. In reviewing pictures I'll make him a target, not to impress somebody else as you do with some of them, but to help him."

In that hour or so I named off all thirty-six Packers, and out of their instant personality profiles there also emerged a profile of the man often described now as the greatest of all football coaches. In the month in camp and a week during the season, I heard the tongue-lashings. I saw men, grown beyond the size of most of us—some of them fathers—cringe, and I heard others swear under their breath. They knew, however, and if they didn't they soon learned, what I knew after that morning in the office. He knew them, not just as football players but as distinct individuals, each of whom he was determined to make into a better player than that man had ever thought he could be, in Vince Lombardi's obsession to create, out of all the parts, one entity greater than any team that had ever been.

"Willie Davis," I said.

"Traded to Cleveland for him," he said. "A hell of a young man. Very excitable under game conditions. A worrier. Before a game he's got that worried look, so I try to bolster his confidence. He's not worried about the team losing—he's got confidence in the team—but he's worried about how Willie Davis will perform . . . about not letting the team down. Fine brain, too. In Willie Davis we got a great one."

Fourteen years later, on our way out to Jim Tescher's in North Dakota, my wife and I stopped off at Green Bay for three days. On that Sunday the Packers would be opening another season—under Bart Starr now—and I wanted to visit with old acquaintances. I hoped to find, in one or another, what still lived of Vince Lombardi six years after cancer took him on September 3, 1970, in Georgetown University Hospital.

"Willie Davis is coming in from California," Tom Miller said. He played end during the mid-forties for the Eagles, Redskins, and the Packers, and he is the Packers' general business manager. "Willie's doing very well. He has a big Schlitz distributorship in L.A., and he's on the board of directors of the Schlitz Brewing Company. You remember Willie, of course."

"Of course," I said. "I remember him very well."

I remember that great smile flashing, and how the others called him "Dr. Feelgood," and I remember that worried look that Lombardi had described and that would shroud Willie Davis in front of his locker before a game. During the week he would be the outward optimist, but he was unable to eat before a game and until the morning after, and once, during that month in camp in '62, we sat in one of those dormitory rooms in Sensenbrenner Hall at St. Norbert, and he told me about his beginnings.

He was born in Lisbon, Louisiana, the oldest of three children of a broken family. He grew up in Texarkana, Arkansas, where his mother cooked at a country club, did catering, and took in laundry. At Grambling College, which has sent so many football players to the pros, he captained the team for two years.

"When I was drafted by the Browns," he said that day, "I was the seventeenth choice when they picked thirty, and I was concerned. I was from a small Negro school, and there were guys with bigger names picked later. Then in camp you find a guy from Notre Dame or Michigan State whom you've read about."

"Well, they didn't run you off the field," I said.

"No," he said, "and pro football has been the difference between me being just another guy and having something today. In fact, I sometimes shake when I think I might not have finished college and not made a pro club."

"There are a lot of guys," I said, "who are lucky enough to be able to play this game but to whom that thought has never occurred."

"Well," he said, "I think the responsibility I had growing up of looking after the young ones helped me. I've never smoked, and I'm not considered a drinker."

"And the coach tells me you're a worrier, always worried about Willie Davis doing his best."

"That's right," he said. "I constantly replay situations where I could have played better. During the off-season I think of them over and over, and I come back thinking, 'I'm not gonna do that again.' What it is, I guess, is that I try to play so that I can live with myself."

He became the Packers' defensive captain, and on those Packer teams that won five NFL championships in seven years and the first two Super Bowls, he was one of the finest defensive ends ever to play the game. He made All-Pro five times, and he retired at the end of the 1969 season.

On the morning after Tom Miller had talked about him, I met Willie, the high forehead a little higher but the smile just the same, at the Packer offices at Lambeau Field on what, in 1968, they renamed Lombardi Avenue. He drove me in his car over to the Midway Motel, and for an hour or so we talked in his room.

"Are you the first black on the Schlitz board of directors?" I said.

"That's right," he said, smiling. "In fact, I'm the second non-family member."

"How did that come about?" I said.

"Well," he said, "long before I quit playing I had started to put together for the day when I could no longer live up to Willie Davis's standards. I wanted to avoid that situation where some coach walks up to you and taps you on the shoulder and says, 'We can't use you any more.' The most fearful thing to me was the day when I couldn't play the game any more.

"My first year in Cleveland I subbed in the school system, but by the second year of subbing I just didn't feel I wanted to be a teacher. I caught on in sales with a brewery out of Pittsburgh, and when I came back to Green Bay the next year I approached the people in Schlitz. I moved to Chicago to work that area, and I enrolled at the University of Chicago, in the business school, and in four years I got my master's in business administration, in marketing. Then, any time the situation warranted, I could leave football."

"And how did you know when it was time to leave?"

"I came back in '69 because of Coach Bengtson," he said. Phil Bengtson, who had coached the Packer defense under Vince Lombardi, had succeeded him. "Coach Bengtson had meant a great deal to me, and I wanted to see him have a winning season. I played that '69 season and when, with four games to go, we were mathematically eliminated, it was the first time since grade school that I walked out onto a field and had trouble scrambling for reasons to play.

"After that game—I believe it was against Minnesota—I said to myself, 'There's no need of me kidding myself. There's no way I'm gonna play.' On the twenty-first of December, Forrest Gregg and I walked out onto the field for our last game, and he said, 'Willie, we've broken a lot of huddles together, and we'll never do it again.' Later, Sid Gillman called me from San Diego, and he said, 'We've studied films, and you can play three or four years.' I told Sid, 'When I walked off that field in Green Bay I walked off a field for the last time. I'm never gonna play again.' A week later I got a call from Schlitz to buy out the company operation in Los Angeles.

"I'd been offered a few coaching jobs, five or six," he said, and only later would I learn that one of them had been at Harvard, "but I said to myself, 'I'm going into the heart of Watts, where I want to be an example.' I mean, I see so many basketballs bouncing in Watts. A kid can identify with that, but why can't I impress them that there's another avenue where maybe they can make it?

"You take the Willie Davis Distributing Company. Maybe people say, 'The guy isn't short of ego.' I didn't name the company a minute on ego. If I say that, I may be kidding myself to some degree, but there's a fine line between ego and pride. If the kids get a chance to see me on parade, maybe that'll help them to reach too. In the evenings, when I get ready to leave the place, many times I don't have to open the gate. Sure, maybe some want a dime or a quarter, but we have a relationship."

He was, he said, president of the Los Angeles Urban League, had been on the board of the West Adams Community Hospital, had served on a public commission to study county government and come up with recommendations to go on the ballot. He worked for the United Way, with Explorer Scouts, with the Watts Festival in Black, and on a career task force with junior high and high schools, and during his first four years there he averaged a speech a week.

"What I'd like to do," I said, "is come out and see you in your environment. Then we can talk at length about you and about the old coach."

"I give one man almost ninety percent credit for whatever I am," he said. "I give Paul Brown credit for two years at Cleveland. I give my college coach, Eddie Robinson, credit for motivation and his approach to education, but right today I have a daughter and a fifteen-year-old son who is playing football, and the one sad thing is that he will never have a chance to play for Vince Lombardi."

In early March I flew out to Los Angeles, and checked into a motel near the airport. It was midafternoon when I called his office.

"Oh, he's out of town for the day," his secretary said.

"What time will he be in tomorrow?" I said.

"Oh, seven thirty," she said. "He's usually here by then."

The next morning, after we spoke on the phone, he sent his younger brother Al out to pick me up. Al looks like Willie, tall and high-waisted, and he has the same walk. On the way out, we talked about some of the great Packer games and, when we got into Watts, where whole city blocks, although cleared of rubble, remain vacant and weed-grown, we talked of the riots in 1965. We talked of promises unkept and dreams left still unfulfilled by a nation that, it seems to me, too often functions as if it is a battalion aid station that has neither the time nor the resources to do more than stop the bleeding.

At the plant he drove through the gate of the eight-foot chain-link fence with the barbed wire on top, and up to the entrance to the two-story, modern red-brick office section that fronts the warehouse. He took me through the warehouse, high-ceilinged and immaculate, the cases stacked in perfect alignment, a white truck, spotless and with the name on the doors, being loaded.

"We usually have a hundred fifty thousand cases in here," he said, "but we're down to about a hundred twenty thousand right now."

While I was still trying to imagine a hundred fifty thousand cases of beer being consumed, all that hoisting of bottles and cans and the aftermath, he opened the door of the refrigerator room, the cold air hitting us. We stepped into an aisle between the stacked aluminum kegs.

"We have the Coliseum," he said, "and the Forum and the Sports Arena, so we move a lot of draft beer."

Back in the office reception room, he led me up a flight of stairs. There were two carpenters working, putting up the studding for new walls, and he said that Willie had just bought an FM radio station that would broadcast from there.

"KACE-FM," he said. "It'll be 103.9 on the dial."

Willie's office is on the ground floor, a windowless interior room, walnut-paneled; on the wall behind the dark oak desk a black-tinted, gold-specked mirror; the carpeting tomato red. On the wall to the left of the desk there was an oil portrait of Lombardi in the dark green Packer coaching jacket and holding a football. On the other walls there were two full-color Packer team photographs, award plaques, and framed certificates.

"I was very sorry to read about Henry Jordan," I was saying.

Willie was sitting behind the desk in a brown-leather swivel chair. He had on a gray shirt, open at the neck, a dark green tie, and dark green trousers. On his left ring finger was the Packer ring with the three diamonds denoting the successive championships in '65, '66, and '67.

"It was a shock to me," he said. "I've been affected. I've been moved."

Ten days before, at the Milwaukee Athletic Club where he had been jogging, Henry Jordan had died of a heart attack. He had been a five-time All-Pro defensive tackle on those teams with Willie, and he was forty-two.

"I went to the funeral," Willie was saying, "and I was one of the pallbearers."

"I saw the picture in the paper," I said, "of you and Bart and Hawg Hanner and Bob Skoronski and . . ."

"Ron Kostelnik and Lionel Aldridge," he said. "After the service they slide the casket out, and you take a hold and you feel this weight. I thought, 'I've lifted tables and I've lifted cases of beer, but this is my friend that I played football with for eleven years.'

"That's a weight," he said, and he leaned back and put his hands behind his head, "and it makes you think. Henry was six months younger than I am, and how much time do any of us have to enjoy life?"

"Never enough, I guess," I said, "and I'm sorry to tell you that you'll have this feeling more often from now on."

"There's so much a man wants to do, and that he can do," he said, "and Henry's passing made me realize again that you have to get about the business of doing it."

"Lombardi got both Henry and you from Cleveland," I said. "I remember how, before Lombardi turned everything around, they used to say in the league that being traded to Green Bay was like being sent to Siberia. What was it like when they told you in Cleveland that you'd been traded?"

"By then the Packers had had their first winning season under Lombardi," he said, "but it was sort of—well—disturbing. I was subbing in the school system on the west side of Cleveland, and that evening I heard it on a sports flash on the car radio."

"What a nice way to be informed," I said.

"Yeah," he said, smiling. "I had started ten ball games for Cleveland as a rookie and played three games both ways, as an offensive tackle and a defensive end. I was in Cleveland last year, and a trivia question there was, 'Who was the last Cleveland player to play a complete game both ways?' I was kind of shocked by the answer: Willie Davis.

"The next year, I'd just signed three weeks before and been told I'd graded out second best to Jim Ray Smith, and I was to start in the old Lou Groza spot. Being traded I was probably as confused as any person could be, but I drove to Green Bay, with just a couple of rest stops, and when I got near I was kind of bug-eyed. I thought I could see what seemed like hay coming across a field toward the road on some kind of a conveyor. I thought it was an optical illusion, but it was a big wagon of hay being pulled by a tractor, and the guy came up and right across Highway 57 in front of me.

"I went off the road, and I thought, 'Where am I going? I get up here and I darn near lose my life.' When I got in, they said the coach wanted to see me, and you know that Coach Lombardi, with all the meanness and toughness that's been written about, had that smile that could melt an iceberg. He said, 'Willie, I want you to know one thing. We really wanted to make this trade. When I was the offensive coach in New York we took advantage of you because it was the defense you were forced to play. I was impressed by your quickness and aggressiveness. If you play like that for us, you'll make it big.' Then he said, 'What were you making in Cleveland?' Now, he knew, and before I could say anything, he said, 'We're increasing it by a thousand dollars.' Well, I was ready to be shown the practice field, and I started behind there for one week and I moved up and started for the next ten years."

"I heard him jump on any number of people," I said, "but never you. Did he ever abuse you?"

"Yeah," Willie said, smiling. "Henry Jordan told about it once. We were in training camp, and nothing seemed to be in Lombardi's style. He'd been after Jordan because he'd come in heavy, and in that seven o'clock meeting he went up and down Henry, and he finally said, 'But Jordan is not a one-man team, so there have to be some other contributors.' I'm sitting there, thinking I'm having my best camp, when he jumped on me and he said, 'Davis, what about you? When are you gonna get with this game?'

"Well, I was shocked, and I almost thought he was kidding. That night, like around midnight, if he'd been on the premises, I think I'd have told him, 'I quit.' The next morning Henry went to Bengtson and he handed in his playbook, and he actually wanted to quit. When Lombardi saw me that morning he said, 'I've got to prove nobody's beyond chewing out.' I said, 'Yeah, coach, but give me some warning.'

"The worst game I ever played in my life was the Sunday we played the 49ers after the Kennedy assassination. Such an attitude pervaded the whole team, but Lombardi hardly said a word. He realized that that thing had taken a lot of starch out of everybody, including himself."

"He had met Jack Kennedy, and he greatly admired him."

"Then, after a Minnesota game he got on me in a deserving way. The frustrations of Fran Tarkenton just left me bewildered. At one of the pro bowls I told Fran, 'I went a whole season saying that, if I ever catch up with you, you're gonna be in a world of trouble.' So Lombardi got on me then, but once Max McGee said, 'This had to be a tough day. He even got on Willie.'

"What he would do was, he would never hit you when you expected it. When we'd win by forty points, he'd take us apart. We'd lose 17 to 14, and he would make a point of why we'd win again. He could walk you out of a defeat, and the next week you'd be absolutely convinced you were gonna win again. He'd pick out two or three essentials, and he'd say, 'If you get back to these basics, it's never gonna happen again.' When we were at the fatigue point, he'd sympathize, but when he thought we were ready to win and we didn't, he took us to task."

"To put it mildly," I said.

"The man knew us," he said. "He told me once, 'Not that I can ever be black, but I can understand. When you reach out, I can understand the reach.' Forrest Gregg was another one he never had to get on."

"Well," I said, "Forrest and you were a lot alike. You were both dedicated guys."

"For ten years," he said, "Forrest and I lined up across from each other day after day, and it was like a . . . a . . ."

"A mirror?"

"Yeah," he said, smiling. "A black and white mirror."

"Speaking of black and white," I said, "I would judge, from walking around the plant and office with Al, that you've got an integrated company here."

"Is that right?" he said, laughing. "Since my favorite color is green, I really don't know. When I came here, there was one black in the office and one black truck driver and a few as salesmen. We're near fifty-fifty now, although I guess there are more black."

"Can you remember," I said, "when, growing up, you first became conscious of the difference between black and white?"

"Growing up in the South," he said, "you're segregated by so many patterns that the sight of a white person denotes the difference. My first real, believe it or not, experience in a black and white situation was when I worked at the club where my mother worked. You really felt like an object. It was the haves and the have-nots, and nothing distresses me more now than going into a restaurant and seeing a guy who has money giving a waiter or a waitress, regardless of color, a hard time.

"When I got up with Cleveland, it was the first time I was functioning as a peer, working with a white guy on the same level. In Cleveland we worked it out, and that made me appreciate Paul Brown, as I did Lombardi."

"But when you went to Green Bay," I said, "there was no real black community, and only two or three other blacks on the ball club. What was that like?"

"My wife was teaching school in Cleveland then," he said, "and the whole thing there was so interesting for both of us that my predisposed instinct was not to go. Being accepted by the Packers, though, was like being accepted into a family, and as to the people, they looked at you on the street kind of in awe. I'm not sure they looked at me as a Packer, or as a black Packer."

"You never found any prejudice?"

"The closest I came," he said, "was my second year, and I was looking for an apartment for the season. I saw something in the paper and I called on the phone, and it was still available. I went by, and it had just been rented. I left, and I had a friend call and it was available again.

"There was an emptiness in me. I thought, 'How can they see you on the street and make you feel so good, and turn around and they won't rent to you?' Then I said to myself, 'That's one person. It's a population of eighty thousand, and let's multiply that person a few times and you're still going to have a chance to meet mostly good people.'

"I went to a service station there and I mentioned it to this guy, Paul, and he got so interested that he got on the phone and turned something up. Then, two years later, I met Fabian Redman, a builder in Green Bay, and he kept an apartment open for me, and I had that every year. I'm sure he missed the income, renting only between times, and in Green Bay I saw people who almost dealt with you with kid gloves. You had to turn down invitations to dinner.

"When I went to Green Bay I went with a lot of resentment on being traded, but I would say right now that, even taking the success and having it someplace else, I honestly enjoyed myself there as much as any place I could be, with the ease in getting to the ball park and the closeness. In Cleveland we saw each other at practice, and then there was a mad exodus. In Green Bay, even if you didn't go out socially with that guy, if you went out you saw him there, anyway.

"When you lost," he said, "some woman would come up to you and say, 'That's all right. You guys will get 'em next week.' You would look at the disappointment on their faces, and it was so strong that you had to win the next time."

His phone had rung, and he picked it up.

"I'll be right out," he said into it, and then to me, "It's my insurance man. I'll be back in a few minutes. I've got some problems with the guy about claims."

On his desk there was a copy of *The Wall Street Journal*. On the coffee table in front of the sofa there were copies of *Nation's Business*, *BusinessWeek*, and *Black Enterprise*, and I looked through those until he came back with the insurance man, whom he introduced as Hector Rexton.

"But look," Rexton said, sitting down, and obviously picking up their previous conversation, "I'm sure that they're all indoctrinated, but what happens between the indoctrination and the execution that results in these claims?"

"Well," Willie said, leaning back in his chair behind the desk, "let me say this. You send a man out with a truck and fifty cases, and he makes stops and unloads. If, somehow, you can motivate each man so that he is accident-proof, then I'm telling you that you're 'Man of the Year' every year."

"I recognize your point," Rexton said, "but if you have another year this year like last year, your premium will be four times what it is now."

"But what are we talking about?" Willie said. "Sixteen cases, but it's only those two. I think you people have to get tough. If you fight these claims, not the legitimate ones but these ones that you and I understand, maybe it would stop.

"The saddest thing in this country," he said, "is that there's not a desire to work, but to get hurt working. It almost makes you ill when you see a guy come to work, and you almost know he's going to figure a way to make a claim."

They talked a few more minutes about coverages, percentages, and alternate plans. Rexton reeled off numbers, Willie nodding, and then he handed Willie some papers in a folder and shook hands and left.

"It's a problem," Willie said. "You hungry? Do you want me to send out for some sandwiches?"

"This problem," I said, after he had phoned the order, "it's not just those few who are looking to cop injury claims. It seems to me, and a lot of other people who remember another time, that there's a growing reluctance everywhere to do a hard day's work, a lack of pride in personal performance."

"You deal with what you see in this country," Willie said, "and you end up with opinions you've heard, as well as your own. You hear about minorities being shiftless, that they don't want to work, but you're being insulting when you generalize. There is a work-ethic problem in this country. To say that every guy should want to be gainfully employed is probably an unrealistic expectation. Today a lot of guys just don't believe they can get a decent job in which they can take pride.

"The problem, if you're the employer, is to impart pride, but that's not easy with some guys. When you tell a guy that, hey, he's not doing the job and he'd better start cuttin' it, he lights up. He's going on unemployment insurance. That's the problem."

"So what do you do about it?"

"With some there's nothing you can do," he said, "but what I try to do here is what Lombardi did at Green Bay, instill pride in the organization. When a new guy walked in there, he got caught up. Chuck Mercein, Ben Wilson, Anderson, the tight end, it was almost like they were saying, 'Hey, you guys really expect to win!' When I set up an incentive, it's How well are we going to do it? I try to make a guy grow in his own position, but always remembering that you can't compare some guy who just doesn't have it with a Dave Robinson. The ability is just not there, but I have brought salesmen in here who have said, 'I can't believe the attitude you guys have.' It's what Coach Lombardi used to say, 'Success is contagious. It breeds.'"

"Seeing you here," I said, "running a sizable operation, and knowing that you sit on the board of the parent company, I have to make an adjustment. I had the same feeling at Green Bay last fall, watching Bart Starr on the practice field ordering people around. I remember you all just taking orders, subservient, and day after day just following commands."

"Yeah," he said, smiling. "I can see what you mean."

"I recall, too, something Jerry Kramer once told me. He said, 'I often think, What am I doing? Here I am, a grown man, with a wife and three kids, and I'm rolling around on the ground like a kid myself.'"

"You know, it is a child's game," Willie said, "but all the years I played, and when I was getting older, I maintained my enthusiasm for it. Only in my last year, in those last four games, did I say, 'What am I doing here?'"

"A fine athlete," I said, "expresses himself in his sport as he can in nothing else, regardless of whatever success he has later in some other endeavor."

"That's right," he said.

"Do you ever miss that moment when you would break through the block and make the perfect tackle, knowing that feeling you can never reproduce in anything else?"

"Yes," he said. "That's right. I do."

"Is that an idea I've just put in your mind?"

"No," he said, "I've thought of that, but what I really miss is being one of the guys."

"As a boss?"

"Right. People look at you in a different way. You want to say, 'Hey! I'm me!' You know?"

"Yes," I said. "I would imagine that maybe there's a sort of fraternity here of, say, drivers. They share experiences."

"Exactly," he said. "I go out, and I see them laughing and talking, and I walk up and something happens. It changes. On the Packers I was kind of a fun guy, a laughing guy. Now I see them standing around, and one guy is telling a story and laughing and they're all listening, and I walk up and I can see the guy's eyes change, and he goes on with the story, but it goes flat. I remember I'd be telling something and laughing, and Coach Lombardi would come up, and it was like it just wasn't that funny any more."

We talked, over the sandwiches and coffee, and between phone calls that he accepted and made, of the changes in professional football. We spoke of players' agents and the rocketing salaries and bonuses in all team sports.

"As long as the money is there," I said, "I'm for it going to the athletes. After all, who would pay to see Wellington Mara kick a football around with Edward Bennett Williams or Art Modell?"

"That's right," he said. "People ask me, 'Don't you really wish you were playing now? Wouldn't you like all that money?' I wouldn't trade my years for anything, though. I played in a period when football reached its maturity in this country, and I'm still so pleased that I'll take my period, the people who played with me, and what it meant to me. That's why it's hard to put away a Henry Jordan.

"Every time I get back to Green Bay it warms my heart all over, because the people reach out and bring me back to left end. They say, 'If you were at left end, this Packer team would have what it needs.' I chuckle, but that's unfair to the guy out there."

"You look like you could almost step in there," I said. "You haven't put on much weight."

"I'm two fifty-five," he said, "and I played last at two forty-seven. I jog in the morning, and there are days when I wake up and I don't feel like getting up and crawling into the office. I say to myself that I own the Willie Davis Distributing Company, and today I'm going to exercise my prerogative and not go in. Then I think, 'What would Lombardi do?' I get up and out of bed. It's six o'clock, and I throw on my sweats and drive here and I jog and do a few wind sprints. They get harder to do. I think that today maybe I'll do six, and then I say to myself, 'Why don't I do two extra?' So I do, and then I take my shower."

"The Lombardi syndrome," I said. "During those terrible grass drills—up and down, up and down—when you guys were ready to collapse, he'd call for more. You remember how Bill Quinlan was always trying to cheat on them, and Lombardi would jump him?"

"Yeah," Willie said, smiling.

"One day Quinlan said to me, 'When I give up this game and start to miss it, I'll have it solved. I've got a film of this grass drill, and I'll run that and sit back and say, "The hell with it!"'"

"The Lombardi syndrome is everywhere," Willie said. "Jerry Kramer and Bob Skoronski and people like that—we'll sit down and share experiences. I'm involved in the school supply business with Bob, and we'll compare notes on motivational speakers at conferences. You not only find that there are those Lombardi principles that work, but you can't believe the admiration they had for the man. Whether the speaker is from IBM, or whatever, you hear them throw back at you again dedication, effort, pride . . ."

"And the importance of winning," I said.

"I've made it a point to clarify that statement," he said. "When Lombardi said that winning is the only thing, it was so expressive in my own mind. If you knew the man, you knew it was the pursuit, and you don't prepare to lose. I say that I hope we never reach the point where we're planning to lose, and that's all Lombardi meant."

"He caught a lot of flak for that," I said, "and he caught some more when we did a couple of pieces in *Look*, and got onto the subject of competitive animosity and the need, each week, to build up a hate for the opponent. Of course, it dissolves the moment the game is over."

"That's right," Willie said. "Gale Sayers lived in the next block from me in Chicago, and he's one of the nicest human beings. We'd have dinner together, but when I'd see him in that Bear uniform, I could take him on with determination and hostility. That's what Lombardi meant."

It was shortly after five o'clock when Willie had finished with phone calls and office appointments and the signing of letters. He said he would drive me back to my motel, and we walked out into the parking space where, although I had failed to notice it coming in, there was an old double-decker London bus. It was painted a dark red, and a sign on it advertised a firm of accountants specializing in preparing income tax returns.

"We just got it today," Willie said. "We're going to have the engine reconditioned and have it reupholstered and repainted, and take it around for the radio station."

"As a sort of mobile unit?"

"That's right," he said. "To take it to the people."

He opened the door and I followed him in, and we climbed to the upper deck. Mounted in front and in back to face into frames were the black scrolls with the white letters that had revealed to those inherently patient and polite British who had queued up at stops six thousand miles away, even amid the rubble of the London Blitz, the destinations: Oxford Circus . . . Regent Street . . . Piccadilly Circus . . . Trafalgar Square.

"I've been meaning to ask you," I said, as we got out, "about your plans for the station."

"Well," he said, "I have felt for some time that one of the most important involvements I could have would be in the community where I'm selling my product. All my life I'd heard, especially in minority communities, of selling products and then going home every night regardless of the quality of life of the people. One thing I knew was that I was going to be able to sleep at night, and so I've worked with the Urban League and those other things, and the radio station can provide me with another opportunity.

"My greatest commitment with the station will be to serve the people. Equal to my profit motive is my motive to provide an outlet for the citizens within the coverage area. KACE will be a station of credibility."

"That's fine," I said, "but how do you accomplish that?"

"We did a survey," he said, "and found crime and unemployment were what were troubling people. You expect that, but I personally went out and I said, 'If you had a station, what would it address itself to? What do you like and dislike?' Now, this is not some computer-derived survey. Maybe we haven't gone through all that I went through at the University of Chicago. I don't care about the randomness or the statistical reliability. I talked with the people, and music and our public service will be what it's about. Music transcends all racial backgrounds, and I want this to be a station that anybody can listen to and one that's sensitive enough to address itself to issues with meaningfulness and impact."

We got into his car. It was a new light gray Cadillac Seville, and he backed it out of the parking space.

"This is the first Cadillac I've ever had," he said. "It's the smaller model, though."

"You don't have to apologize," I said. "You've earned it."

"I don't know if I should say this," he said, "or how you can put it in the written word."

"Try me," I said.

"When I go to white banquets—and I mean basically white motivated—people come up and say, 'I'd like an autograph for my kid.' When I go to a black dinner, nobody comes up. Now, I don't mean that I'm disappointed for myself, that I need that."

"I understand."

"I've wondered about this. I've thought that the black kid is maybe being deprived of the incentive that maybe the white father is trying to stimulate when he takes the autograph home, like, 'Hey! See what you might achieve.'"

"Maybe," I said, "it's because the black community still is not a community of achievers."

"Hey, that could be it," he said. "I don't know."

"It might be something," I said, "that your station might address itself to."

"It might," he said. "I'll think about that."

The décor of the cocktail lounge in the motel was American Anthracite—black banquettes, black tabletops, dark walls and carpeting. Candles were flickering in globes on the tables, and when we ordered, Willie asked for a glass of white wine.

"When you think back over the years," I said, "what games keep coming back?"

We had one of the banquettes. Willie was leaning back, his arms spread along the top, his eyes following the traffic between the tables.

"I know two or three experiences," he said, "maybe four. I know what the first championship meant in '61, when we beat the Giants, 37–0. I don't think any football team in the world could have beaten us that day. Then I think of the first Super Bowl, how uncomfortable it was to represent the NFL against the new kid down the block. How impressive, how convincing would we be? Would we convince the AFL fans?

"One thing Coach Lombardi said to us was, 'If there is any doubt you have about this Kansas City team being good, look at their roster. Look at the All-Americans—Dawson, McClinton.'"

"Did you have a fear of losing?"

"Oh, yeah," he said. "There was the reason to fear we might get beat. It was very uncomfortable for me. I didn't want to get hit by Mike Garrett on a quick trap. I didn't want Curtis McClinton busting one up the middle. That was the reason we played the first half so conservative."

With both CBS and NBC carrying it on television and radio and the press building it for weeks, that first Super Bowl had become the Game of Games, the pride of the old league against the precocity of the new. At the half, the Packers led only 14–10, and then they came out again and turned it into a 35–10 rout.

"When Lombardi huddled everybody for the second half," Willie was saying, "he said, 'Look. I'll tell you what. You went out and played thirty minutes where you adjusted to Kansas City. Now I want you to go out and make Kansas City adjust to you.' The man was so right."

"What about the two Dallas games?" I said.

They were for the NFL title in '66 and '67 and for the right to meet Kansas City in the first Super Bowl and Oakland in the second. They were playing, as it turned out, for winners' shares that added up to $23,000 per player that first year, and $24,700 the second.

"The Dallas games were important," Willie was saying, "in that they made the Packers, and in the same sense they didn't make the Cowboys. Even in preseason we didn't want the Cowboys to think they could beat us."

In '66 in the Cotton Bowl in Dallas, with time running out, and the Packers leading 34–27, Dallas had a fourth down on the Packer 2-yard line when Don Meredith, with Willie Davis chasing and Dave Robinson hanging on to him, lofted the pass that Tom Brown, the Packer left safety, intercepted in the end zone. In '67, in that ice bowl at Green Bay, with time for only one more play and the Packers behind by 17–14, Bart Starr sneaked the ball in from the 1-yard line and the Packers won, 21–17.

"In that second game," I said, "what was it like on the sideline? When Bart came trotting over, and it was all coming down to one single play, were you close enough to hear what he and Vince were saying?"

"I heard," he said, "but I couldn't understand what the play was. As Bart trotted back out, I thought of all the possibilities. You know, a bad snap, whatever? I said to myself, 'Aw, hell.' I turned my head. I didn't want to see it. I waited, until I heard the crowd reaction. When

I looked up, it was just a mass of bodies out there. I didn't know that Bart had run a sneak.

"I think of other games, though," he said. "The Rams playoff in Milwaukee in '67. That was our challenge game, and you didn't challenge us, really—but they did. We'd already won our division, and they beat us out here on a blocked punt in the last minute, and then we started to read all about how they'd broken the Packer mystique and whatnot. Lombardi had those clips on the bulletin board, and he played it low all week."

"In other words," I said, "the Rams and the press dealt him a pair of aces."

"Right," he said. "He didn't have his Wednesday speech, and if he had put his Sunday morning talk, the one he gave us then, on Wednesday, we'd have just bubbled out by game time. He always had great respect for the Rams—Merlin Olsen and trying to handle their inside men—and in the dressing room he said, 'This is the game I wish I could play myself. If I could, I'd be sure how it could be played, but I have to trust it to you guys.'

"Then he got into it. He said, 'There are fifty thousand people out there, waiting for you to come out of this dressing room. They're all your family and your friends. They didn't come here to see the Rams. They came here to see you, and any time you let a team sit in California and say how they've broken your magic and what they're going to do to you, they're challenging you, and if they get away with it, it will be something you'll have to live with the rest of your lives. It's like a guy calling you out before your family and saying, "I'm gonna whip you."'

"Well, Nitschke was growling, and Boyd Dowler ran to the bathroom and threw up. This man had aroused our emotions so much, the guys were so mad that when they ran out, they were running heavy. You could hear their feet pounding, and the first two series, I couldn't adjust, I was so fired up."

"And you clobbered them," I said, for the Packers won that one, 28–7.

"Yeah," Willie said, "and we might have beaten them anyway, but I don't know that. I say it was the man."

We ordered another round, Willie staying with the white wine. We went on talking about the man, his perfectionism, the fear of him that pervaded practices, his temper tantrums, and his tears.

"I remember," I said, "that Lions game in Green Bay in '62, when they had you, 7–6, with less than two minutes to go, and Herb Adderley intercepted the pass and Hornung kicked the field goal with thirty-three seconds left and you won it, 9–7. In the locker room, Vince tried to say something and his voice broke and I looked at him, and his eyes were filling."

"I think I was the last Packer to see him," Willie said. "Norb Hecker was an assistant coach with the Giants then, and I was in San Diego when they were there. He told me, 'The coach is real bad, and he's going.' So I flew from San Diego to Washington, and I called Marie, and we went to the hospital.

"Coach Lombardi must have been down to a hundred fifty pounds. I said, 'Coach, if you'll come back to Green Bay and coach again, I'll come out of retirement.' He smiled, you know?"

"As you said, it would melt an iceberg."

"Yeah," Willie said. "He tried to smile, and the tears started to come out of his eyes and he said, 'Willie, you're a hell of a man.' Then he said, 'Get out of here.' And we left—Marie, too—and we weren't in there for more than a minute and a half. Since then I've wondered if maybe I shouldn't have gone. He cried."

The Greatest, Pound for Pound

There's Only One Sugar Ray

It is when we try to grapple with another man's intimate need that we perceive how incomprehensible, wavering, and misty are the beings that share with us the sight of the stars and the warmth of the sun.

Joseph Conrad, Lord Jim

"WHEN I AM OLD," I wrote more than twenty years ago, "I shall tell them about Ray Robinson. When I was young, I used to hear the old men talk of Joe Gans and Terry McGovern and Kid McCoy. They told of the original Joe Walcott and Sam Langford, of Stanley Ketchel and Mickey Walker and Benny Leonard. How well any of them really knew those men I'm not sure, but it seemed to me that some of the greatness of those fighters rubbed off on these others just because they lived at the same time.

"That is the way," I wrote, "I plan to use Sugar Ray. When the young assault me with their atomic miracles and reject my Crosby records and find comical the movies that once moved me, I shall entice them into talking about fighters. Robinson will be a form of social security for me, because they will have seen nothing like him, and I am convinced that they never will."

I am still sure today that they will never be able to match Robinson because of the social changes that were altering life in this country

---

Chapter 12 of *Once They Heard the Cheers*, 1979.

while he fought. The prejudice that drove the black as before him it drove the Irish, the Jew, and then the Italian to the ring in desperation is becoming a part of our past. In an age of reason fewer men are forced to fight with their fists, the amateurs are not what they used to be, the bootleg circuit, where Robinson received his intermediate schooling, is long gone, and the professional game has been on the decline for twenty-five years.

Ray Robinson—and Archie Moore, the venerable Sage of San Diego and the greatest ring mechanic I ever saw—were the last of the old-fashioned fighters because they fought from the end of one era through the beginning of another, and because they were the products of poverty as well as prejudice. Robinson was eight years old when his mother brought him and his two older sisters from Detroit to New York, and tried to support them on the fifteen dollars a week she made working in a laundry. Robinson sold firewood he gathered in a wagon under the West Side Highway and as far south as the Bowery. On Saturdays and Sundays he shined shoes, and at night he danced for coins on the sidewalks off Broadway. For him, as for all those others of that time, the fight game was a court of last resort.

"You may find this hard to believe," he told me a couple of times, "but I've never loved fightin'. I really dislike it. I don't believe I watch more than two fights a year, and then it has to be some friend of mine fightin'.

"Fightin', to me, seems barbaric," he said. "It seems to me like the barbarous days when men fought in a pit and people threw money down to them. I really don't like it."

"But at the same time," I said, "I must believe that fighting has given you the most satisfying experiences you have ever known."

"That's right," he said. "I enjoy out-thinkin' another man and out-maneuverin' him, but I still don't like to fight."

I believed him then, and I still do, because of something else he once told me and that one of his sisters confirmed. On the streets of Detroit and New York he ran from fights.

"I would avoid fightin'," he said, "even if I had to take the short end. I'd even apologize when I knew I was right. I got to be known as a coward, and my sisters used to fight for me. They used to remark that they hoped that some day I'd be able to take care of myself."

How able he became is in the record. He began fighting when he was fifteen, and he had 160 amateur and bootleg-amateur fights before he turned pro. As a professional he not only won the welterweight championship of the world, but he won the middleweight title for the fifth time when he was thirty-seven and he went fifteen rounds trying for it again when he was forty. He was forty-five when he finally retired in 1965, and in 362 fights, amateur and pro, over thirty years, he failed to finish only once. On that June night in 1952 when he boxed Joey Maxim for the light-heavyweight title, giving away fifteen pounds, it was 104 degrees under the Yankee Stadium ring lights, so brutally hot and humid that Ruby Goldstein, the referee, had to be replaced in the eleventh round. Robinson was giving Maxim a boxing lesson, and seemed on his way to winning yet another title, when he collapsed in his corner at the end of the thirteenth.

While Willie Pep was the greatest creative artist I ever saw in a ring, Sugar Ray Robinson remains the greatest fighter, pound-for-pound and punch-for-punch, of more than a half century, or since Benny Leonard retired with the lightweight title in 1924. Perhaps it is foolish to try to compare them, for Pep was a poet, often implying, with his feints and his footwork, more than he said, as that night when he won a round without even throwing a punch. Robinson was the master of polished prose, structuring his sentences, never wasting a word, and, as he often did, taking the other out with a single punch. That was the Robinson, however, that most Americans, enthralled by him as they were but who came to follow boxing on television, never saw. His talent had peaked between 1947 and 1950, before the era of TV boxing and before it saddened me to watch him years later on the screen struggling with fighters like Gene Fullmer and Paul Pender whom once he would have handled with ease.

"The public don't know it," he told me when I brought it up as far back as 1950, fifteen years before he retired, "but I do. The fighter himself is the first one to know."

"And how does he know it?" I said.

"You find you have to think your punches," he said. "The punches you used to throw without thinkin', you now have to reason."

It is something that happens to all of us, once the instinctive inventions and discoveries have been made. Then we reach back into the library of our experience, and what was once the product of inspiration is now merely the result of reason.

"How are you, old buddy?" he said on the phone, when I called him before flying out to Los Angeles. "When are you comin' out?"

"I'm fine," I said, "and I want to come out next week if you'll be there. How about next Friday?"

"Let me check that," he said, and then, "I'll be here. I'll be lookin' for you, because you're my man."

In his 202 professional fights, he hit fifty or more towns, and I imagine that in most, if not in all, there are still writers today whom he anointed as his "man." He was as smooth outside the ring as he was in it, and under pressing interrogation he was as elusive, but until you found that out he was a charmer.

I met him first in the spring of 1946. Already unquestionably the best welterweight in the world, he was unable to get a shot at the title, and he had hired a press agent named Pete Vaccare. We were sitting, late one morning, in Vaccare's office in the old Brill Building on Broadway, waiting for Robinson as, I was to find out, one almost inevitably did, when we heard singing out in the hall. Then the door opened, and they came in, Robinson and Junius (June) Clark, whom he called his secretary, both of them in heavy road clothes topped off by red knitted skating caps, for they had been running on the Harlem Speedway, and they finished the song. It was "The Very Thought of You," with Robinson carrying the melody and Clark improvising, and they ended it with a soft-shoe step and a hand flourish, and amid the laughter, we were introduced. We talked, with Robinson telling how he once stole so much from a grocery store that the owner gave him a job as a delivery boy to protect his stock, and how the minister who caught him in a crap game on the steps of the Salem Methodist Episcopal took him inside and introduced him to boxing.

"I just met Ray Robinson," I said to Wilbur Wood when I got back to the office that afternoon. "He's quite a guy."

"Oh, no," Wilbur said. "He conned you too."

"What do you mean, conned me?" I said.

"Hang around the fight game a little longer," Wilbur said, "and you'll find out."

In the fight game they like fighters who will fight anybody anywhere at any time and leave the business end to their managers. After he won the welterweight title, with George Gainford doing the dickering, Robinson made his own deals, and I knew a New York boxing writer who had collected two dozen complaints against him from promoters around the country.

"The trouble with Robinson," another one told me one day at lunch in Lindy's, "is that every time I get ready to bomb him, he shows up at some hospital or at the bedside of some sick kid. He's always one move ahead of you."

"As he is in the ring," I said.

There was about him an air of humble superiority, a contrariety that annoyed and frustrated those who tried to come to know him. He would plead humility and reserve a pew in church for Easter Sunday. At big fights, when other notables gathered for their introductions in the ring before the main event, Robinson would wait beyond the ringside rows and receive his applause apart as he came down the aisle and, all grace, vaulted through the ropes. He was a man who was trying to find something he had lost even before he turned professional.

"The biggest thrill I ever got," he told me once, "was when I won the Golden Gloves and they streamed that light down on me in Madison Square Garden and said, 'The Golden Gloves featherweight champion,

Sugar Ray Robinson!' I bought the papers. I read about it over and over. It was more of a thrill than when I won the welterweight championship of the world.

"Once I read," he said—and he even read law, fascinated by its contradictions—"something that King Solomon said. He said, 'The wiser a man gets the less beauty he finds in life.' If I try to explain that to people they don't understand. It's like the first time you go to Coney Island and you ride the Shoot-the-Chute and you get a big thrill. The second time it isn't so much."

Few fighters have been as disliked within their profession and by its press as was Robinson while he was struggling to make his way, and the fight game was, in part, responsible for that. In this country, from the turn of the century on, boxing gave the black man, because it needed him, a better break than he received in any other sport, but it only gave him what it had to. For years, while Mike Jacobs ran big-time boxing, he refused Robinson that chance at the welterweight title.

"Mike explained that to me," Robinson told me once. "He explained that I'd kill the division. He said, 'I got to have two or three guys fightin' for the title. You'd darken the class.' I understand that. That's good business."

I am sure he understood it, but he did not have to like it. In his early days, in order to get fights, he had to take less money than the opponents he knocked out. Once, after he had trained three weeks for a fight, the promoter ran out. A couple of years later, Jacobs promised him $2,000 beyond his small purse if he would box for a Boston promoter to whom Jacobs owed a favor. When, after the fight, Robinson showed up for his money, Jacobs ridiculed him.

"You didn't think I'd go into my own kick," Mike said, "for some other guy's fight."

They tried to do it to him in the ring too. There was the story that Duke Stefano, then a manager of fighters, was telling me one afternoon in Stillman's Gym.

"I remember Robinson one night when he was just starting out as a pro," Duke said. "Just before the fight, Robinson complained that he had a bad ear, and he didn't want to go through with the fight. It was his left ear, and they looked in it, and you could see it was red and swollen.

"The other guy's manager—he was from New Jersey—looked at it and he said, 'Look, my guy is just an opponent. Go through with the fight, and I promise you he won't touch the ear.' Robinson said, 'Okay, long as he stays away from the ear.' Well, the bell rang, and the other guy came out of his corner and winged a right hand at the ear. Robinson just turned his head and looked at the corner. The guy did it a second time, and Robinson looked at the manager again. The third time the guy tried it, Robinson stepped in with a hook and flattened him.

"The manager," Duke said, "turned right around and went back to New Jersey. He didn't even second another kid he had in the next bout."

Fritzie Zivic did it to him too, as he did to many others. He was the recently dethroned welterweight champion of the world when Robinson, in only his second year as a pro, out-pointed him over ten rounds in Madison Square Garden. Ten weeks later he would knock Zivic out in ten.

"Fritzie Zivic," Robinson told me once, "taught me more than anybody I ever fought."

"What did he teach you?" I said.

"He taught me that a man can make you butt open your own eye," he said, and I appreciated the phrasing. He was one of the cleanest of fighters, and what he had learned from Zivic was not something that you did to another man, but that he could do to you.

"And how does a man do that?" I said.

"He slipped one of my jabs," Robinson said, "and reached his right glove around behind my head and pulled my head down on his."

Young Otto, who boxed the best lightweights during the first two decades of this century and was a great student of the science, refereed that first fight. One day in Stillman's I asked him about it.

"In the sixth round," he said, "Robinson said to me, 'He's stickin' his thumbs in my eyes.' I said, 'You ain't no cripple.' After that he give it back to Zivic better than Zivic was givin' it to him. I said to myself then, 'This kid is gonna be a great fighter.'"

So they tried to use him and abuse him, and sometimes succeeded, in and out of the ring. When, in self-defense, he retaliated, he acquired the reputation that provoked *The Saturday Evening Post* to ask me to do a piece they were to entitle, "Why Don't They Like Ray Robinson?"

"This is a tough assignment for me," I said to him.

"How's that?" he said.

We were sitting in his office at Ray Robinson Enterprises, Inc., in Harlem, and he had his feet up on his triangular glass-topped desk. He owned most of the block on the west side of Seventh Avenue from 123rd to 124th streets, and he had $250,000 tied up in the five-story apartment house, Sugar Ray's Bar and Restaurant, Edna Mae's Lingerie Shop, and Sugar Ray's Quality Cleaners, with its five outlets.

"I have to ask you the tough questions," I said.

"That's all right," he said. "Go ahead."

"I will," I said, "but I want to explain something first. I think this piece can do you a lot of good. You're unquestionably the best fighter since Benny Leonard, and there are some old-timers who say you may be the best since Joe Gans, who died ten years before you were born."

"They say that?" he said, as if he hadn't known. "I appreciate that."

"My point is," I said, "that you should be the most popular fighter of your time, but you're not. There are raps against you in the fight game, and they keep bringing up your Army record and you've never made the money that you should. A fighter like Graziano, who's a beginner compared to you and has a dishonorable discharge from the Army while you have an honorable one, has made twice as much as you have."

"That's right," he said.

"Part of that is style," I said. "All his fights are wars, and that's what the public likes, but it's style outside the ring, too. He's open and frank, and you're not, really. What I want to do is explain you. I want you to tell me what it's like to have a fine mind and great physical talents, to be a great artist but to be colored and to have that used against you in the fight game and out of it. It can explain a lot about you, and I'll understand. If I understand, I can make the readers understand, and as I said, that can mean a lot to you, if you'll level with me."

I really believed it. I believed it for about five minutes.

"If you can do that," he said, "I'll appreciate it. Nobody's ever done that for me before. You just ask me the questions, what you want to know."

"All right," I said. "Let's get the Army thing out of the way first."

It wasn't any good. We went around and around, as in a ring, and when Robinson couldn't counter my leads or even slip them, he professed only astonishment that I should hold such documented assertions to be facts.

There was something to be celebrated in his Army record. He had been a member of Casual Detachment 7, known as "The Joe Louis Troupe." Joe and he and four other fighters spent seven months touring camps in this country and putting on boxing exhibitions. In Florida, Robinson refused to box unless black troops were allowed to attend, and he, an enlisted man, faced down a general. At Camp Sibert, Alabama, a white M.P. saw Louis emerge from a phone booth in so-called white territory, and he threatened to club Joe. Robinson took him on, the two rolling on the ground, and there was rioting by black troops before apologies were made to the two fighters.

It was a matter of Army record and common knowledge, however, that when the troupe sailed for Europe, from Pier 90, New York, on March 31, 1944, Robinson was not aboard. It was also in the record that he had previously declared his intention not to go, and that the Articles of War as they applied to the punishment for desertion had been explained to him.

"But why would a man say such a thing?" he said when I had read to him from the affidavit.

"He not only said it," I said, "but he swore to it."

"I can't understand that," Robinson said. "I never met that officer, and he never read me such things."

Years later, in his autobiography, he would state that he had been suffering from amnesia following a fall, and had been hospitalized for that before his honorable discharge as a sergeant on June 3, 1944. It was a book he had wanted me to write after he had retired for the first time in 1952. Because he preferred to avoid using elevators, as he also preferred not to fly, we had met late one afternoon with my agent and another, not in my agent's office on the twentieth floor of the Mutual of New York Building, but in the cocktail lounge of the Park Sheraton.

"I just can't do it, Ray," I said, after we had talked for a while, the others listening, and I had tried again. "There are those conflicting versions of those events in your life, in and out of boxing, and we tried two years ago in your office and we've tried again now, and we still can't resolve them. I'm sorry, but I just can't do the book."

"That's all right, old buddy," he said. "I understand."

I doubt that he did—why couldn't we just put it all down the way he said, and possibly even believed it had been, and ignore the conflicts? And when I would see him after that it would always be in camp before his fights and I would be with others. Now I had heard that he was heading up a youth project in Los Angeles, and at ten o'clock on that Friday morning the taxi driver and I found it, finally, on West Adams Boulevard with the sign—SUGAR RAY'S YOUTH FOUNDATION—fronting the one-story building.

"He's in conference with Mr. Fillmore right now," the woman said across the counter, and I had missed her name when she had introduced herself. "I don't think he'll be long, though."

"That's all right," I said. "I have plenty of time."

"Maybe while you're waiting," she said, "you'd like to look at some of our material."

"That would be fine," I said.

She introduced me then to Mel Zolkover, who had arisen from behind one of the desks beyond the counter. He is a middle-aged retired mechanical engineer and the foundation's administrative director, and we shook hands.

She went back to a desk, and while I waited I could hear the even tones of Robinson's voice, still familiar after all the years, in an office on the left. When she came back she handed me the several sheets of publicity and a folder from the 1976–77 "Miss Sugar Ray Teen Pageant." From a photograph I identified her as Thelma Smith, the executive secretary, and elsewhere I noted that Bob Hope is the foundation's honorary chairman, Robinson the chairman, and Wright Fillmore the president. I read about arts and crafts projects, costume making, karate instruction, talent shows, art classes, and workshops in beauty and personal development, drama, band and combo repertory, and dance.

"Old buddy!" he said, smiling and his face fuller and shaking hands across the counter. "How's my old buddy?"

"Fine," I said. "And you?"

"Just fine," he said. "Come on in here and sit down and we'll talk."

I followed him to the middle desk at the back. He was wearing a blue leisure suit, the jacket over a dark blue-and-fuchsia sports shirt. Once I had checked his wardrobe. He owned thirty-four suits, twenty-six pairs of shoes, nine sports jackets and as many pairs of slacks, six overcoats, and four topcoats, most of which apparel he said he had never worn even once.

"You've gained some weight," I said.

As a fighter he was one of the most lithe and handsome of men. He moved with such grace and rhythm, in the ring and out, that watching him made me think of rubbing silk or satin between one's hands. During his first retirement, in fact, he tried it as a dancer, opening at the French Casino in New York for $15,000 a week. After that, it was downhill.

"Robinson was a good dancer, for a fighter," a Broadway booking agent told me, after Robinson had come back to knock out Bobo Olson and win the middleweight title the second time. "Maybe no other fighter ever danced as well, but the feature of his act was his change of clothes. He looked good in everything he put on."

He was leaning back now in the high-backed desk chair. Not only was his face fuller, but at fifty-six he was a lot heavier across the shoulders and chest and at the waist.

"Yeah, I'm heavier," he said now. "You see, I sit here with something on my mind, and I don't get the exercise I should. Every day, though, I try to take a five-mile walk."

"How heavy are you?"

"Oh, one eighty-three, one eighty-four," he said, and he fought best at 147. "You see, you've got a certain ego about having been a champion, and you'd like to keep like that, but it's so difficult. There are temptations, and it takes will power. When you're fightin' you have to live by the rules, because when that bell rings condition is the name of the game. Even then, in camp, Joe Louis and I would go out in the boat and have quarts of ice cream and our trainers would get mad."

He reached into a desk drawer, and he brought out a package of Danish pastries. He tore one end off the transparent wrapper and took out one and, leaning back again, began eating.

"My breakfast," he said. "You know, the most important meal is breakfast."

"And that's your breakfast?"

"That's right," he said, "and Jack Blackburn used to get after Joe and me."

Blackburn was Louis's discoverer, teacher, and trainer. He developed Louis so precisely in the image of what he himself had been as a fighter that Louis had the same flaw that Blackburn had of dropping the left arm after a jab. It was what made Louis vulnerable to a straight right counter over the jab.

"Blackburn," Robinson was saying, "used to tell us, 'You got to eat breakfast.' Then they used to squeeze blood from the meat, and I'd drink that. From Monday through Friday I'd drink it. You have to get that from a slaughterhouse, and they put this blood in a can and I used to go down there and get it. I'll tell you, that's the most potent thing there is."

"I remember that you used to do that," I said. "Do you ever drink it now?"

"Every now and then I think I'll do it," he said, "but I don't." He had finished the pastry and folded over the end of the package. He put the package back in the desk drawer.

"What brought you out here to California?" I said.

"My wife is from out here," he said. When he was fighting he was married to Edna Mae Holly. She had been a dancer and they had two sons, and I had not known he had remarried. "Joe Louis was goin' with a girl out here, and I met Millie through the recommendation of this other girl. You know, like a dog. You see something, and the ears go bong! We were married in 1965, and that's how I met Mr. Fillmore, and we started this foundation."

"Tell me about that."

"We went to London," he said, "and she was having her thirty-third or thirty-fourth birthday party, and . . ."

"Who was?" I said.

"Queen Elizabeth," he said. "Millie and I, we were invited and we went to the party. It was a wonderful ceremony, and Prince Phillip and I were talkin'. You remember those strikes?"

"What strikes?"

"I think it started in Berkeley," he said.

"The student protests?"

"That's right," he said. "We were talkin', and he said, 'Sugar, I believe you could help that.' I said, 'What do you mean?' He said, 'Youngsters look up to you, and I've got an idea.' I had met Mr. Fillmore, and of all the people I've met—all the Popes and all—I never met a man who believes in God and lives it more than Mr. Fillmore. You never hear the guy say a harsh word, even a loud word, and I want you to meet him."

"I'd like to," I said.

"I came back to New York," he said, "and I was goin' with my present wife. She lived upstairs out here and Mr. Fillmore lived downstairs. I talked with him, and we went to the Council of Churches and asked them to help us, and they gave us money. The county saw the potential and funded us. Now we hope to have the State Junior Olympics, and Jimmy Carter was out and I met with him, and he's a nice guy and likes what we're doing, and we hope for federal funding. We work with the Board of Education and the Department of Parks and Recreation, and there has never been a paid member of the board of trustees. Every dollar goes in, and I'm about the poorest cat on the board."

"What happened to all that property you owned in Harlem?"

"I sold that even at a loss," he said, "just to get out. I fell in love with my wife out here, and Harlem was goin' downhill so bad, and now if you see a white face there, you know it's a cop."

"Did you get clipped?"

One day, sitting in his office in Harlem, he had told me that he felt he was destined to make a great success in business. It was that afternoon in 1950, when he spoke of how he knew his ring skills were starting to decline.

"After a man attains all the things he likes," he had said then, "he has to find some other form of happiness. I feel I'm gonna find that in business. I'm not cocky within myself. I'm an extreme Christian within myself. I just believe. My faith is so strong that I know that someday I'm gonna be the head of some real big business. I thank God for the success I've had, and the investments I've made."

"Yeah, I got clipped," he said now. "It happened to Joe, too, but that's a part of life. I didn't get out with too much, but I didn't lose too much, either."

"As you say," I said, "it happened to Joe, too, and it happens so often. They talk about the dirty fight game, but a fighter makes a fortune in it, and when he gets out into the nice clean world of American business they take it all from him."

"You're so right," he said. "What other fighters are you seeing for the book?"

"I just saw Willie Pep last month."

"He was a great one," he said. "When I beat him in the amateurs in Connecticut, they took me to the police station."

"I remember that story," I said. "Willie's all right. He's working for the Athletic Commission in Connecticut, and he's married for the fifth time."

"You know how that is," he said, smiling. "When Joe was the champion and I used to go to the airport, they came off that plane like it was a parade."

"And I saw Billy Graham," I said. "He's doing fine, working for Seagram's."

"Billy Graham?" he said. "He's my man. He beat me in the first fight I lost."

"When you were ninety-pound kids," I said.

He had reached into the desk drawer again. He brought out the Danish, and started on another one.

"There are so many of your fights I remember," I said. "The night you won the middleweight title from Jake LaMotta in Chicago . . ."

"Jake wasn't smart," he said, "but he was in condition. He was 'The Bull.'"

"I know," I said. "I remember that, after your first fight with him, you were passing blood for days."

"That's right," he said.

"When you fought him in Chicago for the title in '51," I said, "I watched it at a neighbor's house on TV. Ted Husing was announcing the fight, and in the early rounds he was filled with LaMotta. He kept saying that we were seeing an upset, that LaMotta was running the fight."

"He said that?"

"Yes, and I said to my neighbor, 'Husing doesn't know what he's talking about. Watch what Robinson does the next time the referee breaks them, or Robinson backs off from an exchange.' You would back off so far that sometimes you went out of the camera range, right off the screen. I said, 'LaMotta had trouble making the weight, and Robinson is walking the legs off him. When he gets ready to turn it on, Jake won't have much left.' In the thirteenth round you turned it on, and the referee had to stop it."

"That's right," he said, nodding. "That's exactly what I did. You remember that?"

"Another fight I remember," I said, "was the one with Flashy Sebastian, and that one scared me."

"That scared me, too," he said.

On June 24, 1947, Robinson knocked out Jimmy Doyle in the eighth round in Cleveland, and the next day Doyle died of brain injury. At the coroner's inquest, Robinson was asked, "Couldn't you tell from the look on Doyle's face that he had been hurt?" Robinson said, "Mister, that's what my business is, to hurt people." Because he was absolutely frank, he caught the criticism. He set up a $10,000 trust fund for Doyle's mother, and two months later he took little more than his expenses to fight Sebastian, the welterweight champion of the Philippines, on an American Legion show in Madison Square Garden.

"It was right after that Doyle fight," I said now.

"I know," he said. "The night before the Doyle fight I dreamed what was gonna happen, and I got up the next day and I called the commission and I told them. They said that they'd sold all the tickets, and they went so far as to get a Catholic priest to talk to me."

"In that Sebastian fight," I said, "you came out of your corner for the first round and he threw a wide hook, and you brought your right glove up and blocked it. He backed off, and came in again and did the same thing. This time you threw the right hand inside the hook and followed it with a hook of your own, and he went back on his head. Then he tried to get up, and he fell forward on his face, and the photographers at ringside were hollering, 'Get this! Get this! This guy may die, too!'"

"I know," he said. "I said, 'Oh, Lord, don't let it happen again.'"

"In the dressing room later," I said, "Sebastian was hysterical. Whitey Bimstein had seconded him, and he took a towel and soaked it in ice water and snapped it in Sebastian's face to bring him out of it. I said to Whitey, 'What kind of a fighter is this they brought all the way from the Philippines to almost be killed?' Whitey said, 'I never saw him before tonight, but they asked me to work with him. After I got him taped, I told him to warm up. He threw one punch, and I stopped him. I said, "Look, fella. When you throw that hook, don't raise your head. You're fightin' Ray Robinson. You do that with him, and he'll take your head right off your shoulders."'

"Then sometime later I was talking with Ruby Goldstein. You remember Ruby was the referee that night, and Ruby said, 'That Sebastian threw that first hook, and Robinson brushed it away. I was just thinkin' to myself that if he did that again Robinson would cross a right. The next thing I knew he did, and I was saying 'One . . . two . . . three.'"

"I was lucky that night," Robinson said now.

"And Sebastian was, too," I said, "and I'll tell you another night when you were lucky."

"When was that?" he said.

"When you got the title back from Randy Turpin."

In August of 1950 Robinson carried Charley Fusari over fifteen rounds of what was ostensibly a fight for Robinson's welterweight title but was, on Robinson's part, just one of the greatest boxing exhibitions I have ever seen. He gave his entire purse to the Damon Runyon Cancer Fund, of which Dan Parker, the sports editor and columnist of the *New York Daily Mirror*, was president. This act of charity had the effect, however unintended, of silencing Parker who, whenever the word got out that Robinson intended to go to Europe, would recall that he had missed that opportunity when he had failed to sail with "The Joe Louis Troupe."

The following May, Robinson left for Paris—Parker merely pointing out that it was "by boat"—and took along his fuchsia Cadillac and George Gainford's black one. Included in the party of eleven were Robinson's golf pro and his barber, and in Paris they acquired an Arabian midget who spoke five languages. They occupied most of one floor of the Claridge, and seldom left to eat in restaurants. There was an almost constant flow of room-service waiters through the suites, and the bill at the end was staggering.

"You know how the French are," Lew Burston, who had lived for many years in Paris and ran the foreign affairs of the Mike Jacobs boxing empire, said to me one day following Robinson's return. "In the old days they used to see the maharajas arrive with their retinues, and they basically believe that another man's business is his own. At the end of Robinson's stay, though, even the French were somewhat stunned."

Robinson fought a half-dozen times in Europe, in Paris and elsewhere, and on July 10 in London he defended his middleweight title against Randy Turpin, the British and European champion. Turpin out-pointed him over the fifteen rounds in an upset so startling that in the fight game on this side of the ocean they found it hard to believe.

"You may remember," I was saying to him now, "what Lew Burston said after the first Turpin fight. He said, 'Robinson had Paris in his legs.'"

"That was one of the few fights," he said, nodding, "where I took a chance. Remember what I told you—about temptation and will power? Then he had one of the most unorthodox styles, too. You remember the second fight?"

Two months after the London fight they met again in the Polo Grounds in New York. Robinson won the early rounds, but then Turpin, awkward, sometimes punching off the wrong foot, lunging with his jab, chopping with his right in close and eight years younger, began to come on. By the tenth round, Robinson seemed spent, and then a wide cut opened over his left eye and, obviously fearful that the fight might be stopped and with the blood gushing out of the cut, he took the big gamble. He walked in with both hands going. He shook Turpin with a right, pushed him off, and dropped him in the middle of the ring with another right. When Turpin got up at nine, Robinson drove him to the ropes, and there he must have thrown forty punches. Turpin, reeling now and trying to cover, was half sitting on the middle rope, and there were sixty-one thousand people there, and it sounded as if they were all screaming.

"Of course I remember the fight," I was saying now, "and, as I said, you were lucky that night. When you had him on the ropes and he didn't go down, you reached out with your left, put your glove behind his head, and tried to pull him forward. There were only eight seconds left in the round, so if you had pulled him off the ropes and he had gone down, the count would have killed the rest of the round. You had that cut and you were exhausted, and you would never have survived the next five rounds."

"You're right," he said.

"And I'll tell you a night," I said, "when you did outsmart yourself."

"What night was that?" he said.

"That night in the Yankee Stadium when you fought Maxim and it was a hundred and four degrees in there. You were not only licking him, but you were licking him so easily that you made a show of it, dancing around in and out, throwing unnecessary punches. That's why, in that heat, you collapsed at the end of the thirteenth."

"You're right, old buddy," he said. "That was a mistake. I was incoherent all the next day. I never remembered when Goldstein fell out. I had a premonition the night before that fight too. I had a premonition that I would die."

He had finished the pastry and reclosed the package again, and he returned it to the desk drawer.

"There's this Sugar Ray Leonard," I said, "who won a gold medal in the Olympics. There was another one—Sugar Ray Seales. How do you feel about these kids calling themselves Sugar Ray?"

"Bill, you know," he said, sitting back and smiling, "it's a good feeling to think that the kids think that much of me."

It was different when he was a fighter. There was another welterweight at that time named George Costner, and in Chicago in 1945 Robinson knocked him out in two minutes and fifty-five seconds of the first round. Five years later they were matched again, this time for Philadelphia, and in the days leading up to the fight, the other, by then known as George (Sugar) Costner, was quoted on the sports pages as disparaging Robinson.

"Listen, boy," Robinson said to him at the weigh-in, "I've been readin' what you've been sayin' in the papers about what you're gonna do to me."

"Why, there are no hard feelings, are there, Ray?" Costner said. "I just did that to boost the gate."

"That may be all right," Robinson said, "but when I boost the gate I do it by praisin' my opponent."

The logic of publicity, revolving as it does around the build-up of the underdog, was all on Costner's side, but this time Robinson knocked him out in two minutes and forty-nine seconds. While it was succinct, this was, in its scientific precision, one of Robinson's finest performances.

"There's only one 'Sugar,'" Robinson was quoted as saying right after the fight, but I remember another aftermath. It involved still another welterweight who was asked by his manager if he would fight Sugar Costner.

"No thanks," the fighter said.

"But you can lick Costner," the manager said. "Robinson flattened him twice inside of one round."

"I don't want to fight anybody named Sugar," the fighter said.

"I've been remembering," I said to Robinson now, "the first time I ever met you. It was in Pete Vaccare's office in the Brill Building, and we heard you singing out in the hall, and you and June Clark came in wearing road clothes and harmonizing 'The Very Thought of You.' You two did it very well."

"Yeah," Robinson said, smiling. "June Clark, he was a musician—Armstrong was in his band—and he, too, was a believer in God."

"That was a long time ago," I said. "It was in March of 1946."

"Are you sure?" Robinson said. "Didn't we meet before then?"

"I'm certain," I said, "because I didn't start to write sports until I came back from the war."

"You were in the war?" Robinson said.

"Yes," I said, "but only as a war correspondent."

"Where were you?" Robinson said.

"All through northern Europe," I said.

"In the ETO?" he said. "Then how come we didn't meet over there?"

"I don't know," I said. It was as if I had just been stunned by a sucker punch, one you never expect the other to throw, and I was sparring for time.

"We were over there," Robinson was saying now. "Joe Louis and I, we had a troupe, and we boxed in the ETO and everything."

I still didn't know what to say. There were the others at their desks—Thelma Smith and Mel Zolkover and a secretary—who could have heard us, and I didn't want to challenge it there. I am quite sure that, if we had been alone, I would have, just to try again after so many years to understand him, but as I have thought about it since, I believe it was better that I let it ride. He is a man who has his own illusions about his life, as do we all, about the way he wishes it had been, and there is little if any harm, although some sadness, in that now. I shall send him a copy of this book, however, and when he reads this chapter I hope he understands that, as a reporter, my responsibility, as pompous as this may sound, is to draw as accurate and honest a portrait as I can.

"I want you to meet Mr. Fillmore," he was saying now. "Mr. Fillmore can tell you a lot about the foundation."

"I'd like to meet him," I said, and he led me into Fillmore's office and introduced us.

Fillmore, a slim, immaculate man, bald and wearing dark glasses, said that he would be seventy-eight in a couple of months. He had worked, he said, for the Southern Pacific Railroad for forty years, as a waiter and then as an instructor, and he had been retired for seven years when Robinson and he started the foundation in 1969.

"The first time I met Ray personally," he said, "was through his present wife. She was rooming with us, and he was going with her, and then he finally married. We got to talking and got to be buddies, and one day I got a telegram from London that he wanted to see me.

"I wondered, with all the people he knew, why he wanted to see me. I waited, and he and his wife flew in and, it being hot, we sat in the backyard. I asked him what was so important, and he said he'd always wanted to do something for youth. I said, 'What do you want me to do about it, Ray? With all the people you know, you want me to put together something for children? I'm retired.' He said, 'No. You have just started working.' I told him, 'We need money, and we need children. If you can get the money, I can get the children.'

"From the back step we moved to Millie's kitchen, then to the church, and when it got too big for there, we moved here. Since 1969 there's no black mark on this organization, and I challenge anybody to go to the IRS or wherever.

"The Southern Pacific," he said, "had given me a three-year course in human relations, and what we try to do here is make good citizens, not only a Sugar Ray Robinson or a Sandy Koufax. We had these fellas here, and they called themselves 'The Young Black Panthers.' They knew every way to do wrong. There was 'One-Legged Joe' and there was 'Bluefish,' and the one was fourteen and the other was fifteen, and we gained their confidence.

"The news came out one time that a hamburger stand had been held up, and it sounded to me like One-Legged Joe and Bluefish, so I called in Tony, one of the lesser lights. I said to him, 'Where were you on such-and-such a night?' He said, 'I know what you want, but I wasn't in it.' I said, 'I know, but if I could find out where it was and I could find the pistol, I could help out.'

"He told me where it was, where to find the pistol, and it was a toy. One-Legged Joe went to UCLA and stayed there three years and got a job. Bluefish joined the Navy, and that was what Ray Robinson had in mind, and what we try to do."

When I came out of Fillmore's office, Robinson was at his desk, finishing another Danish, and he suggested that we go over to the foundation's annex. We walked up the sidewalk, then through the blacktopped parking area of a shopping center, and at the far side, into what had been a store and was now partitioned into several rooms. He led me into a conference room, and we sat down with Zolkover and with Richard Jackman, a then thirty-two-year-old law graduate who is the program director, and his assistant, Scott McCreary, then twenty-six and a graduate of the University of California at Santa Barbara.

"Tell Bill," Robinson said, at the head of the long table, "what we do here."

"Well, take our baseball program," Zolkover said. "We kind of take the place of the YMCA and the Little League for kids six to sixteen in the lower socioeconomic areas where they can't afford those others. The children are not allowed to pay, and when you think of it, when Ray was a kid his mother couldn't afford it."

"We're not trying to build a Sugar Ray," Jackman said.

"That's right," Robinson said, "and the last thing, that we're just goin' to start now, is the boxing. I didn't want people to think we're a boxing organization."

"At the same time," Jackman said, "it's Mr. Robinson's charisma that makes it go. He has friends all over the world, and if we get the Junior Olympics started here it could include ten to fifteen cities, and we could expand to Europe, too."

"He can open any door," Zolkover said, nodding toward Robinson. "One day the question was, where could we get readership? I said, '*Reader's Digest*.' I looked up the chairman of the board, and Ray called, and it was, 'Hey, Ray!'

"You see," he said, "we're like a church. We pay no money, so we have to have people with dedication like Ray."

"When he was boxing," Scott said, "they called him the greatest fighter, pound-for-pound. We say that, pound-for-pound, we get the greatest distance out of our money."

When Robinson and I left them a few minutes later, we stood for a moment on the sidewalk edging the parking area, looking out over the quadrangle of parked cars. The California climate, unlike that of the Northeast where I abide, is conducive to keeping cars clean, and I was struck by how they glistened, older models as well as new, in the sunlight.

"Are you still on the Cadillac kick?" I said to him.

"No," he said. "No more."

"I remember you turned that chartreuse one in for the fuchsia one."

"The car I drive now," he said, and then pointing, "is that little red Pinto over there."

"That's your car?"

"Yeah," he said, and then, smiling, "but I've been there."

"I'll say you have," I said.

We walked slowly across the parking area. We were dawdling in the warm sunlight.

"While you were fighting," I said, "did you take out any annuities?"

"Nope," he said.

"Did you buy any stocks?"

"A few, and I sold those."

"When you had all those investments in Harlem," I said, "I was always afraid you were going to get clipped."

"That's right," he said.

"So how do you get along now?"

"I've got friends," he said. "I borrow five grand, and I pay back three. I borrow three, and pay two. Then something drops in, and I pay everybody. People say to me about this foundation, 'What are you gettin'?' They can't understand doing something for kids. I've always been a Christian believer in God. I was gifted with a talent that helped introduce me to people, and all that was in preparation for what I'm doin' now."

"And I celebrate it," I said.

When we got back to the office I called for a cab. While I was waiting for it, he said he thought he would take his five-mile walk, and we shook hands and wished each other well. He went out the door and, through the wide front window, I saw him start up the sidewalk, the greatest fighter I ever saw, the one I wanted so much to know.

The Smallest Titan of Them All

Eddie Arcaro Rode to Win

I think no virtue goes with size;
The reason of all cowardice
Is, that men are overgrown,
And, to be valiant, must come down
To the titmouse dimension.

Ralph Waldo Emerson, The Titmouse

"LITTLE GUYS," he said once, "usually don't have it their own way."

His mother was sixteen when he was born, and he weighed three pounds. She told me that for two months the doctor who had delivered him came to the house daily to bathe him in warm water with whiskey in it. She said she didn't know why that was, and until he was four months old her own mother used to wrap him in cotton flannel strips, and they called him "the shoe-box baby."

"The only thing I ever hungered for as a kid," he said, "was the size to play baseball. Those other kids didn't want me. I was always the one left over."

For the month of August of 1955 I was tailing him around Saratoga where, for those four weeks, New York thoroughbred racing moves each year as it has since 1863. Tailing is the right word, for I never

---

Chapter 14 of *Once They Heard the Cheers*, 1979.

took on as elusive a single subject as Eddie Arcaro when he was this country's greatest jockey, or one who, when I could corner him and sit him down, was more of a delight with that quick mind, that frankness, his ability to paint word pictures, and his sophisticated knowledge of his calling.

"On the streets," I asked him once, "did the other kids beat up on you?"

"Hell, no," he said. "I was too small to fight."

"What about that temper of yours?" I said.

"That's an odd thing," he said. "I've asked my mother about that, and she says I was kind of a nice, mild-mannered kid. The temper was what racing did to me."

He came into racing before the day of the film patrols that record every foot of a race and on tracks where rough riding—sawing off an opponent, fighting your way through jams, leg-locking, and holding saddle cloths—was the style of survival. On the backs of those thousand-pound animals and in the heat of those races, that temper of his ignited and he was fined or suspended more than thirty times, once for a year. Over his career he himself survived more than forty falls.

"Even when I caddied," he said, "I didn't weigh seventy pounds, and I couldn't carry doubles like the big kids. I had all I could do to lug singles. Racing was the only thing I ever found where I could be a competitor."

A competitor he was, and more than that. He never grew taller than five feet three, and he rode best at 108 pounds, but in what he did he was as big as the other giants of his time—Joe DiMaggio, Ted Williams, Sammy Baugh, Joe Louis, Ben Hogan—and one for all time. He was the first to win five Kentucky Derbies—Bill Hartack would tie him in that—and the only one to win twice the Triple Crown—the Derby, the Preakness, and the Belmont. When the best of the ballplayers aspired to make $100,000 a year he was making $150,000 and more.

"I'll get into Miami late Thursday afternoon," I was saying on the phone now. "Let's get together on Friday."

"But how much time will this take?" he said.

It was that way in 1955. We had signed a contract with *Look* to do two articles, and I tailed him not only during that month at Saratoga but for another month at Belmont and elsewhere on Long Island, where he and his wife, Ruth, and their young daughter and son lived. There was always somebody who had just got into town or someone with whom he had to discuss a business deal, or there was a date that he and his wife had for dinner.

"I'll make it as painless as I can," I said. "How about lunch Friday?"

"Lunch?" he said. "We'll probably be done by two o'clock, and that's too late to play golf. What am I going to do the rest of the afternoon?"

I don't know, Eddie, I was thinking. Read a book, perhaps? No, I don't ever recall you mentioning a book, and with all that nervous energy, reading wouldn't be the answer. I don't know the answer, because I've never been able to put myself in your place.

"I'll tell you what I'll do," I said. "I'll call you on Friday morning."

"Good," he said.

Then he would surprise me. After the articles had been accepted by the magazine, I phoned him one night at his home.

"Eddie, I hate to ask you this," I said, "but the editors at the magazine want to meet you. You don't have to do it, because they've already bought the pieces."

"What the hell," he said. "They're paying that money, so if they want to meet me I'll come over."

We had lunch at Toots Shor's, and while we were having a drink I got him talking again about riding tactics. On that white tablecloth, before the food came, he started moving the silverware around, demonstrating a blind switch—three horses strung out from the rail and his horse pocketed behind—and how you know the capabilities of all of them and at what point one figures to come up empty and leave the opening. I was getting it from the master, and that is the bonus of the business I am in.

When we finished lunch we still had a few minutes to kill before the appointed hour for the handshaking, so walking him east toward the *Look* building on Madison Avenue, I led him south a block to

Rockefeller Plaza. It was early November, and down on the ice rink in front of the gilded Prometheus statue the skaters were circling.

"What the hell is that?" he said.

"It's a skating rink," I said.

"How long has that been there?" he said.

"For more than twenty years," I said.

"I never knew this," he said. "I've got to bring the kids over here."

He was a man of the world, but of his own world. It was the world of the race tracks across this country, of jockey rooms and racing's millionaires, of fashionable resorts and eating places, of celebrities and hangers-on, and high stakes races and honors, and oil wells coming in and stocks paying off. It was a world I would never know any more than he would know mine.

He and his wife live now at the Jockey Club on Biscayne Boulevard in North Miami. It is an elegant, white, balconied high-rise with gatehouse, and if you can pass muster, they will relieve you of a hundred dollars a night.

"Hell, if you're on your own, as I presume you are," he had said on the phone, "I'd stay at the Holiday Inn across the street for thirty a night."

"I'll do that," I said.

At the motel on Friday morning I called his apartment at nine o'clock. His wife said that he had left for Boca Raton, and to check back later. I called at one and left my phone number, at five, at six, and from a restaurant at seven.

"I haven't heard from him," his wife said. "I don't know where he is, but I know this. When he gets in we're not going to eat dinner here."

"So when you finally get him on the phone," my good and longtime friend Bard Lindeman, who was then the medical writer of the *Miami Herald*, said at dinner, "straighten him out. Tell him you've come all the way down here, and you've got a job to do and a living to make and . . ."

"Come on, Bard," I said. "You've been in this business of ours long enough to know what the basic relationships really are. The subject doesn't need the writer. The writer needs the subject. Eddie Arcaro never needed me."

"I suppose that's right," he said.

"In fact," I said, "I'll never forget the first time I met him."

It was at the old Aqueduct track before they were to tear it down to build the Big A. It was in the jockey room between races, and changing silks he was washing his face from a pail of water that stood on the wooden bench in front of the row of metal lockers. *Cosmopolitan* had asked me to do a piece about a day in the life of a jockey from the time he gets up at six o'clock in the morning to work horses until he has ridden his last race of the day. They said they wanted Eddie Arcaro, and I explained it to him. "I don't want it," he said. "It's not for me."

"But it would be good public relations," I said, "not only for you but for racing."

"You mean publicity?" he said, the towel in his hand and his face wet and turning to me. "You know what publicity does for me? It makes an 8–5 shot even money, and when it behaves like an 8–5 shot and I don't bring it in, they boo my butt off."

I understood that. He was so good and so prominent that they believed he could win on almost anything he rode. When he didn't they booed him unmercifully, abused him with filthy language, and, in letters, threatened his life and his family. Racing crowds are the most avaricious and vicious of the audiences of sport, and for a while the Pinkertons guarded him at the track and he seriously considered giving up riding.

"I called you last night," he was saying on the phone now, when I finally got him at nine o'clock on Saturday morning. "You weren't in."

"I finally went to dinner."

"I've got it right here," he said. "It's 893-4110, Room 419."

"Right. Now when do we meet?"

"Well," he said, "I don't know exactly what you want."

"Come on, Eddie," I said. "I want to ask some questions, and they won't be stupid questions."

"Hell, I know that, Bill," he said. "I mean I have to get my day straightened out, so how long will this take?"

"Let's say an hour."

"Okay," he said, "but let me finish my breakfast and get my day straight, and I'll call you back."

"I'll be waiting by this phone," I said.

I waited, reading the paper and working on and finishing the crossword puzzle, and it was 1955, at Saratoga and Belmont and around Long Island, all over again. When I would finally sit him down, though, in the house he and his wife rented at Saratoga and at their home in Garden City, the flavor and aura of racing would fill the room and my notebooks. I thought of Sherwood Anderson and the way he wrote "I'm a Fool" and the other stories in *Horses and Men*.

He was born in Cincinnati on February 19, 1916, and started to grow up there and across the Ohio River in Southgate, Kentucky. He really grew up around the tracks, though, because he quit school when he was thirteen and came to racing by one of those accidents by which most of us come to do what we do.

"There was some fella I caddied for," he was telling once. "I never remember his name, but he was a good stake. He'd give me a dollar twenty-five when them other kids were only getting that to carry doubles, and he had some connection with the race track. He used to kid me about being a jock, and he'd introduce me to his friends as 'my jockey.' He put the bug in my head."

When he threatened to leave home on his own and change his name, his father took him one day to Latonia. There was a porch there off the jockey room, and he said he stood there for two or three hours just watching the jocks in their colors.

"Then when I heard how they traveled," he said, "and the big races they won, I had to have it."

For three months he kept nagging until one morning his father took him back to Latonia. He introduced him to Rome Respess and Roscoe Goose, who trained horses.

"Rome," he said, "was an old, hard, chew-tobaccy guy, and he looked at my hands and feet and said I'd grow too big to be a jockey. Roscoe just said he'd like to have me, but he already had two boys he was starting. Then we went out by the gap at the five-eighths pole and we watched the horses working, and my old man had a hell of a time getting me away. I know that going home I was a really dejected little man."

"Had you ever been around horses before?" I said.

"I'd seen milk-wagon horses," he said.

"I mean race horses," I said. "Standing there by the rail and watching them go by you so big and with the jockeys on them so small, didn't the thought of riding them scare you?"

"Hell, no," he said. "I was so damned elated how fast they went by that I couldn't wait to get up on them."

He would wait for some time. His father got him a job with the stable of T. H. McCaffrey, and each morning he would leave home at six o'clock to take the three trolleys that would get him to Latonia where he would walk hots, rub horses, fill the buckets, and clean tack.

"The first day," he said, "I bought a pair of boots and then my old man sent me over to Cincinnati to have a pair of English whipcord riding pants made. I was the best-dressed kid walking hots you ever saw, and I was in those things from morning till night. Right now I'd be embarrassed to get on a streetcar with boots and riding pants on, but then it was a thrill just copying somebody who could do something."

McCaffrey had two exercise boys, and they showed him how to saddle and knot the reins and set the stirrups and how to tread the saddle, which off the track is called posting. They put him up on the stable pony and he rode that around the stable area, and then Odie Clelland, who had been a rider and trained for McCaffrey, started to make improvements on him. He pulled the stirrups so Eddie said he felt as if he had no perch at all, and he got him off the horse's back so the weight would be on the withers and he would get more purchase. He used to emphasize getting a deep seat, to be low, and he was the first to start him out of a gate, teaching him how to leave his hold long so that, if the horse bobs, you can give with it. Once a filly ran off two miles with him, with Eddie afraid only of what Odie would say.

"That second winter," he said, "Odie took me to Florida, and any time I'd gallop a horse he'd be with me, and we always worked two at a time, head and head. I lived with him and his wife in a cottage they rented, and Odie would bring home jock's boots and pants and I'd try them on at night. McCaffrey wouldn't go for it, though. When we got back to Latonia he told my old man I should go back to school. He said, 'If your boy ever makes a rider, we'll have a snowy day in July.' After I won a couple of Derbies my mother saw him, and she said, 'Well, Mr. McCaffrey, we've been having a lot of snow in July.'"

He hooked up with Paul Youkilus, who had a three-horse stable, and at Bainbridge, Ohio, he rode his first race. He was fifteen, and he had to borrow the equipment from the other riders. He was all over the horse and lost his cap and finished sixth with the tails of his silks hanging out of his pants. He would ride in forty-five races before he would win one.

Youkilus had A. W. Booker training for him, and when they shipped to Agua Caliente in Mexico, Booker's brother and Eddie went along with them. There were a dozen horses from another stable in the horse car, and the railroad allowed one man to take care of three horses. That man was Booker's brother, so Eddie was stowing away.

"In that car," he said, "there must have been six of us who shouldn't have been on, and they had straw piled up and bales of hay, and when you'd feel that train slow down at any time of day or night we'd be in our holes in the hay. The only schedule we had was to feed the horses at five and eleven in the morning and at five or six at night, so we'd just sleep when we were sleepy. We never got out of our clothes, and while we were still in the cold part of the country we'd have the horse blankets over us. It was amazing, too, how everybody kept clean, washing and shaving in a pail.

"Being only fifteen," he said, "I was all ears. The rest of them would sit around and tell stories and reminisce over races, and Booker's brother had me captured. He was kind of an old man, and he'd tell me about great riders and great races, and whether he was conning me or not he sure was entertaining me. When we got to the desert where it was hot, those people had a knack of opening the door a little and setting up the bales of hay for the air to bounce off. I sat there and looked out at that sand and cactus and listened to their talk by the hour.

"At Caliente," he said, "until Booker and his wife got there and we moved in with them, Booker's brother and I lived at the stable. The tack room was fixed up with a couple of cots, and we used to eat at the track kitchen or make our own breakfast or our own stews over the open fires they used for the water boilers. We'd get up at four thirty or five to water and feed the horses, and I can still remember the smell of that bacon frying and the coffee boiling with the grounds right in the pot."

I can see it all again now, that trip West and the life around the track, and that is what I mean. When I could get him off that merry-go-round that was his life, it made all the tailing, all the waiting, worthwhile.

At Caliente, on Eagle Bird, one of the three horses that Youkilus had, he finally won his first race. It was a long meeting though—107 days that ran right through Christmas and New Year's—and he had no money and he was homesick.

"Booker was supposed to pay me," he said, "but he had no money himself. He was a game little guy, though, and he had the grocery and the feed man on the cuff. I used to just look at those mountains and wonder if I'd ever get back over them again, and many a night I used to cry. When Booker got out of there he had to leave Eagle Bird and another horse to cover the feed bills."

"How did you feel about leaving Eagle Bird?" I said.

"I don't suppose anybody ever forgets the horse he broke his maiden on," he said, "so when I hitchhiked out of there for Tanforan I had to be sad about Eagle Bird. They probably raced him around Mexico until he broke down, and then they destroyed him, because he never showed on an American track again. If he had, I'd have known it."

At Caliente he had talked Clarence Davison into taking him. Davison carried between twenty and thirty horses, and Eddie said that it seemed that every time he looked up, Davison's colors—yellow with blue hoops on the arms and body—were coming down on top.

"Davison and his wife," he said, "were kind of farmer-like people, with their own sense of humor, and not much of it at that, but I'd never have made it without him. I don't know who elects a guy to meet those kind of people in your life, and there's been many a time since when I wished I still had them around.

"When I was a kid at home, everybody was sort of a half-baked hoodlum, seeing who could live the fastest. I'd never had anybody boss me before, and with him there was no staying up until twelve. It was a training proposition, and you worked hard. It gave me a sense of responsibility, and there was no lying, no matter how bad it was. There was no sulking either, and whenever I'd get depressed I'd have to sit down and talk it out with Davison to find the meaning. He'd say, 'I'm the one who's puttin' up the money. You got nothin' to lose. If a lot of people around me start sulking I'll start to sulk, and I don't want to.'"

When Eddie first went with him, Davison used to rig reins onto a bucket in the barn, and he would have Eddie sit on a bale of hay, whipping and practicing how to switch the whip while passing the reins from hand to hand at the same time. Eddie said that some of the prominent jocks, and he named them, still couldn't do it without putting the whip in their mouths while they switched the reins.

"In the mornings," he said, "he was very exact about time, and he was the first one to make me time-conscious. If he told you to work a mile in forty-one, he didn't want you coming down in forty-two."

That is a minute and forty-one seconds, and what they mean when they say a jockey "has a clock in his head." They used to say and write that about Eddie, and I told him that I couldn't understand how, not only during the morning works but during the heat of a race, he could keep track of the time within a second.

"Night after night," he said, "Davison would sit me down with that stopwatch. He'd flip the watch and start talking to me, and then he'd say, 'How much?'"

"But I still don't understand how you can do it," I said.

"You break time down into twelves," he said, "because if a horse runs an eighth of a mile in twelve seconds, he's going pretty good. People who can't do it think it's quite a thing to be able to come within two-fifths of a second, but actually it's four-fifths, because it's two-fifths either side of the second, and not as hard as it seems."

"It would be for me," I said.

"I never rode a race for Davison," he said, "that he didn't tell me everything I did, whether I sawed on his mouth or pulled him up too short. He and his wife watched me from the time I left the paddock until I got back, and now when I see jocks kidding and laughing going to the gate I think of those days. Davison had better not catch me laughing on one of his. I was a solid citizen."

Davison was the first to teach him how to place a horse, how you shouldn't make your run all in an eighth of a mile but gradually, unless it is to save ground. He said that Davison was bugs on saving ground.

"He made me rail conscious," he said. "He had me always looking at that rail first, and if I went around when there was room to come through on the rail, he'd scream, 'I can't run a horse that much the best! You gotta save something on any horse I ever run!' At first he made me lose more races than he helped me win, because he tried to ride every race for me. I rode almost that whole apprentice year and couldn't grasp it, because mentally I didn't know management. I was trying to be a robot for Davison, and he was shouting me into some awful scrapes."

From Tanforan they had moved to Chicago, and Davison also had ten horses stabled up at Devonshire and Kenilworth in Windsor, Canada, just across the border from Detroit. Eddie and LeFoy Cunningham, Davison's other rider, would ride in Chicago and then they would get into Davison's car, and while Davison drove they would sleep in the back seat. The next day they would ride at one of those Windsor tracks.

"That first year I had twelve or fourteen falls," he said, "and I was picking up fines and suspensions at every meeting. Davison would holler, 'Don't get beat no noses on any of my horses!' He was so desperate that if you were on number 8, he'd say, 'Number 6 is the favorite. Now don't give him any of the best of it.' When you put that in a kid's mind you're playing with dynamite. Davison was all for shutting horses off, and when one of his would get beat a head or a nose he'd be so goddamn mad I'd be scared to bring the animal back. He'd holler, 'Why didn't you get ahold of him?'

"It was nothing," he said, "to grab a saddle cloth. The other boy could hardly tell, and if he turned around you just let loose. Riding with your toe in you'd leg lock, hooking your heel in front of his toe. At those Canadian tracks the rail was made of pipe, and where it was joined together there were couplings. You'd get another horse against the rail, and you could hear that fence sing until the jock's boot would hit one of those couplings. There was many a rider got a broken foot up there that way."

One day, while Eddie was trying to take his horse around the leader, the boy on him—a jock named Sielaff—grabbed Eddie's leg. They were about seventy yards from the finish, and Eddie just dropped the reins and grabbed Sielaff by the throat, and that was the way they went across the line with Eddie choking him.

"I won it," he said, "but they disqualified the horse and fined me fifty dollars, and that was a horrible trip back to Chicago that night. I'd just get to sleep in the back seat when Davison would go at me again. 'But have you got any idea why you did it?' he'd say over and over. 'You know how bad-legged that poor old horse is, and you just tossed that race off him. Why did you do it?' Who was thinking of that horse? I was just thinking of choking Sielaff, but Davison had a piece of that rough riding and that temper trouble of mine.

"One day he put me up on a filly, and Joe Guerra, the jock from Cuba, threw me against the fence. When Davison came down he wanted to kill Guerra, and the next day he had five horses entered and he put me on all five. He said, 'I'm gonna give you a fair chance. If Guerra don't go down, home you go.'

"At first I didn't pay any attention. The first two races I didn't get near Guerra, but in the third race he put me on a real speedy filly. He said, 'Here's your chance. You haven't been anywhere near Guerra all day. I don't care how this filly finishes. I want Guerra on the ground.' I nailed him. I threw two horses in that race. I threw Guerra, and some poor innocent guy who was in the middle went down too. I got fined fifty dollars again and came near getting Davison's filly all cut up, but that satisfied Davison."

Waiting for him now in that motel room, I turned on the television. There was a game show in progress, and two losers had just walked off, winners of more than $3,000 each, when the phone rang.

"Bill?" he said. "What the hell kind of a place is this?"

"It's a motel," I said.

"I know that," he said, "but they don't answer the goddamn switchboard. I've been calling for the last half hour but nobody answers, so I came over. I'm down in the lobby."

"So come on up," I said. "Turn right after you get off the elevator. I'm in 419."

I opened the door and waited for him. He came striding down the hall, that little man, and he was wearing a light brown, summer-weight suit and a dark brown sports shirt open at the neck. Around his neck there was a small-linked gold chain with whatever was on it hidden beneath the shirt. That swarthy face was more lined now, but there was that prominent nose and those big dark eyes as quick as ever as he looked around the room and we sat down.

"So what can I tell you?" he said.

"Oh," I said, "about how you're living these days."

"We've got a two-bedroom apartment over there," he said, "and it's nice for Ruth and I. When we moved in nine years ago we had to cut down on a lot of furniture and the trophies and things. Ruth gave a lot to the museums at Saratoga and Lexington. There was a whole trunk—one of them steamer trunks—with articles and scrapbooks and stuff.

"The last race I rode, in Australia in January of '62, when I came back I just had that bag with the saddle and the whip and the boots and pants. I put it in a closet, and I've never been able to find it. I've hunted all over the Jockey Club. The place was new then, and they were moving stuff around, and maybe somebody stole it."

Out of a jacket pocket he had taken an emery board. He was starting to work on his nails.

"I don't have time to get a haircut or a manicure," he said.

"What takes up all your time?" I said. "I see you occasionally on TV doing the commentary on a big race. I've seen you on that RCA commercial in the silks and talking about the colors."

"I just did one for Buick," he said. "I don't know if it'll play up your way or not, but I say, 'I rode two hundred fifty races before I rode a winner, and this is a winner.'

"Don't tell me you say that," I said. "We had it in those two articles we did for *Look*, how many races you rode before you broke your maiden."

"We did?" he said. "I don't know if I ever read those things."

"Of course you did," I said. "You had to approve them before the magazine would accept them."

"I remember at Saratoga you were on my tail for the whole month," he said, "but I don't remember reading the articles."

"After Saratoga," I said, "and when I got back to the city, I spent four hours one afternoon in the library at the *Morning Telegraph*. I got down the chart books and I checked every race at every track you were at when you were breaking in. They'd been writing for years that you'd ridden over two hundred, and I figured that, if I never did anything else in my life as a reporter, I would at least establish how many races Eddie Arcaro rode before he had a winner."

"How many was it?"

"When you won on Eagle Bird at Caliente, it was your forty-fifth race."

"When I did that Buick thing," he said, "the guy in the truck said, 'You rode two hundred fifty before you won?' I said, 'I never rode that many. I couldn't have, but I sure as hell don't know how many it was.'"

"You know now," I said. "So tell me what it was like when you quit."

"I thought I'd go fishing and play golf," he said, "but that became old hat in a hurry. I'd doodle around, and then I got into a couple of businesses and I lost my butt, but I had to keep busy."

In '55 I asked him one evening if he was a millionaire. I never forgot his answer, "To tell you the truth, I don't know. I've never sat down to figure it out."

"I got in a trap with an electric burglar alarm," he was saying now, "and I lost four hundred thousand on that thing."

That's a lot of money to drop, I was thinking, no matter how you make it. When you make it riding, that's an awful lot of races over a lot of years and an awful lot of risks.

"I never got into any serious financial problems," he was saying, "where it curtailed my way of living, and then I got into the horse insurance business and I lost there, but not a lot. I jumped our premiums from three hundred thousand to three million in three and a half years, but you can't make money insuring thoroughbreds. In insurance you hold a claim for a year and make a profit where it's millions of dollars, but you can't do that with horses. I lost a couple of years of my life."

"Speaking of your life," I said, "I was worried when you had that open-heart operation. I heard about it on the morning news on the radio."

"I didn't know I had anything the matter with me," he said. "One evening I was going over some claims to evaluate horses, and Julie Fink came in and he said, 'You don't look good.' I said, 'Man, I don't feel good.' He ran me down to his doctor, and the guy took a cardiogram and told me I had angina. I got out of the insurance business—if that was affecting my health—and I was hitting golf balls one day when the thing hit me.

"Dr. Richard Elias—a hell of a guy—looked at me and took an arteriogram, and he said, 'You need an operation.' He showed Ruth and I the pictures on a TV set like the one there."

"Did that scare you?"

"No. You go to the Heart Institute here and see the people they've done it on, people up to seventy-five, and the loss ratio is so small. I've been operated on from ankles to head, so I've never had that fear. Then the Heart Institute is like living at the Waldorf. I've been on the board there for four or five years, and you've got to see it to believe it.

"They give you a menu, and the night before, the doc said, 'What do you want for dinner?' I said, 'A martini and a big steak.' He walked to the phone, and I said, 'You're kidding.' He said, 'No.' I said, 'What are my chances?' He said, 'Your chances are good, and you better bet on me. The only ones we lose are the ones we take a chance on when it's the only thing to do.'"

He reached for the gold chain around his neck and on it was a small, circular gold pillbox. He opened it, and in it were small pills, some green and some pink.

"I'm a nervous guy," he said, "and I take nine thousand pills a day to slow me down."

He snapped the pillbox shut and put it back inside the open collar of his shirt. He had been smoking, and he lit another cigarette.

"With all the bullets I dodged in my life," he said, and he meant all the jams and those more than forty spills on the track, "I'm not going to worry about lung cancer. All the races you ride, and you have a near miss every day."

At that winter meeting of 1931–32 at Caliente, where he finally rode his first winner, it was a rodeo every day. He was one with Silvio Coucci and Hank Mills and Wayne Wright, whom they called "Cowboy Wright," and Georgie Woolf who, he said, used to holler at you and hit you with the whip at the same time.

"When you got half a length in front of a guy," he was telling me once, "you sawed him off. If a guy bothered you one day you didn't run to the stewards and complain, but you got him the next day. That sort of thing started a chain reaction that never stopped, and we had a couple of falls a week.

"One day Jackie Westrope's brother, Billy, was killed. It happened right after the finish, as he was pulling up at the seven-eighths pole, which was right in front of the jocks' room. The horse stumbled and Rope's brother landed on the point of his chin. We all saw it, but I don't believe it scared any of us, we were such a wild bunch of bastards."

The following year, at Washington Park, in Chicago, he had the fall that almost killed him. All he could remember when he came to in the hospital was leaving the gate and running into a jam.

"I was unconscious for three days," he said, "and when I came to I was still a little groggy and I saw my mom and my old man and my Aunt Libertina from Pittsburgh standing there. On the way up they'd heard I was dead. I had a fractured skull and a punctured lung and a broken nose, and it had me cross-eyed for a while.

"The family tried to talk me out of ever riding again, but I thought I really could ride now, and laying there I never thought I'd be scared. I came back at Hawthorne, and I'd been galloping horses mornings, and I thought I was fine until that first day when we went into a turn and I could see those bastards stepping all over me again. You just don't have any fear of those hoofs until one of them nails you.

"For five or six days I couldn't win a race. I was pulling them up, and a lot of times that's the worst thing you can do. They come together in front of you, and you hit their heels, and that's when you go down. You have to fight them in there, if you can make yourself do it.

"That Davison saved me again. He said, 'I've got to send you home. You've lost your nerve. You're just yellow, and you're no good to me or yourself, and you're gonna get yourself killed.' I know it hurt his wife to hear him bawl me out, and he'd holler, 'You're just yellow! I've got two more years on your contract, and if you pull another of my horses up I'm gonna set you down.'

"When I went to bed I cried all night. I was more scared of being sent home than I was of getting hurt, but I still couldn't do it until I went down on a filly of his named Printemps. There was a jam at the half-mile pole, and I was pulling up when I should have been going. I didn't get a scratch on me, and that cured me. After that, just to prove I wasn't scared, I'd put those sonsabitches up there where they had no chances. I'd put them up there running and just split the field open.

"It's an awful thing," he said, "being scared to ride and having to ride. Young kids laugh at that sort of thing, but they haven't had it. Nick Wall was laid up in a hospital once for fourteen months, between life and death. When he first came back he couldn't do it. He'd scream and holler in a spot where you could put a bunch in sideways. Johnny Gilbert went into the hospital black-haired and came out gray. Alfred Robertson had a fall at Jamaica and said, 'I quit.' Ralph Neves had a fall in California one year, and when they got him to the hospital there was no pulse or heartbeat. They gave him adrenalin, but nothing happened. They pulled a sheet up over him, and after a while he pulled it off and said, 'I'm riding in the fourth race. What am I doin' here?'

"Gilbert Elston had two terrible falls. He was a nice-looking boy, real trim, until a horse stepped on his head and scalped him and popped his eyes. After that he was never exactly right. He never smoked or drank, but then he became an alcoholic and he tried suicide two or three times. I stopped him one night in a hotel in Chicago. I had him living with me, trying to get him to straighten out, and he was trying to get out the window. Then later he shot and killed himself."

"I'll always remember," I was saying now, "something you told me when we were doing those pieces. You said, 'Jockeys are the only athletes who, if you left them alone, would kill one another.' You said that, if it weren't for the stewards and patrol judges and film patrol, you could start out with twenty jocks and at the end of three months of racing there would be only one left, because that's what racing does to you."

"That was right," he said.

"Do you think that, left on their own, jocks would still be that way today?"

"More or less," he said. "It's the nature of the game, and I don't think that's changed, but people have changed."

"In what way?"

"You take Shoe," he said, meaning Willie Shoemaker, and since the day when they first became competitors they have been the best of friends. "I've seen Shoe time and again throw away the race rather than hurt somebody. People are more considerate. It's like you've got a gun on a guy and you pull the trigger.

"They tell me this Cauthen kid in New York," he said—Steve Cauthen was having his sensational apprentice year—"is like that. He'll give a little."

"Do you wish you were him, and starting all over again when you read about him?"

"Hell, no," he said. "I hardly remember riding. I go to the races occasionally because I still get a kick out of seeing a good horse run, and I can hardly conceive of doing what they're doing. He's an awful nice kid though, sixteen going on thirty mentally. He handles himself real well."

"You've met him?"

"I did that race on TV when he rode here. They told me, 'Go interview him. We want him on.' I said, 'Hell. Leave the kid alone. He just rode a race. The press has been bothering his butt off.' I didn't want to do it, but they insisted."

"I know," I said. "Now you're on my end of this business."

"He couldn't have been nicer. He was real nice to me."

"After all," I said, "you're Eddie Arcaro. You're probably a hero of his."

"I don't know about that," he said. "He's just a real nice kid. A fella interviewed me for the paper here. I wasn't derogatory. I just said that, like with all jocks, his butt has got to hit the ground, and if he's busted up you have to see how it bothers him. He wrote an awful article—that I said he's gonna get hurt and he may be chicken."

"The last spill you ever had," I said, "was it in that Belmont?"

It was the 1959 Belmont Stakes, and I was watching it on television at home. It had come up mud, and Eddie, on Black Hills, had started to make his move on the stretch turn when the horse and Eddie went down. Another fell over them, and after the finish a camera closed in on Eddie, lying there like a lifeless doll, facedown in the ankle-deep mud just off the rail.

"That couldn't have been the last time I went down," he said. "I rode four or five years after that and, hell, you can't ride four or five years without falling. I wasn't really hurt."

"It scared *me*."

"A horse hit me in the back of the head, and I was unconscious for four hours and . . ."

"And that's not being really hurt?"

"And there was a photographer there who took a picture of me laying there in that slop. You saw that picture in *Life*?"

"I may have, but I remember it from TV."

"The guy who took the picture saved my life. After he took it he saw I didn't move, and he turned my head out of the slop. If he didn't, I would have suffocated. Then they took an encephalogram, and it would come to one spot and zero up. The doc said, 'There's something wrong.' I had some torn ligament in my back here too, and finally I said, 'Doc, there's nothing the matter. I'm drinking a quart of whiskey a night and dancing.'

"I went fishing in Canada with my dad and my son, and I came back and he gave me another encephalograph. I said, 'It must be the machine.' He said, 'Let's start all over. Did you ever have a fractured skull?' I said, 'Yes, when I was eighteen.' He said, 'That's it.' I said, 'Yeah, that's just great.' I blew the Queen's Plate in Toronto. While we were fishing I heard on the radio what won it, and I said, 'What the hell am I doing here?'"

"Are your folks living and well?"

"My mother's not well now, and my old man is dead. He lived with us for eight years, and died in our house in Garden City. You know, he and my mother split, and when that happens it's hard to take, but when I got to know my old man I came to understand him."

"You told me something about your dad once," I said, "and you asked me never to write it as long as he was alive, and I never did."

"What was that?"

"About the bootlegging."

"You can write it now, if you want to."

His father had a paint store and a taxi business, and then he began buying up houses and putting couples to live in them. He would also put stills in them.

"When I was six, seven, and eight," Eddie had told me, "I remember sitting there at the dining-room table and separating money. I'd separate the fives and tens, and we had a closet full. When I first came on the track as a kid, I had more money than the jocks did."

"Hell," he was saying now, "I was labeling whiskey when I was twelve. I was getting a hundred a week when people were in breadlines, and in that town it was like everybody did it. I had my own car when I was fourteen. Then later my dad had this place in Erlanger, called 'Arcaro's,' and one day Spencer Drayton called me in."

Spencer Drayton was the head of the Thoroughbred Racing Protective Bureau. They police racing and are concerned with the pedigrees and performances of both horses and people.

"Drayton said, 'You're a public figure. You know they're making book down there. I want you to talk to your father.' I said, 'Why don't you go out there and tell him?' I didn't want any part of telling my old man."

"He had that temper you inherited?"

"Hell, he had a boiling point at zero. So Drayton sent a guy out, and after he got done talking, my old man said, 'I'll tell you what you do, fella. You finish your drink and then get the hell out of here, and remember that my name was Arcaro before Eddie's was.'"

When Eddie's temper flared only Red Adair, the fireman of the oil-field blowouts, could have capped it. In 1942, in the Cowdin Stakes at Aqueduct, it almost cost him his career. He was riding a horse named Occupation, and Vincent Nodarse, the Cuban jockey, was on one of the others.

"All Occupation's races had been in front," Eddie had told me, explaining it, "and they wanted somebody on him who could rate him. I said I'd take him back, and I told Nodarse in the gate that I wanted to take my horse back at the start, and to give me time. You'll talk like that with other jocks, and when Occupation broke a neck on the field and I started to take him in, Nodarse got a half-length in front and sawed him off.

"I damn near went over his head, and by the time we hit the chute I didn't have a horse beat. I was on the outside, and I just lost my temper. Nodarse was in front, and I got Occupation gathered up and hit him, and he must have run the quarter in twenty-one seconds. Before we hit the turn I got a neck in front of Nodarse's horse and I nailed him. He saw me coming, and he knew what I was gonna do. He was hollering, 'No could help, Eddie! No could help!' I hollered, 'I'll help you, you sonofabitch! I'll help you right now!'

"I just tried to put him over the fence, and it was lucky he didn't get killed. Even as bad as I rode Occupation, he finished second, but naturally the stewards claimed foul and I walked down that tunnel and up in the elevator. They were trying something new then. They had a microphone to record your claim of foul or your defense, and I sure gave it a great inauguration.

"Marshall Cassidy said to me, 'Eddie, did you do that on purpose?' I said, 'On purpose? I'd have killed the sonofabitch if I could!'"

From Eddie you got an honest answer, and he was grounded for a whole year. For a while he went on drunks for a day or two. He took up golf, and he said that the discipline in learning to control his nerves on the course helped to cure him.

"I'll always remember you," I was saying now, "coming back on the train from Baltimore after you won the Preakness on Citation."

Two weeks before, he had won his fourth Derby on him, and no other jock had ever won more than three. Now he had just won the Preakness, and he would win the Belmont and, with it, his second Triple Crown.

"Arthur Daley and Jimmy Cannon and I," I said, "were sitting in one of the parlor cars, and you came in and sat down. Daley was always carrying around a big manila envelope. I never knew what he had in it, but I figured it was clippings pertaining to the event he was covering, because he often used other people's research in his columns. He used to make notes on those manila envelopes, so he took out his pencil, and he said to you, 'What's it like, Eddie, riding Citation? It must be a thrill.' And you said, 'Actually, it isn't. It's like driving a Caddy. When you want the power it's there, and there's really not much of a thrill to it.'"

"That was right."

"So then Arthur, writing that down, said, 'But you must have got a thrill winning your fourth Derby on him.' And you said, 'Hell, if I'd had any luck, I'd have won a lot of those Derbies.' Arthur was stunned, and I had to laugh."

"That was right, too."

"I know," I said.

In 1942 he was riding for Greentree, and had the choice of Shut Out or Devil Diver. He picked Devil Diver and Shut Out won. In 1947 he was on Phalanx, the best of the three-year-olds, and was beaten by a head by Jet Pilot, and he would tell me later that he bought the movie of that race and played it over and over and that he didn't sleep well for weeks.

"You don't think about those Derbies you've won," he told me. "You've already got those. The ones I think about are the ones I didn't win when I should have."

When I got him to thinking about them, the ones he won, though, there were stories. Four of his five Derby winners—Lawrin in 1938, Whirlaway in 1941, Citation in 1948, and Hill Gail in 1952—were trained by Ben Jones, and B.A., as he was known, starred in Eddie's stories.

"He knew that Louisville track," Eddie said, "better than he knew the back of his own hand, and he knew those horses better than he knew his own relatives."

On those Saturday mornings of the Lawrin and Whirlaway Derbies, B.A. had Eddie come out to the stable early, and he made him walk the track. B.A. was on his stable pony, and Eddie hoofed it alongside while B.A. picked out the best footing and the spots where the track was bad.

"Stomp right there," B.A. would say. "That should be a little soft."

When they got back to the barn, B.A. had a chart of the course and they went over it again. In 1945, though, when Eddie won on Hoop, Jr., he rode him for Fred W. Hooper, and it had rained hard the night before the race. The track was a lake, but when they came out for the Derby, with the band playing "My Old Kentucky Home," Eddie spotted in front of the stands a dry spot about three-sixteenths of a mile long and about fifteen feet wide.

"I got Hoop, Jr. out good," he said, "and I went for that beach. It gave him a three-length lead, and that did it. He didn't get any of that slop thrown in his face, and led all the way and won by six."

He said that, just before he was to win his fifth Derby and set that record on Hill Gail, though, there was a moment in the paddock when he wouldn't have given anything for his chances.

"Hill Gail would usually run as kind as any horse you'll ever see," he said, "but in the paddock he was a wild sonofabitch. When they led him out to put me up he lunged into the stable pony, and when he did, B.A. just reared back and hit that horse a right-hand punch on the soft part of his nose. My eyes must have popped, because I mean that's a hell of a thing to see happen to a horse you're hoping to win the Derby on, but that slowed him, and when I got on him, he was fine."

I got him to tell me, of course, how he rode each one of them, how Lawrin's Derby was one of the roughest, and how he got knocked back to next to last at the start and then played the rail all the way, how the problem with Whirlaway was that once you got him in competition you couldn't hold him, and how Hill Gail, going into the turn coming off the back stretch, started for the outside rail and he had to spin him in midair and then let him open a ten-length lead because he was afraid to stop him. As he told me everything that had happened in those split parts of seconds in one race and then another, he said that thinking alone won't do it for a jockey, that it has to be instinct, and I knew what he meant.

"So what are your days like now?" I was saying.

"I'll be on the course in a little while," he said, "and I keep pretty occupied. I'd like to play golf and be a bum, but they won't let me. Next week I go to New York to do the TV on the Wood Memorial Stakes. I've got to go to Bermuda for a Buick meeting. I come back and I go to the Derby for Seagram's. I do public relations work for them, and then I've got seven more Buick commercials. I haven't done my OTB commercials, and I've got to do them because I've already been paid."

It is New York State's Off-Track Betting. When he was starting to ride into the big money he used to bet $1,000 or $2,000 on a horse.

"At the end of a couple of years," he was telling me once, "I came up empty. My mother said to me one time, 'Eddie, why don't you give me some winners?' I said, 'Mom, if I could beat the races, I wouldn't have to ride.' I might ride a horse for a fella now and go for a story like any sucker and bet a hundred, but never enough to get hurt. I just don't think you can win. If you could, the bettin' jocks would be wealthy. It's the ones who don't bet who have all the money."

We got to talking now about the match race at Washington Park in Chicago, in early September 1955, between Nashua and Swaps. Swaps, with Willie Shoemaker on him, had beaten Nashua, with Eddie on him, a length and a half in the Derby. In the newspapers and on radio and television they made this rematch the equine battle of the century, between the western champion, owned and trained by two ex-cowboys, and the effete eastern challenger, owned by William Woodward, Jr. and trained by old Sunny Jim Fitzsimmons. It was also, of course, a contest between Shoe and Eddie.

They had Nashua in training at Saratoga, and when I wasn't tailing Eddie, I watched some of his works. When he shipped out for Chicago, I went down to the railroad siding to watch them load him, and so I had a subjective rooting interest that, because I was not covering the event, I had no reason to constrain.

"The day of the race," I was saying now, "I was in Philadelphia researching a magazine piece on Bert Bell, who was then the head of the National Football League. He was living at the Racquet Club, and we watched it there. There were a dozen or so others watching, too, and when you came out of that gate first, beating on that horse, and then took Shoe wide on that first turn, I came right up out of my chair. I must have been yelling through the whole thing, and when it was over and you'd come down on top I remember hollering, 'He stole it! He stole it!' There was this white-haired, dignified old gentleman there, and he came up to me and he stuck out his hand and he said, 'I don't know who you are, sir, but let me congratulate you. You've just ridden a great race.'"

"With Shoe," Eddie said now, "he was never jealous of me and I was never jealous of him. In a stakes, if one or the other of us won it, it was just the same. After that race in Chicago, though, he said, 'You'll only do that to me once, buddy.' And that's the way it was."

We talked about some great horses and about some people we both knew who are now gone. When I looked at my watch almost two hours had passed, and I said I would let him off the hook. We stood up and I walked him to the door.

"I've got to tell you something you said once," I said, "that couldn't have been more wrong."

"What was that?"

"Like a lot of other people at the time, I was asking you how long you figured to go on riding, and why you didn't quit right then. You had enough money to retire for the rest of your life. You'd won those five Derbies, and there had been great riders who had never won one. You said, 'But I want the next one, and besides I like being a celebrity. If any sonofabitch tells you he don't like it, you'd better look at his head.' Then you said, 'And when I retire I'll be just another little man.'"

"I said that?" he said, smiling.

"Yes, and when you said it I knew you were wrong."

"I didn't know it," he said, shaking my hand. "Listen, I've got to go."

Somebody Up There Likes Him

The Life and Times of Rocky Graziano

Hey, Ma—your bad boy done it. I told you Somebody up there likes me.

Rocky Graziano, July 16, 1947

HE SAID IT into a radio microphone that had been thrust in front of his face in the ring in the Chicago Stadium. It was 120 degrees under the ring lights, and his hair hung in black streaks, soaked by his own sweat and the water they had sloshed over him between rounds. His right eye was a slit, and over his left eye there was a dark cake of dried blood. In the sixth round of the second of their three vicious fights, he had just knocked out Tony Zale. Now he was the middleweight champion of the world, and it was an event that involved me as did none other among the hundreds I covered in sports.

"You're a tough man to get hold of," I was saying now on the phone.

"Yeah, yeah," he was saying. "I get up early, and then I'm out."

"I know," I said.

I had been calling the apartment in New York for days. Several times I had talked with his wife, Norma.

Chapter 19 of *Once They Heard the Cheers*, 1979.

"He's gone again, Bill," she would say.

"When will he be in?"

"Who knows?" she would say.

"Listen," I was saying to him now. "I'll be in New York on Friday, and I want to see you at your place about eleven in the morning."

"Yeah, yeah," he said. "Good."

"Now, I'm dragging all the way in just to see you," I said, "so you be there."

"Yeah, yeah," he said. "I'll be here, and I'll tell you anything you want to know. You always wrote good about me, Billy. You know?"

"Yes," I said. "I know."

A reporter has an obligation to objectivity, and although we had a racing handicapper who operated as a bookmaker right in the sports department of my paper, I never bet on a horse race, a ball game, or a fight. In every reporter, however, the struggle against subjectivity goes on, and coming up to that second Graziano–Zale fight, I lost that struggle.

It was the night before the fight, and we had been sitting around the living room of the hotel suite in Chicago for an hour or more, listening to a Cubs game on the radio. Rocky was lolling in an armchair, and there were a couple of sparring partners on the sofa. Irving Cohen, who managed him, and Whitey Bimstein, who trained him, had been sitting with a card table between them, counting through batches of tickets, and I saw Whitey look at his watch. I looked at my own, and it was ten o'clock. In twenty-four hours, the fighter would have to climb into a ring once more against the man who, nine months before in Yankee Stadium, in the sixth round and after taking a frightening beating himself, had hit him a right hand in the body and a left hook on the chin to knock him out and end what those who had been around long enough called the greatest fight since Dempsey–Firpo.

"All right," Whitey said. "You better get up to bed now, Rock. It's time you were in."

He got up from the chair and stretched and started out the door. Whitey motioned over his shoulder with his head and I followed them out. Nothing had been said about it, but I knew now why Irving Cohen had asked me to come over to the hotel and why, now, I was a part of this night before this fight.

It had started five months before. In New York they had revoked his license for failing to report the offer of a bribe he had not accepted for a fight that had never been held. There were those of us who had gone to the hearings of the New York State Athletic Commission and who were certain that we could see through this to the politics behind it, and we had been appalled that such a thing could happen in this country.

An uptown Manhattan politician named Joseph Scottorigio had been murdered. Who killed Scottorigio? It is a question that still hasn't been answered, and for weeks the New York papers played it big. For weeks it confounded and plagued the Manhattan police and the District Attorney's office, until they came up with this prizefighter and the bribe offer he had ignored, and Rocky Graziano chased Joseph Scottorigio off the front pages.

As I covered the hearings, what I wrote for the front page was what transpired. What I wrote for my piece on the sports page each day was what I had come to know about this former Lower East Side hoodlum who, it turned out, had been in and out of reform school, jail, and prison, and who had found in boxing a way to make a legitimate living.

I knew it was a tough row to hoe in this garden where I was trying to plant my small seeds of reason. The paper was conservative, resolutely Republican. In my time it had opposed Franklin Delano Roosevelt and Fiorello La Guardia. It stood firm against Harry Truman, organized labor, and any social legislation that, it seemed to me, wasn't current during the administration of Calvin Coolidge. I could never have written politics for it, but it had given me my start and I felt an abiding filial affection for it, and I could write sports.

Two days before a scheduled fight with Cowboy Reuben Shank in Madison Square Garden, Graziano had pulled out, complaining of a bad back. It was the contention of the District Attorney that the problem was not with the fighter's back but with an offer of $100,000 that had been made to him by an unidentified party in Stillman's Gym to take a dive for Shank and that he had failed to report. Graziano admitted that someone had come up to him with an offer that he thought was a gag, and that was the D.A.'s case.

To anyone familiar with boxing, the proposition was absurd. Cowboy Reuben Shank was a journeyman middleweight whose best move against Graziano would have been to take the train out of town and back to Keenesburg, Colorado. Any syndicate trying to place enough money on Shank to profit from a $100,000 payoff would have signaled that a fix was in and driven the fight off the books.

I wrote that and I wrote that you had to know Graziano and you had to know Stillman's Gym to understand how he had looked upon the offer. He was the most exciting fighter, those who had seen them both wrote, since Stanley Ketchel, and Ketchel had been dead by then for thirty-seven years—or since, as John Lardner put it, "he was fatally shot in the back by the common-law husband of the lady who was cooking his breakfast."

When Graziano fought, you could breathe the tension. When he fought in the Garden, you could feel it over on Broadway, and the night he fought Zale for the first time you could sense it two hours before the fight between the cars jammed along the Grand Concourse, half a mile from Yankee Stadium. When he trained at Stillman's, he packed that place to the walls. They would be stacked on the stairway to the balcony, and they would be packed on the balcony, too.

"I'll be glad when that Graziano stops fighting," a fight manager said to me there one day. "It's gettin' so you can't even move in here."

His dressing room would be mobbed, too, and with the characters to cast three road companies of *Dead End*. There was one there, a little guy named Barney, who always wore a dirty cap, the peak to one side, and who played the harmonica. He played it, not by blowing on it with his mouth, but through his nostrils.

"Ain't he a good musician?" Graziano would say, sitting back and listening. "Did you ever see anybody do that before? I'd like to get this poor guy a job."

This minstrel had three numbers in his repertoire—"Darktown Strutters' Ball," "Beer Barrel Polka," and "Bugle Call Rag." While he was playing "Bugle Call Rag," blowing on that harmonica through his nostrils, he would salute with his left hand.

"Ain't that great?" Graziano would say. "Why can't I get this guy a job?"

The virtuoso seemed satisfied because Graziano was staking him. He staked a lot of them. One day I saw him give the shirt he was wearing to some hapless hanger-on. The Christmas of the first year that he had made any real money he bought a six-year-old Cadillac and loaded it with fifteen hundred dollars' worth of toys. He drove it down to his old East Side neighborhood, and he handed out the toys to the kids and another fifteen hundred dollars to their parents. He never mentioned it, but it came out because a trainer at Stillman's who lived in the neighborhood had seen it.

"Look, Rocky," Irving Cohen said to him, "it's nice to do things like that, but you haven't got that kind of money, and you've got to save money. You won't be fighting forever."

"Sure, Irving," Graziano said, "but those are poor people. They're good people. They never done no wrong. They never hurt nobody. They just never got a break."

One day in Stillman's he walked up to Irving. He asked him how much money he was carrying.

"I've got fifty bucks," Irving said.

"Give it to me," Graziano said, "and hustle up another fifty for me."

Irving circulated and borrowed fifty and gave it to him. As you came into Stillman's there were rows of chairs facing the ring, and in one of the chairs a former fighter, still young but blind, was sitting. When Graziano sat down beside him and started to talk to him, Irving sidled up behind them, and he saw Graziano lean over and slip the folded bills into the breast pocket of the other's jacket.

"There's something in your pocket," Graziano said, and he got up.

I wrote that and more, weighing it all against the absurdity of the charges, and I wondered how long I would be permitted that freedom.

After all, how long could a paper, patterned to please stockbrokers, corporate executives, and the ad agencies and their clients that sustained it, afford to speak for a prizefighter, an ex-convict with a fifth-grade education, against the office of the District Attorney and the undoubted integrity of Colonel Edward P. F. Eagan, Yale graduate, former Rhodes Scholar, lawyer, and chairman of the New York State Athletic Commission?

Late one afternoon I found out. When I checked my mail cubicle in the sports department, there was a typed note there from Wilbur Wood.

"Mr. Speed," the note read, and Keats Speed was the managing editor, "suggests that you write no more opinion pieces about Graziano. WW."

I wrote one more. I knew that neither Wilbur nor Speed came in early enough mornings to check the copy going into the first edition that went to press at 10:00 A.M. After the first edition, the piece was yanked.

"Didn't you get my note?" Wilbur said, when I saw him in the office later that day.

"Gee, Wilbur, I didn't," I said. "I was in a hurry to write my piece and catch my train to Connecticut, and I didn't check my mail until this morning."

"Well, that's the end of it," he said. "No more pro-Graziano pieces. That's an order."

"Whatever you say," I said.

"It isn't just what I say," he said. "It's what Speed says and what a lot of other people on this paper are saying."

"You're the boss, Wilbur," I said.

The afternoon that Eagan announced that Rocky Graziano was banned, ostensibly for life, from boxing in New York State, I covered that. In that crowded hearing room, I watched the fighter, who had seemed to have finally found his way in this world, drop his head into his hands, his elbows on the table as he sat there across from Eagan, and I rushed back to the paper and wrote the piece that ran under the eight-column headline that bannered page one.

"Listen," Wilbur Wood said to me, coming back from the city room after the edition had closed. "The city desk wants you to get ahold of Graziano and find out how he's taking this. You're his good friend, so he'll talk to you, and it should make a good piece for tomorrow."

"Sure, Wilbur," I said, thinking that yes, I am his good friend and now you want me to play that friendship you all found so embarrassing, but it is a good piece if I can find him.

With Irving Cohen and Jack Healy, who was another of his managers, I found him. In the fighter's new buff and light blue Cadillac, with "Rocky" on the doors, with Healy at the wheel and Irving beside him, we drove into the Lower East Side. It was early February, and darkness had come by now and there was a mist in the air. At Cooper Square, Healy turned under the El and drove down a side street and parked across from a Chinese laundry on the first floor of an old tenement. Some kids had a bonfire going in the street, piling crates on it, and Healy got out and walked across the street and into the building.

In about ten minutes he came out and Graziano was with him. As they crossed the street toward the car, the wavering light from the bonfire played on them, and then they were silhouetted by the lights of a car turning around in the block.

"Hey, Rocky!" I heard the driver of the car shout, leaning out. "You're still all right!"

Graziano turned around on the wet street and waved his hand, and then he came over to the car and he opened the front door. His face was drawn and his eyes small and Irving Cohen moved over to make room for him on the front seat.

"I been sleepin'," he said. "For three hours I slept at my friend's place."

He started to slide into the front seat. Then he saw me sitting in the back.

"Oh," he said. "Hello."

"Hello, Rocky," I said. "I'm sorry to bother you at a time like this."

"That's all right," he said. "It's a job. I understand."

He was in the car now and he shut the door. Healy got in and drove to the end of the street and started uptown.

"I don't want to pester you, Rocky," I said, "but I have to ask you a couple of questions."

"That's all right," he said. "I understand."

"Were you nervous going in to hear that verdict today?"

"No," he said. "I wasn't nervous. Not nervous."

"How is that?"

"Well, I figured," he said, "I figured that the guy, that Eagan, would say, 'Dismissed.' You know, 'This case dismissed.'"

"But you could tell in the hearings, Rocky," I said, "that they were going to throw the book at you. I mean you could sense it as Eagan began to describe the findings."

"I know," Graziano said, "but I kept on thinkin' the sonofabitch was gonna say, 'But because of the contributions Graziano has made to boxing.' I figured the bastard was gonna say something like that."

"And then what?"

And then it all came out, all of the expletives, all of the vulgarities. The close air in that car was filled with the obscene oaths and the unprintable invectives. He was throwing them wildly, the way he threw punches in the ring where he had found a way to fight back against all the hurts he had invited and that society had inflicted upon him. Now, cornered and wounded again, he was seeing society as his enemy again, personified by Eagan.

"I'll kill the bastard," he was saying. "I'll get a gun. I'll kill the sonofabitch. The sonofabitch should be dead. I'll . . ."

"For Christ sake, Rock!" Healy was saying, and he had slowed the car and he had turned toward him.

"Please, Rocky!" Irving Cohen was saying. "Don't even talk like that!"

"I'll kill him," he was saying.

"Come on now, Rocky," I was saying, and I was leaning forward and I had my hands on his shoulders as he sat there between Healy and Irving. "For God's sake, stop that. You listen to me."

"You listen to Bill, Rocky," Irving was saying. "You listen to Bill. Bill knows."

What did I know? I told him it wasn't the end of his world. I told him that he could fight Zale again, maybe in New Jersey or maybe in Illinois, and that this time he would lick him. When he did, he would be the middleweight champion of the world, and public opinion would turn then on Eagan, and then he would get his license back.

We were at Union Square by now, and Healy turned the car around and drove south again and they dropped me off at my paper on lower Broadway. On the way we kept saying the same things to him over and over again, and when I wrote my piece, of course I left all of that out. They were just words, but some of those he had known had gone to the electric chair and others he had run with were in Sing Sing doing twenty to life, and his whole future was balanced on that pinnacle of public opinion. If I wrote that, there was no way he would ever get his license back, and so I wrote what I could about his hurt and that he would take his wife and Audrey, their small daughter, to Florida while Irving Cohen tried to plan something out.

So the second Zale fight was made for Chicago, and I saw the fighter in training in the East and then out there. Nothing was ever said about the ride from Cooper Square to Union Square and then downtown again, but now, five months later, I was following Whitey and him out into the hallway and up the stairs to the next floor.

They had two rooms there, with the door open between them. In one there were two beds, one for the fighter and the other for Whitey. In the other there were three cots for the sparring partners and Frank Percoco, who would work in the fighter's corner with Irving and Whitey.

"You better try these trunks on," Whitey said.

The fighter undressed. He had been training for two months and he was in great shape, and Whitey handed him the trunks, black with red stripes, first one pair and then the other, and he tried them on, squatting down and then standing up.

"The first ones are too tight," he said, handing the second pair back to Whitey. "These are best."

He got, naked, into one of the beds then, and he pulled the covers up to his chest. He had put two pillows together under his head, so he was half sitting up, and Whitey looked at me and I looked at him, and he walked into the other room.

"So, I'll go now, Rock," I said.

"Okay," he said.

"You have to lick this guy, Rock," I said, and I was standing by the bed, looking down at him. "If you ever had to win a fight, you have to win this one."

"I know," he said, nodding.

"I despise them for what they did to you," I said, "and you hate them, and there's only one way you can get even. If you lose tomorrow night, you're done, not only in New York but everywhere. You have to win, Rock."

"I know," he said.

"You have to stick to it," I said. "You have to win the title, because when you win the title it's yours, and they can't take it away from you outside the ring. You win it and they need it, and as I told you in the car that night, they'll come crawling back, begging you on their hands and knees."

"I know," he said, lying there in that bed and looking up right at me. "If I have to, I'll die in there, tryin'."

We shook hands and he snapped off the light over the bed and I left. I took an elevator down and went out and called a cab, and riding back to my hotel and thinking about it I was embarrassed. They come no more decent than Tony Zale and no tougher than he was inside the ropes, and what was I doing telling someone he would have to take those brutal shots in the belly and to the head while I would just sit there at ringside, looking up into the brutality?

They drew $422,918 for an indoor record and they had them packed to the walls again and up to the rafters. Suddenly, the hot, humid, sweat-smelling air was stilled of sound and then Al Melgard at the Stadium organ started "The Sidewalks of New York," and a roar went up in the back and down the aisle he came. He had the white satin, green-trimmed robe over his shoulders, and Whitey and Irving and Frank Percoco were behind him. The roar, and then the booing, was all over the place now, and Whitey was rubbing his back as they came. Then, two steps from the stairs, he broke from Whitey and took the three steps in one leap and vaulted through the ropes, throwing his arms out into the roar and the boos so the robe slid off.

"Yes," I said to myself, "he'll stick it all right."

He stuck it, and there were times when it looked as if he would have to die doing it. Under his right eye the flesh had swelled so that it shut the eye, and when Zale cut the left eye, the blood flowed into it so that he was stumbling around almost blind and seeing only through a red haze. Snarling, he motioned Zale to come in, and Zale threw all of his big stuff at him and he took it all. There were times in the third round when I said to myself that if this were just a fight, and not bigger than a fight, he would go down. I said to myself that he couldn't win it, and then an odd thing happened.

Between the fourth and fifth rounds, Frank Percoco took a quarter—two bits—and pressing with it between his fingers, he broke the skin of the swelling under the right eye. When the blood came out the swelling came down enough for the fighter to see. In the sixth round, with Zale helpless on the ropes, Graziano, in that frenzy that made him what only he and Dempsey and, I guess, Ketchel, were, was hitting him wherever he could find a place to hit him, and the referee stopped it.

"Well," I said to him, "the world is a big place, and how does it feel to be the middleweight champion of it?"

In that basement of the Chicago Stadium he was standing, naked once more, in the shower stall off the dressing room, his right eye shut again, a metal clip holding the other cut closed. Only a fireman in uniform was with us, guarding the door that Whitey had opened just long enough for me to get in.

"I don't know," he said. He had closed down the flow of the shower so that it barely dripped on him. Cut and bruised and hurt, and leaning back and resting one arm on the shower handles, he was trying to think and to talk. "I don't know. I mean . . . I mean as a kid . . . I mean I was no good. I mean nobody ever . . . you know what I mean?"

"I know what you mean, Rocky," the fireman said suddenly. "You're giving a talk on democracy."

"I mean, I never . . ." the fighter said to me, and then he turned to the fireman and, sort of studying him, he said, "You're a good guy. You're all right. You know what I mean?"

The next day it started in the Chicago papers, as I had told him it would, and it was the same in the New York papers when I got back two days later. Nothing had changed, really, neither the fighter nor the charges against him by those who had called him a liar and a hoodlum, but now those who had been crying out against him were crying out for him as a citizen wronged.

"Well," Wilbur Wood said, a smile on his face and sticking out his hand, when I walked into the office, "we had it all the way."

"All the way?" I said, shaking hands. "What did we have all the way?"

"Graziano," he said, still smiling. "Haven't you seen the other papers?"

"Yes," I said. "I've seen them."

"We had him all the way," Wilbur said. "All the way."

"Good, Wilbur," I said. "I'm real glad."

My gladness was to be short-lived. Just when, it seemed, the pressure of that public opinion and the promise of a big gate for this third fight with Zale would force New York State to restore his license, someone got it out of the War Department that he had gone AWOL from the Army in 1943, had spent nine months in Leavenworth, and had a dishonorable discharge. In this game these misguided patriots were playing with the life of a hounded and tortured human being who had served his time and was trying to make an honest living, he was now back at Square One.

"How did you mess up like that?" I asked him.

"This captain," he said, "he come out from behind his desk. He said, 'You think you're so tough?' He started to take his coat off, like this. What was I supposed to do? I belted him—pow!—and flattened him, and I took off."

And I had misled him. Bending over that bed in that hotel room in Chicago that night, I had told him that once he won the title, they could never take it from him outside the ring but, of course, they did. Because Abe J. Greene, the head of the National Boxing Association, refused to be cowed by them and stood up for him, they let him defend that title against Zale in the ball park in Newark, New Jersey, and they paid him for it, but he was no fighter then. The things they had done to him had taken out of him that which had made him the fighter he had been, and Zale knocked him out in the third round.

Trying to bring him back, Irving Cohen signed him for a fight in Oakland, California, with Fred Apostoli, who, nine years before, had been middleweight champion. Ten days before the scheduled date, riding the train into town, I was checking the sports pages in the morning papers, when I saw the story out of Oakland. Rocky Graziano had disappeared, and Jimmy Murray, the promoter, was threatening to sue him and Irving Cohen. At the paper I tried to write whatever piece I had in mind, but I gave up and called Irving Cohen at his office.

"Where's the fighter?" I said.

"We don't know," he said.

"What are you going to do?"

"I don't know," he said.

"Listen, Irving," I said. "You've got to do something. You know his whole future depends on this. You've got to square this, and you've got to do something right now."

"But I don't know what to do," he said.

"Stay right where you are," I said. "I'll be up there in a half hour."

He had a small office in the Brill Building on Broadway. When I got there it was noon, and I found him with Teddy Brenner, who was making matches for a small club then and later headed boxing at Madison Square Garden.

"Have you found him?" I said to Irving.

"No," he said. "We don't know where he is. We don't know what to do."

"I'll tell you what to do," I said. "Call Terry Young and Lulu and Bozo Costantino and Al Pennino and anybody else you can think of from the old neighborhood. Tell them to form a posse and go out and find him, because he'll be hiding out somewhere in one of his old haunts. Tell them to have him call you, or come up here."

The four I had named were lightweight fighters of the time. Terry Young had brought Graziano, while he was running from the Army, to Irving, and we waited while Irving made some phone calls.

"They'll look for him," Irving said when he came off the phone, "but I don't know."

"Now call the Capitol Hotel," I said, "and reserve a suite for five o'clock. Then tell the Garden to call the news services and all the papers, and tell them that Rocky Graziano will hold a press conference at the Capitol at six o'clock."

"But what if we don't find him?" Irving said.

"Please, Irving," I said, "don't worry about that now. We've got almost six hours, and if he doesn't show, you will."

I went out and had a sandwich, and then I walked over to the boxing office at the Garden to be sure they had made the calls to the sports desks of papers and the news services. It was about three o'clock when I got back to Irving Cohen's office, and we sat around there for another hour, waiting for the phone to ring.

"What do we do now?" Irving said.

"Well, we sit and hope," I said. "We've still got two hours, but if he doesn't show, you will. You'll go over to the Capitol, and you'll speak for him. You know, as well or better than I, that he's not equipped to fight now, and you'll tell them that. You'll say that if he had hurt his hand or had some other injury, a physical examination would reveal that, and the fight would be postponed. The hurt that has been done him outside the ring, however, doesn't show up in an exam, but it has left him so emotionally and mentally disturbed that he is now as ill-equipped to fight as if he had a physical ailment. You'll say it wouldn't be fair to those who'd pay the money to see him fight Apostoli or anyone else right now. You'll say that, and you'll say you'll make whatever amends you have to make to Jimmy Murray for whatever expenses he's had setting up and promoting the fight."

"That's right," Irving said. "We will."

"Good," I said.

"But I don't think I can say all that," Irving said.

"Of course you can," I said.

"No," Irving said, shaking his head. "That's the truth. He's in no condition to fight, but I'll never be able to say it, to explain it like that. I won't get it right."

"All right," I said. "I'll write it out for you."

I sat down at a typewriter there, and I wrote five or six paragraphs and I handed the two pages to him. He read them and folded them and put them in his pocket, and at about five o'clock the phone rang, and Irving picked it up.

"Good!" I heard him say. "Where is he? Good. Now listen. Tell him to be at the Capitol Hotel by six o'clock. We have a suite there in my name. Tell him it's a press conference. Tell him to be sure to be there at six o'clock. You have that? At the Capitol Hotel, across from the Garden, at six o'clock. Good."

He put the phone back on the cradle and he looked up, smiling.

"They found him," he said. "They're going to tell him to be sure to be there. Now I just hope he shows up."

Yes, I was thinking, and he may not. With all he has gone through, and all he has taken, he may just decide that it is hopeless, and go over the hill again.

At 5:30 Irving Cohen left for the Capitol, and just before six o'clock Teddy Brenner and I followed. The suite was at the end of a floor, and they were all there waiting. At 6:30, we were still waiting.

"Come on now, Irving," one of them said, finally. "What's going on? Where the hell is he?"

"He's on his way, I'm sure," Irving said. "I'm sorry to hold you up, but I'm sure he'll be here."

"But when?" somebody else said. "You call us all in here and there's no fighter. We've got deadlines to meet, and we can't sit around here all night. What are we supposed to do now?"

"Well," Irving said, "I've got a statement here, if you'd like me to read it."

"Hell, yes," somebody else said. "Read it. At least give us something."

He took the pages out of his pocket and unfolded them and started to read. Jack Hand of the Associated Press and I were half sitting together on a radiator cover, like all the others taking notes, and he knew how close I was to the fighter and he nudged me.

"Did you write this?" he said.

"Hell no," I said, going on with my note-taking. "I'm a stranger to it too."

"It sure sounds like you," he said.

When Irving finished they started the questions. We were clustered around Irving and the door to the hall was still open, and then I heard someone say it.

"Here he comes now."

He came through the door and into the suite. He had on a beautiful camel's hair polo coat, but there was a growth of several days' beard on his face and under the coat he wore an old woolen shirt and dirty slacks and there were heavy roadwork shoes on his feet.

"I'm with my friends," he said.

Only some of them were his friends, but he had stopped just inside the door, and now he held both hands out. You could hear every breath in the room.

"What happened, Rocky?" one of them said. "What's the matter?"

"It's like I got a scar on my face," he said, staring through them and bringing his right hand up to his right cheek. "Why don't they leave me alone, or put me in jail?"

He always spoke from where he lived, and that did it. It did it in the papers the next day. *Collier's* picked it up from the papers and ran two autobiographical pieces, and the following September, his New York State license was restored. He fought Charley Fusari in the Polo Grounds and stopped him in the tenth round while I, doing a magazine piece about what it is like to be a fighter's wife, walked the streets of Brooklyn with Norma, her mother, and a friend of theirs. On the nights he fought, she could not bear to stay in the house.

They live now in a yellow-brick high-rise apartment house on the southeast corner of Fifty-seventh Street and Second Avenue in what, with the construction that went up there right after World War II, became one of the more fashionable sections of the city. Under the canopy a slim, rather tall woman of late middle years, precise and imperious in a light tan and brown pants suit and wearing a wide-brimmed, buff takeoff—maybe by Don Kline or Adolpho—of a man's fedora, was standing. At her feet were three pieces of matched tan luggage, and the uniformed doorman was walking the street toward the corner, blowing his whistle and waving his right arm and trying to flag down a cab.

I watched him, when he had finally got one, trot along beside the cab to the canopy and then help the cabbie load the luggage into the trunk. Then he ushered the woman into the back seat and shut the door, and I followed him into the lobby.

"Rocky Graziano," I said, and I gave him my name. He picked up the phone and talked into it and turned back to me.

"You can go right up," he said. "It's 16-G, like in Graziano."

Not B, like in Barbella, I was thinking, walking to the elevator. He was born Rocco Barbella, one of seven children, three of whom died in infancy, of an alcoholic, often unemployed father and a mentally and emotionally disturbed mother who was in and out of institutions. While he was running from the Army, he took the name of one of those he used to run with in the streets.

"Whatever became of the original Graziano?" I had asked him the last time I had seen him, some dozen years before now.

"In the can," he said, "doing twenty to thirty. He was like a three-time loser. You know?"

I knew that while he was fighting, Irving Cohen had made him buy annuities, and that, beyond that, he himself had been doing very well. I would catch him occasionally on TV with Martha Raye, once with Cesar Romero and Margaret Truman. His autobiography, *Somebody Up There Likes Me*, had headed the best-seller lists, and off it they had made the movie starring Paul Newman, who caught the sullen moods but not the exuberance that made the fighter exciting just walking down the street.

"I just made The Big One," he told me that day.

"The Big One?" I said. "What's that?"

"A million bucks."

"You're worth a million?" I said.

"Yeah," he said. "My accountant just told me. How about that?"

When I got off the elevator now he was standing there in a black, knitted, short-sleeved sports shirt, gray slacks, and black loafers. The lines in his face were deeper, the full head of hair was still black but graying at the temples. We shook hands, smiling at each other and voicing greetings. He led me down the hall to the apartment where, when he opened the door and led me in, a dog, light brown and knee-high, came toward me, its head going and sniffing at me and blocking my way.

"He won't hurt you," he said. "He's a Lab."

"Labs don't hurt you?" I said, the dog still sniffing at me.

"Yeah," he said. "C'mere, Plumber! The guy who give him to me is in the plumbing business, so I named him Plumber."

He led me through the small foyer and into the living room. Sunlight was coming through sliding glass doors that open onto a terrace, and he motioned me toward the sofa with a coffee table in front of it. As he sat down in a chair across the table from me, we could hear a metallic rattling coming from beyond the dining area in what I presumed to be the kitchen.

"Excuse me," he said, getting up. "It's Plumber. He wants me to give him some water."

He got up, and I could hear him filling the pan. As he came back and sat down I could hear the dog lapping the water.

"Every morning," he said, "he gets me up, six o'clock, six thirty. He wants me to take him out, so I take him out. I go to sleep early, like nine, ten o'clock. You want a beer?"

"No," I said, "but thanks."

"I don't eat," he said, "but I'm drinkin' twenty beers a day. No pasta, no bread, no candy, no ice cream, but I'm drinkin' beer."

"You look good," I said. "I've talked with Norma on the phone. How is she?"

"My Jew?" he said. "Good. She's fine."

"You were lucky," I said. "You married a Jew and you had a Jewish manager, and they made you save your money."

"You're right," he said. "That's right, my wife and my manager."

"How are the girls?" I said.

Audrey must have been about three when he fought Zale in Chicago. She was in a crib in one of the bedrooms of that hotel suite there, and after the fight the noise of the celebration in the sitting room awakened her and she began to cry. When he went in to her and bent over the crib, she looked up at that face with the swelling around one eye and the bandage above the other.

"Daddy, what happened?" she said.

"You see what I mean now?" he said. "Stay out of the gutter."

"Audrey's good," he said now. "Her husband manufactures watches, and they got a boy, two and a half, named Aaron—Aaron Weissman—and they live downstairs. Roxie's husband manufactures cloth in the garment center, and they got a boy, Allen, about ten."

The dog was at the door now, barking.

"Plumber!" he said, and then to me, "Somebody must be in the hallway. He'll stop in a minute, but you got to see this."

He got up and walked toward the glass doors. On the floor, to one side, was a bronze statuette of a boxer, poised to throw a straight right hand.

"It looks like a Joe Brown," I said, kneeling to examine it. "I don't mean the ex–lightweight champ, but the sculptor in residence at Princeton University."

"You got to write this," he said. "Muhammad Ali. They give him this, the Garden did, for somethin'. He said, 'I ain't gonna take it. That's a white man.'"

"It is," I said.

"So he don't take it, and I'm at the Garden and Teddy Brenner tells me the story and I said, 'I'll take it.' I took the plaque off, but it's a guy gettin' ready to throw a right hand, and I used to throw a right hand."

"I'll say you did," I said.

That right hand and the anger he put into it against all those opponents who, to him, personified the society against which he was making his fight made him the fighter he was. He had put it in words in his dressing room in the Chicago Stadium after he had knocked out Zale, and he was still unwinding and they had him in a corner, their pencils and papers out and making notes.

"I wanted to kill him," he said. "I got nothin' against him. He's a nice guy. I like him, but I wanted to kill him."

Sixteen months before, he had fought Marty Servo in the Garden. Servo had just knocked out Freddie (Red) Cochrane to win the welterweight title, but this was over that weight, and now in the second round Servo had already been down twice and Graziano had him against the ropes. With his open left glove under Servo's chin he was holding Servo's head up, and with his right he was clubbing him again and again until Servo went down the third time and they stopped it.

After I had written my piece and got back to the apartment, I still hadn't got rid of it. One of the reasons we write is to try to unburden ourselves of the weight of what we see and hear and feel, to get it all out, but the brutality and viciousness of that haunted me so that for hours I tossed, unable to get to sleep.

Two years later, after that press conference in the Capitol Hotel, Graziano and Irving Cohen and Teddy Brenner and I were going out to eat. The fighter was leading us down Eighth Avenue, walking with those quick, nervous, swinging strides.

"Where are we going?" I said to Irving Cohen.

"We're going to that place where Marty Servo tends bar," Irving said. "Rocky likes him, and he always tries to bring business into the place."

Servo was never a fighter again after that beating. He had to give up his welterweight title and the security it could have brought him without ever defending it, and now, when we walked into the place, he was standing behind the bar. He had on a white jacket, and when he saw us his face brightened and he leaned over the bar to shake hands. When he shook hands with Graziano he smiled and faked as if to hook with his left. Graziano, leaning over the bar, stuck his left hand under Servo's chin as he had that night, and he faked to throw the right. Then the two of them dropped their hands and laughed.

"Every once in a while," I was saying to him now, and we were seated again, "I see you on a TV commercial. Do you do a lot of those?"

"Oh, jeeze," he said, "I done Coldene. I done Brioschi. American Motors. Chrysler Motors. Cadillac. I do Ford Motors. What's that breakfast thing?"

"I don't know."

"Post Cereals," he said. "Lee Myles Transmissions. I do mostly television, so friggin' many. Then I just do verce-over—*voice*-over—for Honeycomb Cereal."

"You must have a good agent," I said.

"I got no friggin' agent," he said. "I'm a freelance. I do *The Mike Douglas Show* twice a month. I got a contract. Let me get a friggin' cigar. You want a cigar?"

"No," I said, "but thanks anyway."

When he came back he had the cigar, lighted, in his mouth. He handed me a glossy print of a picture taken of himself with Richard Nixon in the White House and a leather-bound folio.

"That's a movie I made with Frank Sinatra in 1967," he said. "They give me the script. Then I do a lot of convention shows. Olin Mathieson. Pearl Burey . . ."

"Brewery?"

"Yeah. Country Club Malt Liquor. Commercials, and they have a convention. Then I lecture at colleges and high schools."

The last time I had seen him he had told me that, in schools, he gave talks on juvenile delinquency, and that he had just lectured on criminology at Fordham University. I asked him what he said.

"I spoke to all the kids who were graduatin'," he said, "and a lot of elderly people, like professors and priests."

"But what did you tell them?" I said.

"You know what it is," he said. "I start out, whether I'm talkin' about criminology or juvenile delinquency, and I say, 'You know, I'm so glad my father took the boat, because this is the best country in the world, and if there was another country like this one, I'd be jealous.'"

"Then what do you tell them?" I said.

"I say, 'If you're a juvenile delinquent, two things will solve your problem. All you need is a good alibi and a good lawyer.' Then I tell 'em about the guys I knew went to the chair, and I tell 'em about *Somebody Up There Likes Me*, how they made the movie and about the book."

"So these days," I was saying now, "what do you tell them when you lecture?"

"I say, 'I'm very glad to be here on this occasion. I couldn't be with nicer people.' Then I give a couple of jokes, like a comedian. I'm a comedian. I think I am."

"I'm remembering," I said, "something that Irving Cohen's wife said to me once. I've forgotten her name."

"Jean," he said. "They live in Arizona now."

"It was the night before the Zale fight in Chicago," I said. "She had stopped by the suite in that hotel, and at one point you stood up. You walked across the room to go into the next room, and she said to me, 'You know, there's something about that boy. There's an electricity, a vitality, about him, so I have the feeling that, whatever he does, he'll make a success of it.'"

"She said that?"

"Yes, and she was the first one to spot it. I used to think of that when I'd see you on TV with Martha Raye. You were lucky twice in your life and in two careers. As a fighter you came along in Tony Zale's time, and you two meshed like gears, and made great fights. Then in television, who else could you have made such a partnership with but Martha Raye?"

"Yeah," he said. "That's right."

"How did she discover you?"

"She didn't discover me," he said. "It was her writer, Nat Hiken. A guy calls my manager. I was in Stillman's, and the guy comes over. He says, 'My name is Nat Hiken. You got an agent?' I said, 'I got a friggin' manager named Irving Cohen.' He says, 'We're lookin' maybe to put you on *The Martha Raye Show*. We're looking for a boyfriend for Martha Raye.'

"What Nat Hiken told me was some guy says, 'Get some stupid guy like Rocky Graziano.' Nat says, 'Why not get Rocky Graziano?' The guy says, 'He can't talk. He can't read.' Hiken says, 'I'll go see him.'

"I go to his office. I meet Marlon Brando, and they give me a friggin' stupid script. Big words I can't pronounce. Hiken says, 'Don't worry. The public doesn't know what the script is.' I go on and the guys are sayin', 'Great! Great!' I was playin' myself."

"You always did," I said, "and I've often thought that it all goes back to Frank Percoco, and that two-bit piece. If he doesn't break that swelling under your eye, you don't see. If you don't see, you don't win the title. If you don't win the title, none of this happens."

"Yeah," he said, "and they did the identical same thing in the picture *Rocky*. Since the picture came out, kids nine or ten think I'm that Rocky."

"And I've never heard," I said, "of twenty-five cents that was parlayed into as much as that quarter Frank Percoco happened to have in his pocket. What's he doing now?"

"He's retired," he said. "He's got a little house on Staten Island he bought about thirty years ago."

"And Whitey's gone," I said, "and he saved your life that night."

"Yeah," he said.

It was after the fight, during that celebration in that hotel suite. The fighter had walked into that bedroom when he had heard the child crying, and he had bent over the crib and talked to her. Then, because it was so stifling hot and humid there, he had walked to a window to open it wider. As he tried to raise it, Whitey, walking into the room, started to do it for him. At that moment the window flew up and the fighter fell forward over the sill, and Whitey grabbed him around the thighs as he was about to plunge the ten stories to the street. Had he gone to his death, I am sure they would have surmised in the papers, the climate of public opinion being what it was at the time, that he had double-crossed the mob by beating Zale and been thrown or pushed, because another of his managers was Eddie Coco, who had a record of twelve arrests and known mob connections.

"And Eddie Coco," I said now. "The last I knew, he was doing twenty to life for killing that parking lot attendant in Miami."

"He got out," he said, "but he's back in again."

"What for this time?"

"He got caught shylocking. He was on light parole."

"I'm remembering," I said, "when you ran out on that Apostoli fight in California. No one knew where you were, and I got Irving Cohen to get Terry Young and Lulu and Bozo Costantino and Al Pennino to find you for that press conference. What are they doing now?"

"Terry Young got shot and killed," he said. "Lulu's still got the bar at Thirteenth Street and Second Avenue, and Al Pennino is workin' on the docks."

"And you've moved about three miles north."

"But it's still the East Side," he said. "I say I had three careers. A robbin' career, a fightin' career, and an actin' career. Listen. Can we do this in a restaurant?"

"Sure," I said. "Anywhere you say."

"I got to save my table," he said, getting up.

"But before we go," I said, "can you just show me around for a minute?"

"Sure," he said, sliding open the glass door to the terrace and leading me out. "We got four and a half rooms, and we got this wrap-around terrace, and we got all these plants and these trees here and . . ."

He had led me back through the living room again and into the foyer. He was starting into the bedroom.

"Wait a minute," I said. "I want to see these paintings."

On one wall of the small foyer there were a half-dozen framed oils. One was a copy of Picasso's *Girl Before a Mirror* and there was another of his *Three Musicians*, and there was a French Impressionist street scene.

"Where did you get these paintings?" I said.

"I done 'em," he said, and then, indicating them, "Rocky done this one. Rocky done that one . . ."

"These two are Picasso copies," I said.

"Yeah," he said. "I copied them, when I couldn't afford to buy 'em. I like his painting."

"What about this street scene?"

"Like in Greenwich Village," he said. "My grandmother and grandfather had a place on Bleecker Street, and I done that."

"These are good, Rock," I said. "They really are."

"Yeah," he said. "I draw fairly well, like a fighter, but it comes out good."

"It does," I said, "but I didn't know you could paint."

"When I was in the reformatory," he said, "I went to art school. I learned to mix colors, and I paint friggin' good."

"I'm impressed."

"Then I got all these books," he said, sweeping an arm toward the bookshelves. "I got letters from presidents. I got more plaques than Jesus Christ. I got them all in the what-do-you-call-it—the basement?"

"Right."

"Listen," he said. "We got to go."

"Sure."

He led me out and I followed him to the elevator. He pushed the button and we waited.

"I've just been up to Brockton," I said, because I knew he and Rocky Marciano had been close friends. "I saw his mother and his brother Peter."

"Yeah," he said. "How are they doin'?"

"They're doing all right," I said, and the elevator had come and we got in and started down, "but they can't find Marciano's money."

"What money?" he said.

"All the money he made," I said. "They can't find it, and they think he may have buried it somewhere."

"There wasn't any money," he said.

He was leading me out of the elevator now, and through the lobby and out onto the street. He gave the doorman a wave, and started toward Second Avenue.

"What do you mean, there wasn't any money?" I said.

"Hey, Rock!" someone, passing us, said.

"Hey!" he said, turning and waving, and then to me, "The guy lost his money."

"He lost his money?" I said. "How do you know he lost his money?"

At the newsstand near the corner he stopped and gave the dealer a quick handshake.

"C'mon," he said to me. "We got to make this light."

We crossed the street, hurrying, and we started south on Second Avenue. He was walking with those quick strides, and at Fifty-fifth

Street we turned west. Just before we reached the corner at Third Avenue, he opened the side door of P. J. Clarke's and led me in. P. J. Clarke's is an old saloon and restaurant that has been there for ninety years and looks it, and that, for the last fifteen or so, has attracted a mix of celebrities in politics, entertainment, and the *haute monde*, and those who want to be around them.

He led me to the small table just inside the door where his friend Phil Kennedy, who, Graziano was to tell me, "sells telephones for Electronics, Inc.," was sitting, and he introduced us. Kennedy's jacket was hung over the back of his chair, and he had been making a list on a yellow pad in front of him on the red-and-white checked tablecloth.

"This used to be Frank Costello's table," Graziano said, as we sat down. "We get it every day. I want a beer. You want a drink?"

He waved to a waiter, shirt-sleeved and in a white apron, and he gave him the order.

"Back to Marciano," I said, and then to Phil Kennedy, "We were just talking about Rocky Marciano and . . ."

"Some fighter," Kennedy said. "I'd have liked to have seen him in there with Ali."

". . . and his family," I said, "can't find his money."

"He lost it," Graziano said.

"How do you know that?" I said.

"I was with him," he said. "Out on Long Island. A real-estate deal. He signed for four hundred thousand, and the deal went bust. His name was on the paper, so it was his money."

"They don't know that in Brockton," I said.

"How can they know?" he said. "I mean they're good people up there, but what do they know about things like that? It's different around here than it is in Brockton. You know?"

"But he was so close with his money," I said.

"Yeah," he said. "Listen to this. I'm goin' to California, and when I walk through the plane to the first class, he's sittin' in the coach. The guy just retired. You know? So I say hello, and when I sit down in the first class I say to the stewardess, 'Rocky Marciano is back there.' She says, 'Rocky Marciano? He is?' So I tell the stewardess to tell the captain we got plenty of seats in the first class, and he sits next to me.

"Now we get off the plane, and I get my luggage. I say to him, 'Where's yours?' He says, 'I don't have none. I don't need luggage.' So we walk to get a cab, and I say to him, 'Where are you stayin'?' He says, 'I think I'll stay with you.' I said, 'Great!' I mean, it's good for me too.

"I'm stayin' at the Beverly Hills Hotel, and the guy has just what he's wearin'. I got some nice knits, so now he's wearin' my shirts, and the guy was bigger than I was, so he stretched them so I couldn't wear them no more. He used my toothbrush."

"You're kidding," Kennedy said.

"So help me God," Graziano said, raising his hand. "Then I used to leave to go to work—I was doin' a show—and one day I come back and they call me from the desk. They say, 'You know, Mr. Graziano, your room is free here, but not the long distance phone calls. We have to pay the telephone company for those calls.' I said, 'What calls? I didn't make any long distance phone calls.' She said, 'Oh yes. There's calls to Brockton, Massachusetts, and Florida.' I said, 'Wait a minute. That's the other Rocky.' The guy must have made two hundred phone calls."

"That's almost unbelievable," Kennedy said.

"We'd make personal appearances together," Graziano said. "We'd be sittin' up there at some dinner, and he'd say to me, 'Ask if anybody's got a private plane.' He was a nervous guy. He wanted to get out. Go. Go. Half the time he didn't know where we were goin' next. It used to embarrass me, but I'd have to say, 'If anybody's got a private plane, Rocky Marciano and I want to go to our next appearance.' Then some guy would take us."

"And that's the way he went in the end," I said.

"Yeah," Graziano said. "Too friggin' bad. You want another drink?"

"No, thanks," I said.

He had summoned the waiter, and he ordered another beer.

"You know," Kennedy said, nodding toward him, "this guy is very popular."

"I know," I said, "and I remember when he wasn't."

"Yeah, Bill knows me a long time," he said, "and you know somethin'? Jacqueline Kennedy was in here the other day, and she gave me three kisses and a hug. Here. Right here, in P. J. Clarke's."

"I've seen him," Kennedy said, laughing, "kiss Elizabeth Taylor, Jacqueline Kennedy. He's very huggable."

"Yeah," Graziano said. "Everybody likes me. The black people, all over the country, for some stupid reason, like me."

"He went to Astoria one night," Kennedy said, "and he stood them on their heads. Five hundred drinking Irish cops. The Irish Archie Bunkers with badges."

"All Irish cops," Graziano said, "and I'm an Italian."

"And had your troubles with cops," I said.

"There was a collegiate poll," Kennedy said. "You know who was the most popular in the country? Ralph Nader, and this guy was sixth."

"Yeah," Graziano said. "I was never in San Antonio, Texas, in my life. I get off the plane and they throw a red friggin' blanket out for me to walk on. It just amazes me. I get in a 747 plane to go to California. The captain says, 'I'm flyin' at such-and-such a speed, and we got Mr. Rocky Graziano aboard. Have a drink in honor of Mr. Rocky Graziano.' Yesterday I was sittin' down with the diplomat from Cuba, and I'm goin' there in three weeks. He invited me."

We talked for a while then, while he had two more beers, about fighters and fights we remember. When we were joined by a couple of others, and the conversation became provincial, revolving around their circle of acquaintances who are strangers to me, I got up and shook hands around the table and, when he stood up, with him.

"You got everything you want to know?" he said.

"Everything," I said.

"You sure?"

"I'm sure."

"If there's anything else," he said, "call me at home, but call me before eight o'clock in the morning. After that I'm not there."

"I know," I said.

Out on Third Avenue sunlight bathed the now open street that, in the old days, was roofed and darkened by the El, now long gone. The sidewalk was crowded with office workers, young clerical and junior executive types, in twos and threes, gesticulating as they talked and walked down their lunches, and by secretaries hurrying to get back.

At Fifty-third Street I was one block from the four-story walkup apartment house on the corner of Second Avenue, its exterior bricks painted a battleship gray, where my wife and I lived when I started to write sports after I came back from the war that day and my hand shook so that I had to quiet it before I could press the button in the entry. It was there that we used to battle the mice that came up the two floors from the market on the street level, and it was there that I tossed that night, so appalled by the animalism I had seen in the fighter as he had clubbed down Marty Servo whom he liked. It was there, too, that I brought all my troubles, as I tried to be somebody by being with those who were, and found that their aspirations and their problems became mine.

How many miles I had flown by now and how many miles I had driven to see those I had wanted to see again, I don't know. I had saved Rocky Graziano for last, and I had seen them all now, and so, after all those miles, I didn't walk the last block. Are they still battling the mice? I don't know. My battle would be the same battle it has been for all the years, to try to put it all down—the way it looked and how they looked and what they said and how they said it—and to try to get it as right as I could get it in this book.

AFTERWORDS

SOURCES AND ACKNOWLEDGMENTS

INDEX

Afterwords

by W. C. Heinz

Beau Jack Is Good Customer

He was the primitive in a primitive profession, and he started in the battle royals of Augusta, Georgia. The whites would blindfold a half a dozen blacks in a ring and sound the bell, and the survivor was the winner. It came in after bearbaiting went out, and it was the start of the boxing career of Beau Jack.

"When the bell ring," Beau said, when I asked him to describe it, "you walk into a shot and you don't know where you are. I stay in my corner, and when I feel the wind, I know to get goin'. One time it was only my brother and me left, and I knock him out. Yes, sir."

"And where were the fights held?" I asked him.

"In Augusta, in an auditorium like a car place but the cars are gone, and the guy put in a ring, and it was a nice place."

He had the primitive's basic trust in the niceness and goodness of everything. To Beau Jack, born Sidney Walker in Augusta in 1921, and who would twice win the New York State version of the lightweight championship of the world, everyone was his friend. So filled was his life with those he felt were his friends that it was hard to conceive that he could have an enemy, and yet in and out of the fight game they stripped him of his earnings from his 112 fights, twenty-one of them Garden main events.

Those Garden fights drew $1,578,000 at the gate, and with Bob Montgomery on August 4, 1944, when admission was by purchase of United States War Bonds, $35,864,000 worth were sold. Then, five years after his last fight, and fifteen years after Bobby Jones, Jimmy Demaret, Grantland Rice, and enough other big names to float a bond issue sponsored his trip north to box, he was back shining shoes, this time at the Fontainebleau in Miami Beach.

Twenty-two years later, I found him still there. He was working more than a hundred hours a week, in the barbershop by day and up in one of the men's rooms at night, and still talking about his friends—now Frank Sinatra, Sammy Davis, Jr., and others who played there.

"Beau," I said, "how are you doing?"

He was heavier now but the weight well distributed, the tight curls of the hair gray now. He had on neat gray slacks and an immaculate white T-shirt with the logo of Don King, the boxing promoter, on it.

"Fine," he said. "Just fine."

"You earned a lot of money as a fighter, Beau," I said. "Do you know where it went?"

"No, sir," he said. "I don't know and I don't care. The members of the Augusta Golf Club gave me enough to get started, and I enjoyed it and I thankful. I'd never got out of Augusta but for Bobby Jones, may he rest in peace, and them, and they gave me the money."

"I never knew anyone else," I said, "who seemed to enjoy boxing as much as you did."

"That's right," he said. "I liked that."

"You'd be the first one into Stillman's and the last to leave. As long as there was sparring going on, you'd be there behind the rings watching."

"You remember that?"

"Yes, I do."

"I watched them all," he said. "I love that, and sometimes a boy I lookin' at, I was gonna meet him, and I know exactly what he's doin'. In my lifetime, though, I never want to hurt nobody, just that it be a good fight."

"I know," I said. "You used to ask me if it had been a good fight, and if the crowd had liked it."

"You remember that too?"

I remember it all. While he had been training in Chicago to fight Willie Joyce, his left knee had given way under him. Four months later, after an operation, he was back in Stillman's, getting ready to fight Tony Janiro.

"That doctor that fix that knee," he said, "he a great man. He my friend."

In the fourth round, though, the knee gave out again, and he fell to the canvas. He managed to rise and he tried to go on, but they had to stop it. After a second operation, he fought for five more years, and I remember his last fight at the Garden, when Tuzo Portuguez licked him, and I remember him in the dressing room later.

"I'm sorry, Beau," I said.

He was sitting on a stool, his white terrycloth robe over him, the sweat still on him.

"Were it a good fight?" he said.

"Yes, it was a good fight," I said, and it had been.

"Did the people like it?" he said.

"Oh, yes," I said. "They liked it."

"If the people like it," he said, "that's all that matters. That's good."

2000

Death of a Race Horse

Out of ten years of daily journalism, four of them covering sports, this is the sole piece that I feel deserves an afterlife, although I am not sure. Some months after the column ran, the editors of *Cosmopolitan* wrote to inform me that I had been chosen as one of "twelve leading American columnists," each of us invited to grant reprint rights to his "favorite column" as part of a new monthly feature. As the $500 they were to pay me was more than four times what my impecunious employers were rewarding me for a whole week's labor, this column went out in the return mail. When the reply came back no check fell out, the column rejected because they doubted "that women would understand it."

1982

Brownsville Bum

When I wrote about Bummy Davis I was writing history, for I never met the young man. I saw him in only one fight, and once as he left the offices of the New York State Athletic Commission after a failed attempt to have his boxing license restored. If the piece proves anything, it is that if you are fortunate enough to find the right people who are perceptive enough and sensitive enough, you can still come to know a man.

1982

Punching Out a Living

After fourteen years of it, and 126 fights in which he was never once off his feet, Billy Graham retired. His skills had waned and, as he put it, he had become bored and disenchanted. A diminishing number, who still remember him, think of him as "The Uncrowned Champ," but I will always remember him as the professional, the honest workman who, more than the champions with their great gifts, represented the rest of us. That was why I wrote about him.

Now, their four children grown into adulthood, he and his wife Lorraine live in West Islip, on Long Island. For twenty-five years he has been a distiller's representative, with the same approach to this calling as he had to the old.

"When I was a fighter," he said, "I wanted to give them their money's worth, whether they were for me or against me, and today they don't put the effort in. No matter what I did, I put the effort in, or I wouldn't feel right about it. Today, when I get an order for a case, it makes me feel good. It spurs me, because I'm earning my way."

"But don't you ever miss it?" I said, meaning the boxing. "Ever wish you were young and back in it again?"

"It's a feeling you can't reproduce in any other field," he said. "Not a lot, but two or three times a year, I'll find myself driving into the city, and what comes to mind are not the big fights, but those smaller fights in that scramble to get to the main event. That's where it's all at."

1982

Young Fighter

Billy McNeece is fifty-one years old now, married, with four sons and a daughter, and lives in Oakdale, Long Island, about a dozen miles from where he grew up. All of that money, of which Izzy Grove spoke, wasn't there for him, and after Billy Kilgore stopped him in five rounds in Miami Beach in 1956, he retired with a record of thirty-seven fights, thirty-one wins, and one draw.

"But I loved it," he said. "It was good to me."

"Was it a tough decision then," I said, "when you decided to give it up?"

"No," he said. "Not really. I had a serious car accident—fifty stitches in the head—and after that I didn't feel the same. You know how it is, too, when you're young. You look at your friends. They're goin' out, and you can't. You want to get married and have kids, and for four years I was going to electrician's school, so I had a trade I could go into."

For a while he had his own electrical firm and, at the same time, he ran a sanitation business. Now he works the 4:00 P.M. to midnight shift at the Long Island Lighting Company's nuclear power plant on the north shore of the island. Three years ago he underwent open-heart surgery in Houston with the Dr. Michael De Bakey team doing a triple bypass.

"So I'm lucky," he said. "I've got my health, and a fine family. We're very close, and three of my boys are fighters."

"So I heard," I said.

"You see," he said, "they grew up around it, with the people talking about it. I love the game, so I guess I encouraged them, even though it's difficult for me to see them fight."

"You don't enjoy watching them fight?"

"I go crazy," he said. "You wouldn't believe it. It's much tougher than being in there. I'm a wreck, but it gives them identity. It separates them from being just a face in the crowd, so if that's the avenue they want to pursue, that's great. If I thought they were taking the chance of getting hurt, though, I wouldn't be for it."

1982

Brockton's Boy

Fifteen years later, in September 1969, I heard on the radio that a small private plane had crashed in Iowa and Rocky Marciano was dead. Now another eight years had passed, and I called Peter Marchegiano at the sporting-goods store he owns in Mansfield, just west of Brockton.

"You sound just like your brother," I said, startled by his voice. There was not only the same broad "a," but the same cadence—the same level and the same rhythm—and it was as if I were talking to his brother.

"I know," he said. "Everybody says that."

"How are you and your folks?" I said.

"Pop died three years ago," he said, "but Mom is fine. She's living with my sister Alice now."

"I'm sorry to hear about Pop," I said. "He was a shy and quiet man and a good man."

"You're right, he was," he said. "He was seventy-nine when he went."

I told him that I wanted to visit with Mom and him again, and three days later I drove to Mansfield. It was early afternoon when I got into the town and found the store. It occupied a single-story red brick building on a corner, and when he came out of the office in the back I was startled once more.

"You not only sound like your brother," I said, as we shook hands, "but you look like him, too."

He was wearing chinos and a white T-shirt, his build the same as that of his brother, and his face split into the same smile.

"That's right," he said, "but I'm a little heavy right now."

Not certain how long it would take me to drive to Mansfield, I had arrived more than an hour early. He said that he had some work to finish, and I went out and, following his directions, found a diner. When I returned he was still busy in the back room, and so I waited in the front of the store amid the baseball gloves and bats, the baseballs, basketballs, footballs, and soccer balls, the boxing gloves, track shoes, tennis racquets, fishing poles, and fishing lures.

Several times he came out to serve customers. One was a woman who wanted a baseball glove for her son, had no idea what position he played, and said she would return another day. Two young men were comparison shopping for jogging shoes, and there was a father who led in his son seeking a baseball glove.

"Gee, I'm sorry," Peter said, after these last two had left. "I didn't know I was going to be so tied-up."

"That's all right," I said. "I'm in no hurry."

"My sister Alice is bringing Mom over to our place for dinner, and we can talk then. I have to deliver some bats to the high school in Brockton, though."

"That's fine," I said.

I followed him in my car and parked it in front of his split-level in one of Brockton's newer residential areas. I got into his station wagon, and we started off for the high school.

"How's the business going?" I said.

"Real good," he said, "I started it in '73 and I sell Brown University, and I've probably got a hundred schools and colleges."

"Do I remember that you played some professional baseball?"

"Right," he said. "Three years in the Milwaukee Braves farm system, but I didn't make it."

"That was a big disappointment?"

"Very much so," he said. "Like a ton of bricks. You feel as though you're as good as anybody there, but you look around and see guys who can run faster than you, hit the ball better than you, and do everything better than you. The one thing that kept me going was the love of baseball, like Rocky must have loved boxing.

"I said to myself, 'Should I go home and tell everybody?' I wanted to lie about it, but I figured if I told the truth, I'd be better off in the long run. My dad always told me, 'Tell the truth, and you can't go bad.' Rocky was one in a million, because he never had to make excuses. How do you follow forty-nine straight fights and never lose a fight? It's very difficult."

"But Rocky didn't make it in baseball either," I said. "Boxing saved him. Did you ever want to be a fighter?"

"I boxed in college," he said. "At the University of Miami. I was successful. I loved it next to baseball, and I won a championship. I knocked out two of my opponents in college, but I don't know, I didn't go into it."

"You had a college education, and you didn't have the economic hunger your brother had."

"That's it," he said. "I didn't have to do it. Rocky's answer was that you always have to be hungry."

The Brockton High School is an example of architectural cubism, a huge gray-white block, the upper stories overhanging the first, and we drove down off the road and around one side of it. He parked the car and got out and opened a rear door and picked up the half-dozen bats that were on the back seat.

"I'll be back in a couple of minutes," he said.

Beyond, and down a slight slope, I could see part of the stadium, the back of the concrete stand, and part of the field and the running track bordering it. There were two yellow school buses in the parking space near the stand, some students standing by them.

"When was all this built?" I asked him when he came back.

"In 1970," he said, "right after Rocky died. Armond Colombo is married to my sister Betty, and he coaches football here. In '70, when they named the field Rocky Marciano Stadium, they won every game they played. It was like someone was directing the show."

He had started the car, and he drove slowly around the side of the school and back onto the road. He stopped at the side of the road where we could look down the length of the field, with the concrete stand on one side and, across the football field, the wooden bleachers. There were some runners in warm-up clothes jogging around the track bordering the field and clusters of others here and there. Facing the road was the sign: "Rocky Marciano Stadium." Centered under the sign, resting on the turf, was a large boulder.

"You see the rock there?" he said. "The teams are now called the Boxers, and the mascot is a boxer dog, Rocky. They also have a Rocky Marciano room in the city museum."

"It's an impressive memorial," I said.

"Yes, it is," he said.

He put the car in drive, and we started along the road.

"When he went," I said, "I naturally thought immediately of your folks and you. How did you hear about it?"

"I'm glad you asked that now," he said. "When we get to the house I'd rather you didn't ask Mom. She took it real hard."

"I presumed that," I said. "That's why I asked now. What was he doing in a private plane in Iowa at night?"

"It was sort of a business-pleasure thing," he said. "He was flying from Chicago to Des Moines. The next day was his birthday, September first."

"I had forgotten that."

"He was going to be forty-six. They crashed about ten thirty. I was woke up by Mom, who was home alone with my dad. It was about one thirty or two A.M. She woke me up screaming on the phone. She kept repeating, '*Figlio mio, cuore di mama!*' I understood what she was saying, but immediately I thought of my dad, because it's a kind of idiom in the Italian language. It means, 'My son, heart of my life.' I still had my dad in mind, though, because he wasn't well.

"I said, 'Mom, please settle down.' But she kept repeating, '*Figlio mio, cuore di mama!*' I said, 'Mom, what's happened there?' She said, 'Your brother was killed in a plane crash!' I have another brother—Louis."

"I know."

"I jumped in my car and this close friend, Henry Tartaglia, came up. He said, 'Do you know what's happening? Have you heard anything? I heard that Rocky Marciano or Rocky Graziano was killed in a plane crash.' I said, 'I hope it's Graziano.' Hank drove me over and we went into the house, and then the phone calls started coming and the reporters and so on."

"I hope this isn't going to upset Mom," I said. "I mean my coming back after all these years and reviving memories of Rocky."

"Oh, no," he said. "Mom's all right now, and she'll be glad to see you."

He had pulled up in front of the house, and we went in. His wife, Linda, slim and blond and blue-eyed, met us in the living room and he introduced me and then led me into the kitchen where Mom was standing at the range, stirring something in a pot.

"Mom," he said, "you remember Bill."

She turned, at seventy-five the same sturdy woman. She was wearing a black short-sleeved dress, glasses with hexagonal frames, and her hair had only partially grayed. She was searching my face as we shook hands.

"Oh, now I remember your face," she said. "Now I remember you, Bill."

"You used to call me 'Beel,'" I said.

"That's right," she said, smiling. "Bill."

We each remarked how well the other looked. She said we would be eating soon, and Peter made a drink for me and one for himself, and he and I sat down in the living room.

"As you know," I said, "when Rocky was training at Grossinger's, Mom would be there some of the time, and she called it 'The

Grossinge.' She didn't eat her desserts, so she'd carry them over to the cottage and she kept them in the refrigerator. She's say, 'Beel, you get hungry tonight you come over and have a piece of pie, piece of cake.'"

"That sounds like Mom," he said.

"Her heart was always going out to the acts that appeared in the nightclub on the lower level there. There was a dance team that I think she wanted to adopt. She said to me one night, 'Oh, Beel, they such a lovely couple. They dance so nice, and they have this lovely baby. It's so hard for them to make a living. Why don't you write something about them, Beel?'"

"That's Mom all right," he said.

Mom called us to dinner, and we four sat down.

"So eat now the *pasta e piselli*," Mom said to me. We had the spaghetti and peas, meat loaf, and tossed salad. We had red wine, and I complimented Linda and Mom.

"My father was a real good cook," Peter said. He was looking at me and he winked, and then he looked at Mom.

"Sure, but I teach him," Mom said.

"Come on," Peter said, winking at me again. "Pa told me he taught *you*. He said you couldn't boil water."

"What you say?" Mom said, looking at Peter and then getting it. "You just talk."

"I know Mom's a great cook," I said, "because I had dinner one night at 168 Dover Street. Pop was good at peeling apples, though. After dinner, at the kitchen table, he peeled an apple and cut it up for us."

"That's right," Peter said. "I always liked when he did that."

"Too many memories in that house," Mom said to me, "through Rocky's career and in that park. For four years after Rocky pass away I no good. I give too much trouble my kids. After four years, with my faith, I even had to go to psychiatrist, and then my husband pass away. Fifty-two years together. It took me four years to get over my Rocky, and my husband I over in one year, but I love him very much."

"I know," I said.

"A lot of people, they miss Rocky," she said. "Some people call me regular. Steve Melchior"—the Rock's bodyguard from Philadelphia—"he say, 'How are you, Mom?' They all miss Rocky, but I miss my husband, too. People used to say, 'Rocky, he looks like his mother.' But I say, 'Look at the hands, like his father. The same frame.'

"When Rocky became champ, my husband, he very shy. When Rocky train in the Grossinge, and it be a big fight and I pray he no get hurt, all the people come. He come out and sweat, and he wants to get the shower. He say to the people, 'Why don't you go over there? My father tell you where I born and everything.' My husband see and walk away, and I say, 'Somebody got to do the talking.' I did, and my daughter Alice and Peter.

"My daughter Alice," Mom was saying, "for twenty-two years she answer all the letter, and in Italian I answer to Italy. I send the picture and make Rocky autograph it. I was going to be schoolteacher. My father wanted me to be, but I didn't want to go, and my father he was very upset. You talk about this letter answer in Italian, and in Italy I was very small and in reading I understand very well, in writing not so good."

"How old were you when you came to this country?" I said.

"Maybe you can't write this, Bill," she said, "because he did a wrong thing, my father. My father say I sixteen when I fifteen. He was here, and when he send for me he wrote my mother to say that. On a Saturday me and my sister we land, and on Monday I have job in Millburn, New Jersey. I got a lot of people there from the old country."

"And what was the job?" I said.

"Making flannel nightgown," she said. "I used to make the buttonhole and then I make the puff. You know, the powder puff, and we make by hands. Then we went to New Rochelle, and we stay a little bit."

"What work did you do there?" I said.

"What I used to do there?" she said. "Wait a minute. The same thing. The nightgown in the factory. We move to Bridgeport, and we live over there about three year. I work in the bullets factory, and I don't know if you know. Was a big machine like this table. It go around, and it was a nice job."

"Was it at Remington Arms?" I said.

"That's right," she said. "Then I work where they make the corsets. Then I work in another factory, and a lot of people used to die. In this factory they used to carry this steel and they put it here and carry over there, and they call it The Butch Shop because so many people die. I had a good job with this steel. All men and very few women. I had big surprise, when they give back pay. It was wartime. You know?"

"World War One."

"Yes, and when I get two hundred dollar, I don't know. It was so much money and I give to my father. One time I open envelope to take ten cents, and he almost kill me. He send all the money to Italy, and then he send here my mother and one girl and three boys. We were six in family."

"And then you went to work here?"

"Oh, yes, in shoe factory. They put the little ribbon around, especially the pumps, and I used to put it around, and they liked my work very much. We moved here in March, and in July I meet my husband."

"She never worked after they were married," Peter said.

"Oh, I work when I marry," she said. "Even when I have you I had night job. I nurse my kids all, and with Peter I go to work and only nurse seven months."

"You worked when you had the others too?" Peter said.

"Off and on, so my husband could be home with kids. And then in the war I make bullets in Hingham."

"Hingham, Massachusetts, in World War Two?" I said.

"Yes. Was good money there. There was danger. The powder they put in bullets, there was poison in. You used to break on the skin. In all my hair and my skin it broke out. I had to go to skin doctor, and for fifty-two week I got seventy dollar. They pay me good because they think I poisoned.

"Then Pop was working in shoe shop, and he was getting twenty-one dollar, twenty-five dollar, and thirty-five dollars the most. At wartime he made fifty, sixty dollars, but everything was cheap."

"And the work was hard," I said. "I'll always remember something Rocky told me one afternoon at Grossinger's, after he had won the title. We were sitting by the pool, and he said he had just made an appearance at a convention of shoe manufacturers in Boston. He said, 'When they introduced me I had to say something, and I don't know if I said the right thing or not, but I told them I used to go into the factory where my father worked and I saw how hard he had to work, and then I saw the pay he brought home. I said, "One thing I was sure of was that I was never gonna go into the shoe factories, so I became a fighter, and you men are responsible for me being heavyweight champion of the world."' He asked me if that was all right. I said, 'All right? That was great!'"

"Everybody used to tell me when Rocky become champ," Mom said, "that it gonna hurt Peter, but I don't think so."

"Of course not," I said, looking across the table at Peter. "You have a fine son in Peter."

"When I was playing in Duluth," Peter said, "I was a good catcher—not a Johnny Bench—but I remember one foul-mouthed guy who said, 'It's Rocky's brother, but he's not an inch of his brother.' If I was John Smith's brother it would never have happened. You don't compete with a Rocky Marciano."

"When Rocky first started to fight," I said to Peter, "you were quite young. Do have any early memories of what it was like having a brother who was starting out to be a fighter?"

"I sure have," he said, "in the kitchen at 168 Dover Street, when Rocky lost a fight to Coley Wallace in the amateurs. It was like a bad, bad dream in the kitchen. Mom was in church. She used to go before every fight he had."

"I remember," I said to Mom, "that later, on the nights when Rocky fought, a doctor used to pick you up and drive you around until the fight was over."

"That's right," she said.

"I had to be seven, eight years old," Peter was saying, "and it was the first time that I knew Rocky was a fighter. Somebody said, 'Rocky lost the fight.' It was like the end of the world, and when Mom came in I told her that Rocky lost the fight, and she said, 'He may have lost, but he didn't get hurt.'"

"Always he shouldn't get hurt," Mom said.

"Were you in Philadelphia for the Walcott fight?" I asked Peter.

"I sure was," he said.

"It was some fight," I said. "Some sportswriters, who had seen them all, said it was the greatest heavyweight championship fight since Dempsey and Firpo, and some time later I said to Rocky, 'When Walcott knocked you down with that left hook in the first round, it was the first time you were ever down. What were you thinking when you found yourself on the deck?' He said, 'I was thinking, "Boy, this guy can really hit. This is gonna be some fight." And it was.'"

"I was sitting with a priest in the tenth row ringside," Peter said. "Father McKenzie, and how many times he's been in my house. Father kept saying, 'Keep praying, Peter.' I said, 'No, I got to leave. I don't want to see my brother get beat up.' I left one time, and he brought me back."

Mom was silent. She was just sitting there, looking at her hands folded at the table.

"You tired, Mom?" Peter said. "Do you want to go home?"

"No," she said, straightening up. "I want to talk with Bill."

"Okay," said Peter, smiling. "I just don't want you to get tired."

"When Rocky ten, eleven years old," she said, "he come home from school. I used to make my own bread. He look, and I say, 'What you look?' He say, 'You work all the time.' I say, 'Why don't you help? Wash the dish.' And so he took the cloth and he go like this. He make one slap with it and put it down, and I said, 'What you do?' He said, 'You got the daughter. When they come home from school, let them wash the dish.'

"Then he say, 'What be your wish when I make a lot of money?' I say, 'Rocky, we got nice home, not big but clean.' He say, 'What you like if I make a lot of money? What? You see my arm? I got a lot of strength in my arm. I make a lot of money. What you like to do?' I said, 'I like to travel when my family grow up.' Then he become champ, a big shot, and he send me to Italy."

"I remember that," I said. "You and Pop went over, and it was a great disappointment. You went to Pop's town and everybody wanted money, so you never went to your town."

"Rocky, he give me three, four thousand dollar," she said, nodding. "We should stay three month, but we stay twenty-one days. Too much sadness there. Everybody expect, expect."

"That saddened Rocky, too," I said. "A heavyweight champion is the one athlete who is known and looked up to all over the world, and in Italy, where his parents came from, they wanted money."

"Not everybody want," she said. "We got letter—I threw away now—from Japan, everywhere. They write, 'He's unusual boy. We don't write you because he big shot, but because of what he is. Some people they champ, but nothing else, but that's why we write you, the mother and the father.'"

"And I'm sure," I said, "that letters like that made you and Pop proud."

"Then everywhere he go," she said, "Rocky he leave things. I get package from Waldorf Astoria. Shoes, shirt. I used to thought it was something for me. I say to him, 'I used to teach you, you not like that.' He said, 'When I young boy you used to teach me to try this, do that. But now I got to be the real Rocky. That's why they call me that.' Some people they honest. They send you, and they say, 'Rocky was in this room.' Some people they take."

"It's so odd," Linda said, "how Rocky wanted to make it big since he was a small child. Others would dress to it, but not him."

"He was what he was," Peter said.

We talked on, and at one point Mom got up and left the room and came back with her wallet. From it she took some photographs of Rocky, in one of which he was with Muhammad Ali, and when we all got up from the table I thanked Linda and then Mom.

"So many memories, Bill," she said. "So much to talk."

"But good memories, Mom," I said, "and I shall always remember you and Pop."

"And you give my best to your wife and your daughter," she said.

Peter and I walked out to our cars. He was to lead me to the motel where I had a reservation, and we shook hands.

"I hope it was all right," I said. "I hope I didn't . . ."

"Oh, no," he said. "It's eight years now. For a time it was rough, but it's good for her to talk now. Now Mom lives for one thing, the beautiful memories of Rocky."

"And good luck with the sporting-goods business," I said. "I'm really impressed by how well you're doing."

"I'm doing real well," he said. "It really surprises me how well it's going."

When Rocky was champion all of Brockton ran at him with all kinds of schemes. They wanted him to sign notes for them or lend them money outright or sponsor them on singing or acting careers. One of them wanted to start a band, and another he had never heard of wanted him to go halves with him in a nightclub in Buffalo. They tried to get him into uranium and copper and oil wells, a dairy and a home-oil route, but following the red taillights of Peter's car I closed my mind to that. There was nothing to think about, and I was remembering Mom.

1979

The Rocky Road of Pistol Pete

Twenty years passed before I saw Pete Reiser again, and then I found him in another hospital, St. Anthony's in St. Petersburg, Florida. He had had a heart attack in 1964, but he was with the Chicago Cubs now, working with young ballplayers out of high schools and colleges in an extension of spring training, until, two days before, bronchial pneumonia and a heart murmur put him flat on his back once more.

"What," I asked him, "are these kids like who come up today?"

His breathing was clouded and labored, and when he spoke he exhaled the sentences, his voice husky and almost inaudible. I had suggested that I stop by again when he would be feeling better, but he had said that he would rather talk than just stare at the walls.

"You get all kinds," he said.

"You don't think the world is going down the drain because of the younger generation?"

"Hell, no," he said, stopping for breath. "I see too many good ones. It's so much easier to write about kids doing bad things, than about kids doing good things for others."

"When I wrote about you managing in Kokomo," I said, "I told about the time one of your kids had made a bad throw. You asked him what he was thinking while the ball was coming to him, and he said, 'I was saying to myself that I hoped I could make a good throw.'"

"That's right," he said.

"Then you told him how, when you were playing, you used to be saying, 'Hit it to me. Just hit it to me. I'll make the catch. I'll make the throw. Give me the steal sign. I'll go!'"

"That's right," he said. "You have to think positive. I try to tell them that."

"So after the story ran," I said, "I got a letter from a father. He said that he had sat his own kid down and he'd read that to him, and he thanked me. I wrote him back, saying that I appreciated his letter but that he shouldn't thank me. He should thank Pete Reiser."

"You try to tell these kids," he said, breathing it again, "and one of them said to me, 'I didn't know you played major-league ball.'"

Two days later he left the hospital and flew to Thousand Palms, California, to where he and his wife had recently moved. When, over the years since, we would talk on the phone, I would find him having his good days and his bad and in and out of the hospital. He was still with the Cubs, scouting high schools, junior colleges, and colleges, and covering the professionals in the Pacific Coast League and the

California State League, and always looking, I suppose, for we all do, for an extension of himself.

"So how are you doing?" I asked him the last time we talked. "Have you found a real good one?"

"There's one I've got my eye on," he said, "but other people have their eye on him too. Who knows? It's the luck of the draw."

It would have been some luck and some draw if he had found another Pete Reiser, but it was not to be. He was sixty-two when, on October 25, 1981, that respiratory illness put him down for the last time.

1982

Sources and Acknowledgments

The Top of His Game is a selection from the sportswriting that W. C. Heinz published between March 1947, when he was thirty-two years old, and September 1979, when he was sixty-four. It contains fifteen columns that he wrote as a staff writer for the daily New York *Sun* (1947–49), thirteen pieces that he wrote as a freelance journalist for a variety of American magazines (1947–65), and ten chapters from the volume of profiles and memoirs he called *Once They Heard the Cheers* (1979). It also contains, in an appendix, afterwords to seven of these columns and pieces that were published in books and magazines between 1979 and 2000.

As the texts have been drawn from a number and variety of publications, each of which had its own stylebook, they have been edited here for stylistic consistency. The diction has not been changed but the treatment of dates, numbers, abbreviations, punctuation, and other particulars of style, especially as they occur in dialogue, has been regularized. Titles, unless otherwise noted, are those of the first printings. Subtitles, most of them suggested by phrases in Heinz's texts, have been added throughout. Subheadings and section breaks in newspaper columns and magazine pieces have been deleted in observance of Heinz's practice when collecting his journalism in book form. Typographical errors and misspellings of proper names have been silently corrected.

Many of the columns and pieces printed here were previously collected by Heinz in two volumes of miscellaneous prose, *American Mirror* (Garden City, NY: Doubleday & Company, 1982) and *What a Time It Was: The Best of W. C. Heinz on Sports* (Cambridge, MA: Da Capo

Press, 2001). *Once They Heard the Cheers* was published by Doubleday in 1979.

Out of the War

"Transition" first appeared, under the title "Transition (Autumn 1945)," as the introductory chapter of *Once They Heard the Cheers* (1979). Excerpts from "Transition" were reprinted in *What a Time It Was* (2001) and *When We Were One: Stories of World War II*, by W. C. Heinz (Cambridge, MA: Da Capo Press, 2002). The text from *Once They Heard the Cheers* is used here.

On the Beat

"Memories of a Great Jockey" first appeared in the New York *Sun* for Thursday, March 25, 1947, and was collected in *What a Time It Was* (2001). The text from the *Sun* is used here.

"Beau Jack Is Good Customer" first appeared in the New York *Sun* for Wednesday, February 18, 1948, the source of the text used here.

"Down Memory Lane with the Babe" first appeared, as "Down Memory Lane with Babe," in the New York *Sun* for Monday, June 14, 1948. It was collected, under its present title, in *What a Time It Was* (2001). The text from the *Sun* is used here.

"About Two Guys Named Joe" first appeared in the New York *Sun* for Monday, August 30, 1948, the source of the text used here.

"German Heavyweight Checks In" first appeared in the New York *Sun* for Wednesday, January 19, 1949, the source of the text used here.

"'They Used to Fight Dogs'" first appeared in the New York *Sun* for Monday, February 28, 1949, the source of the text used here.

"Rumpus in the Living Room" first appeared in the New York *Sun* for Wednesday, March 23, 1949, the source of the text used here.

"Uncle Mike Is Back" first appeared in the New York *Sun* for Tuesday, April 5, 1949, the source of the text used here.

"Late Afternoon on the Harlem" first appeared in the New York *Sun* for Thursday, April 7, 1949, the source of the text used here.

"How They Told Charlie Keller" first appeared in the New York *Sun* for Thursday, May 19, 1949, the source of the text used here.

"Jake Steals the Show" first appeared in the New York *Sun* on Thursday, June 23, 1949, the source of the text used here.

"Death of a Race Horse" first appeared in the New York *Sun* for Thursday, July 28, 1949. It was collected, as "Death of a Racehorse," in *American Mirror* (1982) and reprinted in *What a Time It Was* (2001). The text from the *Sun* is used here.

"The Psychology of Horse Betting" first appeared in the New York *Sun* for Monday, September 19, 1949, the source of the text used here.

"'The Lost Leader'" first appeared in the New York *Sun* for Wednesday, October 12, 1949, the source of the text used here.

"Retired Undefeated Heavyweight Champion" first appeared in the New York *Sun* for Wednesday, November 23, 1949, the source of the text used here.

Out in the World

"Brownsville Bum" first appeared in *True*, June 1951. It was reprinted in *Best Sports Stories 1952*, edited by Irving T. Marsh and Edward Ehre (New York: Dutton, 1952), and shared the editors' E. P. Dutton Prize for the best magazine story of 1951. (The co-winner was "Frozen Terror," a Lake Michigan survival story by Ben East.) It was collected in *American Mirror* (1982) and reprinted in *What a Time It Was* (2001). The text from *American Mirror* is used here.

"The Day of the Fight" first appeared in *Cosmopolitan*, February 1947. (The kernel of the piece had been published, as the column "They All Told Rocky That He Would Win It," in the New York *Sun* for September 28, 1946.) It was reprinted in *Best Sports Stories 1948*, edited by Irving T. Marsh and Edward Ehre (New York: Dutton, 1948), and was awarded the editors' E. P. Dutton Prize for the best magazine story of 1947. Heinz collected the piece in *American Mirror* (1982) and chose it to represent his work in *The Book of Boxing* (1999), an anthology that he co-edited, with Nathan Ward, for Total Sports Publishing's "Sports Illustrated Classics" series. The text from *American Mirror* is used here.

"The Fighter's Wife" first appeared, as "Fighter's Wife," in *Cosmopolitan*, December 1949. (The kernel of the piece had been published, as the column "The Fighter's Wife," in the New York *Sun* for September 15, 1949.) It was reprinted in *Best Sports Stories 1950*, edited by Irving T. Marsh and Edward Ehre (New York: Dutton, 1950), and was awarded the editors' E. P. Dutton Prize for the best magazine story of 1949. Heinz chose the piece to represent his work in *The Fireside Book of Boxing* (1961), an anthology that he edited for the publishers Simon & Schuster. It was also collected, under its present title, in *American Mirror* (1982), the source of the text used here.

"Punching Out a Living" first appeared in *Collier's*, May 2, 1953. It was reprinted in *Best Sports Stories 1954*, edited by Irving T. Marsh and Edward Ehre (New York: Dutton, 1954), and was awarded the editors' E. P. Dutton Prize for the best magazine story of 1953. It was collected in *American Mirror* (1982), the source of the text used here.

"Young Fighter" first appeared in *Esquire*, July 1955. It was reprinted in *Best Sports Stories 1956*, edited by Irving T. Marsh and Edward Ehre (New York: Dutton, 1956). It was collected in *American Mirror* (1982), the source of the text used here.

"Brockton's Boy" first appeared in *Cosmopolitan*, June 1954. It was reprinted in *Best Sports Stories 1955*, edited by Irving T. Marsh and Edward Ehre (New York: Dutton, 1955). The text from *Best Sports Stories 1955* is used here.

"Scouting for the Yankees" first appeared, as "I Scout for the Yankees," in *Collier's*, July 11, 1953, the source of the text used here.

"The Rocky Road of Pistol Pete" first appeared in *True*, March 1958. It was reprinted in *Best Sports Stories 1959*, edited by Irving T. Marsh and Edward Ehre (New York: Dutton, 1959), and was awarded the editors' E. P. Dutton Prize for the best magazine story of 1958. It was collected in *American Mirror* (1982) and reprinted in *What a Time It Was* (2001). The text from *American Mirror* is used here.

"The Ghost of the Gridiron" first appeared in *True*, November 1958. It was collected in *What a Time It Was* (2001), the source of the text used here.

"Work Horse on Ice" first appeared, as "War Horse on Ice," in *The Saturday Evening Post*, January 10, 1959. It was reprinted, under its current title, in

Best Sports Stories 1960, edited by Irving T. Marsh and Edward Ehre (New York: Dutton, 1960). The text from *Best Sports Stories 1960* is used here.

"The Happiest Hooligan of Them All" first appeared in *True*, October 1959, the source of the text used here.

"The Rough and Tumble Life" first appeared, as "Rough and Tumble Life of a Top Bronc Buster," in *True*, February 1965, the source of the text used here.

"The Twilight of Boxing" first appeared in *The Saturday Evening Post*, January 7, 1961, the source of the text used here.

Among the Monuments

"The Shy One" first appeared as Chapter 1 of *Once They Heard the Cheers* (1979) and was reprinted in *What a Time It Was* (2001). It incorporates reporting first published in "The Tender-Hearted Champ," *The Saturday Evening Post*, July 27, 1957 (reprinted in *Best Sports Stories 1958*); "A Visit with the Champion," *The Saturday Evening Post*, February 28, 1959; and "The Floyd Patterson His Friends Know," *Sport*, November 1960 (reprinted in *Best Sports Stories 1961*). The text from *Once They Heard the Cheers* is used here.

"The Man Who Belongs in Blue Jeans" first appeared, in somewhat different form, as Chapter 3 of *Once They Heard the Cheers* (1979). For its appearance here, 850 words have been cut to avoid word-for-word overlap with "The Rough and Tumble Life," of which it is a sequel. The text from *Once They Heard the Cheers* is used here.

"So Long, Jack" first appeared as Chapter 4 of *Once They Heard the Cheers* (1979) and was reprinted in *What a Time It Was* (2001). It incorporates reporting first published in the New York *Sun*, 1946–49; "The Man Who Makes Fighters," *Esquire*, May 1952; and "The Last Campaign of Boxing's Last Angry Man," *The Saturday Evening Post*, February 11, 1967. The text from *Once They Heard the Cheers* is used here.

"The Fireman" first appeared as Chapter 8 of *Once They Heard the Cheers* (1979). It incorporates reporting first published in the New York *Sun* in 1946–49 and notes collected for "Ballplayer's Wife," an abandoned profile of Katie Carrigan Page commissioned by *Life* magazine in 1950. The text from *Once They Heard the Cheers* is used here.

"The Artist Supreme" first appeared as Chapter 9 of *Once They Heard the Cheers* (1979) and was serialized, as "Willie Pep, Boxing's Running Legend," in *The Ring*, November 1979. The text from *Once They Heard the Cheers* is used here.

"The Coach, Relived" first appeared as Chapter 11 of *Once They Heard the Cheers* (1979). It incorporates reporting done for *Run to Daylight!*, a diary of one week with the Green Bay Packers "by Vince Lombardi, with W. C. Heinz" (New York: Simon & Schuster, 1963). The text from *Once They Heard the Cheers* is used here.

"The Greatest, Pound for Pound" first appeared as Chapter 12 of *Once They Heard the Cheers* (1979) and was reprinted in *What a Time It Was* (2001). It was also serialized, as "Sugar Ray: Boxing's Greatest, Pound for Pound," in *The Ring*, February 1980. It incorporates reporting first published in "Why Don't They Like Ray Robinson?," *The Saturday Evening Post*, December 9, 1950. The text from *Once They Heard the Cheers* is used here.

"The Smallest Titan of Them All" first appeared as Chapter 14 of *Once They Heard the Cheers* (1979). It incorporates reporting first published in "You Have to Ride Rough," *Look*, April 17, 1956, and "How to Win the Derby," *Look*, May 1, 1956, a two-part memoir "by Eddie Arcaro, as told to W. C. Heinz." The text from *Once They Heard the Cheers* is used here.

"Somebody Up There Likes Him" first appeared as Chapter 19 of *Once They Heard the Cheers* (1979). It incorporates reporting first published in the New York *Sun*, 1946–49; "Goodbye, Graziano," *Sport*, March 1952 (collected as "So Long, Rock," in *American Mirror*, 1982, and *What a Time It Was*, 2001); and "Rocky Graziano Revisited," *Sport*, September 1966 (reprinted in *Best Sports Stories 1967*). The text from *Once They Heard the Cheers* is used here.

Afterwords

The postscript to "Beau Jack Is Good Customer" is an eight-hundred-word abridgment of "Beau Jack," a thirteen-hundred-word tribute published in *The Ring*, July 2000. (Beau Jack had died the previous February, at the age of seventy-eight.) "Beau Jack" incorporates reporting first published in "The Primitive," Chapter 15 of *Once They Heard the Cheers* (1979). The text from *The Ring* is used here.

The postscript to "Death of a Race Horse" first appeared as an addendum to the piece as collected in *American Mirror* (1982). It was reprinted, in the same fashion, in *What a Time It Was* (2001). The text from *American Mirror* is used here.

The postscript to "Brownsville Bum" first appeared as an addendum to the piece as collected in *American Mirror* (1982). The text from *American Mirror* is used here.

The postscript to "Punching Out a Living" first appeared as an addendum to the piece as collected in *American Mirror* (1982). The text from *American Mirror* is used here.

The postscript to "Young Fighter" first appeared as an addendum to the piece as collected in *American Mirror* (1982). The text from *American Mirror* is used here.

The postscript to "Brockton's Boy" is a four-thousand-word abridgment of "I Remember, Mom," a thirteen-thousand-word sequel first published as Chapter 17 of *Once They Heard the Cheers* (1979). "I Remember, Mom" incorporates reporting first published in "Brockton's Boy" and in "How It Feels to Be Champion of the World," a memoir "by Rocky Marciano, with W. C. Heinz," *Collier's*, May 13, 1955. The text from *Once They Heard the Cheers* is used here.

The postscript to "The Rocky Road of Pistol Pete" first appeared as an addendum to the piece as collected in *American Mirror* (1982). The postscript incorporates reporting first published in "The Man They Padded the Walls For," Chapter 16 of *Once They Heard the Cheers* (1979). The text from *American Mirror* is used here.

The editor and publisher of *The Top of His Game* are indebted to Gayl Heinz, the author's daughter and literary executor, and Andrew Blauner, her agent, for the enthusiasm, imagination, and expertise they have brought to this project. Grateful acknowledgment is also made to the generosity and good wishes of Roger Kahn, Mike Lupica, Jeff MacGregor, David Maraniss, John Schulian, and Glenn Stout.

Index

About the Author

WILFRED CHARLES HEINZ was born on January 11, 1915, in Mount Vernon, New York. He attended Middlebury College, in Middlebury, Vermont, where he studied political science, edited the sports page of the school paper, and met Elizabeth Bailey, who would later become his wife and the mother of their two daughters. After graduation he worked as a messenger for the New York *Sun* and quickly moved up the paper's editorial ladder, first as a copy boy and then as a city reporter and rewrite man. In the fall of 1943 he was sent to Europe as the *Sun*'s junior war correspondent. (The best of his dispatches were collected in 2002 in *When We Were One: Stories of World War II.*) Upon returning to the *Sun* offices in the summer of 1945, he wrote about sports every weekday until the paper's demise in early 1950. By then he was also publishing short fiction and contributing sports stories to *Cosmopolitan* and *Collier's*. In the 1950s and '60s he was a freelance writer, mainly on boxing and baseball, for American weeklies and men's magazines including *The Saturday Evening Post*, *Life*, *Look*, *True*, *Esquire*, and *Sport*. During this period he wrote *The Professional* (1958), a novel about a prizefighter; edited *The Fireside Book of Boxing* (1961), an anthology of reporting, essays, fiction, and verse; and co-wrote *Run to Daylight!* (1963), Vince Lomabardi's first-person account of coaching the Green Bay Packers. In the early 1960s he moved beyond sports to write profiles of, among others, a test pilot, the Selma-to-Montgomery civil rights marchers, a Navajo shaman, and a thoracic surgeon. This last piece inspired two novels set in the world of medicine, *The Surgeon* (1963) and *Emergency* (1974), and brought him into contact with Dr. H. Richard Hornberger, a physician who, during the Korean War, had worked for the 8055th Mobile Army Surgical Hospital. Together, under the name "Richard Hooker," they wrote *M*A*S*H* (1968), a novel inspired by Hornberger's war experiences that provided source material for a successful Hollywood feature and a long-running television series. In 1979 he published the retrospective *Once They Heard the Cheers*, a volume of sports profiles based on three decades of magazine reporting and on late-life visits with the athletes he admired most. This was followed by *American Mirror* (1982), a collection of his favorite journalism, and *What a Time It Was: The Best of W. C. Heinz on Sports* (2001). He also co-edited, with Nathan Ward, *The Book of Boxing* (1999). He died on February 27, 2008, near his longtime home in Dorset, Vermont.

This book is set in 10 point Whitman, a relatively new typeface created by book designer Kent Lew, who was inspired by the typography of W. A. Dwiggins (1880–1956) and Eric Gill (1882–1940), and honored with a Type Directors Club Type Design Awards in 2002. The paper is acid-free lightweight opaque and meets the requirements for permanence of the American National Standards Institute. The binding material is Arrestox, a cotton-based cloth with an aqueous acrylic coating manufactured by Holliston, Church Hill, Tennessee. Text design by David Bullen Design. Composition by Publishers' Design and Production Services, Inc. Printing and binding by Edwards Brothers Malloy, Ann Arbor.